A Guide to Site and Environmental Planning

THIRD EDITION

HARVEY M. RUBENSTEIN

A Wiley-Interscience Publication

JOHN WILEY & SONS

New York Chichester Brisbane Toronto Singapore

Library of Congress Cataloging in Publication Data:

Rubenstein, Harvey M.
A guide to site and environmental planning.

"A Wiley-Interscience publication."
Bibliography: p.
Includes index.
1. Building sites—Planning. 2. Site and environmental planning. I. Title.
NA2540.5.R83 1987 720 87-2048
ISBN 0-471-85033-0

Printed in the United States of America

10 9 8 7 6 5

To Lynne and Steven

Preface to the Third Edition

This book has continued in use as both a textbook and a professional reference on site planning for over 18 years. Since moving to the Dallas/Fort Worth Metroplex in 1983 where many exciting projects have been recently completed or are presently under construction, I have looked forward to adding new material to this book.

Existing chapters such as Details in the Landscape have been revised, renamed, and expanded and four new chapters have been added on Specifications, Sports Facilities and Playgrounds, Roof top Gardens, and Development Design Guidelines.

Additional tables and illustrations (now over 560) help to explain and illustrate the concepts presented.

This revised text will be useful particularly to those in the fields of architecture, landscape architecture, urban planning, and civil engineering.

Harvey M. Rubenstein

Dallas, Texas
March 1987

Preface to the Second Edition

For more than 10 years this book has continued in use as a textbook for site planning courses and a professional reference for practitioners.

In this revised edition I have added more in-depth material on many aspects of resource analysis; circulation relating to the automobile, bicycle, pedestrian, and handicapped; visual design factors and contextual elements; earthwork calculations; storm water drainage, erosion control, and soil loss; alignment of horizontal and vertical curves; and site details. Of the two chapters added, one contains data on trees that can be used in site planning and provides a detailed list of specific trees. The other outlines residential development concepts, highlighting design elements to consider in site planning.

Additional tables, sample problems, and illustrations (now over 360) work together to explain and illustrate the concepts presented.

I hope this revised text will be useful for many years to come.

Harvey M. Rubenstein

Clarks Summit, Pennsylvania
July 1979

Preface to the First Edition

Both creative ability and imagination are essential to site and environmental planning. It is my purpose in *A Guide to Site and Environmental Planning* to present an approach to design based on factual information so that creative talent may be used to its utmost advantage. This book has evolved out of the need for a reference text that combines a design approach with the background of technical information necessary for design development. By providing sufficient technical data I have tried also to keep the tedious task of searching for information in other references to a minimum.

Chapters follow phases in the development of a site plan and include material explaining site selection and analysis, land use and circulation, visual design factors and natural elements in site organization, contours, grading and earthwork calculations, site drainage, alignment of horizontal and vertical curves, and details in the landscape.

Students and practicing professionals in architecture, landscape architecture, civil engineering, city and regional planning, and environmental design will find this book useful for varying scales and types of project in site planning work. Numerous diagrams, sample problems, and photographs of actual projects are of particular value as visual supplements.

This book has developed from research for my site planning courses in the School of Architecture and Urban Design of the University of Kansas, but many ideas discussed here were generated by the landscape architecture departments of Pennsylvania State University and the Harvard Graduate School of Design.

Harvey M. Rubenstein

Lawrence, Kansas
December 1968

Contents

A Guide to Site and Environmental Planning

FIG. 1-1 Fallingwater by Frank Lloyd Wright has long been known for its unity of building and site.

Chapter One
Introduction

Site planning is the art and science of arranging the uses of portions of land. Site planners designate these uses in detail by selecting and analyzing sites, forming land use plans, organizing vehicular and pedestrian circulation, developing visual form and materials concepts, readjusting the existing landforms by design grading, providing proper drainage, and finally developing the construction details necessary to carry out their projects. (See Fig. 1-1.) Although they may determine the overall uses of their sites, such is not always the case. The planners, however, do arrange for the accommodation of the activities clients have specified. They must relate these components to each other, the sites, and structures and activities on adjacent sites—for whether sites are large or small, they must be viewed as part of the total environment. Site planning is professionally exercised by landscape architects, architects, planners, and engineers. (See Fig. 1-2.)

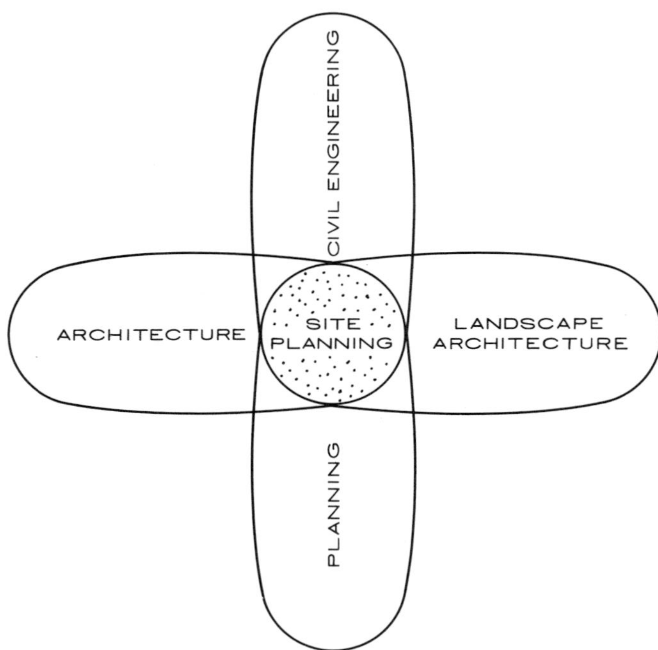

FIG. 1-2 Practicing site planners.

CRITICAL THINKING PROCESS

In site planning, as in other forms of problem solving, the critical thinking process of research, analysis, and synthesis makes a major contribution to the formation of design decisions. Research material may be gathered from existing projects, books, photographs, or experiments. The designer must formulate a program and list the elements required to develop the project. Being open-minded is essential to creativity. Site planners must constantly strive to ward off preconceived thoughts or influences that might close their minds to worthwhile ideas. First intuitive thoughts should be recorded and shown graphically whenever possible since they are often pertinent to the development of the program.

Analysis of the site should consider all existing features, both natural and man-made, to determine those inherent qualities that give a site its "personality." A topographical analysis of its existing features is mandatory. Emphasis should be placed on the site's relationship to the total environment and its special values or potentials.

Sample Student Problem: A Community Center

Program

1 Pedestrian and vehicular access.
2 Parking—10 visitors, 10 staff, 100 members.
3 Softball field and touch football field.

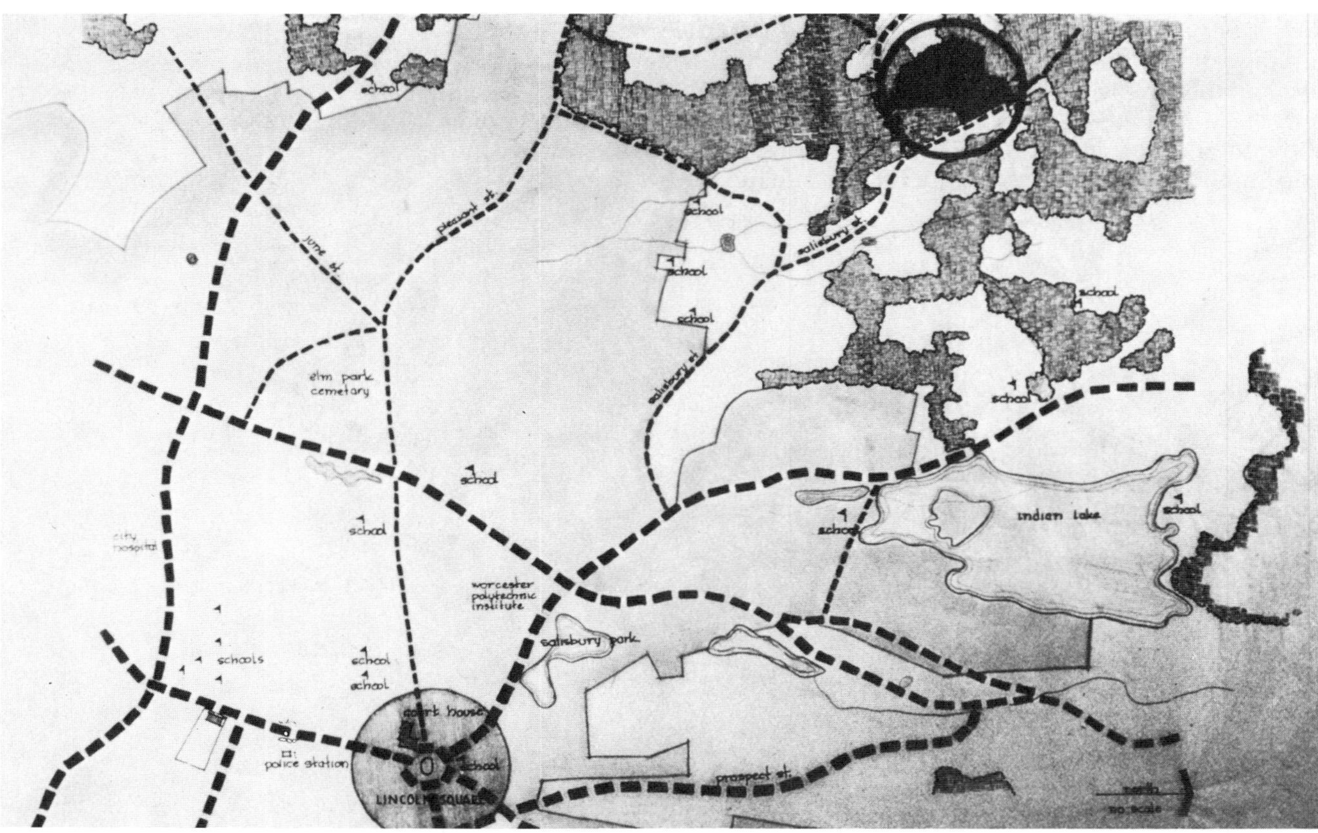

FIG. 1-3 Site environs: the community center is emphasized by the circle at the upper right. Salisbury Street is the primary route to the site.

4 Two tennis courts and basketball court.
5 Tot-lot and bike parking.
6 Crafts area.
7 Truck service.

Site Factors

1 The character of the site is steep and open, except where foliage is dense and large existing boulders occur.
2 The site is essentially split in half by foliage and steep slopes.
3 It has a northeast exposure—cold, but good for winter sports. Most of it is well protected from the wind.
4 Soil condition is glacial till with large boulders at depths averaging 8 ft, except where exposed in woods.
5 Drainage is adequate from stream upward (west).
6 The first 250 ft fronting on Salisbury Street is very low and wet.
7 Views expand as elevation increases.
8 The pond is a very important feature.
9 The pines to the north are very dense and attractive.
10 Except for the northwest and southeast boundaries, the site is entirely surrounded by a single family residential development.
11 Public water and sewage lines run along Salisbury Street.
12 The strongest entry is from Salisbury Street; second strongest from Moreland Street; the third from entry to Temple Sinai; and the fourth from the residential road to the west. (See Figs. 1-3 and 1-4.)

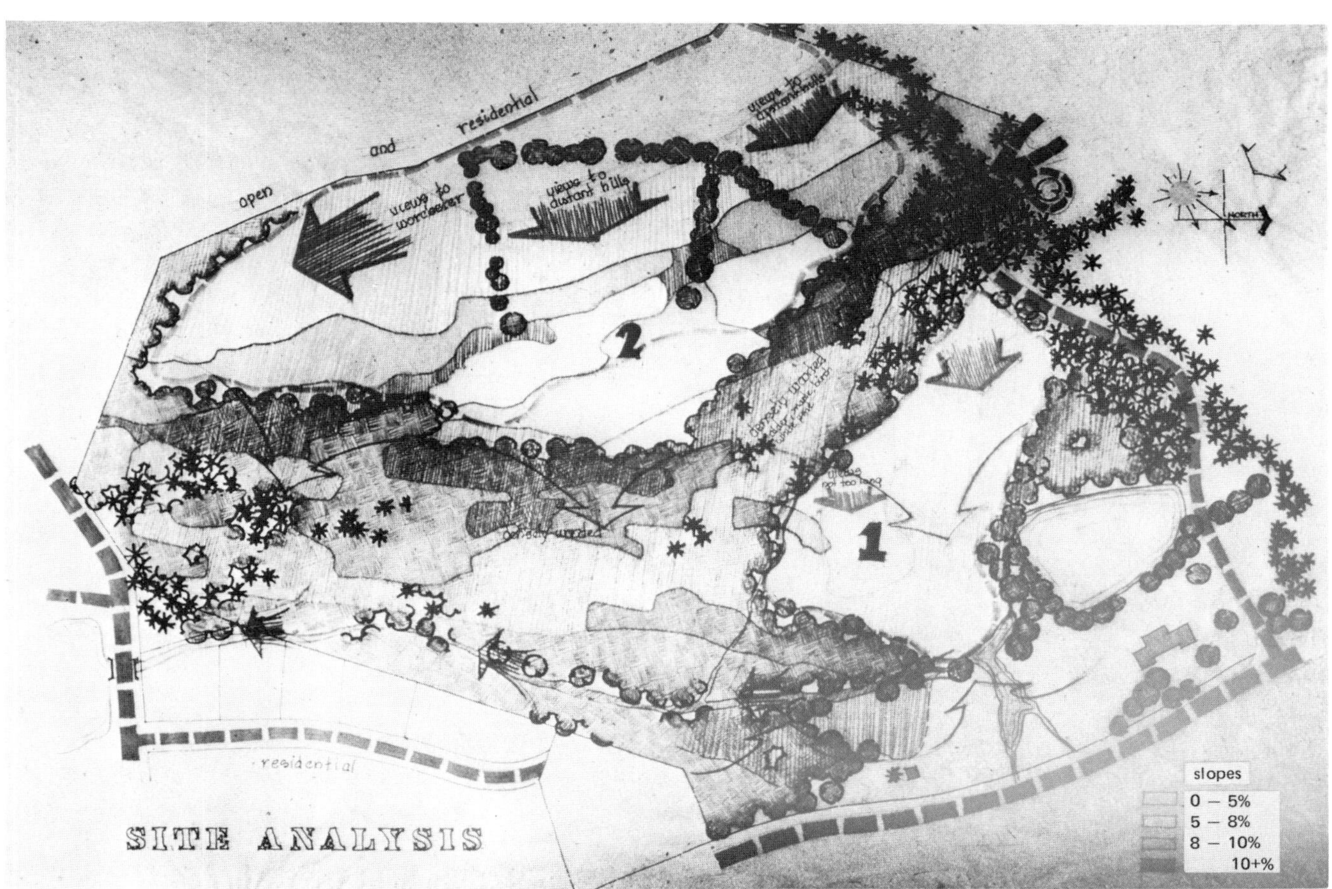

FIG. 1-4 Site analysis: the natural, cultural, and aesthetic factors of the site are graphically illustrated and the two possible building sites are numbered.

Synthesis, based on a land use plan, evolves from the analytical phase. The land use plan is developed from abstract relational diagrams that are rearranged by warping, shifting, stretching, or rotating them to adapt to physical conditions; they are not arbitrary. Therefore test as many alternatives as possible and list negative and positive points in order to choose the best diagram. The design synthesis will be an interpretation and articulation of factors into a design that fits the site without seriously altering functional relationships. (See Figs. 1-5 and 1-6.)

FIG. 1-5 Abstract relational diagram.

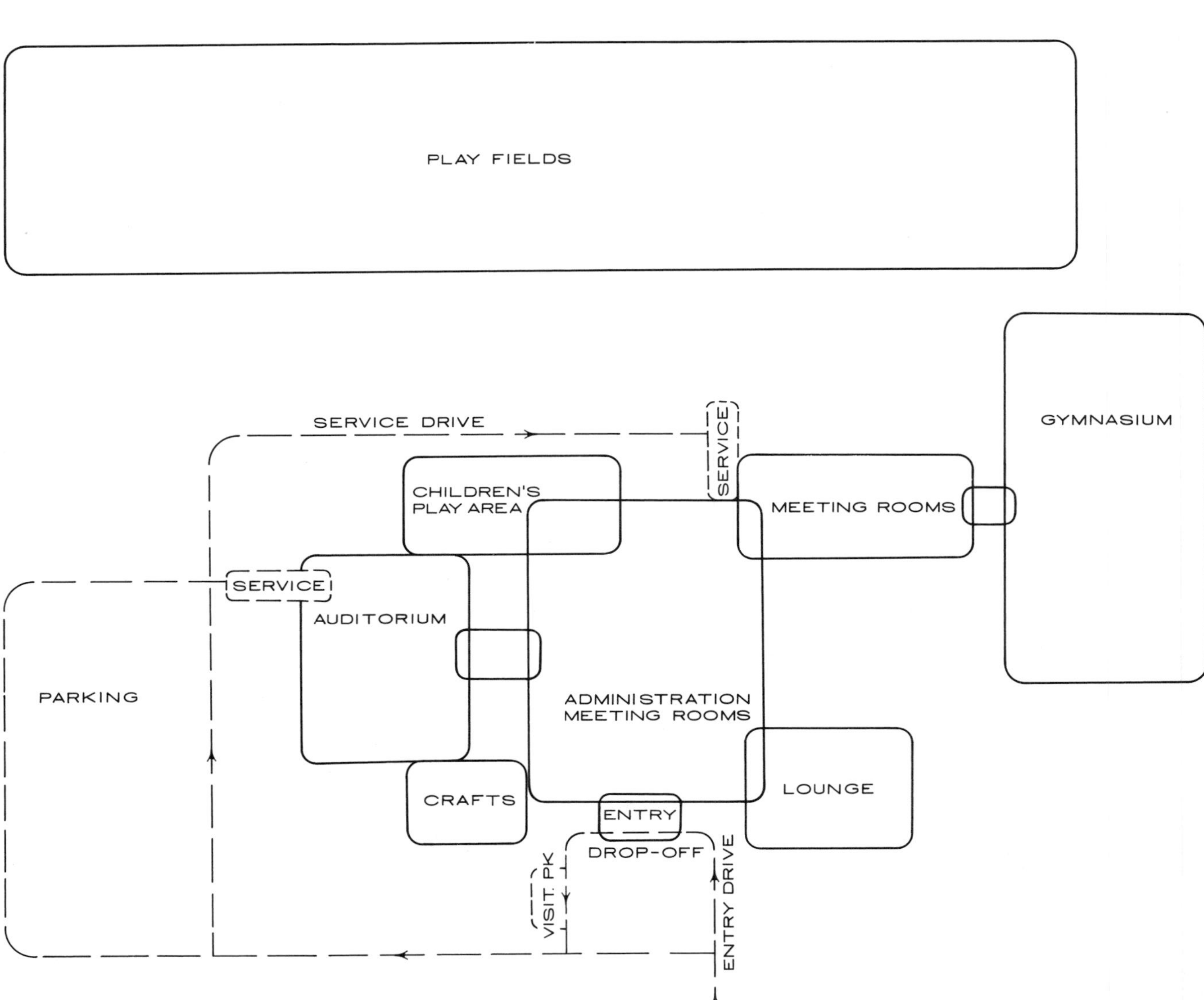

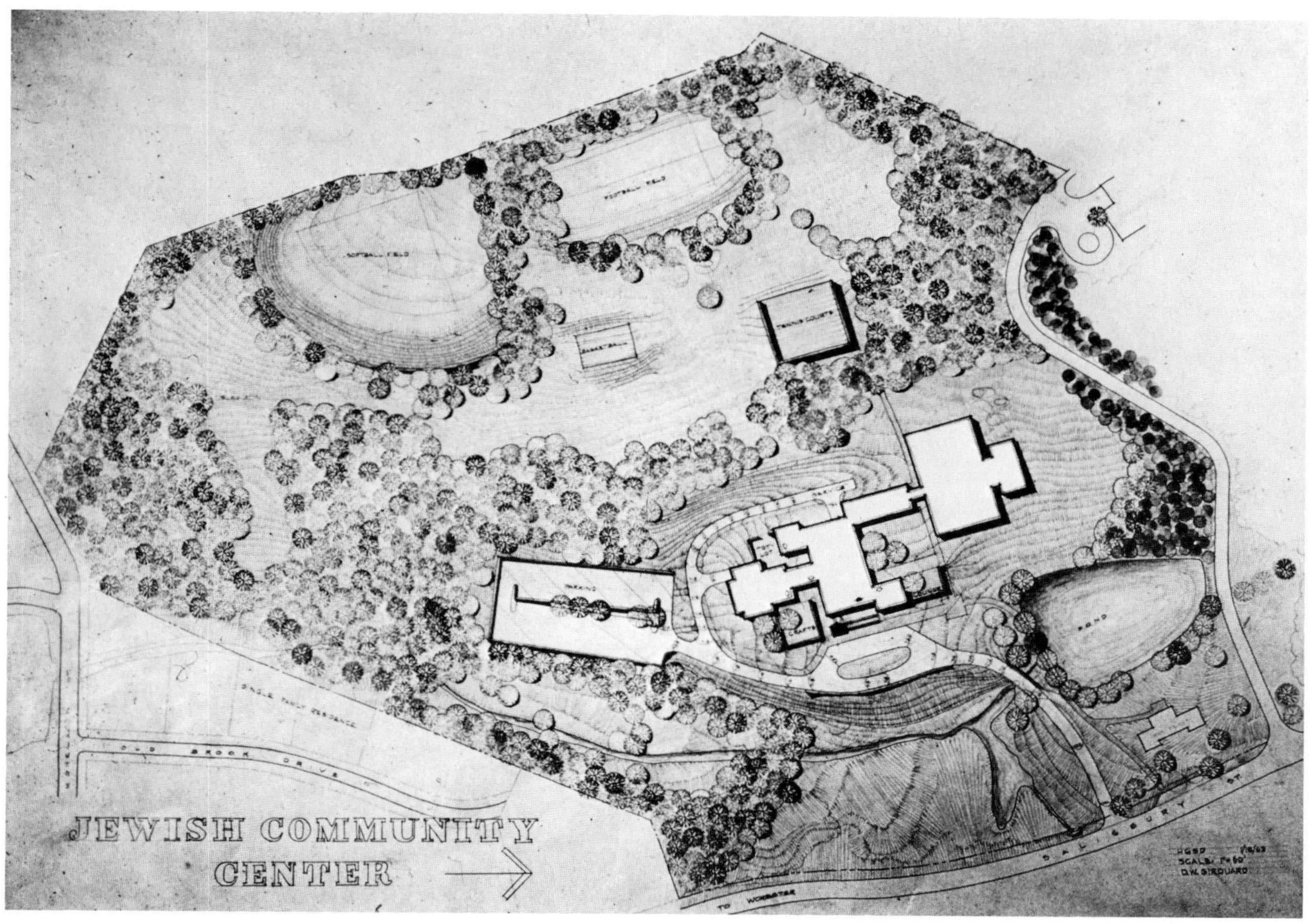

FIG. 1-6 Design development: building site one was chosen for development. In this location harmony is established between the community center and the existing landform on the site. There are good views of the building from Salisbury Street and the entry drive adapts well to topography. People approaching the building have a choice of using the drop-off area or driving directly to parking facilities.

FIG. 2-1 Nature within the urban fabric of the city: Central Park, New York City.

Chapter Two
Site Selection and Resource Analysis

Site investigation made concurrently with the formulation of program objectives insures the flexibility of the site's potential and the integration of its natural and cultural features with the design. To develop the best possible site for accommodating project objectives, a program must be carefully prepared. Because the program develops from specific needs, these needs determine the overall objectives.

Program development is based on the study of factors such as site requirements and sizes, types of building and site construction, and the uses of materials. The program is in a constant process of refinement as these factors are studied. The completely developed program will include a schedule of required facilities, their times of completion, and their priority for construction.

In the first of two methods of establishing a site alternative sites are considered within a general location and a choice is made of the one best meeting the preliminary objectives. This is a good approach to design. In the second method the site location is chosen by a client before the establishment of a program or even before a use for the site has been determined. An inappropriate site or factors of cost may lead to a forced site solution, one that often creates unnecessary problems, for example, excessive grading due to a forced solution may raise the estimated construction costs of a project, thereby compromising other program requirements, and it may well destroy the natural site features that could have been the primary reason for choosing the location.

On large projects such as campus planning, shopping centers, parks, or planned community developments site selection may require a detailed analysis of potential sites. The following method is a useful aid not only in selecting a site but also in analyzing one that has already been chosen. The analysis of the site and its environs includes all natural, cultural, and aesthetic factors that affect it. These features influence final site selection and provide clues to site personality that will be helpful in establishing guidelines for later development.

Any information inventoried should be illustrated graphically. On these illustrations important factors may be abstracted, or isolated and emphasized, to build a firm foundation from which to interrelate all known elements.

Natural Factors

1 Geology—bedrock and surficial.
2 Physiography—geomorphology, relief, topography.
3 Hydrology—surface and groundwater.
4 Soils—classification of types and uses.
5 Vegetation—plant ecology.
6 Wildlife—habitats.
7 Climate—solar orientation, wind, precipitation, and humidity.

Cultural Factors

1 Existing land use—ownership of adjacent property and off-site nuisances.
2 Traffic and transit—vehicular and pedestrian circulation on or adjacent to site.
3 Density and zoning—legal and regulatory controls.
4 Socioeconomic factors.
5 Utilities—sanitary and storm water systems, water, gas, steam, electricity, and telephone.
6 Existing buildings.
7 Historic factors—historic buildings, landmarks, and archaeology.

Aesthetic Factors

1 Natural features.
2 Spatial pattern—views, spaces, and sequences.

RESOURCE ANALYSIS PROCESS

In reviewing natural or ecological processes the characteristics of surface features, vegetation, and wildlife should reflect the sum of the components or layers below. These factors include geology, physiography, soils, and hydrology.

Overlay Mapping System

An overlay method of mapping natural determinants is often used to determine the suitability of a particular site for prospective land uses. In this process each natural factor such as geology is illustrated on black line prints, reproducible vellum, or acetate.

Matrix. A matrix can be developed of specific land use needs in relation to natural factors. (See Fig. 2-2.) For each land use desired the inventory maps (see Fig. 2-3) are interpreted for opportunities they offer. This interpretation may follow the Soil Conservation Service designation of limitations as slight, moderate, or severe. *Slight* soil limitation is the rating given to soils that have properties favorable for the rated use. Good performance and low maintenance can be expected. Areas rated with *moderate* limitations have characteristics moderately favorable to development but may require more planning or maintenance than areas rated slight. The third category called *severe* has one or more properties unfavorable for site use such as steep slopes, little depth to bedrock, or high water table. The limitations may require major site work to compensate for the degree of limitation.

FACTOR		VALUE TO SOCIETY				MINIMUM FOUNDATION			ON-SITE COSTS MAINTENANCE				WATER SUPPLY		MAXIMUM DESIRABILITY FOR LOCATION					ACTIVITY				
HYDROLOGY		HAZARDOUS TO HUMAN LIFE	HAZARDOUS TO HUMAN LIFE AND HEALTH BY SPECIFIC HUMAN ACTIONS	IRREPLACEABLE, UNIQUE OR SCARCE RESOURCE.	VULNERABLE RESOURCE REQUIRING REGULATION TO AVOID SOCIAL COSTS	PAVED SURFACES	LIGHT STRUCTURES	HEAVY STRUCTURES	SITE DRAINAGE	PAVED SURFACES	LAWNS	ON-SITE SEWAGE DISPOSAL	DOMESTIC USE	INDUSTRIAL USE	FAVORABLE MICROCLIMATE	TOPOGRAPHIC INTEREST	LONG VIEWS	SENSE OF ENCLOSURE	WATER RELATED VIEWS	RECREATION – FISHING	SWIMMING			
STREAM	GOOD QUALITY				● 3				●							●	●		●	●				
	MODERATE QUALITY		● 2		● 3																			
	UNKNOWN				● 3																			
	WETLANDS		● 2		● 4														●					
	FLOOD PRONE	● 1			● 5																			

1 SUBJECT TO 100 YEAR FLOOD.
2. VULNERABLE TO POLLUTION.
3. DEGRADATION OF RESOURCE WILL LEAD TO LOSS OF RECREATION VALUE.
4. ALTERATION OF THIS FACTOR WILL RESULT IN LOSS OF FLOOD STORAGE CAPACITY.
5. ANY OBSTRUCTION WILL RESULT IN ALTERATION AND DEGRADATION OF STREAM BEHAVIOR.

FIG. 2-2 Matrix of land use need and/or constraints in relation to a typical natural factor such as hydrology.

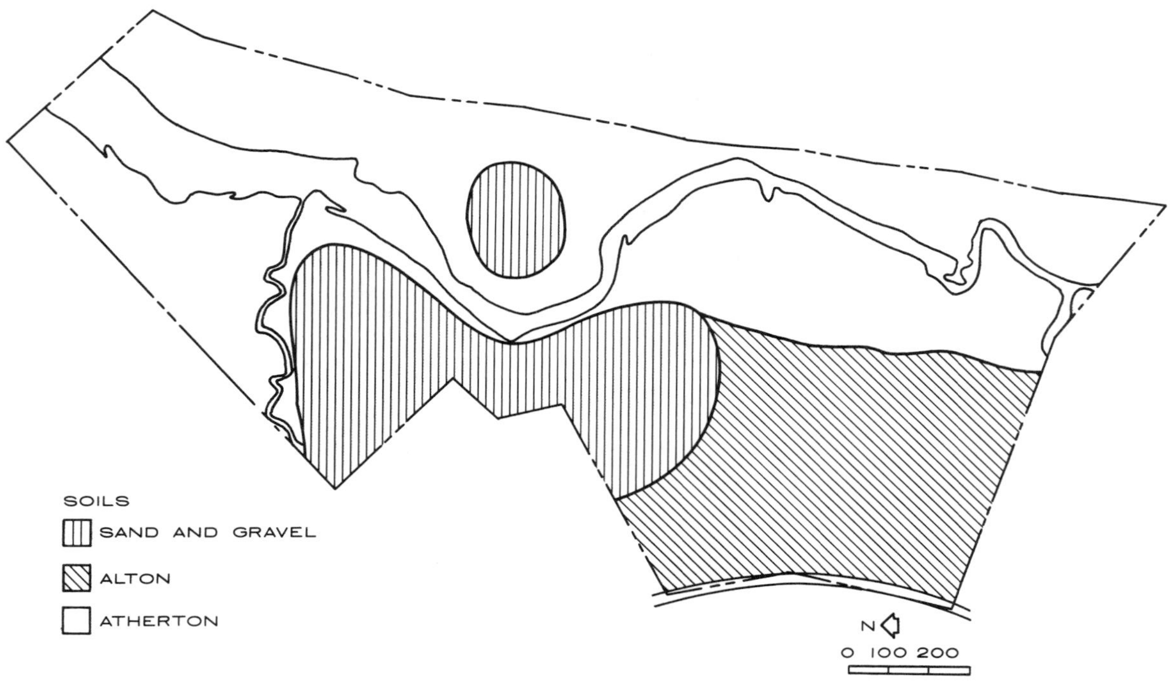

FIG. 2-3 Soils inventory map.

FIG. 2-4 Opportunity map based on slopes.

Opportunity Maps. The opportunity maps are overlaid to produce a composite map. (See Fig. 2-4.) This is done by use of a light table or by converting reproducible vellums onto acetate sheets by means of professional printing processes. Information, which is in black and white on the vellums, can be reproduced in various colors on the acetate sheets for ease of viewing.

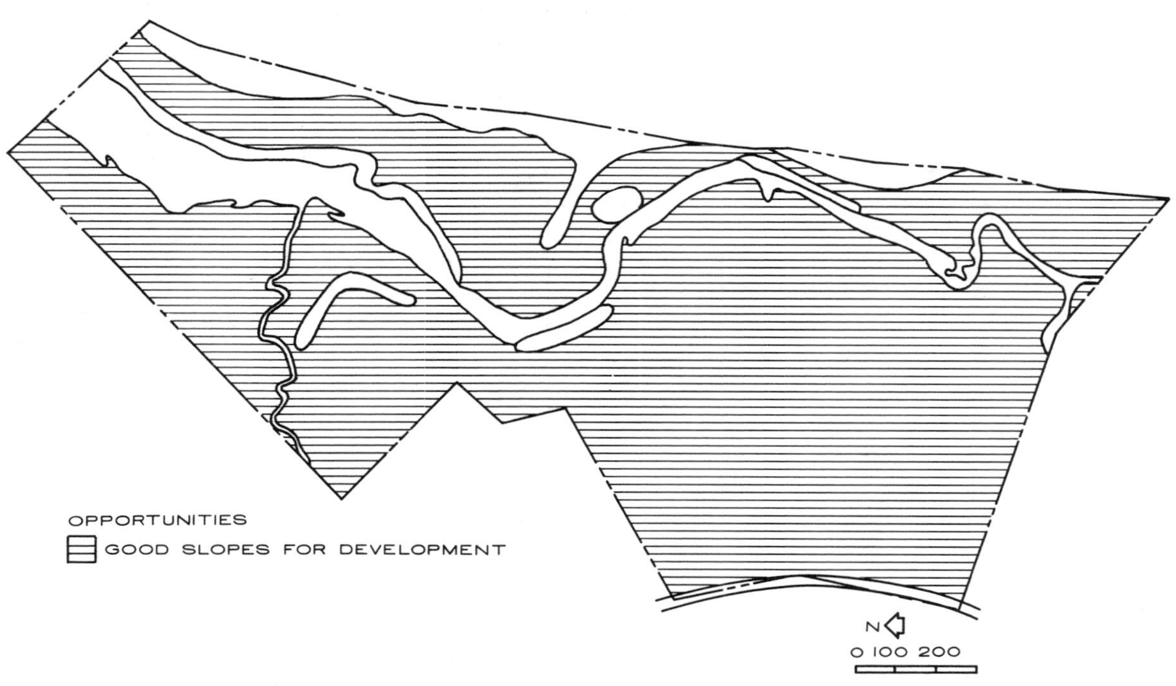

Constraint Maps. Constraints to development must also be mapped for each component to show their influence on development. (See Fig. 2-5.) These constraints are best expressed by the National Environmental Policy Act (NEPA) or by additional state or local regulations. These include areas (*a*) hazardous to life and health; (*b*) hazardous to human life and health by a specific human action; (*c*) having unique, scarce, or rare resources; and (*d*) having a vulnerable resource requiring regulation to avoid social cost. Where these constraints are identified, action may be necessitated by a community.

Suitability Maps. Constraint maps are now overlaid to form a composite map. From the previously discussed composite maps a synthesis of op-

FIG. 2-5 Constraints to development as a composite map.

FIG. 2-6 Suitability map: this is a composite of natural component overlays with opportunities for development in relation to areas with constraints.

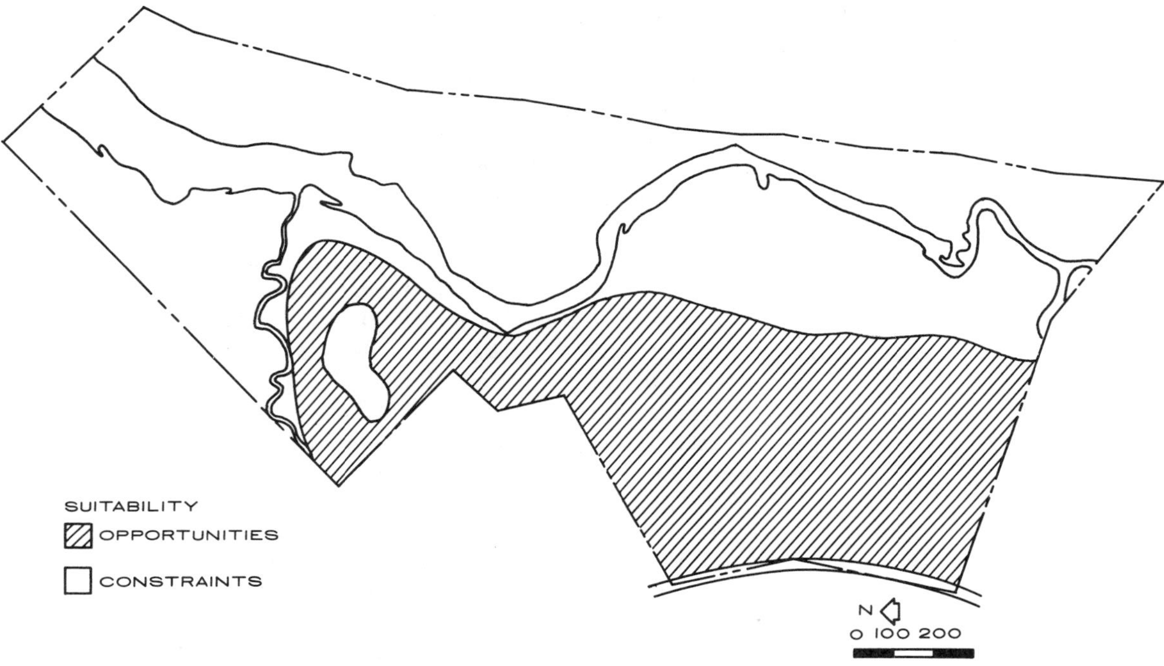

portunities and constraints is formed to produce a suitability map for a prospective use. (See Fig. 2-6.) In some cases there may be primary suitability for one use. In other cases several suitabilities may be present. User need and social, economic, or legal factors will help determine how the site is developed.

Computer mapping is being used with increased frequency to inventory and analyze resource data. The computer is particularly useful on large sites of many thousands of acres where data can be stored and recalled for many types of comparisons.

Considering these basic objectives the site planner should review each of the natural, cultural, and aesthetic factors applicable for site selection or for the development of a given site. How detailed these items are investigated depends on the project's complexity and size.

NATURAL FACTORS

In reviewing natural factors one can begin with historical geology and the interior of the earth, with its dense core of about 4224 miles in diameter and a mantle 1863 miles, which is less dense. The earth's crust ranges from 6.2 to 7.5 miles under the ocean basins to 18.5 to 25 miles under the continents. From bedrock geology one can work up to the earth's surface through the components of surficial geology, physiography, hydrology, and soils to study plant ecology, wildlife, and the effects of climate.

Geology

Which geologic processes have affected the site, its formation, and the type of bedrock below the surface of the soil? To understand the processes that have occurred in the past it is useful to review the historical evolution of a region. (See Fig. 2-7.)

Bedrock. *Bedrock* is consolidated rock material lying at various depths below all points of the earth's surface. The type and depth of bedrock presents many questions of its adequacy as a base for foundations of buildings, walls, or roads. Test borings taken at several locations on the site will provide the answers. These borings are located and plotted on topographic maps. The site planner may consult with a soils engineer to facilitate interpretation of the borings. (See Fig. 2-8 and Fig. 2-9.)

Surficial Geologic Materials. Above bedrock, surficial geologic materials extend to the surface soil. These materials may be porous and serve as acquifers. (See p. 19.)

Mass Movement of Land Surface. Some regions of the country are prone to movement of the earth's surface by tectonic movement through crustal stress, shock by earthquakes, or movement caused by surficial processes, including rockfalls, landslides, mudflows, and soil creep.

Tectonic movement may be caused along faults, often accompanying earthquakes. Many people live in unstable tectonic regions such as the earthquake belt, which includes the cities of Los Angeles and San Francisco.

Surficial processes also power mass movement of material by the force of gravity. These are often started by heavy rain or sudden thaws that saturate rock and soil with water to the point where gravity can cause movement. Shock, for example, by an earthquake can also cause movement.

In limestone areas subsidence may be caused as rock dissolves in solution. Subsidence also occurs when subsurface materials have been re-

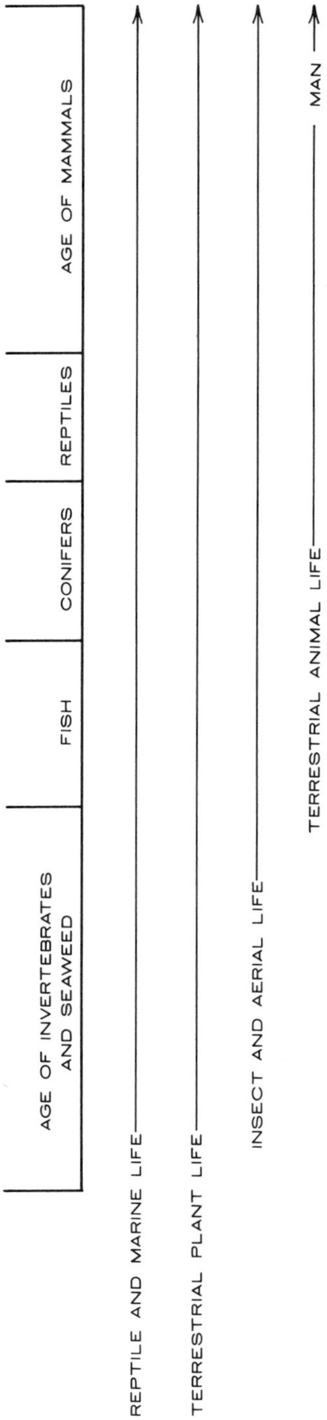

AGE OF MAMMALS
REPTILES
CONIFERS
FISH
AGE OF INVERTEBRATES AND SEAWEED

REPTILE AND MARINE LIFE
TERRESTRIAL PLANT LIFE
INSECT AND AERIAL LIFE
TERRESTRIAL ANIMAL LIFE
MAN

ERA	PERIOD		EPOCH	AGE IN MILLIONS
CENOZOIC	NEOGENE	QUATERNARY	RECENT	0.01 M
			PLEISTOCENE	1 M
			PLIOCENE	13 M
			MIOCENE	25 M
	PALEOGENE	TERTIARY	OLIGOCENE	36 M
			EOCENE	58 M
			PALEOCENE	65 M
MESOZOIC	CRETACEOUS			135 M
	JURASSIC			180 M
	TRIASSIC			230 M
PALEOZOIC	PERMIAN			280 M
	CARBON-IFEROUS	PENNSYLVANIAN		310 M
		MISSISSIPPIAN		350 M
	DEVONIAN			405 M
	SILURIAN			425 M
	ORDOVICIAN			500 M
	CAMBRIAN			600 M
ARCHEOZOIC PROTEROZOIC	PRECAMBRIAN		4.5 BILLION	
AZOIC	FORMATION OF EARTH		6 BILLION	

FIG. 2-7 Geologic time scale.

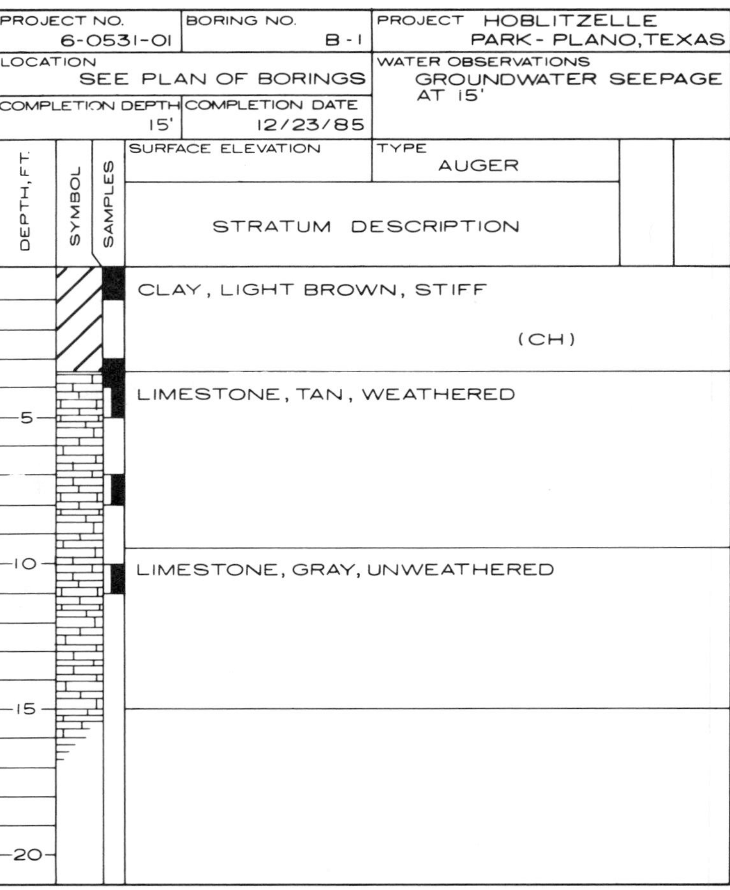

PROJECT NO.
6-0531-01
BORING NO.
B-1
PROJECT HOBLITZELLE PARK - PLANO, TEXAS
LOCATION
SEE PLAN OF BORINGS
WATER OBSERVATIONS
GROUNDWATER SEEPAGE AT 15'
COMPLETION DEPTH
15'
COMPLETION DATE
12/23/85
SURFACE ELEVATION
TYPE
AUGER
DEPTH, FT.
SYMBOL
SAMPLES
STRATUM DESCRIPTION
CLAY, LIGHT BROWN, STIFF
(CH)
LIMESTONE, TAN, WEATHERED
LIMESTONE, GRAY, UNWEATHERED
5
10
15
20

FIG. 2-8 Auger boring.

moved. An example is if liquid is pumped from weakly consolidated sediments or into areas where there has been coal mining. Movement by water, ice, and wind can also cause mass movement.

Special consideration must be given to development in permafrost areas where the surface is perennially frozen. If the surface is composed of silt, clay, or peat and it thaws by removal of the organic material called "muskeg," flow and creep can result. Transfer of heat during construction from structures built on frozen ground is a problem in permafrost areas and special engineering techniques are necessary.

Sources of Data. The U.S. Geological Survey provides Engineering Geology Maps of many areas showing various characteristics such as (*a*) distribution and thickness of rock formations; (*b*) terrain, slope, and slope stability; (*c*) drainage, permeability, and water table; (*d*) frost susceptibility; (*e*) suitability for foundations; (*f*) earthquake stability; (*g*) excavation characteristics; and (*h*) suitability for subgrade fill or borrow and compaction.

State Geologic Surveys also have data available with in-depth studies of some areas. This information can be ordered from state agencies or book stores, and university geology departments often have much data.

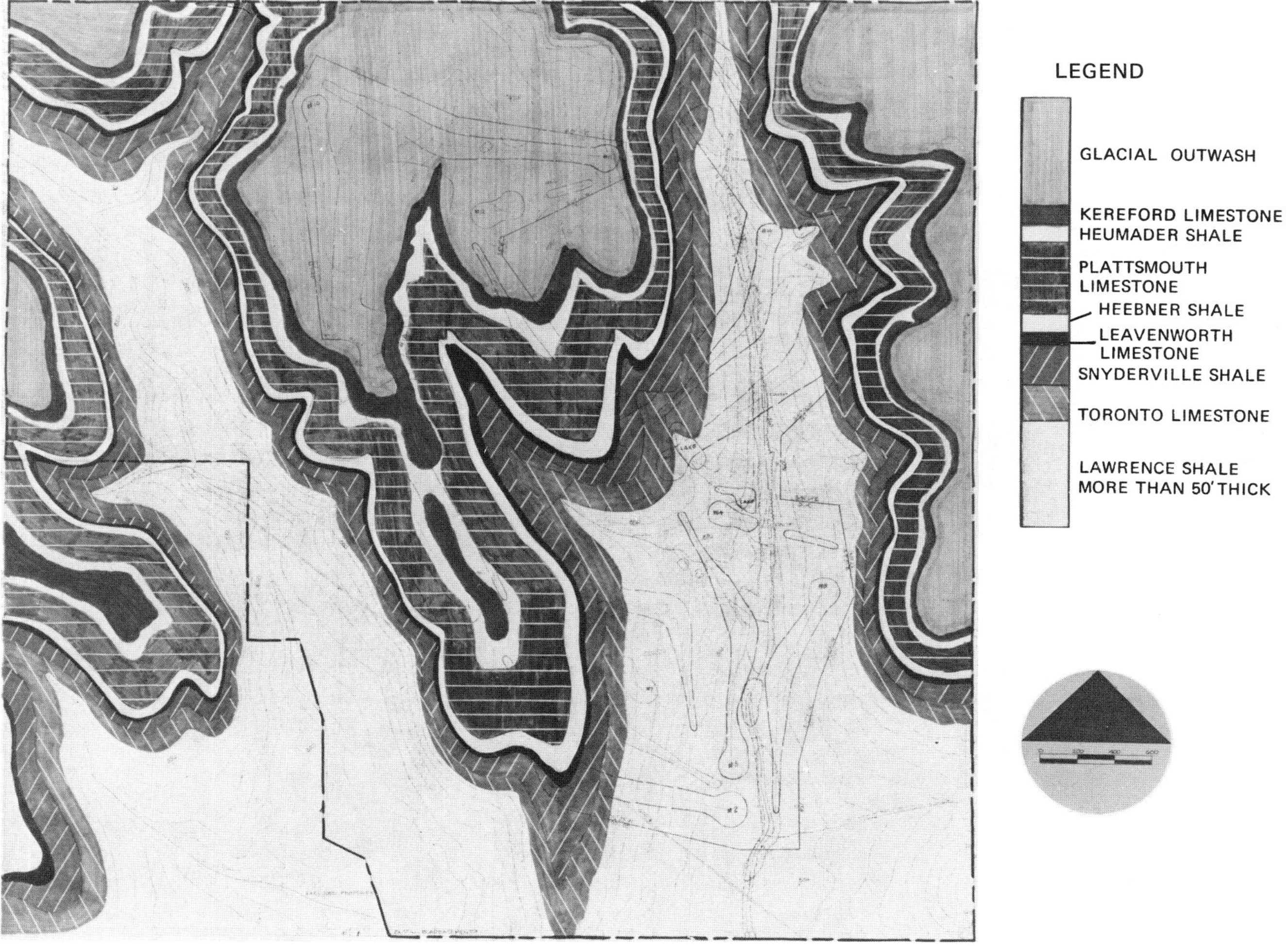

FIG. 2-9 Geologic base: the depth and type of rock below the soil's surface are significant factors in site development.

Physiography

The branch of geology dealing with the origin and nature of landforms is *geomorphology.* The description of landforms is *physiography.*

Landforms. Irregularities of the earth's surface are *landforms.* Knowledge of their kinds and characteristics will influence design if the site is part of, or encompasses, such an irregularity. Landforms are derived from volcanic, glacial, or erosional processes. They should be examined for their origin, topography, drainage, vegetation, and—when photographed for aerial identity and characteristics—tone. We will examine the characteristics of alluvial fans as an example. Alluvial fans occur, particularly in mountainous areas, where a stream discharges onto a plain or valley floor. The result is the formation of a fan-shaped landform. The fan shape varies in proportion to the size of the watershed. It develops as one or more divisions of the main stream channel deposit coarse sediments in the channel and the slope decreases. As the channel becomes choked and overflows, it builds up in elevation until the stream finds another location in a lower portion of the fan. This process is repeated until a symmetrical fan is formed over 90° or more.

The surfaces slope smoothly in all directions from the apex of the fan, which is the origin of the stream from the mountain. Slopes vary in relation to the texture of materials. They are relatively flat wherever fine materials are deposited. In fans formed from coarse materials the surface is marked with distributary channels. Alluvial fans may vary from a radius of several inches to several miles.

Young alluvial fans usually do not contain a surface drainage system, but older fans that have ceased to grow may have some surface runoff as floods overflow the parent stream. During periods of low water virtually all flow filters into the alluvial fan near the apex and moves as groundwater to the edge of the landform.

Vegetative cover in arid areas is principally grass with a few scattered trees. At the edge of the landform, heavier vegetation may be evident if seepage water is present. Being heavier in association with distributary channels, vegetation in humid areas may cover the entire alluvial fan.

Tone of the landform is generally light with radiating lines of darker tones coinciding with the abandoned channels.

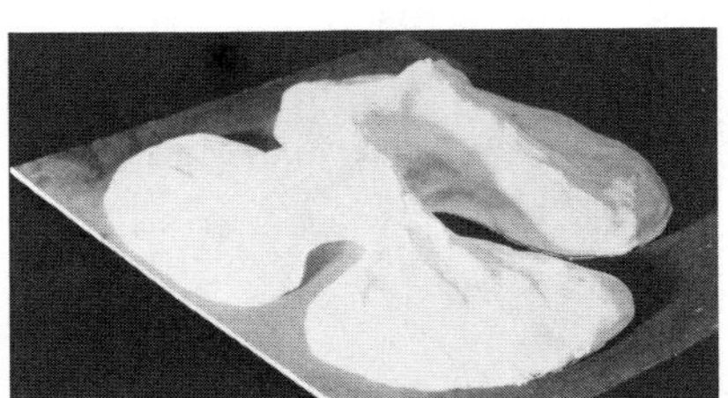

FIG. 2-10 Alluvial fan abstracted in model.

The importance of alluvial fans is based on their being well drained and adaptable to development of all types. They have good air drainage, views, and groundwater. In times of storm, however, the unstable distributary channels may shift, thereby eroding a new channel or completely covering a developed area with a new layer of debris brought down by a newly formed system of distributaries. (See Fig. 2-10.)

By use of aerial photographs viewed stereoscopically, geologic and physical features become distinguishable to the educated eye, and patterns influencing future land use may evolve. A site planner untrained in aerial photo interpretation may consult a geologist.

Topographic Surveys

The analysis of a site and its environs presupposes that topographic maps have been obtained. These maps, available from the U.S. Geological Survey, show locations and elevations of natural as well as man-made features, relief, and vegetation. They cover most areas of the United States at a scale of 1:24,000 or 1 in. = 2000 ft. They come in the 7.5 minute series, with a 10 ft contour level. Specific characteristics such as relief, hydrography, roads, buildings, and features such as bogs, swamps, and marshes are indicated.

When a more detailed topographic map such as 1 in. = 40 ft is required for an area that has not already been surveyed, the site planner should employ a registered surveyor to obtain the necessary data. Methods of surveying may differ; however, aerial surveys are often used for sites covering large areas such as city or state parks, university campuses, or housing subdivisions. (See Fig. 2-11.)

Information Required on Topographic Maps

1 Title, location, owner's name, engineer, certification, and date.
2 True and magnetic north, scale.
3 Property and building lines.
4 Existing easements, rights of way on or adjacent to site.
5 Names of property owners on adjacent sites.
6 Location of structures on site, basement and first floor elevations of buildings, as well as walls, curbs, steps, ramps, tree wells, drives, and parking lots.
7 Location and sizes of storm and sewage systems; manhole, catch basin, and curb inlet drains with rim and invert elevations.

FIG. 2-11 Aerial photography aids in obtaining an overall view of the site.

8 Outline of wooded areas, location, elevation on ground, and type and size of trees with 3–4 in. trunk caliper or larger.
9 Hydrographic features—rivers, lakes, streams, swamps.
10 Location of telephone poles, light standards, fire hydrants.
11 Rock outcrops or other outstanding site features.
12 Road elevations at intervals of 50 ft.
13 Grid system of elevations at intervals of 50 ft.
14 Contour interval—1, 2, or 5 ft.

Slope Analysis

A slope analysis aids in recognizing areas on the site that lend themselves to building locations, roads, parking, or play areas. It may also show if construction is feasible. A parking lot, for example, should have a grade of under 5%. If no available land meets this requirement, regrading will be necessary. The cost of grading may determine whether the development of a site is feasible.

A typical breakdown of grades would be 0–5, 5–8, 8–10, 10–15, 15–20, 20–25, and 25+. These grades are established by measuring the distance between contours at a given scale and contour interval. The formula is D = contour interval ÷ % grade × 100, where D is the distance between contours at a particular grade to be set. To set a 5% grade at a contour interval of 2 ft the equation would be

$$D = \frac{\text{contour interval}}{\%\ \text{grade}} \times 100$$

$$D = \frac{2\ \text{ft}}{5\%} \times 100$$

$$D = 40\ \text{ft}$$

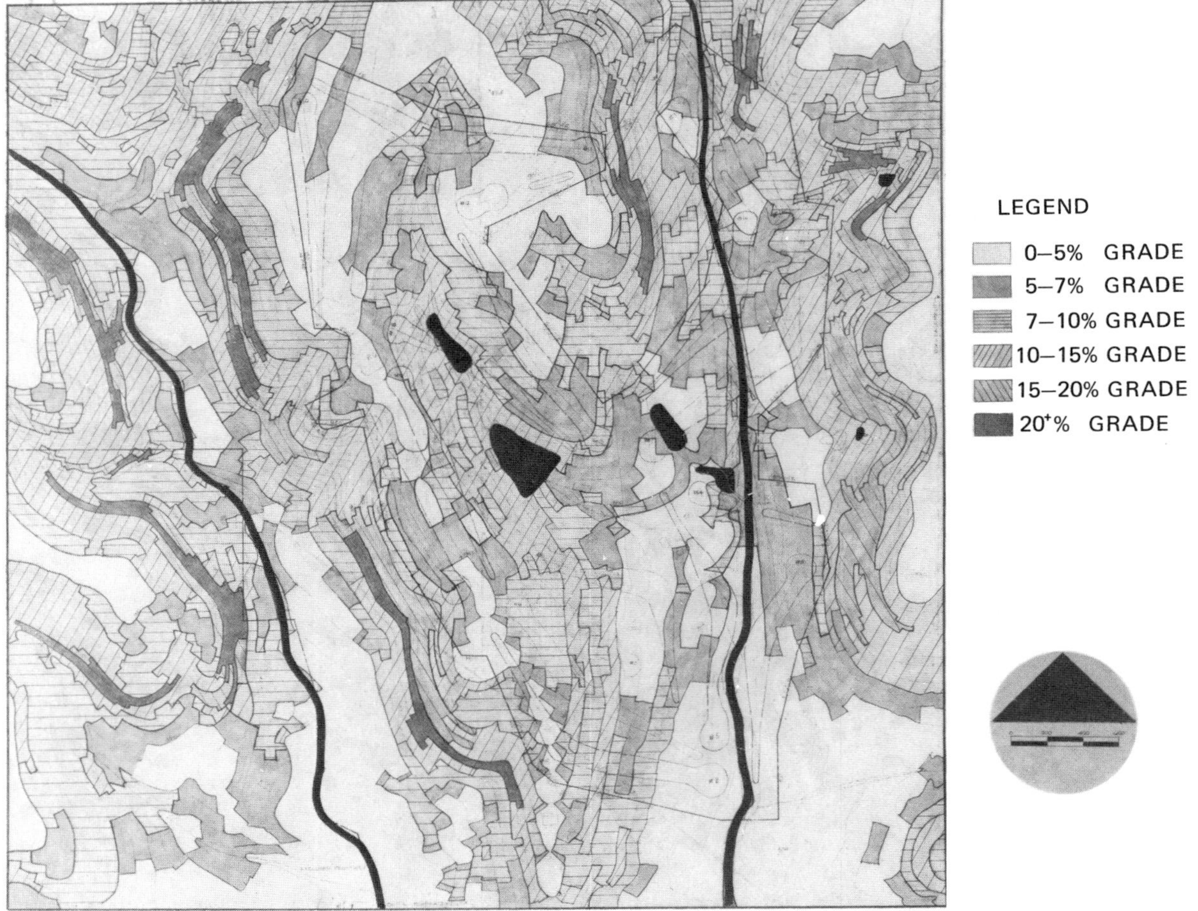

FIG. 2-12 Slope analysis.

The overall pattern of slopes will emerge through slope analysis, which helps the site planner determine the best land uses for various portions of the site, along with feasibility of construction. (See Fig. 2-12.)

Hydrology

Both the surface and subsurface drainage patterns on a site may greatly influence land use. All water bodies—rivers, streams, drainage channels, marshes, or wetlands, floodplains, and acquifers—must be inventoried and analyzed for their opportunities or constraints. Hydrologic features have a bearing in relating activities to the land and are of primary importance in developing a system for site drainage that makes use of existing watershed drainage patterns. (See Fig. 2-13.) In the United States over half of the precipitation runs over land surfaces and into water bodies or wetlands. The rest either percolates through the soil or is intercepted and taken up by vegetation.

Marshes. In some locations a resource such as a marsh may be a scarce or unique feature requiring protection. Some fresh and salt water marshes provide wildlife habitat of much value. For example, when the New Jersey Sports and Exposition Complex was constructed in the Hackensack Meadowlands several areas of marshland were preserved. A small stand of oak trees and other species was also relocated because of their unique qualities.

Floodplains. Floodplains must also be studied carefully for 50 year and 100 year storms to see if all development should be excluded or if a land use such as recreation may be located that would receive little damage by flooding. In building adjacent to streams or rivers detailed flood studies and special permits may be necessary from state agencies. Information on floodways or those areas adjacent to streams and rivers inundated by 100 year storms may be available from the U.S. Army Corps of Engineers or the Geological Survey, the best source of data. Floodplain mapping for insurance may also be available from planning agencies.

Acquifers. Acquifers are water-bearing strata of rock, gravel, or sand in which groundwater is stored. Located by use of geologic maps, acquifers are a very valuable resource of potable water. These resources should be protected from uses such as septic systems that may pollute the acquifer. Even sewer lines may leak pollutants and be hazardous.

Acquifer recharge areas are the points where surface water meets or interchanges with an acquifer. The movement of groundwater contributes to the surface water in streams and rivers especially in periods of low flow. Polluted rivers or streams can therefore contaminate acquifers.

In areas where an acquifer has porous strata above it, percolation from the surface drainage will recharge it. Percolation of pollutants can also pollute it. The acquifer can be recharged and protected by carefully impounding clean streams crossing it.

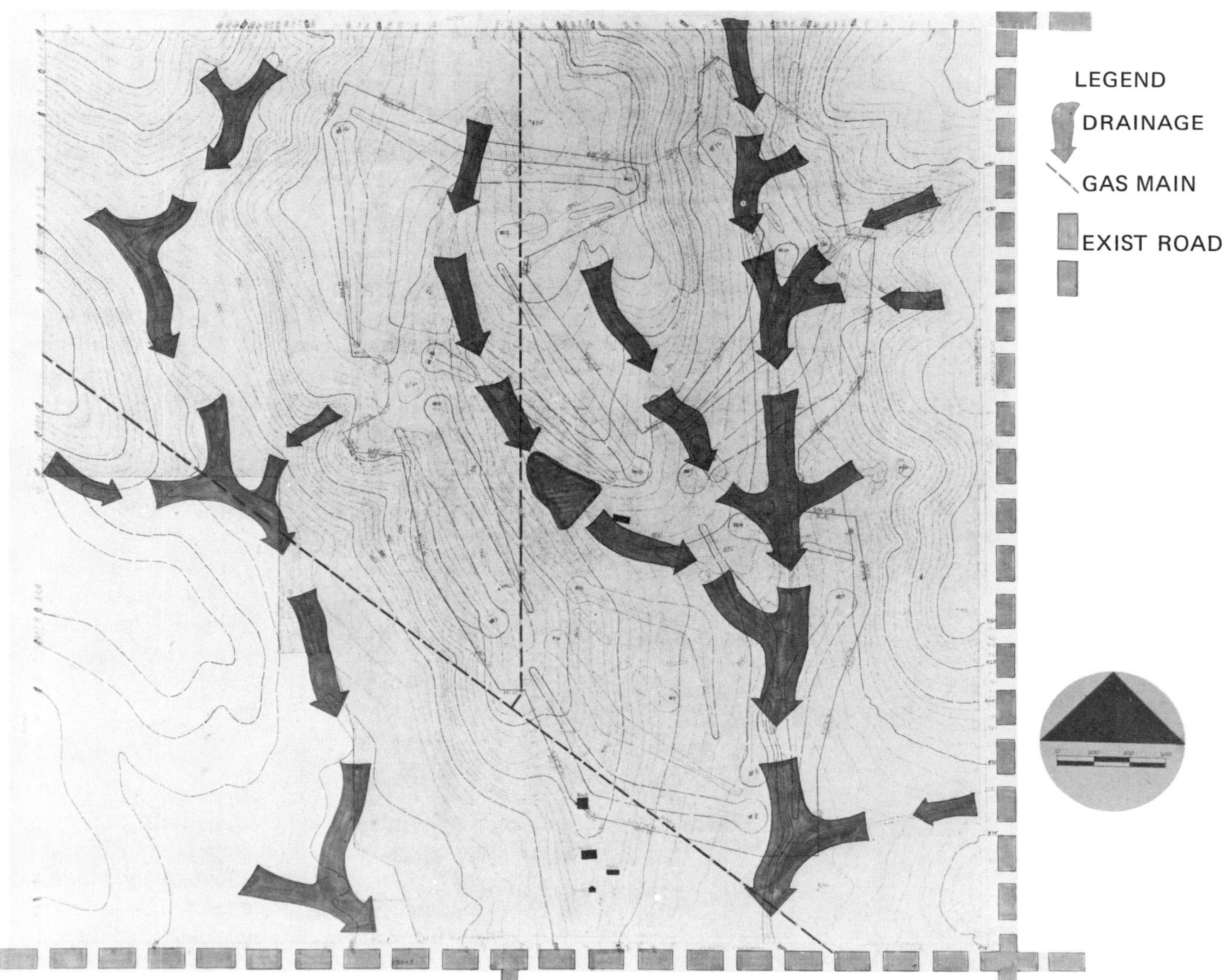

FIG. 2-13 Drainage patterns.

Soils

What types of soils exist on a particular site? What types of land uses are suitable? The U.S. Soil Conservation Service has offices in most counties throughout each state. Many of the counties have published soil surveys classifying each soil and provide soil properties significant to site planning. The surveys are 80% accurate or to 1.1 acres. Data are available on factors such as depth to bedrock, seasonal high water table, permeability, shrink-swell potential, and vegetation. Suitability for land uses such as absorption fields for septic tanks, sewage lagoons, streets and parking, dwellings with basements, pond or reservoir areas, recreation facilities such as athletic fields, campsites, golf fairways, topsoil, sand terraces, diversions, crops, and pasture.

Other information is provided on vegetation related to soils and wildlife habitat. Soil pH, its alkalinity or salinity, is also indicated, but special tests may be made by sending a soil sample to the agricultural department of state universities or to a soils lab.

The data in the soil surveys for a particular site are valuable in determining suitability for land uses. For example, the depth of water table is important. If it is too close to the surface ±6 ft, there will be adverse effects on a building basement, and the project cost will rise as increased waterproofing, pumping, and the use of pilings become necessary. If the water table is too low, problems of water supply and cost may occur.

In areas where septic tanks are to be used in conjunction with residential development, the ability of soils to absorb and degrade sewage effluent quickly must be studied. If the soil is not suited for this use, problems such as water pollution and the smell of raw sewage will occur. Test pits to study the percolation of water into the soil are usually required for on-lot septic systems. These tests are monitored by community inspectors to make sure the site has adequate capacity to absorb effluent.

Vegetation

On small sites existing vegetation must be reviewed before development takes place. Trees take a long time to reach maturity and preserving existing vegetation can be most important to the overall design of a project and to its economy since many small trees will not have to be purchased and subsequently require many years to reach maturity.

Note the name, size, and location of large existing trees 3–4 in. or more in caliper. Observe their form, branch structure, foliage color, and texture. If a site is heavily wooded, a carefully planned thinning of the trees may open potential vistas.

Review the ecology of the surrounding area to find which trees or shrubs are native and which varieties may be added for wind protection, shade, buffer zones, screens, or backdrops. Having previously reviewed soil characteristics, the analyst should also research which, if any, nutrients must be added for improved plant growth. (See Fig. 2-14.)

Plant Ecology

The plant ecology on a large site must be studied carefully. A plant ecologist who knows about the types, pattern, and distribution of plants can contribute much information about their environments. Vegetation is a good indicator of soil and microclimate. For example, certain types of trees such as red maples grow in wet areas while others like well-drained sites such as the oak and hickory association.

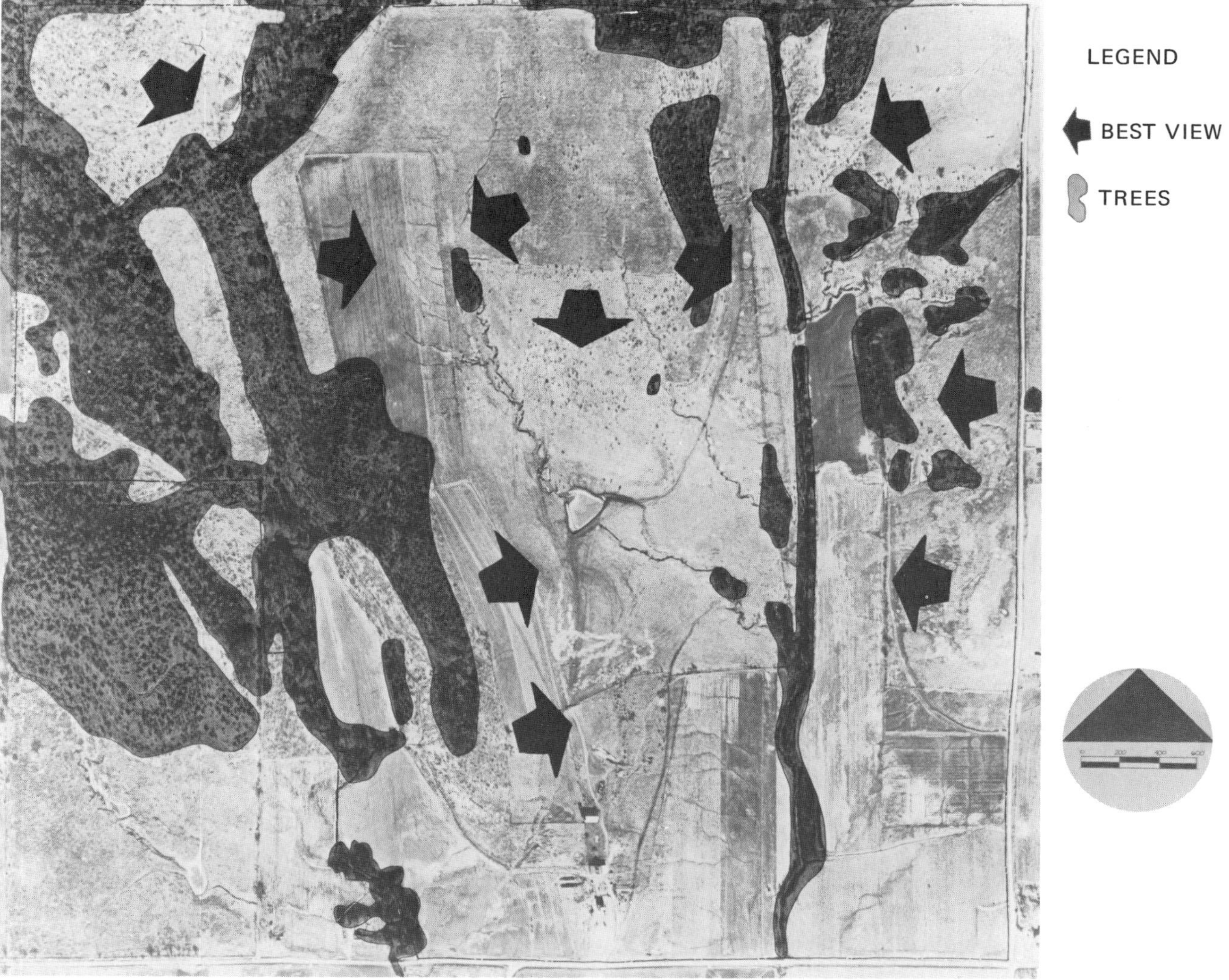

FIG. 2-14 Vegetation: the location and identification of vegetation on a site help to preserve and take advantage of native plant material.

Ecosystems

Earth, water, air, and sunlight are abiotic (nonliving). They provide the base in which plants and animals may grow. Biotic or living elements combine in complex relationships with abiotic elements to produce ecosystems. Two broad classes of ecosystems are terrestrial (land related) and aquatic.

Terrestrial Ecosystems. Ecosystems may vary with location because of physical circumstances that encourage development of plant and animal relations best adapted to a set of conditions. The basic biologic building blocks are plants. Only plants, using the process of photosynthesis in the presence of sunlight, can remove carbon dioxide from the air and return oxygen to it to sustain life and growth. Interaction between climate, geologic materials, water, plants, and animals inhabiting an area produce distinct communities.

Communities often cover large areas exhibiting many similar characteristics, with the largest area or "major life zone" being the biome.

The biome is based on the general character of mature vegetation and animal life associated with the plant community. Biomes include tundra, northern coniferous forest, moist temperate coniferous forest, temperate deciduous forest, broad-leaved evergreen subtropical forest, temperate grassland, tropical savanna, desert, chaparral, piñon-juniper, tropical rain forest, tropical scrub and deciduous, and zonation in mountains.

Biomes are distributed based on climatic, topographic, and geographic characteristics. Within an area of a dominant formation of plants such as a deciduous forest there may be smaller formations of a different type.

The species of trees and shrubs comprising an association such as oak-hickory or beech-maple may be found singly in pure stands or combined with plants of other associations, especially contiguous to the border zone of dominant associations. Plant communities making up an association are called types.

Plant communities found in an association, a formation, or a biome represent the end product of vegetational development called "climatic climax" for a specific set of physical conditions called "succession." Several plant communities may occupy a site, each to be displaced consecutively by a new community until the climax appears. The climax condition is capable of self-perpetuation and is not subject to displacement by other pioneering plants.

Secondary succession takes place when an established climax community is eliminated by natural disaster such as forest fire or by action taken in clearing and cultivating the land. The return to climax condition may take many stages of succession.

Under conditions limiting tolerance such as topography, soil, water, or fire, a plant community may never develop to a climax stage, undergoing instead "edaphic climax." This state occurs when sites are too wet or dry or have poor soil. An example is the New Jersey pine barrens where the oak-yellow poplar climatic climax does not develop, but an edaphic climax of pitch pine and scrub oak occurs. This takes place because of dry soils and periodic fires.

Succession may also be restrained by timber management, grazing, or crops. This stage is "disclimax." If these activities are stopped succession to climatic climax will eventually occur.

Wildlife

Wildlife relates closely to habitats provided by plant communities. Various habitat elements are essential to the different species of wildlife. The Soil Conservation Service divides these elements into three groups: openland, woodland, and wetland.

Openland Wildlife. Openland wildlife includes birds and mammals commonly associated with crop fields, meadows, pastures, and nonforested overgrown lands. Habitat elements essential for openland wildlife include combinations of (*a*) grain and seed crops, (*b*) grasses and legumes, (*c*) wild herbaceous upland plants, and (*d*) hardwood woody plants.

Woodland Wildlife. These species need various combinations of (*a*) grasses and legumes; (*b*) wild herbaceous upland plants; (*c*) hardwood woody plants as just mentioned; and (*d*) cone-bearing shrubs such as pines, cedars, and yews.

Wetland Wildlife. Wetland species include birds and mammals needing habitats with (*a*) wetland food plants or wild herbaceous plants of moist to wet sites, exclusive of submerged or floating aquatic plants; (*b*) shallow water development with impoundments for the control of water where the depth generally does not exceed 5 ft; (*c*) excavated ponds of impounded areas with ample supplies of water of suitable quality and depth for fish and wildlife such as one quarter acre ponds of 6 ft average depth; (*d*) streams.

Wildlife is an important consideration, especially when choosing sites for park or recreation areas. Since fishing and hunting are major recreational activities, choosing land for these uses depends on wildlife as a natural resource.

Wildlife also adds color, form, and movement to the landscape. Existing wooded areas inhabited by wildlife may be preserved as parkland, along with residential subdivisions.

Climate

Local climatological data are available for many areas from the U.S. Department of Commerce, National Oceanic and Atmospheric Administration, Asheville, North Carolina. Information is recorded daily, with some localities having monthly summaries. Daily records include daily minimum and maximum temperature and precipitation and monthly summaries.

Data summaries for each year include average temperature, degree days, precipitation, relative humidity, wind speed and direction, total precipitation, and snowfall. (See Fig. 2-15.)

Humidity is the amount of water vapor in the air. *Relative humidity* is the amount of vapor the air is holding expressed as a percentage of the amount the air can hold at a particular temperature.

If at a particular temperature air is saturated with water vapor it has 100% relative humidity. Warmer temperatures are capable of holding more water vapor before saturation is reached.

Degree day is a unit based on temperature difference and the time used in estimating fuel consumption and specifying the nominal heating load of a building in the winter. For any one day, when the mean temperature is less than 65°F, there exists as many degree days as the difference in degrees below 65°F. For example, if the temperature dropped to 30°F, there would be 35 degree days.

For each 300 ft rise in height from the earth's surface, temperature decreases approximately 1°F in the summer. Certain cities (Brazilia, for example) are located at higher altitudes in the otherwise hot climate of the tropics. Differing height in topography also affects microclimate; cool air flows toward low points or valleys at night, but higher side slopes remain warmer.

Precipitation and temperature are the two major factors affecting vegetation, although wind, humidity, and soil characteristics are also important influences.

In cool and temperate climates vegetation may be used to block winter winds. Sometimes trees have adjusted to being part of a forest area and, if left to stand alone as a single element, may die because of strong winter winds. Wooded areas can also be opened or thinned to allow sunlight pockets for residential or other developments in cool climates. Deciduous trees are used to provide shade and may alter microclimate several degrees in summer. This can be important for energy conservation.

Water bodies also influence the climate of the site. Oceans and large lakes retain their heat in winter months as land masses cool and they are cool in summer as land masses warm. The water bodies adjacent to land, therefore, moderate temperature. This influence decreases with the distance inland from the water body.

Climates can be divided into four general types—cool, temperate, hot

NORMALS, MEANS, AND EXTREMES

DALLAS – FORT WORTH, TEXAS

LATITUDE: 32°54'N LONGITUDE: 97°02'W ELEVATION: FT. (grd) 551 (msl) 596 TIME ZONE: CENTRAL WBAN: 03927

	(a)	JAN	FEB	MAR	APR	MAY	JUNE	JULY	AUG	SEP	OCT	NOV	DEC	YEAR
TEMPERATURE °F:														
Normals														
-Daily Maximum		54.0	59.1	67.2	76.8	84.4	93.2	97.8	97.3	89.7	79.5	66.2	58.1	76.9
-Daily Minimum		33.9	37.8	44.9	55.0	62.9	70.8	74.7	73.7	67.5	56.3	44.9	37.4	55.0
-Monthly		44.0	48.5	56.0	65.9	73.7	82.0	86.3	85.5	78.6	67.9	55.5	47.8	66.0
Extremes														
-Record Highest	31	88	88	96	95	99	113	110	108	105	102	89	88	113
-Year		1969	1959	1974	1972	1980	1980	1980	1964	1953	1979	1955	1955	JUN 1980
-Record Lowest	31	4	9	15	30	41	51	59	56	43	29	20	5	4
-Year		1964	1978	1980	1973	1978	1964	1972	1967	1984	1980	1959	1983	JAN 1964
NORMAL DEGREE DAYS:														
Heating (base 65°F)		651	469	313	85	0	0	0	0	0	56	300	533	2407
Cooling (base 65°F)		0	7	37	112	275	510	660	636	408	146	18	0	2809
% OF POSSIBLE SUNSHINE	6	53	58	59	64	64	71	81	77	74	61	62	56	65
MEAN SKY COVER (tenths)														
Sunrise - Sunset	31	6.1	5.7	5.9	6.0	5.8	4.8	4.2	4.2	4.7	4.7	5.1	5.6	5.2
MEAN NUMBER OF DAYS:														
Sunrise to Sunset														
-Clear	31	9.8	9.9	9.6	8.6	8.3	11.3	15.3	15.0	13.1	13.7	12.3	11.4	138.4
-Partly Cloudy	31	5.6	5.8	7.6	7.9	10.9	11.4	9.4	10.0	8.5	7.5	6.0	6.3	97.0
-Cloudy	31	15.5	12.5	13.7	13.5	11.8	7.3	6.4	6.0	8.4	9.8	11.7	13.4	129.9
Precipitation .01 inches or more	31	7.0	6.4	7.3	8.2	8.7	5.9	4.9	4.7	6.8	6.1	5.7	6.1	77.8
Snow, Ice pellets 1.0 inches or more	31	0.6	0.4	0.1	0.0	0.0	0.0	0.0	0.0	0.0	0.0	0.*	0.1	1.2
Thunderstorms	31	0.9	1.7	4.1	6.0	7.3	5.9	4.7	4.6	3.5	2.9	1.5	1.0	44.1
Heavy Fog Visibility 1/4 mile or less	31	2.7	1.7	1.1	0.7	0.4	0.1	0.0	0.*	0.1	0.9	1.4	2.5	11.8
Temperature °F														
-Maximum														
90° and above	21	0.0	0.0	0.2	0.7	3.7	19.7	27.8	26.7	14.1	2.7	0.0	0.0	95.6
32° and below	21	1.9	0.5	0.0	0.0	0.0	0.0	0.0	0.0	0.0	0.0	0.0	0.7	3.1
-Minimum														
32° and below	21	15.8	10.0	2.8	0.1	0.0	0.0	0.0	0.0	0.0	0.*	2.5	9.6	40.8
0° and below	21	0.0	0.0	0.0	0.0	0.0	0.0	0.0	0.0	0.0	0.0	0.0	0.0	0.0
AVG. STATION PRESS. (mb)	12	999.6	997.8	993.3	993.2	991.7	992.8	994.2	994.2	994.8	996.5	997.4	998.3	995.3
RELATIVE HUMIDITY (%)														
Hour 00	21	73	71	70	73	79	73	66	67	75	73	73	73	72
Hour 06 (Local Time)	21	79	79	79	82	87	85	80	81	85	82	80	78	81
Hour 12	21	61	58	57	57	60	55	48	50	56	55	56	59	56
Hour 18	21	59	53	51	53	57	50	44	45	54	55	58	59	53
PRECIPITATION (inches):														
Water Equivalent														
-Normal		1.65	1.93	2.42	3.63	4.27	2.59	2.00	1.76	3.31	2.47	1.76	1.67	29.46
-Maximum Monthly	31	3.60	6.20	6.39	12.19	13.66	7.85	11.13	6.85	9.52	14.18	6.23	6.99	14.18
-Year		1968	1965	1968	1957	1982	1981	1973	1970	1964	1981	1964	1971	OCT 1981
-Minimum Monthly	31	0.13	0.15	0.10	0.59	0.99	0.40	0.09	T	0.09	T	0.20	0.17	T
-Year		1976	1963	1972	1983	1977	1964	1965	1980	1984	1975	1970	1981	AUG 1980
-Maximum in 24 hrs	31	2.39	4.06	4.39	4.55	4.86	3.11	3.76	4.05	4.76	5.91	2.83	3.10	5.91
-Year		1975	1965	1977	1957	1965	1966	1975	1976	1965	1959	1964	1971	OCT 1959
Snow, Ice pellets														
-Maximum Monthly	31	12.1	13.5	2.5								5.0	2.6	13.5
-Year		1964	1978	1962								1976	1963	FEB 1978
-Maximum in 24 hrs	31	12.1	7.5	2.5								4.8	2.5	12.1
-Year		1964	1978	1962								1976	1963	JAN 1964
WIND:														
Mean Speed (mph)	31	11.1	11.9	13.0	12.7	11.1	10.8	9.5	9.0	9.4	9.6	10.6	11.1	10.8
Prevailing Direction through 1963		S	S	S	S	S	S	S	S	S	S	S	S	S
Fastest Obs. 1 Min.														
-Direction (!!!)	31	28	36	29	32	14	32	36	36	11	27	34	32	36
-speed (MPH)	31	53	51	55	55	55	52	65	73	53	44	50	53	73
-year		1979	1962	1954	1970	1955	1955	1961	1959	1961	1957	1957	1968	AUG 1959

FIG. 2-15 Meteorological summary for Dallas–Fort Worth. Reproduced from "Local Climatological Data," Dallas–Fort Worth: U.S. Department of Commerce, National Oceanic and Atmospheric Administration, 1984.

METEOROLOGICAL DATA FOR 1984

DALLAS – FORT WORTH, TEXAS

LATITUDE: 32 °54′ N LONGITUDE: 97 °02′ W ELEVATION: FT. (grd) 551 (msl) 596 TIME ZONE: CENTRAL WBAN: 03927

	JAN	FEB	MAR	APR	MAY	JUNE	JULY	AUG	SEP	OCT	NOV	DEC	YEAR
TEMPERATURE °F:													
Averages													
-Daily Maximum	49.9	63.8	66.8	75.2	84.8	93.1	97.2	97.4	86.5	75.6	64.6	61.7	76.4
-Daily Minimum	28.7	37.9	45.8	52.1	62.5	71.8	73.7	74.2	65.6	58.4	44.6	43.4	54.9
-Monthly	39.3	50.9	56.3	63.7	73.7	82.5	85.5	85.8	76.1	67.0	54.6	52.6	65.7
-Monthly Dewpt.	27.4	33.2	42.7	44.8	58.9	66.2	62.9	64.0	57.5	57.8	41.7	44.8	50.2
Extremes													
-Highest	74	76	81	91	95	103	104	106	99	90	83	76	106
-Date	29	14	26	24	5	23	16	19	14	6	9	29	AUG 19
-Lowest	10	21	32	40	49	61	64	67	43	42	30	28	10
-Date	19	6	1	5	9	1	30	15	30	1	28	7	JAN 19
DEGREE DAYS BASE 65 °F:													
Heating	789	401	281	89	11	0	0	0	38	66	322	389	2386
Cooling	0	0	20	60	288	531	644	652	376	135	16	12	2734
% OF POSSIBLE SUNSHINE	61	75	58	69	68	74	81	72	66	44	63	41	65
AVG. SKY COVER (tenths)													
Sunrise – Sunset	5.6	3.7	5.5	4.3	4.5	3.9	3.7	4.5	4.5	7.0	5.6	7.5	5.0
Midnight – Midnight	5.0	3.4	5.2	3.7	4.2	3.6	3.4	4.4	4.2	6.5	5.2	7.2	4.7
NUMBER OF DAYS:													
Sunrise to Sunset													
-Clear	11	16	10	15	13	15	15	14	15	6	9	5	144
-Partly Cloudy	6	5	10	8	10	10	13	11	5	8	11	5	102
-Cloudy	14	8	11	7	8	5	3	6	10	17	10	21	120
Precipitation .01 inches or more	4	5	9	5	5	4	3	4	3	17	6	11	76
Snow, Ice pellets 1.0 inches or more	0	0	0	0	0	0	0	0	0	0	0	0	0
Thunderstorms	0	5	7	4	4	3	2	4	1	8	3	1	42
Heavy Fog, visibility 1/4 mile or less	2	1	1	0	0	0	0	0	1	2	2	5	14
Temperature °F													
-Maximum													
90° and above	0	0	0	2	9	20	30	29	16	1	0	0	107
32° and below	2	0	0	0	0	0	0	0	0	0	0	0	2
-Minimum													
32° and below	20	9	1	0	0	0	0	0	0	0	2	5	37
0° and below	0	0	0	0	0	0	0	0	0	0	0	0	0
AVG. STATION PRESS. (mb)	1002.7	994.9	993.2	989.2	992.9	992.6	993.7	993.4	995.9	994.2	998.0	998.0	994.9
RELATIVE HUMIDITY (%)													
Hour 00 (Local Time)	72	61	68	60	68	68	56	58	62	82	71	82	67
Hour 06 (Local Time)	79	72	77	69	82	82	69	73	76	87	80	88	78
Hour 12 (Local Time)	58	47	58	45	53	52	39	44	50	69	56	70	53
Hour 18 (Local Time)	54	40	51	40	47	48	34	36	43	68	56	71	49
PRECIPITATION (inches):													
Water Equivalent													
-Total	1.07	3.11	4.92	1.41	3.04	2.79	0.43	1.47	0.09	6.50	2.97	6.09	33.89
-Greatest (24 hrs)	0.77	1.05	1.65	0.76	1.70	1.51	0.31	1.14	0.05	2.15	1.20	1.91	2.15
-Date	8- 9	11	23	7	1	6	5	11-12	28	20-21	17-18	17-18	OCT 20-21
Snow, Ice pellets													
-Total	0.0	0.0	0.0	0.0	0.0	0.0	0.0	0.0	0.0	0.0	0.0	0.0	0.0
-Greatest (24 hrs)	0.0	0.0	0.0	0.0	0.0	0.0	0.0	0.0	0.0	0.0	0.0	0.0	0.0
-Date													
WIND:													
Resultant													
-Direction (!!)	352	249	139	268	158	173	155	167	147	159	195	192	174
-Speed (mph)	3.1	3.6	0.6	2.0	6.3	10.3	6.0	5.7	3.9	3.4	2.5	1.8	3.1
Average Speed (mph)	10.1	13.4	12.9	14.3	12.6	12.9	10.2	9.5	12.1	9.9	11.6	11.2	11.7
Fastest Obs. 1 Min.													
-Direction (!!)	36	33	32	27	01	09	14	09	36	20	18	31	32
-Speed (mph)	31	37	37	33	31	35	23	35	33	36	30	35	37
-Date	9	27	28	29	27	28	12	14	25	18	7	15	MAR 28
PEAK GUST													
-direction (!!)	N	N	NW	W	N	E	NE	E	N	S	NW	NW	NW
-Speed (mph)	41	51	52	48	39	53	35	41	43	41	55	43	55
-Date	10	27	28	29	27	28	28	14	25	18	1	15	NOV 1

arid, and hot humid. In each the site planner should investigate the solar orientation for buildings, the best facing slopes, and the part of the slope that makes use of air flow for warmth in cool climates or for breezes in temperate or hot climates. Each factor is important in energy conservation.

Figures 2-16 to 2-19 represent factors for each climatic zone; residences are placed to receive the best solar orientation for each climatic region. (See Figs. 2-20 to 2-22.)

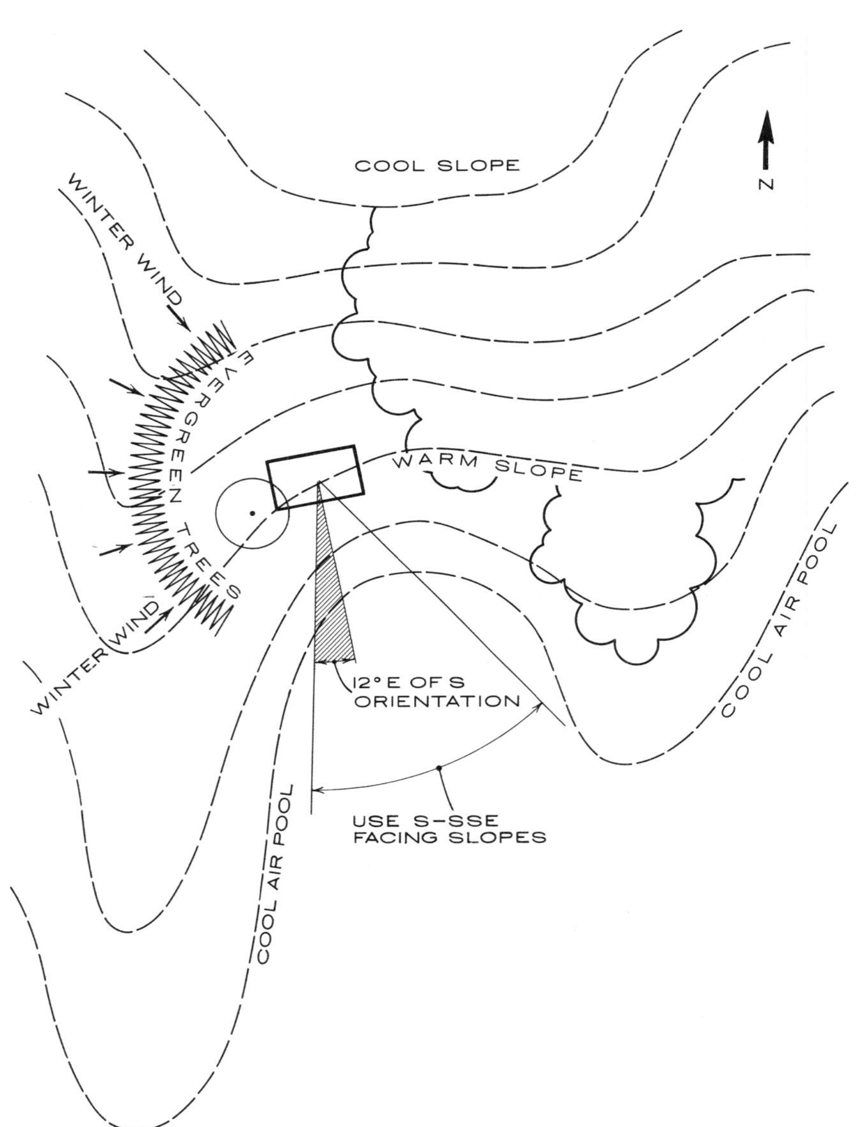

FIG. 2-16 Cool climates.

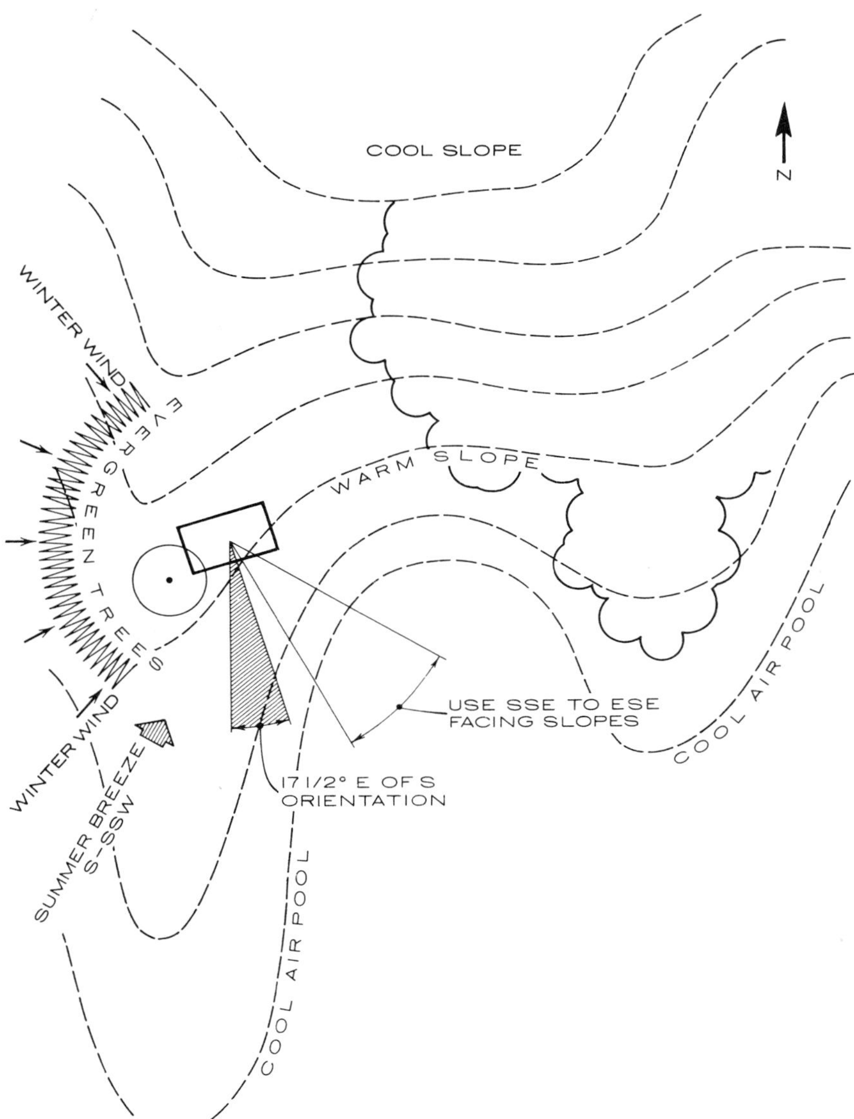

FIG. 2-17 Temperate climates.

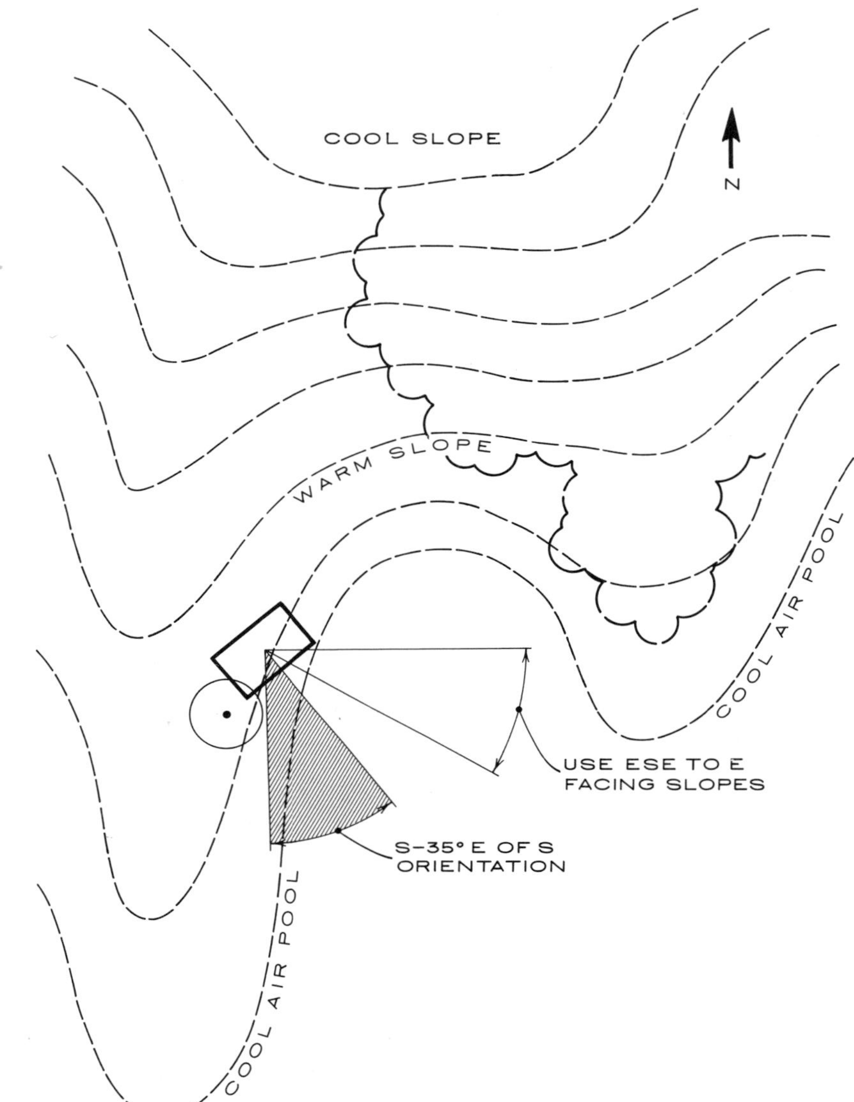

FIG. 2-18 Hot arid climates.

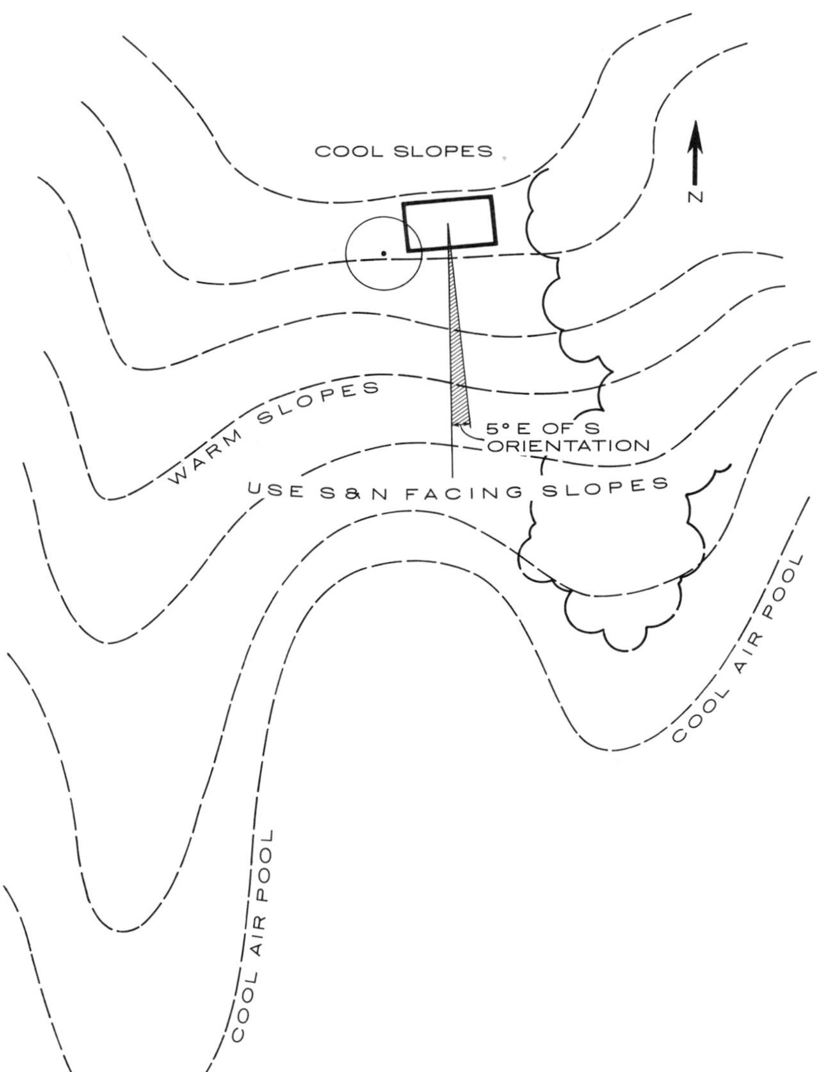

FIG. 2-19 Hot humid climates.

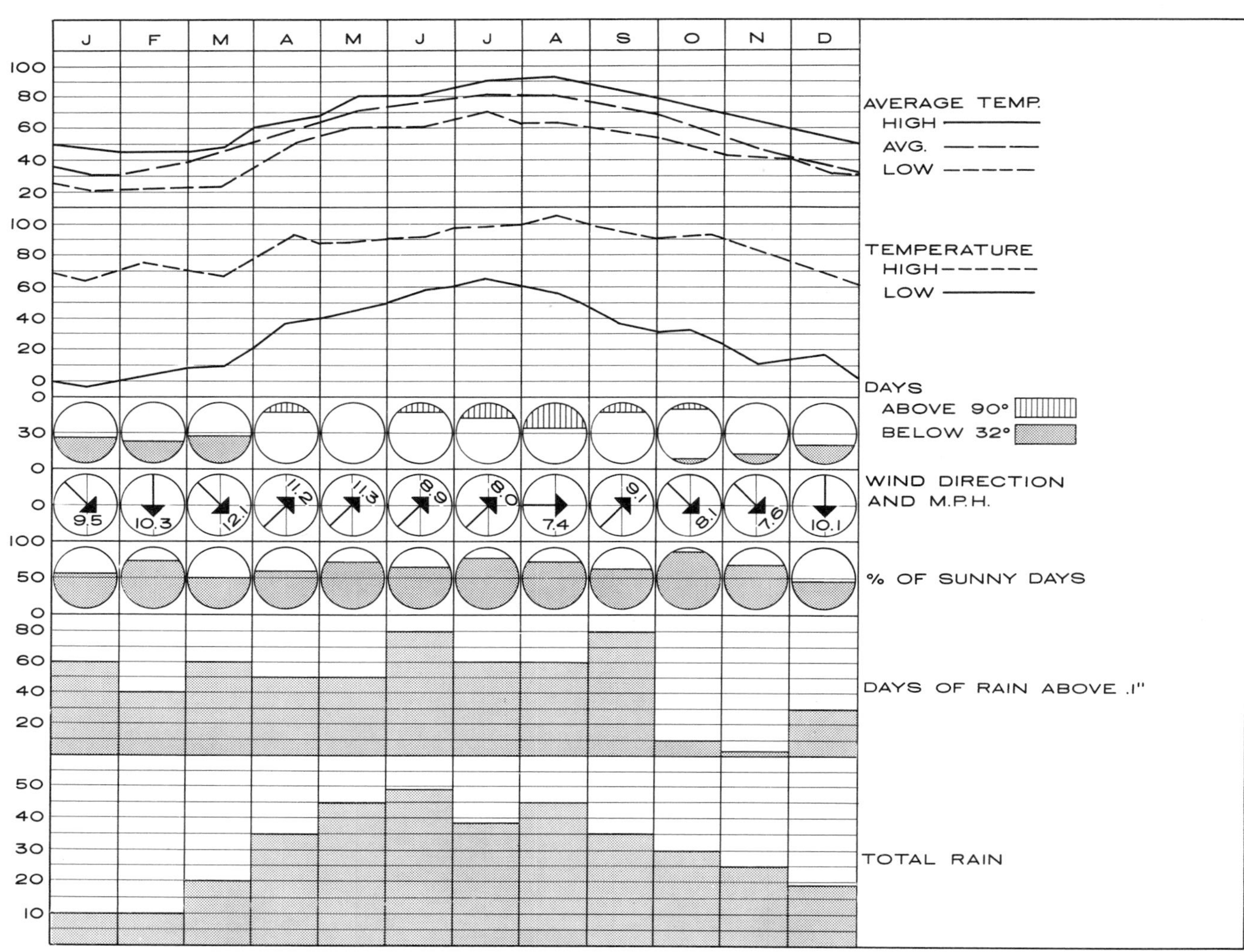

FIG. 2-20 Climatic data: information from the weather bureau can be illustrated in charts or graphs for easy interpretation.

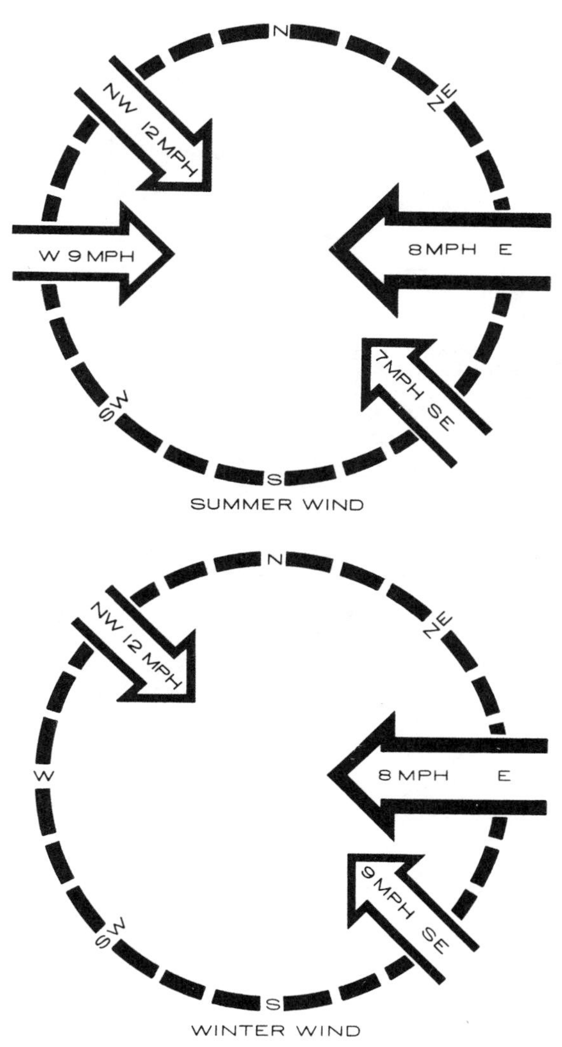

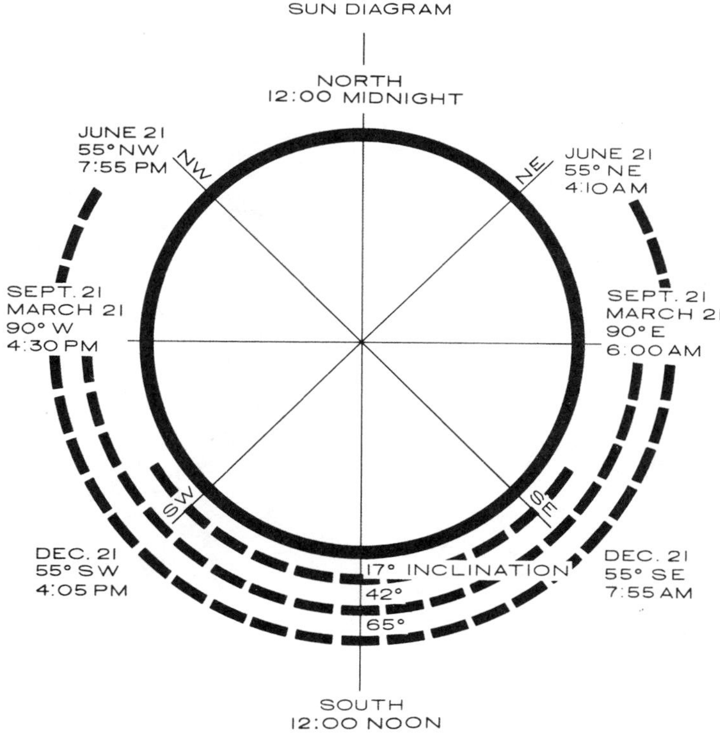

LOWEST DAILY TEMPERATURE 20 MINUTES BEFORE SUNRISE.

HIGHEST DAILY TEMPERATURE 2:30 IN THE AFTERNOON.

FIG. 2-21 Wind and sun diagrams: Vancouver, Canada.

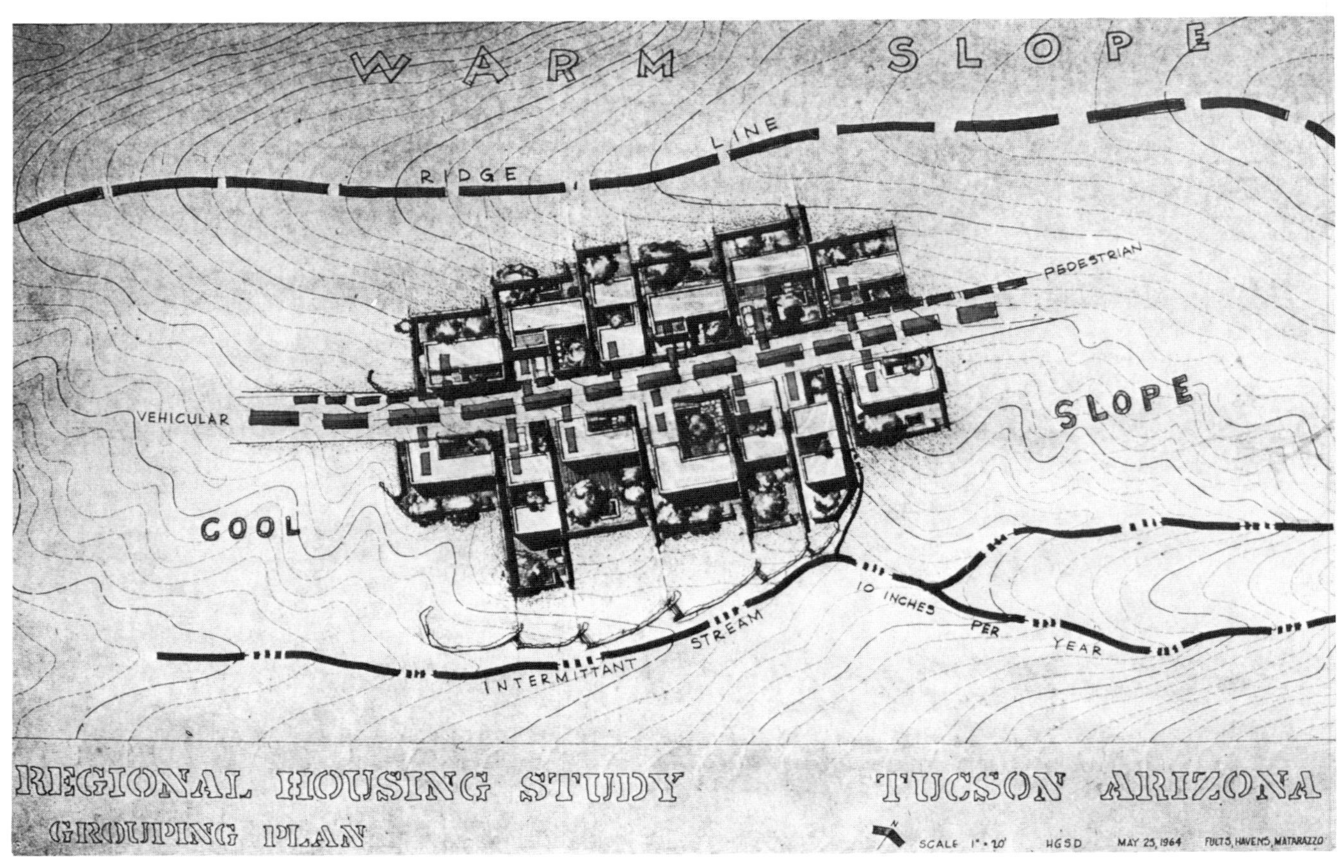

FIG. 2-22 A typical study for grouping housing: the hot arid climate of Tucson, Arizona.

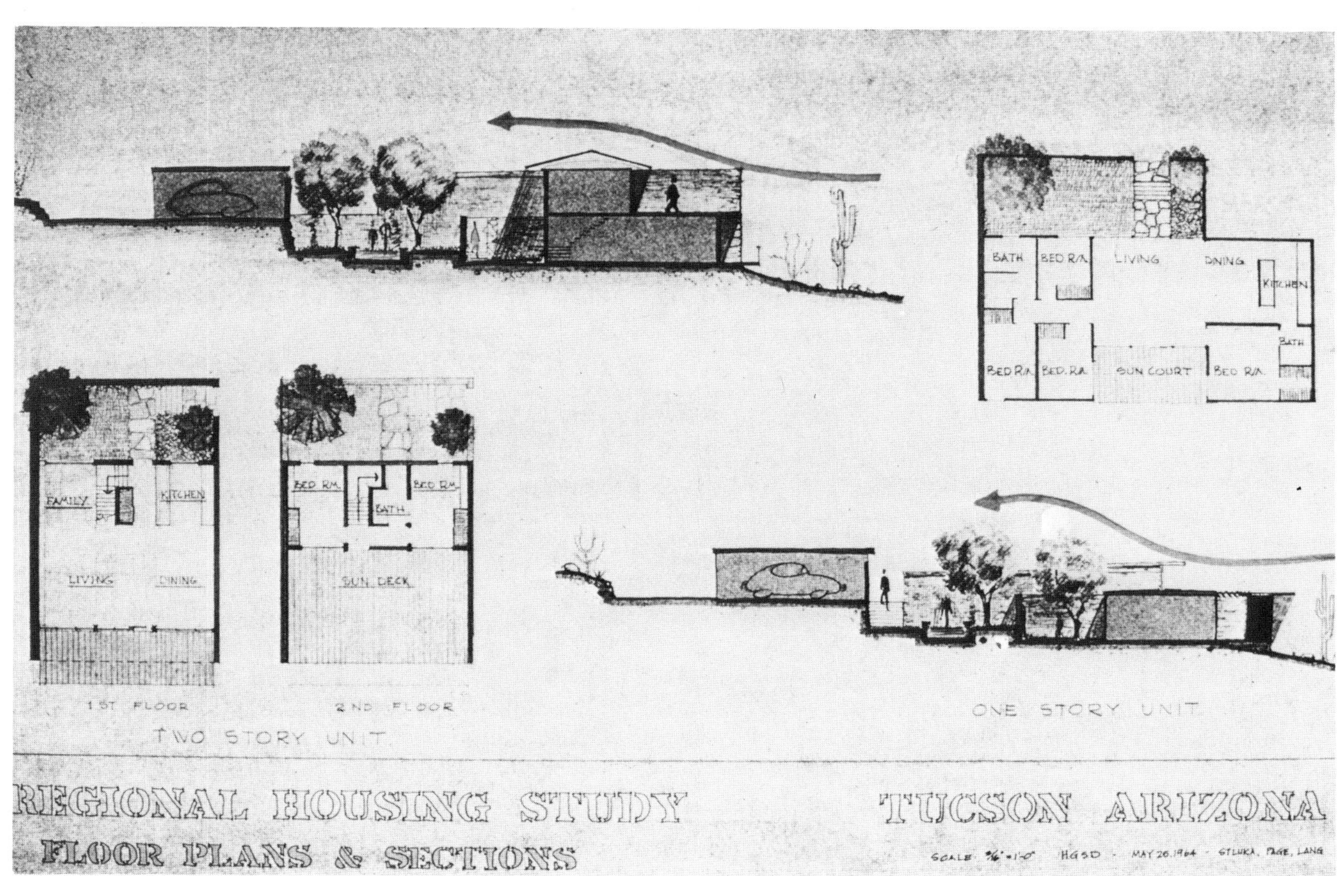
BATH
BED R/M.
LIVING
DINING
KITCHEN
BATH
BED R/M.
BED R/M.
SUN COURT
BED R/M.
FAMILY
KITCHEN
LIVING
DINING
BED R/M.
BATH
BED R/M.
SUN DECK
1ST FLOOR
2ND FLOOR
TWO STORY UNIT
ONE STORY UNIT
REGIONAL HOUSING STUDY
TUCSON ARIZONA
FLOOR PLANS & SECTIONS
HGSD · MAY 20, 1964 · STLUKA, PAGE, LANG

Fog

For some types of uses such as road locations fog areas should be studied. Fog is formed when the relative humidity of the air is increased to the saturation point by cooling or by the addition of moisture. On clear nights land loses heat by radiation; the ground may cool lower layers of air enough to create fog. This type of fog is generally located in low areas.

Persistent fog results when moist air passes over cooler land or water. These advection fogs are prevalent in summer over cold ocean currents in coastal areas. During winter and spring the flow or advection of humid air from the ocean traveling over land areas may also cause dense fogs. Additionally, fogs can form when rain adds moisture to cool air or when moisture is added during the movement of cold air over warm water (called steam fog).

Over urban areas air pollution is linked to temperature inversion during which air near the ground does not rise to be replaced by moving air. The inversion is characterized by clear nights with little wind; the earth is cooled by long-wave radiation, and air near the ground is cooled. Air movement is limited and in cities pollution becomes concentrated. Areas with temperature inversions must be studied to limit land uses that will further add to pollution.

CULTURAL FACTORS

Existing Land Use

The pattern of existing land use must be designated in relation to the site. Community facilities both public and semipublic, residential, commercial, industrial, and recreational are inventoried to denote overall trends in

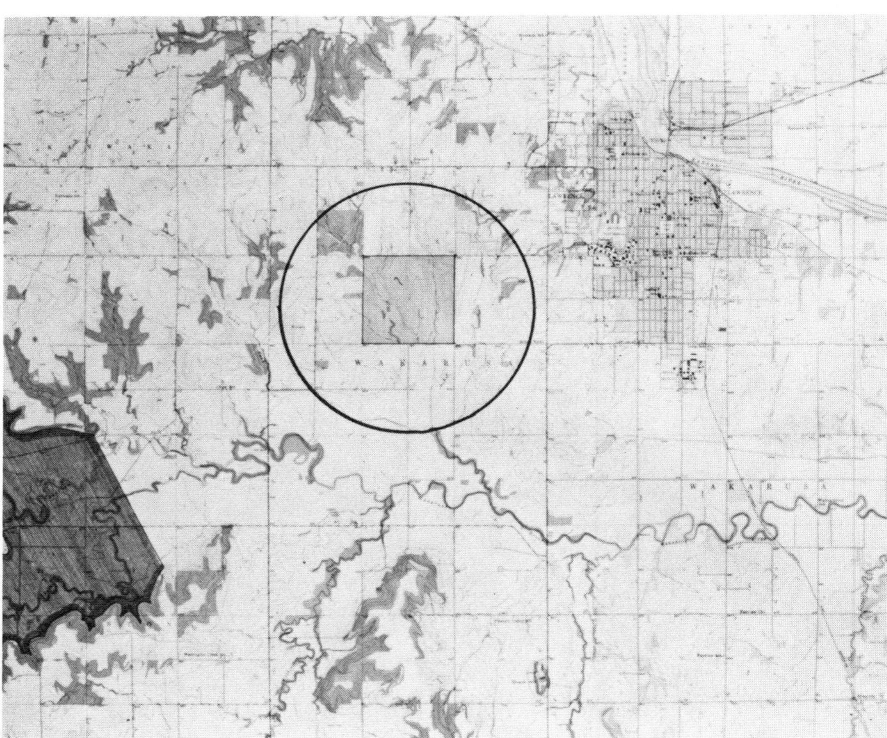

FIG. 2-23 Site location: a site should be located in relation to the larger environment. The site encircled in this photograph is an area of a proposed planned unit development in Lawrence, Kansas.

development that may have bearing on uses of land adjacent to and including the site under study. (See Figs. 2-23 and 2-24.)

Along with the study of existing land use, the site planner should meet with the adjacent property owners to find out, if possible, what future development of their sites may be under consideration and whether this development will be in conflict with uses planned on the new site.

Off-Site Nuisances. Off-site nuisances—whether visual, auditory, or olfactory—and safety hazards must be investigated. If one or more of these problems is uncontrollable, an alternative site may have to be chosen. Among visually disruptive elements are power lines, water towers, certain industrial complexes, highways, billboards, and junkyards. Possible auditory nuisances include heavy automobile, rail, or air traffic, or noise made by large numbers of people. Olfactory nuisances originate in dumps or in chemical and other wastes. Safety hazards result from the lack of linkages in areas of heavy traffic. Severe and sudden changes in land, such as a steep cliff at the edge of a site, may be a safety hazard. Air pollution, another safety hazard, may be caused by traffic in congested areas.

Linkages

While studying the location of the site and its relation to adjacent properties and to the community, all existing ties or linkages, if any, should be specified. Linkages may involve the movement of people, goods, com-

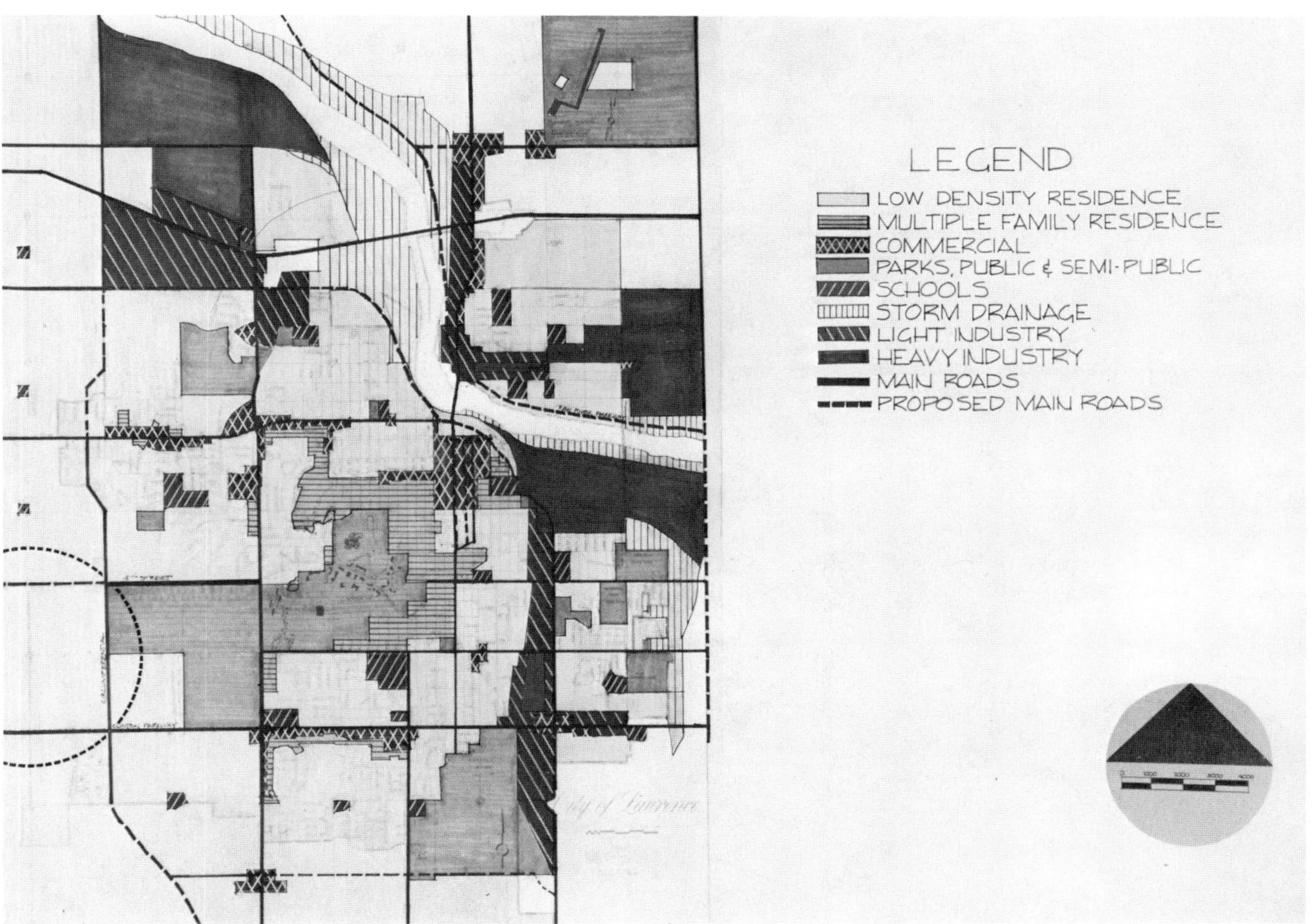

FIG. 2-24 Existing land use.

munication, or amenities. Now ask whether, by the addition of parkways, parks, or pedestrian overpasses or underpasses, these linkages need strengthening? Community facilities such as nearby shopping centers, employment hubs, residential areas, churches, schools, parks, and playgrounds should be inventoried in relation to the site. Determine whether adequate linkages exist, and, if not, decide how they can be established or improved by future development.

Traffic and Transit

What is the relationship of traffic patterns to each other and to the site? Are there adequate roads in the vicinity? If the site is urban, does public transportation service the area? Depending on the complexity of the problem, automobile, bus, railroad, and air circulation should be reviewed to show if, and how, these facilities will integrate with future site development. (See Fig. 2-25.) In inventorying existing vehicular networks, trips—including their origin and destination, purpose, time of day, and volume—should be considered. Graphically plot transportation systems and their location or routes when they are available. Check the volume of traffic or frequency of flights to determine whether additional routes

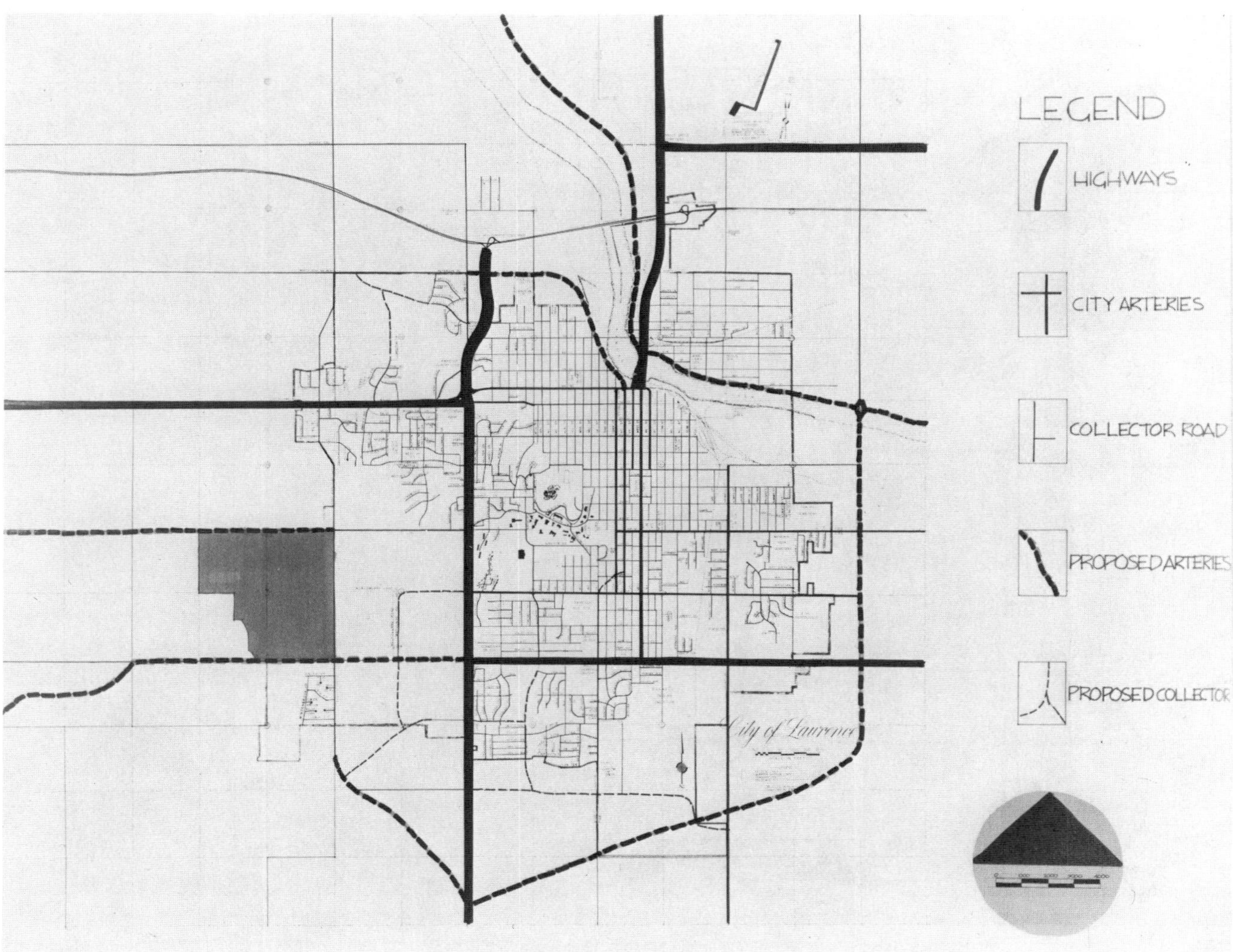

FIG. 2-25 Existing and proposed road pattern.

are necessary. If sites are within 15 miles of airports, check noise zones and building height restrictions for airport hazard. The Federal Aviation Administration office or military agency in charge of the airport should be contacted.

Density and Zoning

Density is an important sociological and legal element in most types of development. In residential development, it is expressed in numbers of families or dwelling units per acre. Density may also be used to express floor area ratio or gross floor area covering the site—if all floors were spread out and assumed to be one story in height as compared with total site acreage. (See Fig. 2-26.)

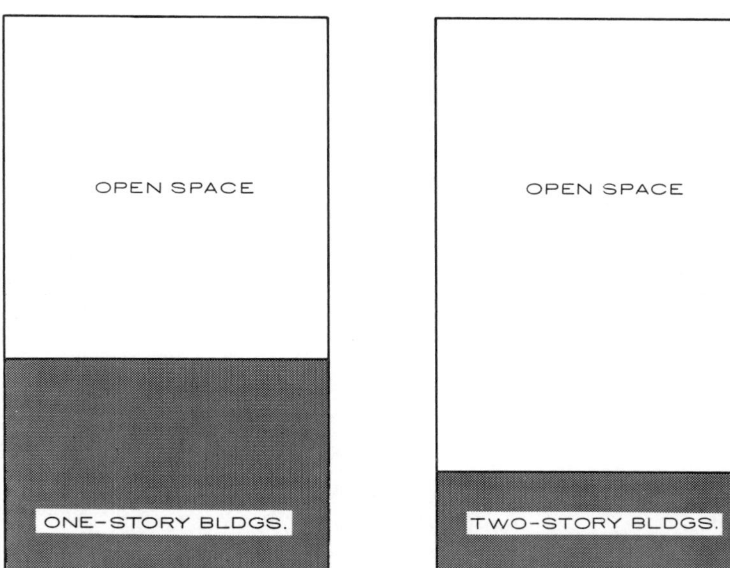

FIG. 2-26 Floor area ratio.

Cities have zoning regulations concerning standards of density because of economic, social, and functional implications. Zoning with over 50 years of supporting legal opinions is a form of legal regulation. Zoning provides for the division of a municipality into land use areas that are designated by height, building coverage, open space, or density of population. Density may influence privacy, freedom of movement, or social contact among people. Zoning regulations, easements, codes, and mineral rights must be checked before a site is developed. This is necessary to work within regulations set or to determine if changes would be desirable when possible. Information concerning zoning and much of the other information on codes, regulations, and names of property owners is available at city hall or other municipal offices such as townships. (See Fig. 2-27.)

Socioeconomic Factors

The study of a community and its social and economic structure is important in determining the feasibility of a project. Who is the user of a project? Are the user's needs being programmed into the project? Public opinion surveys can provide answers to some of these questions.

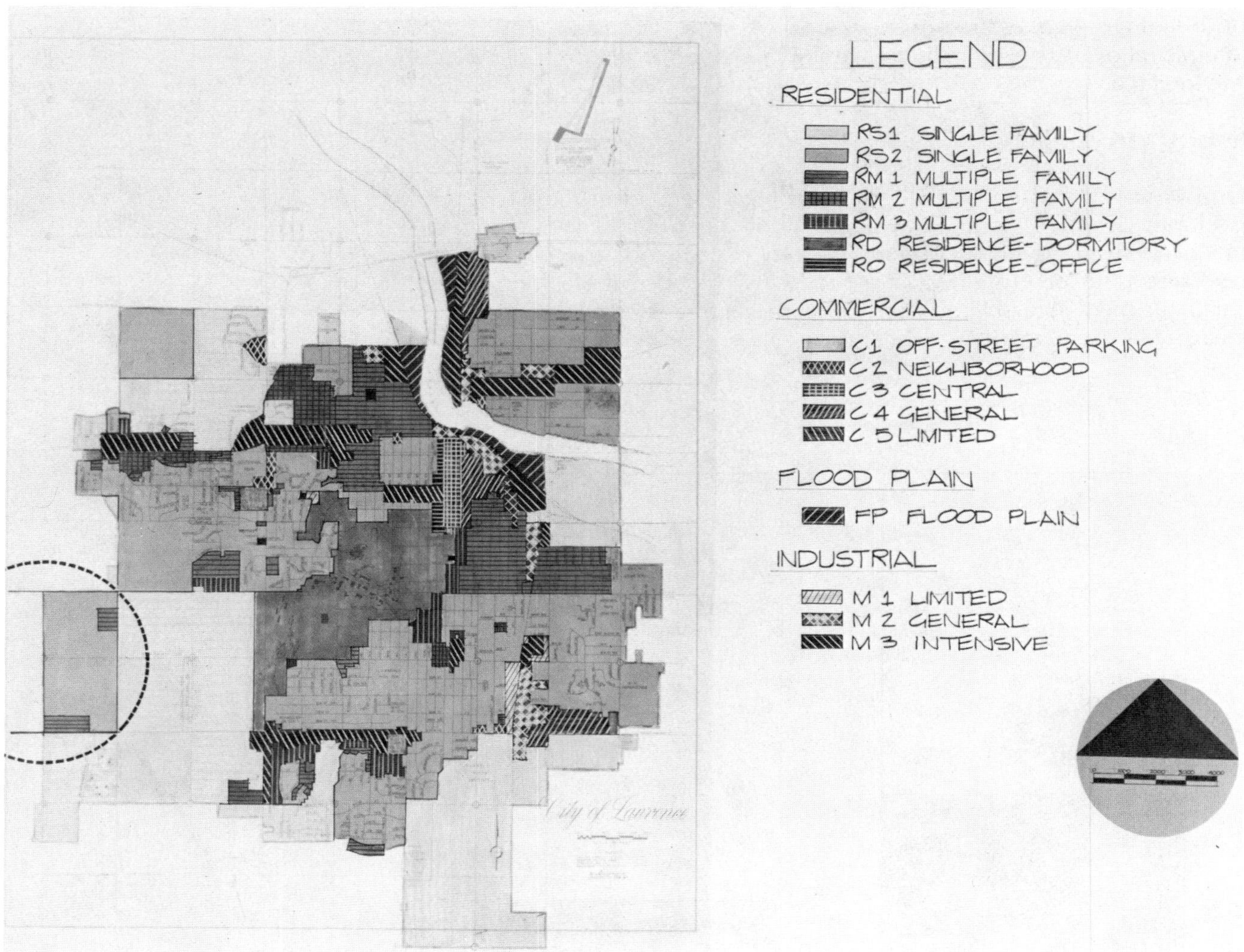

FIG. 2-27 Zoning.

Social factors have a broad range of effects on community facilities and services. Sometimes new facilities displace homes, businesses, or other community activities. For example, a new highway may cut through an area severing its cohesion by creating visual or physical barriers and affecting business and property values.

Market Analysis

Socioeconomic feasibility is based on a market analysis. The metropolitan region or an entire local area is the unit on which the analysis is carried out.

Population. Population is the base of many planning decisions. Population characteristics within an area can identify the potential user or consumer. These characteristics include population change by births, deaths, migration, age, sex. race, family size, occupation, income levels, housing accommodations, tax rates, and assessments. This information is important, to show, for example, who the urban consumers are or the direction of urban growth.

Local sources of data on socioeconomic factors are planning commissions, zoning boards, utility companies, and universities. Regional data are available from the U.S. Department of Commerce, Bureau of Census; U.S. Department of Labor; Bureau of Labor Statistics; and Censuses of Population and Housing.

Utilities

All utilities located on or adjacent to the site under study should be shown graphically for consideration in site development. (See Fig. 2-28.) Utility companies should be contacted early in the site planning process to see if project needs can be met. Generally utilities are located in open areas adjacent to streets or under streets for easy maintenance.

Potable Water. Water is the most critical utility for growth at the community level. Primary sources of water are rivers, lakes, springs, and subsurface supplies such as acquifers. There are several types of distribution systems such as gravity from a reservoir, where water is stored and distributed by the force of gravity; and direct pressure, where water is pumped

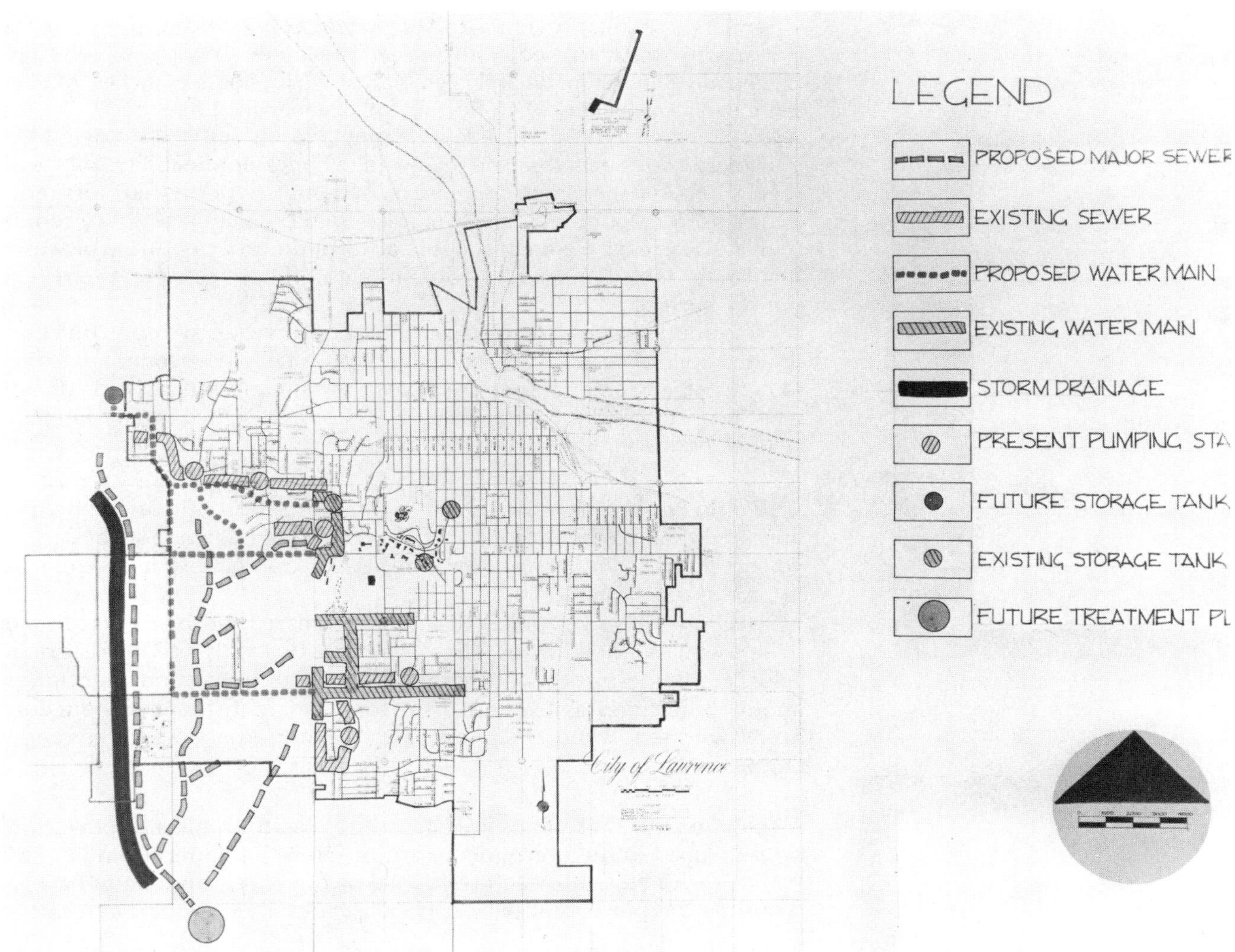

FIG. 2-28 Utilities.

into a main. Most large urban systems use combinations of these. Waterlines are generally adaptable to most site layouts, and mains are located adjacent to roads where they can be serviced easily. Laterals carry water directly from the main to buildings.

Most water systems supply domestic, fire, and industrial users from a distribution system. In high-density areas high-pressure fire mains are sometimes used. Water supply systems are often in branch or grid patterns. Grid patterns can have a loop that provides service from two or more directions. Mains used for water supply have size requirements set by fire protection use and minimums are 6 in. for residential areas, 8 in. for high value areas. Valves are placed in the mains so that breaks will affect no more than about 500 ft of pipe, which are placed below frost level to prevent problems due to freezing.

Fire hydrants are spaced from about 150 to 600 ft apart. They are at the closer spacing in high value areas.

User need for water varies from 50 to 75 gal/person per day in cities. In rural areas wells are often used but should be a minimum of 100 ft from sanitary absorption fields.

Sanitary. Sewage is usually disposed of in systems separate from storm water and carried to a disposal plant where it is treated into effluent, which may be discharged into a river, stream, or other natural body of water. Sanitary pipe systems often work by gravity, but may require pumping stations to reach a common point of discharge.

Sanitary systems provide a closed system connected to sinks and toilet drains with traps to keep out odors. The minimum size of sewer pipe is generally 8 in. for mains and laterals and 6 in. for house branches. Minimum self-cleaning velocities when flowing full is generally 2 ft/second.

In areas such as residential developments where septic systems are being considered soils data must be reviewed to check permeability. Subdivision regulations set lot sizes where septic systems are permitted; lots require a minimum of one half acre to a full acre. Percolation tests are required to make sure each lot has a suitable absorption capacity. Areas of seasonal high water table can create problems with effluent causing it to rise near the soil surface.

Well-drained soils are usually suitable for septic systems, but poorly drained soils or soils with seasonal high water table have limitations. Depth to bedrock and steep slopes are also important considerations in deciding whether septic systems are feasible. Grades over 15% create limitations as does bedrock close to the soil surface.

Electric Power. Electric power is transmitted on primary high-voltage lines and then by the use of transformers stepped down to secondary low-voltage lines. Secondary systems often use a loop pattern in case of failure in part of the system.

Traditionally power poles about 120 ft apart have been placed along streets with overhead wires. These wires are unsightly and in areas of high value are being placed underground. While underground distribution is about three times as expensive in front end cost, there is reduction of breakage due to wind and elimination of interference with trees and the clutter of wires.

Telephone. These lines are placed overhead on electric power poles or are placed in underground conduits. From the underground conduits service is directed into each residence or building. Some states have laws requiring the placement of telephone utilities underground in residential areas.

Gas. Gas is piped in an underground system similar to water distribution. Gas transmission lines have pressures ranging from 100 to 500 lb./in.^{2} (psi) while service pressures range from 10 to 100 psi. Pipe size varies from 12 to 36 in. for transmission and $1\frac{1}{4}$ to 20 in. for high- and medium-pressure distribution.

Steam. Steam is suitable in urban areas where a large number of customers can be served. The mains are large and add to the cost of installation. The cost of operation is high with return on investment low during the summer.

Storm Water. Storm water systems pick up surface water and carry it to local streams or lakes where it can be discharged safely. Storm pipe is often a minimum of 15 in. to prevent clogging with manholes 300 to 500 ft apart for cleaning and changing direction or size of pipe. Catch basins placed in roads or other areas pick up the water. Pipes are set below frost level and generally have a self-cleaning velocity of about 2.5 to 3 ft/second. (See p. 134 for pipe size calculations.)

Existing Buildings

If a project is to be expanded buildings on the site must be shown graphically and their uses and facilities studied. Size, floor area, and existing conditions must be inventoried. Existing buildings will strongly influence the physical layout of the new site plan and will help to establish the grading and drainage pattern on the site. They also may determine the choice of future architectural expression in building type, color, facade, texture, materials, window type, and roof style to insure coherence and unity in design.

History

A campus plan or other large project may have a meaningful background that influences future expansion. It is then pertinent to ask, "Will historic factors be of consequence to the project?" The history of these projects should be investigated and shown graphically so that relevant influences may be considered in the design phase. The investigation may show, for example, that specific buildings should be preserved within the redevelopment of a campus, as should other historic buildings or landmarks in other projects. (See Fig. 2-29.) On large sites archaeology should also be reviewed to see if artifacts are present and need to be preserved.

AESTHETIC FACTORS

Sites on which future development is planned must be analyzed to determine significant aesthetic factors. Natural features and spatial patterns are all important in relating design elements.

The character of many sites is distinguished by the arrangement of these elements. This is true, for instance, in the following examples of sites that have a unique character in the midst of an industrial area of Pittsburgh or within an urban residential area in San Francisco. (See Figs. 2-30 and 2-31.)

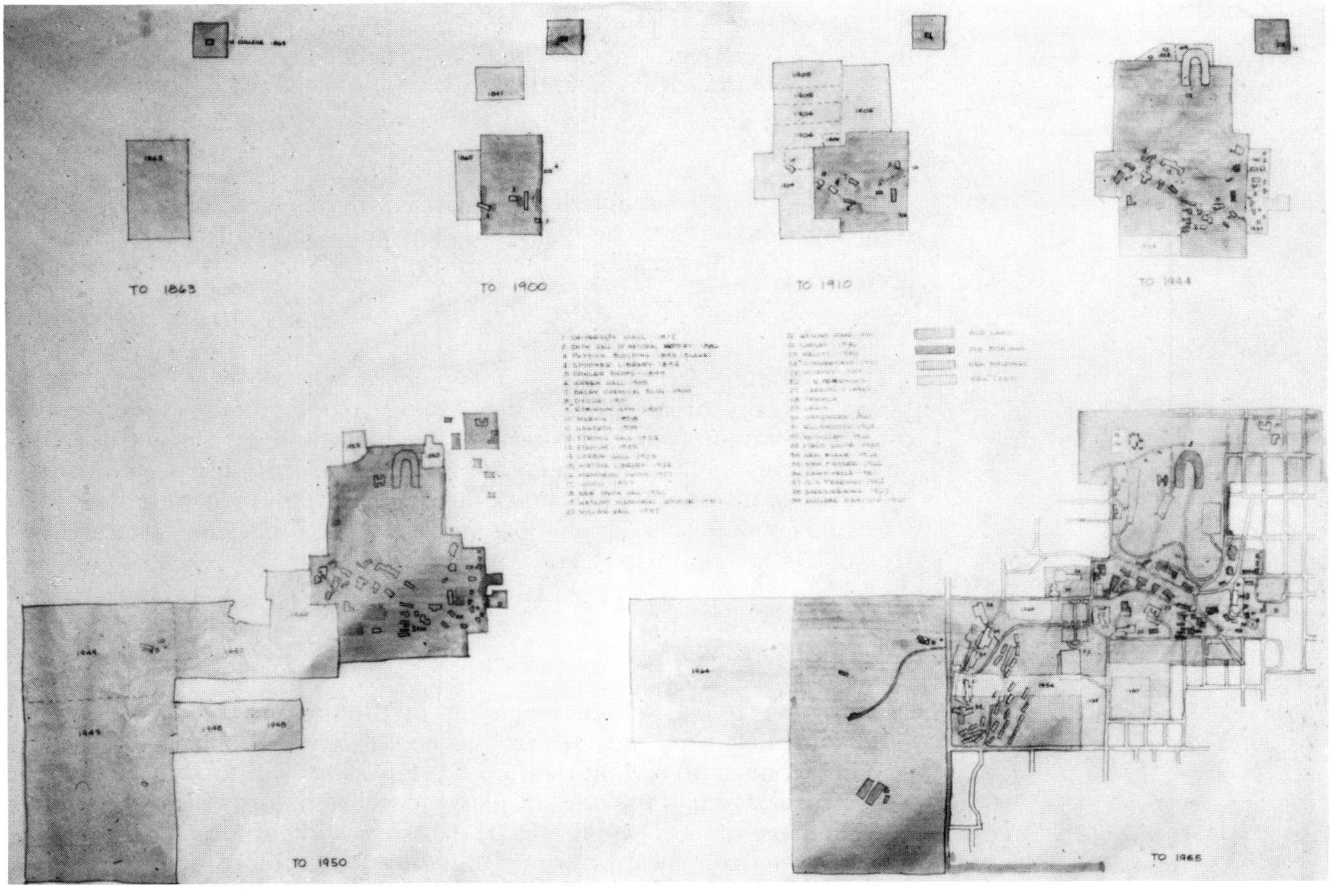

TO 1863

TO 1900

TO 1910

TO 1944

TO 1950

TO 1965

FIG. 2-29 History: the historic growth of Kansas University since 1865 may influence its future development.

FIG. 2-30 Industrial character of Pittsburgh, Pennsylvania.

FIG. 2-31 Residential character of San Francisco, California.

Natural Features

Sites may be endowed with outstanding natural features of earth, rock, water, or plant material. Landforms, rock outcrops, ledges, boulders, lakes, streams, bogs, or wooded areas have scenic value and may be incorporated, along with architecture, in site development. One of these features, for aesthetic value alone, may be sufficient reason for designating an individual site for construction. The designer must use them to advantage rather than reducing their impact through improper site treatment. (See Figs. 2-32 and 2-33.)

Spatial Patterns

Views. Views on a site may be pleasing or objectionable. They may bear heavily on the orientation of a building and therefore should be carefully studied. An outstanding view must be handled properly to be preserved or accentuated. Views are framed, open, enclosed, filtered, or screened. Be sure to note their sequence. Do they seem static or do they, as if by mystery, attract attention and draw movement toward them? A view should be completely revealed only from its best vantage point, not given away at first glimpse. An observer can be made to anticipate a view and then see it from its best location for its fullest impact. When studying views on sloping sites, the site planner should also consider the angle of vertical view.

Views on a site must be compatible with proposed activities and their relation to each other because nuisances both on or off site may disrupt them. In many cases it is possible to use vegetation, fences, or walls to

FIG. 2-32 Natural character of the Cowanesque River in Tioga County, Pennsylvania, where the Army Corps of Engineers is developing a flood control and recreational project. (See p. 45.)

screen objectionable visual, auditory, or olfactory elements. Billboards, power lines, junkyards, or parking lots, for example, may be handled so that they present no visual problem. Power lines may be placed underground, and junkyards and large parking lots may be depressed below grade level.

Visual Barriers. In some cases, elements such as an elevated highway cut off views of parts of a community or a natural feature such as a river. In studying urban sites these factors must be reviewed.

FIG. 2-33 Bog.

Vistas. A vista may be a natural or completely man-made view. It has a dominant focal point or terminus that is strongly emphasized and is framed and balanced by minor elements forming masses to enclose the vista and screen out conflicting objects from its composition. The open space or line of sight of the vista is a strongly directional element leading the observer toward the focal point for closer observation. (See Figs. 2-34 to 2-38.)

FIG. 2-34 A framed view from the walk approaching a dormitory complex at the University of Colorado, Boulder.

FIG. 2-35 A filtered view through trees.

FIG. 2-36 The line of sight to the Charles River is a strong directional feature at Harvard Married Student Housing, Cambridge, Massachusetts.

FIG. 2-37 An open view from the overlook area at Grand Canyon National Park.

FIG. 2-38 A vista at Parco Reale, Caserta, Italy.

An example of a resource analysis that was carried out for the Baltimore District Corps of Engineers in 1975 is the study entitled "Cowanesque Lake Master Plan," Tioga County, Pennsylvania. This plan concerns a 3183 acre site that is to provide both flood control and recreational facilities. (See Figs. 2-39 to 2-49.)

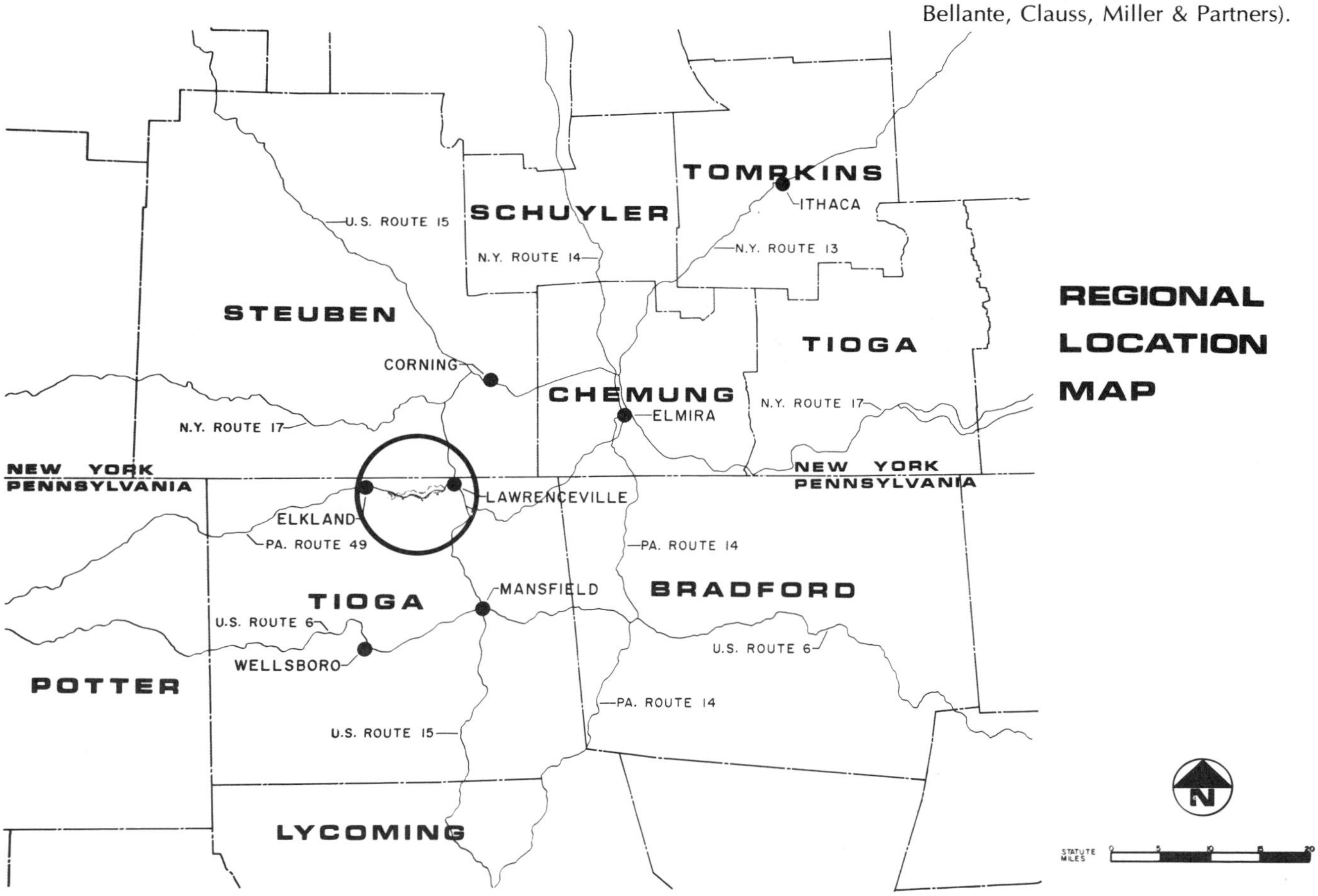

FIG. 2-39 Regional location map of the Cowanesque Lake flood control and recreation project (photographs courtesy Bellante, Clauss, Miller & Partners).

REGIONAL
LOCATION
MAP

TOMPKINS
ITHACA
SCHUYLER
U.S. ROUTE 15
N.Y. ROUTE 14
N.Y. ROUTE 13
STEUBEN
TIOGA
CORNING
CHEMUNG
ELMIRA
N.Y. ROUTE 17
N.Y. ROUTE 17
NEW YORK
PENNSYLVANIA
NEW YORK
PENNSYLVANIA
LAWRENCEVILLE
ELKLAND
PA. ROUTE 49
PA. ROUTE 14
TIOGA
MANSFIELD
BRADFORD
U.S. ROUTE 6
U.S. ROUTE 6
WELLSBORO
POTTER
PA. ROUTE 14
U.S. ROUTE 15
LYCOMING
N
STATUTE MILES 0 5 10 15 20

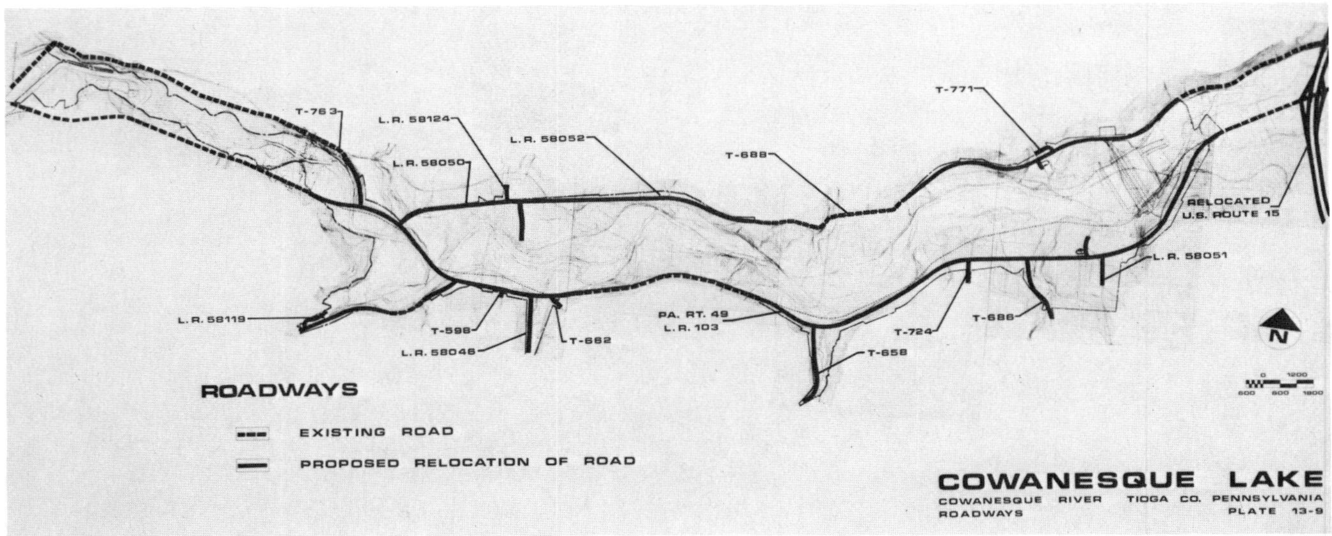

FIG. 2-40 Roadways around the 3183 acre site that will have a 410 acre lake for recreation.

FIG. 2-41 Geology: depth to bedrock is important in locating buildings and utilities.

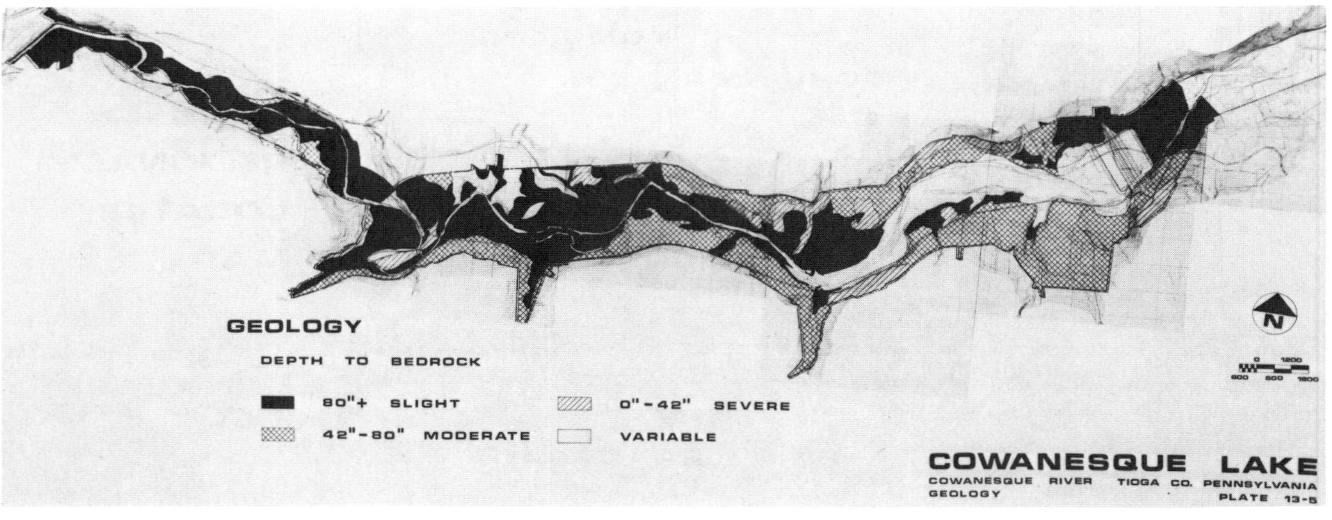

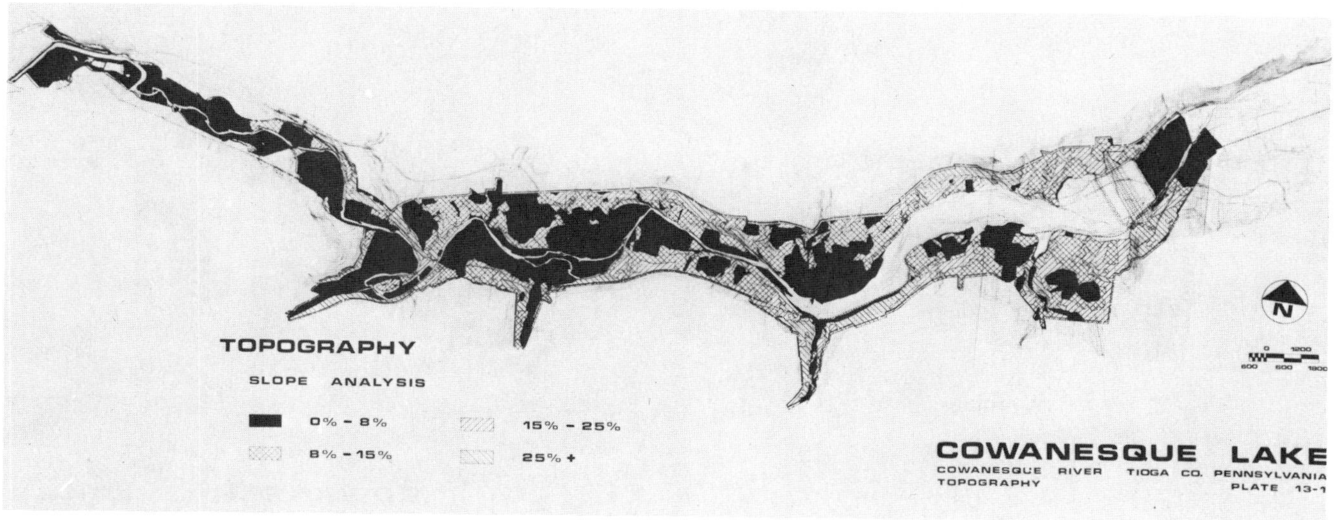

FIG. 2-42 Topography.

FIG. 2-43 Soil permeability is studied to determine what type of sanitary system is feasible on the site.

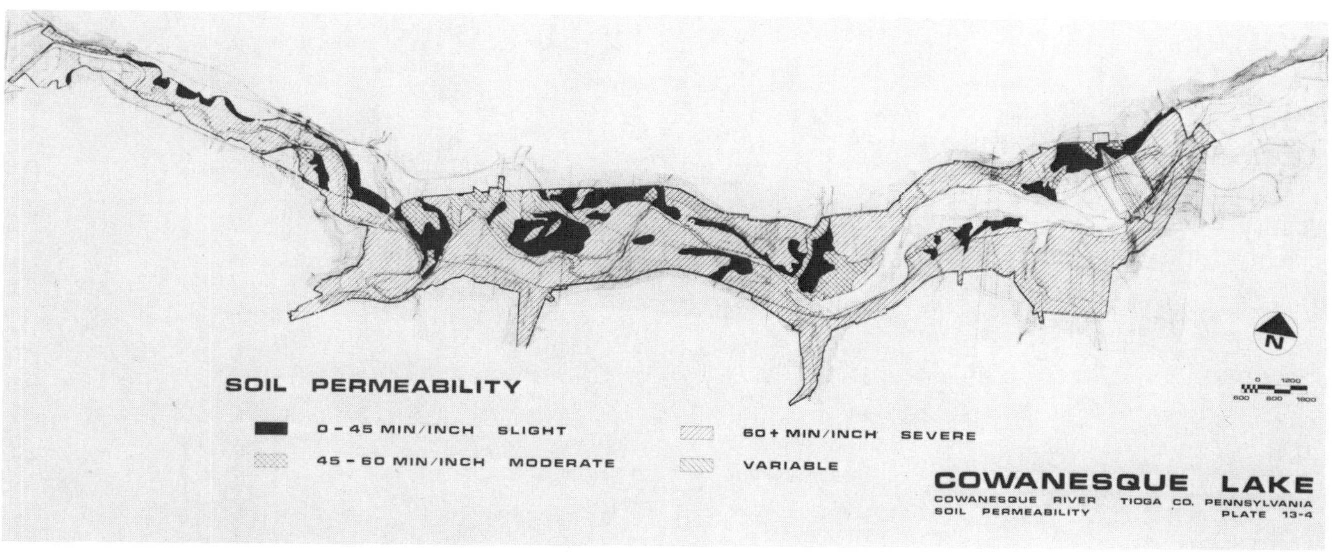

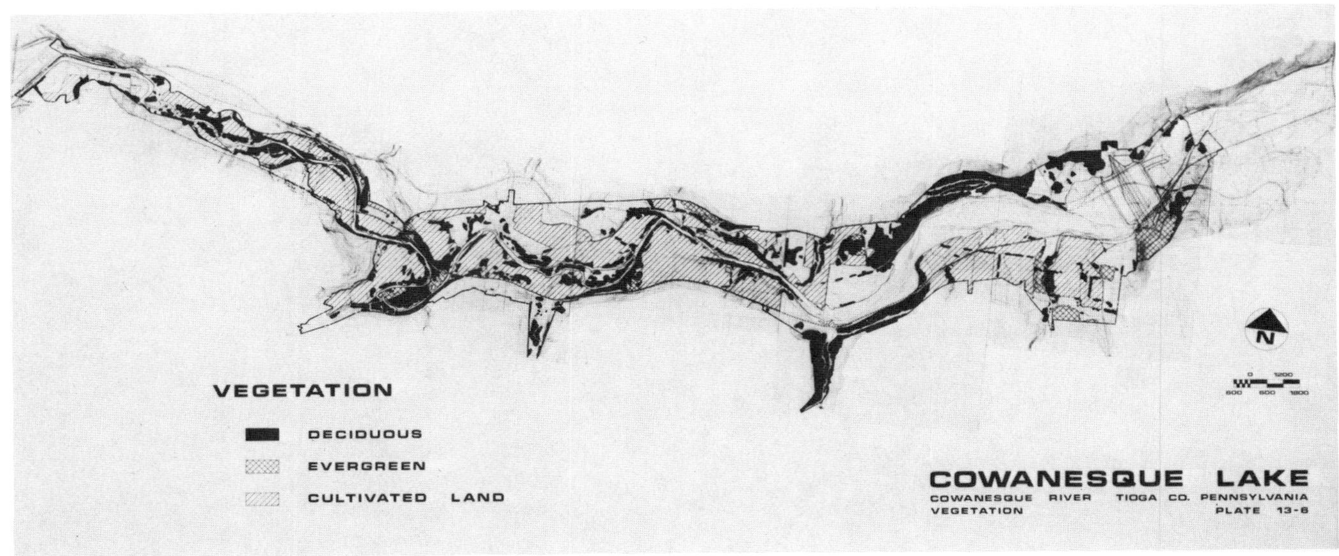

FIG. 2-44 Vegetation was inventoried for its relation to existing wildlife, proposed recreation facilities, and to keep the better cultivated farmland above the recreation waterline of the lake in production.

FIG. 2-45 An ecological profile was developed through the project area.

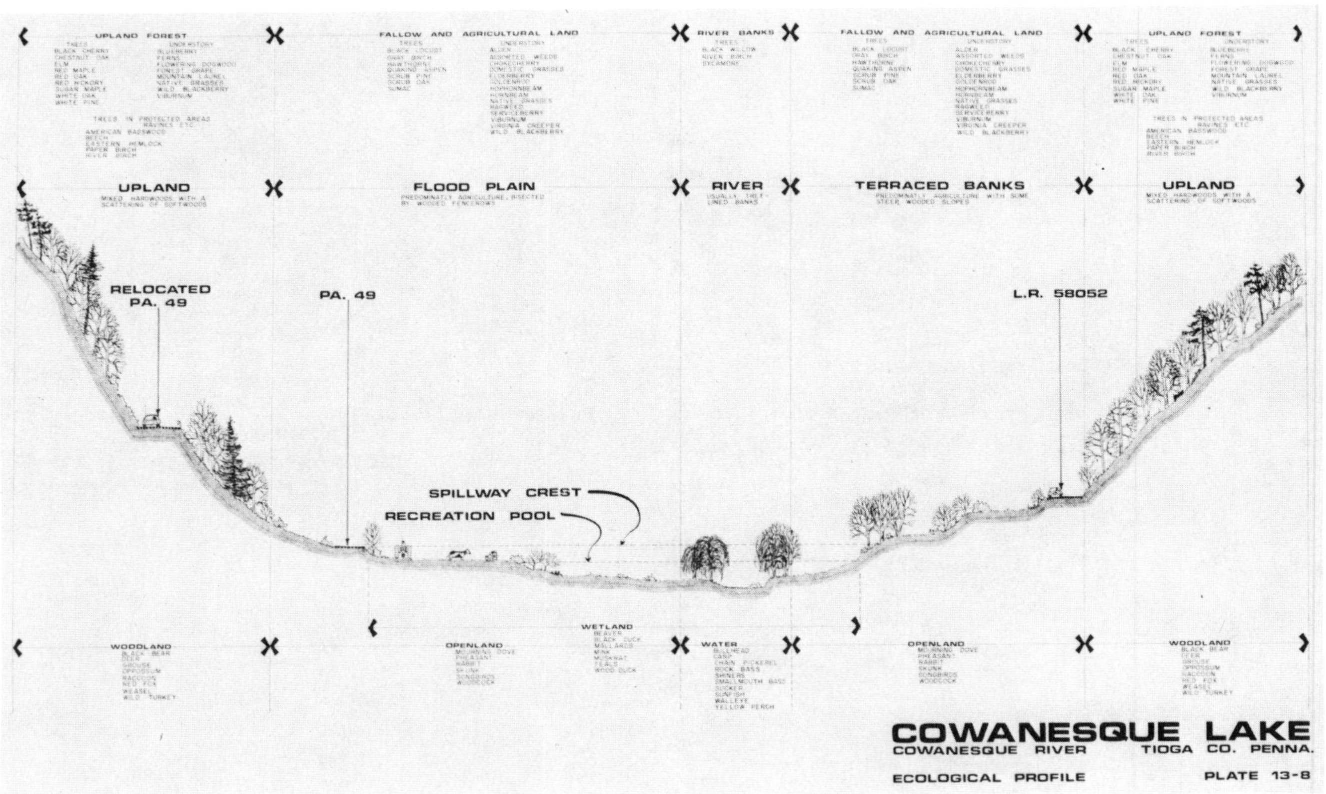

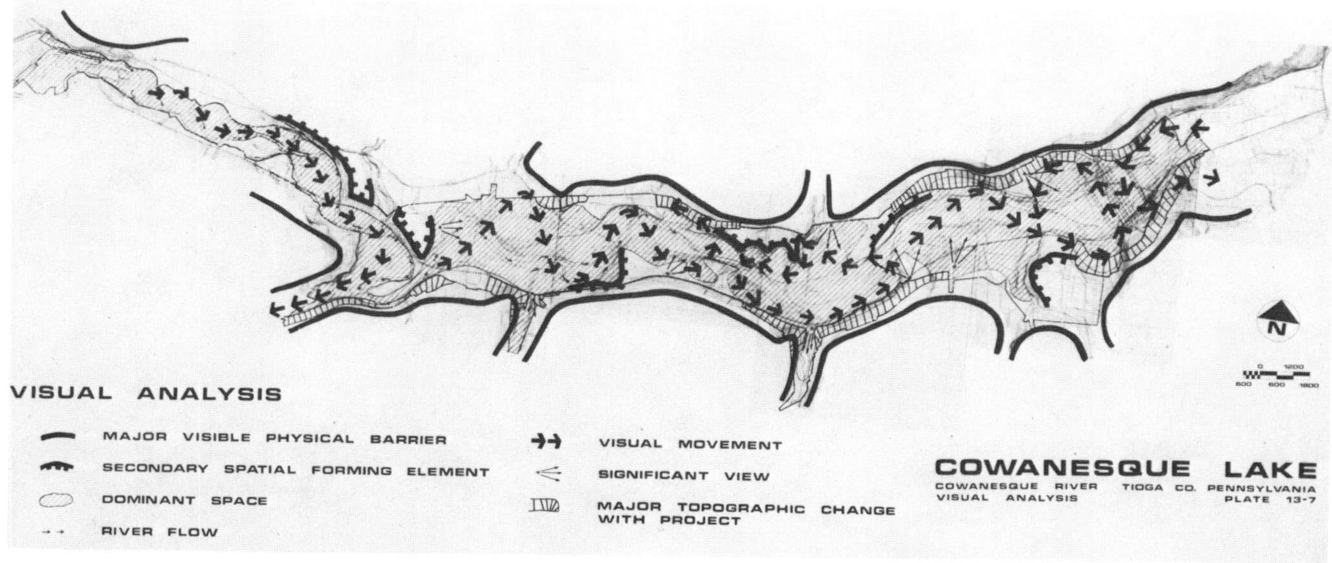

FIG. 2-46 Visual analysis.

FIG. 2-47 The natural component overlays of opportunities and constraints were made into composite maps from which this map of areas of limitation or suitability was developed.

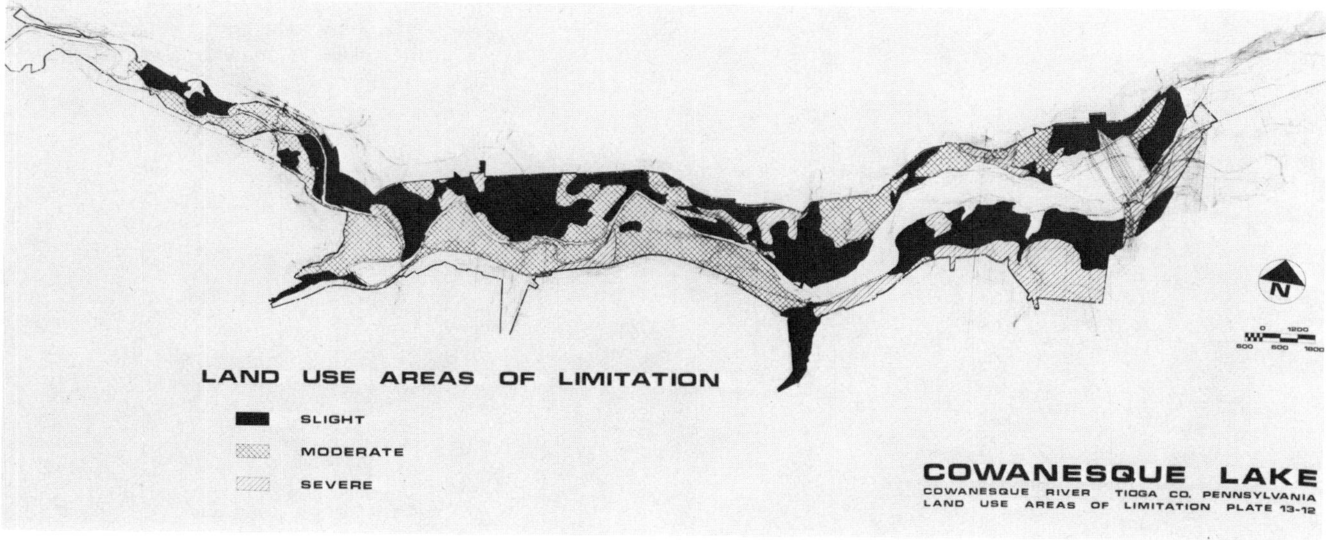

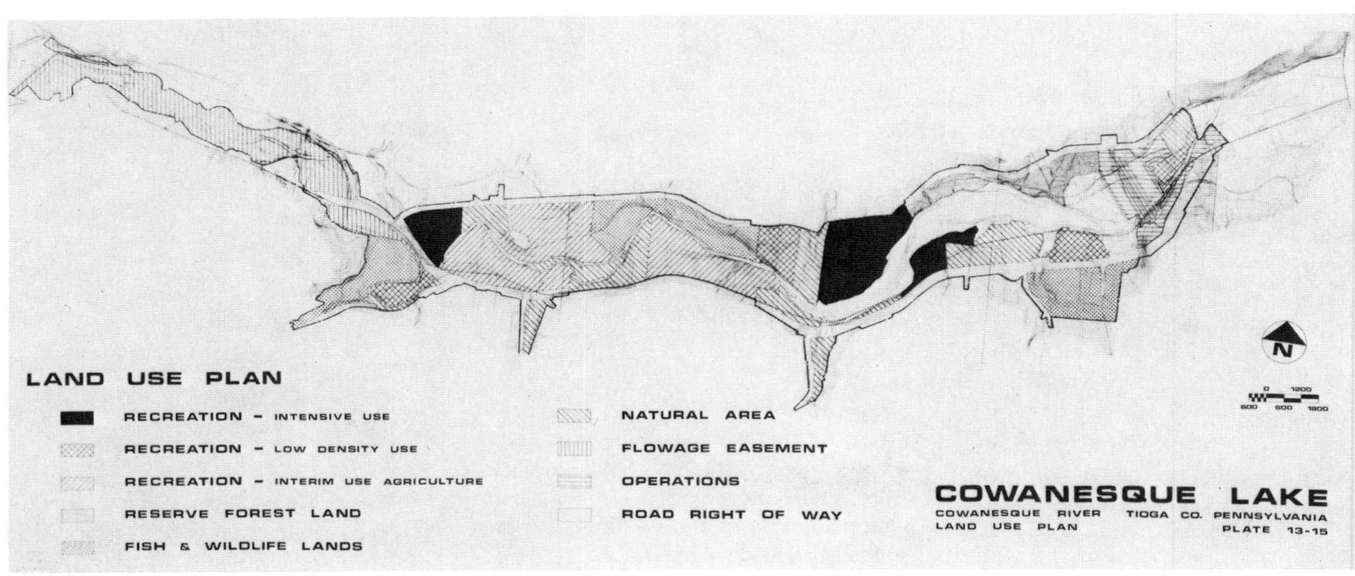

FIG. 2-48 The land use plan based on the resource analysis was then developed.

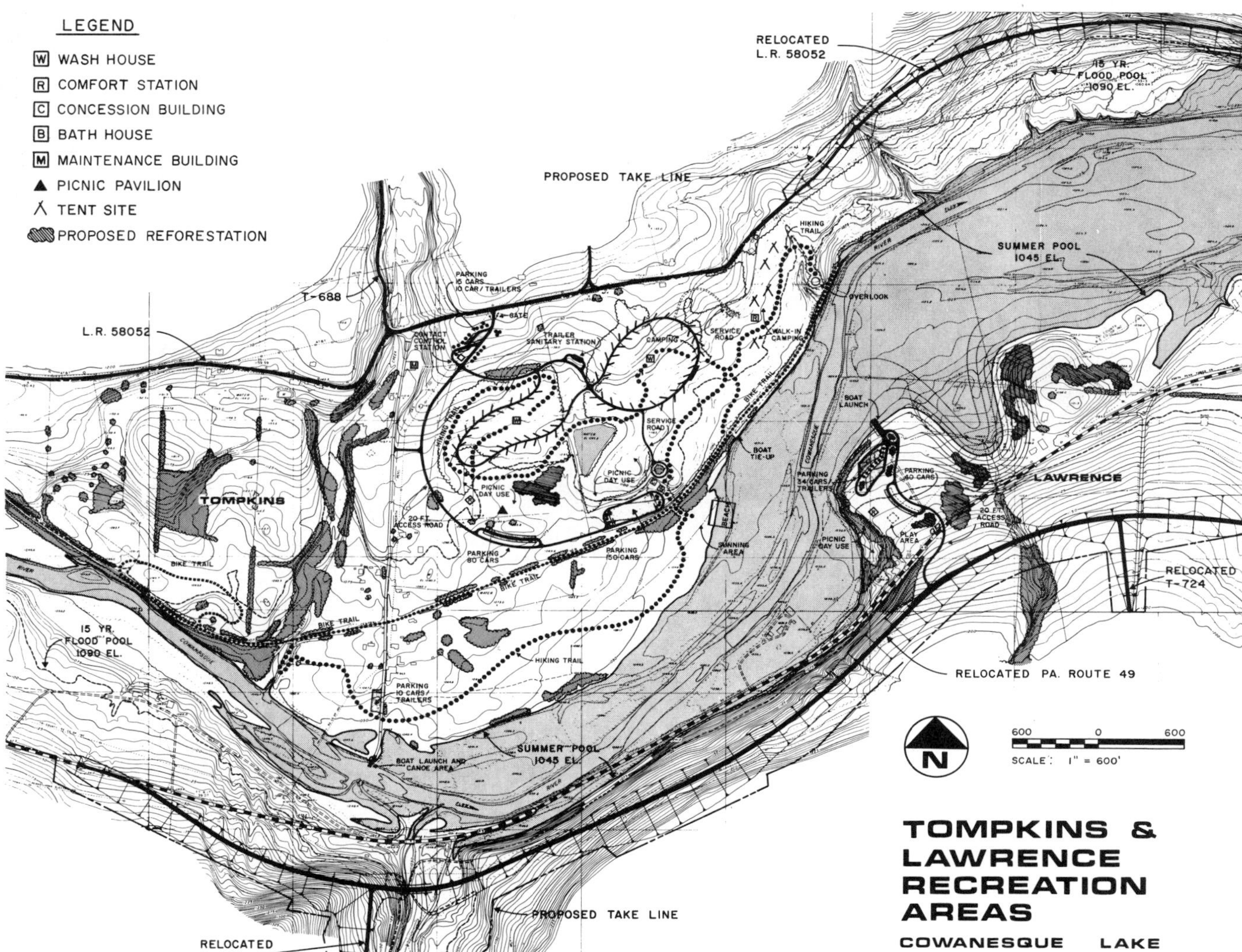

FIG. 2-49 Schematic site plans were developed for the Tompkins and Lawrence Recreation areas.

FIG. 3-1 Pedestrian circulation as a major structuring element at Foothill College, Los Altos, California (Photograph courtesy of Sasaki Associates).

Chapter Three
Land Use and Circulation

LAND USE

The land use plan evolves from the analytical phase. (See Fig. 3-2.) It shows the general functional arrangement of a plan in terms of types of activities, linkages, and densities. Activities must be grouped so they will function in relation to each other. When land uses have been established, the linkages between them must be evaluated. Linkages may be the movement of people, goods, or wastes, communication networks, or a connection of amenity such as views. Land use also involves the concept of density or number of families per acre. In community development plans, density standards must be adhered to.

The activities and linkages are summarized in abstract relational diagrams. Alternative diagrams must be evaluated to obtain a good solution. Value judgment, creativity, and imagination must be used to develop these diagrams, which may be judged on linkages between activities and a sense of form and organization. If diagrams are drawn in scale with land areas, their accommodation to the actual site will become apparent. The land uses shown in abstract relational diagrams must be considered in relation to natural site features and with a general visual form in mind. They should not be forced on the site, but should develop by manipulation or rearrangement of uses that keep functional relationships and linkages and also adapt to physical site conditions.

The type of construction will also influence the land use plan. If a plan is not economically feasible because of excessive site work, an alternative may be necessary. On the other hand, the type of construction may be a major factor in determining a particular land use and may require a specific type of site, which is flat, rolling, or hilly. (See Figs. 3-3 to 3-5.)

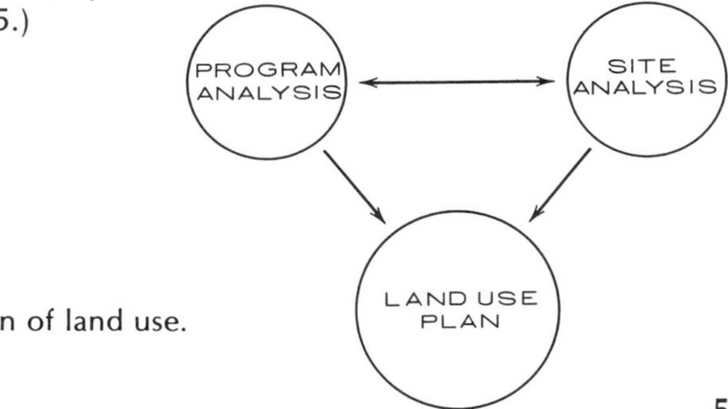

FIG. 3-2 Evolution of land use.

FIG. 3-3 Type of construction may influence the land use plan. Habitat, Expo 67.

FIG. 3-4 At Oakford Glen Condominiums in Abington Township, Pennsylvania, the buildings step down a steep site (Photograph courtesy of Bellante, Clauss, Miller & Partners).

FIG. 3-5 At McCoy Park in Independence, Missouri, playground areas step down the site giving an amphitheatre effect from the shelter pavilions on the upper level.

CIRCULATION

Circulation systems are vital linkages that relate activities and uses on the land. The vehicular circulation system in particular produces one of the primary structuring elements of a land use plan. This system forms a hierarchy of flow or change of scale from major to minor roads within a project and also connects with off-site networks bringing people and goods to the site. On the site, and in conjunction with buildings or recreational activities, the circulation pattern must solve the difficulties of approach, drop-off and parking, and service, all in a clear and organized sequence.

One of the site planner's major concerns is the development of the vehicular and pedestrian circulation systems, but utility and communication networks are directly related to road and walk patterns. For a unified comprehensive design to be achieved, pipelines for water and sewage, gas, oil, power, and telephone transmission must be interrelated with all elements on the site. Often utility and communication lines are placed underground; however, telephone and electric power lines are frequently elevated. Economics may influence the final decision between alternatives.

After the overall importance of circulation is examined patterns and criteria of arrangement and development should be pursued in depth. The following examples show some of the analysis studies that were made for the expansion of an existing university. Among them were existing vehicular and pedestrian circulation plans that influenced the land use plan. Alternative circulation plans were then reviewed in order to structure the land use plan. (See Figs. 3-6 to 3-10.)

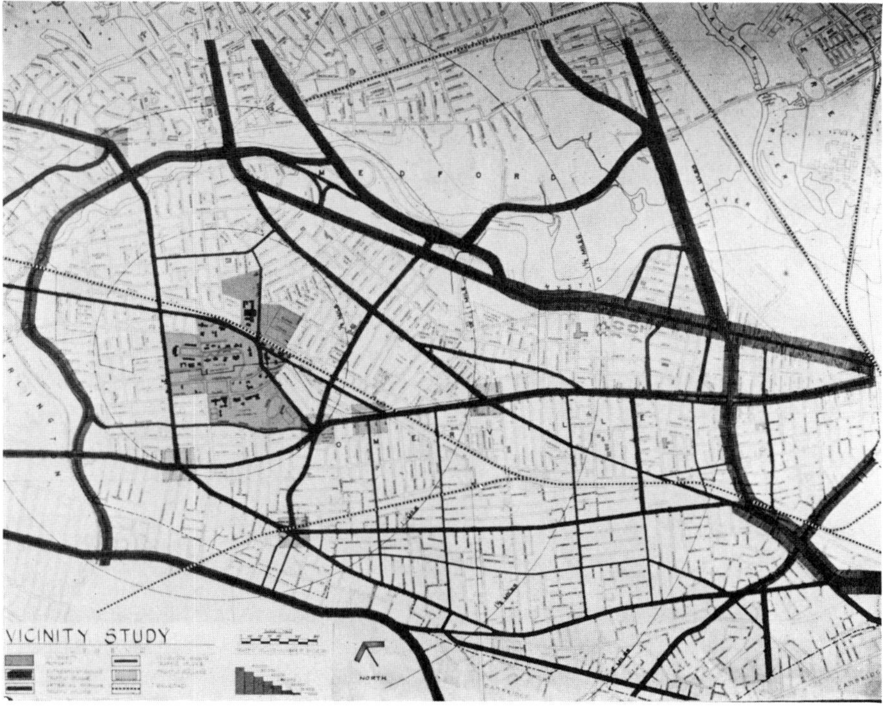

FIG. 3-6 Study map of vicinity vehicular circulation: the width of streets on this map shows the hierarchy of their use.

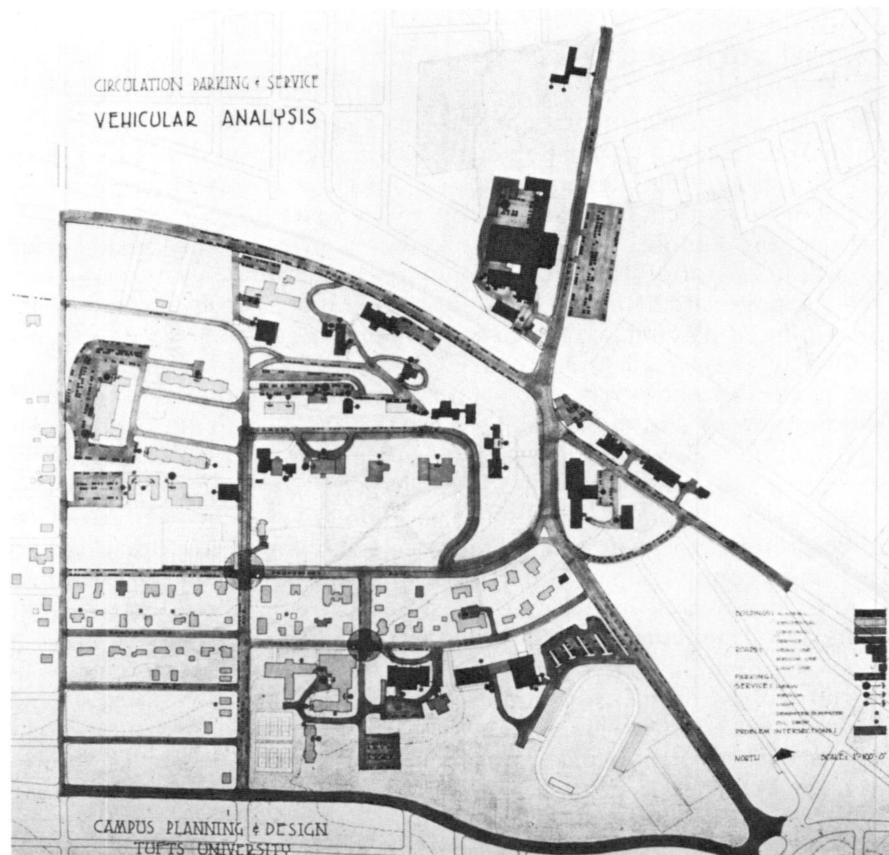

FIG. 3-7 Inventory of vehicular circulation: existing roads, parking, and service must be analyzed before future expansion proceeds.

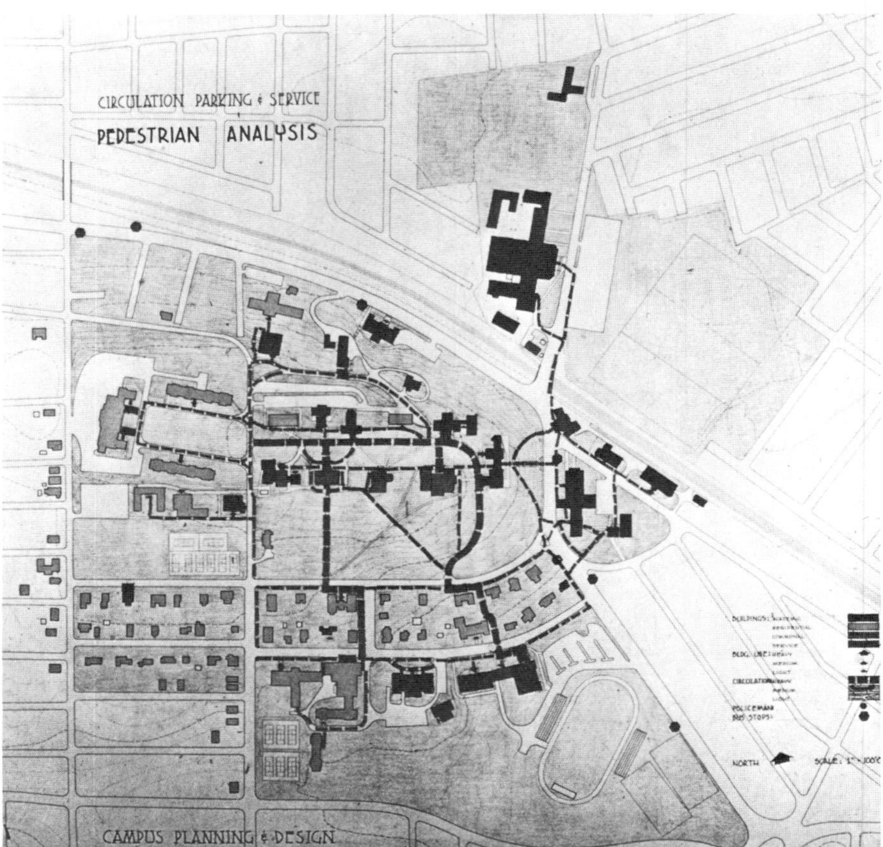

FIG. 3-8 Inventory of pedestrian circulation: an objective of this study is to determine if adequate separation exists between pedestrian and vehicular circulation.

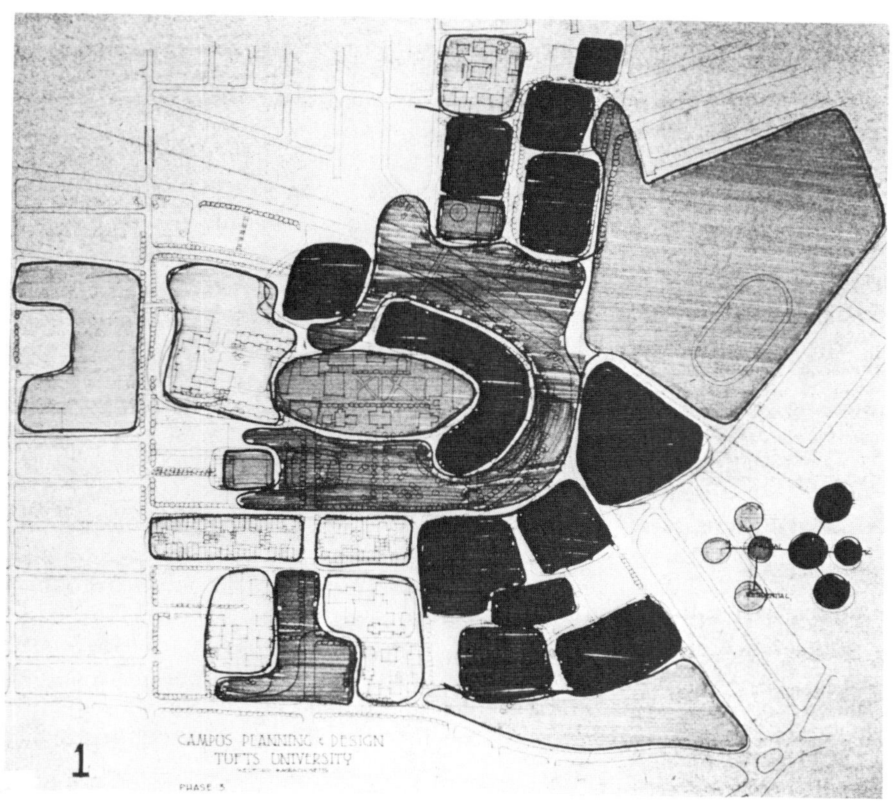

FIG. 3-9 Future land use plan: this plan developed from the analysis phase. Designated areas are related to existing facilities and natural site features.

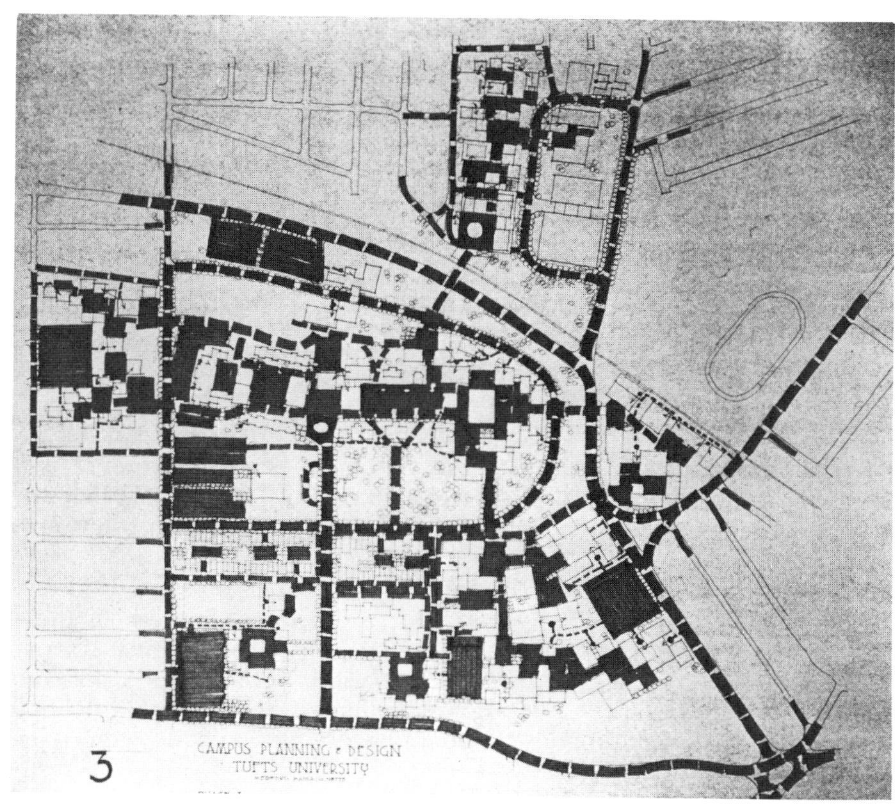

FIG. 3-10 Future vehicular and pedestrian circulation study: this plan develops linkages necessary to carry out the land use plan.

FIG. 3-11 Grid system.

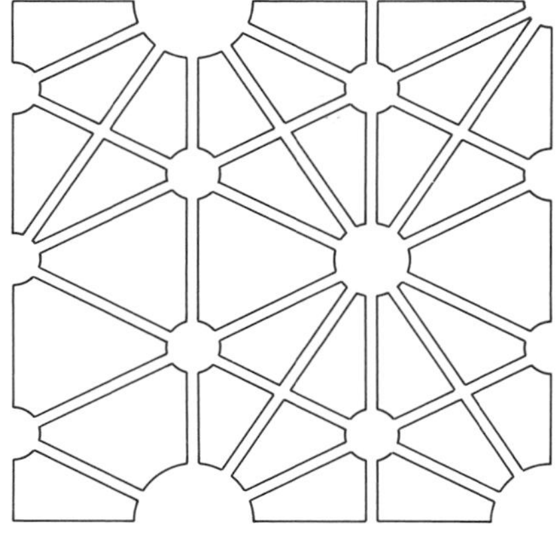
FIG. 3-12 Radial system.

FIG. 3-13 Linear system.

Vehicular Circulation Patterns

Circulation systems are not simply haphazard; they fall into categories or classifications—grid, radial, linear, or curvilinear systems and various combinations of these.

Grid System. The grid system is usually comprised of equally spaced streets running perpendicular to each other. Generally used on flat or slightly rolling land, it is often poorly applied and results in visual monotony or unsympathetic handling of topography.

Since grids are easy to follow, they may be used for complex distribution of flow if a hierarchy of channels is established. This hierarchy is frequently neglected, leading to confusion and overloading of some arteries. By adapting the grid to fit topography through bending, warping, varying size of blocks, and establishing a hierarchy of flow for streets, a more interesting and workable pattern may be attained. (See Fig. 3-11.)

Radial System. A radial system directs flow to a common center; where high levels of activity exist, however, the center may become hard to manage. Since its center is fixed and therefore is not easily adaptable to change, this system is not as flexible as the grid.

Rings may be added to the system allowing for bypassing of movement, and additional flow may branch out from points other than the center. Streets branching out from points along the main artery permit collection of minor distribution of flow at the local level and its direction toward the center. (See Fig. 3-12.)

Linear System. The linear system of circulation connects flow between two points and is illustrated by railroad lines or canals. An adaptation for this system is the use of loops on either side of the main artery to aid local flow. (See Fig. 3-13.)

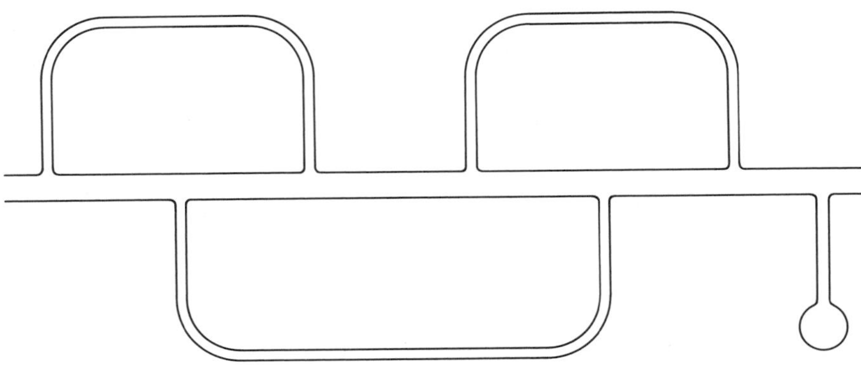

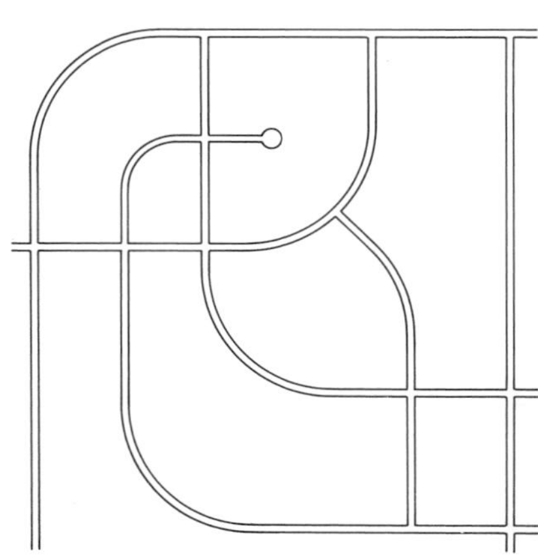
FIG. 3-14. Curvilinear system.

Curvilinear System. The curvilinear system takes advantage of topography by following the land as closely as possible. This system is closely related to traffic at the local level and may have a variety of street alignments readily adaptable to topography. In a curvilinear system, there are fewer through streets as compared with the grid. *Cul-de-sacs,* dead-end streets having a maximum length of 500 ft, are commonly used. All these elements have a tendency to slow traffic down. With a curvilinear system, streets are more interesting because of varied views, street types and lengths, and adaptability to topographic change. Increasingly, planned unit residential developments are adapting the curvilinear system. (See Fig. 3-14.)

Organization of Vehicular Circulation

In organizing vehicular circulation on the site, consider alternative designs to arrive at both a viable and aesthetically harmonious solution. Note the type of people who will be using the site. Are they employees, students, or visitors or are they providing a service? How many will there be and will they be arriving by car, bus, or truck?

On the approaches to the site there should be a good unobstructed view of the entry drive from either direction on the highway. Sight distance varies with speed and the number of lanes of highway; for example, a minimum of 200 ft is desirable at 30 mph, 275 ft at 40 mph, and 350 ft at 50 mph. Strive for a natural feeling of entry and take advantage of existing site features. Explore the site to determine whether an entry drive can be situated between large existing trees, two knolls, or other topographic forms that lend themselves to such an entry.

The alignment of roads must follow existing topography as closely as possible. Road alignment should also make use of pleasing views and existing site features on the approach drive, rather than ignoring them as often happens. Do not allow the observer's eye to slip by a building. Provide a good direct view of the building and its entry. (See Figs. 3-15 and 3-16.)

FIG. 3-15 The entry drive to John Deere, Moline, Illinois, by Sasaki Associates uses a pleasing road alignment and allows glimpses of the building on the approach by Sasaki Associates (Photograph courtesy of Kurt Youngstrom).

FIG. 3-16 The natural landscape flows uninterrupted by elevating the road over existing landforms on the site at John Deere, Moline, Illinois, by Sasaki Associates (Photograph courtesy of Kurt Youngstrom).

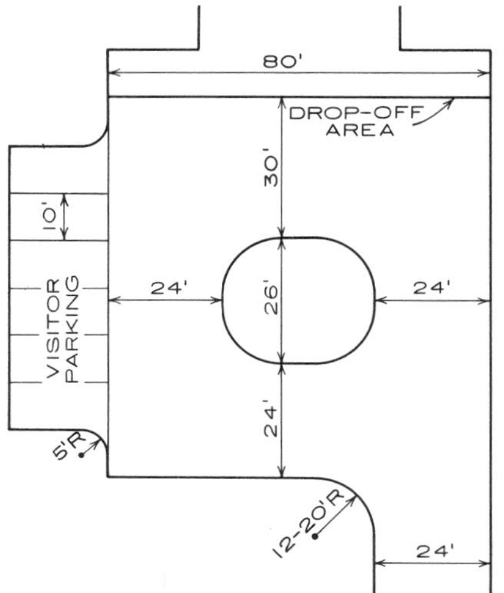

FIG. 3-17 Rectilinear drop-off area.

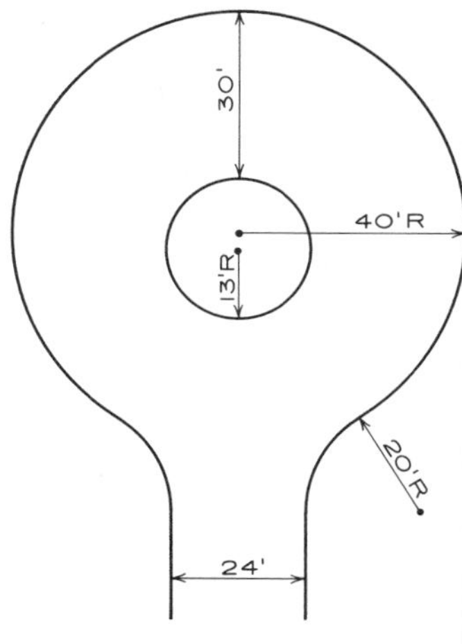

FIG. 3-18 Curvilinear drop-off area.

FIG. 3-19 Master plan of Kansas City International Airport, Missouri. The penetration of the landscape into the terminal areas plays a significant part in giving passengers pleasant views on the approach to their gates. Three passenger terminals, each with 15 gates, will be constructed in the first phase of development. This concept also provides for ease of vehicular and pedestrian circulation, which includes a short walking distance from parking to terminals (Photograph courtesy Kivett & Myers).

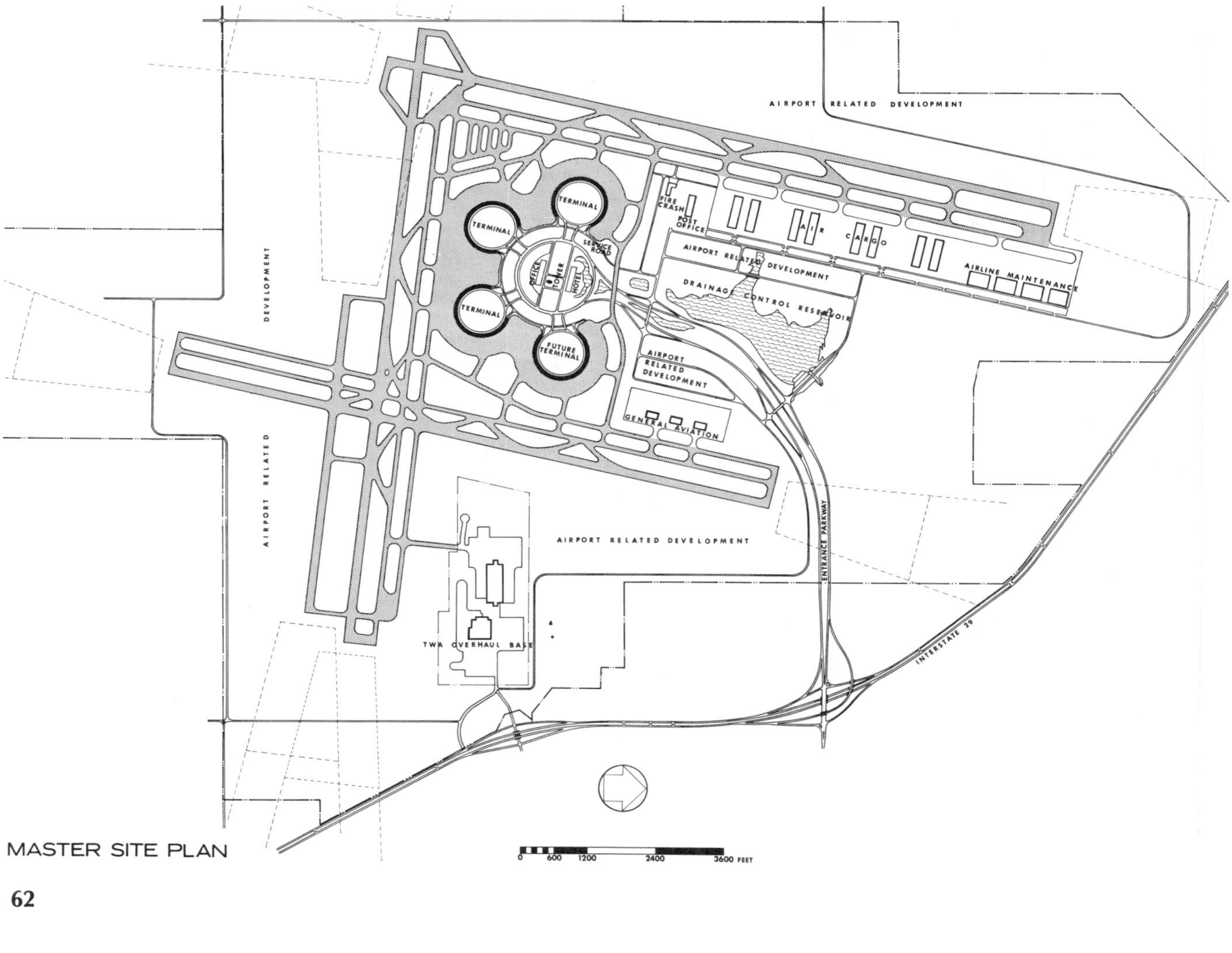

MASTER SITE PLAN

The arrival and turnaround area should be designed for a right-handed drop-off. (See Figs. 3-17 and 3-18.) This permits passengers to arrive at the building entry without having to cross any roads. The drop-off area must be in scale with the building and designed for vehicles using it. Eighty feet is the minimum diameter desirable for automobile turnaround and drop-off areas, while 100 ft or more may be desirable where buses are used. The drop-off area can be covered for protection from rain or snow, as is often done on public buildings, especially schools. (See Figs. 3-19 to 3-23.)

FIG. 3-20 This model of a typical terminal area clearly shows the sequence of approach, drop-off, and parking at Kansas City International Airport. The drop-off area is covered to protect passengers from rain or snow. Parking areas are depressed 4 ft below grade. This, along with a retaining wall, provides a screening element. Five pedestrian walks radiate from the center of the parking area, giving a maximum walking distance of about 200 ft to the terminal (Photograph courtesy of Kivett & Myers).

FIG. 3-21 This model of Kansas City International Airport shows in further detail the design of the terminal buildings, the passenger drop-off area, the connection of the parking and terminal areas, and the use of trees to soften and add scale to the project (Photograph courtesy of Kivett & Myers).

FIG. 3-22 Circulation is handled very well at Dulles International Airport, Washington, D.C. There are separate levels for the enplaning and deplaning of passengers and complete separation of pedestrian and vehicular circulation from the parking level.

FIG. 3-23 New Jersey Sports & Exposition Complex: parking is provided for over 20,000 cars and 400 charter buses. Pedestrian malls provide ease of circulation to both Giant Football Stadium and the race track grandstand (Photograph courtesy of DiLullo, Clauss, Ostroski, & Partners).

When insufficient transition areas occur between roads and buildings, walls, walks, steps or trees other than at drop-off areas, visual and physical crowding results. A minimum distance between paved areas and existing trees is 6 ft; this may vary, however, depending on the size of trees and existing site conditions. If not given adequate space, trees may die because of altered site conditions to which they have not adapted. (See Figs. 3-24 and 3-25.)

Visitor and Other Parking. To meet program requirements, visitor parking should link with building approach and drop-off areas and be within short walking distance of the building it serves. It should not be combined with turnaround islands or other areas that obstruct the view of a building. Visitors should not be required to arrive at a building by first driving through a parking lot. Public parking areas must have a clear connection to the entry, but those people who simply wish to park their

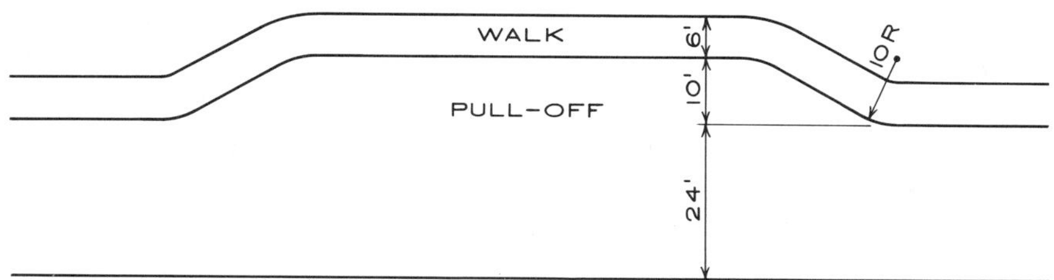

FIG. 3-24 Pull-off area.

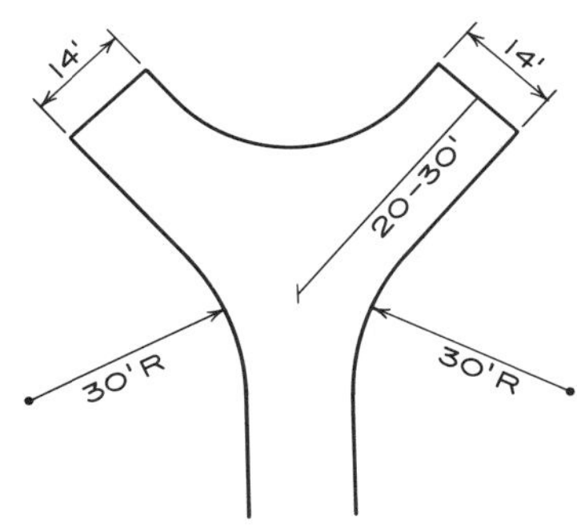

FIG. 3-25 Backup and turnaround.

cars directly without dropping anyone off should not have to drive past the drop-off area. Walking distance from any parking area to a facility must be as short and convenient as possible.

In shopping centers large asphalt areas can be softened by depressing paving below grade and using trees and other plant material. In estimating parking areas the site planner can use 300 ft² per car as a standard. This figure includes the parking stall, plus aisles. In shopping centers about 3 or 4 ft² of parking space is used for each square foot of gross floor space.

Service Areas. Service areas can work in conjunction with parking facilities; it is always better, however, to separate parking and service to reduce conflict of use. Since there must be adequate maneuvering space, design for the largest service vehicle using the site. Locate service areas so that they do not block any major views. Do not block entry and turnaround areas by close proximity of truck service. (See Figs. 3-26 and 3-27.)

Street Widths	
Minor streets	9–11 ft per lane
Major streets	10–14 ft per lane
Collector streets such as boulevards	10–18 ft per lane
Parallel parking in addition to street	8–10 ft per side
Private drives	8– 9 ft per lane
Service drives	12–14 ft in width

Residential Streets	
Collector streets, plus emergency parking	36 ft in width
Multifamily, plus parking	32 ft in width
Single family, plus parking	26 ft in width
Cul-de-sacs, plus parking on one side	20 ft in width

Turning Radii	
Minor streets	$12\frac{1}{2}$–15 ft radius
Major arteries used by large trucks	35 –50 ft radius

Street Intersections. Street intersections are shown in Figs. 3-28 to 3-33.

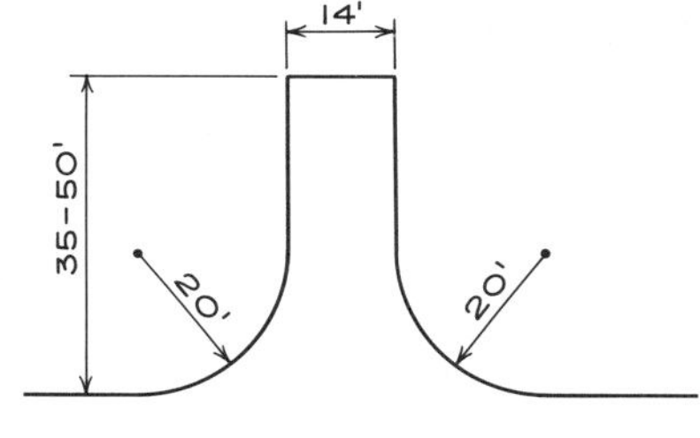

FIG. 3-26. Service area.

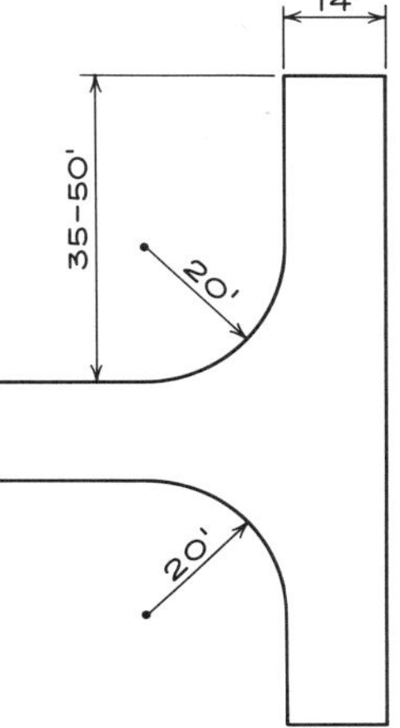

FIG. 3-27 Service area.

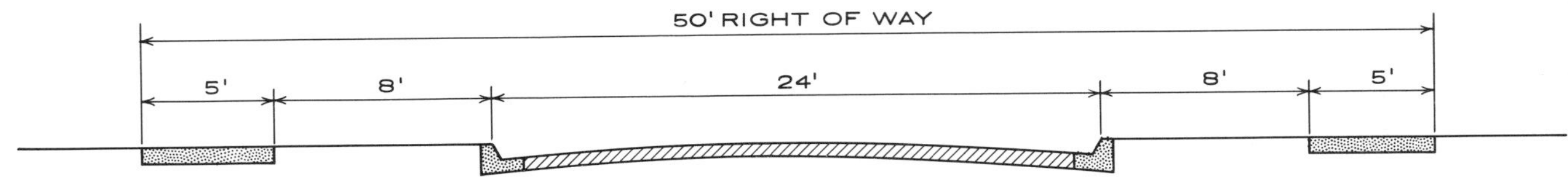

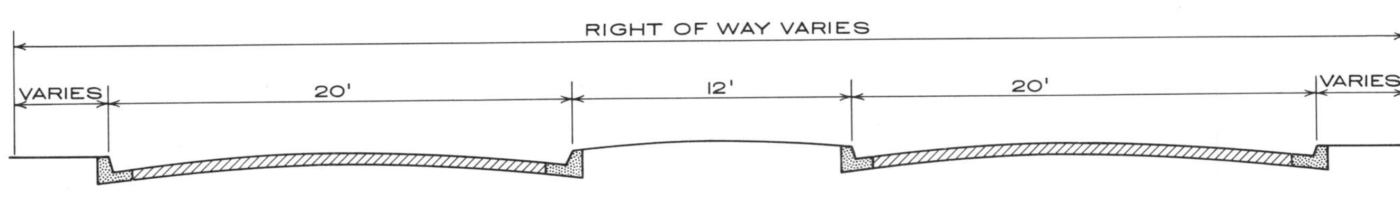

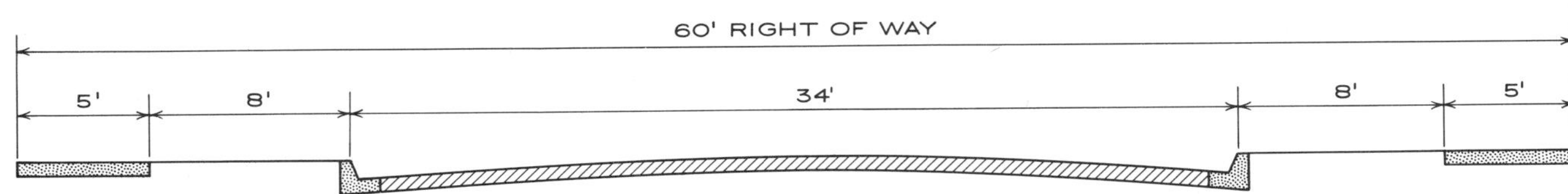

FIG. 3-28 Typical street sections.

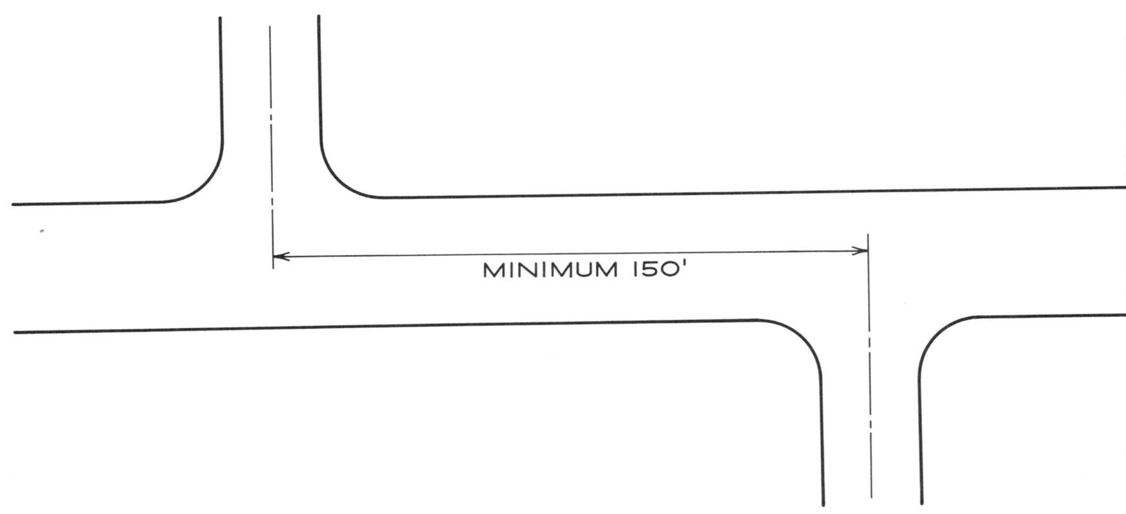

FIG. 3-29 Street intersections should be a minimum of 150 ft apart.

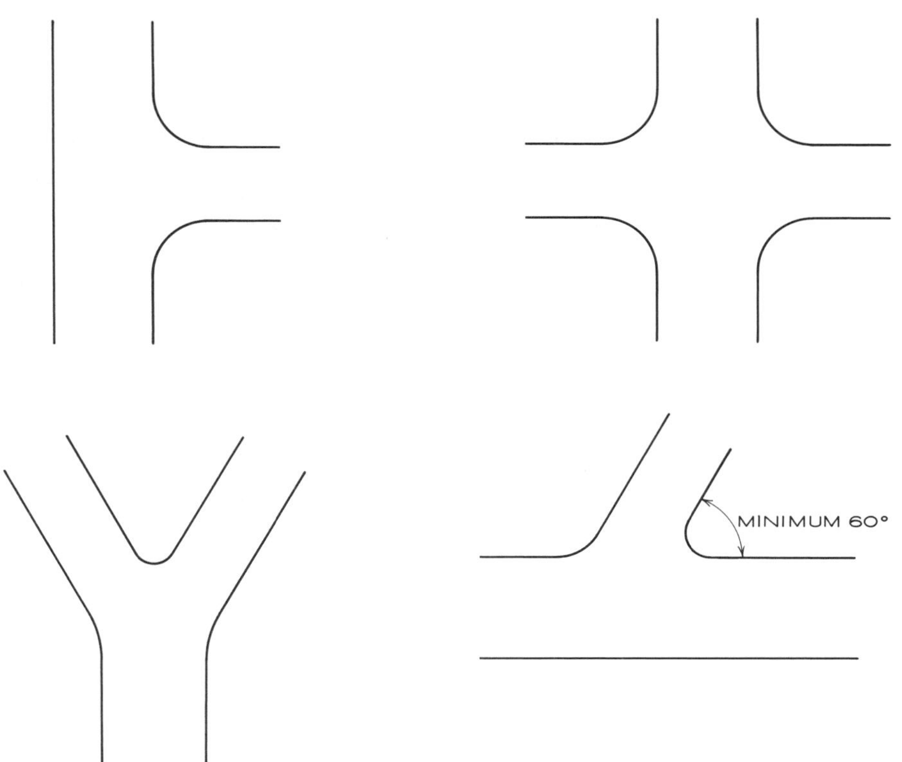

FIG. 3-30 The T-junction is good for minor road connections.

FIG. 3-31 The four-way intersection is often used for both minor and major road connections. There are more possible contact points for accidents with this type of intersection than with the T-junction.

FIG. 3-32 The Y-junction is dangerous and should be avoided.

FIG. 3-33 The angular intersection may be used where the angle is a minimum of 60°.

Organization of Pedestrian Circulation

The primary objectives of pedestrian circulation are safety, security, convenience, coherence, comfort, and aesthetics. Pedestrian circulation forms an important linkage in relating activities on a site. It may be a principal structuring element, particularly where the pedestrian is given primary consideration in projects such as college campuses, shopping malls, and recreation areas.

Pedestrians will generally follow the most direct path; if, however, a walk system is developed with points of visual interest, the pedestrian may take a longer route because of its added aesthetic enjoyment. When existing paths are circuitous, new ones may be worn through grass or planted areas. They may eventually be paved, but proper study of pedestrian flow would have prevented this problem.

In a pedestrian circulation system, the width of walks or plazas depends on their capacity, scale, and relation to other design elements. Although 5 ft is the average width for sidewalks and is also the desirable minimum for wheelchairs, they may vary from 8 to 12 ft in width at vehicular drop-off areas or where volume or use make it necessary. On a pedestrian plaza or mall, large paved areas may be 40 ft or more to accommodate circulation.

Alignment of walks, the visual approach to a building, and the spatial sequence along the walk are significant factors in the design of pedestrian circulation. Fitting walks to topography and using natural site features to best advantage make for an aesthetically pleasing solution. Walks with long curves and short tangents are most desirable. There must also be a hierarchy of walk widths to distribute varying volumes of pedestrian traffic to its destination.

In establishing pedestrian circulation, studying these factors along with the texture and color of paving materials will lead to a harmonious relationship with other site elements. (See Figs. 3-34 to 3-41.)

FIG. 3-34 Curvilinear walkway systems may direct pedestrian flow through campus areas and provide interest from varying alignment and sight lines: Foothill College, Los Altos, California.

FIG. 3-35 Angular walk systems also have interest from varying widths and sight lines: Northwest Plaza, St. Louis, Missouri.

FIG. 3-36. Angular entrance courtyard at Bushkill Headquarters Building, Delaware Water Gap National Recreation Area (Photograph courtesy Bellante, Clauss, Miller & Partners; photographer, Otto Baitz).

FIG. 3-37 A rectilinear format is used at Northeastern Bank Plaza, Scranton, Pennsylvania (Photograph courtesy of Bellante, Clauss, Miller & Partners).

FIG. 3-38 A rectilinear podium formed by walls and reflecting pools defines the pedestrian areas at the Kimbell Art Museum in Fort Worth, Texas.

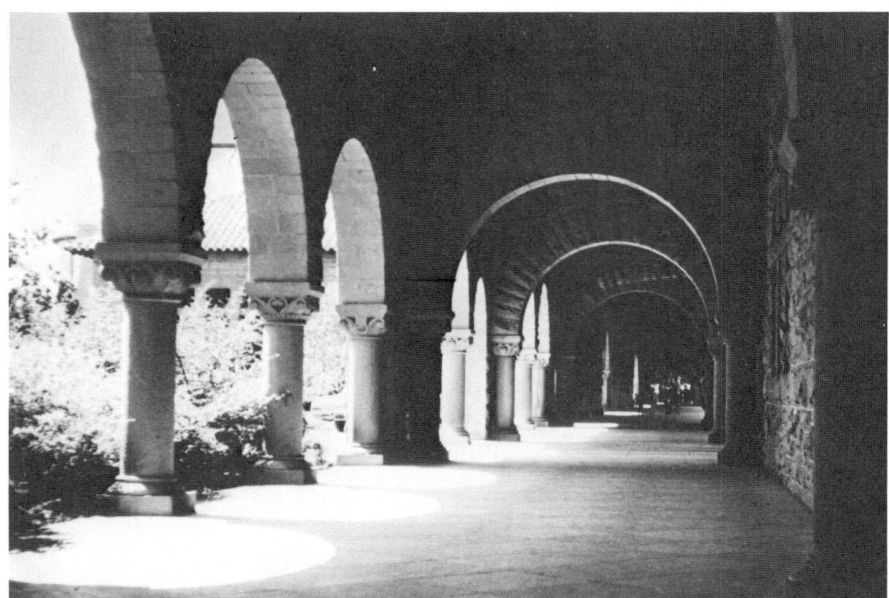

FIG. 3-39 Covered pedestrian walkways offer protection from precipitation and the direct heat of sunlight at Stanford University, Palo Alto, California.

FIG. 3-40 This footbridge separates pedestrian and vehicular circulation in Farsta, Sweden.

FIG. 3-41 A footbridge links drop-off to intensive use area at McCoy Park, Independence, Missouri.

Determining Pedestrian Flow

The formula for calculating pedestrian flow volume (P), in pedestrians per foot width of walkway per minute (PFM) is the following:

$$P = \frac{S}{M}$$

where P = pedestrian volume
S = average pedestrian speed per minute
M = average number of square feet per pedestrian

For example, if the average pedestrian speed per minute is 270 ft and there is an average pedestrian area of 30 ft^2, the pedestrian volume equals 9 PFM:

$$\frac{270 \text{ ft/minute}}{30 \text{ ft}^2\text{/pedestrian}} = 9 \text{ PFM}$$

Surveys show the average free flow walking speed for males as 270 ft/minute, for females 254 ft/minute, and for all pedestrians combined 265 ft/minute. Mean speeds for dense pedestrian flows are generally normal, up to about 25 ft^2/person. Below this square footage speed usually declines quickly. (See Tables 3-1 and 3-2.) The minimum normal walking speed of 145 ft/minute is attained with an occupancy of 7 ft^2/person.

Table 3-1 Level of Service on Walks[a]

Ft^2/Person	Average Flow (PFM)	Speed and Bypassing
35	7 or less	Free selection of speed Can bypass freely No severe peaks
25–35	7–10	Normal walking speed Can bypass others No severe peaks
15–25	10–15	Walking speed is restricted slightly Inability to bypass freely
10–15	15–20	Majority have normal walking speed restricted Difficulty in bypassing
5–10	20–25	All pedestrians have speed restricted Much difficulty in bypassing
5 or less	up to 25	Extremely restricted Frequent unavoidable contact with people and no bypassing

[a]Reproduced from John J. Fruin, *Pedestrian Planning and Design*. New York: Metropolitan Association of Urban Designers and Environmental Planners, Inc., 1971.

Table 3-2 Level of Service on Stairs[a]

Ft^2/Person	Average Flow (PFM)	Speed and Bypassing
20^+	5 or less	Free selection of speed Can bypass No severe peaks
15–20	5–7	Free selection of speed Some difficulty in passing slower pedestrians
10–15	7–10	Speed restricted slightly Inability to bypass slower pedestrians
7–10	10–13	Speed restricted for majority Inability to bypass majority of pedestrians
4–7	13–17	All persons have normal speed reduced Inability to bypass others Intermittent stopping may occur
4 or less	up to 17	Breakdown in traffic flow with much stopping

[a]Reproduced from John J. Fruin, *Pedestrian Planning and Design*. New York: Metropolitan Association of Urban Designers and Environmental Planners, Inc., 1971.

At an average speed of 145 ft/minute at 7 ft^2/pedestrian the pedestrian volume equals 145 divided by 7 or 20^+ PFM. Assuming a 3 ft walkway, this would provide 60 pedestrians/minute. The time spacing interval can be determined as follows:

$$\frac{60 \text{ seconds/minute}}{60 \text{ pedestrians/minute}} = 1 \text{ second/pedestrian}$$

The distance between pedestrians is found by dividing the 145 ft/minute speed by 60 pedestrians/minute calculated earlier for an interval of 2.4 ft.

Example

If 1000 pedestrians in a 10 minute period at 25 ft^2/person with a speed of 250 ft/minute use a walk, how wide is the walk? Using the average walking speed of 250 ft/minute divided by 25 ft^2/person equals 10 PFM. Setting up the following equation we can find the walk width:

$$\frac{1000 \text{ pedestrians}}{10 \text{ minutes} \times 10 \text{ pedestrians/minute}} = 10 \text{ ft walk width}$$

Generally $1\frac{1}{2}$ ft is added to each side of the walk for side clearance from buildings or the street for an additional width of 3 ft. This would actually allow for a 13 ft walk width in the example provided.

Steps and Ramp

Where grades become excessive, ramps or stairs must be used. The maximum number of risers per set is 10 or 12 (*risers* are the vertical surface of the step, *treads*, the horizontal). It is best to have a set of stairs no higher than eye level so that the pedestrian may judge the distance to the top of a landing safely. To prevent tripping over one or two stairs not easily seen, provide at least three risers. Handrails are used for five or more risers, especially where wet or icy conditions prevail.

A general rule to follow in establishing the size of risers and treads is 2 risers + tread = 26 in. This rule has evolved from the length of the average person's stride. Step dimensions commonly used are $5\frac{1}{2}$ in. riser with 15 in. tread and 6 in. riser with $13\frac{1}{2}$ to $14\frac{1}{2}$ in. tread. Risers are seldom over 6 in. outdoors because a small tread would appear out of scale. Cheek walls are used for maintenance purposes and often lighting is incorporated with them. Illuminate tops of stair landings for safety.

Ramps. Ramps usually have an absolute minimum length of 5 ft; $6\frac{1}{2}$ ft, however, has become a desirable minimum length based on a person's stride. Ramp grades under 6% are easier for people to use. The stated desirable maximum is 10%, although ramps up to 15% are sometimes used. (See Figs. 3-42 to 3-45.)

Handicapped Ramps. Handicapped ramps should have a maximum grade of 8.33% (1 : 12 slope). On long steep slopes, flat resting areas are needed at about 30 ft intervals or where changes in direction occur. Flat areas should also extend beyond the width of building doorways where ramps are used to allow room for maneuvering the wheelchair. Curbs 2 in. or more in height are often used on both sides of a ramp for safety in keeping the wheelchair on the ramp. Adult size wheelchairs are 27 in. wide and 42 in. long. The minimum width of a ramp should be 4 ft, which allows one person in a wheelchair and one pedestrian to pass. A 5 ft wide ramp is desirable and allows two persons using wheelchairs to pass.

FIG. 3-42 Steps work with the change in grade along the sidewalk at the Neighborhood Facilities Center, Scranton, Pennsylvania (Photograph courtesy Bellante, Clauss, Miller & Partners).

FIG. 3-43 An outdoor stairway at the University of California, Los Angeles, acts as a focal point in the landscape.

FIG. 3-44 These steps in combination with architecture have a strong directional movement and establish an entrance sequence leading to the quadrangle above at Wellesley College, Wellesley, Massachusetts.

FIG. 3-45 Lighting and handrailings promote safety and are incorporated with these steps at the University of California, Santa Cruz.

Handrails are often used by people in wheelchairs to help themselves up ramps. These handrails should be rounded with a lower handrail about 19 in. from the ramp to the top of the rail. A clearance of $1\frac{1}{2}$ in. should also be provided between the handrail and a wall. Upper handrails are usually 33 in. above the ramp and 36 in. above a flat walk or pad leading to the ramp or to a set of steps. If handrails are not present on public walks, the grade should not exceed 5% on at least one entrance.

Ramps at curb cuts providing access to cross walks should have a maximum grade of 8.33% (1 : 12 slope) where possible, but up to 16.66% (1 : 6 slope) is allowable on narrow walks. If a curb cut is used at cross walks or where a ramp meets the street, there should be no more than $\frac{1}{2}$ in. of curb projecting above the street for ease of use.

Bikeways

Bicycle paths have become popular in the United States. These paths have been designated into three classifications.

Class 1
Class 1 has a completely separated right-of-way for the exclusive use of bicycles. Cross-flow by pedestrians or automobiles is limited and a physical separation is placed between cars and bicycles on protected street lanes.

Class 2
This class has restricted right-of-way for either the exclusive or semiexclusive use of bicycles. This system is often referred to as a bike lane. Though travel by pedestrians or automobiles is not permitted, cross-flows are allowed for access to driveways or parking facilities.

Class 3
In this class a shared right-of-way is designated by signs and is referred to as a bike route.

Separating bicycle paths from pedestrians is desirable because bicycle speed is often three to four times as fast as pedestrian walking speed. Pedestrians also can change direction unpredictably and small children often play on sidewalks causing possible safety problems for the bicyclist.

Design Criteria

Bicycle speeds average about 10 mph, with potentials of 30 mph or more. The average speed on slight downgrades is about 20 mph. At these speeds sufficient lane width, radii of curves, stopping sight distance, and appropriate grades must be provided for the bicyclist to avoid safety problems. The bicycle itself takes up about a 24 × 70 in. area of space. Allowing a minimum of 8 in. on either side of the handle bars gives a width of 40 in. for operation. While 4 ft is the minimum bicycle path acceptable, it does not provide room for passing. For paths along streets, 6 ft lane widths are better as a minimum and passing is possible, but 8 ft lanes, especially on separate pathways are desirable for passing or side-by-side bicycling.

The desirable grades on bikeways should not exceed 5% over distances of about 300 ft with maximum desirable grades of 7%. Flat grades of 2–3% are desirable over long distances.

In Oregon, the State Highway Division uses a 20 mph design speed for grades between +3 and –7%. On grades over –7% a 30 mph design speed is used. A formula that relates curve radius to design speed for bicycles has been developed at the University of California at Davis:

$$R = 1.25V + 1.4$$

where V = speed (mph)
R = curve radius (ft)

Maximum desirable radii are about 20 ft. If the speed is 20 mph for example, the radius would be 1.25 × 20 + 1.4 = 26.4 ft.

A formula for calculating the stopping sight distance (ft) for bicycles is

$$S = \frac{V^2}{30f \pm G} + 3.67V$$

where S = stopping sight distance (ft)
V = velocity (mph)
f = coefficient of friction (use 0.25)
G = grade, ft/ft (rise/run)

Parking

Parking is one of the most important land uses on a site. It can be visually disruptive if it is not properly placed in relation to the topography and to other activities or uses. To organize parking, site planners must be aware of the dimensions of the vehicles for which they are designing to provide adequate spaces. Include the overall length, width, front and rear overhang, and minimum turning radii for both inside and outside front and rear bumpers.

Site planners must devise schemes for the largest vehicle using a site (whether cars, buses, or trucks). These factors that affect parking should be investigated. (See page 173.)

1. Size of parking area in square feet and the dimensions.
2. Angle of parking—90, 60, or 45°.
3. Direction of traffic flow to the site.
4. Type of parking—self or attendant.
5. Width of parking spaces—8½, 9, 9½, or 10 ft, with parking spaces for the handicapped at 12 ft.
6. Width of access drive.
7. Organization of circulation within parking area, both vehicular and pedestrian—position of possible points of entrance and exit to minimize crossing movements and turns.
8. Aesthetic factors—depressing parked cars below eye level, planting, lighting, paving material.
9. Drainage of parking area.
10. Maximum walking distance from parking to building.
11. Separation of customer parking and service areas.
12. In shopping centers, parking index—amount of parking for each 1000 ft^2 of gross leasable area, including all basements, mezzanine, and floor area, 3000 to 4000 ft^2.

In some cases width of usable land determines the type of parking. A greater number of cars can be parked at 90° using same stall width than at 60 or 45°. On the other hand, 60, 45, and 30° parking establish a one way traffic system and make it easy to pull into a space. It is more convenient and less hazardous, however, to back out of a space at 90° because of the larger aisle width. (See Table 3-3.)

Table 3-3 Commonly Used Parking Dimensions (ft)[a]

Angle	Width	Curb Length	Length of Space	Aisle Width	Total
90°	9 stall	9	19	24	62
60°	9 stall	10.4	21	18	60
45°	9 stall	12.7	19.8	13	52.6

[a]Reproduced from Geoffrey Baker and Bruno Funaro, *Parking*, by permission of Reinhold Book Corporation, a subsidiary of Chapman-Reinhold, Inc., New York, 1958.

Acute angle parking provides fewer spaces because of the curb length of the stall and the length of the space. Furthermore, there are triangular areas left over at the end of each stall and at the end of each row. If access roads and size of stalls are a minimum width, it takes a longer time to park. One way access roads should be at least 11 ft wide, whereas two way access should be 24 ft wide. Roads leading to parking should not be lined with cars. When people must back on to the road when leaving their parking spaces, traffic is impeded.

To open car doors easily, parking spaces 9 to 10 ft wide should be used in self-parking areas. Spaces 8 to $8\frac{1}{2}$ ft in width make it necessary to squeeze in and out and are simply inconvenient. (See Figs. 3-46 to 3-54.) For handicapped parking spaces a 12 ft wide space is desirable close to buildings on flat grades.

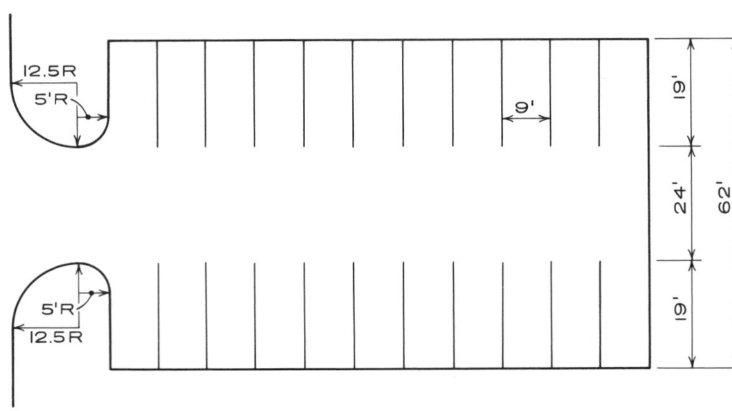

FIG. 3-46 Ninety-degree parking.

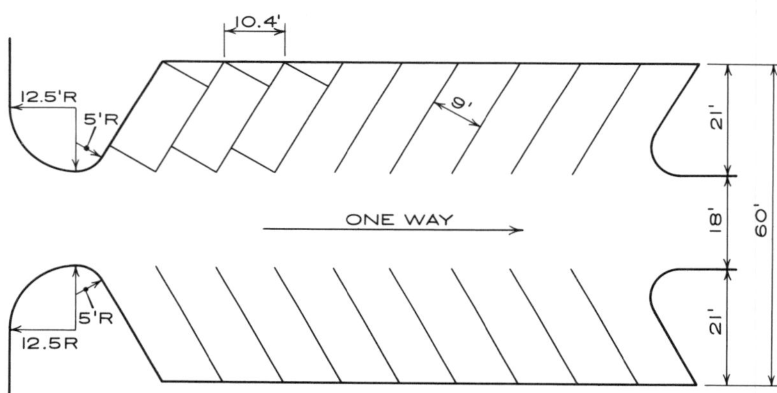

FIG. 3-47 Sixty-degree parking.

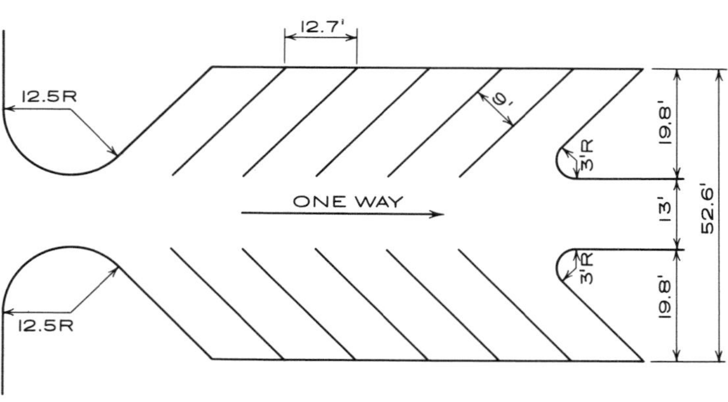

FIG. 3-48 Forty-five-degree parking.

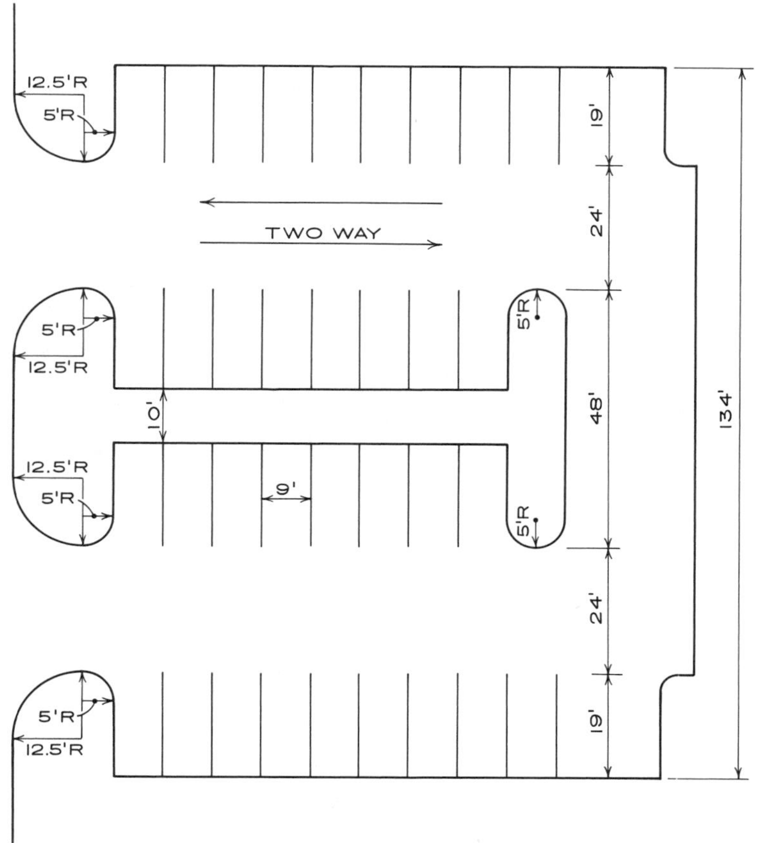

FIG. 3-49 Multilaned 90° parking.

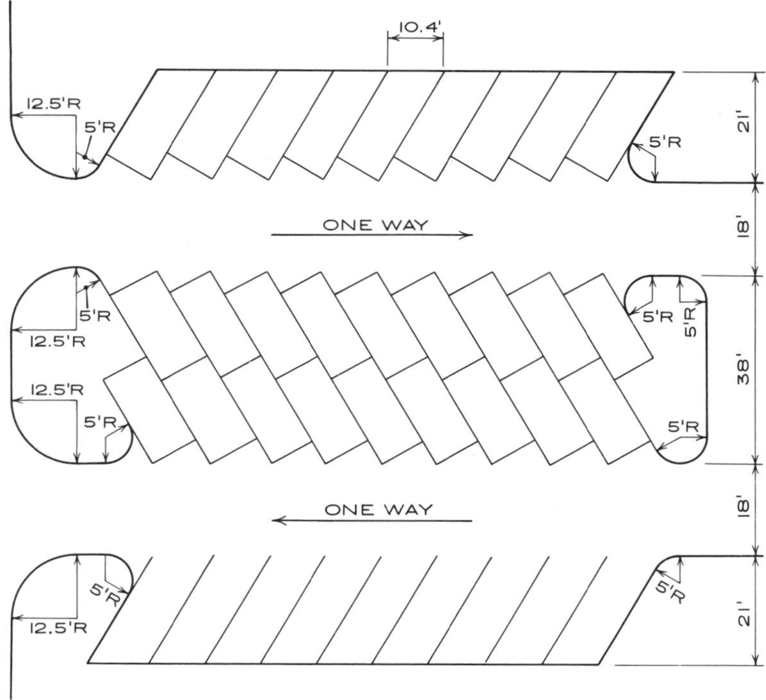

FIG. 3-50 Multilaned 60° parking.

FIG. 3-51 Parking is stepped down the site at the Las Colinas Sports Club, Irving, Texas.

FIG. 3-52 Planting along the stepped parking lot helps to filter the views of cars at the Las Colinas Sports Club, Irving, Texas.

FIG. 3-53 The front overhang of automobiles is considered in designing the pedestrian circulation at the Colonnade, Addison, Texas. Planting and interlocking concrete pavers also give the areas added interest.

FIG. 3-54 Mounding and planting at the Colonnade, Addison, Texas, provide screening of much of the parking from view along the Dallas Parkway.

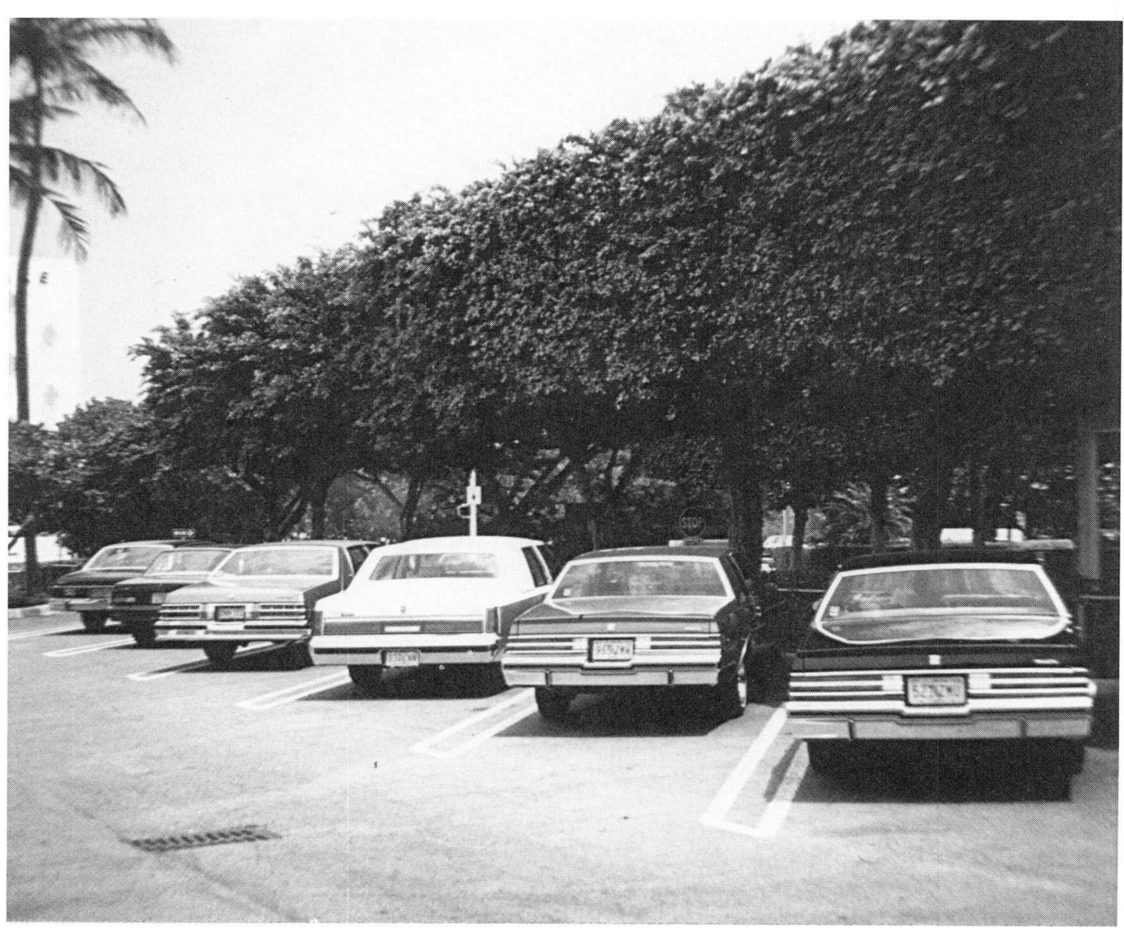

FIG. 3-55 A hedge of small evergreen trees along with a hedge of shrubs provides a strong entrance effect and screens the parking at the Bal Harbour Shopping Center in Miami Beach, Florida.

FIG. 3-56 Parking spaces can be given more interest and shade by providing tree planting islands throughout a parking area. At Market Hall in Dallas, Texas, live oak trees are used for shade.

Both motorcycle and bicycle parking must be considered when designing circulation systems for schools, parks, and other public facilities. (See Figs. 3-57 to 3-59.)

FIG. 3-57 Motorcycle parking: University of California, Los Angeles.

FIG. 3-58 Bicycle parking: Northwest Plaza, St. Louis, Missouri.

FIG. 3-59 Bicycle parking: University of Colorado, Boulder.

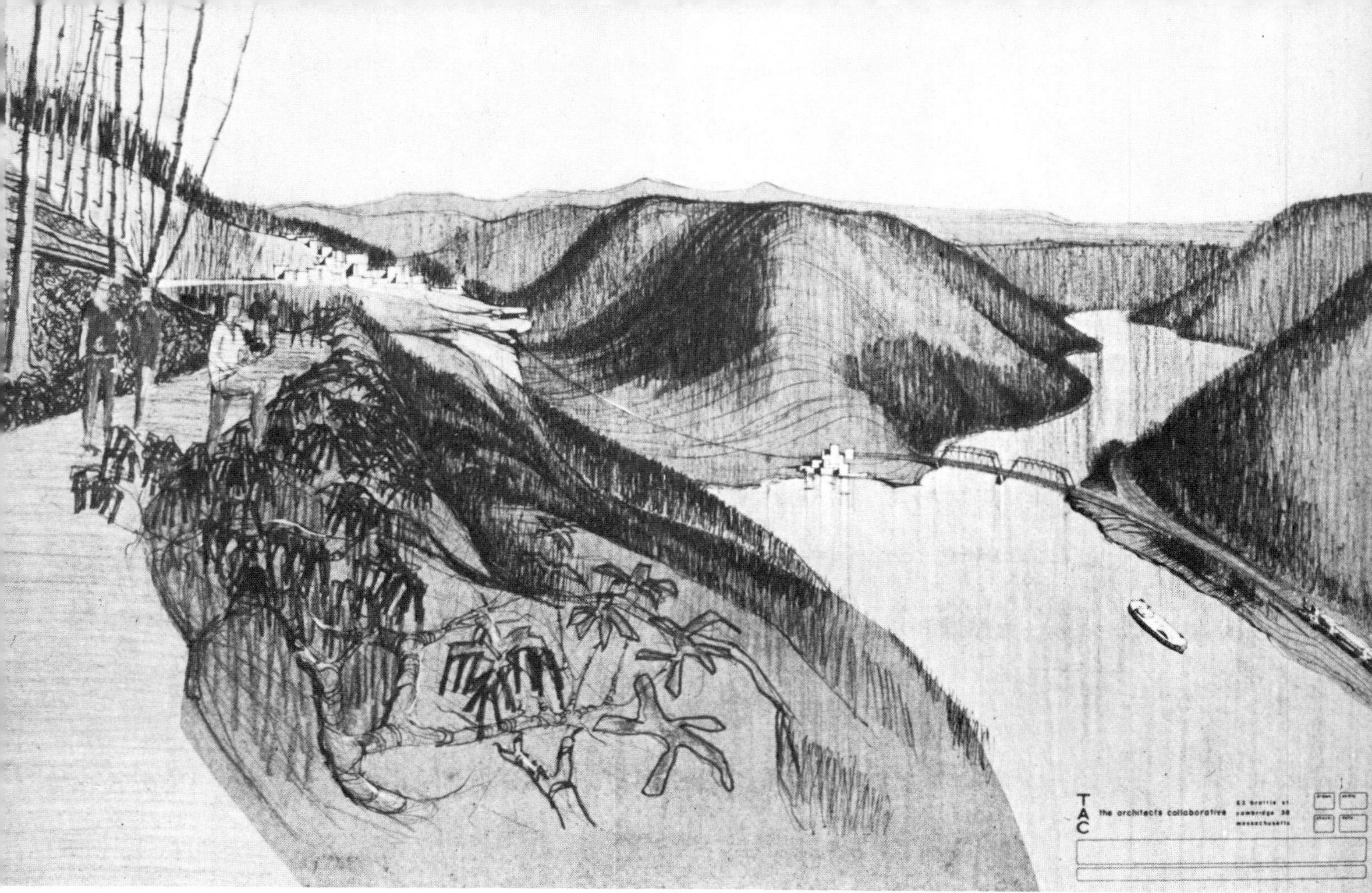

FIG. 4-1 Studies of visual form must be made in conjunction with the land use plan (Photograph courtesy of The Architects Collaborative).

Chapter Four
Visual Design Factors, Context, and Natural Elements

VISUAL DESIGN FACTORS

Along with land use and circulation, visual design and contextual factors and natural elements must be studied in structuring the site plan. (See Fig. 4-1.) The plan should be viewed as a total organization of space formed with buildings, earth, rock, water, and plant material. It must be structured so that its parts not only work together, but also are visually unified and coherent.

Form Characteristics

Figure-Ground. The contrast of an object to the ground is *figure-ground.* An element appears as a figure if it stands out against undisturbed ground. For example, a tree or sculpture can stand out as figure against the sky as ground. Figure-ground is often referred to as positive and negative elements. One organizes spaces by the use of positive elements (figure) in relation to negative elements (ground).

Continuity. A series of coherent parts provides continuity. The parts may be related by providing a common scale, form, texture, or color for an area. An example is using a particular paving material such as brick throughout a series of spaces that provides continuity in shape, size, color, and texture.

Sequence. Spaces are experienced by persons moving through them. The observer, in analyzing existing spaces, may find a planned sequence to be a very strong organizational device. *Sequence* is continuity in perception of spaces or objects arranged to provide a succession of visual change. It may create motion, a specific mood, or give direction. Each element in a sequence should lead to the next without necessarily revealing it.

Repetition and Rhythm. The simplest kind of sequence is repetition, which may involve color, texture, and shape; however, only a single factor must be reiterated for it to occur. (See Fig. 4-2.)

If a sequence of repetitive elements is interrupted at recurring intervals, rhythm is established. Rhythm gives variety in contrast to total repetition, which may prove monotonous. An example in an existing paving pattern would be the recurrence of brick bands between concrete squares. (See Fig. 4-3.)

Balance. The next element of order is balance. Are the objects in a space in symmetrical or asymmetrical balance? In symmetry, equal and like elements are balanced on either side of an axis. *Asymmetry* is the balance of unequal and unlike elements on opposite sides of an axis. In occult balance an optical axis or center of gravity is implied and opposing elements may be symmetrical or asymmetrical. An example of asymmetrical occult balance would be trees appearing to balance a hill on an implied visual axis. When opposing elements or structures develop tension among themselves to the extent that there seems to be a total balance of the elements with the surrounding space, a dynamic form of balance has occurred.

Shape, Size, Scale. The characteristics of objects in the landscape determine the quality of a space and its enclosure. What is the shape or

FIG. 4-2 Repetition of design elements: One Preston Park South, Plano, Texas.

FIG. 4-3 Rhythm in the paving pattern at Flora Street in the Arts District, Dallas, Texas.

form of the space? Is it rectilinear, curvilinear, or triangular? What is the size of the space? The size of an object or space is relative; it is large or small according to the standard with which it is compared. Size also depends on the distance of an object from the observer while scale denotes relative size. Scale is therefore generally based on the size of the average observer—5 ft 9 in.

In viewing a building, the eye has an angle of vision of about 27°. To see an entire building at this angle, one must view the building from a distance equal to twice its height.

Outdoor space has a good relation to buildings when the space has a width equal to the height of a building or twice the building height. If the outdoor space or plaza exceeds four times the height of the building, balance between building and space dissipates. As spaces become larger than about 150 × 200 ft in size, a feeling of intimacy is difficult to retain.

Proportion. Proportion is also a vital design factor. It is the ratio of height to width to length and may be studied in drawings or models. Ratios have been developed to achieve a series of dimensions that relate to each other. Simple ratios such as 3:5 have been used in architectural design. The Greeks used a ratio of 1.618:1 to build their temples. By forming a golden-mean rectangle the rectangle has a ratio of 1.618:1. (See Fig. 4-4.)

Pattern, Texture, and Color. Whenever one cannot determine the size and shape of specific parts as they form a continuous surface, there is texture, which may be perceived by touch or by sight. When one can differentiate among the parts forming a whole, there is pattern. All materials used on a project have texture whether they are rough surfaced granite or smooth polished marble. Inherent in the use of materials is color. Materials must be carefully chosen to relate textures, patterns, and colors. On expansion of existing projects try to match existing materials in color and texture to achieve harmony. (See Fig. 4-5.)

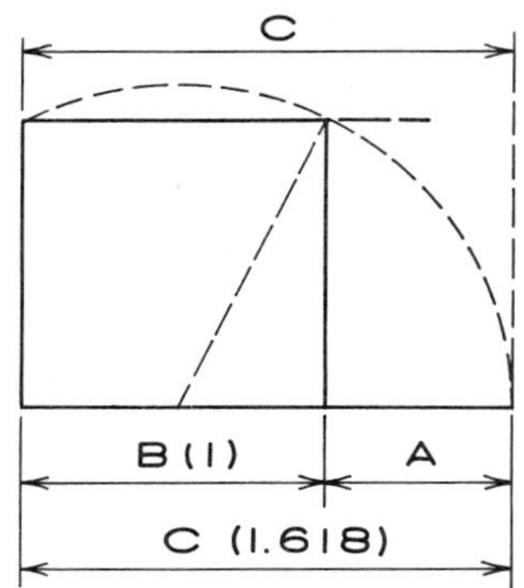

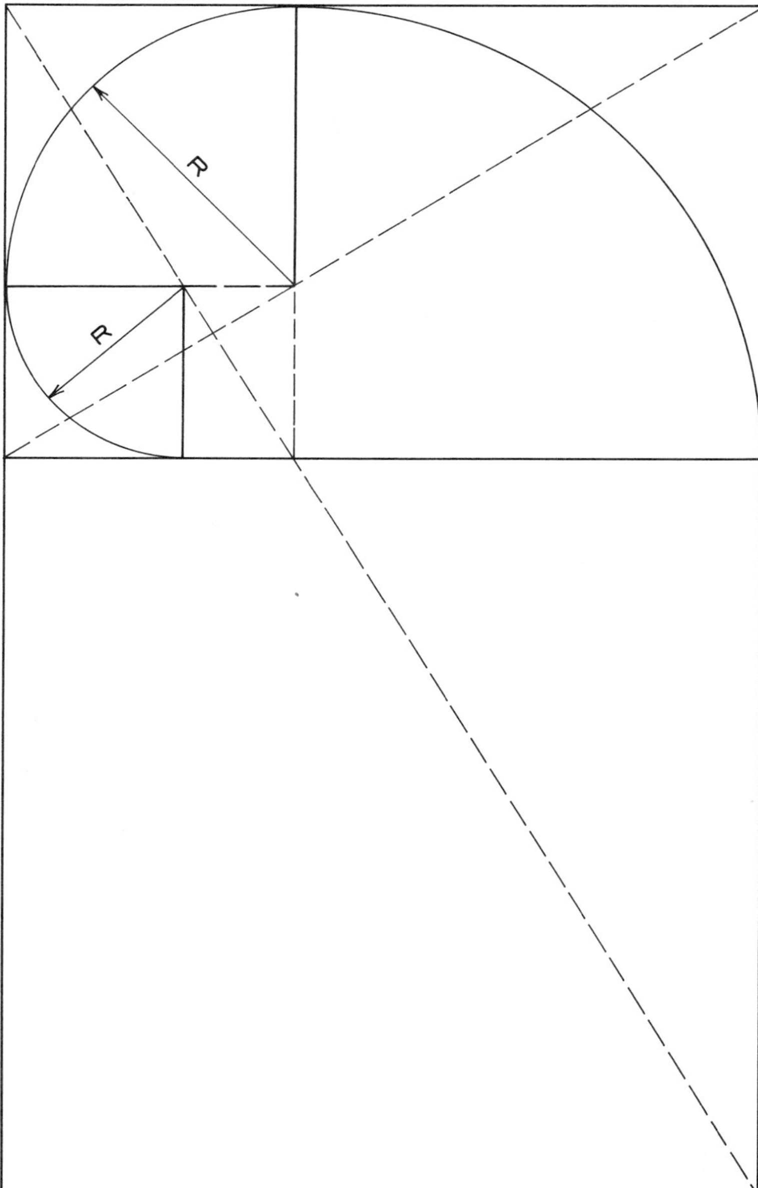

FIG. 4-4 Golden-mean rectangle: the diagonal of half a square is the beginning radius. The shape can form an endless sequence of squares spiraling logarithmically using the radius from the corners of each square to form the arc to spiral to the adjacent square.

FIG. 4-5 Harmony is achieved in Florence, Italy, by the repetition of design elements and the use of color.

Hierarchy. Hierarchy may be used to rank sizes or colors. For example, a hierarchy in the sizes of spaces is a sequence of spaces that progressively change in size of importance until one comes to a dominant or central space. Another example of hierarchy is its use in determining the width of walks according to the volumes of pedestrian traffic anticipated. A third example is in ranking colors of paving material to give added importance to a dominant feature within a space, such as a fountain or sculpture. Often a darker shade or color of material is used as a subtle transition to emphasize the paving around the feature. (See Fig. 4-6.)

Dominance. Dominance denotes importance by having the largest size or most prominent location, feature, or activity. Where a sequence of spaces is developed, one space may have dominance over the others by having one of the forementioned features.

Transparency. Transparency gives depth by overlaps or penetration of vision. It can occur in paving patterns when elements overlap and color changes occur at the overlaps.

Direction. This is a line along which objects lie or a reference toward a point or area that gives order. A north-south direction, for example, is often used for orientation.

Similarity. The grouping of like elements is similarity. Elements can by repetition or color, shape, size, and texture create this chaı acteristic.

FIG. 4-6 Hierarchy in sizes and importance of spaces (Photograph courtesy Kansas University School of Architecture & Urban Design).

Motion. A process of moving or changing time or position is *motion*. It reinforces direction or distance and can give a sense of form in motion as one views a space from changing positions or locations.

Time. Time is the sequential relationship that any event has to any other, past, present, or future. Continuity can be achieved over a period of time and preserving old structures and adding new additions provides continuity with the past.

Sensory Quality. The sense of a place—its visual impression and appeal to one's senses of sound, smell, and touch—adds a further dimension to the design of spaces.

Volumes and Enclosure

To achieve clearly defined spaces, consider enclosure or space-forming elements and the volumes contained by the space. Exterior volumes are formed by three enclosing or space-forming elements—the base, overhead, and vertical planes.

Base Plane. The base plane is our greatest concern in determining land use. It is the surface of the earth and therefore must be properly planned for uses and their linkages before further development can take place. Through treatment of the base plane, one relates and articulates all elements on its surface. A strong land use plan must exist beforehand.

Overhead Plane. The sky is our greatest overhead plane. Man-made planes may be used for further definition in the height of a space. Overhead planes may be solid, translucent, or perforated, but this is generally not as important visually as the type of articulation they provide. (See Fig. 4-7.)

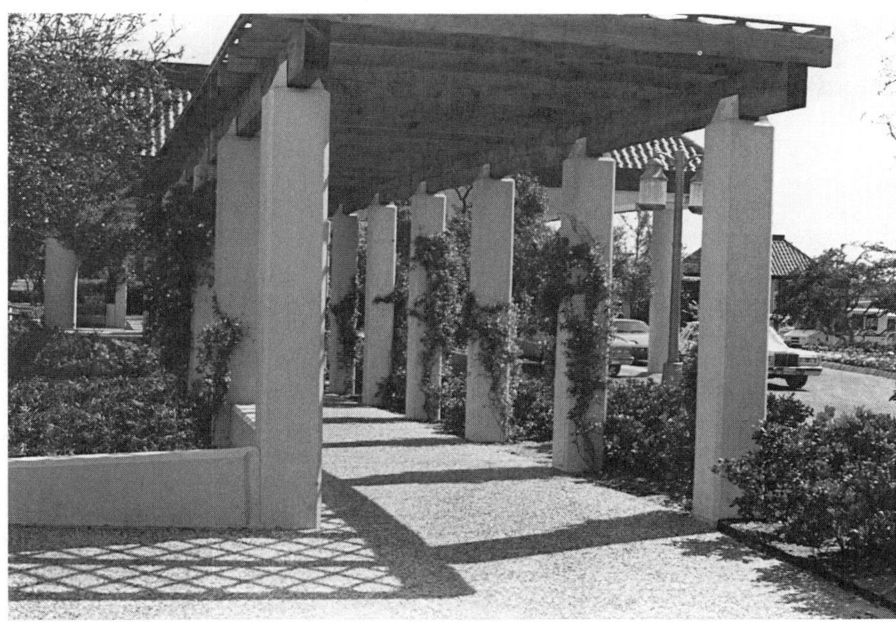

FIG. 4-7 Overhead planes define this walkway leading to the Four Seasons Hotel in Las Colinas, Irving, Texas.

Vertical Plane. Vertical planes have the most important function in defining the uses of spaces. Buildings are usually the dominant vertical elements that form space and with which the site planner must work. The placement of these buildings and other vertical elements will determine the degree of enclosure of a space.

Vertical elements also have great visual impact and may act as points of reference or landmarks. A vertical element such as a sculpture may also become the dominant feature within a volume. Vertical planes can act as screens to eliminate objectionable views, thereby framing good views. These planes also serve as buffering elements for noise in the form of plant material and they may control sunlight or wind. (See Figs. 4-8 and 4-9.)

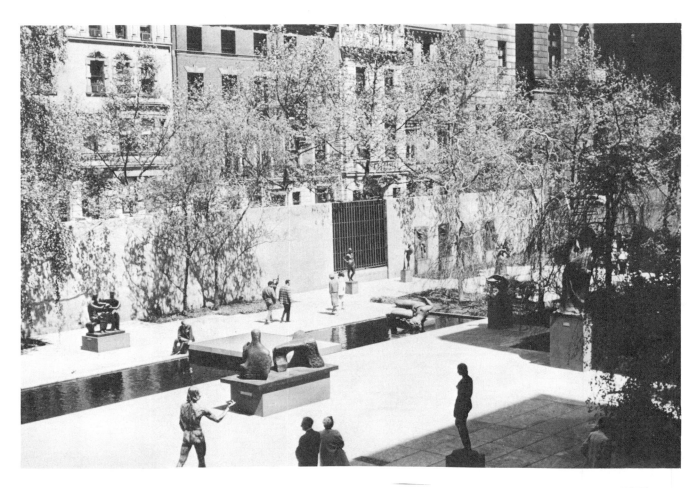

FIG. 4-8 This garden is distinguished by its use of architectural elements, pools, paving, and planting that define the space and act as a backdrop for sculpture: Museum of Modern Art, New York City.

FIG. 4-9 Vertical elements such as walls, planters, and fountains define this outdoor restaurant, Dakotas, at Lincoln Plaza in Dallas, Texas.

CONTEXT

Image

In developing plans for urban areas the overall context of an area must be studied. A city's image or identity is based on its shape, color, texture, arrangement, and sensory quality. This gives an observer clues to the city's identity and structure.

Image has been classified into five elements—paths, nodes, edges, districts, and landmarks.

Paths. The circulation routes or lines along which people move are *paths*. They are streets, walks, and transit and rail lines. (See Fig. 4-10.)

FIG. 4-10 Path along the Riverwalk tourist area in San Antonio, Texas.

Nodes. These are centers of activity. They are junctions or crossings of paths or points of concentration such as transportation centers. (See Fig. 4-11.)

Edges. Linear boundaries or edges distinguish one area or region from another. An edge may be a river, a row of buildings forming the outline of an area, or an elevated roadway separating two parts of a community. (See Fig. 4-12.)

Districts. These large to medium parts of a city have common characteristics. Identifiable from the inside, districts can be used for exterior reference if viewed from the outside. They can be useful in giving direction and may have such names as North Side or Hill Section.

FIG. 4-11 Node: Spanish Steps, Rome, Italy.

FIG. 4-12 Edge: along Grand Canal, Venice, at Doges Palace and Piazza San Marco.

Landmarks. Physical objects such as a tower, building, sign, mountain, or hill make up landmarks, which aid in the identification of points of choice and direction. Landmarks may be objects familiar to observers giving them cues so that they may decide, for example, which road junction to use.

Of these elements just discussed paths rank highest in providing order. Each path should have some quality distinguishing it from others. This can be the color or texture of paving, building facades, lighting, planting design, or activities that give continuity to the path. (See Fig. 4-13.)

FIG. 4-13 Landmark: Parma, Italy.

NATURAL ELEMENTS

Early in the development of site plans, planners must relate a materials concept to their spatial concept. As the spatial concept is refined, so is the materials concept. Materials have inherent characteristics that must be expressed. They are also used along with other materials and must be carefully chosen in relation to each other.

Natural elements studied in the materials concept may be earth, rock, water, or plant material. These elements are perpetually undergoing change. Variety resulting from their size, shape, texture, or color can produce an appreciable emotional effect when properly used.

Earth

Earth, the base plane upon which we build, is a plastic element and can be molded to enhance a design, especially where the topography is level or shapeless. Steep slopes left as undeveloped woodland tend to organize space and form linkages with areas adjacent to the site. In a new development existing topography often must be changed, but transition between new and existing landforms is essential. Design grading may change these existing forms to screen objectionable views or gain privacy; or by sinking or depressing roads, walks, and parking, it may make land appear to flow undisturbed. Level and uninteresting topography can be given variety by mounding.

Studying topography in model form, whether in cardboard, clay, or some other material, is extremely valuable, for landform is difficult to interpret in a two-dimensional plan. Creating site models is a worthwhile aid to studying buildings in their relation to the land, each other, and influences on adjacent sites.

Rock

Because of its symbolic, structural, and aesthetic qualities, rock is a prominent element in design. It may be used as a natural feature or a sculptural element. Rock composed in courtyards or gardens should have the same soil line as it had in its natural state and, if moss is present, the same orientation, moisture, and shade. (See Fig. 4-14.)

Rock indigenous to a site can be used to great advantage in its natural state as outcrops, ledges, or boulders as well as in walls, sculptures, podia, or buildings themselves. Taking the naturalistic approach, if the stone is used for both a structure and other site elements the building may become unified with the site through proper handling. On the other hand, the man-made approach can be emphasized by placing the building on a podium and having the natural landscape lead to the man-made structure. Either approach may work; it is up to the planner to decide which method is appropriate on the given site.

FIG. 4-14 A natural rock outcrop as a feature in the landscape.

Man-made materials such as brick or concrete created from natural elements can also be classified as rock. These are widely used in construction and detailing.

Water

Water, the most flexible of natural elements, assumes the shape of its container. It is like a magnet in the landscape, drawing people toward it. Giving a cooling and reflective effect in large still pools, it conveys a sense of quietude and repose. Essential to the balance of life, water, in hot arid climates, makes living bearable. Differences in sound also make its use appealing. Water in fountains or pools may splash, drip, gurgle, trickle, foam, flood, pour, spurt, ripple, surge, spray, or jet. Fountains of various sizes may be designed to take advantage of a particular sound. Sunlight and night-lighting add other qualities and are important considerations in fountain design. Finally, water may produce a feeling of coherence in a design when used or found naturally in large bodies, for it acts as a unifying element. (See Fig. 4-15.)

Plant Material

Plants constantly undergo change, especially during peaks of seasonal variation; this makes the use of plant material most challenging. They have climatic, environmental engineering, architectural, and aesthetic uses. Trees help control solar radiation, reduce glare, and control wind. They also help clean the air through the process of photosynthesis. Additionally, they help filter out particulate matter, absorb unwanted sound, and minimize erosion.

In architectural and aesthetic uses plants can provide enclosure, overhead canopies, control views, and privacy. They can stand out as sculptural elements in the landscape and serve as backdrops.

FIG. 4-15 Fountain at Boston City Hall.

Trees and shrubs, in their variety of forms, provide color and texture in the landscape. So do the seasonal variations with flowers in the spring and colorful leaves in the fall. Not to be overlooked either is the variety of bark color and texture of trees and shrubs or the colorful fruits some of them provide.

FIG. 5-1 Architecture in a refined setting at the Bushkill Headquarters Building, Delaware Water Gap National Recreation Area, Pennsylvania (Photograph courtesy of Bellante, Clauss, Miller & Partners; Photographer, Otto Baitz).

Chapter Five
Contour Lines

Planners must understand the characteristics of contours to develop a given site plan. Contours facilitate their visualization of land in the third dimension. They show existing elevations of topography and comprise a contour map that will reveal site characteristics.

The primary purpose for changing existing contours is to direct runoff water away from structures or activity areas and to adapt man-made structures to existing topography. This process is called grading and is discussed in Chapter 6. The following definitions introduce the nature of contour lines; plotting contours is also described in this chapter.

CONTOUR CHARACTERISTICS

Contours are lines of equal elevation above the same reference plane. The *datum plane* is the reference generally referred to and is located at mean sea level. A *contour interval* is the vertical distance between contours, and the choice of a suitable interval results from the purpose for which a topographic map is to be used. Common intervals are 1, 2, and 5 ft.

Knowledge of the characteristics of contours is essential for their interpretation. A list of them follows:

1 A uniform slope is indicated by evenly spaced contours. (See Fig. 5-2.)
2 Slope increases with closeness of contours. Lines close at the top of a slope and wider apart at the bottom indicate a concave slope. The reverse situation indicates a convex slope. (See Fig. 5-3.)
3 Contour lines point up stream valleys. (See Fig. 5-4.)
4 Contour lines point down ridges. (See Fig. 5-5.)
5 With the exception of an overhanging shelf or cave, contours never cross; they merge only at vertical walls or cliffs.
6 Contours along the highest points of ridges or the lowest points of valleys are always found in pairs, for each contour is a continuous line that closes on itself either on or off the drawing and never splits or stops. (See Fig. 5-6.)
7 High points on summits or low points within a depression are indicated by spot elevations.

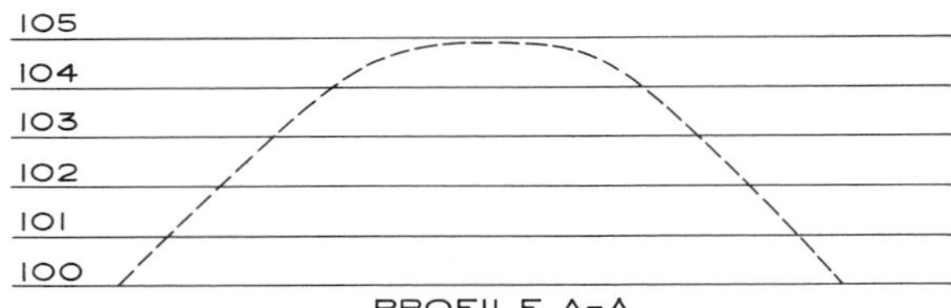

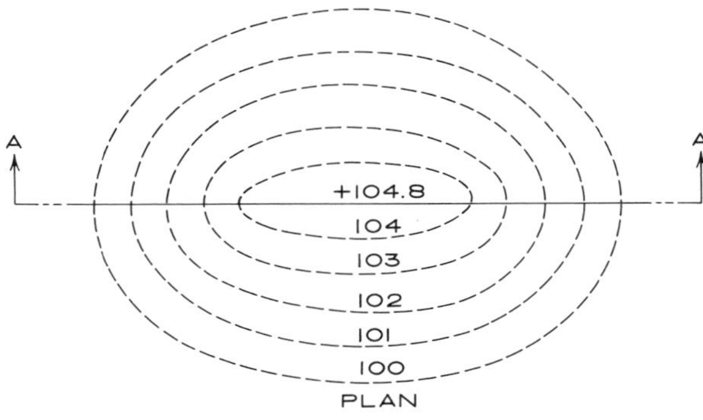

FIG. 5-2 Contours show uniform slopes.

106
105
104
103
102
101
100
PROFILE A-A

A
A
+105.8
105
104
103
102
101
100
PLAN

FIG. 5-3 Contours show concave slopes.

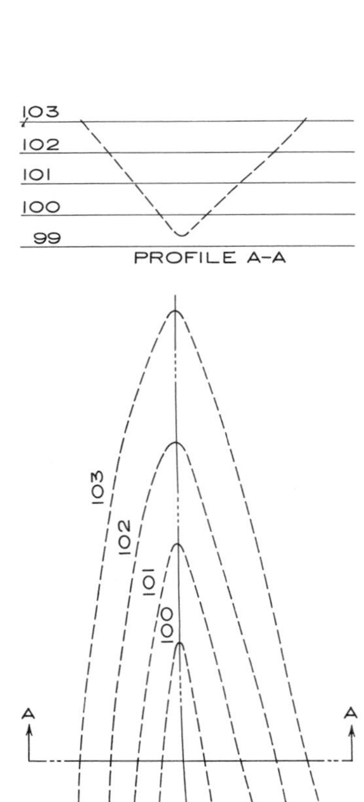

FIG. 5-4 Contours show streams.

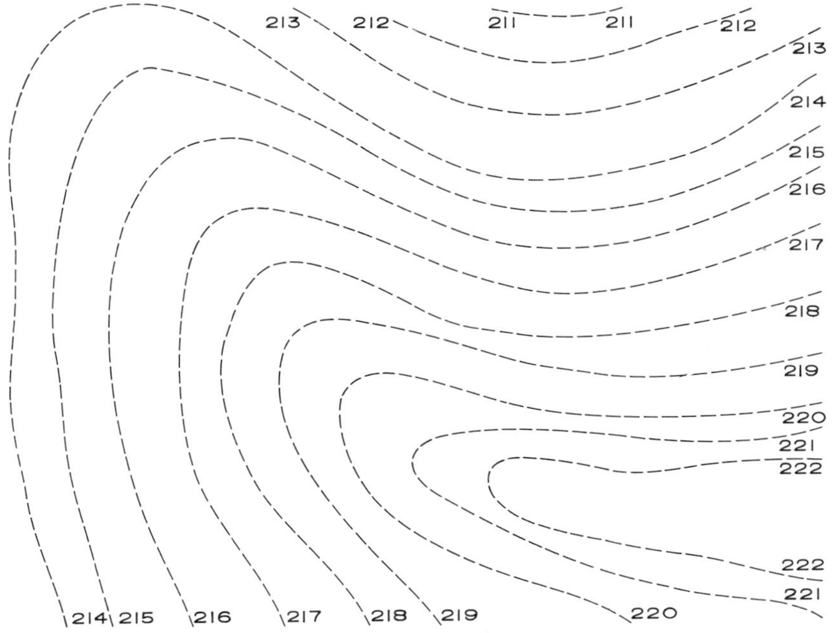

FIG. 5-5 Contours show ridges.

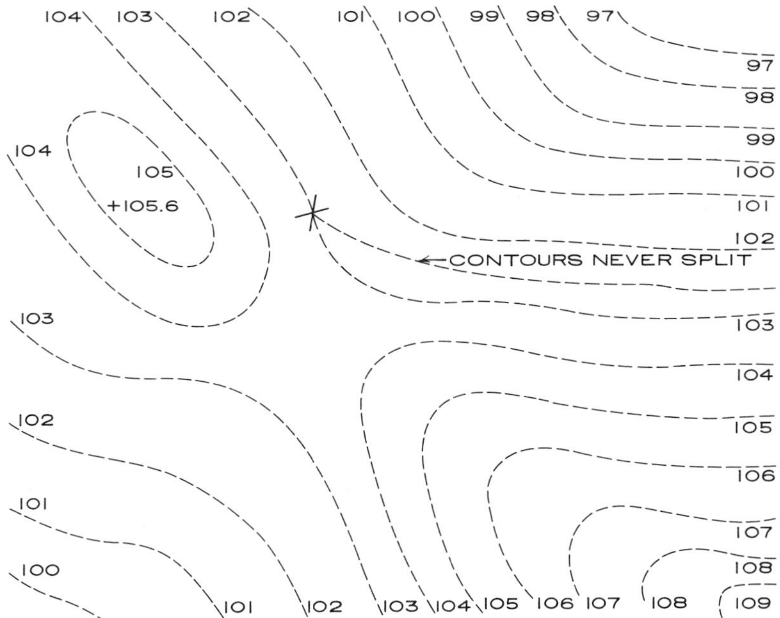

FIG. 5-6 Contours never split and merge only at vertical walls or cliffs.

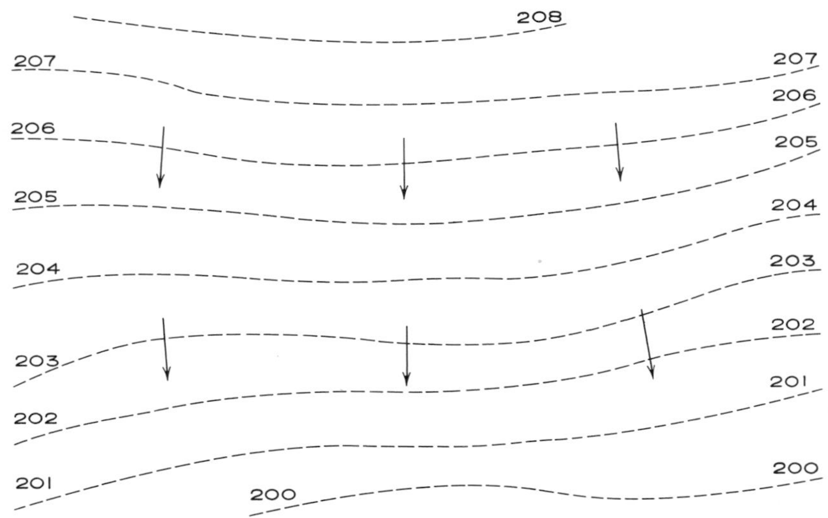

FIG. 5-7 Contour lines show flow of runoff water.

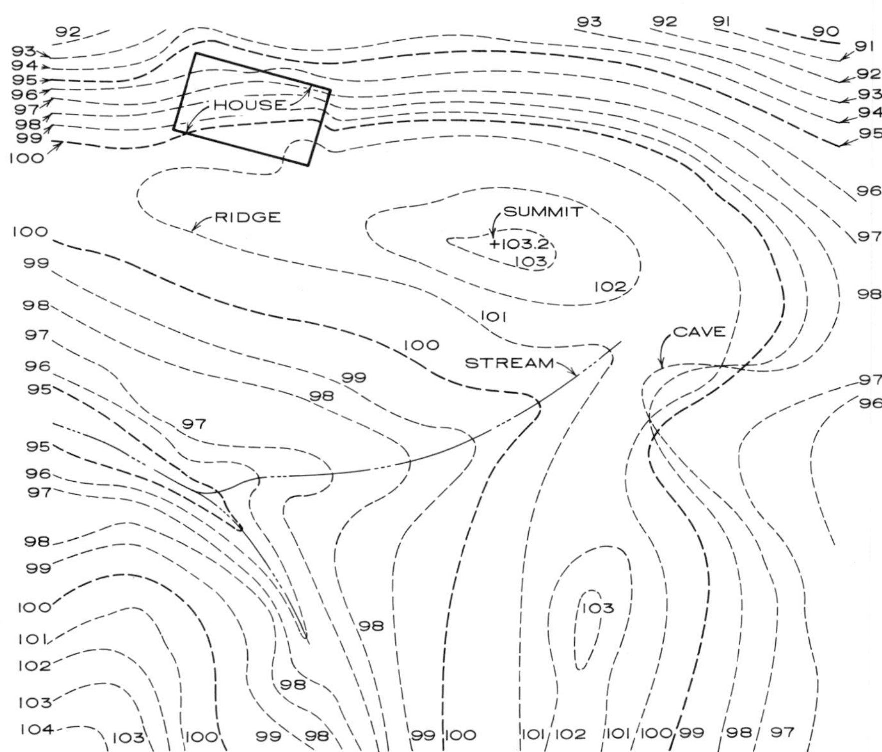

FIG. 5-8 Existing contour map.

8 Runoff water flows downhill perpendicular to contour lines. (See Fig. 5-7.)

9 Existing contours are shown as dashed lines with every sixth line in a 1 ft contour interval drawn heavier. Contours are numbered either in the mass of the contour line or on the uphill side. New contour lines for proposed grades are shown as solid lines. (See Fig. 5-8.)

INTERPOLATION OF CONTOURS

Interpolation of contours is the process of establishing even numbered contours from a grid system of spot elevations measured by a surveyor. In some cases this has already been done; however, the site planner may need additional elevations and these are found by interpolation either with a scale (see Figs. 5-9 and 5-10) or by calculation (see Figs. 5-11 and 5-12).

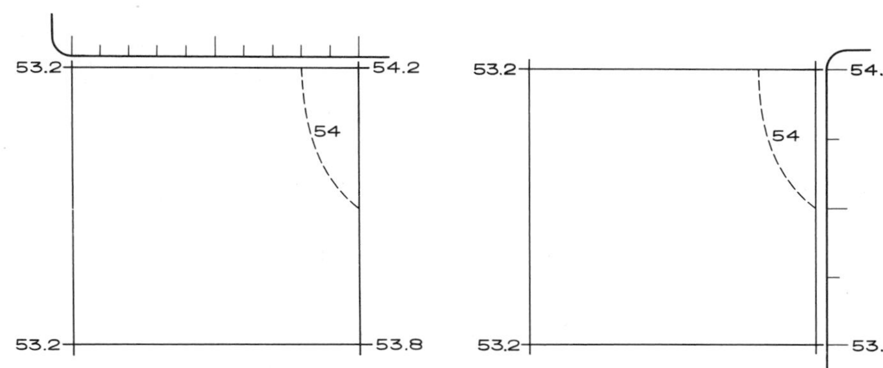

FIGS. 5-9 and 5-10 Interpolation by scale.

Example—Find location of contour 54. Difference in elevation

$$\begin{array}{r} 54.00 \\ -53.20 \\ \hline 0.80 \end{array}$$

Total difference in elevation

$$\begin{array}{r} 54.20 \\ -53.20 \\ \hline 1.00 \end{array}$$

Proportion of total horizontal distance (50 ft) between 53.20 and 54.00 is

$$\frac{0.80}{1.00} \times 50 = 40.00 \text{ ft}$$

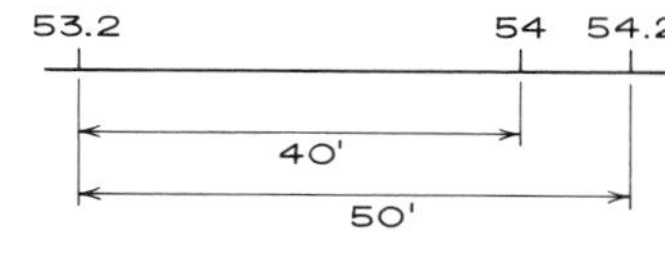

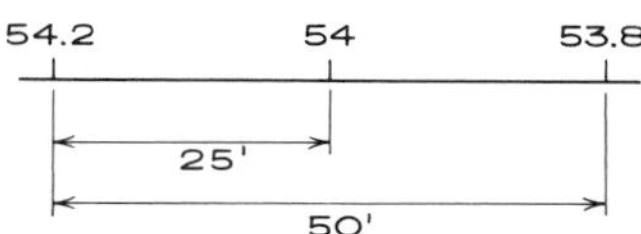

FIGS. 5-11 and 5-12 Interpolation by calculation.

Find location of contour 54. Difference in elevation.

$$\begin{array}{r} 54.20 \\ -54.00 \\ \hline 0.20 \end{array}$$

Total difference in elevation

$$\begin{array}{r} 54.20 \\ -53.80 \\ \hline 0.40 \end{array}$$

Proportion of total horizontal distance (50 ft) between 53.80 and 54.00 is

$$\frac{0.20}{0.40} \times 50 = 25 \text{ ft}$$

FIG. 6-1 Mounding created in Prospect Park, Brooklyn, New York, provides a strong directional movement in the space.

Chapter Six
Grading and Earthwork Calculations

GRADING

A concept of design grading is essential in developing the physical form of the site. This grading concept must strengthen the overall project rather than detract from it as often happens. Positive drainage, an important concept in grading, allows storm water runoff to flow away from structures and activity areas. When water flows away from structures toward drainage channels, flooding is prevented. Studying existing and proposed topography in model form will aid in relating buildings or activities to the land. It is also especially helpful in observing the relationship between ground forms such as mounds when this type of treatment is desired. (See Figs. 6-1 to 6-8.)

Definitions of Terms Commonly Used in Grading

Grade: Percentage of rise or fall per 100 ft. (See Fig. 6-9.)
Crown: Provides for runoff of water on roads or walks. Symbol *x* in Fig. 6-10 indicates crown; it may be in inches per foot or a whole number (6 in. crown).
Cross Slope or Pitch: Provides for runoff on paved areas and is given in inches per foot or a whole number.
Wash: Provides for runoff on steps and is given in inches per foot ($\frac{1}{8}$ to $\frac{1}{4}$ in.). (See Fig. 6-11.)
Batter: Amount of deviation from vertical such as 2 in./ft for a vertical surface such as a wall—2:1 batter. (See Fig. 6-12.)
Slope: The ratio of horizontal to vertical. (See Fig. 6-13.)
Maximum Slopes:

Solid rock	$\frac{1}{4}$:1	Firm earth	$1\frac{1}{2}$:1
Loose rock	$\frac{1}{2}$:1	Soft earth	2 :1
Loose gravel	$1\frac{1}{2}$:1	Mowing grass	3 :1

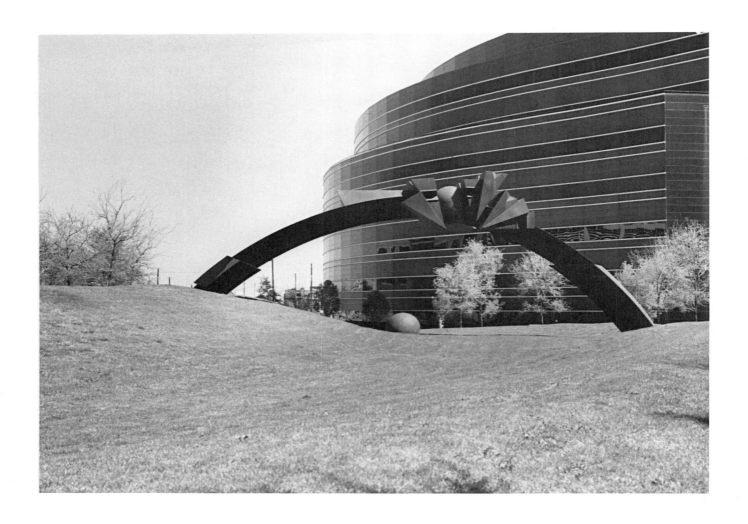

FIG. 6-2 These mounds and sculpture act as the focal point in the landscape infrastructure at the Quorum, Addison, Texas, by the HOK Planning Group, Dallas.

FIG. 6-3 The mounds are defined by the coping at seating height. They also permit trees to be planted above the parking garage at Constitution Plaza, Hartford, Connecticut.

FIG. 6-4 Mounds act as islands floating on the paved areas at Southern Illinois University, Edwardsville. Their placement also provides a feeling of entry.

FIG. 6-5 The use of mounds at Northeastern Bank Plaza, Scranton, Pennsylvania, allows sufficient depth of soil for trees to grow above the concourse level. The mounds also define the sequence of spaces through the plaza (Photograph courtesy of Bellante, Clauss, Miller & Partners).

FIG. 6-6 The base plane slopes so that runoff water may flow toward catch basins located in the paved drainage swale. This swale becomes part of the overall paving pattern at Southern Illinois University, Edwardsville.

FIG. 6-7 The performing Arts Center at Saratoga Springs, New York, makes use of the natural slope of the land for the seating area; the raised pedestrian walkway allows the landscape to flow undisturbed.

FIG. 6-8 The grading of this slope is too steep and has caused erosion.

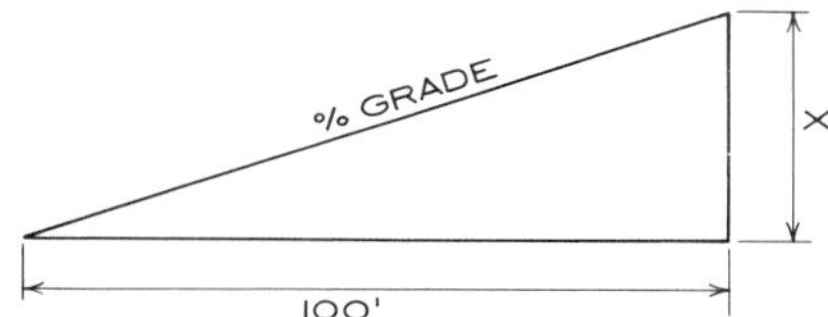

FIG. 6-9 Grade.

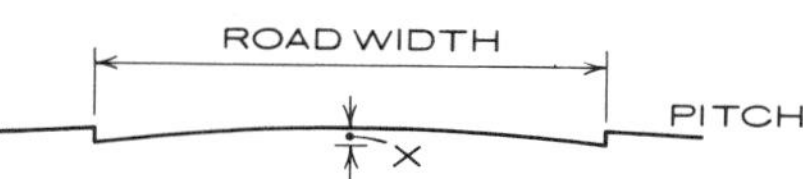

FIG. 6-10 Crown and pitch.

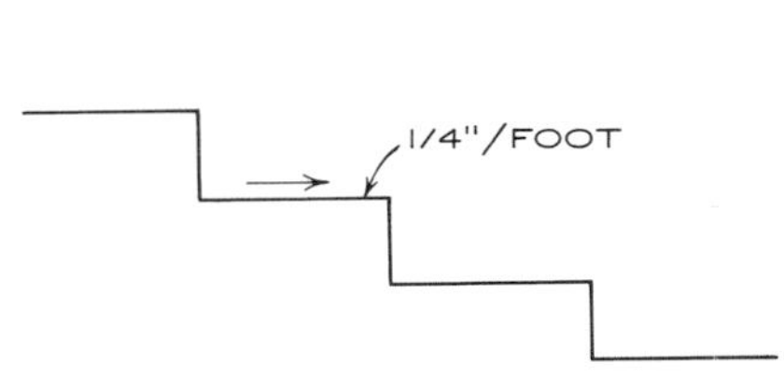

FIG. 6-11 Wash.

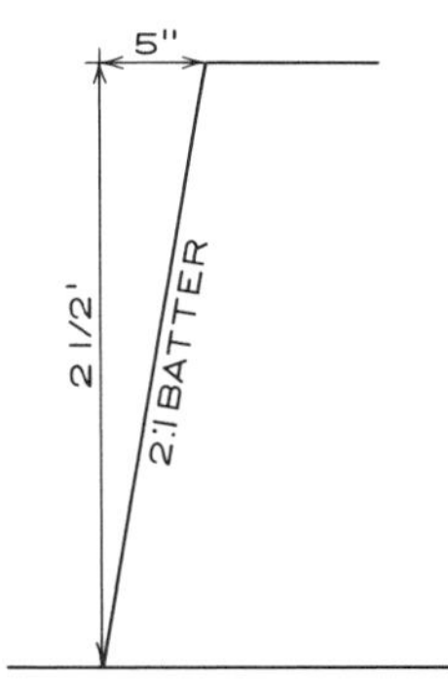

FIG. 6-12 Batter.

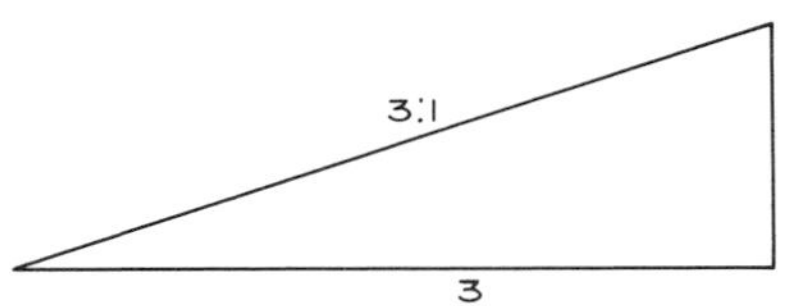

FIG. 6-13 Slope.

Cut and Fill: When a proposed contour is moved back into an existing slope, cut is indicated. When a proposed contour is moved away from an existing slope, fill is indicated. It is the purpose of earthwork calculation to determine if a balance exists between cut and fill or whether material will have to be added to or carried away from the site. (See Fig. 6-14.)

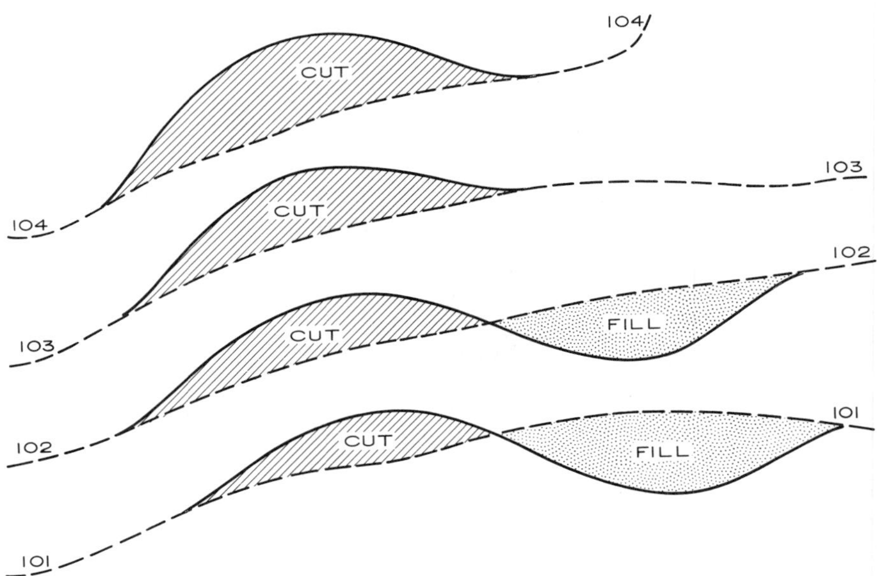

FIG. 6-14 Cut and fill.

Spot Elevations

The grading plan is significant in the technical development of the site plan. The major consideration in a grading plan is to set trial or preliminary spot elevations in order to achieve a positive drainage pattern. This study follows development of the land use and circulation plans, along with studies in visual form, and is done on the topographic map with requirements established in Chapter 2. Before the grading study begins the project's layout has already been drawn on the topographic map, used as the base sheet. This study may lead to changes in placement of the building or circulation.

Factors to Consider in Setting Preliminary Spot Elevations

1. Setting the first floor elevations of buildings, generally a minimum of 6 in. above grade.
2. Meeting existing building elevations and relating grading to adjacent properties so as not to disturb by regarding or diversion of runoff.
3. Relating elevations of roads, walks, parking, and other activities to building elevations to achieve positive drainage.
4. Saving good trees by taking their elevation into consideration or planning on the use of tree wells in cuts of 6 in. or fills over 8 in.
5. Avoiding rock or drainage problems by careful examination of the site.
6. Saving the cost of unnecessary retaining walls where other types of grading concepts may be used.
7. General balancing of cut and fill areas to avoid having to haul material to or from the site.

After preliminary spot elevations are studied in relation to each other, preliminary contour lines are drawn on the grading plan at a chosen contour interval such as 1, 2, or 5 ft. When the proper balance of cut and fill has been obtained, final spot elevations and contour lines are set.

Finished Spot Elevations Are Placed at the Following Locations

1 First floor elevations of buildings.
2 All corners of buildings and door stoops or landings.
3 Corners of parking areas, terraces, or other paved areas.
4 Corners at the top of landings and bottom of steps.
5 Top and bottom of walls, curbs, and gutters.
6 On rock outcrops and bases of large trees (3-4 in. cal).
7 Rim and invert elevations of drainage structures—catch basins, manholes, drain inlets, and invert elevations of sanitary sewers and water lines.

Gradients

	Desirable Grades	Maximum (%)	Minimum (%)
1	Streets (concrete)	8	0.50
2	Parking (concrete)[a]	5	0.50
3	Service areas (concrete)	5	0.50
4	Main approach walks to buildings	4	1
5	Stoops or entries to buildings	2	1
6	Collector walks	8	1
7	Ramps	10	1
8	Wheelchair ramps	8.33	1
9	Terraces and sitting areas	2	1
10	Grass areas for recreational use	3	2
11	Swales	10	2
12	Mowed banks of grass	3:1 slope	—
13	Unmowed banks	2:1 slope	—

[a]The minimum desirable grade for bituminous areas such as parking lots is $1\frac{1}{2}$%.

Setting Grades for Positive Drainage

The formula $G = D/L$ is of major importance in manipulation of contours. Here G = percent of grade, D = difference in elevation × 100, and L = horizontal length between two points. For example, $G = D/L$ as in Fig. 6-15:

$$G = \frac{2 \text{ ft}}{200 \text{ ft}} \times 100$$

$$G = 1\%$$

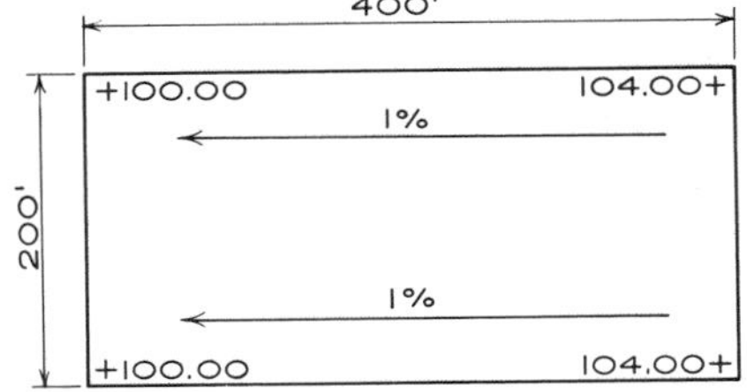

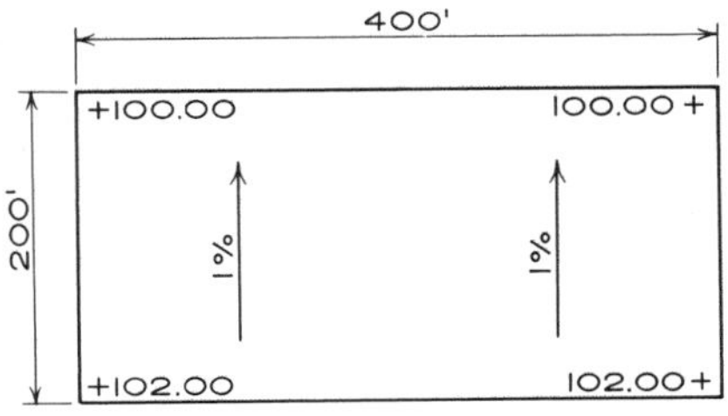

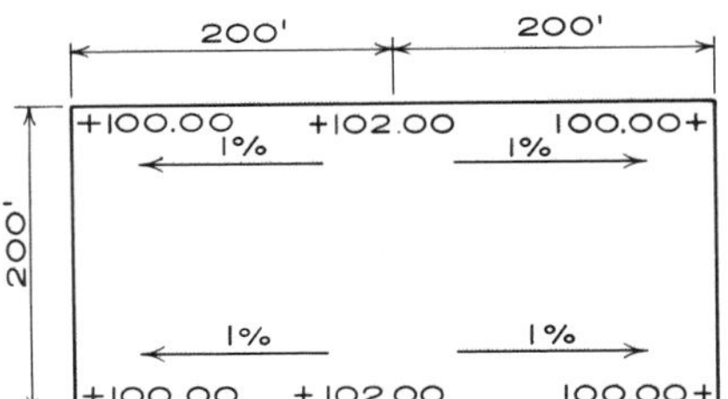

FIG. 6-15 Spot elevation diagrams as used for positive drainage.

Establishing Contours

Set the contours at a 1 ft contour interval on Fig. 6-16. In setting contours D = the distance between contours at a particular grade and contour interval. (See pages 122 to 125.)

$$D = \frac{CI}{\%G} \times 100$$

where CI = contour interval
$\%G$ = percent of grade
$D = 1\text{ ft}/2.4 \times 100$
$D = 41.6\text{ ft}$

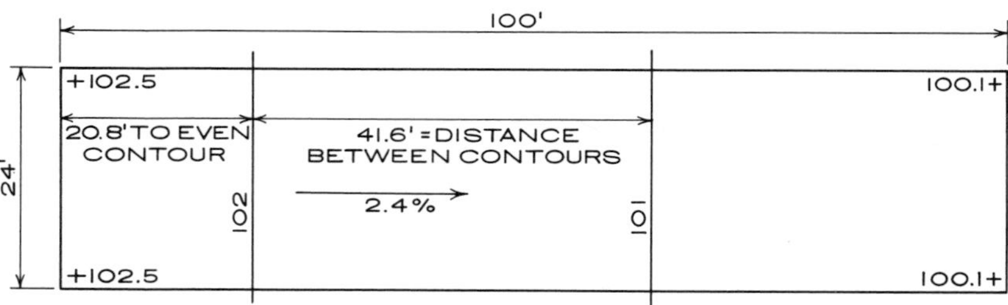

FIG. 6-16 Example of establishing contours.

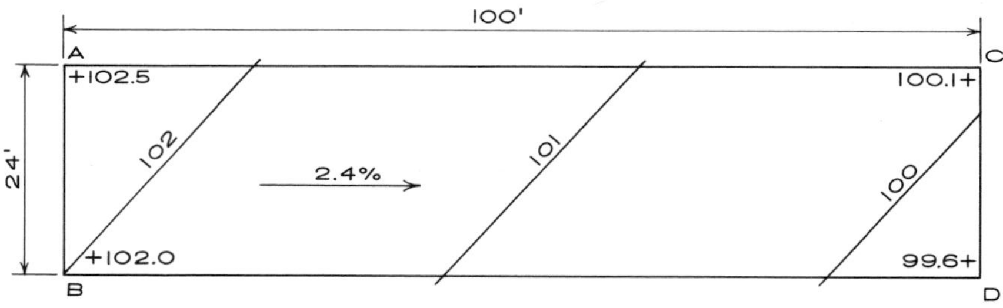

FIG. 6-17 Example of establishing contours with a cross slope.

In Fig. 6-17 corner A has an elevation of 102.5 ft with a $\frac{1}{4}$ in./ft cross slope toward corner B, and corner C has an elevation of 100.1 ft with a $\frac{1}{4}$ in./ft cross slope toward corner D. Set the contours. The distance between contours is 41.6 ft as in Fig. 6-16. Now calculate corner B = ($\frac{1}{4}$ in./ft for 24 ft = 6 in.) 102 ft and corner D = 99.6. Draw in contours. (See pages 122 to 125.)

Contours on Slopes. See Figs. 6-18 to 6-23.

FIG. 6-18 Contours are 3 ft apart for 3:1 slopes at a 1 ft contour interval.

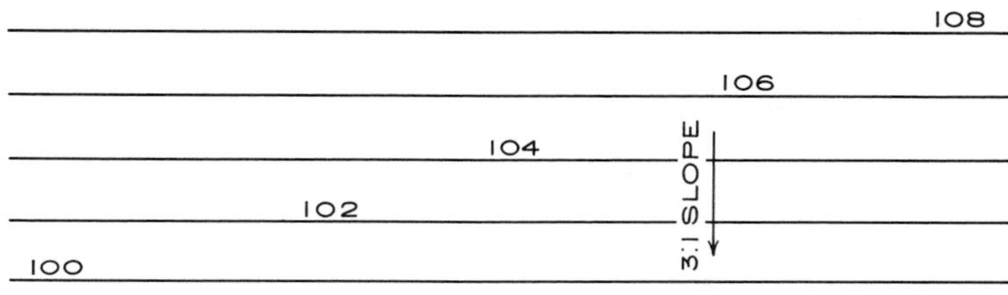

FIG. 6-19 Contours are 6 ft apart for 3:1 slopes at a 2 ft contour interval.

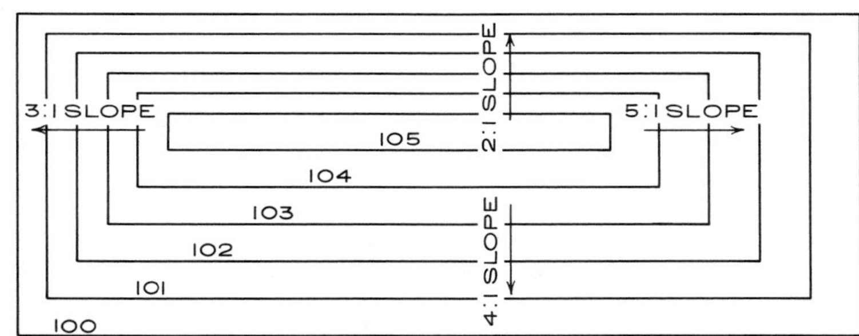

FIG. 6-20 Comparative slopes.

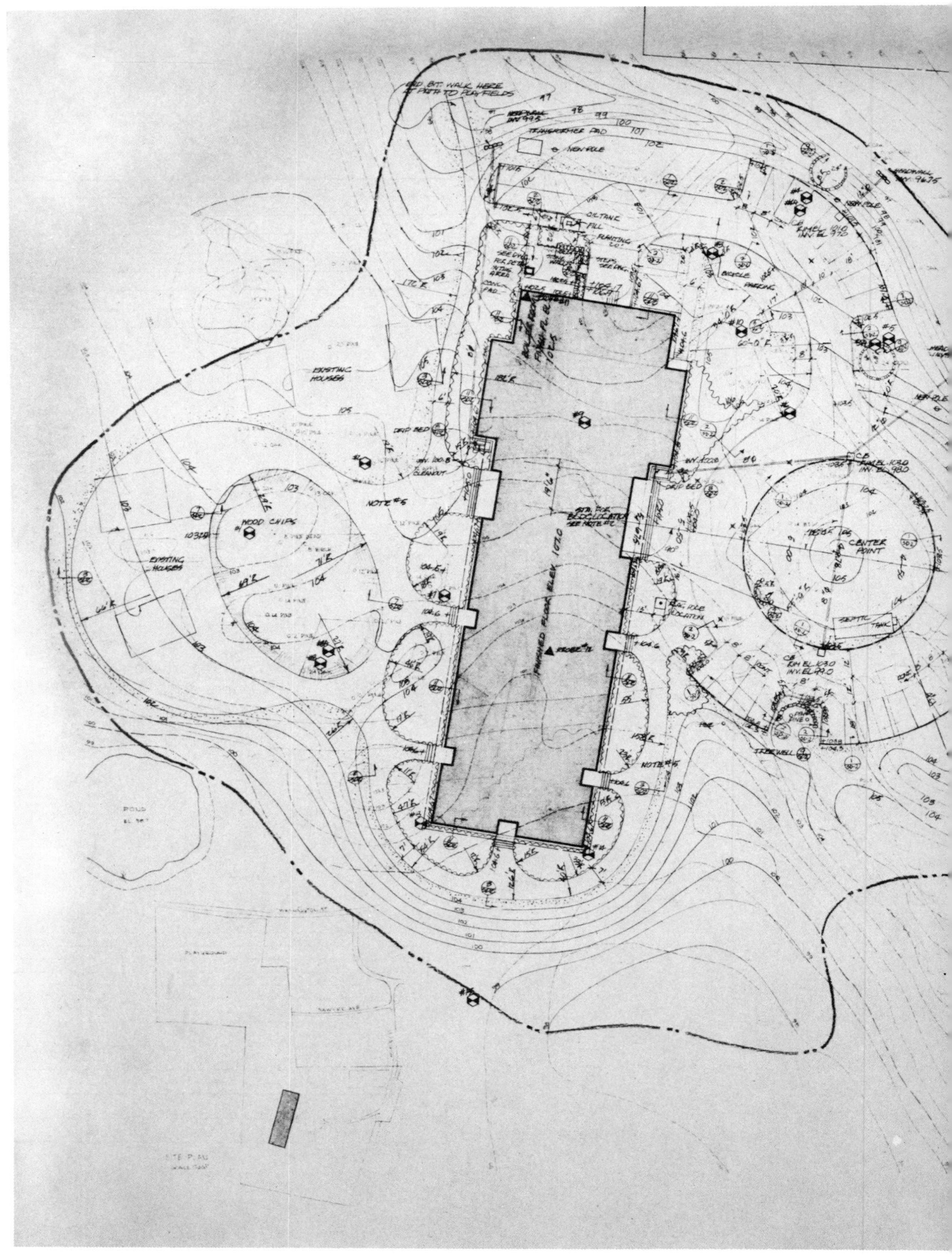

FIG. 6-21 Plum Cove Elementary School, Gloucester, Massachusetts. This layout and grading plan illustrates the use of spot elevations and refined grading. The school was placed to take advantage of natural site features. The location gives the building good orientation and approach views from the entry drive. Circulation was developed to handle cars, buses, and service vehicles, and parking requirements for both staff and visitors. Since existing trees were of particular importance on the site, special attention was given to working

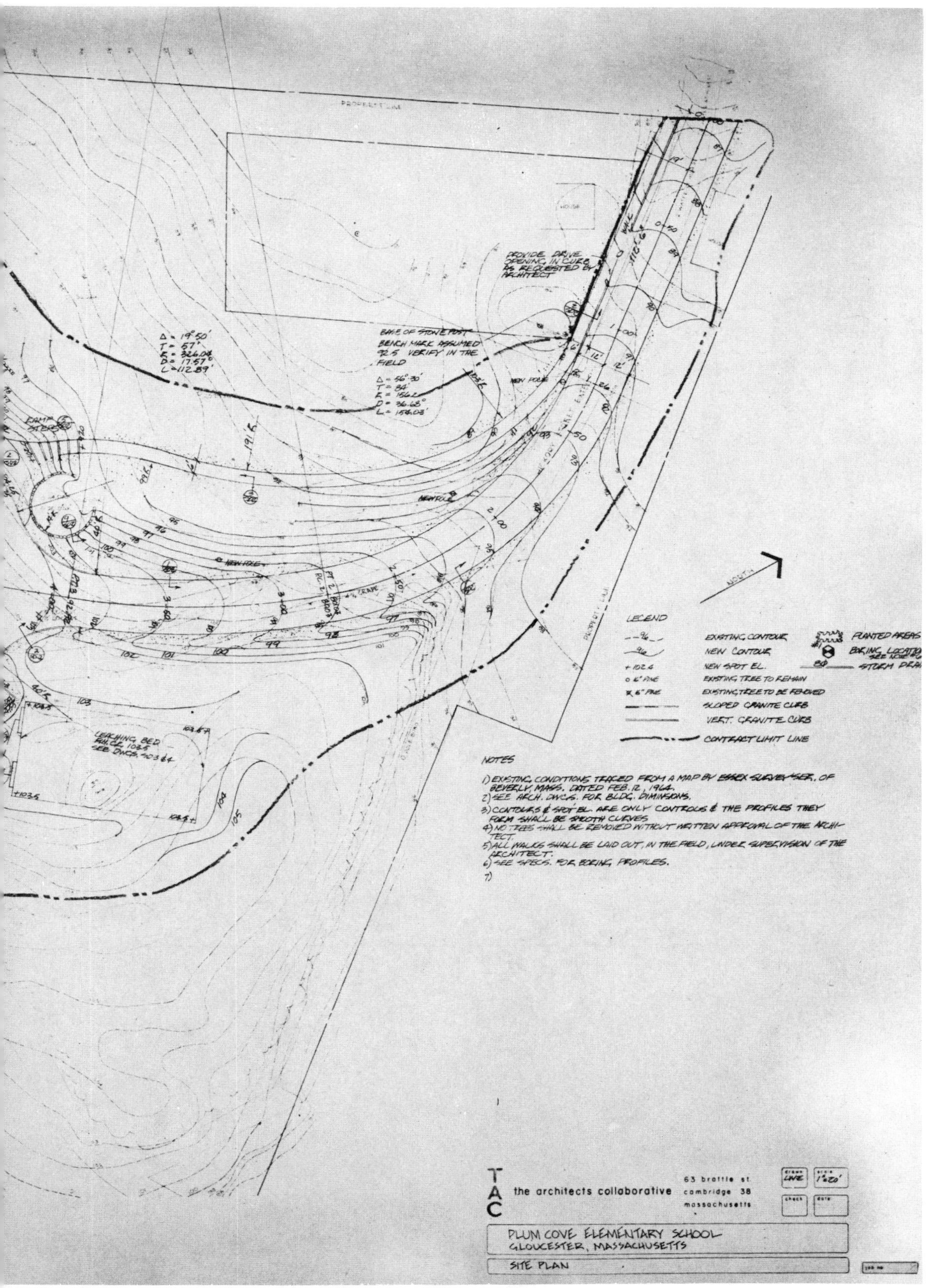

with them as design elements. Before grading was started a surface drainage flow study was made to determine positive drainage. From this study trial grading plans were developed until all grades achieved the purposes of the design plan. The refined grading on the site reinforces the design and uses 3:1 slopes to blend into the existing grade on either side of the entry drive (Plan courtesy of The Architects Collaborative).

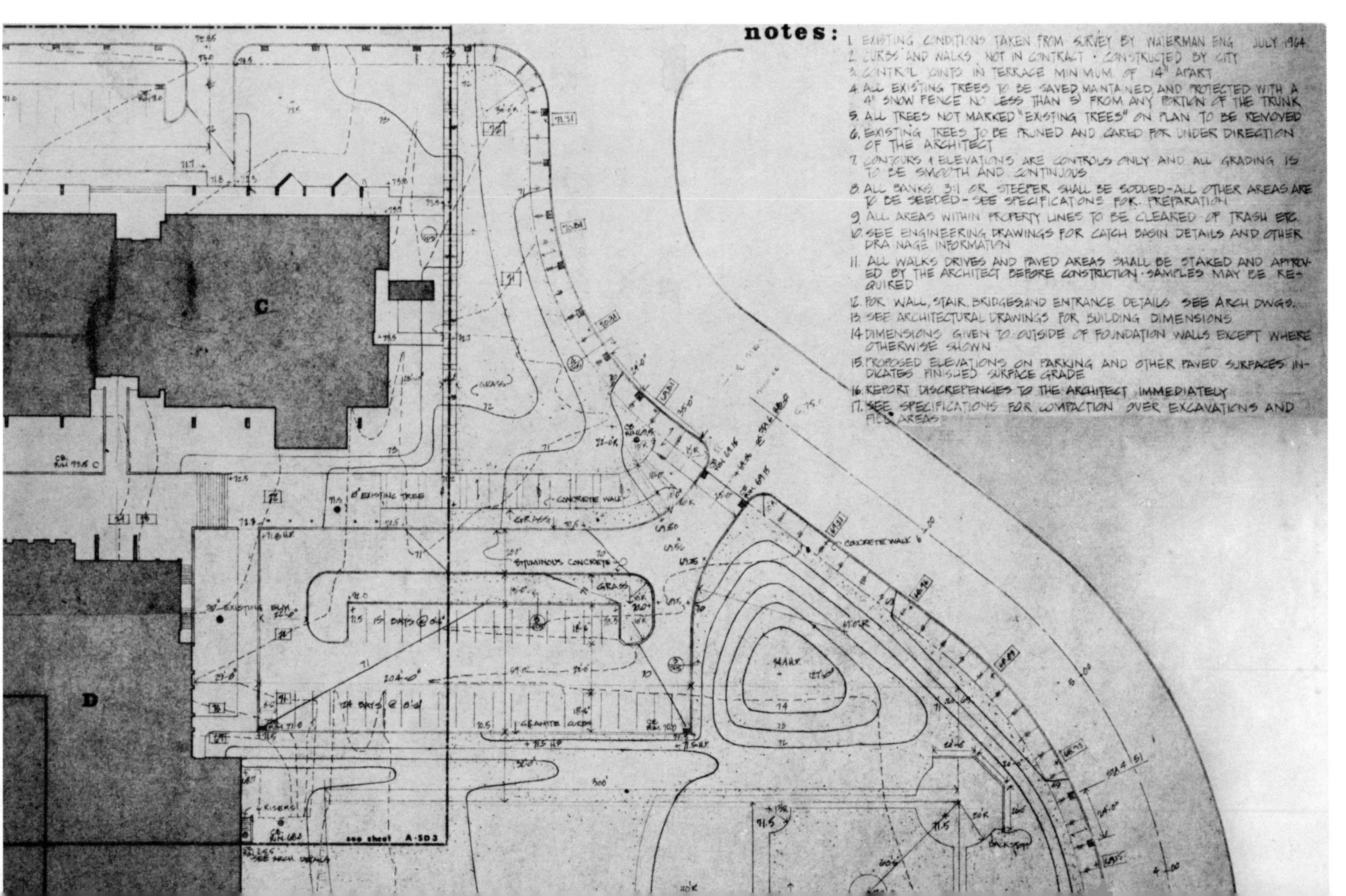
notes:
1. EXISTING CONDITIONS TAKEN FROM SURVEY BY WATERMAN ENG. JULY 1964
2. CURBS AND WALKS NOT IN CONTRACT · CONSTRUCTED BY CITY
3. CONTROL JOINTS IN TERRACE MINIMUM OF 14' APART
4. ALL EXISTING TREES TO BE SAVED MAINTAINED AND PROTECTED WITH A 4' SNOW FENCE NO LESS THAN 5' FROM ANY PORTION OF THE TRUNK
5. ALL TREES NOT MARKED "EXISTING TREES" ON PLAN TO BE REMOVED
6. EXISTING TREES TO BE PRUNED AND CARED FOR UNDER DIRECTION OF THE ARCHITECT
7. CONTOURS & ELEVATIONS ARE CONTROLS ONLY AND ALL GRADING IS TO BE SMOOTH AND CONTINUOUS
8. ALL BANKS 3:1 OR STEEPER SHALL BE SODDED - ALL OTHER AREAS ARE TO BE SEEDED - SEE SPECIFICATIONS FOR PREPARATION
9. ALL AREAS WITHIN PROPERTY LINES TO BE CLEARED OF TRASH ETC.
10. SEE ENGINEERING DRAWINGS FOR CATCH BASIN DETAILS AND OTHER DRAINAGE INFORMATION
11. ALL WALKS DRIVES AND PAVED AREAS SHALL BE STAKED AND APPROVED BY THE ARCHITECT BEFORE CONSTRUCTION · SAMPLES MAY BE REQUIRED
12. FOR WALL, STAIR, BRIDGES AND ENTRANCE DETAILS SEE ARCH DWGS.
13. SEE ARCHITECTURAL DRAWINGS FOR BUILDING DIMENSIONS
14. DIMENSIONS GIVEN TO OUTSIDE OF FOUNDATION WALLS EXCEPT WHERE OTHERWISE SHOWN
15. PROPOSED ELEVATIONS ON PARKING AND OTHER PAVED SURFACES INDICATES FINISHED SURFACE GRADE
16. REPORT DISCREPENCIES TO THE ARCHITECT IMMEDIATELY
17. SEE SPECIFICATIONS FOR COMPACTION OVER EXCAVATIONS AND FILL AREAS
C
D
CONCRETE WALK
BITUMINOUS CONCRETE
GRASS
GRANITE CURB
15 BAYS @ 8'-6"
24 BAYS @ 8'-6"
see sheet A-SD3

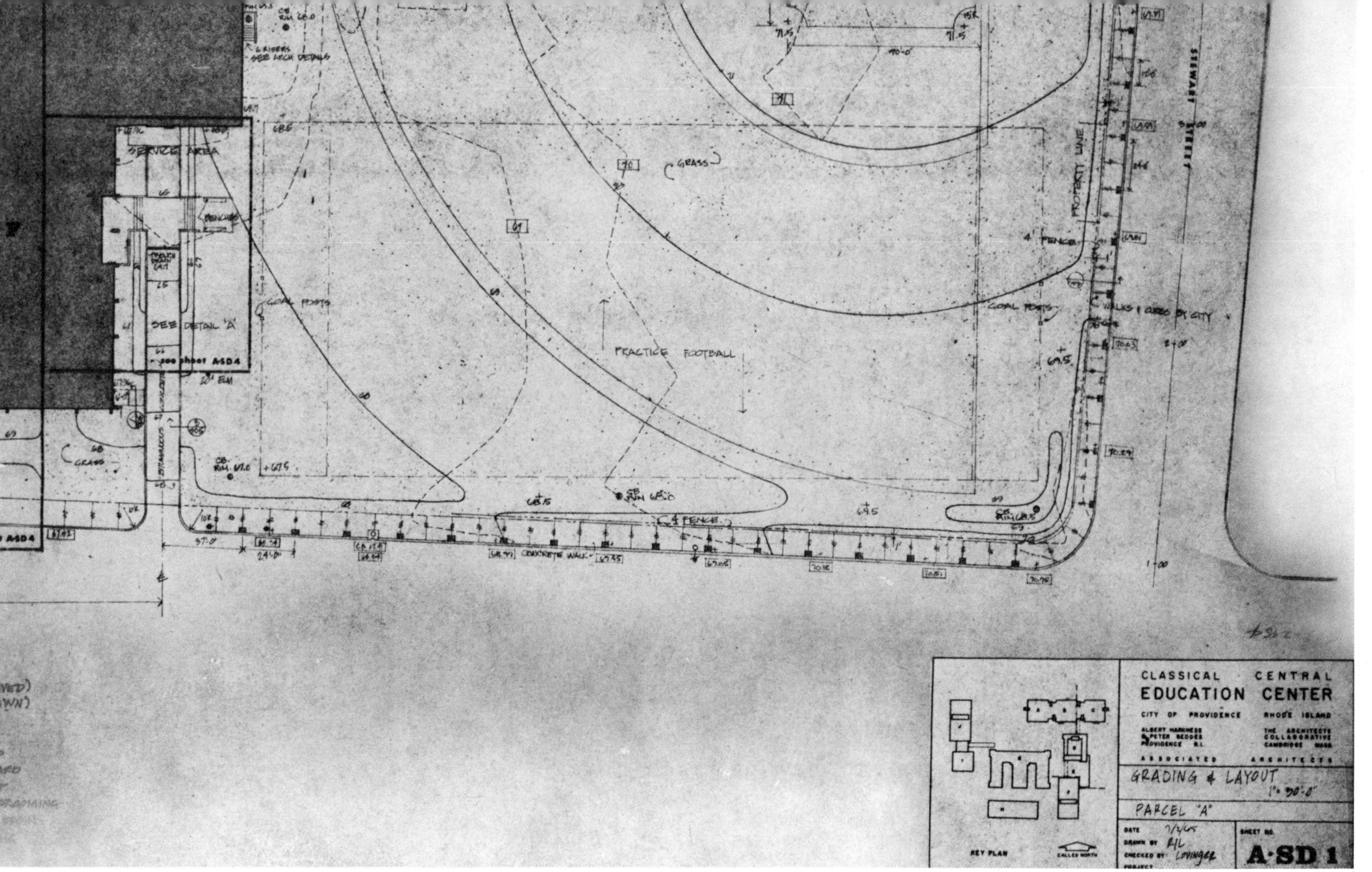

FIG. 6-22 Classical Central Education Center, Providence, Rhode Island. Note the use of spot elevations and grading on this plan. Existing contours were changed to develop adequate surface drainage for both paved and grass areas. Grass areas should have a minimum grade of 2% for surface drainage. This is particularly important on play fields to avoid puddles (Plan courtesy of The Architects Collaborative).

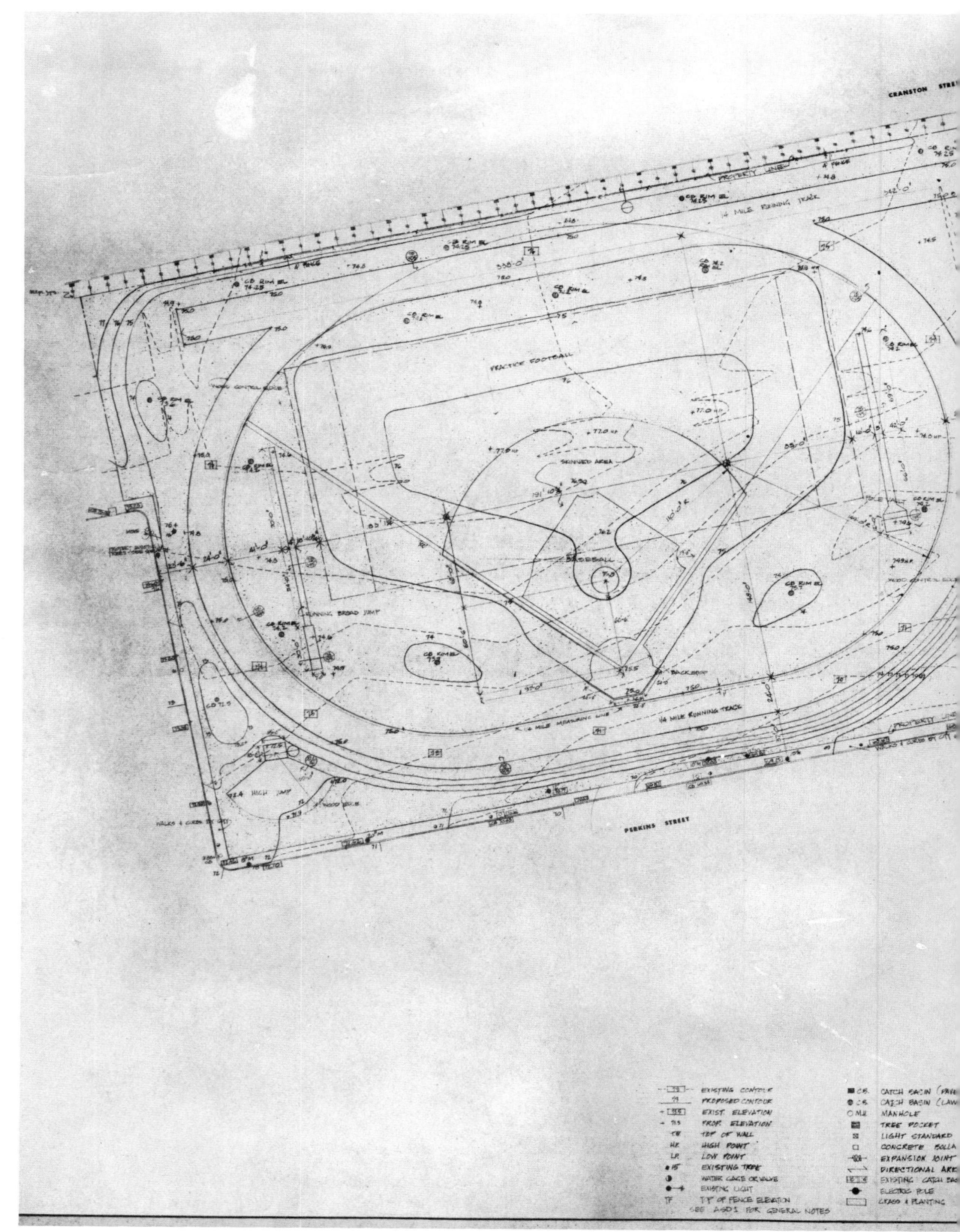

FIG. 6-23 Classical Central Education Center, Providence, Rhode Island. Space was limited for play fields and a combination track and practice football and baseball field was developed. Existing contours were changed to achieve proper

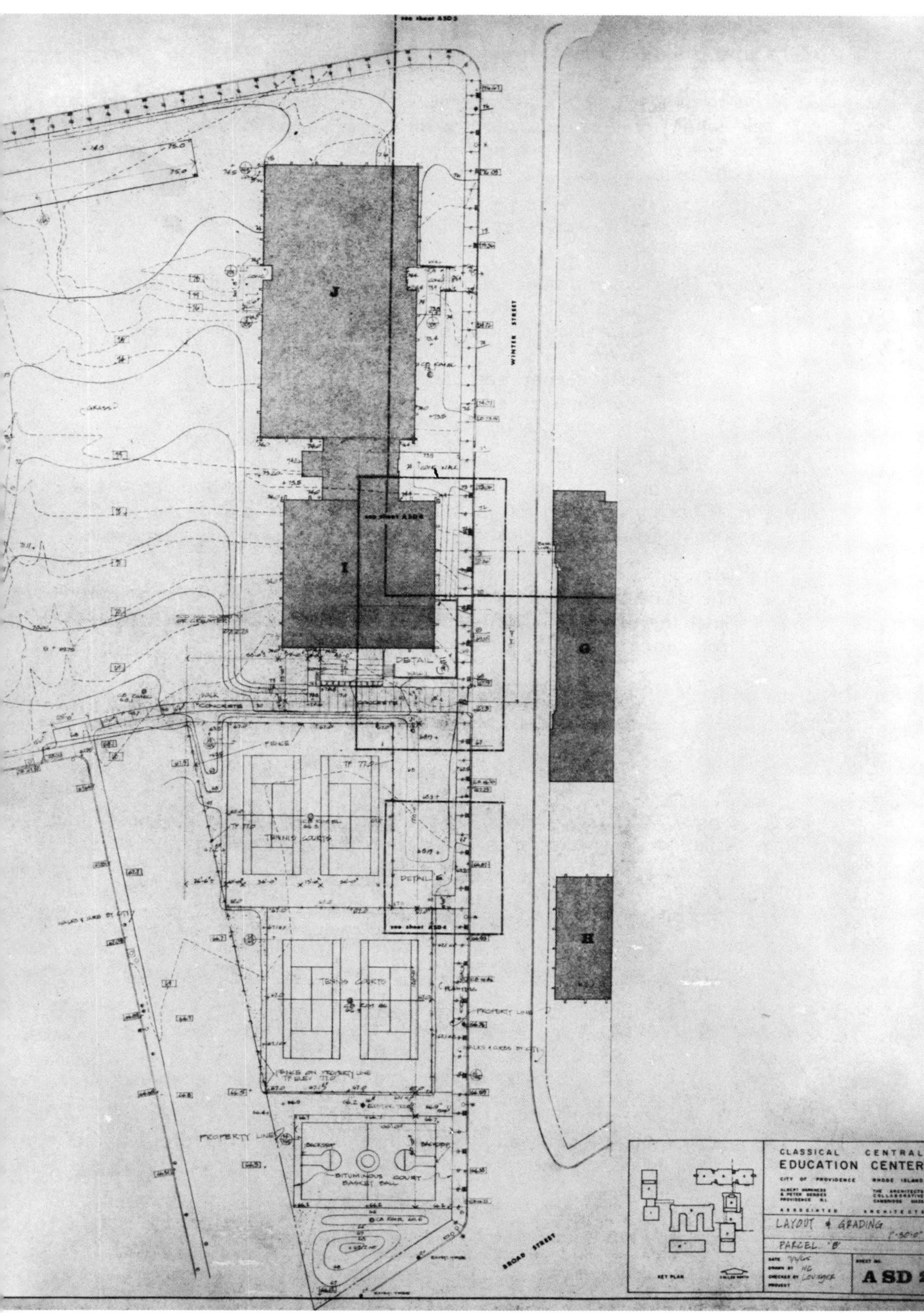

layout and drainage for these facilities, and runoff water was diverted to catch basins wherever possible before it washed over walks (Plan courtesy of The Architects Collaborative).

Contours on Roads

The formulas $G = D/L$ and $D = CI/\%G \times 100$ are used extensively in calculating contours on roads. Roads may have a crown or cross slope for drainage of storm water runoff. To calculate crown, shoulder, or ditch, use the following formula:

$$\frac{X}{CI} = \frac{TD}{D} \quad \text{or} \quad TD = \frac{X \times D}{CI}$$

where TD = travel distance, the measurement needed to indicate contours for crown, shoulder, or ditch
X = difference in elevation due to cross slope, ditch depth, and so on
D = distance between contours at a particular grade and contour interval
CI = contour interval

The following examples will illustrate the use of these formulas. A road 20 ft wide has a crown of $\frac{1}{2}$ in./ft, a 7% grade, a 5 ft shoulder with a $\frac{1}{4}$ in./ft pitch away from the road, a ditch 6 ft wide and 6 in. deep, and a contour interval of 1 ft. Plot the crossing of three contours on the road.

1. Draw a plan of the road at a scale of your choosing.
2. The grade is given as 7%; establish the distance between contours. Since this example is not related to topography, pick any point to start from along the road center line.

$$D = \frac{CI}{\%G} \times 100$$

$$D = \frac{1\text{ ft}}{7} \times 100$$

$$D = 14.28\text{ ft}$$

3. Establish crown—crown = $\frac{1}{2}$ in./ft for half the road width of 20 ft:

crown = 5 in.

Find the travel distance for the crown:

$$TD = \frac{X}{CI} \times D$$

$$TD = \frac{5\text{ in.}}{12\text{ in.}} \times 14.28\text{ ft}$$

$$TD = 5.95\text{ ft}$$

The crown, which points downhill, is now set.

4. Draw shoulder width on the plan. The shoulder = $\frac{1}{4}$ in./ft for 5 ft and slopes away from the road:

shoulder = $1\frac{1}{4}$ in.

Now find the travel distance for the shoulder and set it on the plan:

$$TD = \frac{X}{CI} \times D$$

$$TD = \frac{1.25\text{ in.}}{12\text{ in.}} \times 14.28\text{ ft}$$

$$TD = 1.49\text{ ft}$$

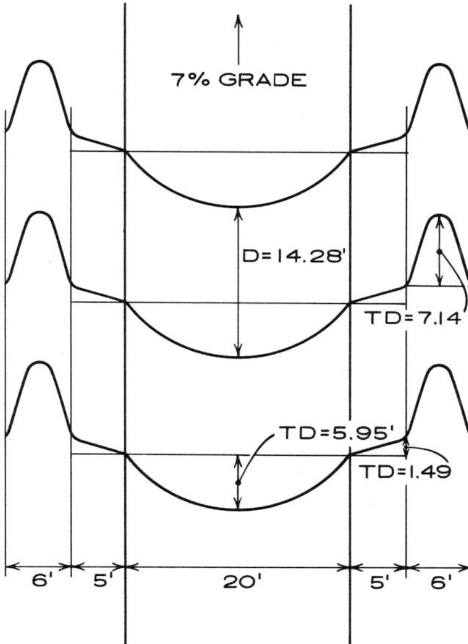

FIG. 6-24 Contours on roads.

5. Draw the ditch width on the plan. The ditch depth was given as 6 in.:

$$\text{ditch} = 6 \text{ in.}$$

We must now find the travel distance for the ditch and set it on the plan. (See Fig. 6-24.)

$$TD = \frac{X}{CI} \times D$$

$$TD = \frac{6 \text{ in.}}{12 \text{ in.}} \times 14.28 \text{ ft}$$

$$TD = 7.14 \text{ ft}$$

A road 20 ft wide has a 6 in. crown, 6 in. curbs, and 6 ft walk (left side) with $\frac{1}{4}$ in. cross slope away from the road. The side slopes along the road are 3:1. Plot 2 ft contours on the road. The scale is 1 in. = 20 ft and station elevations are given.

1. Start at station 3 + 00 and elevation 24.35 ft given on the plan. Determine the grade:

$$G = \frac{D}{L}$$

$$G = \frac{24.35 \text{ ft} - 9.1 \text{ ft}}{200 \text{ ft}} \times 100$$

$$G = 7.62\%$$

2. Now find the distance between contours:

$$D = \frac{CI}{\%G} \times 100$$

$$D = \frac{2 \text{ ft}}{7.62} \times 100$$

$$D = 26.24 \text{ ft}$$

3. Starting at station 3 + 00 and elevation 24.35 ft we must find the first even contour, the 24 contour:

$$TD = \frac{X}{CI} \times D$$

$$TD = \frac{24.35 \text{ ft} - 24 \text{ ft}}{2 \text{ ft}} \times 26.24 \text{ ft}$$

$$TD = 4.6 \text{ ft}$$

We can now step off the distance between contours 26.24 ft from contour 24.

4. Establish crown, given at 6 in.:

crown = 6 in.

We must now find the travel distance for the crown:

$$TD = \frac{X}{CI} \times D$$

$$TD = \frac{6 \text{ in.}}{24 \text{ in.}} \times 26.24 \text{ ft}$$

$$TD = 6.55 \text{ ft}$$

5. Establish curb, given at 6 in.:

curb = 6 in.

Find the travel distance for the curb and set it on the plan:

$$TD = \frac{X}{CI} \times D$$

$$TD = \frac{6 \text{ in.}}{24 \text{ in.}} \times 26.24 \text{ ft}$$

$$TD = 6.55 \text{ ft}$$

6. Draw the walk on the plan. The cross slope or pitch is given as $\frac{1}{4}$ in./6 ft:

walk = $1\frac{1}{2}$ in.

We must now find the travel distance for the walk and set it on the plan:

$$TD = \frac{X}{CI} \times D$$

$$TD = \frac{1.5 \text{ in.}}{24 \text{ in.}} \times 26.24 \text{ ft}$$

$$TD = 1.64 \text{ ft}$$

7. Establish 3 : 1 side slopes and blend new contours into the existing grade. (See Fig. 6-25.)

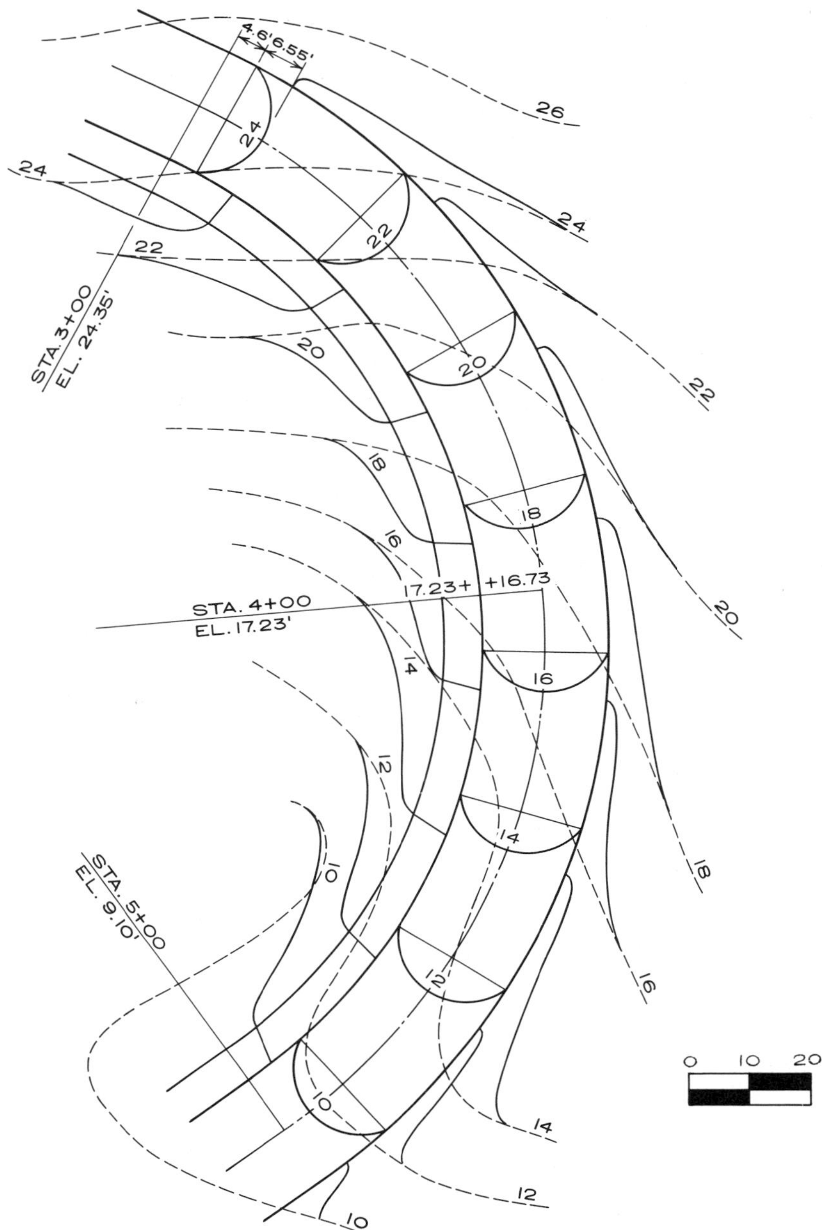

FIG. 6-25 Contours on roads.

EARTHWORK CALCULATIONS

Two types of grading that reshape existing contours are rough grading (before construction) and finished grading (after construction). Before rough grading is begun existing topsoil should be stripped from the area to be graded and stockpiled away from the construction area. Topsoil of good quality can be reused in the process of finished grading. Consider the kind of soil, how it reacts in cut and fill situations, and its bearing capacity. Allow approximately 10% for loss in weight and volume in moving soil and from shrinkage by spillage or excessive compaction. To determine amount of cut or fill we use the methods discussed next.

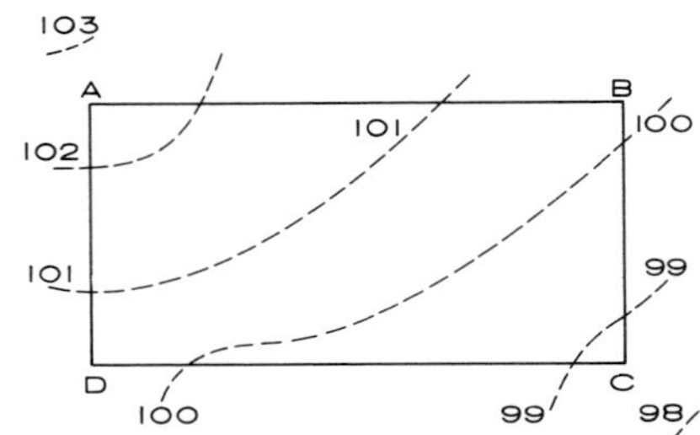

FIG. 6-26 Excavation: cut and fill.

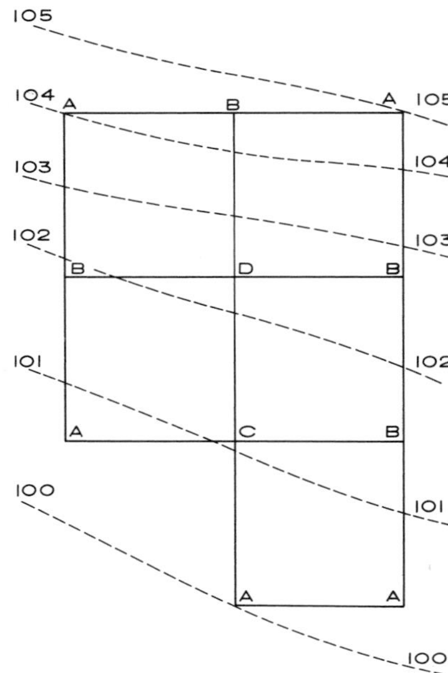

FIG. 6-27 Extensive excavation problem: cut and fill.

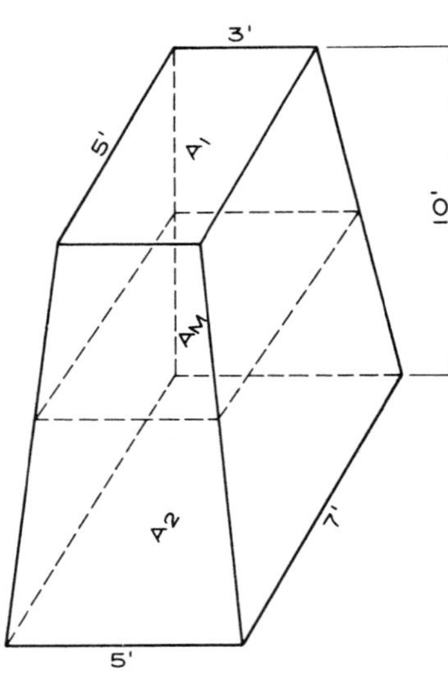

FIG. 6-28 Geometric volume computed by average end or prismoidal formula.

Computing Cut and Fill by Borrow-Pit Method

To compute excavation of material for a rectangular building, see the following example and Fig. 6-26, a 10 × 20 ft rectangular excavation, the bottom of which is 95.3 ft.

A		*B*		*C*		*D*	
102.5 ft		100.2 ft		98.8 ft		100.4 ft	
−95.3 ft		−95.3 ft		−95.3 ft		−95.3 ft	
7.2 ft	+	4.9 ft	+	3.5 ft	+	5.1 ft	= 20.7 ft

Average height = 20.7 ft/4 = 5.2 ft. Volume = average height multiplied by the area of the excavation and divided by 27 to arrive at cubic yards:

$$V = \frac{5.2 \text{ ft} \times 10 \text{ ft} \times 20 \text{ ft}}{27} = 38.5 \text{ yd}^3$$

When building excavations are more extensive, calculate the volume in the following manner.

1. Area is divided into a grid of squares of any convenient size.
2. Letter *a* corners which occur on one square, *b* corners common to two squares, *c* corners common to three squares, *d* corners common to four squares.
   All *a*'s, *b*'s, *c*'s, and *d*'s. (See Fig. 6-27.)
3. Compute the heights of corners of excavation and the sum of heights of all *a*'s, *b*'s, *c*'s, and *d*'s. (See Fig. 6-27.)

Bottom of excavation = 95.0 ft.

a's:	104.0 ft		105.0 ft		100.6 ft		100.0 ft		100.4 ft	
	−95.0 ft		−95.0 ft		−95.0 ft		−95.0 ft		−95.0 ft	
	9.0 ft	+	10.0 ft	+	5.6 ft	+	5.0 ft	+	5.4 ft	= 35 ft
b's:	104.5 ft		101.8 ft		102.6 ft		101.5 ft			
	−95.0 ft		−95.0 ft		−95.0 ft		−95.0 ft			
	9.5 ft	+	6.8 ft	+	7.6 ft	+	6.5 ft	sum of *b*'s = 30.4 ft		
c's:	101.1 ft									
	−95.0 ft									
	6.1 ft	sum of *c*'s = 6.1 ft								
d's:	102.2 ft									
	−95.0 ft									
	7.2 ft	sum of *d*'s = 7.2 ft								

$$\text{volume} = \frac{\text{area of 1 square}}{27} \times \frac{\text{sum } a\text{'s} + 2 \text{ sum } b\text{'s} + 3 \text{ sum } c\text{'s} + 4 \text{ sum } d\text{'s}}{4}$$

$$\text{volume} = \frac{20 \times 20}{27} \times \frac{35.0 + 2(30.4) + 3(6.1) + 4(7.2)}{4}$$

$$\text{volume} = 529.3 \text{ yd}^3$$

Average End Area Formula. Where cross sections occur through longitudinal cuts and fills, the average end area method is used to compute volume. The volumes obtained are not exact and tend to be in excess; however, since this formula is easily computed, it is often used. (See Fig. 6-28.)

$$V = L\frac{(A_1 + A_2)}{2} = \text{ft}^3 \text{ divided by } 27 = \text{yd}^3$$

where V = volume
A_1, A_2 = areas of two parallel faces
L = horizontal distance between cross sections

Prismoidal Formula. The prismoidal formula is used for computations of volume where accuracy is required and the geometric solid is a prismoid (a solid with parallel but unequal bases with its other faces quadrilaterals or triangles).

$$V = L\frac{(A_1 + 4A_m + A_2)}{6}$$

where V = volume
A_1, A_2 = areas of successive cross sections or parallel faces
A_m = area of section midway between A_1 and A_2
L = horizontal distance between A_1 and A_2

Planimeter. A *planimeter* measures irregular areas. It converts the answer to square inches on a drum and disc while a tracing point is moved over the outline of the area to be measured. This instrument consists of two metal arms joined by a ball and socket joint. The pole arm is weighted and has an anchor point; the tracer arm has a tracer point, finger grip, recording wheel, and measuring scale. The measuring scales are usually calibrated to read in square inches to the nearest $\frac{1}{100}$ of a square inch. (See Fig. 6-29.)

The anchor point is set at a spot outside the area to be measured. See if the arm will cover the whole area or if the anchor point must be changed. The tracer point is now set over the starting point, the vernier set to zero, and the tracing point moved clockwise around the area to be measured until it arrives at the starting point. A reading is now taken on the vernier. Enter four figures to eliminate possible errors in placing the decimal point. Now retrace the outline a second time and record a second reading, which should be approximately twice the first. Divide the second

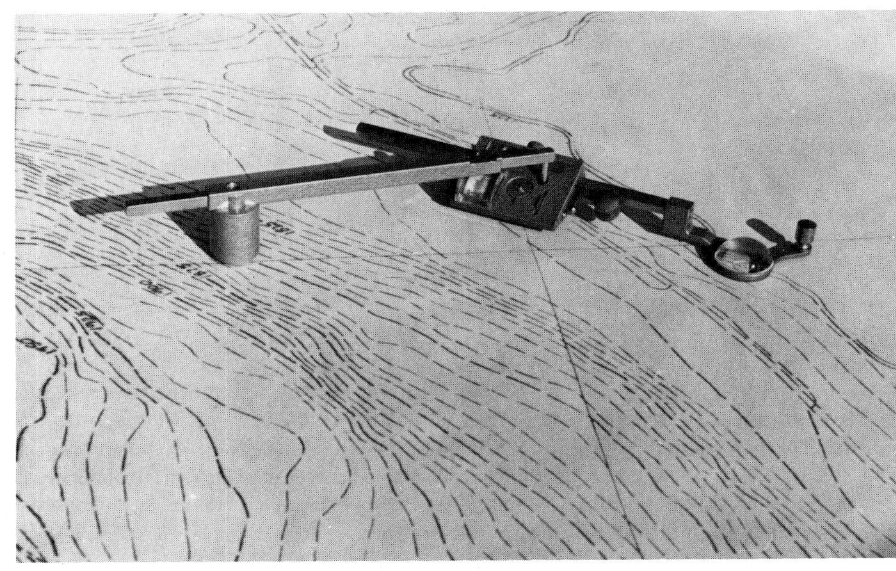

FIG. 6-29 Planimeter.

reading by two and obtain the average of both readings. They should be within 1% of each other. If the instrument is carefully used, there should be no error greater than $\frac{1}{2}$ to 1%.

Be careful to protect the instrument from bumps. Do not rub fingers over the recording wheel. Keep the instrument clean.

Example

1.25 in.^{2} was the reading on the planimeter. 1 in. = 50 ft is the scale of the drawing. The area of 1 in.^{2} on the planimeter ($L \times W$) = 50 × 50 ft. To find the volume we use the formula $V = L \times W \times H$. Therefore

$$1.25 \times 50^2 = 3125 \text{ ft}^2$$

V = 3125 ft^2 × 2 ft (height varies; it is the contour interval in this example)

V = 6250 ft^3

$$V = \frac{6250 \text{ ft}^3}{27 \quad \text{ft}^3/\text{yd}^3} = 231.5 \text{ yd}^3$$

The Cross-Sectional Method

The cross-sectional method for computing cut and fill is the simplest of any others for determing earthwork quantities. It was used to compute cut and fill in Table 6-1.

Table 6-1 Sample Cut and Fill Planimeter Chart with Cut and Fill Computations[a,b]

	Cut			Fill			Area		Length	Volume	
Station	1st	2nd	Cor.	1st	2nd	Cor.	Cut	Fill	C/F	Cut	Fill
0 + 00							—	—			
0 + 50				1.15	2.30	1.15	—	46.00	0/50		1150
1 + 00				0.74	1.47	0.74	—	29.60	0/50		1890
1 + 50	0.45	0.92	0.46	0.13	0.27	0.14	18.40	5.60	25/50	230	880
2 + 00	1.32	2.68	1.34				53.60	—	50/13	3600	36.4
2 + 50	1.02	2.04	1.02				40.80	—	50/ 0	2360	
3 + 00				0.99	1.99	1.00	—	40.00	20/30	408	600
3 + 50				2.14	4.26	2.13	—	85.20	0/30		1878
4 + 00				1.87	3.74	1.87	—	74.80	0/50		4000
4 + 50				1.12	2.23	1.12	—	44.80	0/50		2990
5 + 00	0.03	0.06	0.03	0.13	0.13	0.13	1.20	5.20	5/50	3	1250
5 + 50	0.46	0.90	0.45				18.00	—	50/ 7	480	18.2
6 + 00	1.55	3.11	1.56				62.40	—	50/ 0	2010	
6 + 50	2.47	4.93	2.47				98.80	—	50/ 0	4030	
7 + 00	1.37	2.76	1.38				55.20	—	50/ 0	3850	
7 + 50	0.09	0.16	0.08	0.10	0.10	0.10	1.60	4.00	50/ 3	1420	6
8 + 00				2.08	4.15	2.08	—	83.20	2/50	1.6	2180
8 + 50				0.94	1.88	0.94	—	37.60	0/50	120	3020
9 + 00	0.23	0.47	0.24	0.02	0.04	0.02	9.60	0.80	25/50	1000	960
9 + 50	0.75	1.51	0.76				30.40	—	50/22		0.8

[a]See road alignment, p. 174.

[b]Horizontal scale of sections 1 in. = 10 ft. Vertical scale of sections 1 in. = 4 ft. One square inch on planimeter = 40 ft^2. $V = L\ (A_1 + A_2)/2$ = ft^3 divided by 27 = yd^3. Total cut = 19,512.6 ft^3 = 722.9 yd^3. Total fill = 20,859.4 ft^3 = 772.6 yd^3. The figures in Table 6-1 were computed by first taking two consecutive planimeter readings to arrive at the readings for each cut or fill area. The two readings were then averaged and the corrected figure used in computing areas of cut or fill. One square inch on the planimeter as previously shown from the horizontal and vertical scales of the sections was 40 ft^2/1 in. Each corrected planimeter reading was multiplied times 40 ft^2/1 in. to compute the areas. On station 0 + 50, for example, to find the area, 1.15 in. × 40 ft^2/1 in. = 46.00 ft^2. To compute the volume, the formula $V = L\ (A_1 + A_2)/2$ = ft^3 is used. The length of the cut or fill between sections was determined from the sections and profile (see Fig. 8-22), and figures are given in the chart. The volume of fill between stations 0 + 00 and 0 + 50 = $L\ (A_1 + A_2)/2$ = 50 ft (0 + 46.00)/2 = 1150 ft^3.

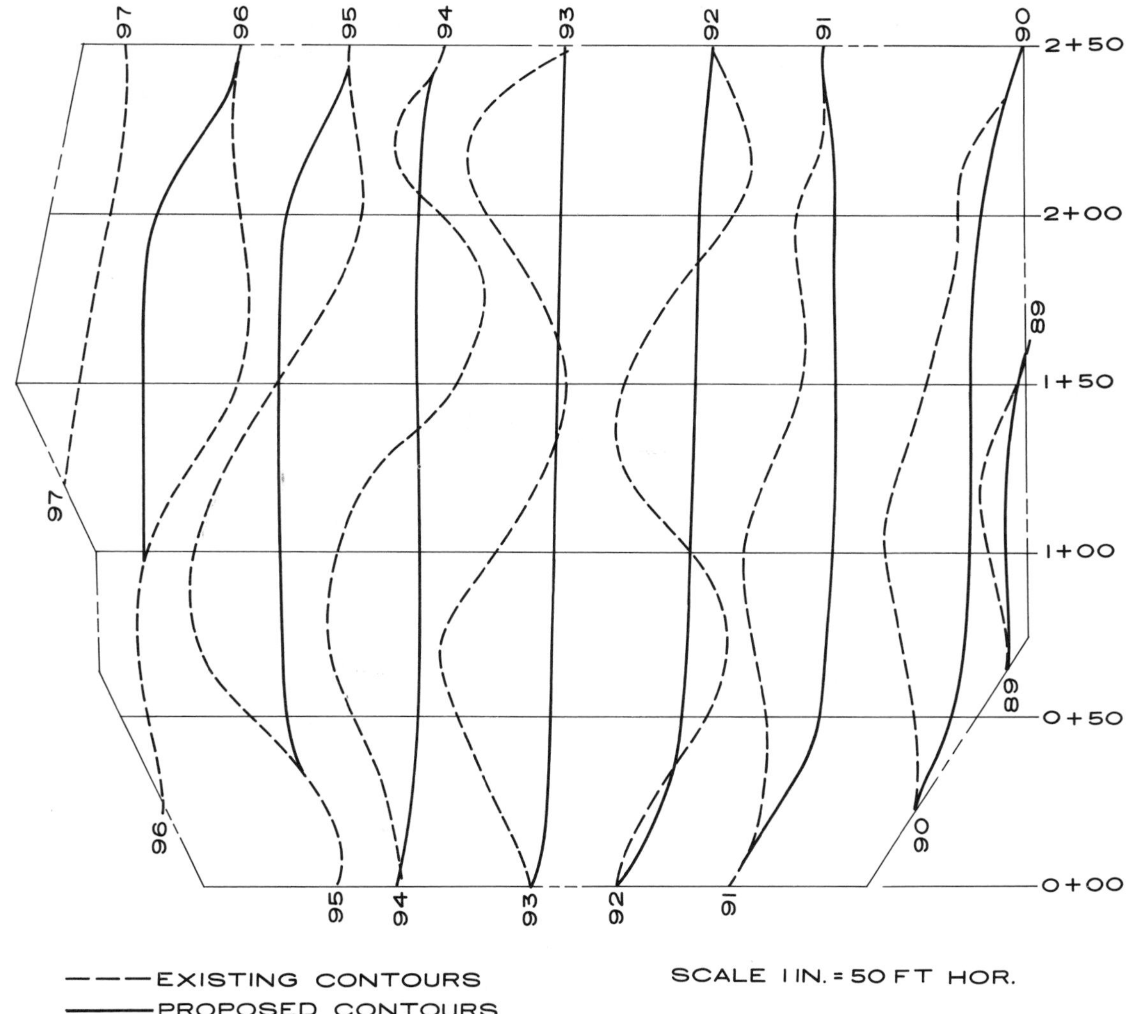

FIG. 6-30 Section method: cut and fill problem.

Parallel section lines are drawn through a grading plan usually at 50 ft intervals. The cut and fill along each section or station is then measured with a planimeter and the area of cut and fill recorded. This is referred to as the cut and fill for each end area. The average end area formula is then used to determine the cut or fill between each successive set of stations such as between station 0 + 50 and 1 + 00 or 1 + 00 and 1 + 50. Excavation areas for building basements are best calculated separately in this method for more accuracy. Table 6-1 shows how the cross-sectional method is used to determine cut and fill for the sample road sections in Fig. 8-22.

In the sample grading plan in Fig. 6-30 a site has been regraded for use as a play field. The grade across the field is $2\frac{1}{2}\%$. To determine the cut and fill we can use the section method. Sections are drawn every 50 ft perpendicular to the contour lines. A planimeter is used to determine the cut or fill along each end area. The average end area formula is then used to determine the cut or fill between stations. The total cut and fill can then be added together. (See Fig. 6-31 and Table 6-2.)

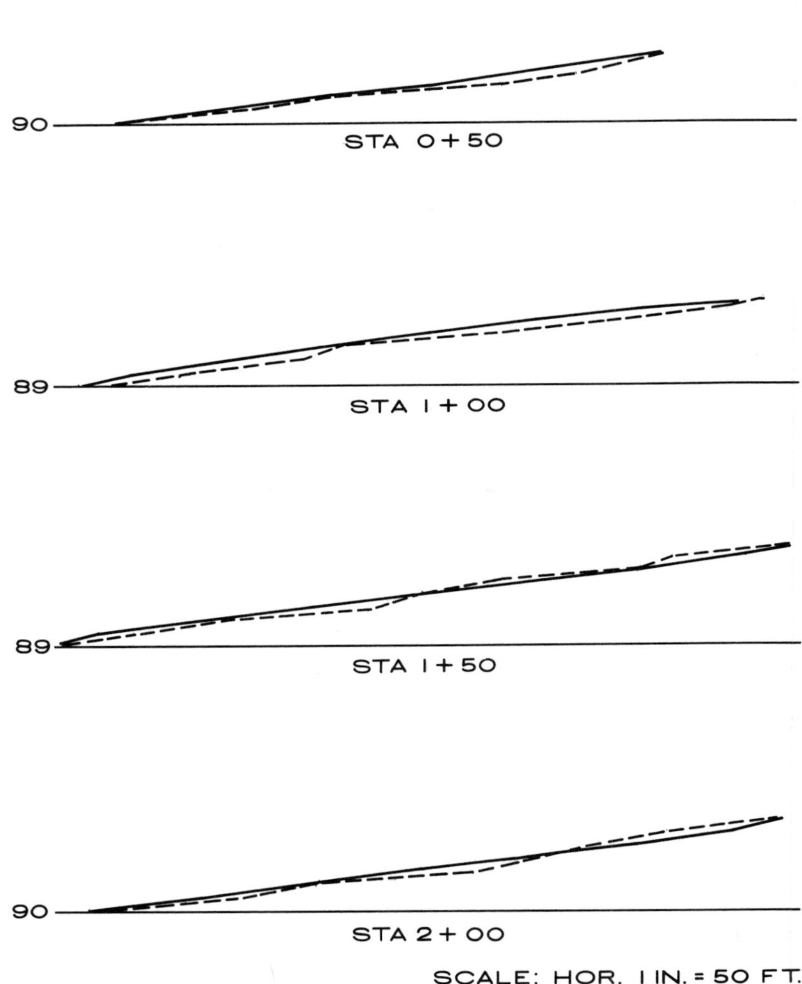

FIG. 6-31 Sections through grading plan.

Table 6-2 Cut and Fill Chart for Sample Grading Plan[a]

	Cut			Fill			Area (ft^2)			Volume (ft^3)	
Station	1st	2nd	Cor.	1st	2nd	Cor.	Cut	Fill	Length (ft)	Cut	Fill
0 + 00											
0 + 50				0.13	0.26	0.13		65	50		1,625
1 + 00				0.28	0.60	0.30		150	50		5,375
1 + 50	0.12	0.22	0.11	0.13	0.26	0.13	55	65	50	1375	5,375
2 + 00	0.06	0.12	0.06	0.12	0.24	0.12	30	60	50	2125	3,125
2 + 50									50	750	1,500
										4250	17,000

[a]In computing cut and fill for Fig. 6-30 sections do not have to be drawn for stations 0 + 00 or 2 + 50, since these end areas are at the beginning and end of the new grading (or where new grades have been blended into the existing topography). Horizontal scale of sections 1 in. = 50 ft. Vertical scale of sections 1 in. = 10 ft. One square inch on planimeter = (50 × 10 ft) = 500 ft^2. $V = L(A_1 + A_2)/2$ = ft^3 divided by 27 = yd^3. The volume in Table 6-2 was computed between end areas (stations) 0 + 00 to 0 + 50 for its 50 ft length, 0 + 50 to 1 + 00 for its 50 ft length, and so on, for both cut or fill areas. For example, to compute the fill from station 0 + 00 to 0 + 50

$$V = 50\left(\frac{0 + 65}{2}\right) = 1625 \text{ ft}^3$$

Total cut = 4250 ft^3 + 27 = 157 yd^3. Total fill = 17,000 ft^3 + 27 = 629.6 yd^3. This cut and fill study shows that 472.6 yd^3 of fill are needed to regrade the site unless a closer balance of cut and fill can be achieved in the grading plan.

FIG. 7-1 Drainage flows into this lake, which acts as a feature element with its aerated fountain jets at Lincoln Centre, Dallas, Texas.

Chapter Seven
Site Drainage

SITE DRAINAGE

Surface Drainage

Storm water runoff includes both man-made and natural systems. Often a storm drainage system is composed of a closed or piped system and natural drainage areas such as swales or streams that pick up the water from the closed system. Drainage swales are also used to guide and carry water to a closed system.

In residential areas natural systems should be used as much as possible as well as be considered in the design and layout of housing. The use of natural systems should be used to keep the cost of the storm water system down, since this system can be one of the higher cost items in site development. Doing so allows water to percolate into the soil recharging the ground water system.

Controlling storm water runoff is a major factor in preparing a grading plan. To prevent problems caused by erosion or flooding, the principle of positive drainage is used—that is, diverting storm water away from a building or area and carrying it away from a site in a storm drainage system. Spot elevations are set at critical points adjacent to a building to provide drainage. Advantageous points must be chosen for placement of catch basins, and their connection to existing drainage channels in the area or to an existing storm drainage line must be considered. (See Figs. 7-1 to 7-3.)

Surface drain lines are called storm sewers and are constructed with tight or closed joints. Surface drainage can be provided by adjusting ground slopes to allow for runoff of storm water and its interception at various intervals in catch basins.

The design of a drainage system is based on the amount of rainfall to be carried away at a given time. Runoff is that portion of precipitation that finds its way into natural or artificial channels either as surface flow during the storm period or as subsurface flow after the storm has subsided. Runoff is determined by calculating the volume of water discharged

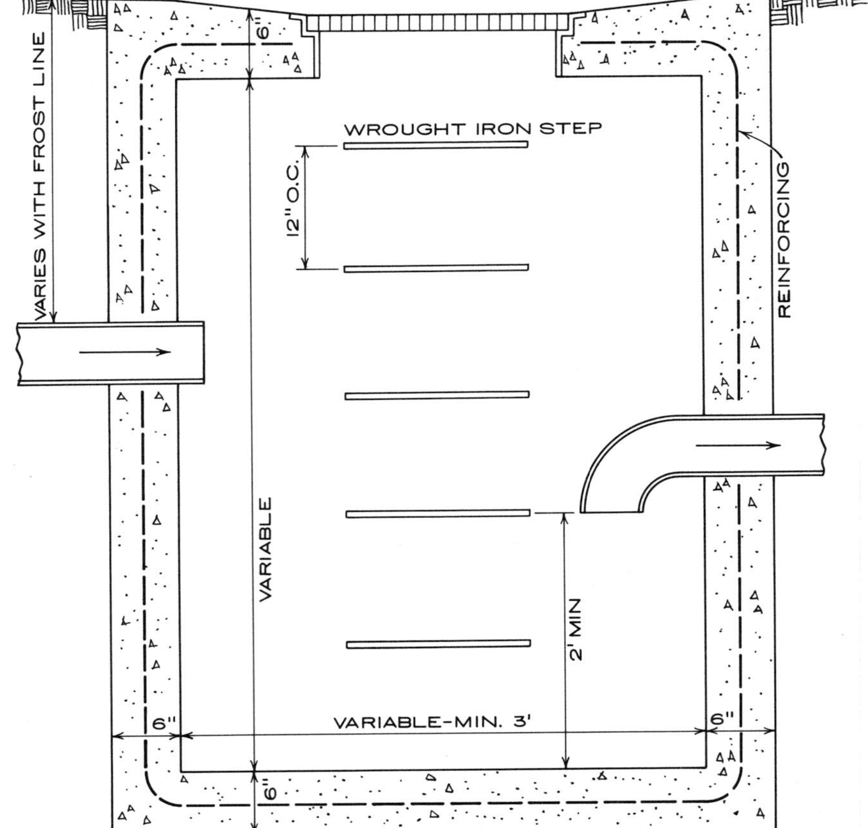

FIG. 7-2 Catch basins intercept storm water and sediment is retained before water enters the outlet line of the drainage system. For this reason they must be cleaned periodically to prevent flooding.

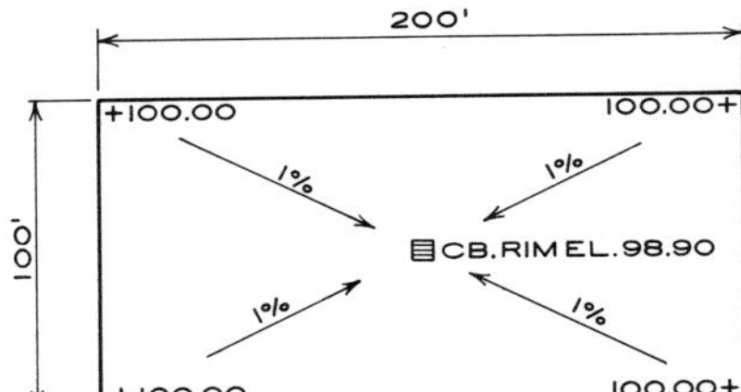

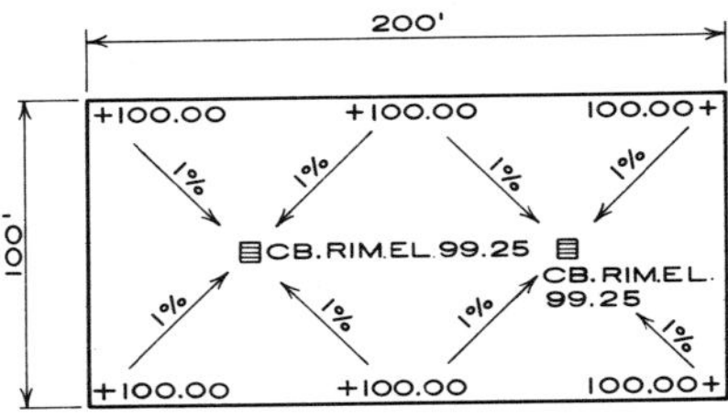

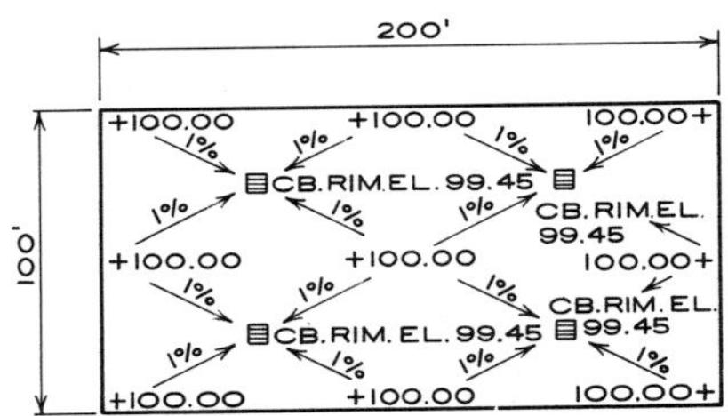

FIG. 7-3 Examples of catch basin locations on paved areas. Surface drainage influences design decisions in the initial layout of a project and is affected by type of surface material, soil, vegetation, size of area, and location of existing drainage channels or watershed areas. Excessive surface water must be removed by natural or constructed channels or carried away by subsurface pipe systems.

from a given watershed area and is measured in cubic feet of discharge per second.

To calculate runoff, we use the rational formula:

$$Q = CIA$$

where Q = storm water runoff from an area (ft^3/second)

C = coefficient of runoff (percentage of rainfall that runs off depending on the characteristics of the drainage area)

I = average intensity of rainfall (in./hour) for a duration equal to the time of concentration for a selected location and rainfall frequency

A = area (acres)

The rational method makes two assumptions:

1. Time of concentration (TOC) is based on the average rainfall rate during the time required for water runoff to flow into the nearest inlet from the most remote point (inlet time), plus the time of flow in the storm line from the furthest inlet to the outlet point.
2. The peak rate of rainfall occurs during the time of concentration. Average rainfall intensities used in the foregoing have no relation to the actual rainfall pattern during the storm.

The rational method can be used for drainage areas less than 5 square miles and is most frequently used on areas up to $\frac{1}{2}$ square mile.

In urban areas the frequency of rainfall generally designed for is the 10 year storm. (See Figs. 7-4. to 7-7. for one hour rainfall maps. These maps are not used for TOC method calculations where shorter durations than one hour are needed). In residential areas this may be reduced to a 2 or 5 year storm. Inlet times of 5 to 15 minutes are generally used. To determine the design storm to be used various communities have established design criteria which must be followed. Rainfall intensity duration curves in inches per hour are available from the weather bureau or city engineering office. These curves have 2, 5, 10, 25, 50, and 100 year storms. For example, in Newark, New Jersey, a 10 year storm is designed for with an inlet time of 6 minutes.

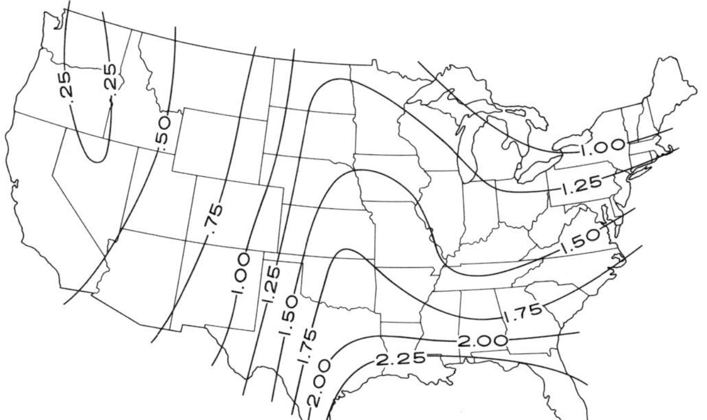

FIG. 7-4 Two year storm: one hour rainfall in in. per hour. D. L. Yarnell, "Rainfall Intensity-Frequency Data," U.S. Department of Agriculture Miscellaneous Publication 204, 1935.

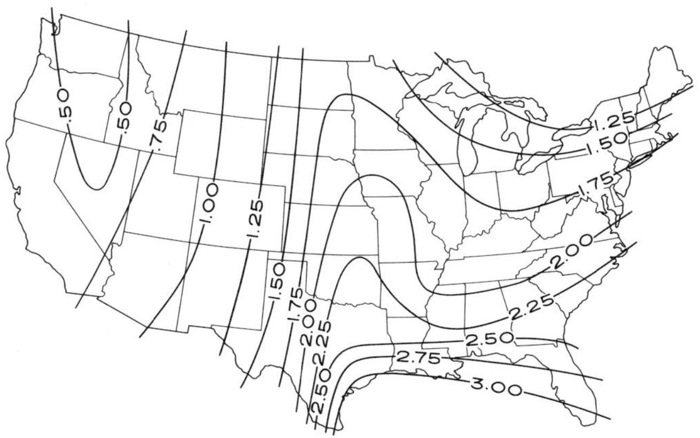

FIG. 7-5 Five year storm: one hour rainfall in in. per hour. D. L. Yarnell, "Rainfall Intensity-Frequency Data," U.S. Department of Agriculture Miscellaneous Publication 204, 1935.

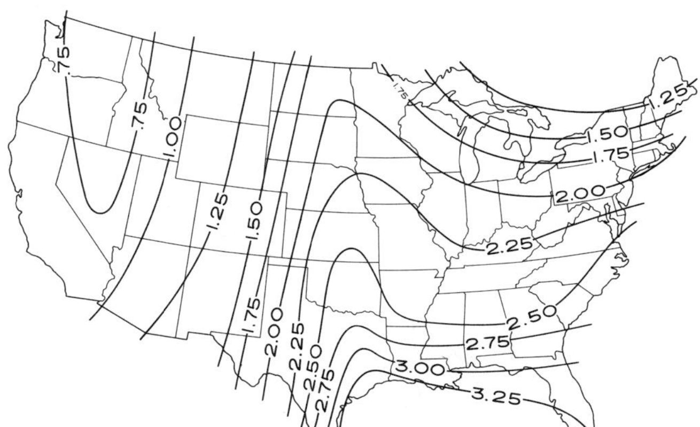

FIG. 7-6 Ten year storm: one hour rainfall in in. per hour. D. L. Yarnell, "Rainfall Intensity-Frequency Data," U.S. Department of Agriculture Miscellaneous Publication 204, 1935.

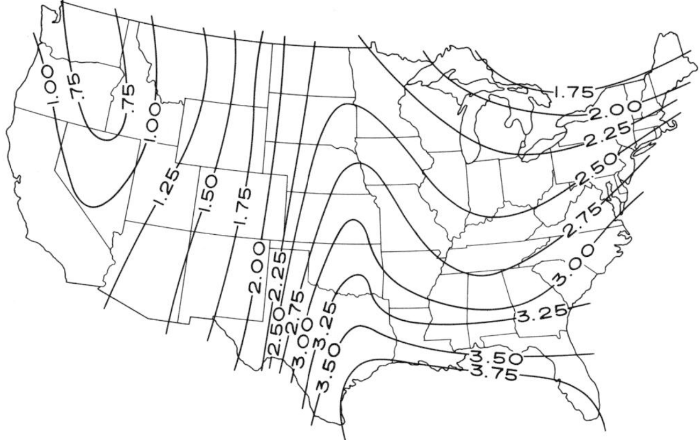

FIG. 7-7 Twenty-five year storm: one hour rainfall in in. per hour. D. L. Yarnell, "Rainfall Intensity-Frequency Data," U.S. Department of Agriculture Miscellaneous Publication 204, 1935.

Catch Basins and Drop Inlets

Catch basins intercept storm water and sediment is retained before water enters the outlet line. The catch basins must be cleaned periodically to prevent clogging.

Drop inlets do not have sediment traps below the outlet line and must be designed with self-cleaning velocities to function properly. Drop inlets are often used in low maintenance areas where sediment would clog improperly maintained catch basins.

Both these structures use cast iron grates to allow water to enter the structure. Grate openings must be large enough to permit water to enter, but in areas where pedestrian or bicycles use is predominant, grate openings should be a minimum size for safety.

Catch basins or drop inlets are generally placed 100 to 200 ft apart on roads and closer where swales have been developed around buildings.

Manholes

Manholes are used as a means of inspecting and cleaning sewer lines. They are placed at these points:

1 Changes of direction of pipe lines.
2 Changes in pipe sizes.
3 Change in pipe slope.
4 Intersection of two or more pipe lines.
5 Intervals not greater than 300 to 500 ft.

Pipe

Pipe used in closed systems is generally concrete, vitrified clay, cast iron, or galvanized corrugated metal pipe. In some cases where corrugated metal pipe is used it has a paved invert for flow where the slope of the pipe is small such as 0.5% or 0.005 ft/ft. Pipe slope is generally desirable at 1% or 0.01 ft/ft. Pipe inverts are set below frost level so that flow will not stop in the winter. Roughness coefficients are shown in Table 7-1.

In selecting the size of pipe for the storm drainage system the site planner can follow the sequence presented here.

1 Develop the layout of catch basins or inlets, manholes, and any leaders from building roof drains.
2 Calculate the area in acres draining into each catch basin and the coefficients of runoff for each part of the area if they vary—grass, paving, roofs, and so on, must be determined. (See Table 7-2.)
3 Multiply the areas times each material coefficient to arrive at totals for each catch basin.
4 Obtain the time of duration charts for the community in which the site is located. Find out the design storm and the time of concentration for which the system must be designed.
5 Multiply rainfall intensity (I) determined from the charts just mentioned times ($A \times C$) to give runoff (Q) in cubic feet per second.
6 Measure the length of pipe between catch basins.
7 Determine the slope of pipe for self-cleaning velocity. The self-cleaning velocity is 2.5 ft/second. Rim and invert elevations must be known to determine the needed slope of the pipe. The charts in Figs. 7-11 and 7-12 will show if the flow has a self-cleaning velocity.

Table 7-1 Manning Roughness Coefficients, *n*

	n Values
Pipe	
Concrete pipe 24 in. and under	0.015
Concrete pipe over 24 in.	0.013
Vitrified clay pipe	0.012
Cast iron pipe, uncoated	0.013
Galvanized corrugated metal pipe (rivited)	0.024
Galvanized corrugated metal pipe with paved invert	0.021
Open channels, lined	
Concrete pavement	0.015
Asphalt pavement	0.015
Concrete bottom, sides as indicated	
Random stone in mortar	0.017–0.020
Rip-rap	0.020–0.030
Rubble masonry	0.020–0.025
Gravel bottom, sides as indicated	
Concrete	0.017–0.020
Random stone in concrete	0.020–0.023
Rip-rap	0.023–0.033
Brick	0.014–0.017

Table 7-2 Values of C in $Q = CIA$

Types of Drainage Areas or Surfaces	Runoff Coefficients, C
Roofs	0.95
Pavements, concrete or bituminous concrete	0.75–0.95
Pavement, macadam or surface treated gravel	0.65–0.80
Compacted gravel	0.70
Loose gravel	0.30
Sandy soil, cultivated light growth	0.15–0.30
Sandy soil, woods, or heavy brush	0.15–0.35
Gravel, bare or light growth	0.20–0.40
Gravel, woods or heavy brush	0.15–0.35
Clay soil, bare or light growth	0.35–0.75
Clay soil, woods or light growth	0.25–0.60
Central business districts	0.60–0.80
Dense residential	0.50–0.70
Suburban residential	0.35–0.60
Rural areas, parks, and golf courses	0.15–0.30

8. The charts for determining pipe size must be used for the roughness coefficient of the pipe being used.
9. Use the charts to determine velocity in feet per second and diameter of the pipe in inches. If the chart shows a size between 18 and 24 in. for example always use the larger size.
10. Determine flow time by dividing velocity in feet per second into the length of pipe and add this figure to time of concentration for flow time. (See Fig. 7-8 for a sample data sheet.)

SUBJECT ______ SHEET NO. ______ OF ______

BY ______ DATE ______ JOB NO. ______ CHKD. BY ______ DATE ______

FROM	INLET NO.	TO	AREA ACRES	RUNOFF COEFF. (R)	A × R ACRES	A × R Σ ACRES	TIME OF CONCENT. MIN-UTES	RAINFALL INTENS. (I) IN./HOUR	RUNOFF (Q) C F S	LENGTH FT	SLOPE FT/FT	SIZE IN.	VELOCITY F P S	FLOW TIME MIN-UTES	CAPACITY C F S	INV. ELEV.	
																UPPER END	LOWER END

FIG. 7-8 Sample data sheet.

Sample Problem
This problem (see Fig. 7-9) is an example of a method used to compute storm water runoff in cubic feet per second so that pipe sizes may be determined from the Manning formula chart or the nomograph for computing the size of circular drains.

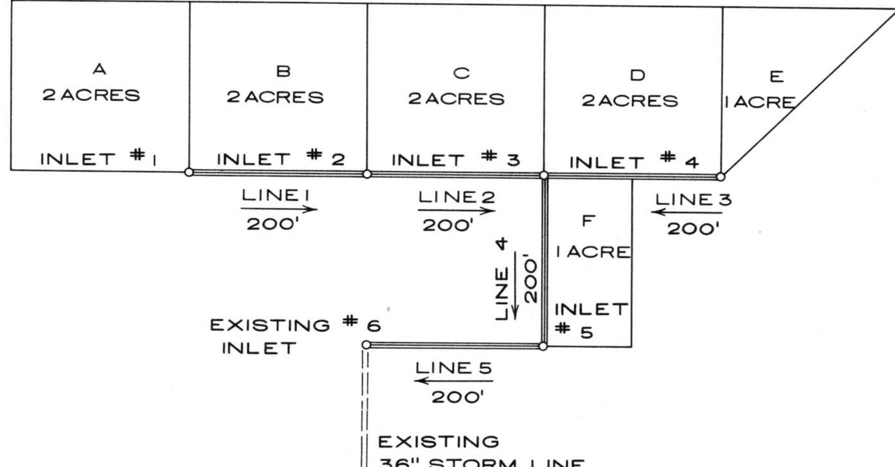

FIG. 7-9 Drainage areas and storm lines for sample problem.

The example area is located in Scranton, Pennsylvania. The design storm frequency is 10 years with a 6 minute duration. (See Fig. 7-10.) Assume a roughness coefficient value *n* of 0.015 (concrete pipe) with a desirable slope of 0.01 ft/ft or a grade of 1%. Also, assume that no drainage outside the site area is picked up by the inlets and that the site is sloping with a 2–7% grade.

Beginning with area *A* (see Fig. 7-9), which drains into inlet #1, assume 1 acre is grass and 1 acre is bituminous paving. For the coefficient of runoff for grass use 0.15 and for bituminous use 0.90 as determined from Table 7-2. Since half of the area has either coefficient the sum of the coefficients $0.15 + 0.90 \div 2 = 0.525$ or 0.53 rounded off. Rainfall intensity from Fig. 7-10 = 5.8 in. for a 6 minute duration for a 10 year storm. Using the formula $Q = CIA$, $0.53 \times 5.8 \times 2 = 6.14$ ft^3/second. Now using the nomograph in Fig. 7-11 or the Manning formula chart in Fig. 7-12 for 0.01 ft/ft with a roughness coefficient of 0.015 for concrete pipe for pipe line 1, we project a pipe size above 15 in. We therefore use the next size or an 18 in. pipe. The velocity from the chart is 4.6 ft/second. The flow time for the 200 ft pipe length ÷ 4.6 ft/second = 43 seconds. This flow time is added to the 6 minute time of concentration and gives a figure of 6 minutes and 43 seconds for the flow time from start to inlet 2 in line 1. (See Fig. 7-13.)

If it is desired to have a smaller gradient on the pipe line to keep the depth of the pipe invert a minimum of 3 ft for frost protection a minimum gradient of 0.002 ft/ft can be used to achieve a self-cleaning velocity of 2.5 ft/second.

Area *B* drains to inlet #2. Assume $\frac{3}{4}$ of the area is in grass and $\frac{1}{4}$ is in bituminous paving. Seventy-five percent of the runoff will have a coefficient for grass of 0.015 and 25% of the runoff will have a coefficient of 0.90 for bituminous paving. The combined coefficient is 0.34. Now add the sum of area times runoff coefficient 0.68 to 1.06 to get the total drain-

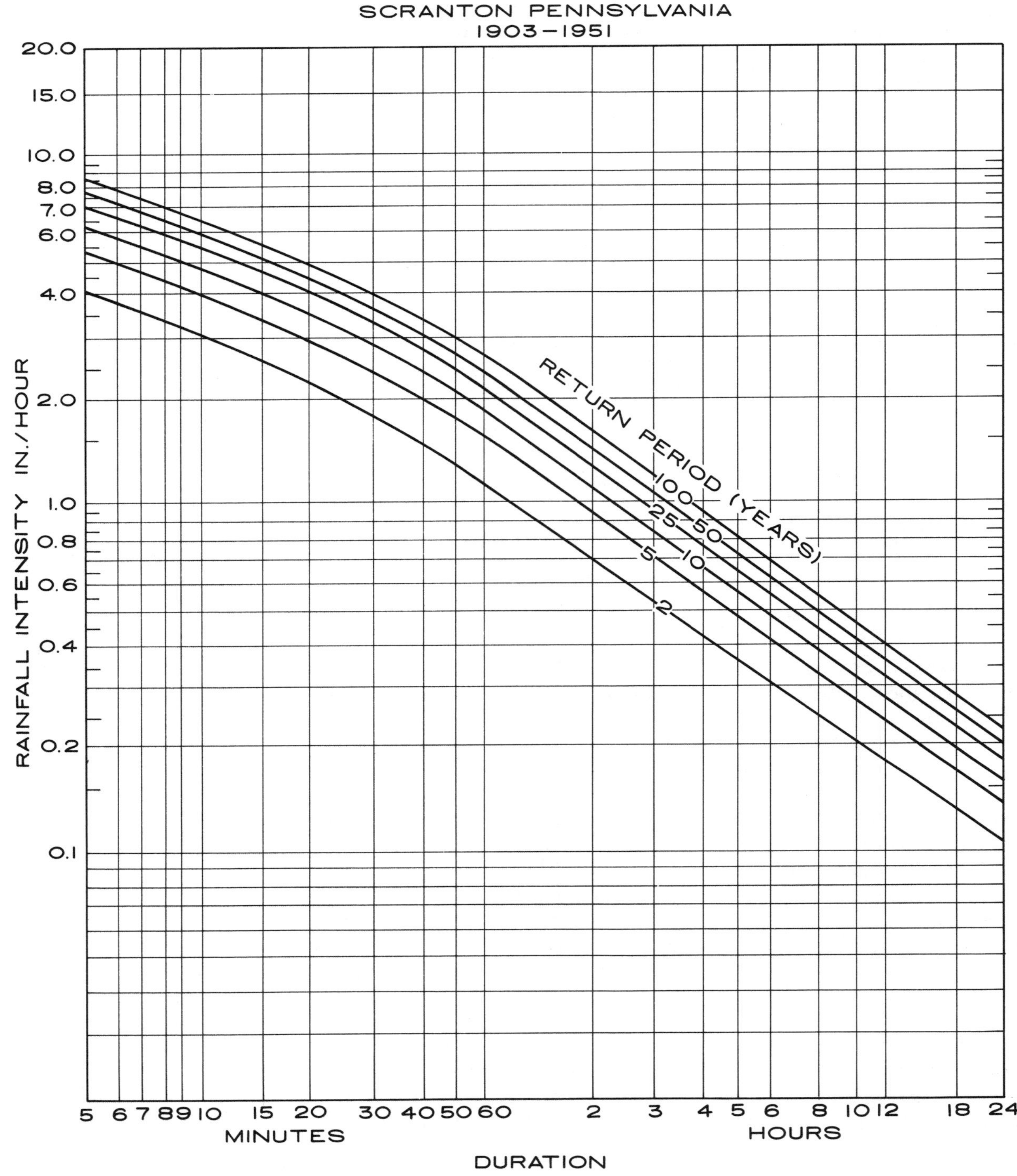

FIG. 7-10 Rainfall intensity curves for Scranton, Pennsylvania.

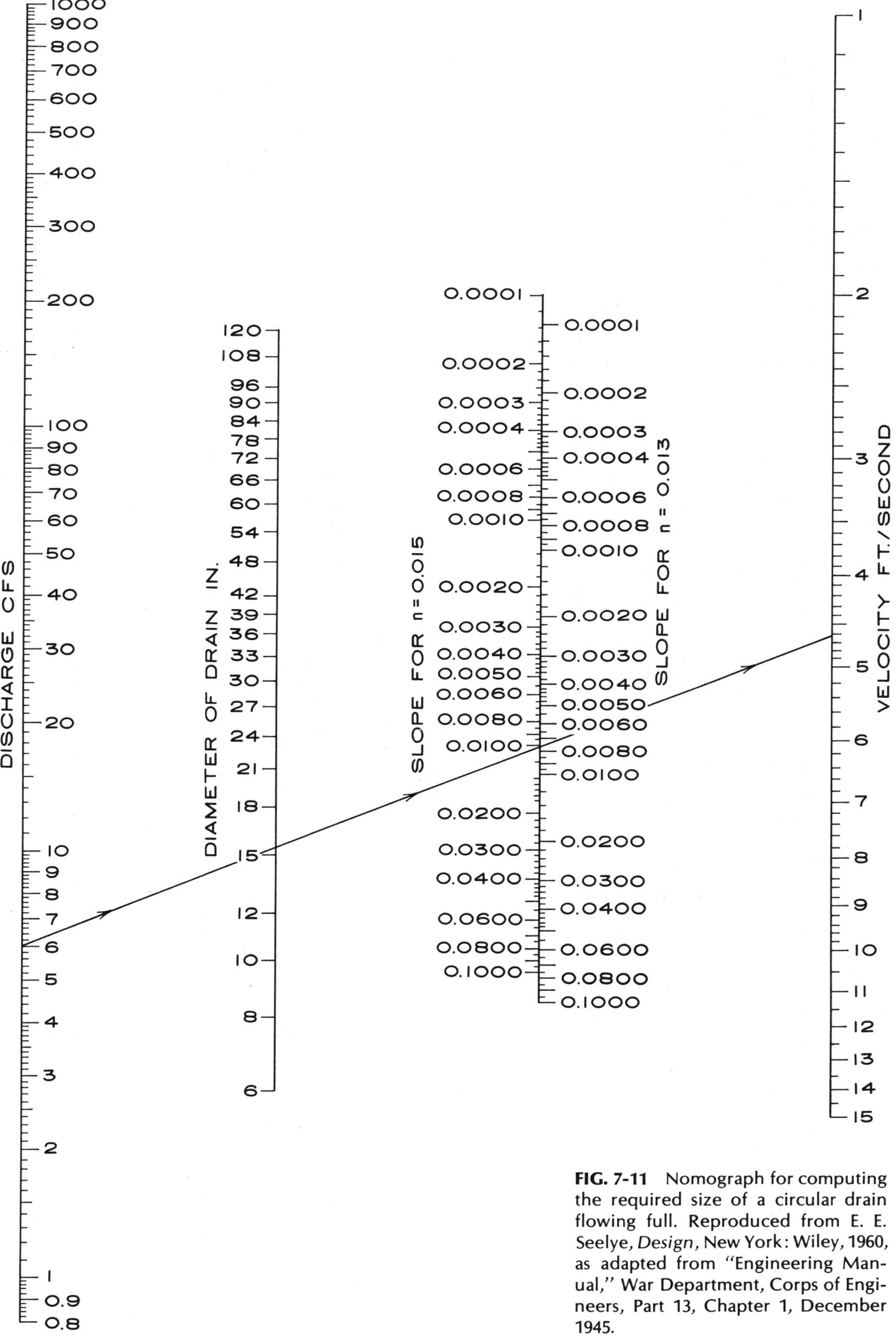

FIG. 7-11 Nomograph for computing the required size of a circular drain flowing full. Reproduced from E. E. Seelye, *Design*, New York: Wiley, 1960, as adapted from "Engineering Manual," War Department, Corps of Engineers, Part 13, Chapter 1, December 1945.

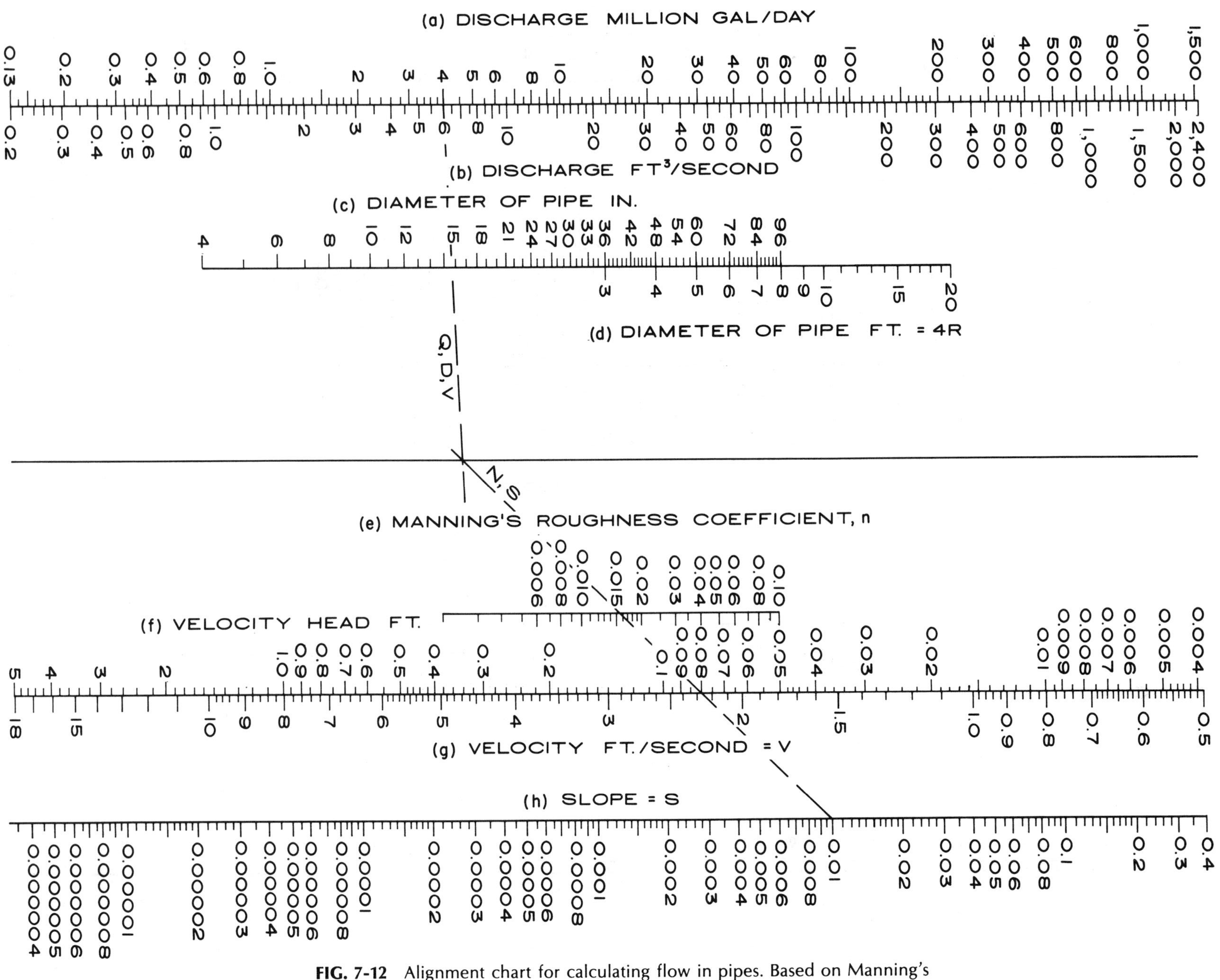

FIG. 7-12 Alignment chart for calculating flow in pipes. Based on Manning's formula from ASCE Manual No. 37, *Design and Construction of Sanitary Storm Sewers*, New York, 1960, the American Society of Civil Engineers and the Water Pollution Control Federation, Page 89.

SUBJECT ______ SHEET NO. ______ OF ______

BY ______ DATE ______ JOB NO. ______ CHKD. BY ______ DATE ______

FROM	INLET NO.	TO	AREA ACRES	RUNOFF COEFF (R)	A × R ACRES	A × R Σ ACRES	TIME OF CONCENT. MIN-UTES	RAINFALL INTENS. (I) IN./HOUR	RUNOFF (Q) C F S	LENGTH FT	SLOPE FT/FT	SIZE IN.	VELOCITY F P S	FLOW TIME MIN-UTES	CAPACITY C F S	INV. ELEV. UPPER END	INV. ELEV. LOWER END
A	1	INLET # 2	2	0.53	1.06	1.06	6'	5.8	6.14	200	0.01	18"	4.6	6'-43"	9.2		
A + B	2	INLET # 3	2	0.34	0.68	1.74	6'-43"	5.5	9.57	200	0.01	21"	5.2	7'-21"	14		
C	3	INLET # 3	2	0.15	0.30	0.30	6'	5.8	1.74	—	—	—	—	—	—		
D E	4	INLET # 3	3	0.15	0.45	0.45	6'	5.8	2.6	200	0.01	12"	3.7	6'-54"	3		
ABCDE	3	INLET # 5	9	—	—	2.49	7'-21"	5.5	13.74	200	0.01	21"	5.3	7'-59"	14		
F	5	INLET # 6	1	0.15	0.15	2.64	7'-59"	5.2	13.89	200	0.01	21"	5.3	8'-37"	14		

FIG. 7-13 Data sheet for sample problem.

age flowing into inlet #2. Total 1.06 × 5.5 ft³/second now equals 9.57 ft³/second for 5.5 in./hour based on a 6 minute and 43 second time of concentration. From the nomograph we determine a 21 in. pipe size with a velocity of 5.2 ft/second. For a 200 ft pipe length the flow time is 38 seconds, giving us 7 minutes and 21 seconds to inlet #3 in pipeline 2 from the start of rainfall. (See Fig. 7-13.) Area *C* of 2 acres in grass is picked up by inlet #3. The runoff coefficient for grass is 0.15. This area begins with a 6 minute time of concentration and has a rainfall intensity of 5.8 in./hour from Fig. 7-10. The area times runoff is 0.30. $Q = 0.30 \times 5.8 = 1.74$ ft³/second.

Areas *D* + *E* flow to inlet #4 and have 3 acres in grass. The runoff coefficient for grass is 0.15. This is also the beginning of a new pipeline and we begin again with a 6 minute time of concentration. The area times runoff is 0.45 at the 6 minute time of concentration and gives a rainfall intensity of 5.8 in./hour from Fig. 7-10. $Q = 0.45 \times 5.8 = 2.6$ ft³/second. At 0.01 ft/ft gradient we have a pipe size of 12 in. with a velocity of 3.7 ft/second as determined from the nomograph in Fig. 7-11. Flow time for line 3 is 200 ft ÷ by 3.7 ft/second = 54 seconds. (See Fig. 7-13.)

Areas *A*, *B*, *C*, *D*, and *E* flow into line 4, which picks up 9 acres with a time of concentration of 7 minutes and 21 seconds from inlets #1 to #3. From Fig. 7-10 the rainfall intensity is 5.5 in./hour. The sum of area × runoff coefficient = 2.49 × 5.5 in./hour × 13.74 ft³/second. A flow time of 38 seconds is determined from the nomograph Fig. 7-11. for line 4. This gives a total flow time through line 4 of 7 minutes and 59 seconds from the time the storm started. (See Fig. 7-13.)

Area *F* of 1 acre drains into inlet #5. Assume the area is grass. From Fig. 7-10 the time of concentration for 7 minutes and 59 seconds for a 10 year storm frequency gives a rainfall intensity of 5.2 in./hour. $Q \times 13.89$ ft³/second for a sum of 2.64 *A* × runoff coefficient of 5.2 in./hour. From the nomograph the pipe size is 21 inches with a 5.3 ft/second velocity. Flow time for inlet #5 to inlet #6 is 200 ft ÷ by 5.3 = 38 seconds. Total flow time—the time the storm started—is 8 minutes and 37 seconds through pipe line 5. (See Fig. 7-13.)

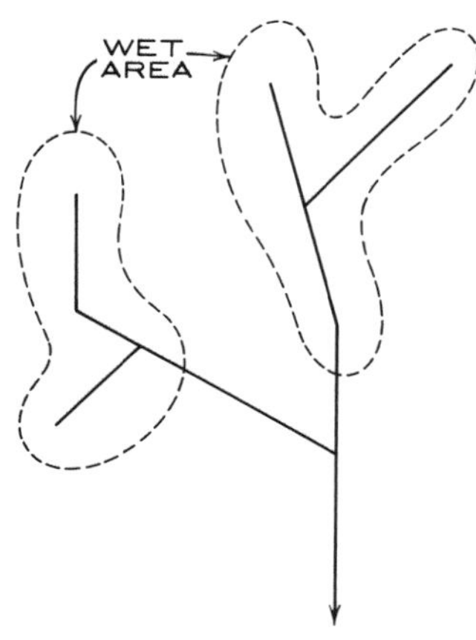

FIG. 7-14 Natural system.

Subsurface Drainage

Subsurface drainage involves the control and removal of soil moisture; it is concerned with the following:

1. Carrying water away from impervious soils, clay, and rock.
2. Preventing seepage of water through foundation walls.
3. Lowering water tables for low flatland.
4. Preventing unstable subgrade or frost heaving.
5. Removing surface runoff in combination with underground drainage.

Subsurface drainage may be accomplished by providing a horizontal passage in the subsoil that collects gravitational water and carries it to outlets. Subsurface drain lines either have open joints or use perforated pipe. Flow into subsurface drains is affected by soil permeability, depth of drain below soil surface, size and number of openings into the drain, drain spacing, and diameter.

Types of Systems

1. Natural: Used for areas that do not require complete drainage. (See Fig. 7-14.)
2. Herringbone: Used in areas of land with a concave surface with land sloping in either direction. This system should not have angles over 45°. (See Fig. 7-15.)

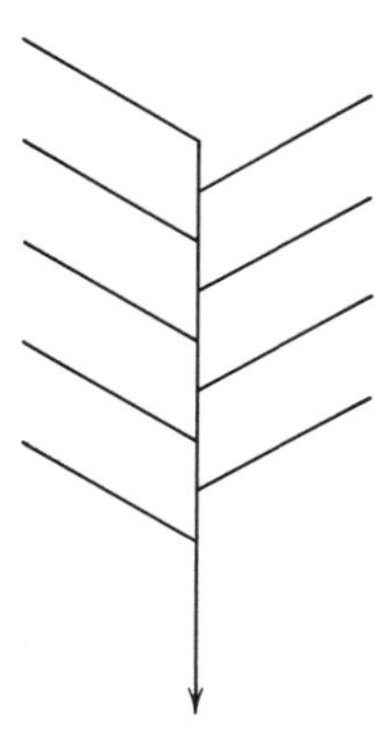

FIG. 7-15 Herringbone system.

3 Gridiron: Used where laterals enter the main from one side. Mains and laterals may intersect at angles less than 90°. (See Fig. 7-16.)
4 Interceptor: Used near the upper edge of a wet area to drain such areas. (See Fig. 7-17.)

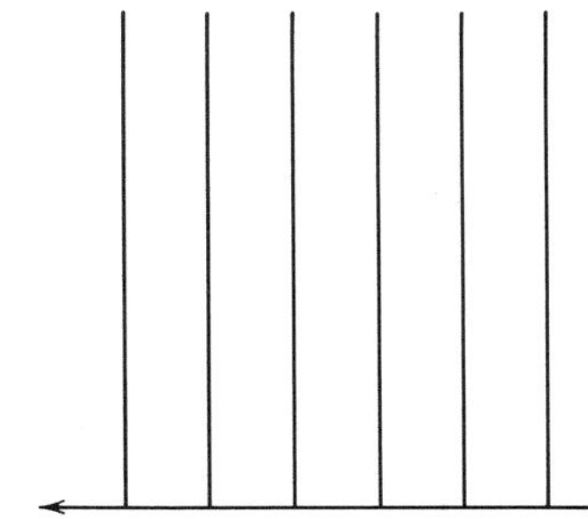

FIG. 7-16 Gridiron system.

Outlets should discharge flow without erosion and prevent flooding when they are submerged. Tile lines should be placed $2\frac{1}{2}$ to 5 ft below the soil surface. In moderately permeable soils a space approximately 24 ft wide should be used for each foot of depth below soil surface. In general, depth varies with soil permeability.

The slope of tile may vary from a maximum of 2 to 3% for a main to a desirable minimum of 0.2% for laterals. A minimum velocity of 1.5 ft per second is sometimes used. Drainage tile varies in size—4 in. is a minimum; 5 or 6 in. is used more frequently. Figure 7-18 may be used to calculate underdrainage pipe size based on the formula $Q = CIA$. Rainfall intensities as shown in Fig. 7-4 to 7-7 are based on a rainfall of 1 hour in duration.

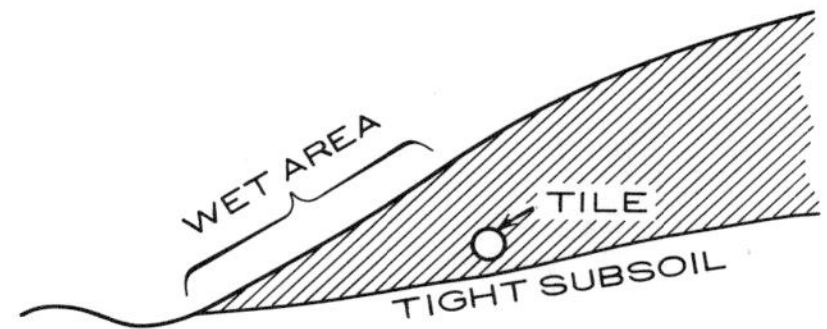

FIG. 7-17 Interceptor system.

Swales and Ditches

Water causes scouring action when left uncontrolled. Drainage swales, usually under 10% grade, must be properly designed and stabilized to prevent erosion. The shape of the swale and its side slopes are vitally important. Velocity differs with the type of grass or other material used to line a swale. Minimum gradient for grass swales is 2%; the minimum for paved channels is 0.5 to 1%. To calculate the capacity of a channel, we must know the cross-sectional size, frictional factors, and volume and velocity of the water.

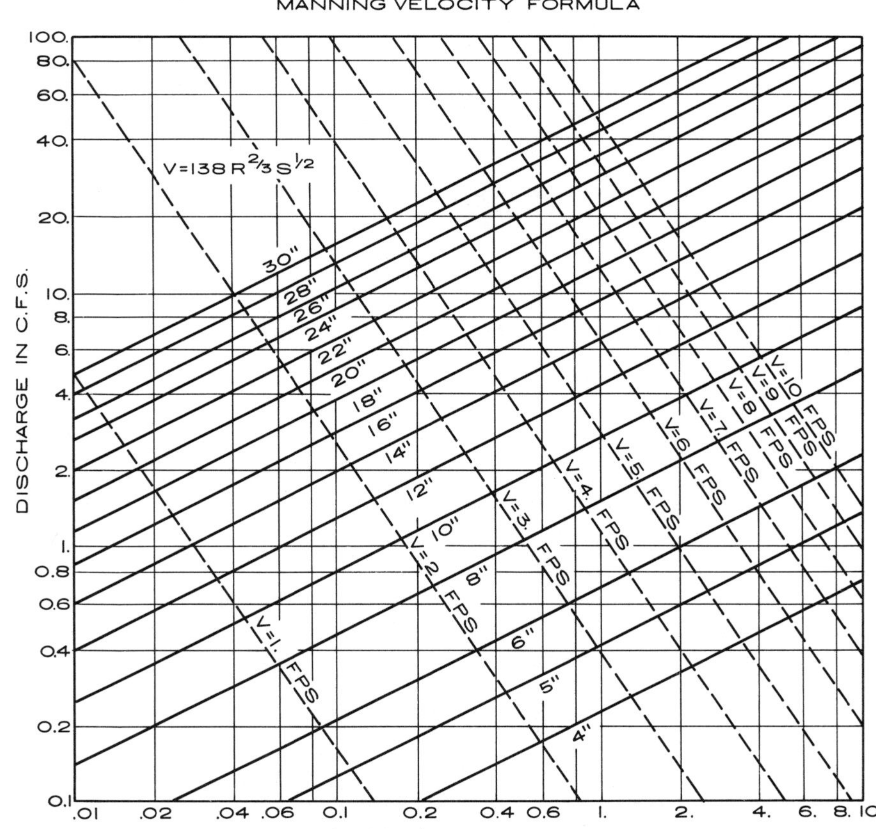

FIG. 7-18 Size of tile drain pipes. This chart can be used to calculate subsurface tile lines based on storms of one hour duration. (See Figs. 7-4 to 7-7.) Reproduced from D. L. Yarnell, "The Flow of Water in Drain Tile," U.S. Department of Agriculture Bulletin 854, 1920.

The shape and size of swales and ditches depend on the storm water to be carried. The most common ditch shape used is trapezoidal. Storm water runoff is determined as previously described using the formula $Q = CIA$ to determine Q in cubic feet per second. Charts can then be used to select the channel size.

Velocity in a swale or ditch formula:

$$V = \frac{Q}{A}$$

where V = velocity of water in ft/second
A = cross-sectional area (ft^2)
Q = discharge of water (ft^3/second)

The capacity of drainage facilities is measured in terms of discharge and determined by the equation

$$Q = \frac{A}{V}$$

where Q = discharge of water (ft^3/second)
A = net effective area (ft^2) provided by the structure; it may not be desirable to use the entire cross-sectional area of the structure to carry water
V = velocity of water (ft/second). (See Table 7-3).

Table 7-3 Mean Velocities That Do Not Erode[a]

Swale or Ditch Surface	Maximum ft/second
Pebbles or broken stone	4
Sod	5
Cobble not grouted or bituminous	7.5
Stone masonry	15
Concrete	—

[a]Velocities are reduced for depths under 6 in.

The velocity is determined by Manning's equation:

$$V = \frac{1.486}{n} R^{\frac{2}{3}} S^{\frac{1}{2}}$$

where R = hydraulic radius; it is equal to the net effective area (A) divided by the wetted perimeter (WP). The wetted perimeter is the linear feet of the drainage structure cross section that is wetted by water.
S = slope of energy line (use water surface slope in stream and streambed in dry steam)
n = roughness coefficient

A nomograph for the solution of the Manning equation is presented in Fig. 7-19. Design charts for open channel flow (Figs. 7-20 and 7-21) are available from the U.S. Department of Transportation, Federal Highway Administration.

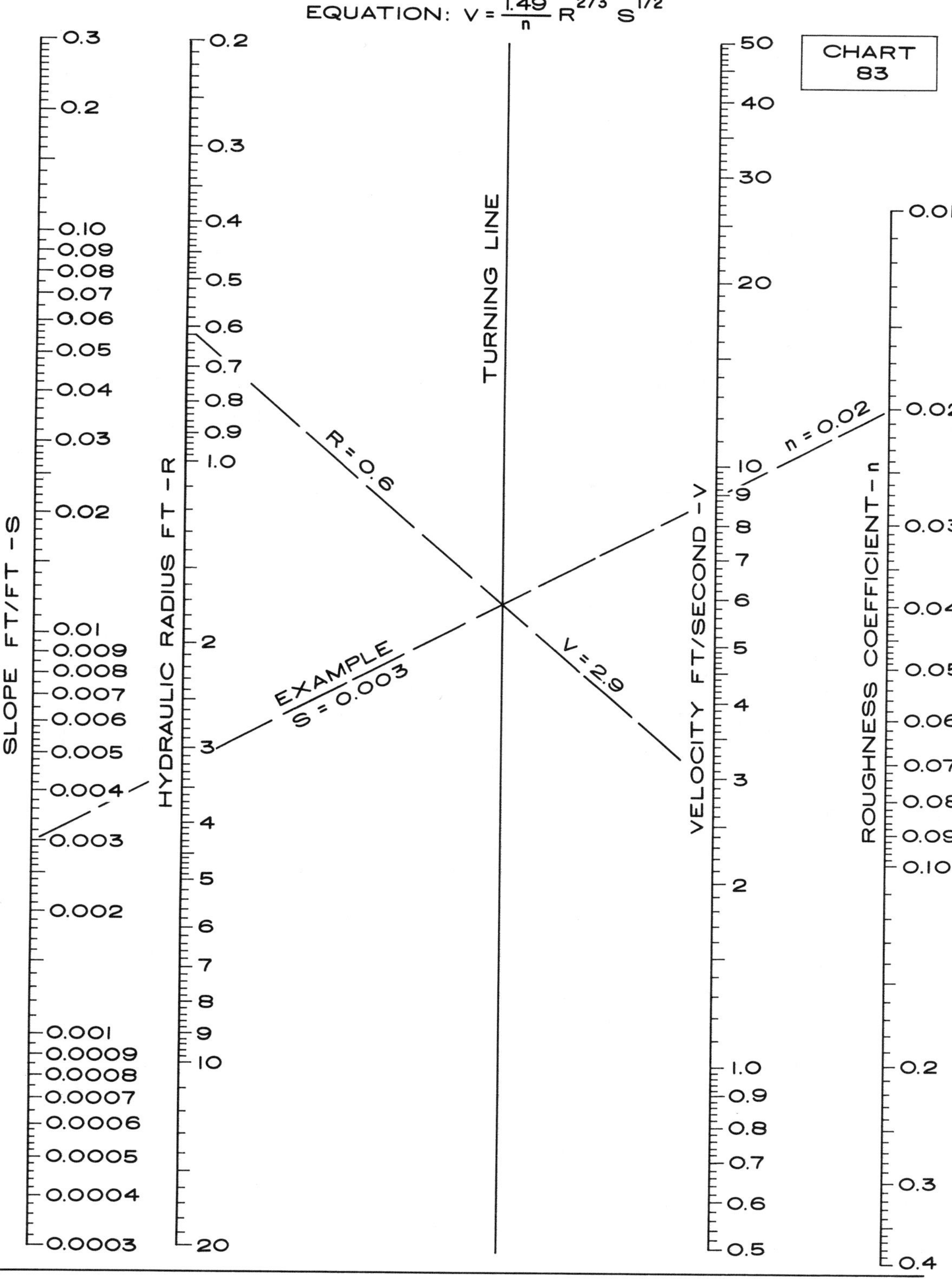

FIG. 7-19 Nomograph for solution of Manning Equation. Reproduced from "Design Charts for Open Channel flow," U.S. Department of Transportation, Federal Highway Administration.

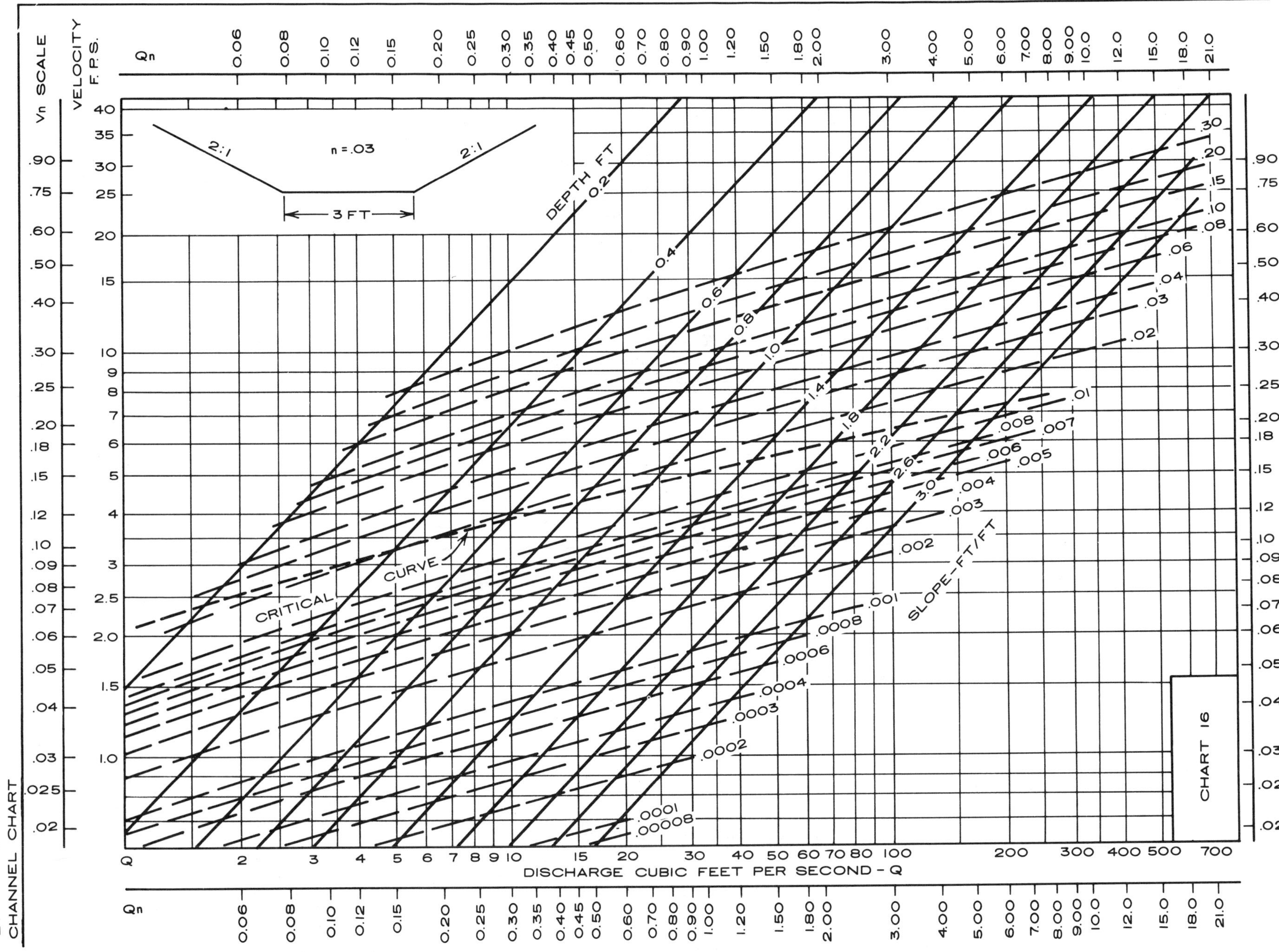

FIG. 7-20 Channel chart. Reproduced from "Design Charts for Open Channel Flow," U.S. Department of Transportation, Federal Highway Administration.

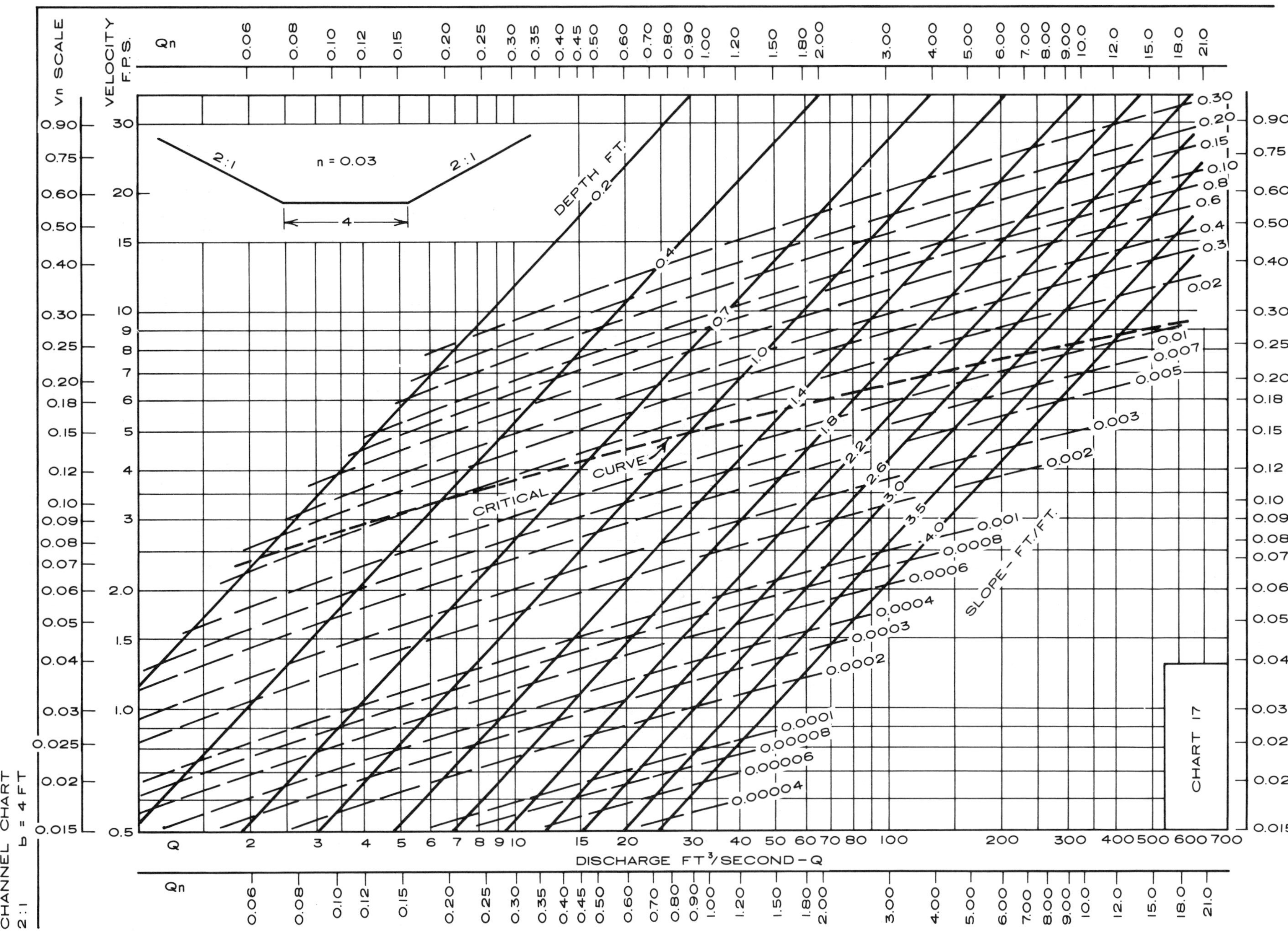

FIG. 7-21 Channel chart. Reproduced from "Design Charts for Open Channel Flow," U.S. Department of Transportation, Federal Highway Administration.

EROSION CONTROL

When vegetation is removed during construction, accelerated erosion occurs. Sediment creates an unhealthy habitat for fish and carries with it fertilizers that accelerate the aging of lakes and ponds and pesticides that have a toxic effect on aquatic organisms. Sediment also reduces water carrying capacity of water courses.

In areas with easily erodible soils, erosion control procedures are important during development of a site. Soil erosion due to storm water runoff can be severe when a site is stripped of its vegetation during construction. Vegetation stabilizes soil, increasing its resistance to erosion. For example, sandy loam soils stripped of vegetation are highly erodible. Erosion losses on construction sites can be calculated by the Soil Conservation service universal soil-loss equation:

$$A = RKLSCP$$

where A = computed soil loss per unit area
R = rainfall factor
K = soil erodibility factor
L = slope length factor
S = slope gradient factor
C, P = crop management and erosion control practice factor, not considered in soil losses on nonagricultural land

This method applies to construction sites and similar unvegetated areas. Losses estimated are for sheet erosion generally occurring on short slopes. This method, however, does not account for said loss by rill and gully erosion from heavy concentration of runoff water. Values for the equation are available for the eastern half of the United States for various counties from the Soil Conservation Service. For purposes of this example, Delaware County, Pennsylvania, is used. (See Tables 7-4 to 7-7.)

The erosion class and norm for the class are based on the following:

Class	K Range	Norm
Low	0.10–0.20	0.17
Medium	0.24–0.32	0.28
High	0.37–0.49	0.43
Very high	0.55–0.78	0.64

Reproduced from *Erosion & Sediment Control Handbook,* Delaware County, Pennsylvania, Soil Conservation Service, 1973.

Problem 1

Assume an unvegetated construction site. The disturbed area is 30 acres. The average slope is 6% and the slope length is 500 ft. The soil is aldino and the most exposed material is from the 10–24 in. layer of subsoil. Find the estimated soil loss from the unprotected construction area of the site for a 12 month period.

K for aldino silt clay loam from Table 7-4 is medium range, 0.24–0.32; use the norm 0.28. RLS from Table 7-6 is 228. $A = 0.28 \times 228 \times 30$ acres $= 1915$ yd^3

Using a silty clay loam as shown in Table 7-7 gives a factor of 1.06, which when multiplied times 1915 = 2030 yd^3.

Table 7-4 Soils Mapped in Delaware County, Pennsylvania[a,b]

Soil Series	Depth (in.)	Normal Textures	K Value	Class	Norm
Aldino	10–36	Silty clay loam, silt loam	0.39	Medium	0.28
	36–60	Silt loam, loam	0.49	High	0.43
Beltsville	9–50	Silty clay loam, silt loam	0.32	Medium	0.28
	50–72	Sandy loam	0.24	Medium	0.28
Brandywine	8–12	Loam	0.28	Medium	0.28
	12–48	Loamy sand, sand	0.17	Low	0.17
Brecknock	8–36	Silt loam, silty clay loam	0.28	Medium	0.28
	36–46	Loam	0.17	Low	0.17
Butlertown	10–49	Silt loam	0.49	High	0.43
	49–60	Silt loam	0.64	Very high	0.64
Calvert	13–36	Silty clay loam, silt loam	0.37	High	0.43
	36–43	Clay	0.17	Low	0.17
Chester	8–42	Loam	0.32	Medium	0.28
	42–62	Loam	0.43	High	0.43
Chewacla	8–58	Silty clay loam, silt loam, loam	0.37	High	0.43
	58^{+}	Loamy sand	0.10	Low	0.17
Chrome	7–15	Silty clay loam	0.17	Low	0.17
	15–30	Clay loam	0.10	Low	0.17
Congaree	8–38	Loam	0.28	Medium	0.28
	38–80	Silty clay loam, clay loam	0.24	Medium	0.28
Conowingo	9–32	Silty clay loam, clay loam	0.32	Medium	0.28
	32–56	Silt loam	0.20	Low	0.17
Glenelg	6–24	Silt loam, loam	0.32	Medium	0.28
	24–60	Loam	0.32	Medium	0.28
Glenville	9–40	Silt loam	0.49	High	0.43
	40–48	Sandy loam	0.24	Medium	0.28
Manor	10–60	Loam	0.43	High	0.43
Melvin	7–60	Silt loam, silty clay loam	0.37	High	0.43

[a]Reproduced from *Erosion & Sediment Control Handbook*, Delaware County, Pa: Soil Conservation Service, 1973.
[b]Erodibility values (K) for subsoil by textural layer, Pennsylvania.

Table 7-5 Erosion Index Values for Annual Rainfall and Expected Magnitudes of Single-Storm EI Values at Key Locations in Pennsylvania[a,b]

Location	Annual Average	Probability 1 year in		Single Storm Normally Exceeded Once in		
		5	20	5 Years	10 Years	20 Years
Erie	100	181	331	—	—	—
Franklin	125	135	184	35	45	54
Harrisburg	150	146	199	35	43	51
PHILADELPHIA	*175*	*210*	*282*	*55*	*69*	*81*
Pittsburgh	125	148	194	45	57	67
Reading	150	204	285	55	68	81
Scranton	150	140	188	44	53	63

[a]Reproduced from *Erosion Sediment Control Handbook.* Delaware County, Pa.: Soil Conservation Service, 1973.
[b]It is important to note the average annual erosion-index value in the Philadelphia area. It is the highest in the state. This factor increases the amount of potential sediment loading. For instance, a Glenelg soil found in the Philadelphia area will have a greater potential for erosion than the same soil found in the Reading area.

Table 7-6 Rainfall-Slope Effect Table (cubic yards of silt loam per acre per year per unit of K; $R = 175$)[a]

Slope Length (ft)	RLS Values and Percent Slope														
	4	6	8	10	12	14	16	18	20	25	30	35	40	45	50
50	46	76	107	152	198	244	304	365	457	655	913	1203	1538	1918	2,345
100	61	107	152	213	274	350	426	518	639	929	1294	1705	2192	2725	3,304
150	76	122	183	244	335	426	533	639	766	1142	1583	2101	2680	3334	4,050
200	91	137	213	289	396	502	624	731	898	1325	1827	2421	3091	3837	4,674
250	107	152	244	335	442	563	685	822	1005	1477	2040	2710	3456	4293	5,237
300	107	183	259	365	472	609	761	898	1096	1629	2238	2969	3791	4704	5,725
350	122	183	274	396	518	655	822	974	1188	1751	2421	3197	4095	5085	6,181
400	122	198	304	411	548	700	868	1035	1264	1873	2588	3426	4370	5435	6,623
450	137	213	320	442	578	746	929	1096	1355	1994	2740	3624	4644	5770	7,019
500	137	228	335	472	609	792	974	1157	1416	2086	2893	3821	4887	6075	7,399
550	152	244	350	487	639	822	1020	1218	1492	2192	3030	4019	5131	6379	7,749
600	152	244	365	502	670	868	1066	1264	1553	2299	3167	4187	5359	6653	8,100
650	167	259	381	533	700	898	1111	1325	1614	2390	3304	4370	5572	6927	8,435
700	167	274	396	548	731	929	1157	1370	1690	2482	3425	4522	5785	7186	8,754
750	167	274	411	563	746	959	1203	1416	1736	2558	3547	4689	5983	7445	9,059
800	183	289	426	579	776	990	1233	1462	1797	2649	3669	4842	6181	7689	9,348
900	183	304	457	624	822	1050	1309	1553	1903	2817	3882	5131	6562	8145	9,927
1000	198	320	472	655	868	1111	1385	1644	2010	2969	4095	5405	6912	8587	10,460

[a]Reproduced from *Erosion & Sediment Control Handbook*. Delaware County, Pa: Soil Conservation Service, 1973.

Table 7-7 Factors for the Conversion of Cubic Yards of Silt Loam Soil to Cubic Yards of Other Textures[a]

Textures	Factor[b]
Clay	1.22
Clay loam	1.13
Fine sandy loam	0.85
Loam	0.94
Loamy sand	0.77
Sand	0.77
Sandy clay	0.94
Sandy clay loam	0.94
Sandy loam	0.80
Sandy silt loam	0.94
Silt loam	1.00
Silty clay	1.06
Silty clay loam	1.06

[a]Reproduced from *Erosion & Sediment Control Handbook*. Delaware County, Pa: Soil Conservation Service, 1973.
[b]Multiply by this factor to convert silt loam to other textures.

Problem 2

Estimate the soil loss for a 6 month period from April through September. From Fig. 7-22 curve 30 for Delaware County, Pennsylvania

% EI October 1	= 85	
% EI April 1	= 5	
Difference	= 80	(0.80% occurs April through September)

From problem 1 multiply 1915 yd^3 $\times$ 0.80 = 1532 yd^3 of loam loss from April through September.

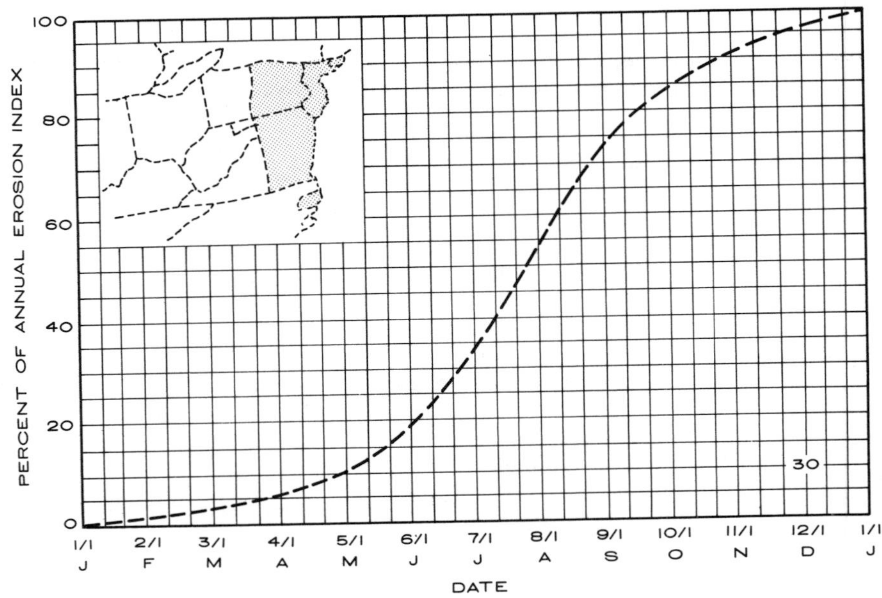

FIG. 7-22 Erosion index distribution curve for eastern Pennsylvania. Reproduced from *Erosion & Sediment Control Handbook*. Delaware County, Pa; Soil Conservation Service.

Problem 3

Compute the estimated soil loss for 1 year in 5 when rainfall intensity will exceed the average annual value of 175 for Philadelphia in Delaware County.

From Table 7-5 R = 210. Using the correction factor R = 210/175 = 1.2. 1915 yd^3 × 1.2 = 2298 yd^3 loss 1 year in 20.

Problem 4

Compute the soil loss for a single storm with a magnitude that may be exceeded once in 10 years.

From Table 7-5 R = 69. Using the correction factor R = 69/175 = 0.39. 1915 yd^3 × 0.39 = 747 yd^3 from a single storm.

Erosion Control Plans

Many states require erosion and sedimentation control plans during site construction. Factors to consider in developing these plans are the type of soil on the site, topographic features of the site, type of development, amount of runoff, staging of construction, temporary and permanent control facilities, and maintenance of control facilities during construction.

During construction, minimizing the area and time of exposure of disturbed soil is important. If earthmoving activities are not to be completed for more than about 20 days, interim stabilization measures should be carried out, such as temporary seeding and mulching or mulching during cold weather. (See Figs. 7-23 and 7-24.)

Storm Drainage System and Sediment Basins. The storm drainage system can be effective in controlling sediment by using straw bale barriers that are cleaned after each storm or a sediment basin can be constructed to collect runoff. The basins either can be a temporary control during construction or cleaned out and turned into a feature upon completion of construction. Ponds have been created for several schools as nature study areas, supplements for fire protection, and recreation sources—such as winter ice skating in cool climates. For example, in Pennsylvania, the use of sediment basins requires a capacity of 7000 ft^3 of storage for each acre of project area tributary toward it.

To estimate the number of acres of drainage for each acre foot of storage for a permanent pond the U.S. Soil Conservation Service has developed the map in Fig. 7-25.

In parts of the East Coast 2 acres of land draining toward a pond are needed for each acre foot of storage. In eastern Kansas, however, 20 acres are needed for each acre foot of water. One acre foot equals 325,851 gal of water.

To have a permanent water supply, the water depth must be adequate to offset probable seepage and water loss from evaporation. Deeper ponds are needed where seepage exceeds 3 in./month or where a permanent water supply is essential throughout the year. (See Fig. 7-26.)

The spillway of a pond should be designed for a 50 year storm where failure would affect buildings or roads. A 10 year storm may be adequate in other areas for a drainage area below 25 acres. Permissible velocities on grass spillways are less than 5.5 ft/second and should not exceed 6 ft/second. The alignment of the exit channel should be straight with flow confined so that water released will not damage the downstream toe of the dam.

A drop inlet trickle tube with holes drilled in the riser pipe is used in sediment ponds during construction. (See Fig. 7-27.) The pipe barrel under the embankment has antiseep collars as shown in Fig. 7-28. If a

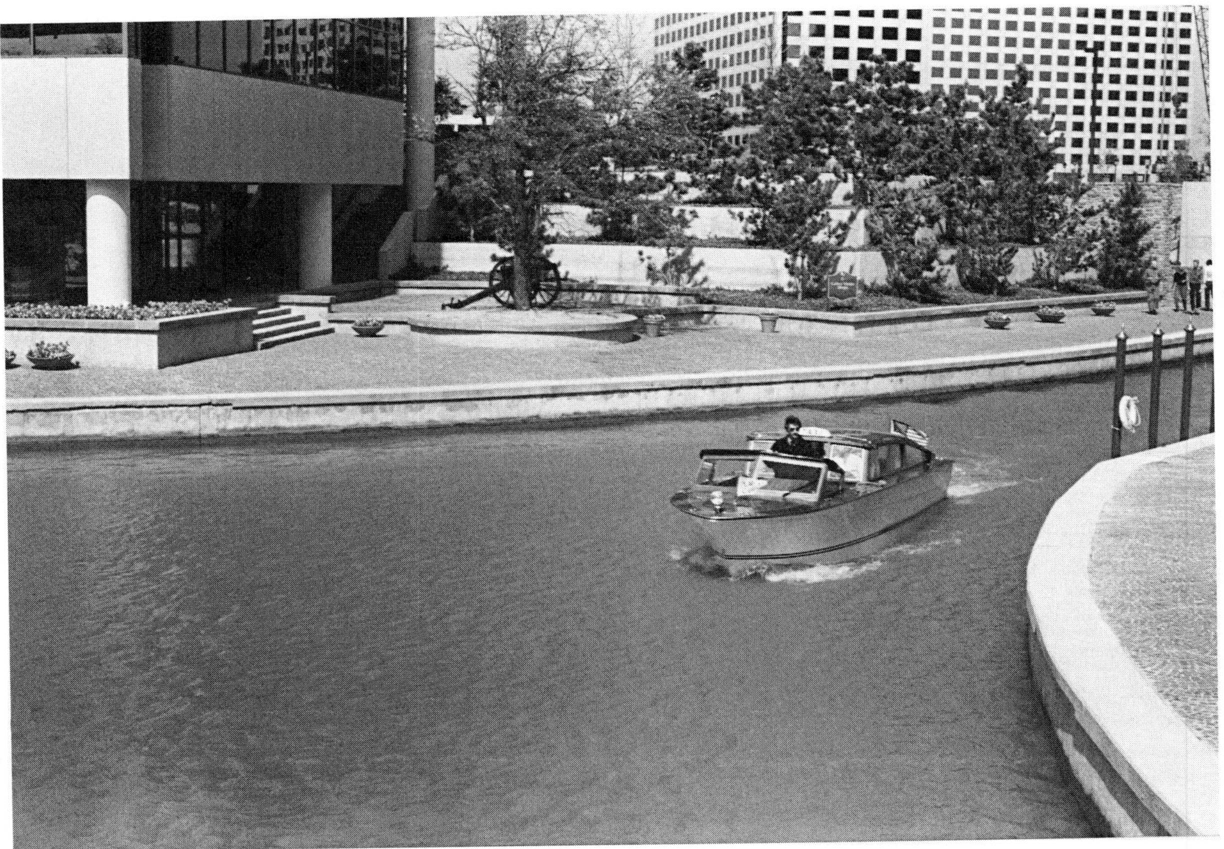

FIG. 7-23 To control erosion and form the canal system in the Urban Center at Las Colinas in Irving, Texas, a hard edge formed by concrete walls is used.

FIG. 7-24 The spillway for this lake at Cityview in Fort Worth, Texas, is paved in irregular fitted stone. The spillway and concrete wall that forms the lake limit erosion along the water's edge.

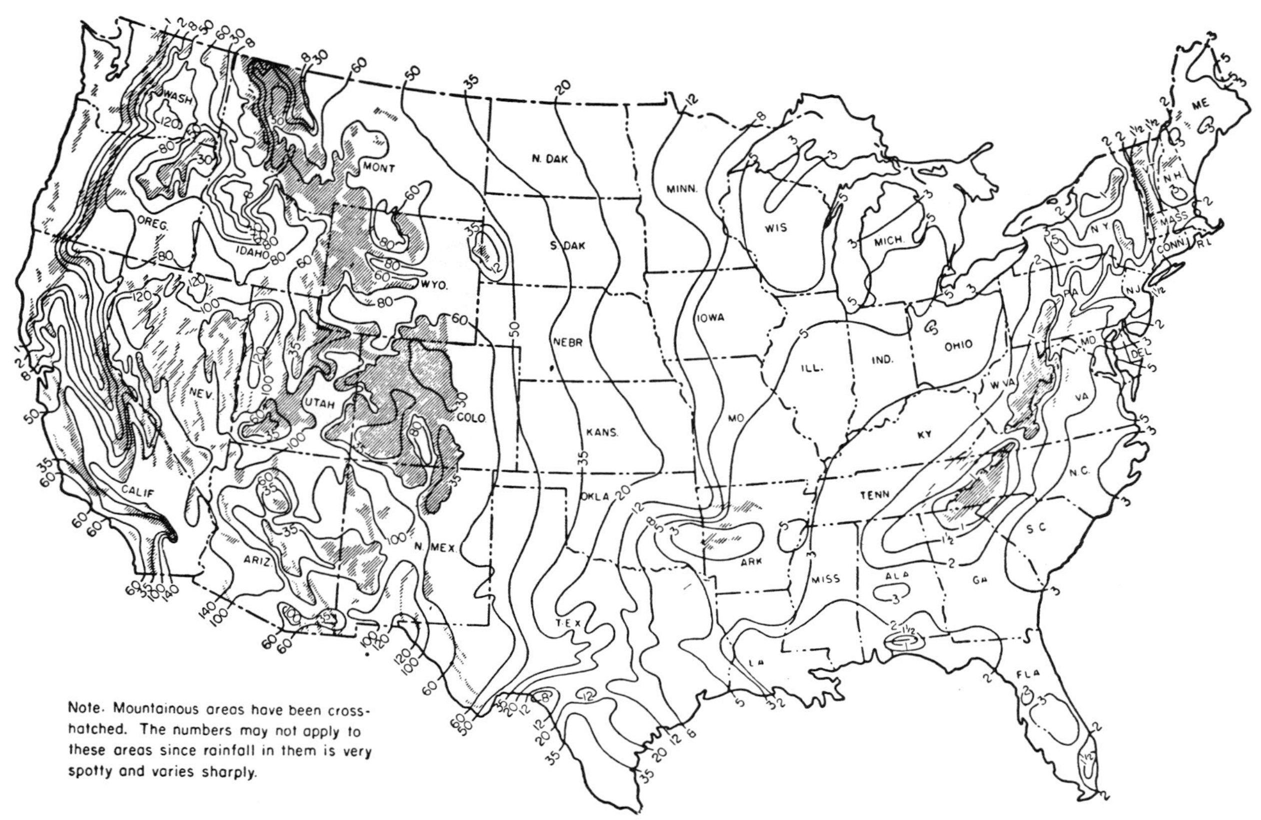

FIG. 7-25 A guide for estimating the number of acres of drainage for each acre-foot of storage for a permanent pond in the U.S. Reproduced from "Ponds for Water Supply & Recreation," *Agriculture Handbook No. 387*. Washington, D.C.: Soil Conservation Service, U.S. Department of Agriculture, 1971.

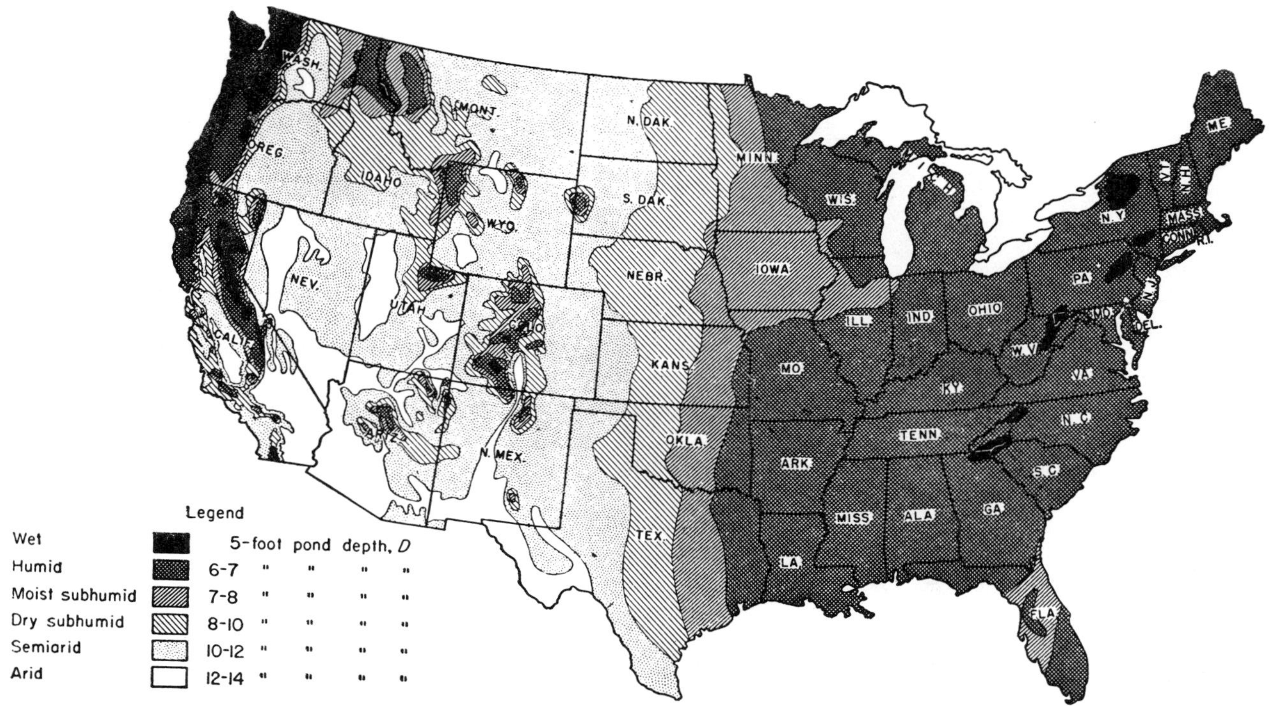

FIG. 7-26 United States. Reproduced from "Ponds for Water Supply & Recreation," *Agriculture Handbook No. 387*. Washington, D.C.: Soil Conservation Service, U.S. Department of Agriculture, 1971.

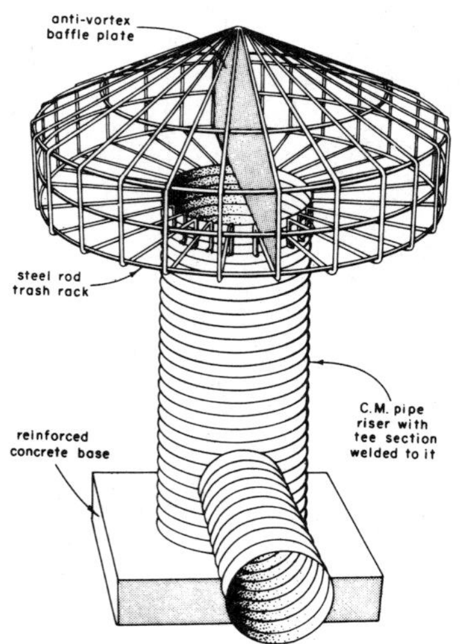

CORRUGATED METAL PIPE RISER
WITH CONICAL TRASH RACK AND BAFFLE

FIG. 7-27 Corrugated overflow pipe riser with trash rack. Reproduced from "Ponds for Water Supply & Recreation," *Agriculture Handbook No. 387*. Washington, D.C.: Soil Conservation Service, U.S. Department of Agriculture, 1971.

FIG. 7-28 Section through an earth embankment showing a drop inlet trickle tube with riser pipe and trash rack. Also shown is the pipe barrel under the dam with antiseep collars. An extension pipe can be connected to the riser pipe with a gate valve and handwheel for draining the pond.

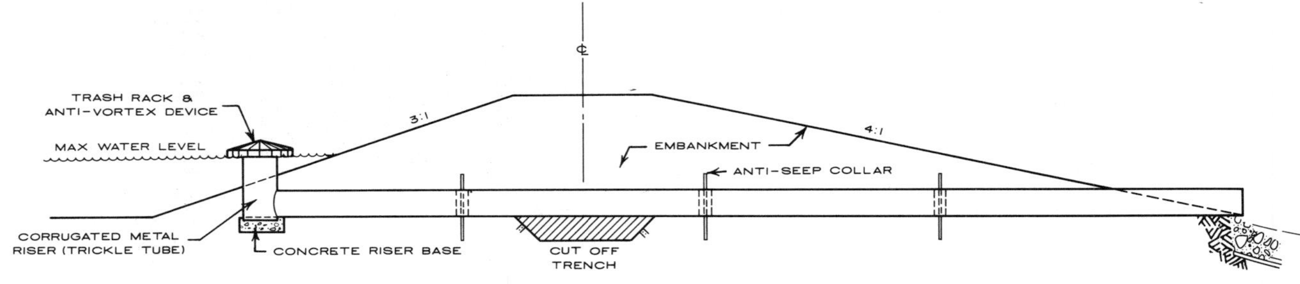

Table 7-8 Discharge Values Q (ft³/second) for Various Sizes of Drop-Inlet Trickle Tubes of Corrugated Metal Pipe[a,b]

Total head (ft)	Ratio of Barrel Diameter to Riser Diameter (in.) 6 : 8 Q	8 : 10 Q	10 : 12 Q	12 : 15 Q	15 : 21 Q	18 : 24 Q
6	0.85	1.73	3.1	5.1	8.8	14.1
8	0.90	1.85	3.3	5.4	9.4	15.0
10	0.94	1.96	3.5	5.7	9.9	15.9
12	0.98	2.07	3.7	6.0	10.4	16.7
14	1.02	2.15	3.8	6.2	10.8	17.5
16	1.05	2.21	3.9	6.4	11.1	18.1
18	1.07	2.26	4.0	6.6	11.4	18.6
20	1.09	2.30	4.1	6.7	11.7	18.9
22	1.11	2.34	4.2	6.8	11.9	19.3
24	1.12	2.37	4.2	6.9	12.1	19.6
26	1.13	2.40	4.3	7.0	12.3	19.9

[a]Reproduced from "Ponds for Water Supply & Recreation," *Agriculture Handbook* No. 387.: Soil Conservation Service; U.S. Department of Agriculture, 1971.
[b]Length of pipe barrel used in calculations is based on a dam with a 12-ft top width and 2.5 : 1 side slopes. Discharge values are based on a minimum head on the riser crest of 12 in. Pipe flow based on Manning's $n = 0.025$. Total head is the vertical distance between a point 1 ft above the riser crest and the center line of the pipe barrel at its outlet end.

permanent pond is desired, a solid pipe can be placed inside the riser pipe after sediment control is completed. (See Table 7-8). A valve can also be designed into the system to allow for draining the pond for cleaning or repairs.

Diversion Terraces and Interceptor Channels. Diversion terraces may be constructed upgrade of a project site to convey runoff around the disturbed area. Interceptor channels may also be used within a project area to reduce the velocity of flow and thereby limit erosion.

Steep Slopes. Whenever possible steep slopes should be avoided. A desirable maximum is 3 : 1 slopes, which may be planted with grass and can be mowed with a tractor.

Swales. Depending on the type of soil, drainage swales may have to be lined with jute netting to prevent washouts or planted with sod pegged in place. In some areas paved channels may even be necessary.

Energy Dissipators. Where water runoff from an outlet pipe is discharged, energy dissipators may be required to control the velocity of runoff. (See Fig. 7-29.)

Endwalls with outlets into streams may need a paved bottom and rubble riprap around them for protection from undercutting during periods of high water. (See Figs. 7-30 and 7-31.)

Sequence of Construction. Phasing construction helps limit erosion. Stockpiling topsoil in the construction area and using temporary seeding limits erosion. Another way is to construct the storm water system as early as possible. Also base courses can be placed for roads and parking so that if needed construction workers can park in these areas until surfacing is started. This limits disturbance of other areas, thereby limiting erosion.

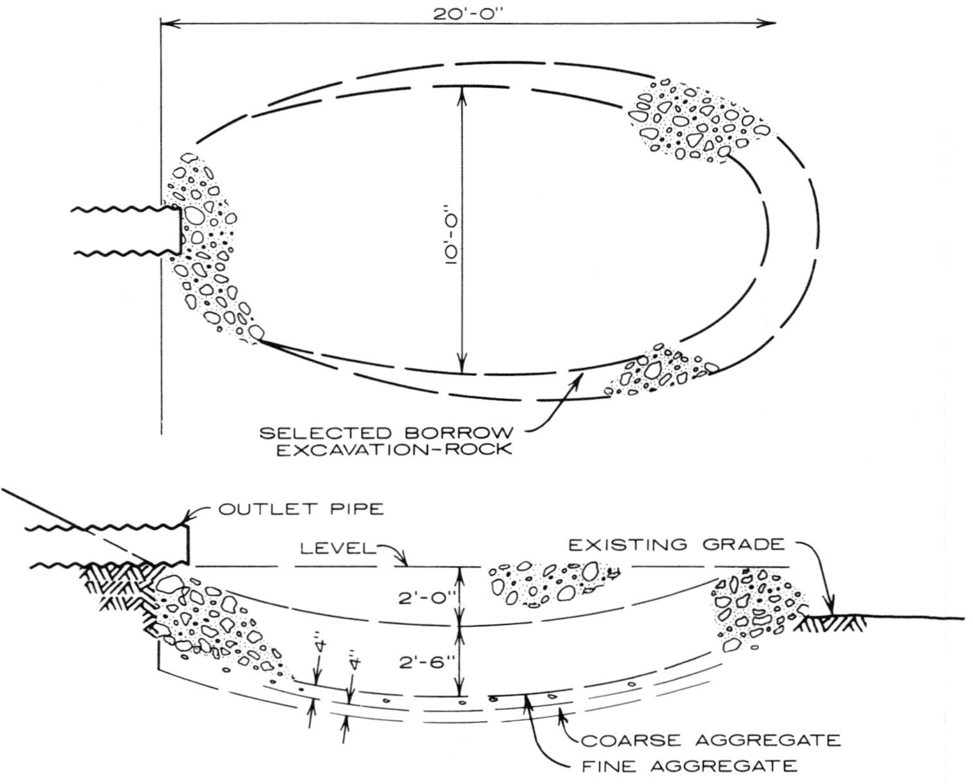

FIG. 7-29 Energy dissipator.

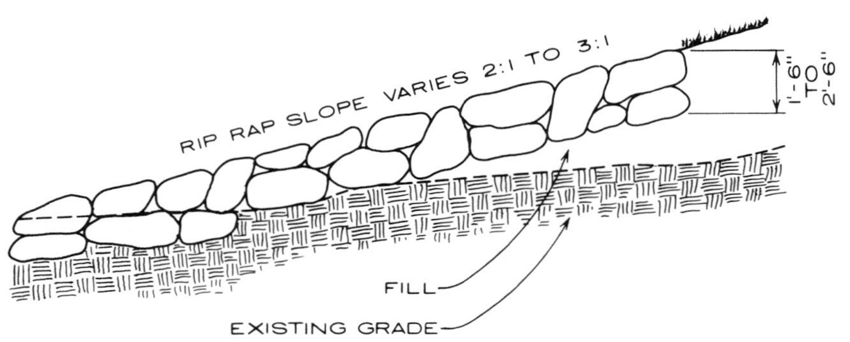

FIG. 7-30 Rip-rap detail.

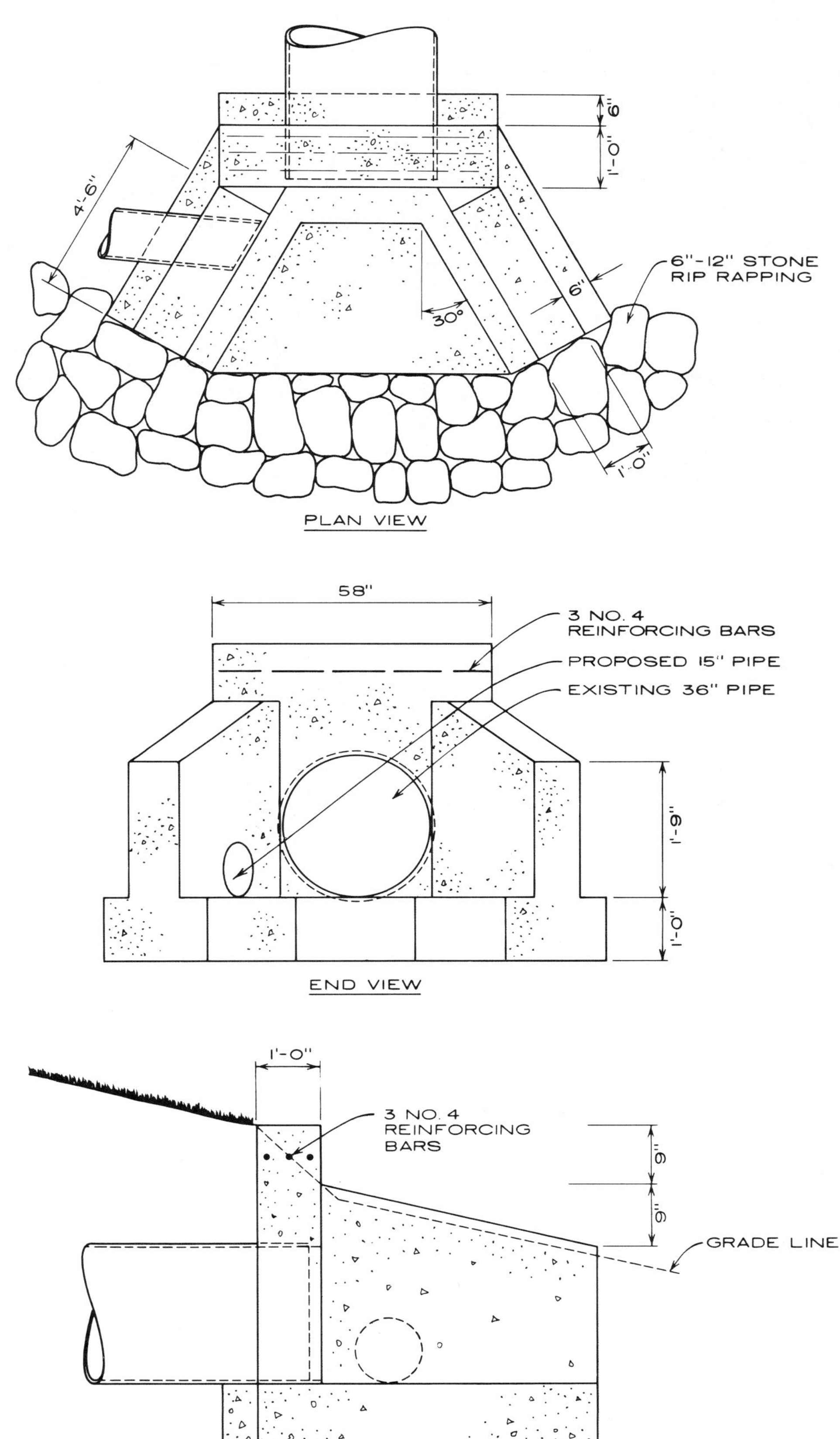

FIG. 7-31 Concrete end wall detail.

FIG. 8-1 Alignment of this park road at Lackawanna State Park, Pennsylvania, is in complete contrast to the design requirements of heavily traveled highways (Photograph courtesy Bellante, Clauss, Miller & Partners).

Chapter Eight
Alignment of Horizontal and Vertical Curves

ALIGNMENT

Although a straight line is the shortest distance between two points, it can be monotonous if aesthetic features are not considered. Road or walk alignment has two planes—horizontal and vertical. Curvature of this alignment gives the site planner an opportunity to fit a road to natural topography, while taking advantage of natural site features and keeping the road economically feasible. (See Fig. 8-1.) Good road design should attain a balance between curvature and grade to insure smooth flow of traffic and to avoid misleading a driver by sudden variation in alignment or sight distance.

The center line of a road is used for reference to relate horizontal and vertical alignment and is measured in 50 ft intervals called stations. Center lines are comprised of tangents and straight lines joined by curves.

The following topics under alignment present technical data for solving the problems presented by horizontal and vertical curves and superelevation. A step-by-step outline procedure for laying out horizontal and vertical alignments in relation to each other is also presented. The calculations shown involve the conventional methods generally used by site planners, especially in smaller offices; however, computers can be programmed to make these calculations and are often used by engineers to design major highways.

Horizontal Alignment and Computation

The following are three types of horizontal curves.

1 Arcs of a circle
   a Simple curve: circular arc connecting tangents at each end. (See Fig. 8-2.)
   b Compound curve: two circular arcs of differing radii tangent to each other at the same side of a common tangent. (See Fig. 8-3.)

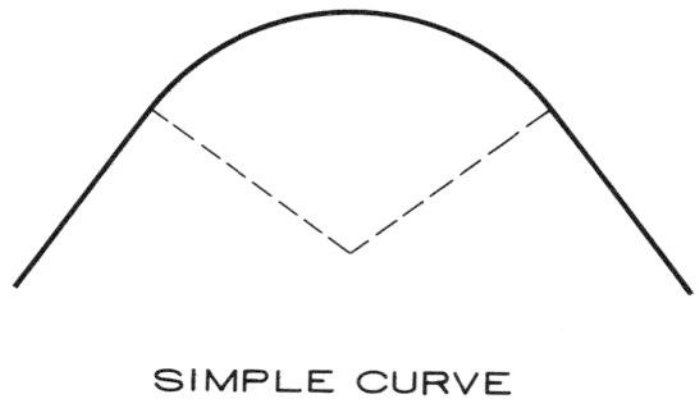

SIMPLE CURVE

FIG. 8-2 Simple curve.

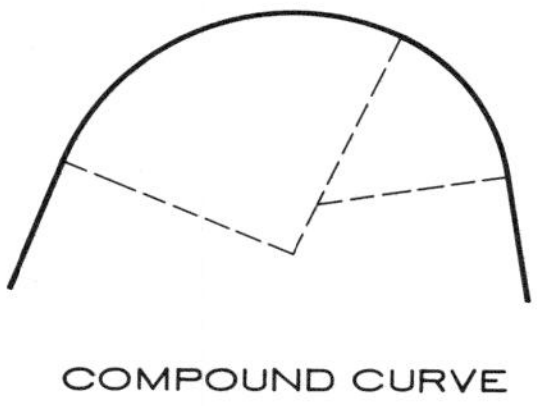

COMPOUND CURVE

FIG. 8-3 Compound curve.

   c Reverse curve: curves on opposite sides of a common tangent. (See Fig. 8-4.)
   d Brokenback curve: short length of tangent connecting circular arcs with centers on the same side. (See Fig. 8-5.)

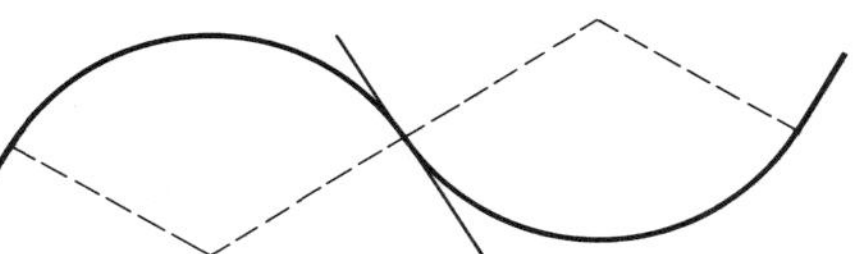

FIG. 8-4 Reverse curve.

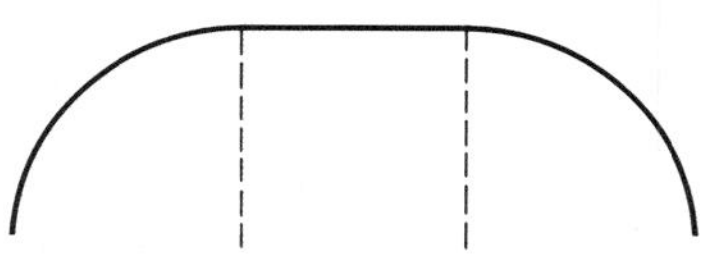

FIG. 8-5 Brokenback curve.

2 Arcs of spiral or easement curve: a curve of varying radius based on the cubic parabola, used at ends of circular curves and between segments of compound curves.
3 Parabolic arcs: arcs generally used for vertical curves.

In drafting a road, sketch the center line of the road freehand, recognizing road design criteria. When the center line is established, redraft the road using tangents and curves calculated from the following formulas. (See Figs. 8-6 and 8-7.)

Measure Δ and T. Then calculate R.

$$R = \frac{T}{\tan \frac{1}{2}\Delta} \quad \text{or} \quad R = 5730 \div D$$

$$D = \frac{5730}{R} \qquad L = \frac{100\Delta}{D}$$

$$C = 2R \sin \frac{\Delta}{2}$$

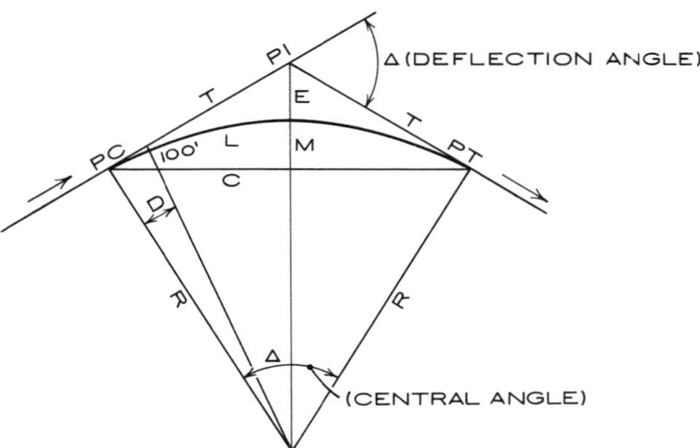

FIG. 8-6 Figure 8-6 presents functions of a simple curve.

PC = Point of curvature or beginning of curve.
PT = Point of trangency or end of curve.
PI = Point of intersection or intersection of two tangents.
Δ = Central or deflection angle.
T = Distance from PI to PC or PT.
R = Radius.
D = Degree of curve or angle at the center subtended by an arc of 100 ft.
L = Length of curve or arc length.
M = Middle ordinate or distance from center of curve to center of long chord.
C = Long chord or distance between PC and PT.
E = External distance or distance from PI to center of curve.

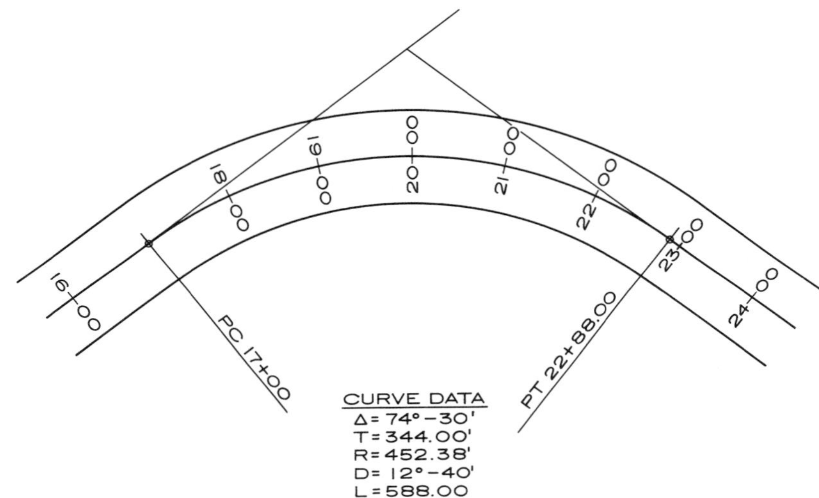

FIG. 8-7 Horizontal curve problem. Problem: Compute the following horizontal curve.

Measure Δ

$$\Delta = 74^\circ\ 30'$$

$$R = \frac{T}{\tan \frac{1}{2}\Delta^\circ} \qquad L = \frac{100\ \Delta}{D}$$

$$R = \frac{344.00'}{37^\circ\ 15'} = \frac{344.00'}{.76042} \qquad L = \frac{100 \times 74.5}{12.67}$$

$$R = 452.38' \qquad L = 588.00'$$

Measure *T*

$$T = 344.00'$$

$$D = \frac{5730}{R} \qquad C = 2R \sin \frac{\Delta}{2}$$

$$D = \frac{5730}{452.38} \qquad C = 2 \times 452.38 \times .60529$$

$$D = 12^\circ\ 40' \qquad C = 547.74'$$

Roadway Widening on Curves

Widening is sometimes needed on highways with narrow pavements and wide curves. Widening is costly and little is accomplished unless a minimum of 2 ft is used. Where smaller widths are shown they should be disregarded. No widening is suggested for roads 24 ft wide where curves are 10° or flatter. (See Table 8-1.)

Widening should be developed gradually on approaches to a curve to insure a smooth alignment on the edge of pavement.

Sight Distance on Horizontal Curves

A factor in horizontal alignment is the sight distance across the inside of curves. Where there are obstructions to sight distance adjustment of the alignment may be required. (See Fig. 8-8.)

Table 8-1 Calculated and Design Values for Pavement Widening on Open Highway Curves; Two-Lane Pavements, One-Way or Two-Way[a,b]

Degree of Curve	Widening (ft) for Two-Lane Pavements on Curves for Width of Pavement on Tangent of: 24 feet						22 feet					20 feet			
	Design Speed (mph)						Design Speed (mph)					Design Speed (mph)			
	30	40	50	60	70	80	30	40	50	60	70	30	40	50	60
1	0.0	0.0	0.0	0.0	0.0	0.0	0.5	0.5	0.5	1.0	1.0	1.5	1.5	1.5	2.0
2	0.0	0.0	0.0	0.5	0.5	0.5	1.0	1.0	1.0	1.5	1.5	2.0	2.0	2.0	2.5
3	0.0	0.0	0.5	0.5	1.0	1.0	1.0	1.0	1.5	1.5	2.0	2.0	2.0	2.5	2.5
4	0.0	0.5	0.5	1.0	1.0		1.0	1.5	1.5	2.0	2.0	2.0	2.5	2.5	3.0
5	0.5	0.5	1.0	1.0			1.5	1.5	2.0	2.0		2.5	2.5	3.0	3.0
6	0.5	1.0	1.0	1.5			1.5	2.0	2.0	2.5		2.5	3.0	3.0	3.5
7	0.5	1.0	1.5				1.5	2.0	2.5			2.5	3.0	3.5	
8	1.0	1.0	1.5				2.0	2.0	2.5			3.0	3.0	3.5	
9	1.0	1.5	2.0				2.0	2.5	3.0			3.0	3.5	4.0	
10–11	1.0	1.5					2.0	2.5				3.0	3.5		
12–14.5	1.5	2.0					2.5	3.0				3.5	4.0		
15–18	2.0						3.0					4.0			
19–21	2.5						3.5					4.5			
22–25	3.0						4.0					5.0			
26–26.5	3.5						4.5					5.5			

[a]Reproduced from *A Policy on Geometric Design of Rural Highways*, AASHTO, Washington, D.C., 1965.
[b]Values less than 2.0 may be disregarded. Three-lane pavements: multiply above values by 1.5. Four-lane pavements: multiply above values by 2. Where semitrailers are significant, increase tabular values of widening by 0.5 for curves of 10 to 16°, and by 1.0 for curves 17° and sharper.

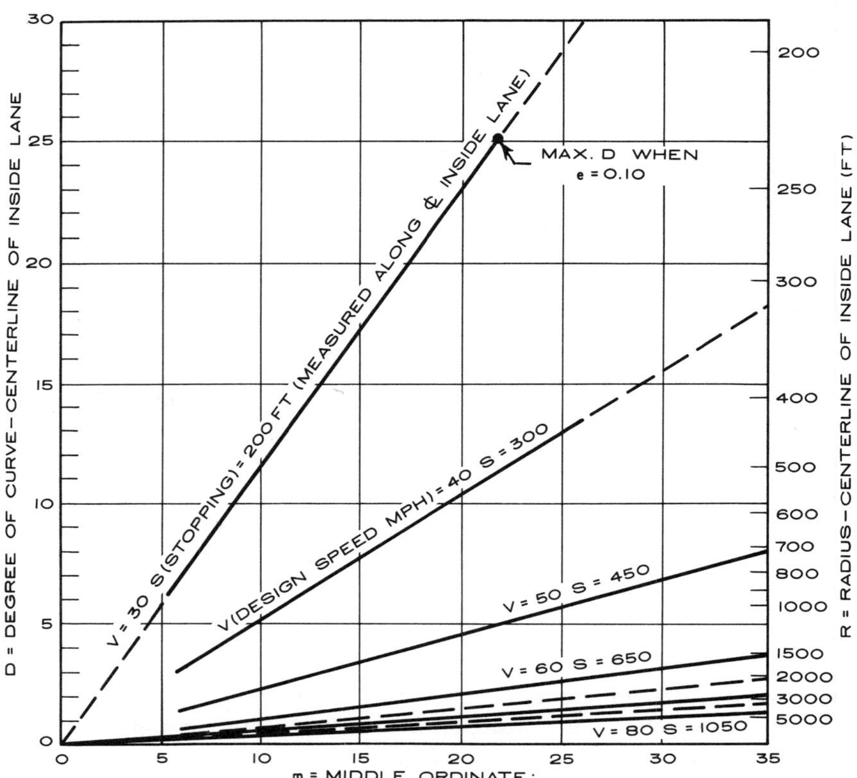

FIG. 8-8 Desirable stopping sight distance on horizontal curves for open road conditions. Reproduced from "A Policy on Design Standards for Stopping Sight Distance," AASHTO, Washington, D.C., 1971.

Vertical Alignment Computations

In vertical alignment, two fixed points or grades must be assured to maintain existing road grades, grades of buildings, or other fixed conditions. The apex point of two grade tangents, therefore, is calculated.

From fixed apex *A*, a tangent line is projected to point *D*, which is directly above fixed apex *C*. Grades of tangent lines *AB* and *BC* are set from study profiles, examples of which are shown further on in the text. We then calculate elevation of point *D*, an extension of tangent line *AB*, by multiplying percent of grade times horizontal distance and adding (or subtracting) to the elevation of apex *A*. Now calculate *h*, the vertical distance between *D* and *C*. Then determine the distance *x* where tangent lines *A*-*D* and *B*-*C* intersect.

$$x = \frac{h\,100}{A}$$

where x = horizontal distance from a given station to apex
h = vertical distance between two grades of given stations
A = algebraic difference

Calculate station of intersection point and its elevation; multiply percent of grade of *BC* by horizontal distance *x* and add (subtract) to elevation of apex *C*. (See Fig. 8-9.)

Vertical curves are parabolic rather than circular and are used for all changes of vertical alignment.

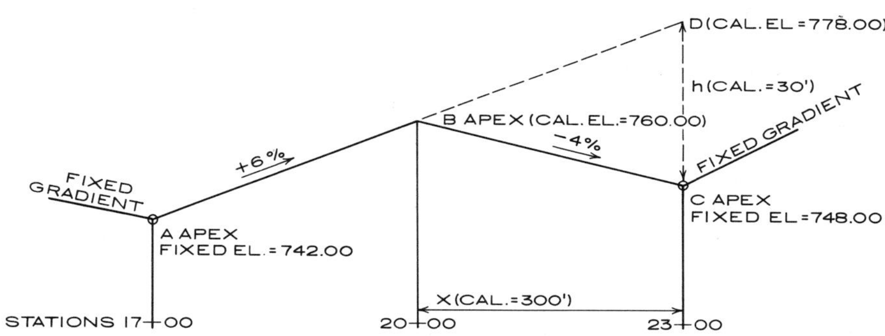

FIG. 8-9 Vertical alignment calculation.

Mathematical Principles of a Parabola

1 Middle ordinate is bisected by the vertical curve.
2 Offsets from tangent lines vary as square of distance from point of tangent.
3 The second differences of the elevation of points at equal horizontal intervals are equal.

Figure 8-10 presents vertical curve functions. (See also Fig. 8-11 and Table 8-2.)

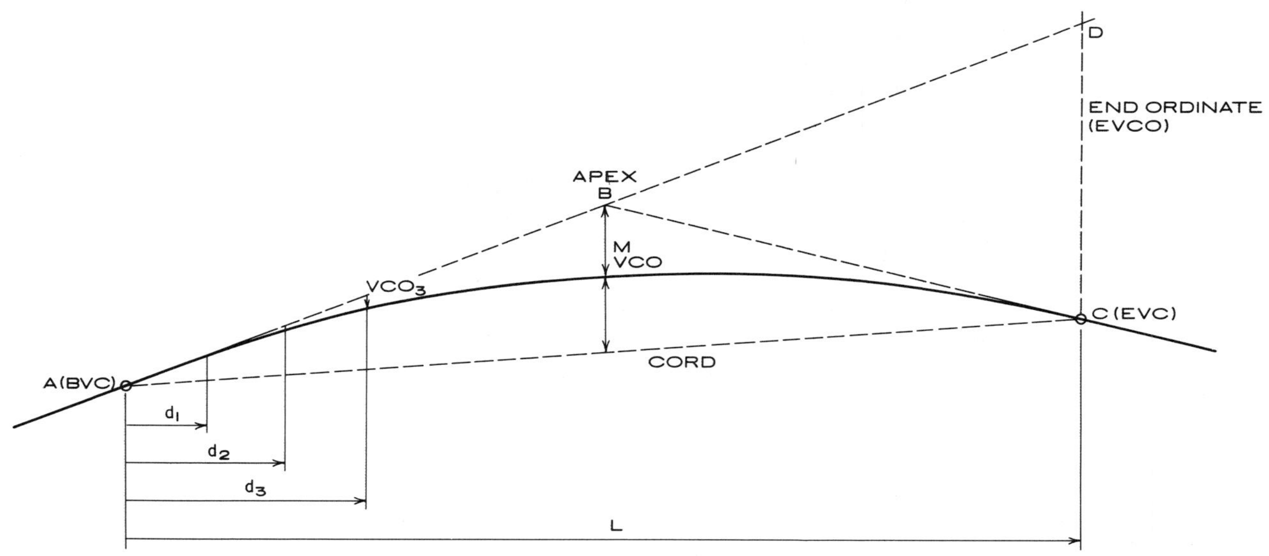

FIG. 8-10 Vertical curve functions.

BVC = Beginning of vertical curve
EVC = End of vertical curve
M = Middle ordinate
A = Algebraic difference—entering grade minus leaving grade—
Eq. -(+6%) - (4%) = 10%
d = Horizontal distance of vertical curve ordinate from BVC
EVCO = End VC ordinate at EVC
L = Length of VC
VCO = VC ordinate offset from tangent

$$VCORD = \frac{(d)^2\ EVCO}{L^2}$$

Table 8-2 Vertical Curve Data Form

Compute apex stations		20 + 00 elevation 760.00′
Compute algebraic difference	+6% entering grade − (−4% leaving grade) =	10%
Compute BVC Station		17 + 00 elevation 742.00′
Compute EVC station		23 + 00 elevation 748.00′
Compute elevation of entering grade line at EVC (D)		778.00′
Compute end ordinate = $\frac{\text{algebraic difference} \times \text{curve length}}{200}$ =		30.00′
Compute middle ordinate = $\frac{\text{algebraic difference} \times \text{curve length}}{800}$ =		7.5′

Station	Distance from BVC	Tangent Rise or Drop from BVC @ +6%	Tangent Grade Elevations	Square of Distance from BVC	VC Ordinates	VC Elevations
17 + 00	0.00′	0.00′	742.00′	0.00	0.00	742.00′
17 + 50	50.00′	3.00′	745.00′	2500.00	0.20	744.80′
18 + 00	100.00′	6.00′	748.00′	10000.00	0.83	747.17′
18 + 50	150.00′	9.00′	751.00′	22500.00	1.87	749.13′
19 + 00	200.00′	12.00′	754.00′	40000.00	3.33	750.67′
19 + 50	250.00′	15.00′	757.00′	62500.00	5.21	751.79′
20 + 00	300.00′	18.00′	760.00′	90000.00	7.50	752.50′
20 + 50	350.00′	21.00′	763.00′	122500.00	10.21	752.79′
21 + 00	400.00′	24.00′	766.00′	160000.00	13.33	752.67′
21 + 50	450.00′	27.00′	769.00′	202500.00	16.87	752.13′
22 + 00	500.00′	30.00′	772.00′	250000.00	20.83	751.17′
22 + 50	550.00′	33.00′	775.00′	302500.00	25.21	749.13′
23 + 00	600.00′	36.00′	778.00′	360000.00	30.00	748.00′
20 + 60 HP	360.00′	21.60′	763.60′	139600.00	11.63	751.97′

Formulas: tangent rise or drop = VC ordinates = $\frac{\text{algebraic difference } (\underline{\text{BVC}})^2}{2 \times \text{curve length}}$

d Values times entering high or low pt. = $\frac{\text{entering grade} \times \text{curve length}}{\text{algebraic difference}}$

Grade %

VC elevations (add or subtract each VC ordinate to tangent grade elevations)

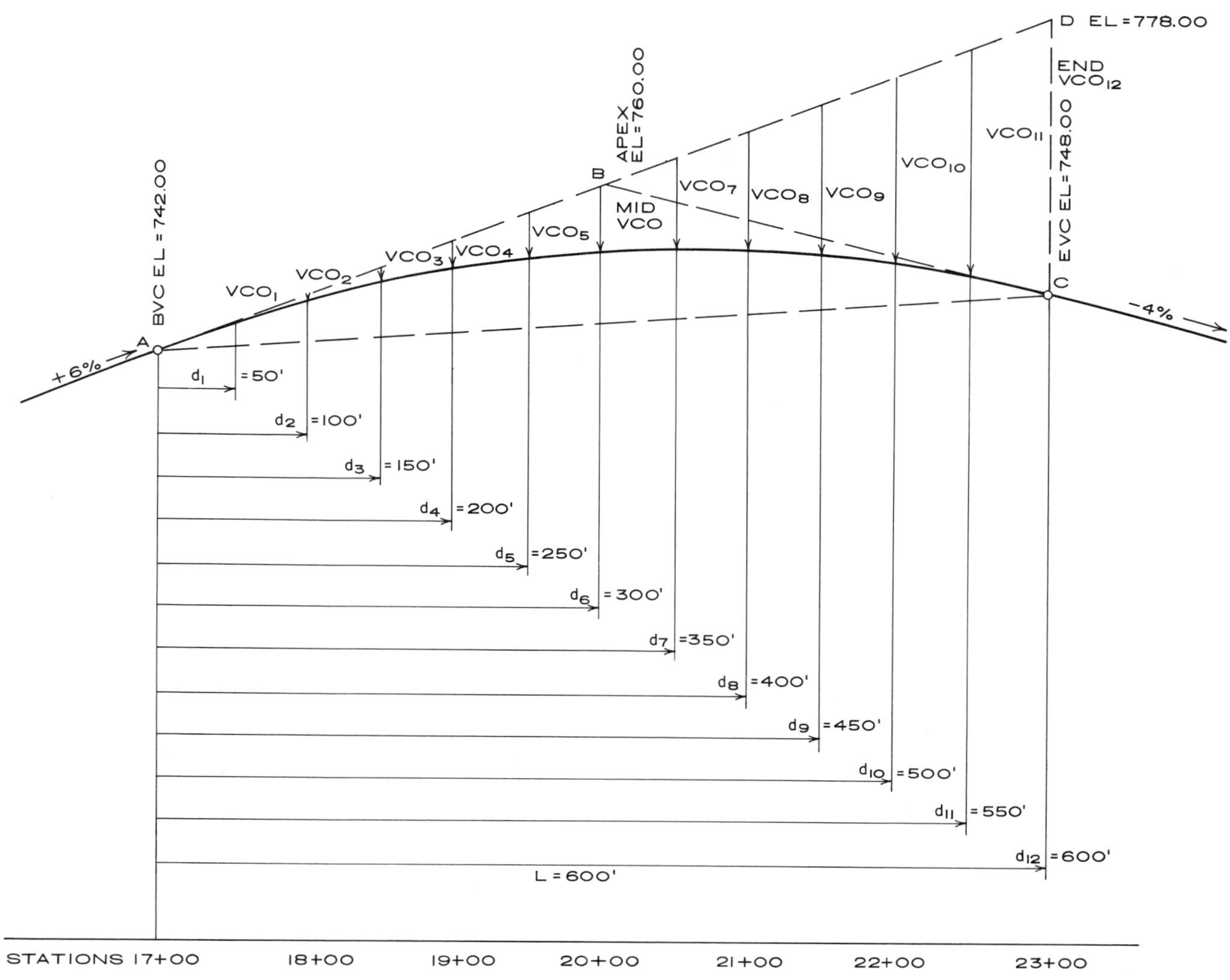

FIG. 8-11 Vertical curve problem. Compute the following curve: A +6% grade meets a −4% grade at station 20 + 00, elevation 760.00 ft. What are elevations at stations and half stations for the 600 ft curve?

$$VCORD = \frac{(d)^2 \times EVCO}{L^2}$$

EVCO = "D" − "C"

EVCO = 778 − 448 = 30

Find VCO_4

$$VCO_4 = \frac{(d_4)^2 \times EVCO}{L^2}$$

$$VCO_4 = \frac{(200)^2 \times 30}{(600)^2}$$

$$VCO_4 = 3.33'$$

Find VCO − Middle ordinate

$$VCO = \frac{(d_6)^2 \times EVCO}{L^2}$$

$$VCO = \frac{(300)^2 \times 30}{(600)^2}$$

$$VCO = 7.5'$$

Superelevation

Superelevation compensates for centrifugal force. It reduces the danger of skidding on curves and induces traffic to keep toward the right side of the road.

Superelevation is accomplished by revolving the surface of the road about the center line as an axis. The amount of tilting depends on the expected speed of the vehicle and radius of the curve. Full superelevation begins at the *PC* and continues the entire length of the curve to *PT*. The transition length required to acquire full superelevation is called runoff distance. The runoff distance is the same length back from the *PC* as from the *PT*. The transition from the normal crowned section on a tangent to the fully superelevated section should be comfortable for safe operation of vehicles at highway design speed. There is no set method for this. Superelevation varies from $\frac{1}{4}$ to $\frac{3}{4}$ in per ft. A minimum effective rate is twice the crown.

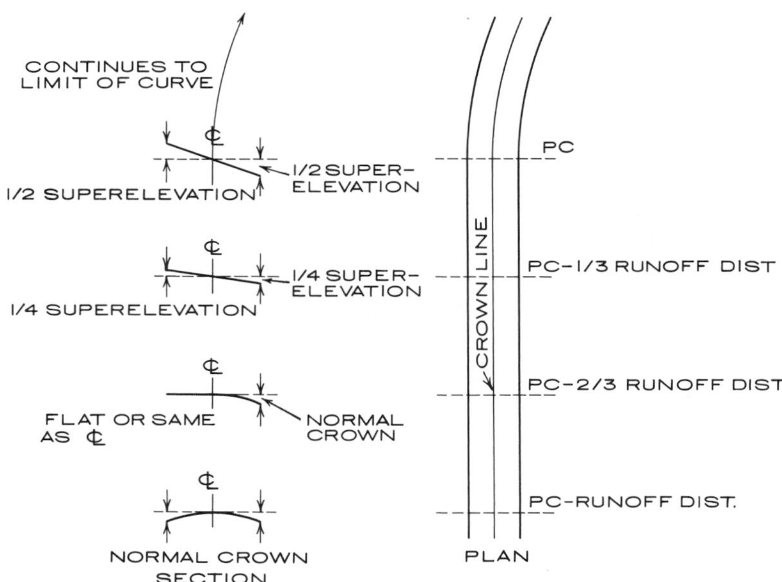

FIG. 8-12 Superelevation.

Table 8-3 Superelevation for 30, 40, and 50 mph; e max = 0.08[a]

Radius	Degree of Curve	30 mph	40 mph	50 mph
5730	1	NC	RC	0.018
2865	2	0.016	0.025	0.035
1910	3	0.023	0.035	0.050
1432	4	0.029	0.044	0.062
1146	5	0.035	0.053	0.070
955	6	0.041	0.060	0.076
819	7	0.045	0.066	0.079
716	8	0.050	0.071	0.080 max
637	9	0.054	0.074	
573	10	0.058	0.077	
521	11	0.061	0.079	
477	12	0.065	0.080 max	
441	13	0.067	NC = normal crown	
409	14	0.070	section	
358	16	0.074	RC = remove adverse	
318	18	0.077	crown and super-	
286	20	0.079	elevate at normal	
260	22	0.080 max	crown slope	

[a]Elwyn E. Seelye, *Design: Data Book For Civil Engineers*, New York: Wiley, 1960.

Runoff distance is divided into three equal parts; the minimum distance used is 150 ft. (See Fig. 8-12.)

Formula for superelevation:

$$e + f = \frac{0.067V^2}{R} = \frac{V^2}{15R}$$

where e = superelevation (ft/ft) of road width
V = vehicle speed (mph)
R = radius of curve (ft)
f = side friction factor: 0.16 for 30 mph and less, 0.15 for 40 mph where e = maximum of 0.08 ft/ft

Rates on areas subject to snow and ice: 0.08 ft/ft.
Maximum for areas subject to snow and ice: 0.10 ft/ft or where slow speeds are required on curves.
Where traffic density and marginal development tend to reduce speeds: 0.06 ft/ft. (See Table 8-3.)

Length of Vertical Curves

To satisfy minimum stopping sight distance, comfort, and aesthetics the length of vertical curves in feet should not be less than three times the design speed in miles per hour.

Crest Vertical Curves. The minimum length of crest vertical curves as determined by safety, comfort, and aesthetics can be determined by basic formulas with a 4.5 ft height of object.

When S is less than L,

$$L = \frac{AS^2}{100\,(\sqrt{2h_1} + \sqrt{2h_2})^2}$$

When S is greater than L,

$$L = 2S - \frac{200\,(\sqrt{h_1} + \sqrt{2h_2})^2}{A}$$

where L = length of vertical curve (ft)
S = sight distance (ft)
A = algebraic difference in grades (%)
h_1 = height of eye above roadway surface (ft)
h_2 = height of object above roadway surface (ft)

Where the height of eye is 3.75 ft and the height of the object is 6 in. the formulas for stopping sight distances are as follows:

When S is less than L,

$$L = \frac{AS^2}{1398}$$

When S is greater than L,

$$L = 2S - \frac{1398}{A}$$

(See Fig. 8-13 and Table 8-4.)

Passing Sight Distance. Passing sight distance of crest vertical curves differs because of height of object criteria. The general formulas apply, but based on a 4.5 height of object become as follows:

When S is less than L,

$$L = \frac{AS^2}{3295}$$

When S is greater than L,

$$L = 2S - \frac{3295}{A}$$

(See Table 8-5.)

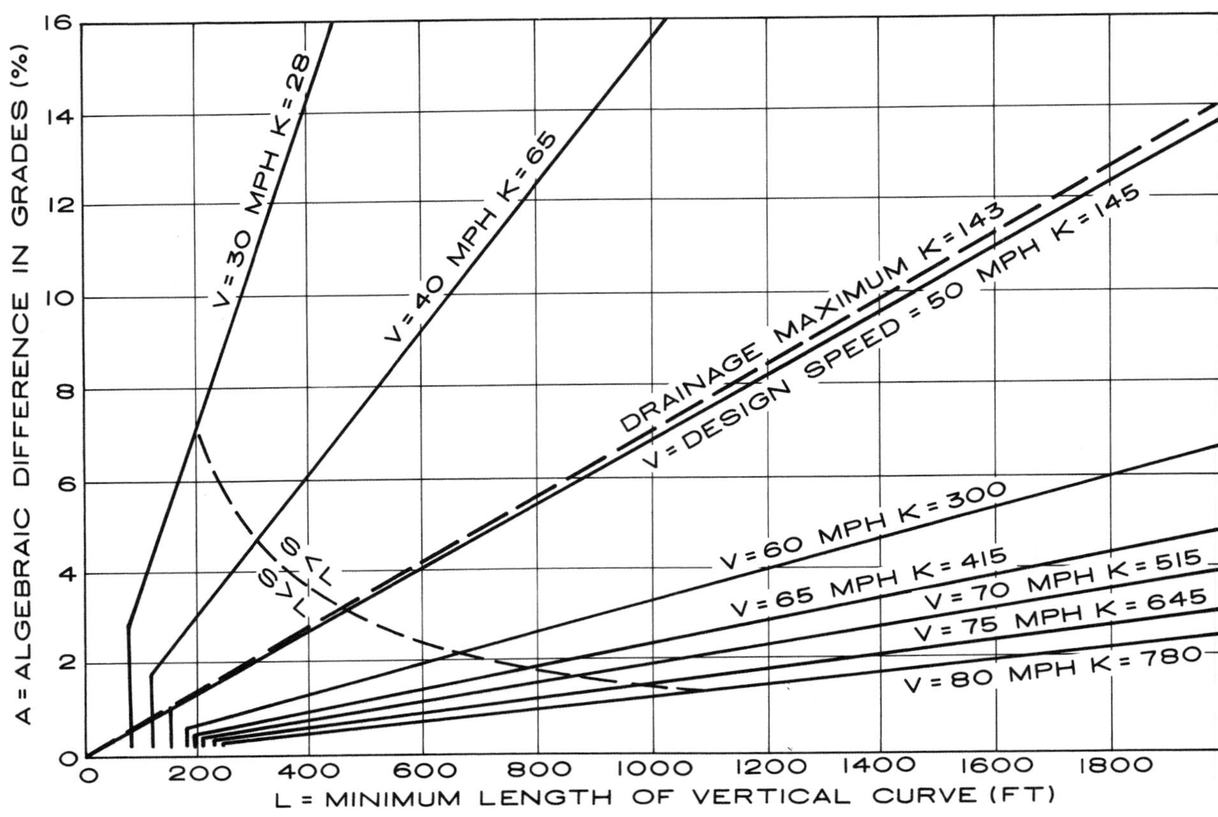

FIG. 8-13 Design controls for crest vertical curves. Reproduced from "A Policy on Design Standards for Stopping Sight Distance," AASHTO, Washington, D.C., 1971.

Table 8-4 Design Controls for Crest Vertical Curves Based on Desirable Stopping Sight Distance[a]

Design speed mph	Desirable Stopping Sight Distance (ft)	K = Rate of Vertical Curvature, Length (ft/percent of A)	
		Calculated	Rounded
30	200	28.6	28
40	300	64.4	65
50	450	144.8	145
60	650	302.0	300
65	750	402.4	400
70	850	516.8	515
75	950	645.6	645
80	1050	788.6	780

[a]Reproduced from "A Policy on Design Standards for Stopping Sight Distance," AASHTO, Washington, D.C., 1971.

Table 8-5 Minimum Sight Distance (ft)[a]

Design Speed (mph)	20	30	40	50	60
Stopping sight distance					
Minimum stopping sight distance (ft)	150	200	275	350	475
K value for[b]					
Crest vertical curve	16	28	55	85	160
Sag vertical curve	24	35	55	75	105
Desirable stopping sight distance (ft)	150	200	300	450	650
K value for[b]					
Crest vertical curve	16	28	65	145	300
Sag vertical curve	24	35	60	100	155
Passing sight distance					
Passing distance (ft)					
Two-lane		1100	1500	1800	2100
K value for[b]					
Crest vertical curve		365	686	985	1340

[a]Reproduced from "A Policy on Design Standards for Stopping Sight Distance," AASHTO, Washington, D.C., 1971.
[b]*K* value is a coefficient by which the algebraic difference in grade may be multiplied to determine the length in feet of the vertical curve which will provide minimum sight distance.

Sag Vertical Curves. Three criteria for establishing lengths of sag vertical curves are headlight sight distance comfort, drainage control, and aesthetics. The general headlight height used is 2 ft, with a 1° upward divergence of light beam from the vehicle.

When S is less than L,

$$L = \frac{AS^2}{400 + 3.5S}$$

When S is greater than L,

$$L = 2S - \frac{400 + 3.5S}{A}$$

where L = length of sag vertical curve (ft)
S = light beam distance (ft)
A = algebraic distance in grade (%)

(See Fig. 8-14 and Table 8-6.)

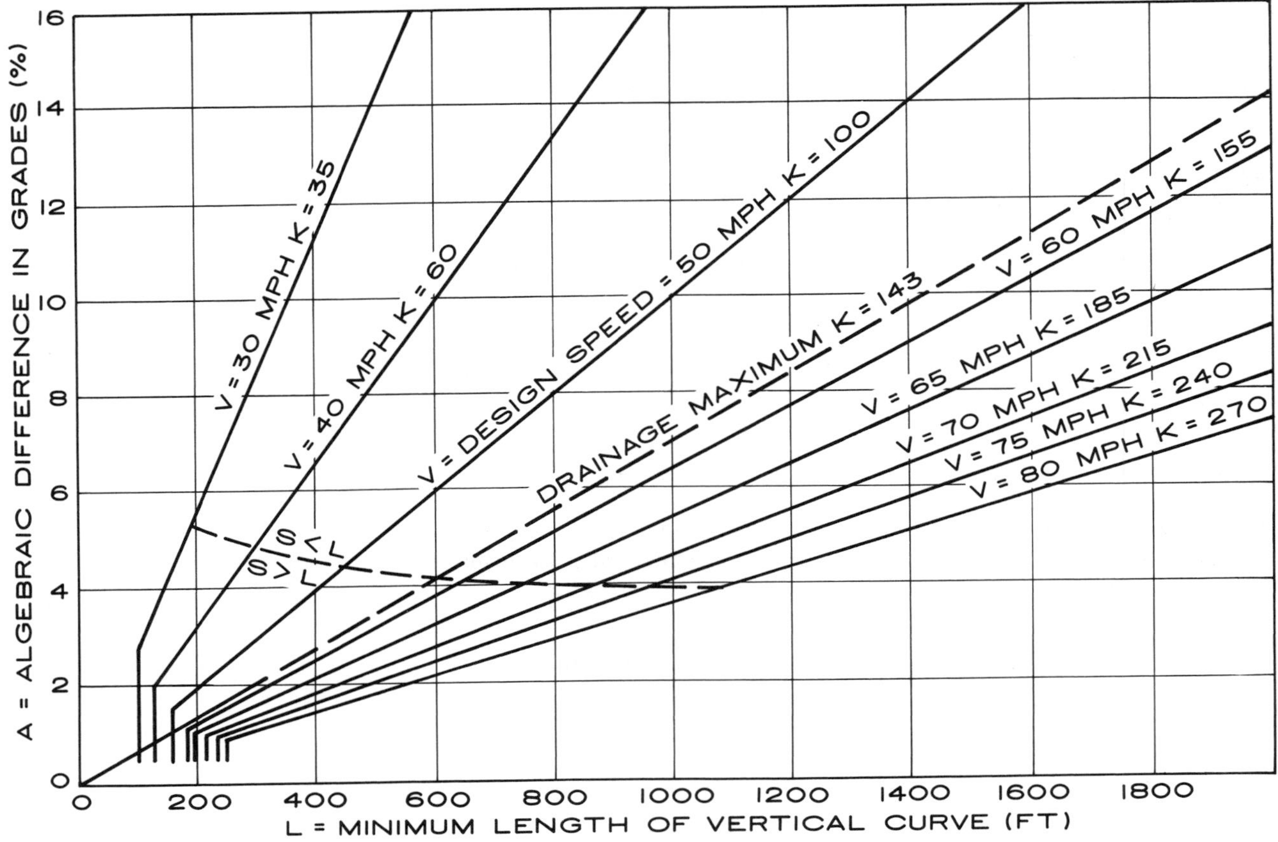

FIG. 8-14 Design controls for sag vertical curves. Reproduced from "A Policy on Design Standards for Stopping Sight Distance," AASHTO, Washington, D.C., 1971.

Table 8-6 Design Controls for Sag Vertical Curves Based on Desirable Stopping Sight Distances[a]

Design Speed (mph)	Desirable Stopping Sight Distance (ft)	K = Rate of Vertical Curvature, Length (ft/percent of A)	
		Calculated	Rounded
30	200	36.4	35
40	300	62.1	60
50	450	102.5	100
60	650	157.9	155
70	850	214.0	215
75	950	242.3	240
80	1050	270.6	270

[a]Reproduced from "A Policy on Design Standards for Stopping Sight Distance," AASHTO, Washington, D.C., 1971.

General Procedure for Alignment of Horizontal and Vertical Curves

1. Field reconnaissance of terrain for approximate location of road.
2. Preliminary topographic surveys are made if not already available.
3. List the design criteria for the road, including speed, type, volume of traffic it can accommodate, number and width of lanes, and degree of curve permitted to carry out road design. (See Fig. 8-15.)

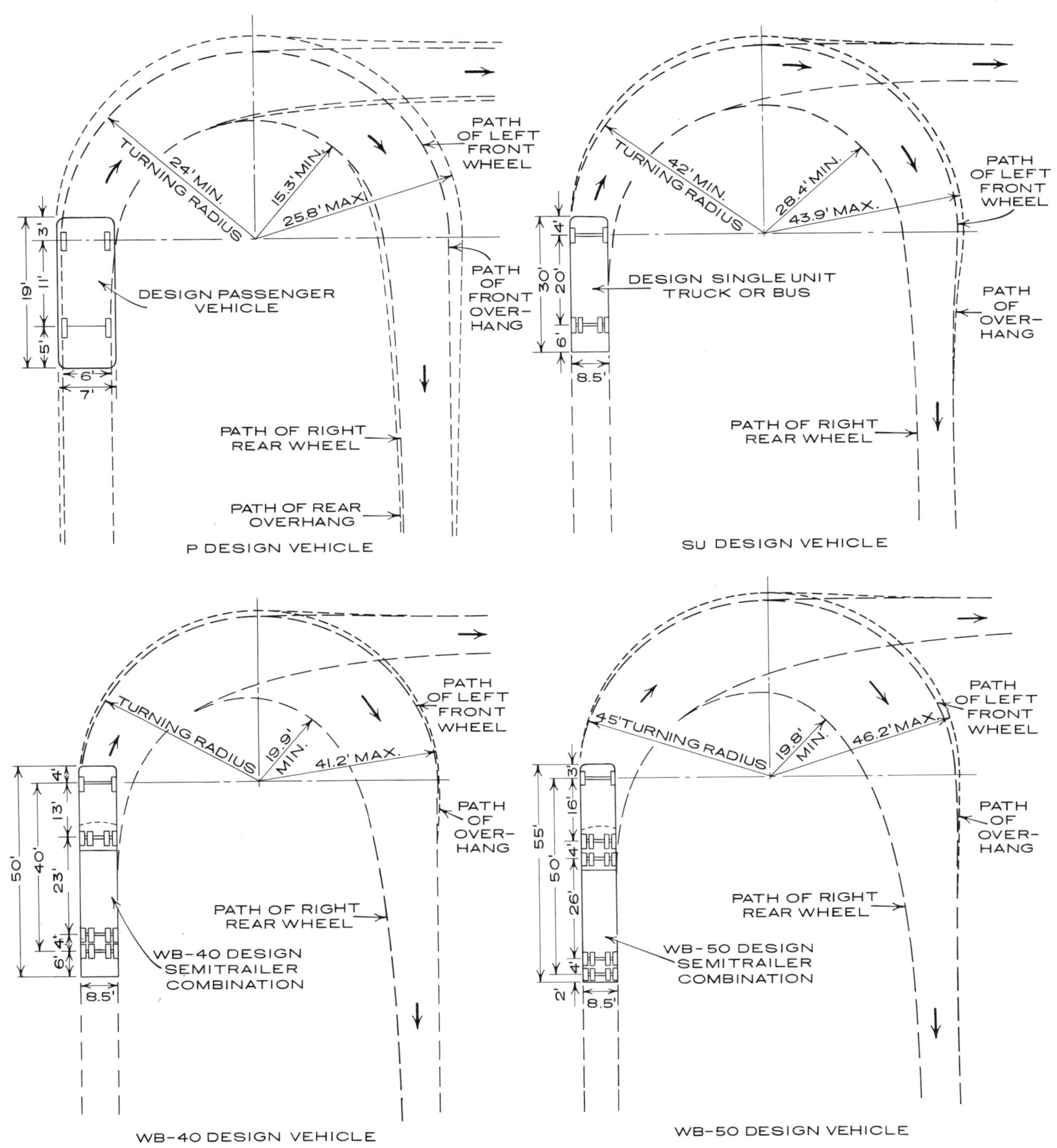

FIG. 8-15 Minimum vehicle turning radii. Reproduced from *A Policy on Geometric Design of Rural Highways, 1965.* Washington, D.C.: AASHO Offices, 1966.

4 Using dividers, establish maximum desirable grade in order to study possible placement of road on steeper portions of topography. Paper locations should always be checked by field reconnaissance.
5 Draw a freehand line representing the center line of road trying various locations and taking existing site features into consideration. Start from an existing point of known elevation such as the center line of a road. (See Fig. 8-16.)

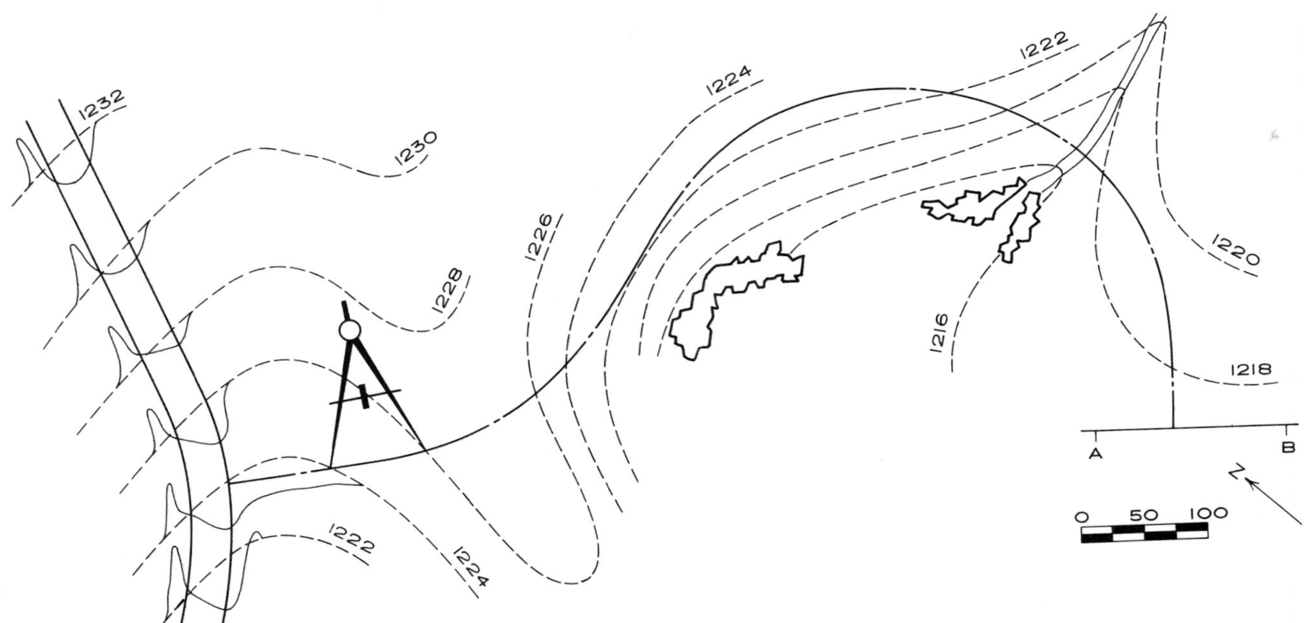

FIG. 8-16 Freehand road alignment.

Horizontal Alignment Principles. Horizontal alignment must be as directional as possible with long flowing curves fitted to topography instead of long tangents that slash artificially across the land. Closely spaced short curves should be avoided, along with brokenback and reverse curves. The sharpest curves permitted by a design speed should only be used at critical locations. Strive for consistent alignment to avoid making a driver hesitate, for this causes accidents. Engineer the line by dividing the proposed alignment into tangents and arcs. Change for correction of degree of curve and use compound curves where necessary to achieve the nearest approach to the proposed alignment. Now redraw the more precise alignment. (See Fig. 8-17.)

6 Compute values for Δ, T, R, L, and C as shown on p. 158.
7 Check each curve by comparing the long chord distance C with its computed *PC-PT* value.
8 Carefully measure and label the stations along the center line of the road. Label *PC, PT, PCC* for compound curves.
9 *Profile.* Draw a tentative profile, using it to adjust cut and fill and to set grades of vertical curves. A profile usually has an exaggerated vertical scale of 1 in. = 10 ft.

Vertical Curve Principles. The profile should be smooth flowing with long vertical curves and not have numerous breaks with short grades. Avoid sag vertical curves on straight horizontal alignment.

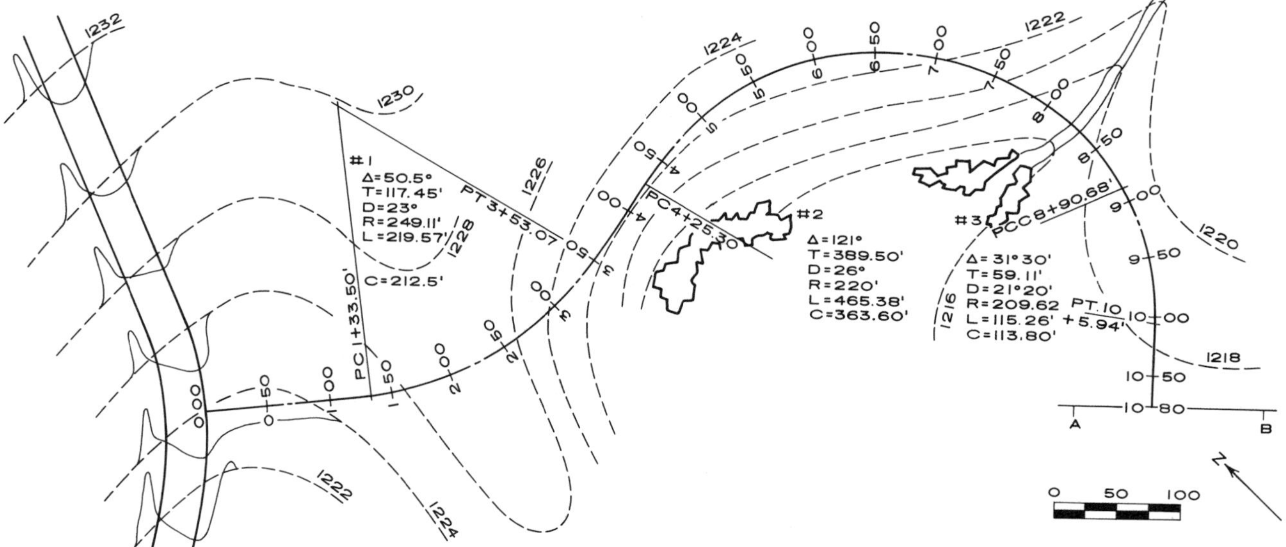

FIG. 8-17 Engineered alignment.

On long grades place steep grades at bottom of ascent. A change in horizontal alignment should be made at a sag vertical curve where a driver will be aware of change, and if there is a horizontal curve at a crest of a vertical curve, change in direction should precede the change in profile. (See Fig. 8-18.)

10 A profile is plotted by first transferring information from the horizontal curve to the profile. To do this a tick strip is prepared to mark off the relation of existing contours and stationing.
Existing contours are ticked off and labeled where they cross the center line of the road by superimposing stationing of the tick strip on the road nearest to the contour being marked. (See Fig. 8-19.)

11 Transfer all information to the datum plane and establish horizontal stations and vertical axis as in Fig. 8-20.

12 Place the tick strip on the profile sheet and accurately locate the points representing contours crossing the center line of horizontal alignment.

13 Connect the points freehand or with a straight edge and use a dashed line since this represents existing topography.

14 Roll up and save the tick strip for further use.

15 Triangles are good for studying trial grades and the proposed grades can be tentatively drawn. A balance of cut and fill should be achieved.

16 Compute the vertical curves; plot and draw the profile hardline.

17 Label the finished grades representing the proposed station elevations on each station line of the profile sheet.

18 Beneath each profile draw the diagrammatic horizontal alignment and label. (See Figs. 8-20 and 8-21.)

19 *Cross Sections.* Cross sections are prepared using a vertical line in the center of the sheet representing the center line and horizontal lines representing the stations. Label left and right sides and each station. A scale of 1 in. = 10 ft is usually used for both horizontal and vertical planes.

20 Taking each station in order and keeping on the same side of the road, scale the distance on plan from the center line to where each contour crosses. Place the information about each contour and its distance from the center line in fraction form on the cross-sectional plotting sheet.

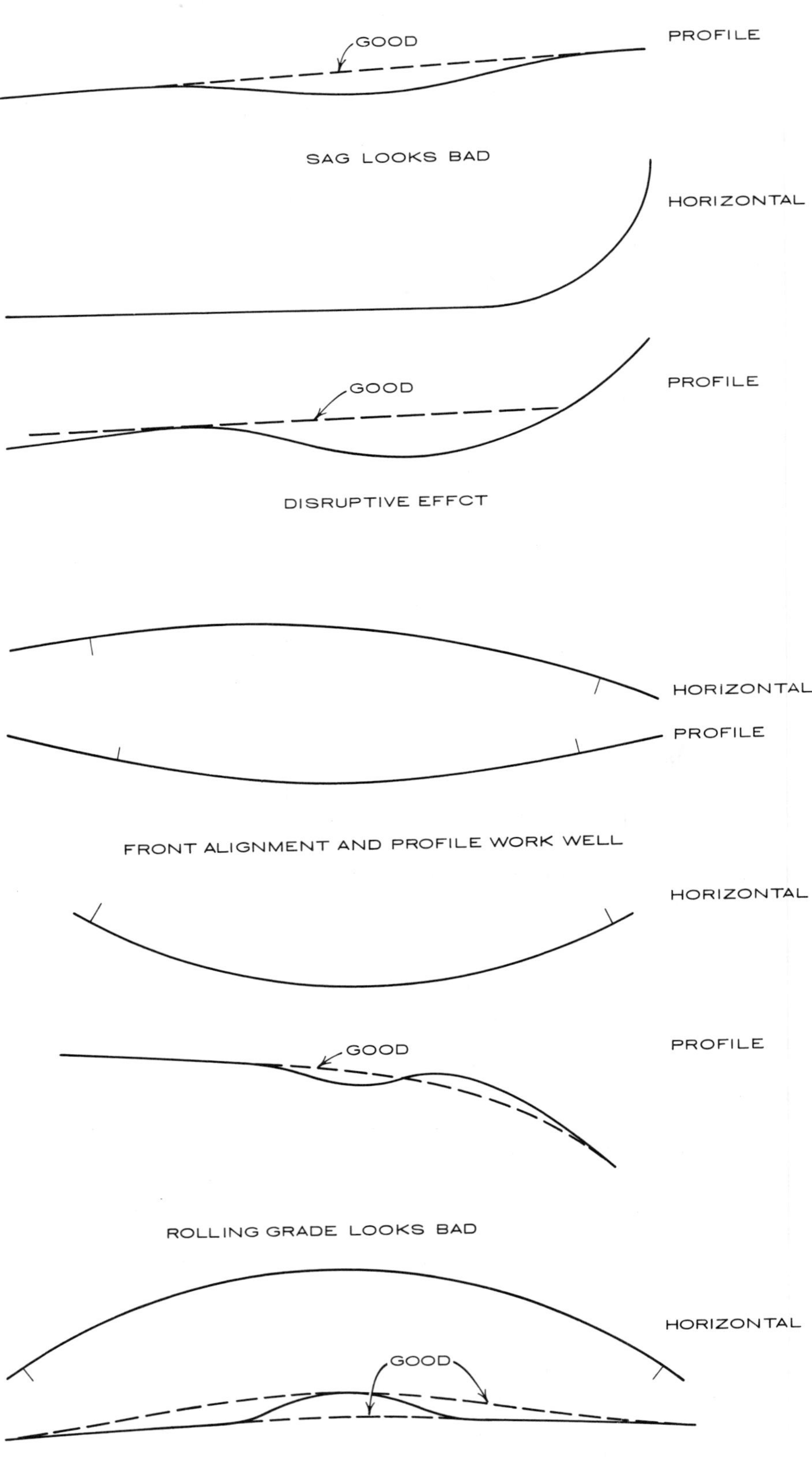
GOOD
PROFILE
SAG LOOKS BAD
HORIZONTAL
GOOD
PROFILE
DISRUPTIVE EFFCT
HORIZONTAL
PROFILE
FRONT ALIGNMENT AND PROFILE WORK WELL
HORIZONTAL
GOOD
PROFILE
ROLLING GRADE LOOKS BAD
HORIZONTAL
GOOD
HUMP IN GRADE HAS APPEARANCE OF
A BROKEN BACK
PROFILE

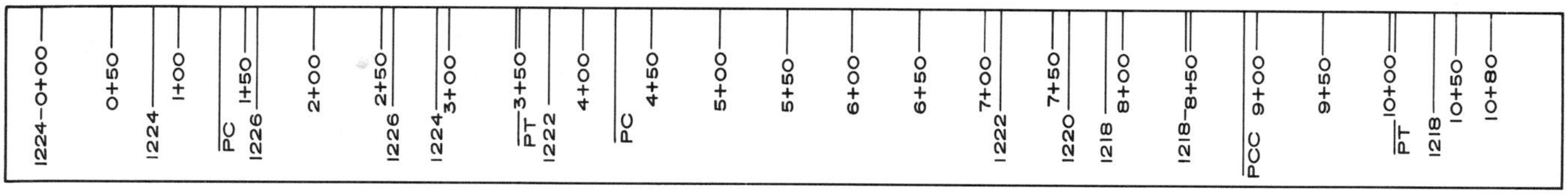

FIG. 8-19 Sample tick strip.

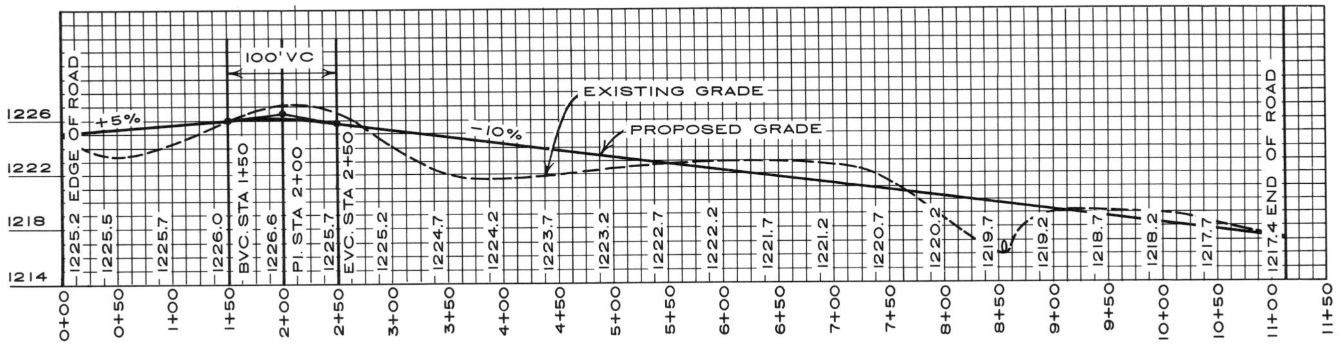

FIG. 8-20 Profile.

FIG. 8-21 Diagrammatic horizontal alignment.

21 Prepare a template of the road cross-sectional design. Label all pitches, slopes, and so on, on the template.

22 Place the template at the proposed station elevation and draw the proposed sections on the cross-sectional sheet. (See Fig. 8-22.)

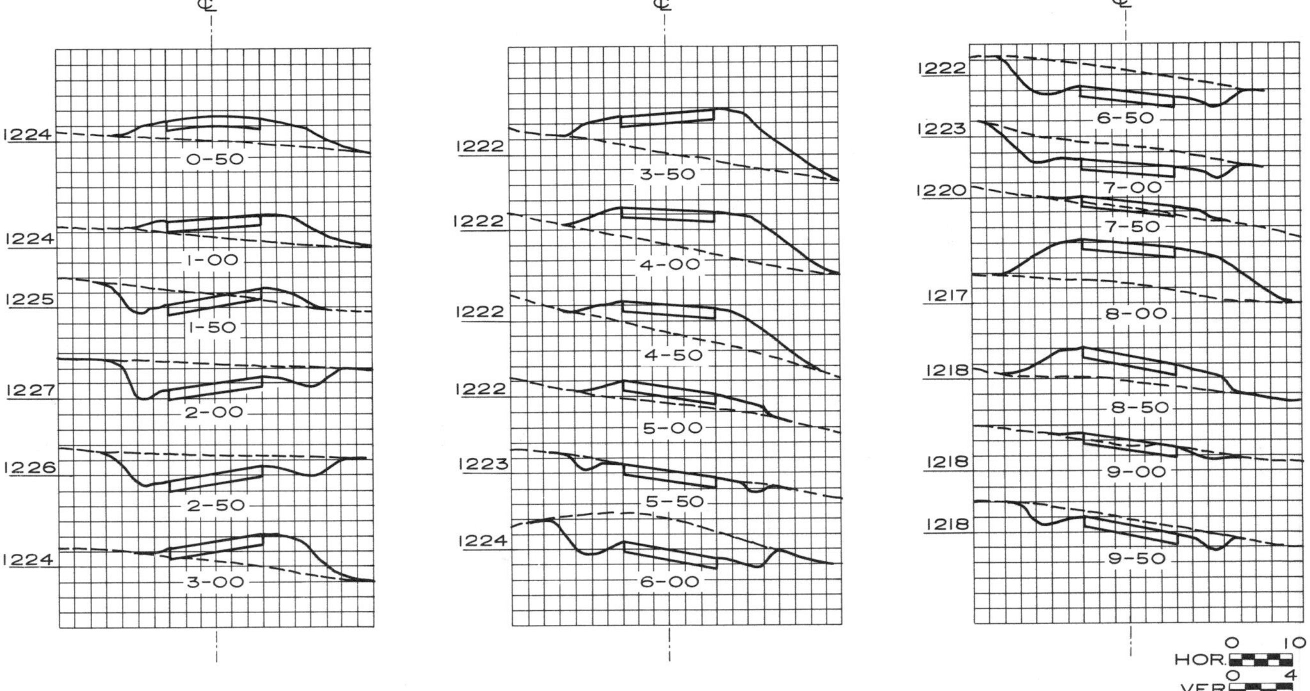

FIG. 8-22 Cross sections.

23 For superelevated sections, plot both the center line proposed elevation and the elevation of the road edge and extend the line through both points for full road width.

24 Blend the proposed line to existing ground for each cross section.

25 Check cross sections for agreement with the profile.

26 *Adjustment of Contours.* Going back to the plan draw the edges of the road, shoulder, and ditches.

27 Plot the proposed center line crossing of each contour on the plan by using the tick strip again and marking these first on the tick strip and then on the plan.

28 Compute the travel distance for crown, superelevation, shoulder, and ditch for each percent of grade.

29 Draw in proposed contours in accordance with travel distance computations.

30 Make necessary blends with existing contours. Where possible use sections to determine location of the contour along the section of a station. (See Fig. 8-23.)

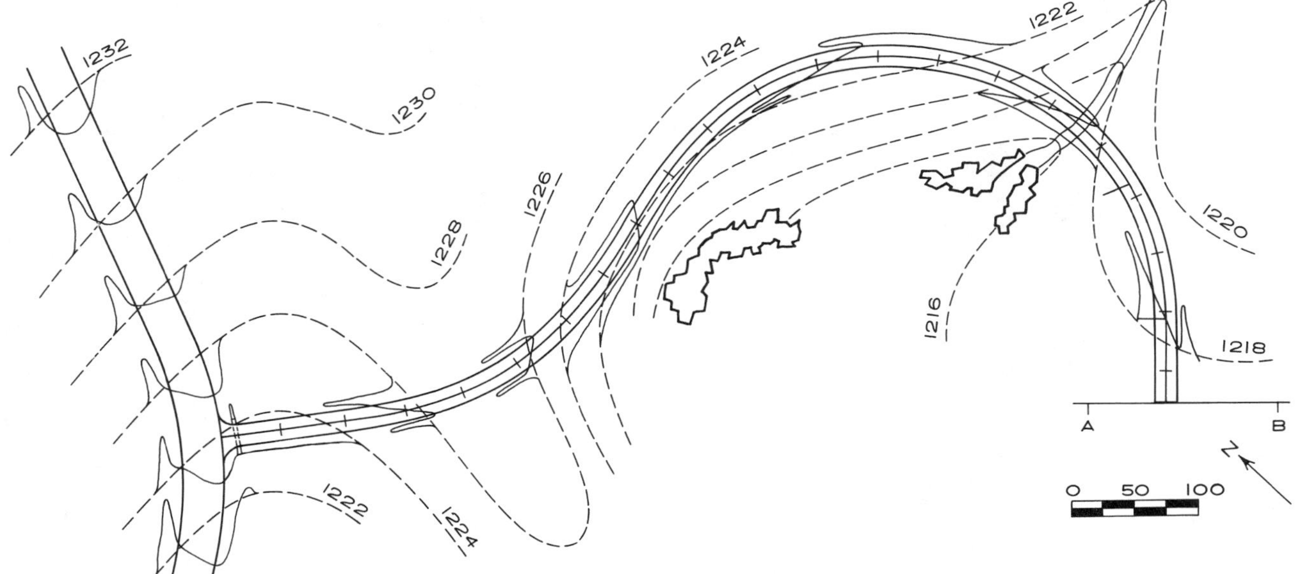

FIG. 8-23 Contours on the road.

FIG. 9-1 The concept of the natural landscape meeting a man-made stone podium is illustrated at Brandeis University, Waltham, Massachusetts.

Chapter Nine
Site and Landscape Construction Details

To be carried to completion, successful design depends on good detailing and supervision. Lack of good detailing may turn an otherwise good design into a mediocre looking project. The site planner must see not only that details are well designed, but also that they are properly built during the construction phase. (See Fig. 9-1.)

Through photographic illustrations and drawings this chapter shows examples of details from many site planning projects, including campus planning, urban plazas, shopping centers, parks, housing, civic centers, and office building complexes. Appropriate proportion, texture, and color are essential in the design of these details. Materials must be chosen in relation to each other and must be thought of in the context of the total design concept of a project. This is important not only for design continuity, but also for durability and ease of maintenance.

Paving Materials

Originally, paving materials were used to eliminate hazards from mud and dust and to form a smooth surface for ease of circulation. They are available today in a wide variety of textures and colors.

Stone. Stone, one of the oldest paving materials, offers a durable, long-wearing surface with a minimum of maintenance. Rubble and ashlar masonry are the two forms of stone used for paving. As taken from the quarry rubble masonry is rough stone, but may be trimmed somewhat where necessary. Ashlar masonry is hewed or cut stone from the quarry and is used much more often than rubble for the surfacing of walks. (See Figs. 9-2 to 9-9.)

FIG. 9-2 Irregular fitted flagstone is used at the Morris & Stiles Dormitories at Yale University, New Haven, Connecticut. Flagstone is generally more than 2 in. thick and grouted with portland cement when an impervious surface is required.

FIG. 9-3 Granite sets with slots for trees are used to give textural variety at the Los Angeles Civic Center, California.

FIG. 9-4 Granite sets are used to form this curvilinear paving pattern at the New Town of Vallingby, Sweden.

FIG. 9-5 Cobblestones are used in this children's play area at the New Town of Cumbernald, Scotland (Photograph courtesy of John Morley, University of Kansas).

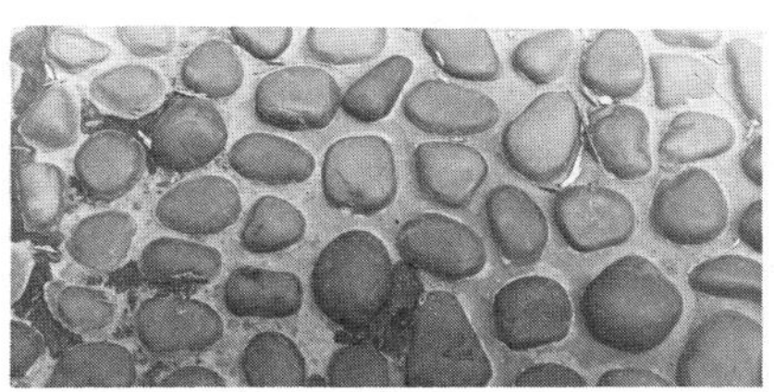

FIG. 9-6 Pebbles can be laid in concrete where an interesting texture is desired. Walking on this surface will be discouraged when the pebbles are laid on edge but encouraged when laid flat.

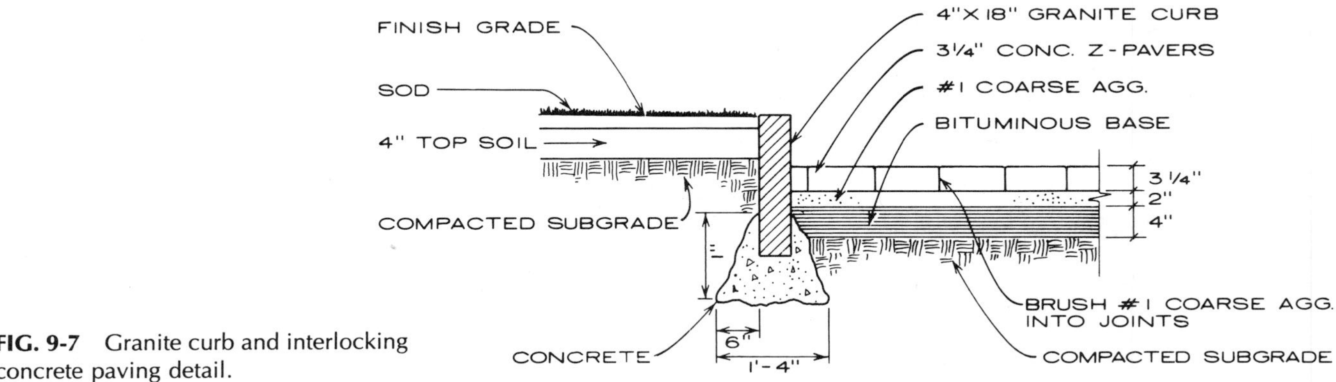

FIG. 9-7 Granite curb and interlocking concrete paving detail.

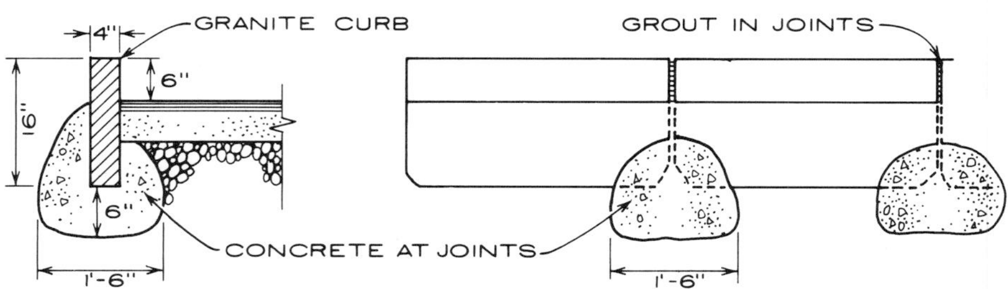

FIG. 9-8 Granite curb detail.

FIG. 9-9 A radial paving pattern is used in conjunction with the fountain in Lincoln Center, New York City (Photograph courtesy of John Morley).

Granite. A very hard igneous rock, granite is a good material to use for curbs along city streets and for special features such as planter pots, steps, bollards, or other elements. This material is available in several colors with different textures. Textures available are created by a thermal or sanded finish or by honing. A honed finish is very smooth while a thermal finish brings out the natural qualities of the stone, but may be rough to sit on. Granite can be saw cut as on the top of curbs, which also have a split face. It is a dense material with a compressive strength of from 26,000 to 30,000 psi and is resistant to chemicals such as salt.

Bluestone. Formed by sedimentary processes, bluestone is a softer stone that can be easily cut and used in irregular fitted patterns. It is often used in residential design for walks and patio areas.

Brick. The oldest artificial building material in use today is brick. It offers a great variety of textures and colors as well as flexibility in its use. Composed of hardburned clays and shales, brick is available in many colors because of the variation in the chemical content of clay.

Three processes of making bricks are the sand-struck, wire-cut, and dry-press methods. The dry-press method forms bricks under high pressure and gives them a smooth surface with true edges and corners. Because they have a hard surface and resistance to wear and cracking, these bricks are best for outdoor paving.

Brick sizes follow:

Standard	$2\frac{3}{8} \times 3\frac{3}{4} \times 8$ in.
Norman	$2\frac{1}{4} \times 3\frac{3}{4} \times 12$ in.
Roman	$1\frac{5}{8} \times 3\frac{3}{4} \times 12$ in.
Baby Roman	$1\frac{5}{8} \times 3\frac{3}{4} \times 8$ in.

Brick may be laid in sand bases or on concrete slabs. The most common brick patterns used are running bond, herringbone, and basket weave. (See Figs. 9-10 to 9-15.) Outdoor brick pavers are available in $1 \times 4 \times 8$ in. size for use on concrete slabs. A dimensional paver size of $1\frac{1}{2} \times 3\frac{5}{8} \times 7\frac{5}{8}$ in. is easier to install in herringbone patterns because it requires less cutting.

FIG. 9-10 Brick pavers used in a fan pattern.

FIG. 9-11 Brick pavers used in a herringbone pattern.

FIG. 9-12 Brick and concrete paving pattern used at Northeastern Bank Plaza (Photograph courtesy of Bellante, Clauss, Miller & Partners).

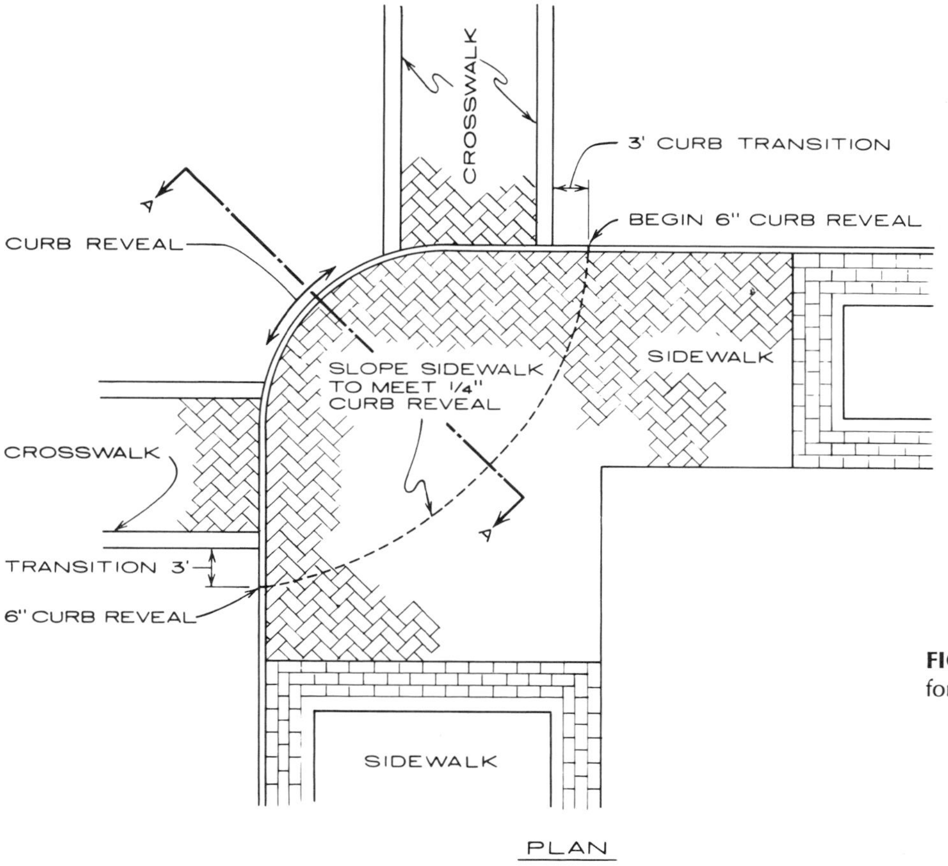

CROSSWALK
3' CURB TRANSITION
BEGIN 6" CURB REVEAL
CURB REVEAL
A
SIDEWALK
SLOPE SIDEWALK
TO MEET 1/4"
CURB REVEAL
CROSSWALK
A
TRANSITION 3'
6" CURB REVEAL
SIDEWALK
PLAN

FIG. 9-13 Plan of brick paving pitched for a wheelchair ramp.

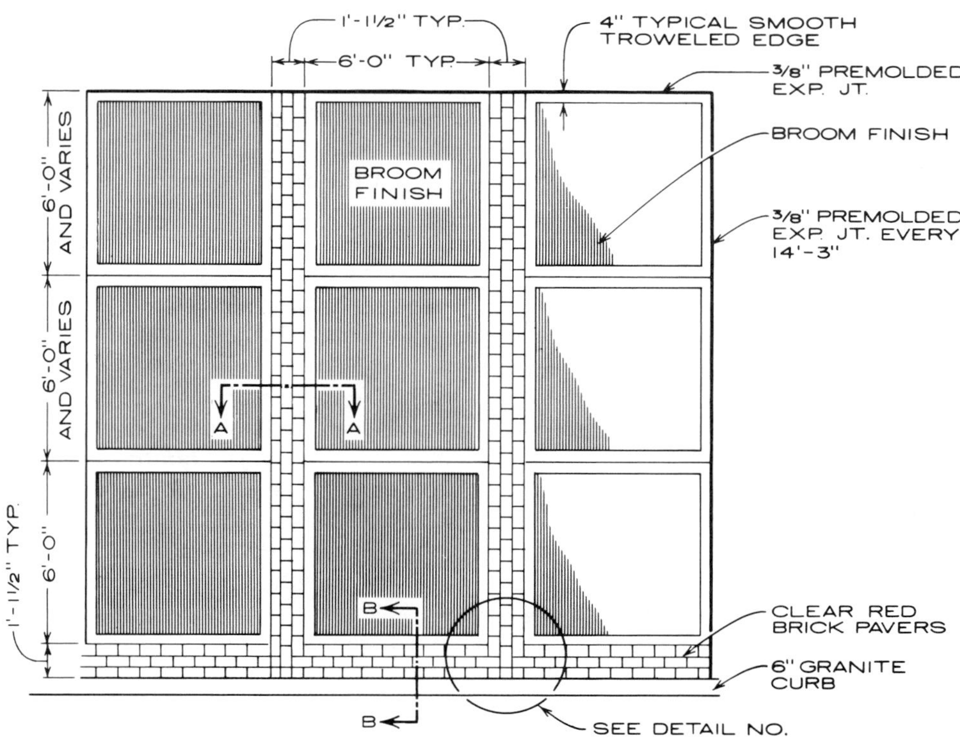

FIG. 9-14 Plan of brick and concrete paving pattern.

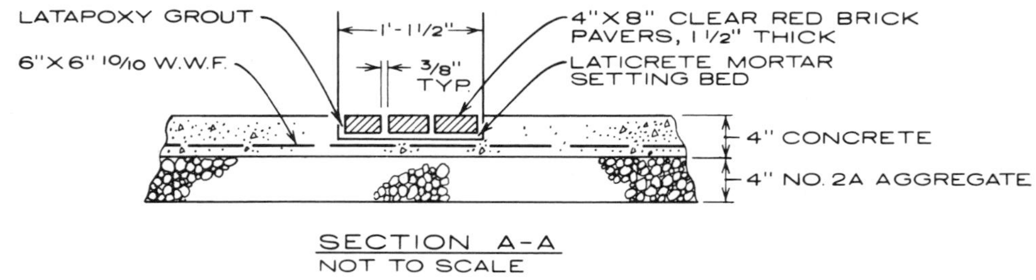

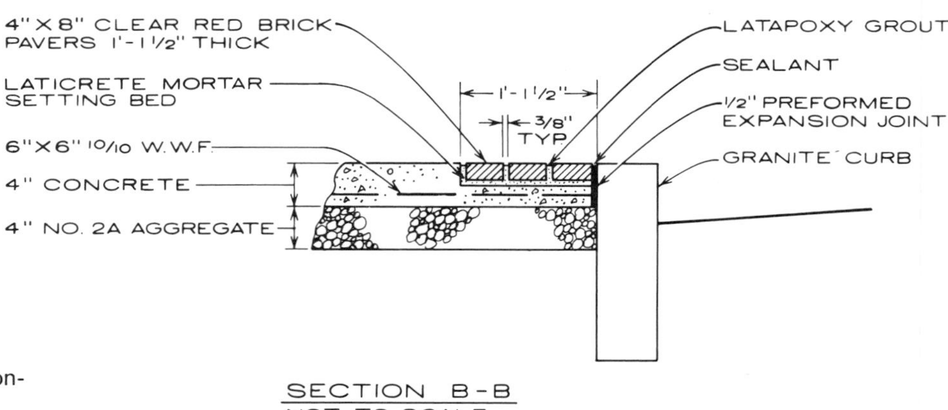

FIG. 9-15 Section of brick and concrete paving.

Concrete. Because it may be poured in place, has variety in texture and color, and forms a durable walking surface, concrete has been used extensively as a paving material. It is a mineral aggregate bound together by a cementing material, generally portland cement. And it lends itself to variations in finish and may be smooth or rough, with aggregates exposed when desired. (See Figs. 9-16 to 9-28.)

Concrete mixtures vary depending on the ratio of cement to sand to gravel; a sample mixture is one part portland cement, two parts sand, and three parts gravel. Fine and coarse grained aggregates are used in the mixture for concrete. Fine aggregates or sand generally range up to $\frac{1}{8}$ in. in diameter, while coarse aggregate is over $\frac{1}{4}$ in. in diameter and consists of crushed stone, gravel, or other inert materials. The maximum size of aggregates used in reinforced concrete is $1\frac{1}{4}$ in.

A technique for improving the durability of concrete in cold climates from freezing and thawing and from chemicals such as salt is air-entraining. Air-entrained concrete contains minute air bubbles throughout the mixture. This is produced by using an air-entraining cement or an air-entraining admixture during the mixing of concrete.

Joints in concrete walks or paved areas are very important. Isolation or expansion joints are used to separate pavement from buildings and other elements such as steps and to permit horizontal or vertical movement during the freeze-thaw cycle. In special locations where, for example, steps meet a walk slip dowels are used to permit horizontal movement while stopping vertical movement, which could cause a safety problem as a result of someone tripping in a place where frost heaving has occurred.

Generally, isolation joints are placed between buildings and concrete

FIG. 9-16 This paving pattern of smooth concrete bands with aggregate concrete infill acts as an integral part of the design of the student union at MIT, Cambridge, Massachusetts.

FIG. 9-17 The texture of smooth concrete blocks adjacent to aggregate concrete produces an interesting rhythm.

FIG. 9-18 Interlocking Z-pavers in conjunction with aggregate concrete pavers produces contrast in color and texture, along with rhythm, at the University of Scranton, Pennsylvania (Photograph courtesy of Bellante, Clauss, Miller & Partners).

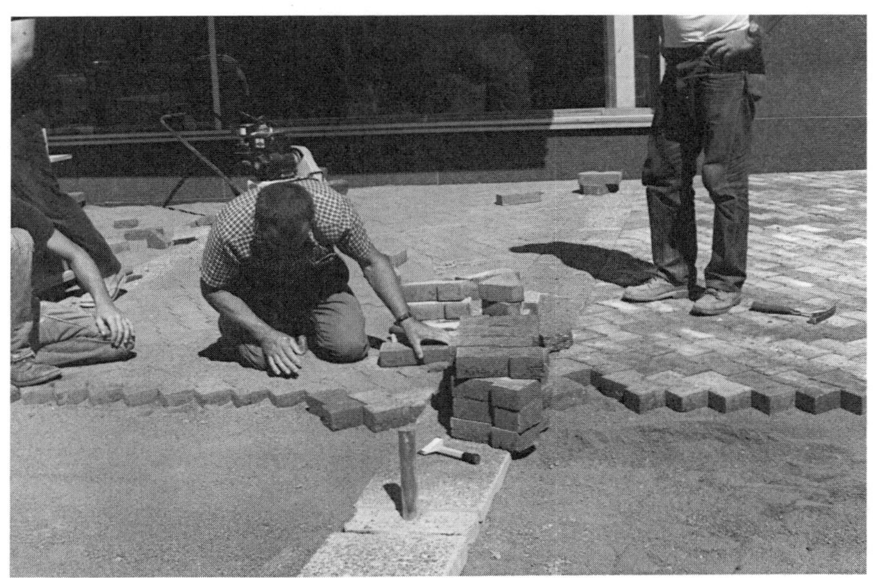

FIG. 9-19 Installation detail of interlocking concrete pavers placed on a coarse aggregate setting bed.

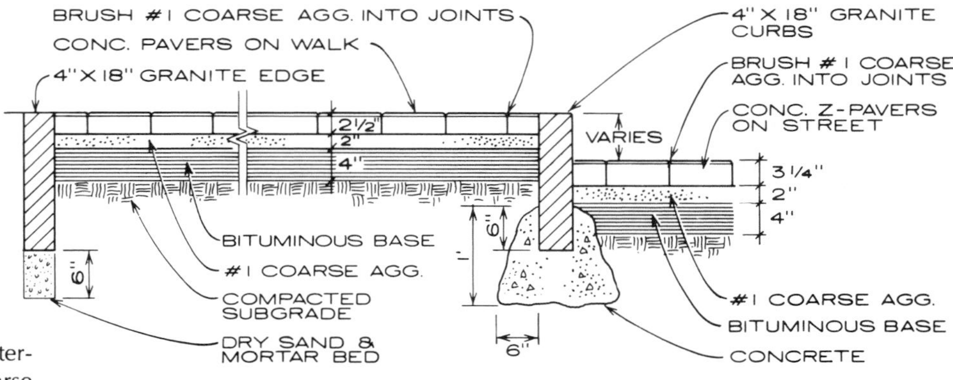

FIG. 9-20 Section of walk with interlocking concrete pavers set on a coarse aggregate bed over a bituminous base coarse.

FIG. 9-21 Varying colors of aggregate are used in this triangular paving pattern at Mellon Square, Pittsburgh, Pennsylvania.

FIG. 9-22 A scoring pattern is placed in this aggregate concrete paving at Constitution Plaza, Hartford, Connecticut.

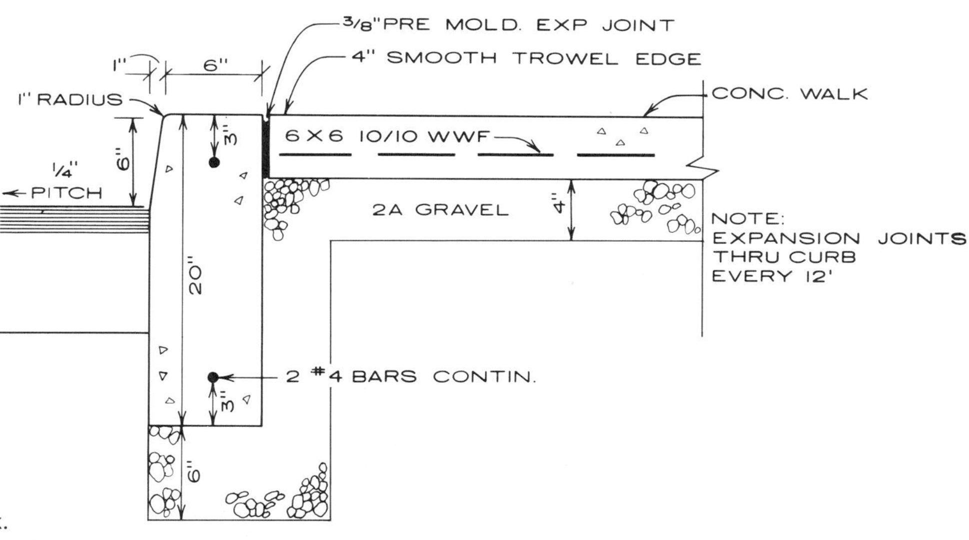

FIG. 9-23 Concrete curb and walk.

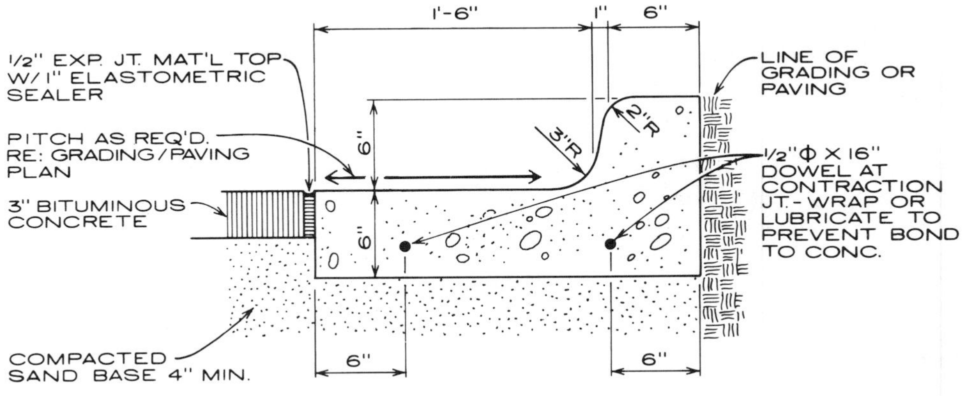

FIG. 9-24 Concrete curb and gutter detail.

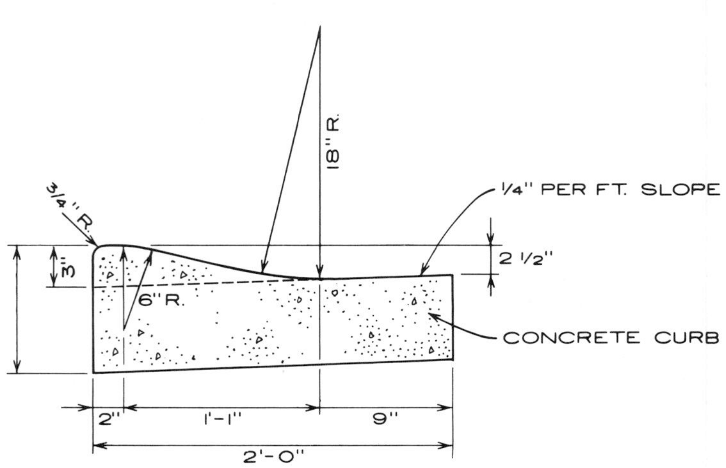

FIG. 9-25 Rolled concrete curb.

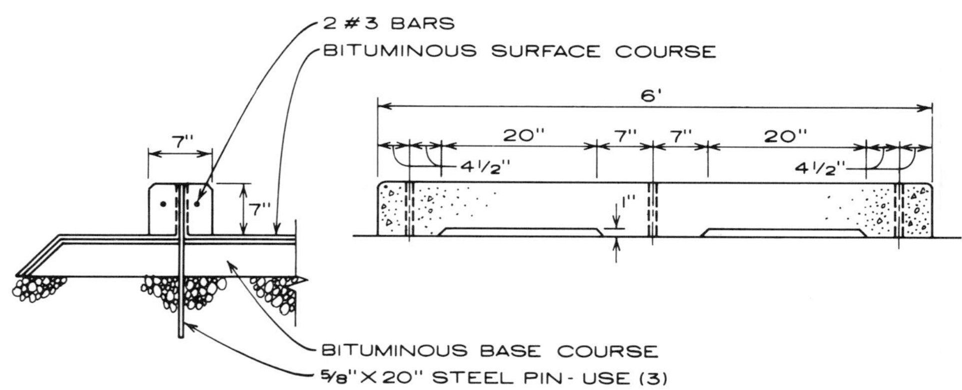

FIG. 9-26 Precast concrete wheel stops.

plazas, around columns adjacent to concrete paving, and every 20 to 30 ft between paving blocks. Material used such as preformed filler comes in various thicknesses such as $\frac{3}{8}$ or $\frac{1}{2}$ in. sizes.

Control or contraction joints are used to allow for contraction caused by drying or shrinkage. If control joints are not used random cracks will occur in paved areas. Generally, control joints are placed each 15 to 25 ft in both directions and are $\frac{1}{5}$ to $\frac{1}{3}$ the slab thickness. They can be formed by a trowel edging tool or by a saw cut.

Construction joints allow for no movement and are the stopping place in the process of building concrete pavement. They can perform as control joints where necessary. There are preformed keyed construction joints, or steel dowels can be used.

Concrete pavers are available in many shapes, sizes, and textures. Some types look like brick and have interlocking shapes for added stability. This material may be placed on sand above a compacted gravel base. Some pavers are available with an 8000 to 9000 psi and are resistant to salt.

Concrete may also be poured in place and may be finished in a variety of textures such as rough board finish or with exposed aggregate. Exposed aggregate can be constructed by use of a water process before the concrete has set, a retardant, acid and wire brush or sand blasting.

In heavily used pedestrian areas where an aggregate concrete texture is desired the aggregate size should be about $\frac{3}{8}$ in. in diameter.

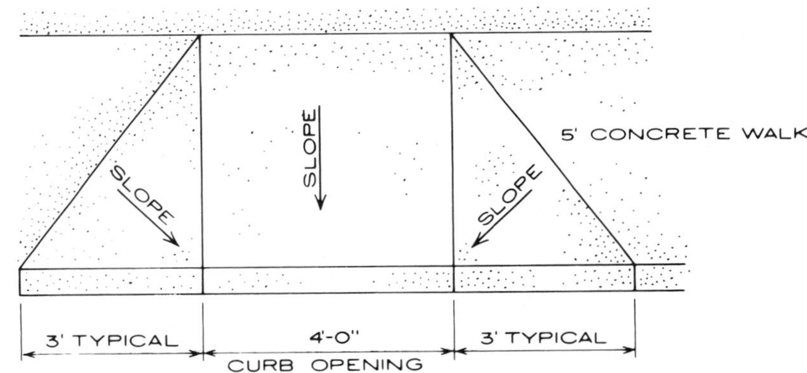

FIG. 9-27 Plan of concrete wheelchair ramp.

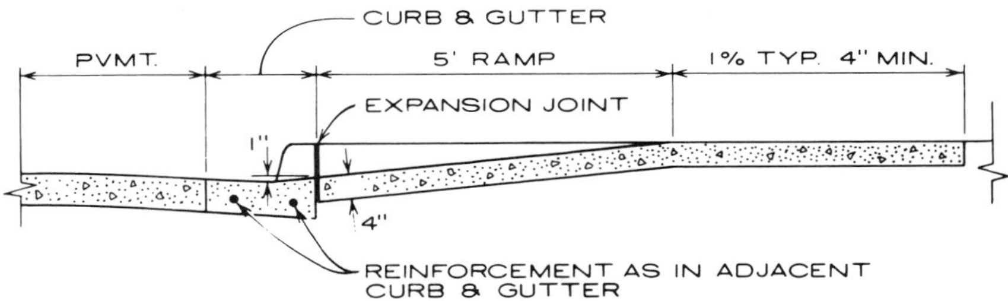

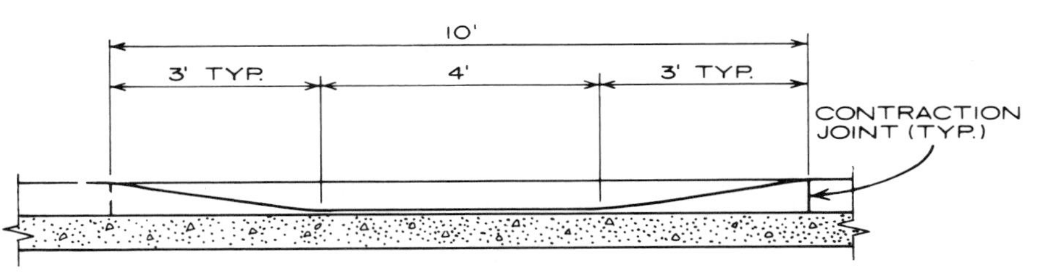

FIG. 9-28 Section and elevation of wheelchair ramp.

Asphalt. Although it gives a softer walking surface, asphalt lacks the variety of textures concrete has. It is not as durable as concrete, but it is less expensive and is used extensively for walk systems on college campuses and in park and recreation areas as well as in the construction of roads and parking areas. (See Figs. 9-29 to 9-32.)

Paving Color

The color of paving material is an important aesthetic and functional design consideration. Color adds interest in areas overcast with limited sunshine during winter months. Conversely, areas that provide the reflection of sunlight from light colored materials are uncomfortable to pedestrian's vision and must be a consideration when the choice of paving materials is made. Also of importance in color selection is the context of the project and the compatibility or contrast with materials used on existing buildings or other structures.

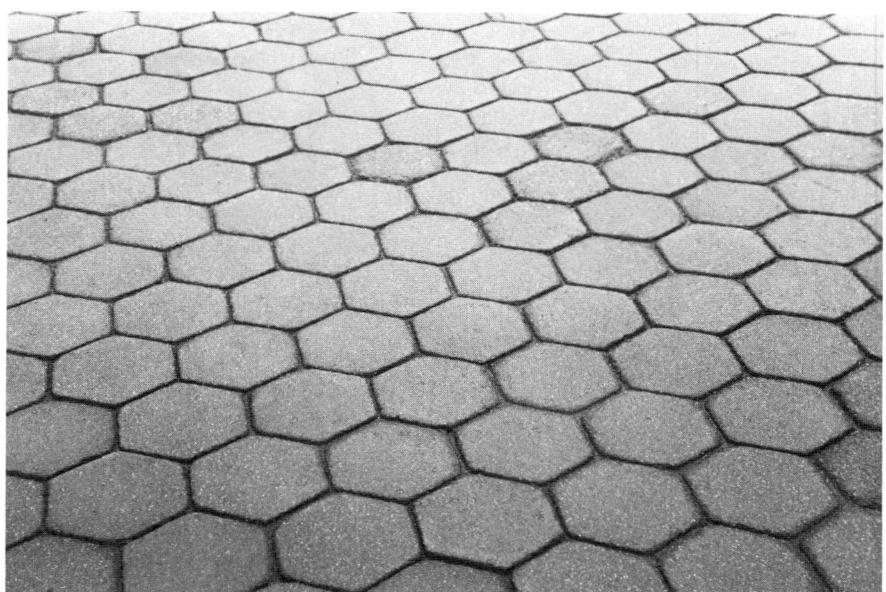

FIG. 9-29 Hexagonal pavers are used for pedestrian walks or plaza areas.

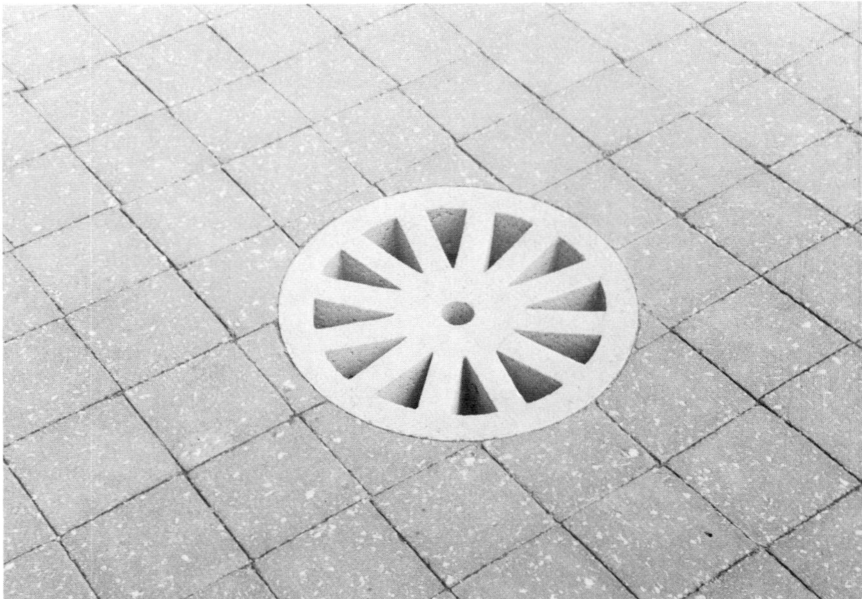

FIG. 9-30 Precast concrete drain and square bituminous pavers.

FIG. 9-31 Precast concrete grates allow water to be absorbed by trees and provide added interest in the paving pattern.

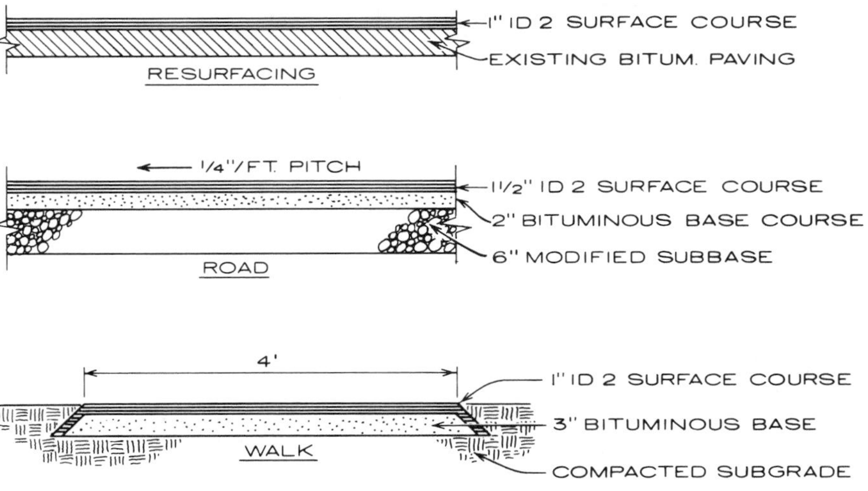

FIG. 9-32 Typical bituminous paving details.

Durability and Maintenance

Durability and ease of maintenance are necessary considerations in the choice of paving materials and curbs. A low initial cost of material may not be the prime consideration. In cold climates materials resistant to snow melting chemicals should be reviewed. For example, granite is quite dense and when used for curbs lasts much longer than concrete.

Tree Grates

Tree grates when used in paved areas can become part of the paving pattern. Grates are used where trees are planted directly in the base plane of a project. They allow air and moisture to reach the tree while limiting compaction.

Tree grates also provide a wider expanse on which to walk adjacent to trees and add interest in scale, pattern, color, and texture. Night-lighting can also be incorporated in the tree grates to give added appeal at night. (See Figs. 9-33 and 9-34.)

FIG. 9-33 Cast iron expandable tree grates are often used in urban areas. This grate was adapted for use with Z-pavers at the Wyoming Avenue Plaza, Scranton, Pennsylvania.

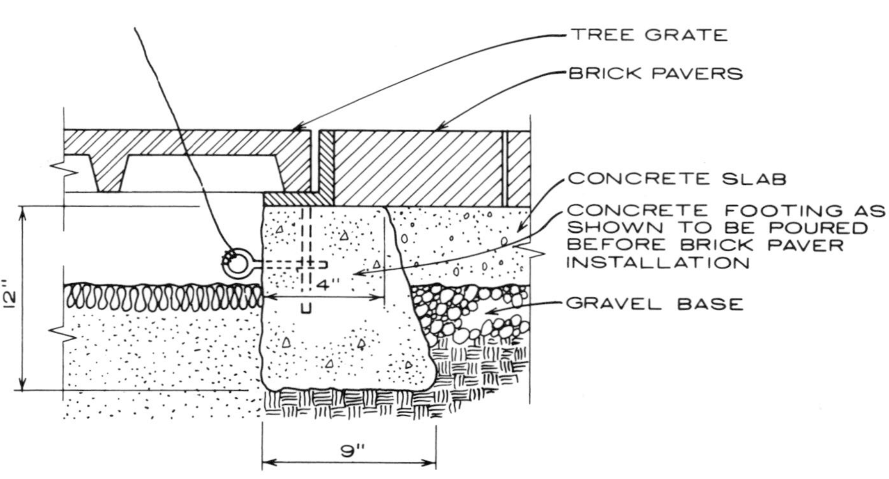

FIG. 9-34 Detail, section of tree grate.

Walls

Walls may be used to provide enclosure, articulate a space, or act as retaining elements. Brick, stone, and concrete are the materials most commonly used. The height and type of walls vary with their use in the overall design concept of a project. They may be at seating height or may be up to 6 ft or more to provide privacy.

Used most extensively in high density projects where land is expensive, retaining walls may save usable areas that would otherwise be occupied by banks. Walls may also act to reinforce and strengthen the design concept for a site; for example, on a steep site, they may reinforce an architectural concept by stepping up sloping land in conjunction with a building, or they may penetrate into the landscape and act as directional elements guiding people to a building. Determining the necessity of walls is therefore a site design and/or grading problem. (See Fig. 9-35.)

Generally, reinforced concrete is the most economical material for constructing retaining walls; however, dry stone masonry may also be used where good quality stone is available. Dry stone walls generally have a maximum height of 3 to 5 ft and need not have a footing greater than 12 to 18 in. below finished grade. On the other hand, reinforced concrete walls have a footing that may vary from 30 to 36 in. or more below grade for frost protection. (See Figs. 9-36 to 9-53.)

FIG. 9-35 This brick retaining wall steps up the sloping site at Wellesley College, Wellesley, Massachusetts.

FIG. 9-36 This brick wall with rod iron segments at transition areas works well in stepping down the site in Fort Worth, Texas.

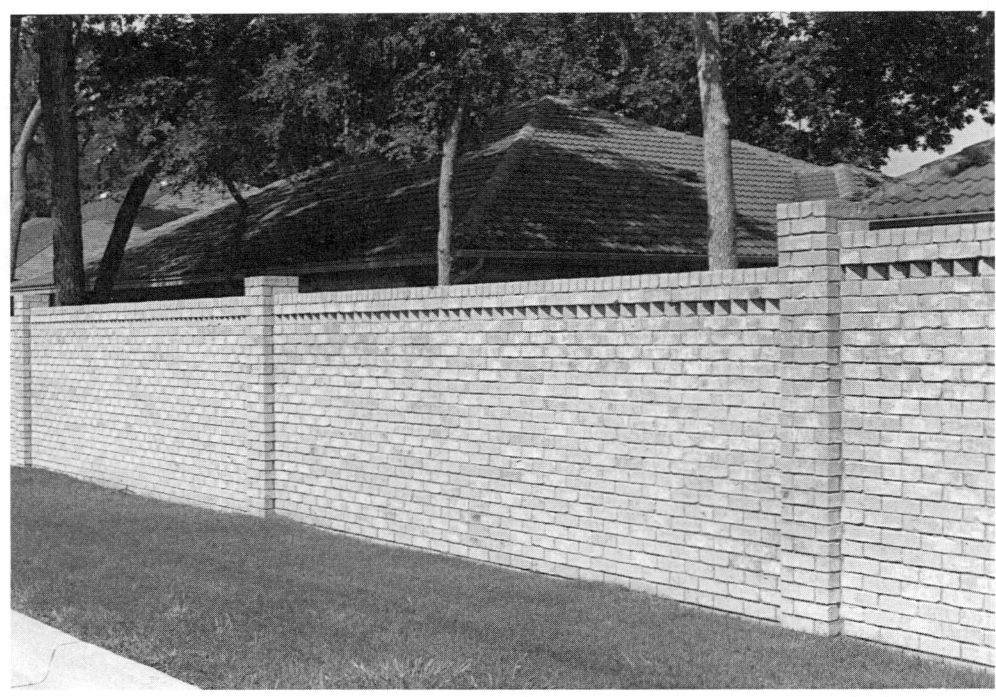

FIG. 9-37 Brick screen wall in a running bond pattern.

FIG. 9-38 This brick screen wall follows the boundary line of the site. The reveal/expansion joint also adds interest to the wall design.

FIG. 9-39 This brick screen wall steps down the site and is designed with niches to save existing trees.

FIG. 9-40 This serpentine brick wall winds its way around existing trees to form an outdoor terrace at the Loeb Drama Center, Cambridge, Massachusetts.

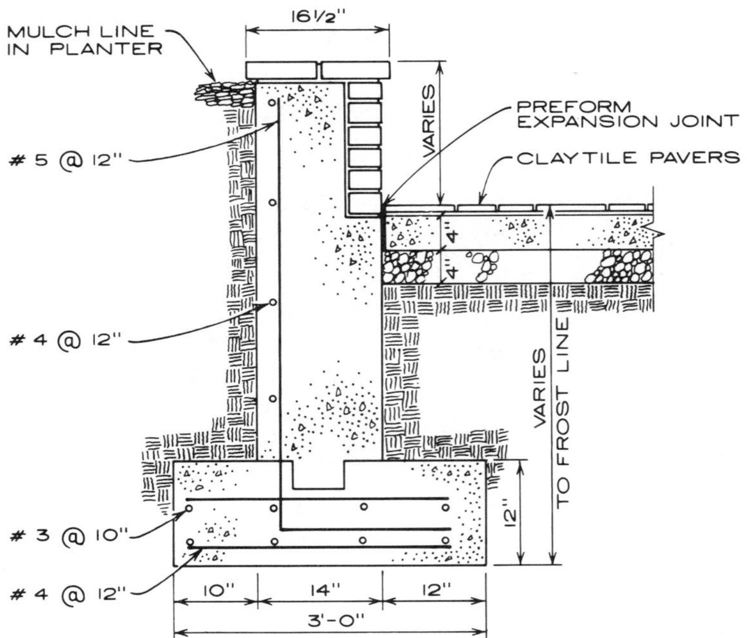

FIG. 9-41 Brick retaining wall. Wall design should be checked by a structural engineer.

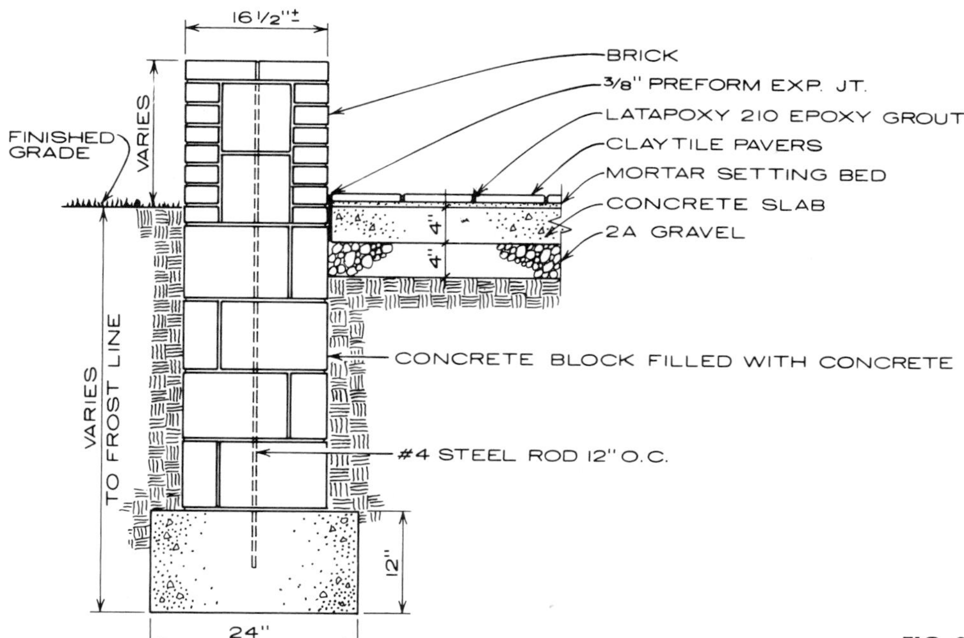

FIG. 9-42 Freestanding brick wall.

FIG. 9-43 Irregular fitted stone retaining wall.

FIG. 9-44 Rubble stone retaining wall.

FIG. 9-45 Marble retaining wall at Georgia Plaza, Atlanta, provides an interesting use of texture.

FIG. 9-46 Dry stone retaining wall.

FIG. 9-47 This dry stone retaining wall extends the building outward to form an entry courtyard at the Bushkill Headquarters Building in the Delaware Water Gap National Recreation Area (Photograph courtesy Bellante, Clauss, Miller & Partners).

FIG. 9-48 Milsap stone retaining wall.

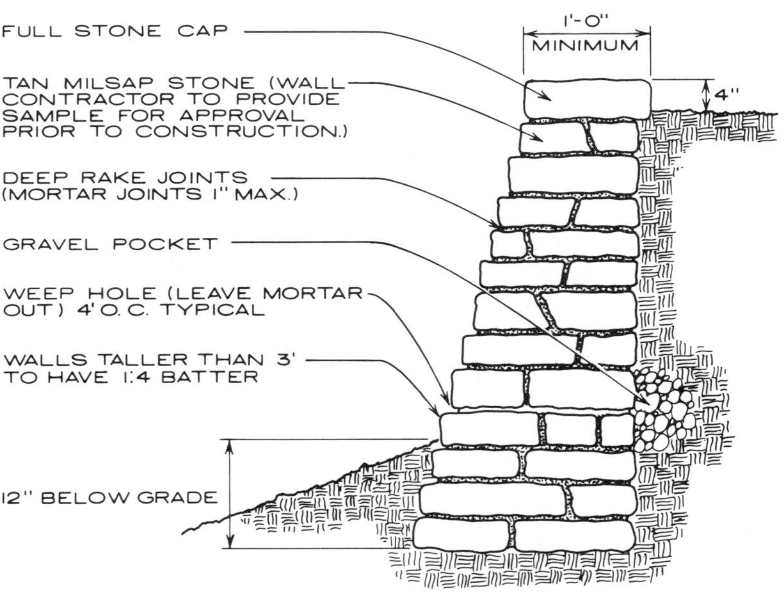

FIG. 9-49 Stone wall details should be checked by a structural engineer if higher than 3 ft.

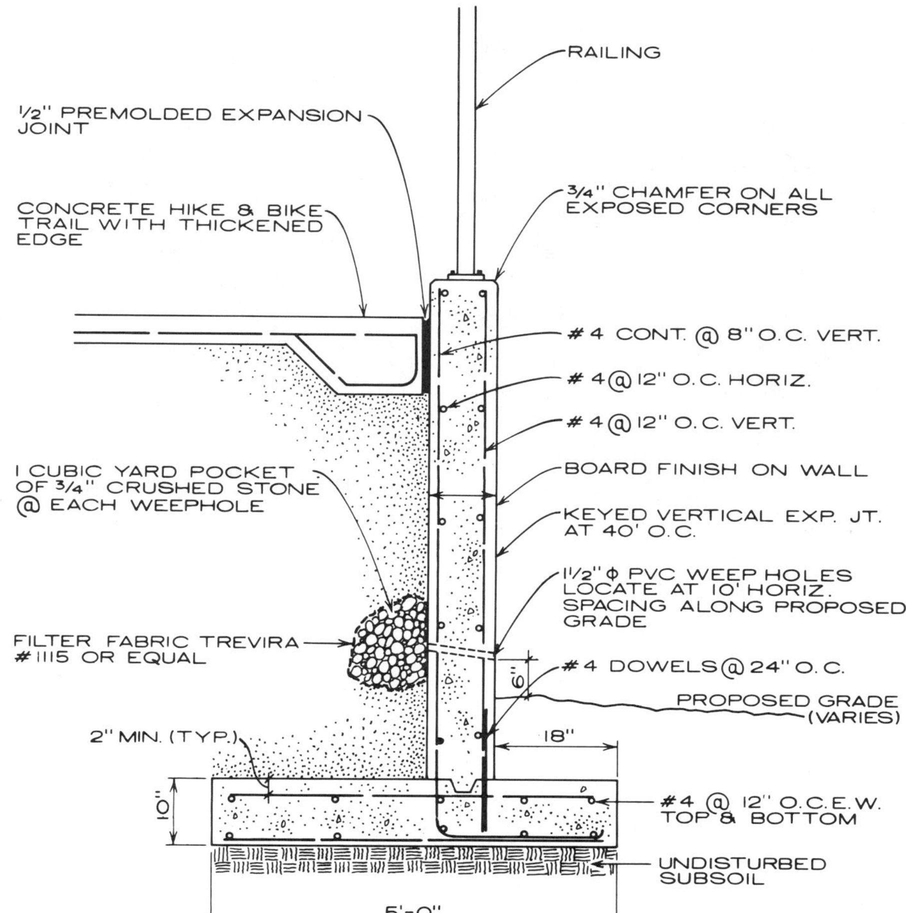

FIG. 9-50 Cross section of a typical concrete retaining wall detail, maximum height 5 ft. Wall design should be checked by a structural engineer.

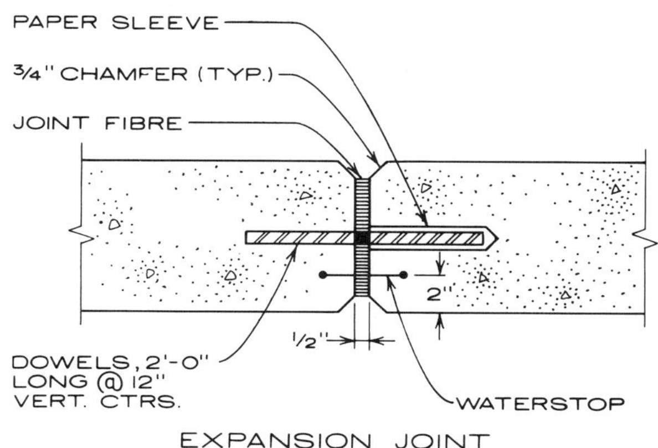

FIG. 9-51 Detail of retaining wall joints.

FIG. 9-52 Typical railroad tie retaining wall. These should be checked by a structural engineer if over 4 ft high.

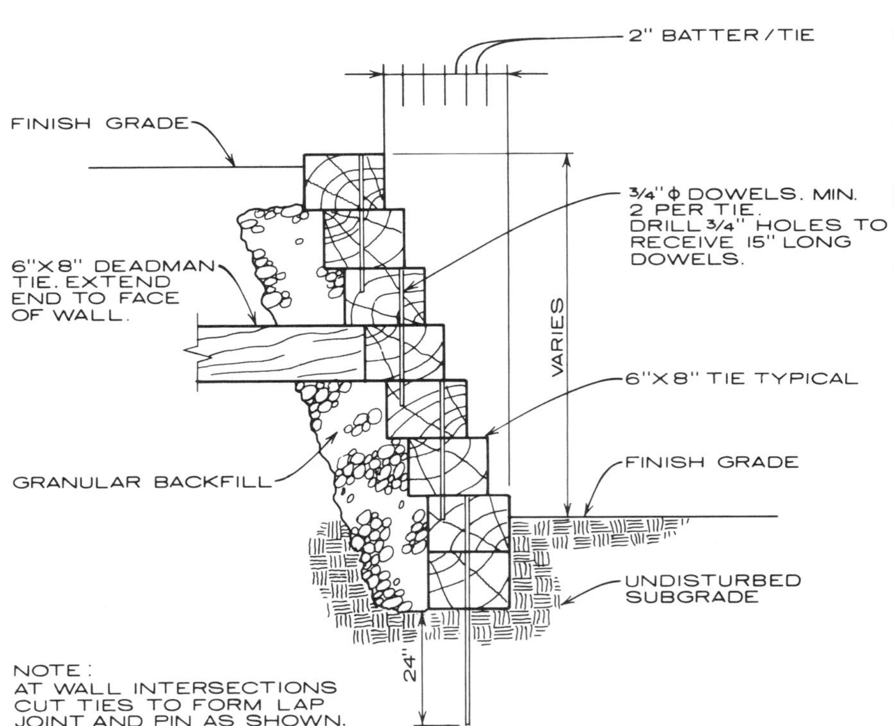

FIG. 9-53 Detail of railroad tie wall.

Steps

Steps act as a connection between levels where grades are excessive. They may also be used to give prominence to entry areas or areas containing features such as fountains or sculpture. Steps should be designed for comfort with a riser and tread ratio best fitting the slope, considering the use of the area. (See p. 73.) Steps should be built into the slope and have a foundation that goes below frost level. They are constructed of various materials such as concrete, brick, stone, or a combination of these. (See Figs. 9-54 to 9-63.)

FIG. 9-54 The detail of these steps at the University of California, Los Angeles, has a high degree of refinement because of choice materials, reveals, and shadow patterns.

FIG. 9-55 These board finished concrete steps form an integral part of the architectural character of the University of Colorado, Boulder.

FIG. 9-56 These steps made of stone have a ramp as part of their design.

FIG. 9-57 Perrons at Kimbell Art Museum, Fort Worth, Texas.

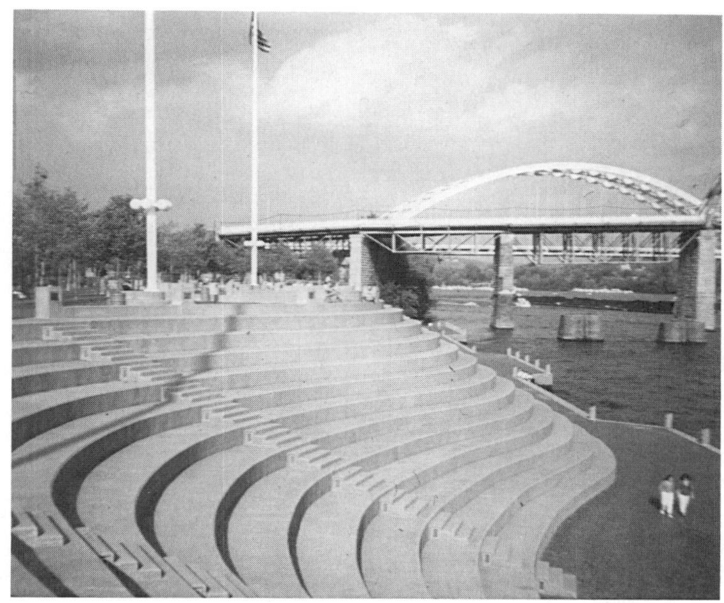

FIG. 9-58 These concrete steps form a strong edge along Riverfront Park in Cincinnati, Ohio.

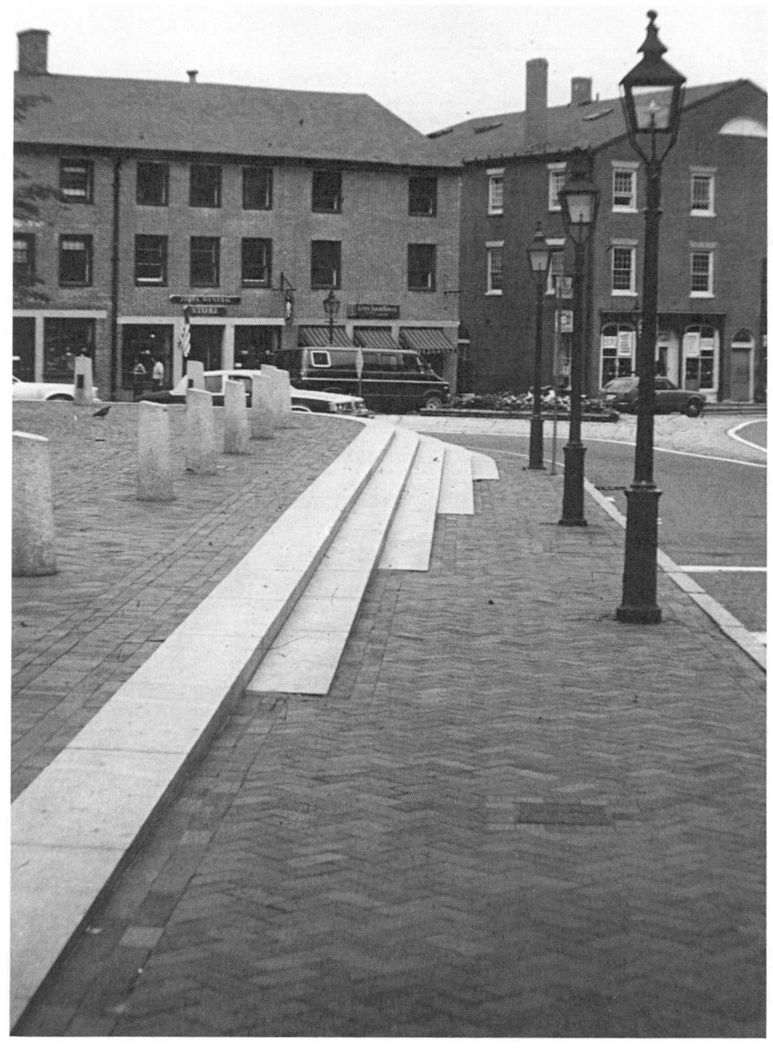

FIG. 9-59 Steps at Newburyport, Massachusetts.

FIG. 9-60 Concrete steps and terraces at Essex Mall, Salem, Massachusetts.

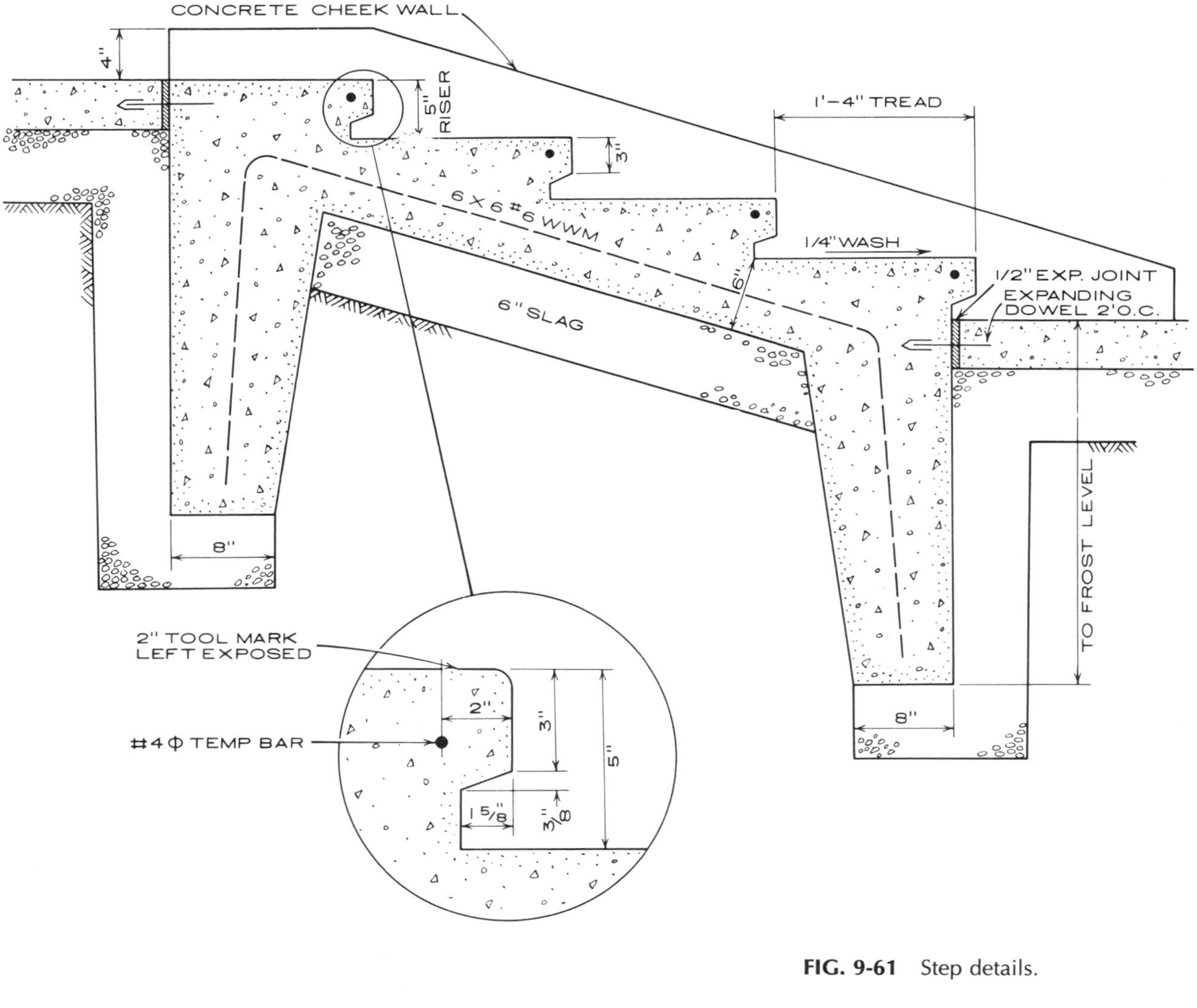

FIG. 9-61 Step details.

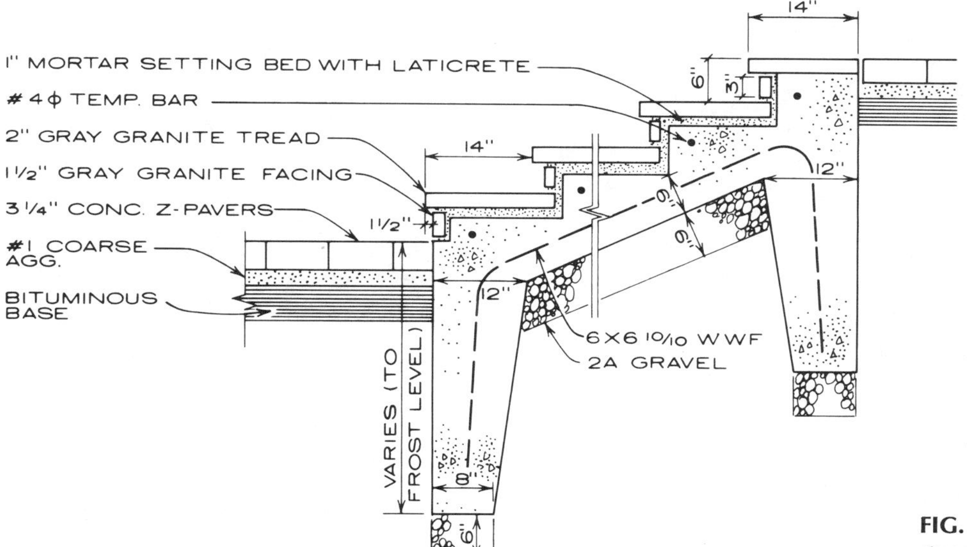

FIG. 9-62 Section of granite-capped steps.

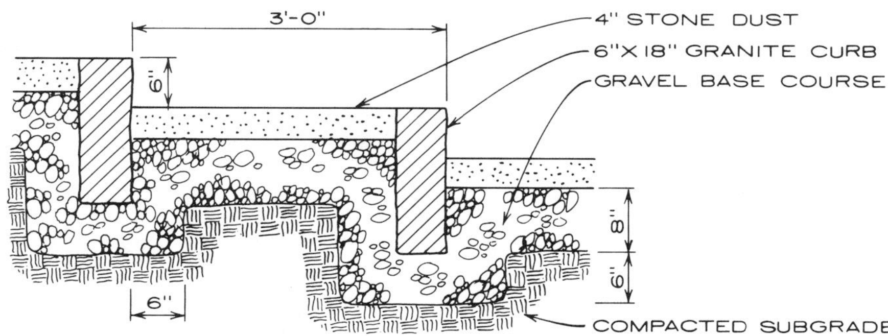

FIG. 9-63 Section of perron steps with granite riser.

Sculpture

Sculpture and other artworks such as wall reliefs are important design elements that act as focal points in outdoor spaces. They improve the sensory quality of a place and help to create an environment people enjoy.

Landscape architects and architects should meet in the early stages of a project with a sculptor to discuss a proposed sculpture's setting, scale, form, mass, and color. Outdoor sculpture requires sufficient mass to stand out against an appropriate background.

The size and scale of a sculpture should relate to its setting. A sculpture must be large enough to have an impact on its environment. The form of a sculpture will either complement or contrast with its setting. An infinite variety of forms can be expressed in such materials as stone, metal, wood, or plastic. (See Figs. 9-64 to 9-78.)

FIG. 9-64 This sculptural stone bench is used at Levi Plaza, San Francisco, California.

FIG. 9-65 Sculpture composed and oriented to be seen easily against a wooded backdrop of the Connecticut General Insurance Building.

FIG. 9-66 This sculpture by Noguchi takes advantage of sunlight and shadow patterns.

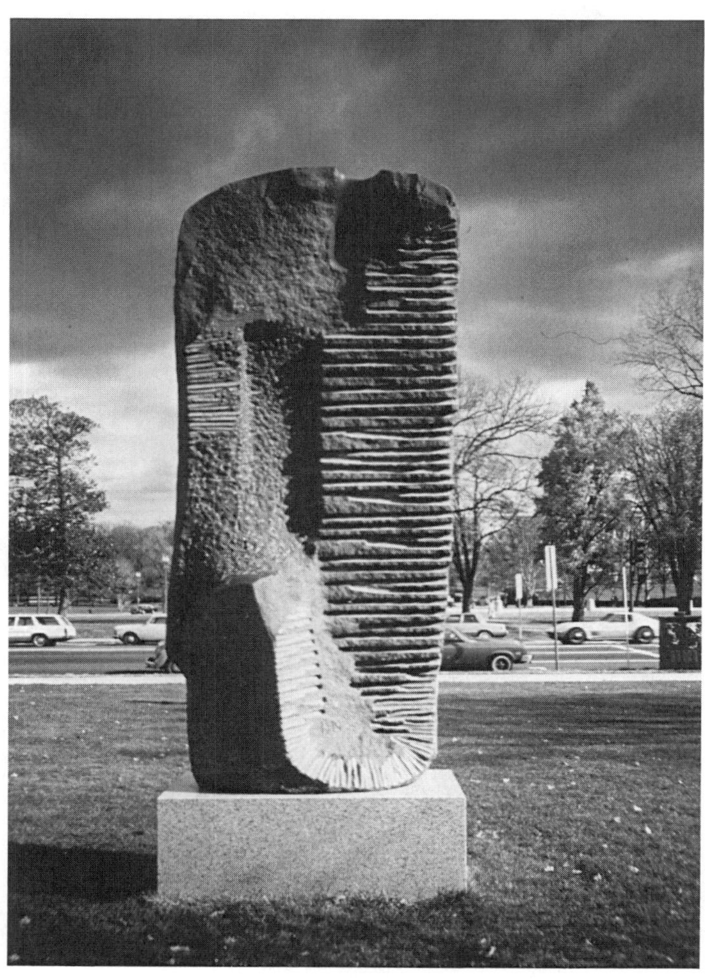

FIG. 9-67 Stone sculpture at National Gallery, Washington, D.C.

FIG. 9-68 Charles Perry's sculpture, "Early Mace," is located on Peachtree Street in Atlanta, Georgia.

FIG. 9-69 Steel sculpture at Lincoln Centre, Dallas, Texas.

FIG. 9-70 This sculpture by Calder acts as the focal point in this space at MIT, Cambridge, Massachusetts.

FIG. 9-71 Steel sculpture by Calder at Lincoln Plaza, Dallas, Texas.

FIG. 9-72 Steel sculpture at Princeton University, Princeton, New Jersey.

FIG. 9-73 Sculpture by Henry Moore.

FIG. 9-74 Bronze sculpture by Henry Moore at Amon Carter Museum, Fort Worth, Texas.

FIG. 9-75 Sculpture in front of water wall at Dallas Art Museum, Dallas, Texas.

FIG. 9-76 This sculpture also acts as a sundial at the Quorum, Addison, Texas.

FIG. 9-77 Sculpture at the Spectrum, Dallas, Texas.

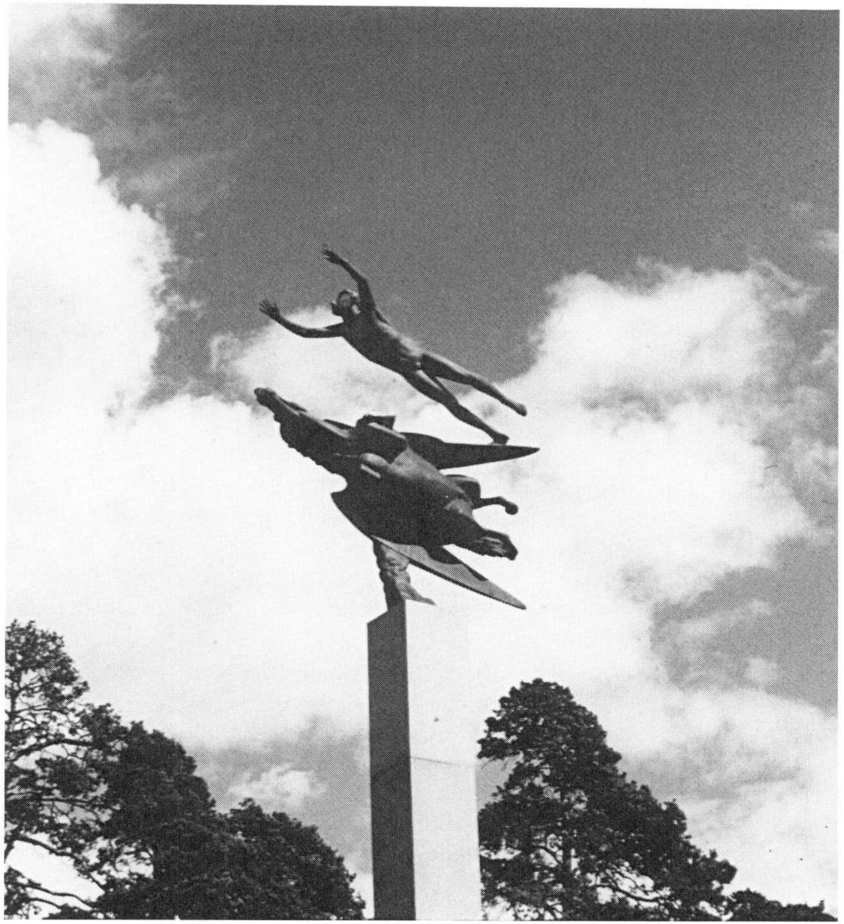

FIG. 9-78 Bronze sculpture at the Milles Garden, Stockholm, Sweden.

The color of a sculpture is often related to the type of material, such as granite, bronze, stainless steel, or weathering steel. Metal can also be painted in a wide variety of colors.

Sculpture is often experienced from several viewpoints or directions and the treatment of the foreground as well as the background should be considered in placing the sculpture. There should also be adequate space adjacent to the sculpture for viewing from varying sight lines, for example, as one walks around it or views it while sitting.

Orientation must also be studied in the placement of a sculpture. Sunlight and shadow patterns vary during different times of the day and with seasonal change. It is therefore advantageous to position a sculpture so it benefits the greatest from sunlight and shadow patterns.

How a sculpture meets the ground is also important to the work's height and the way it is viewed. Sculpture may extend from the base plane or be placed on an elevated base or in a planter or fountain. It may also be anchored to a building.

The installation of a sculpture is another consideration. Special foundations or equipment may be necessary such as a crane to set the sculpture in place.

A sculpture gets added appeal from night-lighting. Important considerations are the location, type, angle, and amount of illumination. Light may be directed from above, or below, foreground, background, or a combination of these.

Fountains and Pools

Fountains and pools are often the focal elements of outdoor spaces. Water, a natural element, can be a prominent feature in the landscape. It may be used in fountains or pools for its reflective qualities, differences in sound, or cooling effect. (See Figs. 9-79 to 9-117.)

Fountains often have sculptural elements, which, in cool climates, act as the focus during winter months. Orientation plays an important part in the reflection of sunlight on the sculpture or off the water feature.

Pool Size. Generally the minimum radius of a pool is equal to the spray height under normal wind conditions of up to 10 mph. Beyond this size the pool should be increased 10% for every additional 5 mph of wind speed designed for, or a wind control system can be used.

Pool Depth. Water depth is generally 16 in. with the wall height or freeboard above water level designed at 6 in. Where wave action or splash is minimal less freeboard may be used but 4 in. is the smallest height recommended. In pools with waterfalls greater freeboard may be needed in the lowest pool to contain larger waves. Also in waterfalls both wall height and water level controls must be designed to consider the volume of water recirculated to upper pools when the pumps begin operating and the volume of water stored in the lowest pool when the pumps are turned off.

Water Effects. Many effects can be used in the design of a fountain such as sprays, jets, waterfalls, and reflecting pools. Nozzles, available in a wide variety of sizes and effects, may generally be rotated about 15° in all directions to aim the water properly. The amount of water flowing through various nozzles can vary from as little as one gallon per minute to hundreds of gallons per minute.

There are two basic waterfall designs: smooth-sheet waterfalls and aerated waterfalls. Generally a minimum water depth of $\frac{1}{2}$ in. is needed for waterfalls, but additional depth can be more effective. Metal attached to the waterfall weirs produces a smooth sheet and can be adjusted to be level. Where a metal edge is used on a weir as little as $\frac{1}{4}$ in. of water can produce a sheet effect. Flat weirs can also be effective in creating a smooth sheet of water.

FIG. 9-79 Water flows from a bowl in this fountain at the University of Colorado, Boulder.

FIG. 9-80 A seating area overlooks this gushing fountain by Sasaki Associates at the University of Colorado, Boulder.

FIG. 9-81 Water gushes in this fountain adjacent to the Travelers Insurance Building at Hartford.

FIG. 9-82 Water pours from spouts in concrete elements at Northwest Plaza, St. Louis, Missouri.

Aerated waterfalls that create a foamy flow can be produced where at least three steps are used. The water flowing over the first step gives a sheet-flow effect but by the third step the water becomes aerated. Generally, the water flowing over the first step is one-eighth of the step height. Therefore a $\frac{1}{2}$ in. depth of water would require a 4 in. step height or riser while a $1\frac{1}{2}$ in. depth would need a 12 in. riser. Step width or treads should generally be equal to or 25% greater than the step riser.

Fountain Details. The bottoms of fountains are often painted black to add reflective qualities to the surface of a pool and to the feeling of depth. Pool bottoms are also often paved with brick or stone.

Edges, Coping, or Steps. Some fountains are designed for people to wade or walk through while others are for viewing only. Coping, when used, acts as a safety barrier, provides a place for sitting, and limits the view of fountain equipment.

Materials. Fountains must be built of weather and crack resistant materials. Often concrete, which is poured in place is used. Brick or tile can be placed over the concrete as a base.

A material's color and its resistance to stains are also important considerations. For example, knowing that weathering steel stains plain concrete, it is necessary to avoid that combination. Precase concrete, which is durable and crack resistant, can be used for fountain elements such as copings and bowls.

FIG. 9-83 Water works along with the sculpture in this fountain at Northwest Plaza, St. Louis, Missouri. Steps leading to the fountain give it prominence and may be used for seating.

FIG. 9-84 Weathering steel elements form this sculptural fountain at Northeastern Bank Plaza, Scranton, Pennsylvania (Photograph courtesy of Bellante, Clauss, Miller & Partners).

FIG. 9-85 Night-lighting effect at Northeastern Bank Plaza, Scranton, Pennsylvania.

FIG. 9-86 Bronze sculpture with horses at Williams Square, Las Colinas, Irving, Texas.

FIG. 9-87 Fountain with bronze figures at Girardelli Square, San Francisco, California.

FIG. 9-88 Fountain at Fountain Square, Cincinnati, Ohio.

Waterproof Membranes. These are used to prevent water from leaking from the fountain and causing problems on places like rooftop plazas. They can be sprayed on or applied from rolls as is felt roofing material.

Mechanical Systems. Generally, mechanical engineers experienced in fountain design plan these systems, which are usually equipped with more than the minimum capacity needed to operate the fountain. Pumps, piping, and storage tanks for water recirculation are generally made larger than needed to allow the system built-in flexibility. The pump, for example, can be throttled down to avoid its having to operate at maximum capacity.

Pipe. Piping for fountains is often copper with brass fittings. If galvanized pipe is connected to copper, electrolysis will result in thermal decomposition where the materials are joined. Dielectric fittings help limit this problem.

Drains are placed in the pool bottom for draining; afterward, the pool can be cleaned or winterized. There are also filtering systems, chlorine injectors, wind and automatic controls that can be used to add water wasted by spillage or evaporation. Completely automatic equipment is available to turn a fountain on or off and to control other equipment.

An adequate mechanical equipment room must be provided beneath the fountain or in an adjacent building. Also space for servicing this equipment must be provided.

FIG. 9-89 Granite elements form fountain at the Main Street Mall, Charlottesville, Virginia.

FIG. 9-90 Civic Center Forecourt Fountain, Portland, Oregon, by Lawrence Halprin & Associates has a very exciting use of water and was designed for participation by people.

FIG. 9-91 Waterfall and plaza area at Lovejoy Fountain, Portland, Oregon, by Lawrence Halprin & Associates.

FIG. 9-92 Lovejoy Fountain, Portland, Oregon.

FIG. 9-93 This fountain at the Water Garden in Fort Worth, Texas, is an abstraction of the Grand Canyon. It was designed by Johnson/Burgee Architects.

FIG. 9-94 Water Garden, Fort Worth, Texas.

FIG. 9-95 Spray pool at the Water Garden in Fort Worth, Texas, is set below grade to keep water from spraying onto plaza areas.

FIG. 9-96 Fountain with water stair at Lincoln Centre, Dallas, Texas.

FIG. 9-97 Fountain at Levi Plaza, San Francisco, California. Architect of buildings Hellmuth, Obata & Kassabaum, Inc., landscape architect Lawrence Halprin & Associates.

FIG. 9-98 Fountains at Tampa City Center Esplanade, Tampa, Florida.

FIG. 9-99 Water wall at Thanksgiving Square, Dallas, Texas.

FIG. 9-100 Fountain at Aquarium, Boston, Massachusetts.

FIG. 9-101 Fountain and waterfalls at Paseo del Alamo in San Antonio, Texas, in the Riverwalk tourist area.

FIG. 9-102 Water pouring in streams at the fountain at Paseo del Alamo in San Antonio, Texas.

FIG. 9-103 Waterfalls at Paseo del Alamo in San Antonio, Texas.

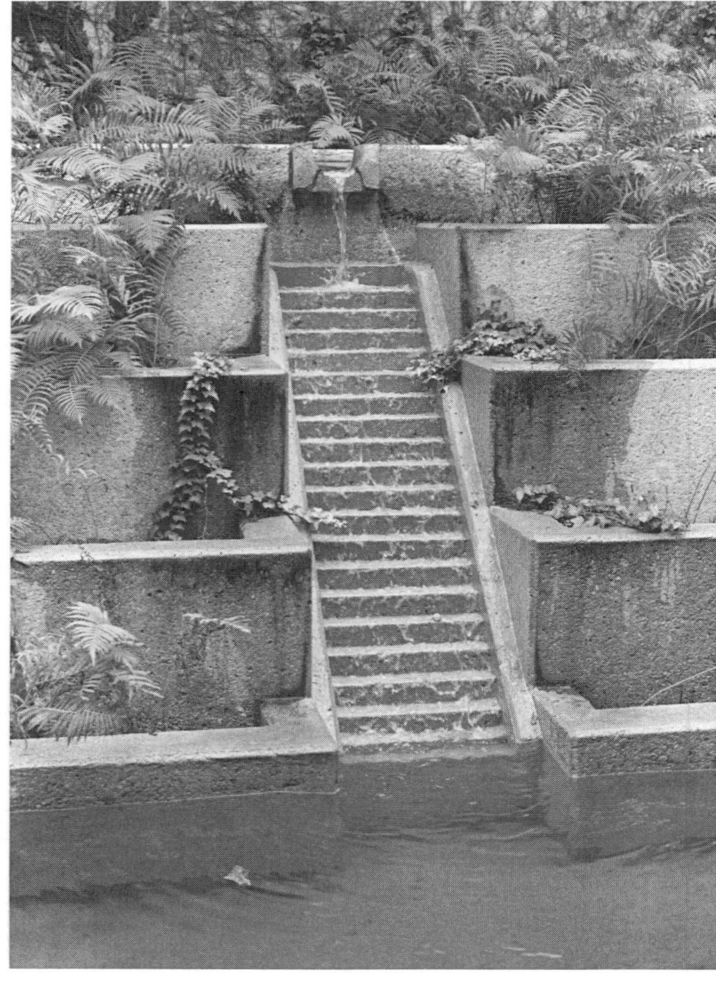

FIG. 9-104 Water stair at Paseo del Alamo, San Antonio, Texas.

FIG. 9-105 Jets of water at St. Louis Station by Hellmuth, Obata, and Kassabaum, Inc. (Photo courtesy of Lynne Rubenstein)

FIG. 9-106 Fountain at Burnett Park, Fort Worth, Texas, by the SWA Group.

FIG. 9-107 Aerated jets and water stair at Penn Square, Reading, Pennsylvania.

FIG. 9-108 Fountain with aerated jets at Lincoln Centre, Dallas, Texas.

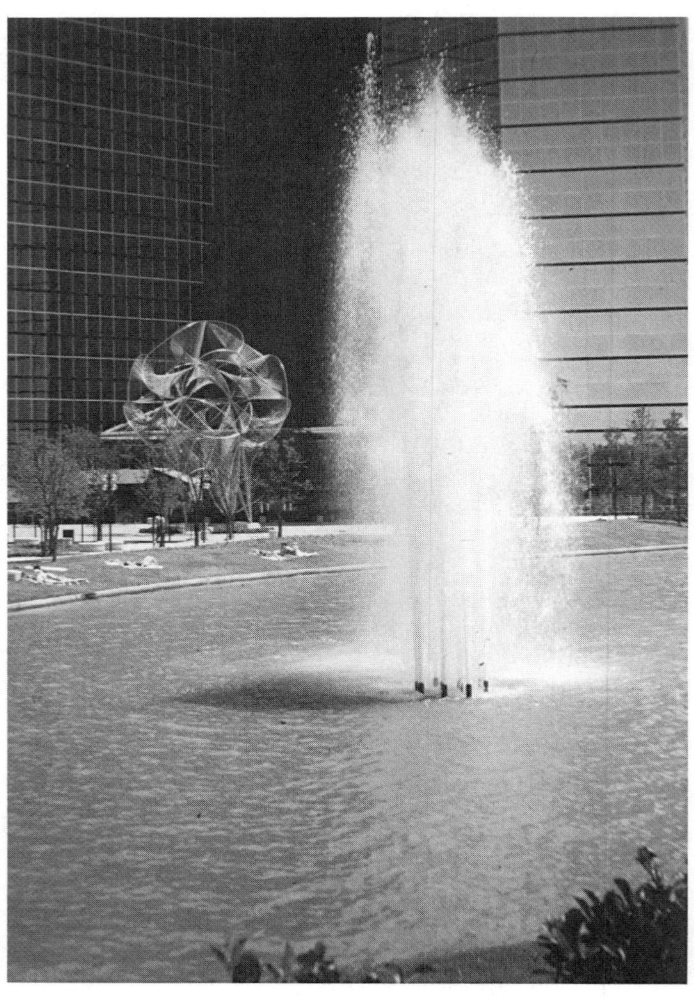

FIG. 9-109 Fountain at Harbour Place, Tampa, Florida.

FIG. 9-110 Los Angeles Civic Center, California.

FIG. 9-111 Los Angeles Civic Center, California.

FIG. 9-112 Los Angeles Civic Center, California.

FIG. 9-113 Los Angeles Civic Center, California.

FIG. 9-114 Los Angeles Civic Center, California.

FIG. 9-115 Water in a pool may be used for its reflective qualities.

FIG. 9-116 Reflecting pool at Christian Science Church, Boston, Massachusetts.

FIG. 9-117 Gravel pool bottoms add interest in shallow water, but if the appearance of depth is desired, a pool bottom may be painted black.

Fountain Lighting. Night-lighting can provide dramatic effects for fountains. The lights can be placed flush with pool bottoms, but they must generally be winterized in cool climates. Protective covers are made for some lights while others must be drained and water-tight gaskets used to seal the light housings. Also, lights set flush in pool bottoms need a minimum of 2 to 3 in. of water in the pool bottom for cooling the lights.

Niche lights can be placed on pedestals and raised to within two in. of the water surface. Good lighting can be achieved in this manner. An important consideration in designing or selecting lighting or other fountain equipment is how the fountain looks when the water is off. Is the equipment ugly? Is it placed beneath protective grating, or is it integrated with the pool walls or floor?

Night-Lighting

Lighting often extends the time for participation in outdoor activities. It provides safety and security and adds interest by accenting feature elements such as fountains or sculptures.

The development of lighting design is often done by landscape architects or architects working with electrical engineers. (See Figs. 9-118 to 9-137.)

In selecting an outdoor lighting fixture the following should be done.

1. Ask for a sample luminaire.
2. Check the housing for tightness at the light source.
3. Do a scratch test on the finish to see how durable it is.
4. Make sure the photometrics are from an independent testing lab that is not owned by the manufacturer.

Illumination. For the feeling of comfort and security, one must have adequate light to illuminate details and to make objects brighter than the sky. If brightness becomes excessive, it becomes glare, which interferes with vision and causes loss of contrast between detail and background.

The unit lumen measures the luminous output of lamps. It is the rate light falls on a 1 ft^2 surface area, with all points being 1 ft from a surface having the intensity of 1 candle.

Illumination on a surface is measured in a footcandle, which is the illumination on 1 ft^2 over which 1 lumen is evenly distributed. Therefore 1 footcandle = 1 lumen/ft^2. The footcandle is the unit used in calculating lighting installations.

Light Sources. Some light sources available for night-lighting are incandescent, fluorescent, and high density discharge lamps such as mercury, metal halide, and high pressure sodium.

Incandescent light has a warm reddish color. Objects are accentuated when this light is used and texture is distinguishable. Using a typical 100 watt A-19 bulb, lamp life is 750 hours with a 1750 lumen output. Extended service bulbs are available that last 2500 to 8000 hours, but have a lower lumen output.

Because of its warm color, incandescent light is best on yellow, red, and brown objects and is very desirable in pedestrian areas where warm color is important.

Fluorescent lamps produce a dull flat light with dark objects viewed in silhouette. Fluorescent bulbs come in bluish, yellowish, or pinkish colors. A 100 watt fluorescent bulb has a lamp life of 12,000 to 18,000 hours and produces about 6300 lumens. Cool white lamps produce a neutral to moderately cool effect with good color acceptance.

While fluorescent lamps have increased efficiency over incandescent

FIG. 9-118 Outdoor street lighting used at the Wyoming Avenue Plaza, Scranton, Pennsylvania, has bronze anodized poles and luminaries with high pressure sodium bulbs (Photograph courtesy of Bellante, Clauss, Miller & Partners).

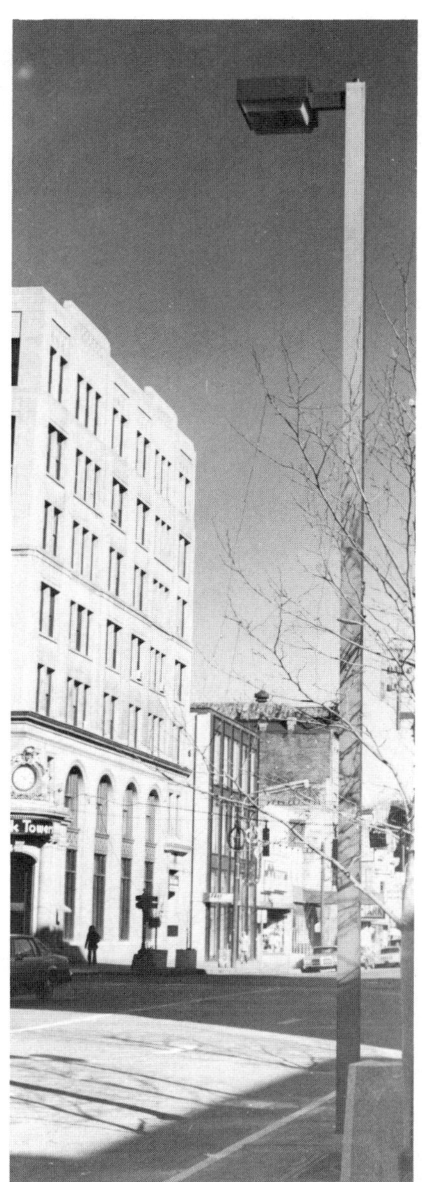

FIG. 9-119 Lighting used on the Essex Mall, Salem, Massachusetts.

FIG. 9-120 Lighting used to work with the entrance design at Allegheny Center, Pittsburgh, Pennsylvania.

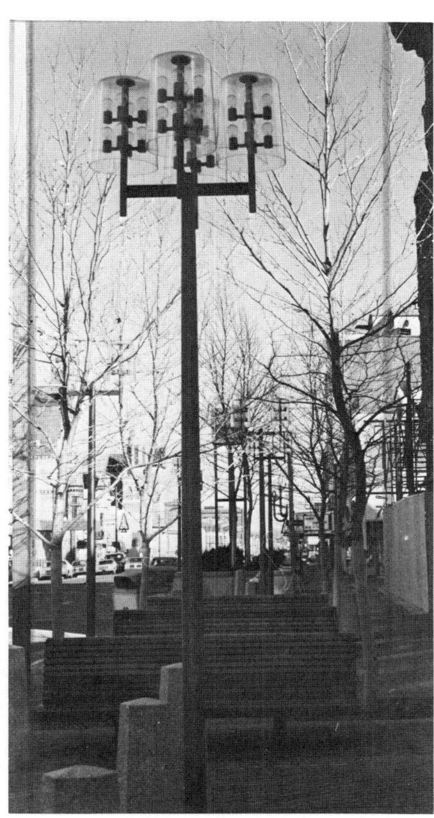

FIG. 9-121 This light uses both clear incandescent traffic signal bulbs and acrylic plastic shades at the Wyoming Avenue Plaza, Scranton, Pennsylvania.

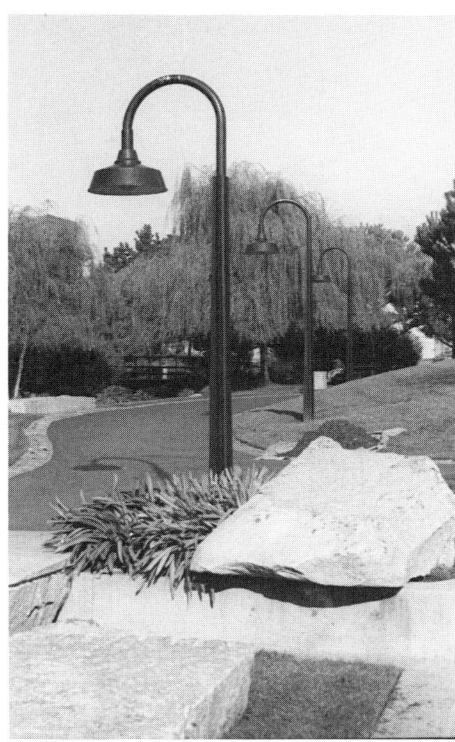

FIG. 9-122 Lighting used at Levi Plaza, San Francisco, California.

FIG. 9-123 Reflected mercury light in clear acrylic luminaire.

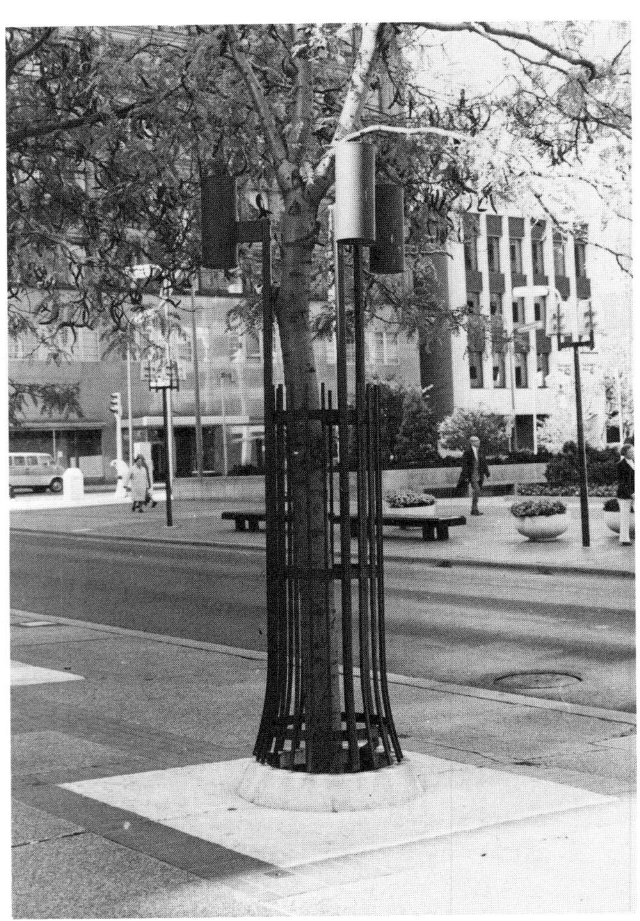

FIG. 9-124 Tree guard and up-lighting at Nicollet Mall, Minneapolis, Minnesota.

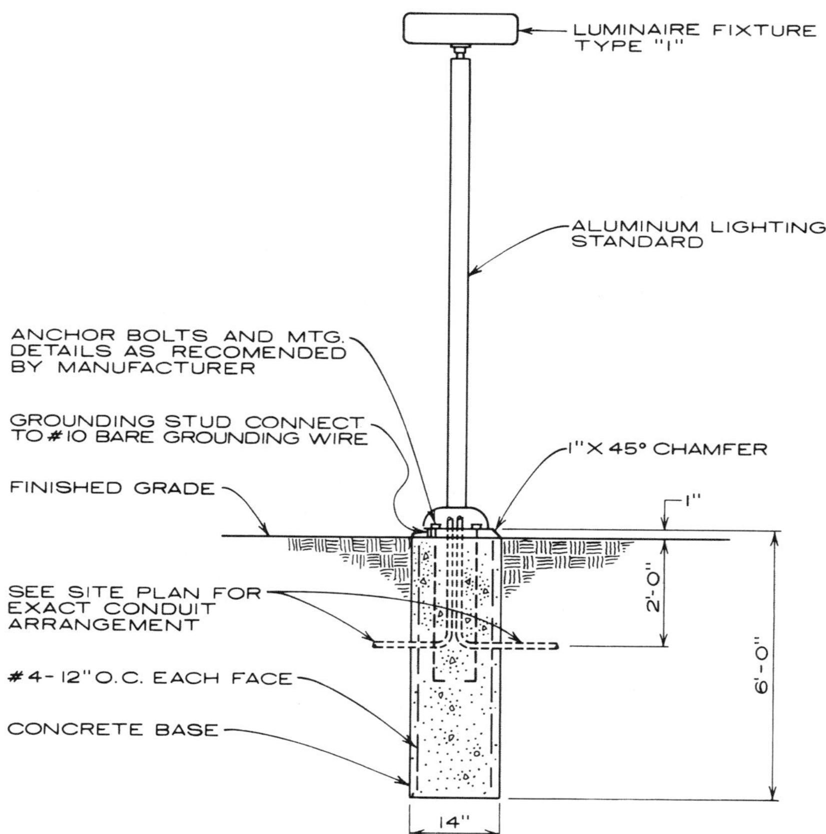

FIG. 9-125 Lighting installation detail.

FIG. 9-126 Lighting at Lincoln Centre, Dallas, Texas.

FIG. 9-127 Lighting at John Fitzgerald Kennedy Library, Boston, Massachusetts.

FIG. 9-128 Lighting at Harbour Place, Tampa, Florida.

FIG. 9-129 Clear globes are used at Faneuil Market in Boston, Massachusetts.

FIG. 9-130 Clear globes at Lincoln Centre, Dallas, Texas.

FIG. 9-131 Clear globes are used at the visitor parking area at Lincoln Centre, Dallas, Texas.

FIG. 9-132 Bollard lighting at Penn Square, Reading, Pennsylvania.

FIG. 9-133 Bollard lighting at the Colonnade, Dallas, Texas.

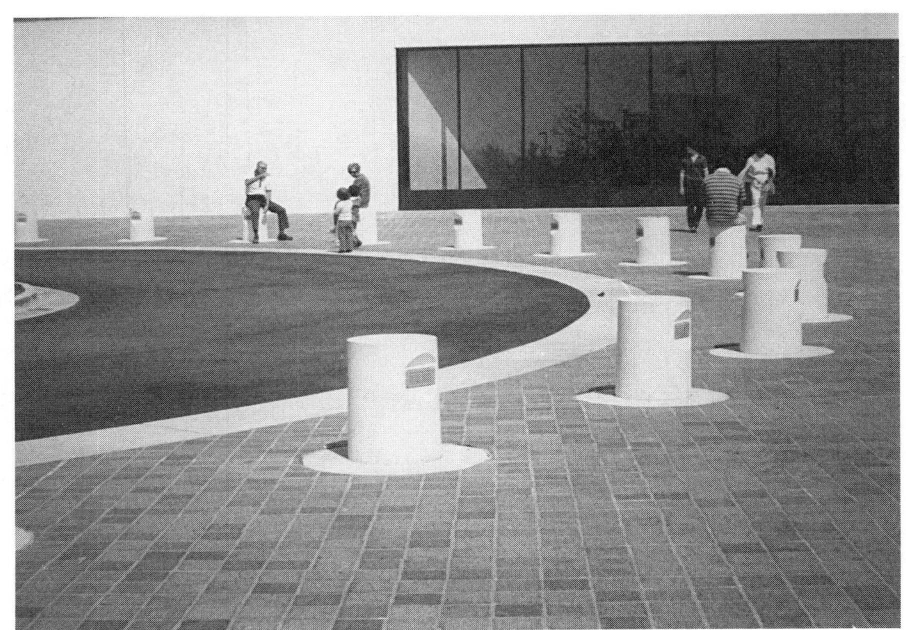

FIG. 9-134 Seating bollards with lighting at the John Fitzgerald Kennedy Library, Boston, Massachusetts.

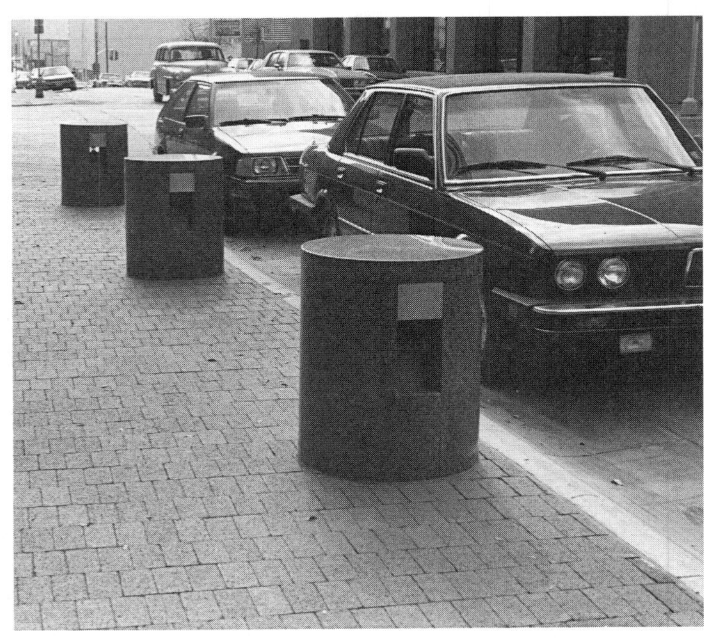

FIG. 9-135 Granite bollards with lights at Lincoln Plaza, Dallas, Texas.

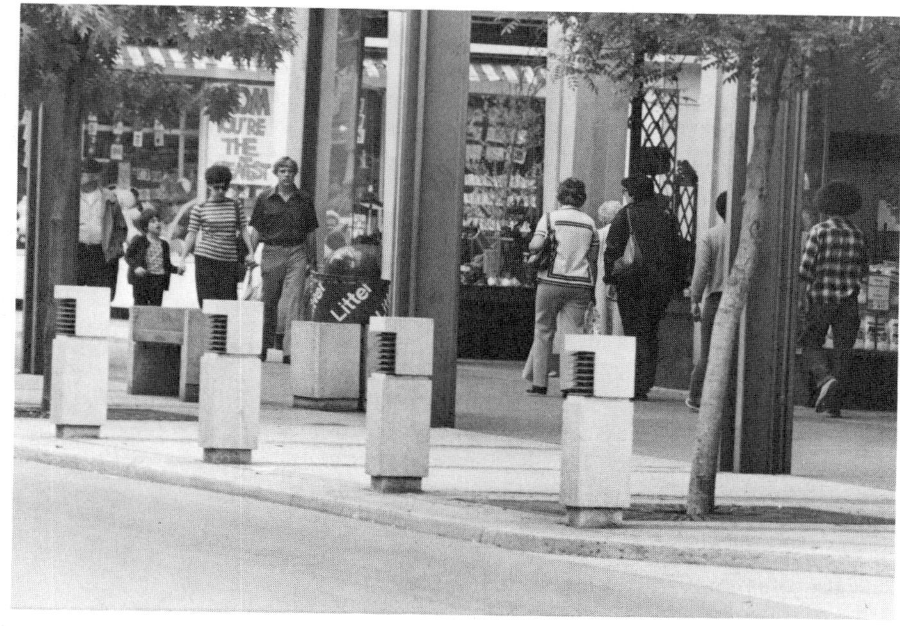

FIG. 9-136 Concrete bollards with built-in lighting at Hamilton Mall, Allentown, Pennsylvania.

FIG. 9-137 Lights used in conjunction with walls usually have metal covers to prevent breakage.

lamps, lamp efficiency varies with cold temperatures unless a cold weather ballast and enclosed fixtures are used.

Mercury Vapor has a sparkling quality. It gives two and a half times more light than incandescent lamps for the power used. A 100 watt mercury bulb has a lamp life of 24,000 hours with an output of 4200 lumens. Mercury also maintains a high output of lumens over its lamp life. Clear mercury lamps have a cool greenish color good for lighting plants while delux mercury lamps have improved red and yellow color with the blue strengthened. Delux lamps have good color acceptance and are often used to light pedestrian or street areas.

Metal Halide is similar to mercury. It is very efficient, giving about an 8000 lumen output at 100 watts with a 10,000 hour life.

High Pressure Sodium has a small lamp size and good light control. It has a very high efficiency and for 100 watts provides about a 9500 lumen output with a 12,000 hour life. It gives a warm yellowish light and is used for street lighting.

Pedestrian Lighting. Lighting is usually placed about 12 ft high in pedestrian areas to stay in scale with people.

Where mercury lighting is used with clear acrylic globes, it is best to use 75 watt lamps with a refractor over it. There are also reflective light sources easier on the viewer's eyes. These light fixtures use 100 to 175 watt lamps.

Benches

Benches have varying design, but the two major types are those with or without backs. They are usually made of wood, concrete, or stone. Concrete or stone benches, particularly those without backs, may act as sculptural elements, are easily maintained and less susceptible to vandalism. Benches, especially those with backs, are most comfortable. Seating height above the ground should be 15 to 16 in. (See Figs. 9-138 to 9-151.)

FIG. 9-138 Wooden benches are used in a sitting area on Constitution Plaza, Hartford, Connecticut.

FIG. 9-139 This bench is used at Northwest Plaza, St. Louis, Missouri.

FIG. 9-140 Contour bench at Lincoln Plaza, Dallas, Texas.

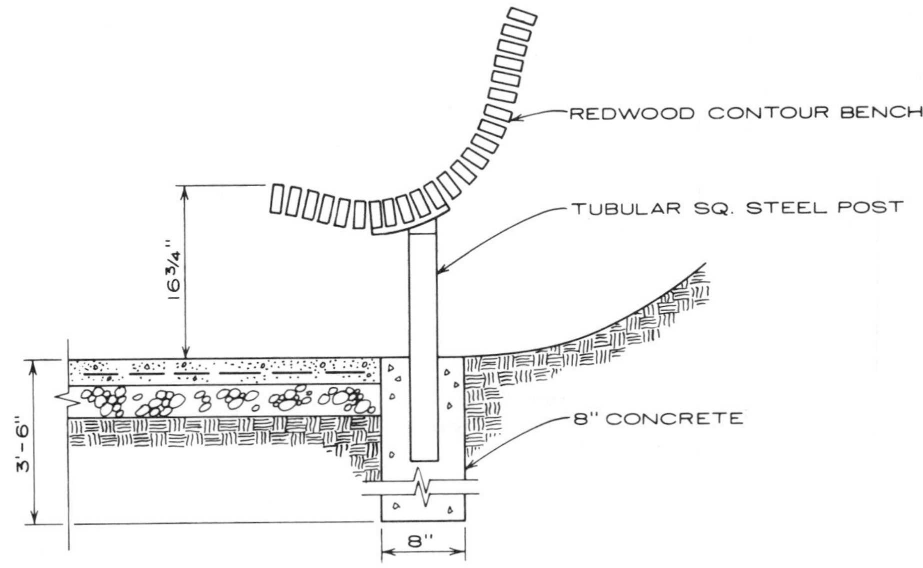

FIG. 9-141 Contour bench detail.

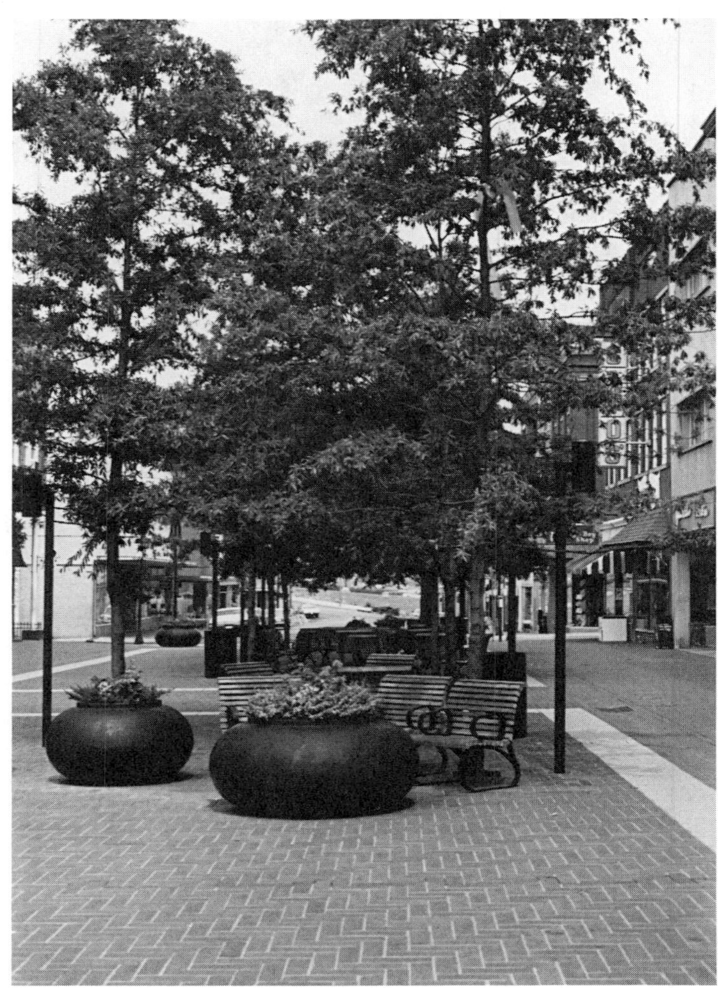

FIG. 9-142 Seating on the Main Street Mall in Charlottesville, Virginia, is movable and people can turn the benches for small conversation groups.

FIG. 9-143 This bench provides room for many people at the University of California, Los Angeles.

FIG. 9-144 Redwood bench used at Northeastern Bank Plaza, Scranton, Pennsylvania (Photograph courtesy of Bellante, Clauss, Miller & Partners).

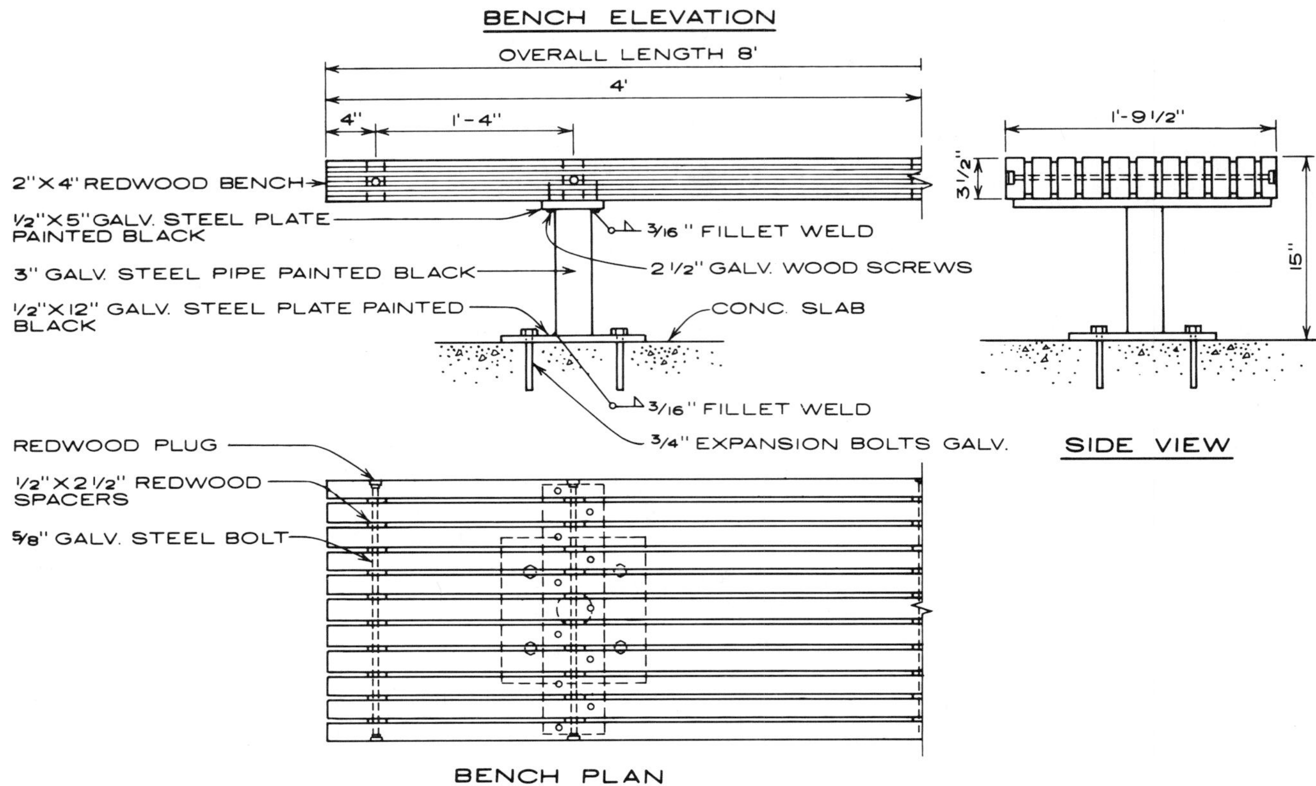

FIG. 9-145 Redwood bench detail.

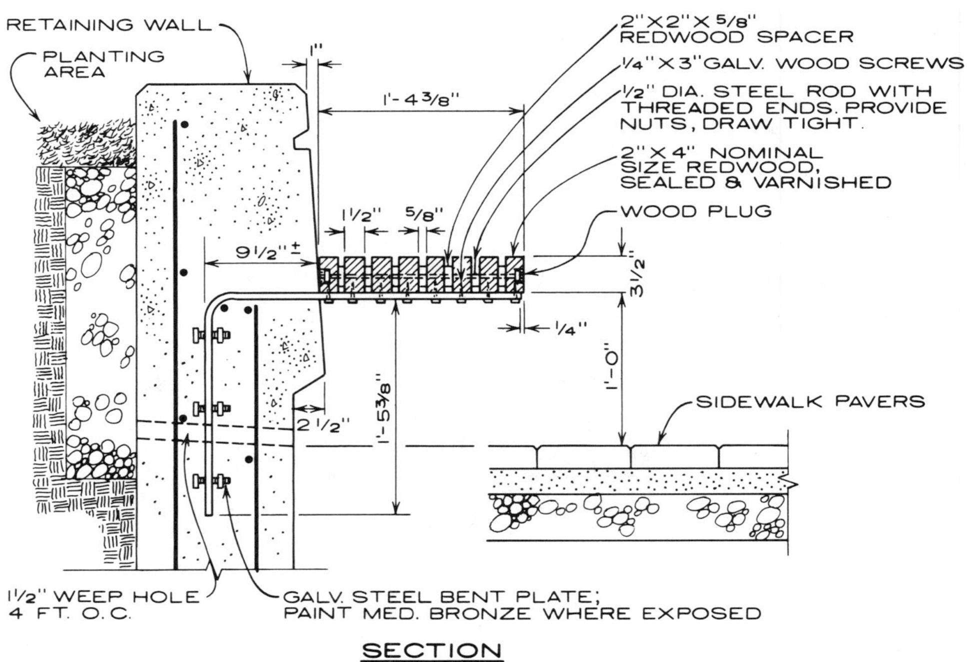

FIG. 9-146 Detail of redwood bench built into a planter wall.

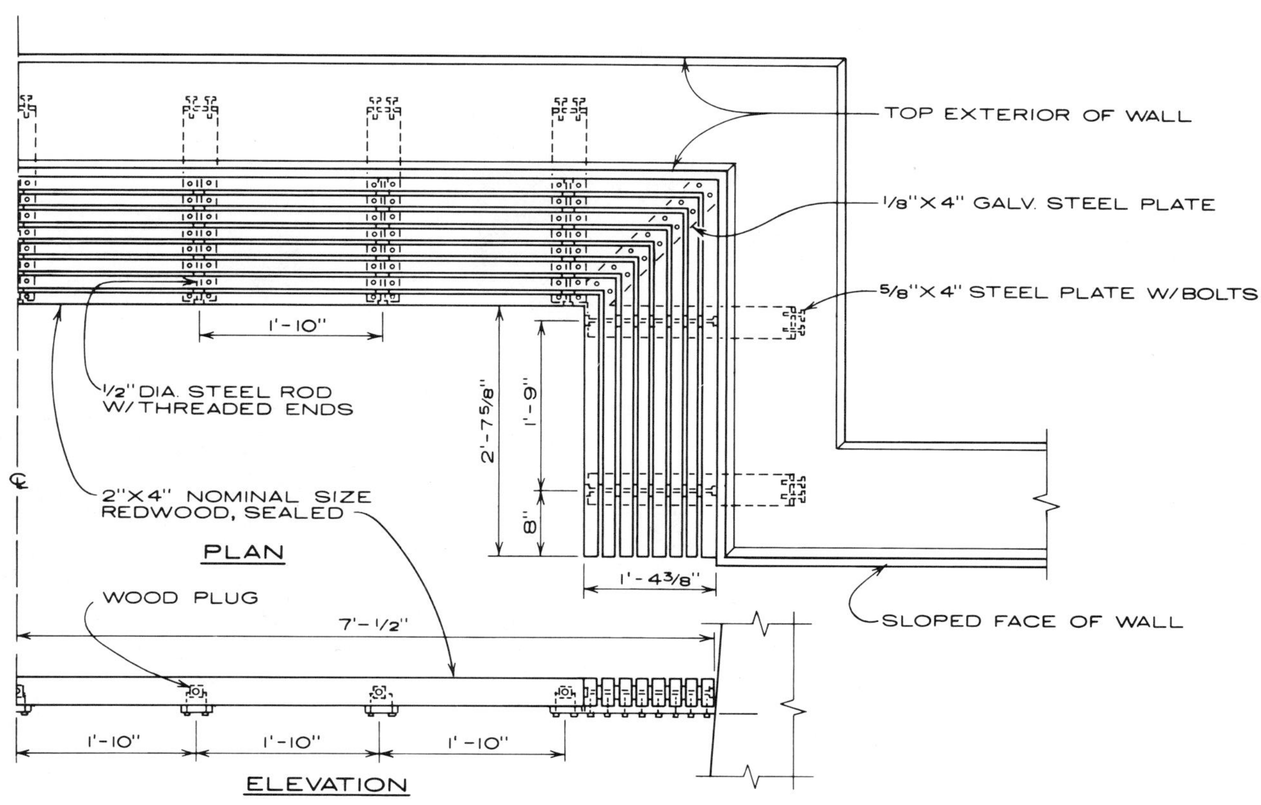

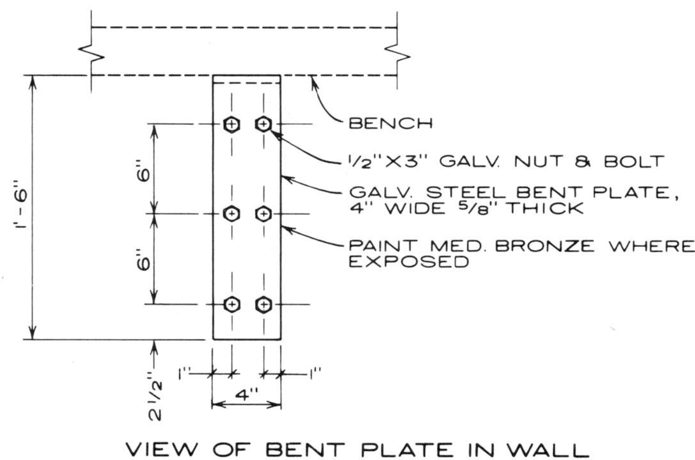

FIG. 9-146 Detail of redwood bench built into a planter wall. (*Continued*)

FIG. 9-147 Bench made from a cut stone slab at Constitution Plaza, Hartford, Connecticut.

FIG. 9-148 Seating used in a small courtyard.

FIG. 9-149 This bench is made of cut stone supported by a steel frame at Skidmore College, Saratoga Springs, New York.

FIG. 9-150 This bench extends from the paving at Southern Illinois University, Edwardsville.

FIG. 9-151 Curved steel bench set on a granite pedestal on Flora Street in the Arts District, Dallas, Texas.

Seating and Outdoor Lecture Areas

Outdoor lecture areas may act as the dominant feature of a space and provide varying amounts of seating. They may also act as theaters-in-the-round. (See Figs. 9-152 and 9-154.)

Seating in Conjunction with Raised Tree Planters

Seating is often combined with tree planters. The height of the planter depends on whether the tree is planted directly in the ground or on the top of a parking garage or other structure.

FIG. 9-152 Outdoor lectures can be given at Marywood Memorial Commons, Scranton, Pennsylvania (Photograph courtesy of Bellante, Clauss, Miller & Partners).

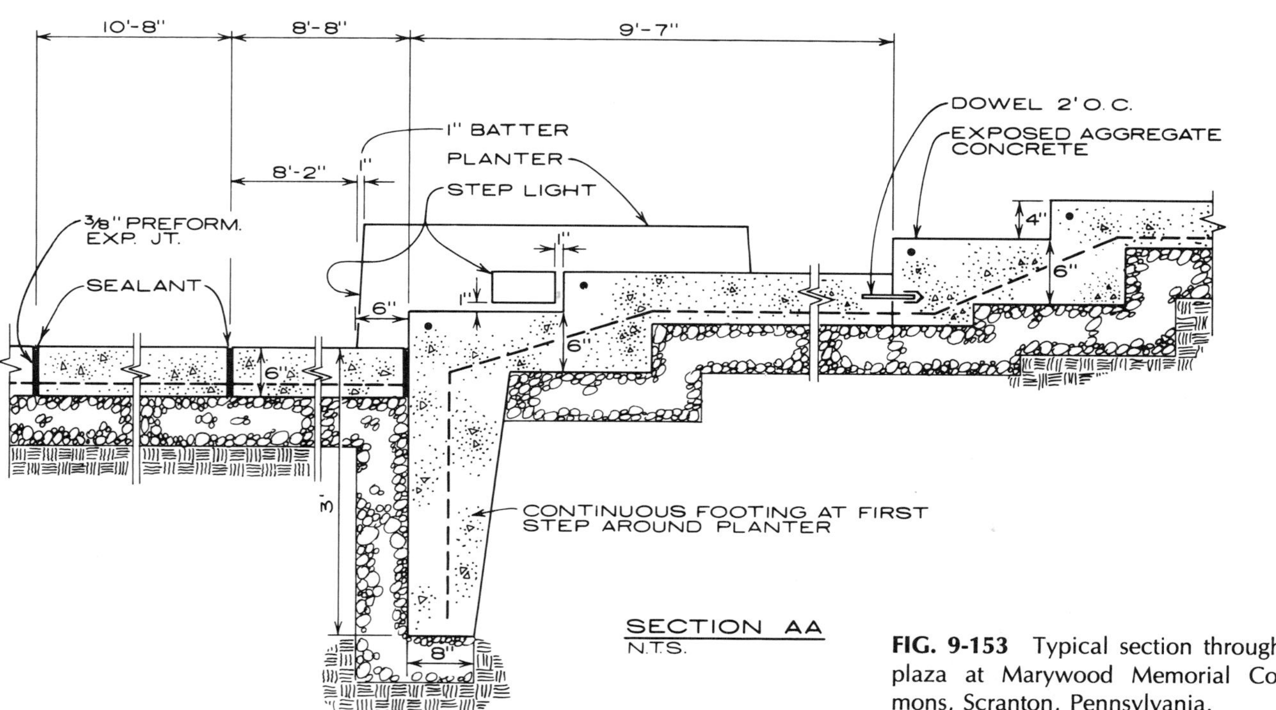

FIG. 9-153 Typical section through a plaza at Marywood Memorial Commons, Scranton, Pennsylvania.

FIG. 9-154 Amphitheatre in downtown Atlanta, Georgia.

Tree Planters and Pots

Tree planters must be of appropriate size to enable trees to grow above structures such as parking garages. Much better growth results where trees are planted directly in the ground. Pots are versatile and some may be moved or arranged for displays.

Planters can be made of a variety of materials, including wood, concrete, stone, or asbestos concrete. It is important to provide good drainage in the planters by the use of weep holes or drainage in rooftop areas. To help drain the planters about 4 in. of gravel are placed in the bottom of the planter with a fiberglass matt between the gravel and the soil mix. (See Figs. 9-155 to 9-166.)

FIG. 9-155 Seating and raised tree planter at Northeastern Bank Plaza, Scranton, Pennsylvania.

FIG. 9-156 Seating and raised tree planters set up a rhythm adjacent to Travelers Insurance Building, Hartford, Connecticut.

FIG. 9-157 Seating and raised tree planter in courtyard adjacent to Travelers Insurance Building, Hartford, Connecticut.

FIG. 9-158 Seating and raised tree planters at the University of California, Berkeley.

FIG. 9-159 Seating and raised tree planters become an integral design feature at the Wyoming Avenue Plaza, Scranton, Pennsylvania (Photograph courtesy of Bellante, Clauss, Miller & Partners).

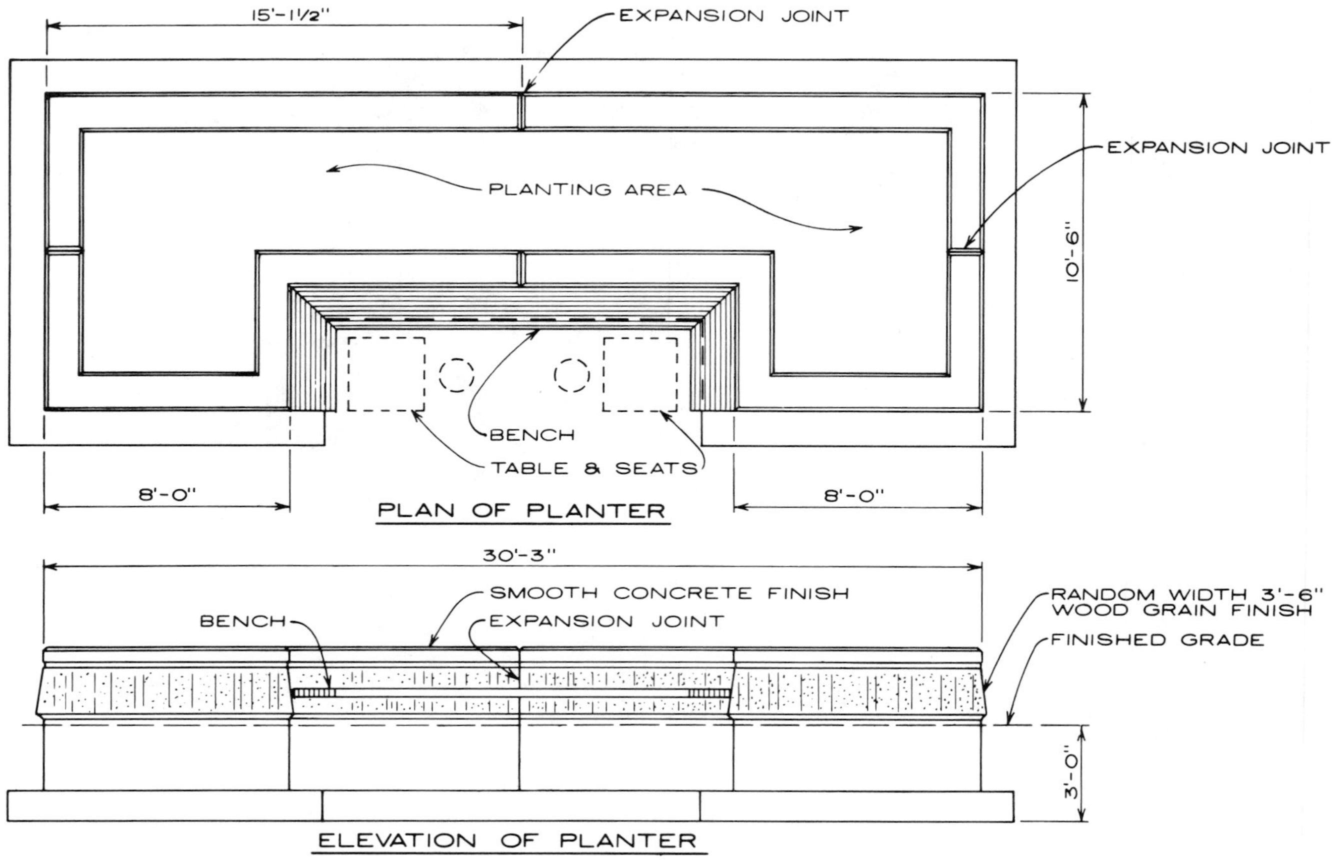

15'-1½"
EXPANSION JOINT
EXPANSION JOINT
PLANTING AREA
10'-6"
BENCH
TABLE & SEATS
8'-0"
8'-0"
PLAN OF PLANTER
30'-3"
SMOOTH CONCRETE FINISH
BENCH
EXPANSION JOINT
RANDOM WIDTH 3'-6"
WOOD GRAIN FINISH
FINISHED GRADE
3'-0"
ELEVATION OF PLANTER

18" SQ.
½" GALV. STEEL PLATE,
PAINT MEDIUM BRONZE
2'-6"
3"
3"
4"
3"
12"
2'-6"
PLAN OF SEATS AND TABLE

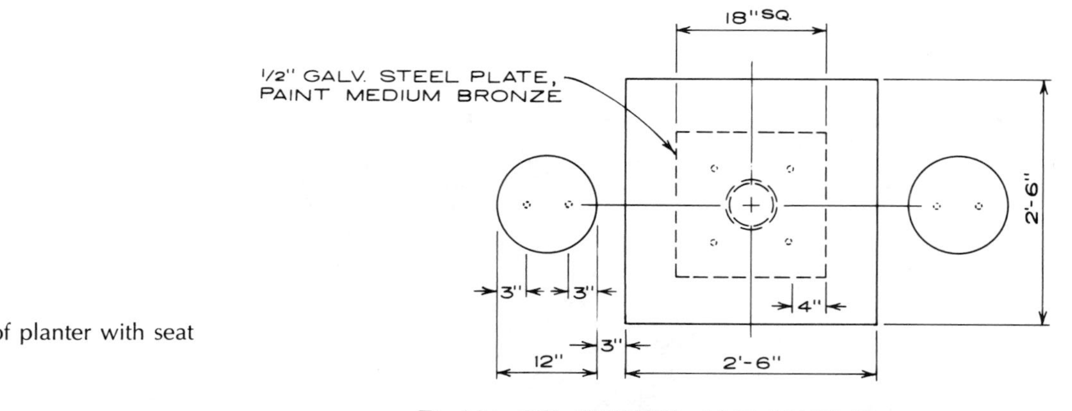

FIG. 9-160 Detail of planter with seat and tables.

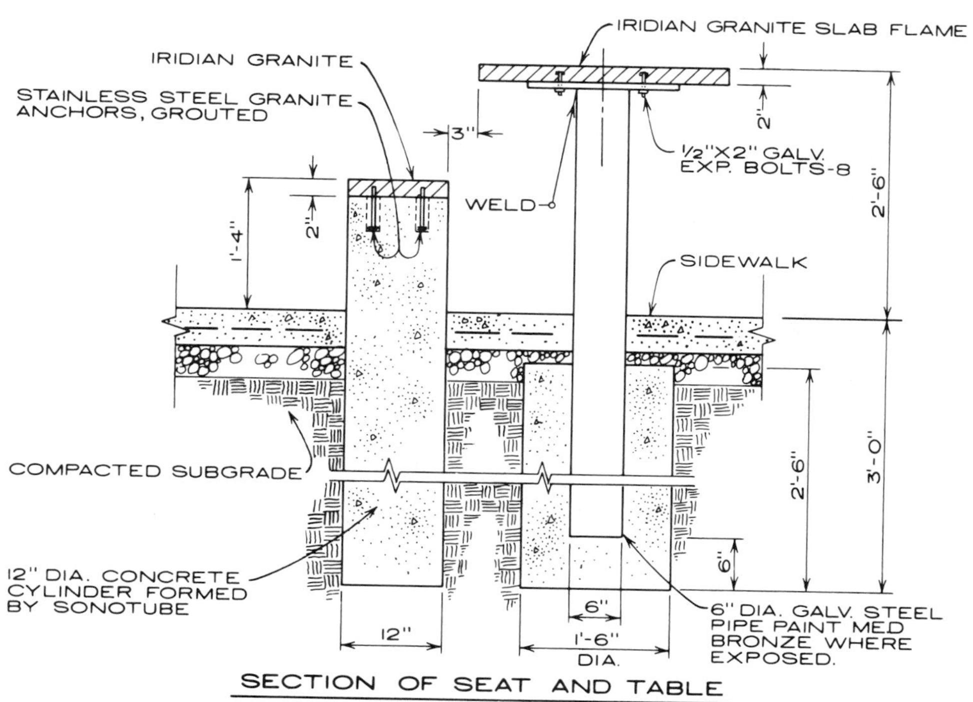

FIG. 9-160 *(Continued)*

FIG. 9-161 These precast concrete planters are used above the parking garage at Constitution Plaza, Hartford, Connecticut.

FIG. 9-162 Planters must be large enough for the variety of plants grown in them.

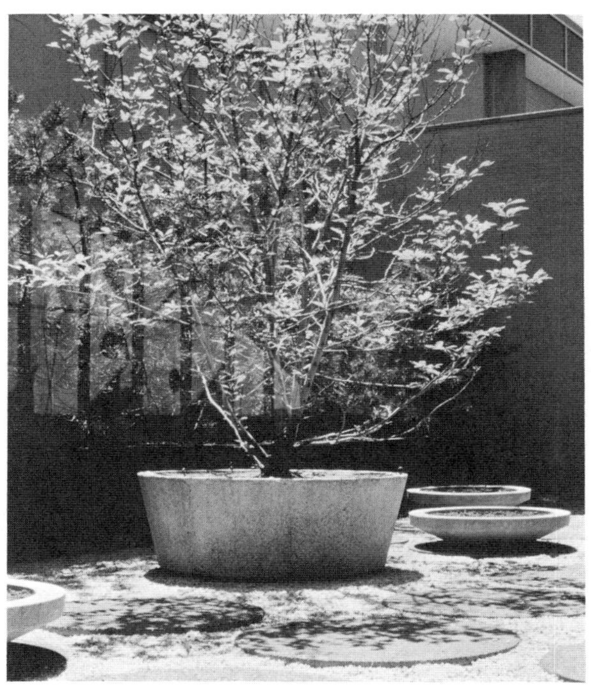

FIG. 9-163 Tree planter and pots used in a small court.

FIG. 9-164 Flower pots used at Main Street Mall, Charlottesville, Virginia.

FIG. 9-165 Flower pots used at Nicollet Mall, Minneapolis, Minnesota.

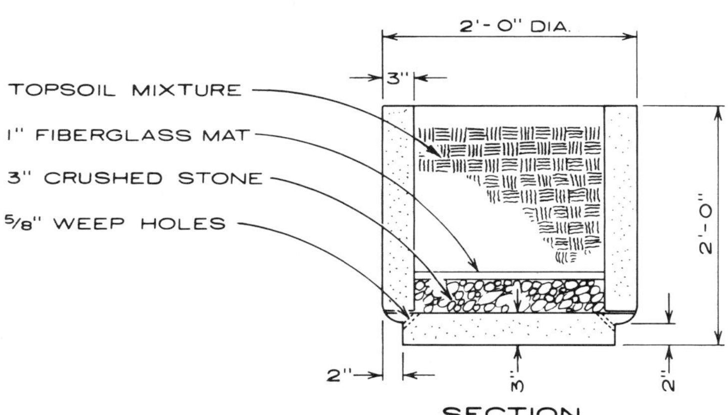

FIG. 9-166 Granite pots on Wyoming Avenue Plaza, Scranton, Pennsylvania.

Bollards

Bollards act as a barrier separating traffic from pedestrian areas or provide or imply a visual transition between areas. They also provide rhythm, give scale, texture, and color.

Bollards can be combined with chain to reinforce the feeling of separation or to help form a barrier. They are also often combined with lights for night-lighting of pedestrian areas. (See Figs. 9-167 to 9-171.)

FIG. 9-167 Granite bollards used on Wyoming Avenue Plaza, Scranton, Pennsylvania.

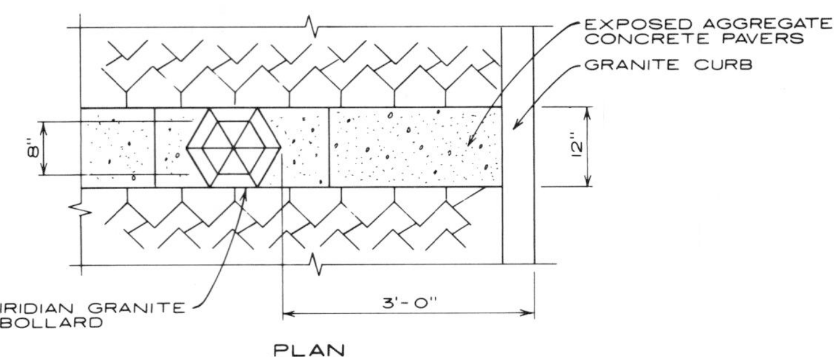

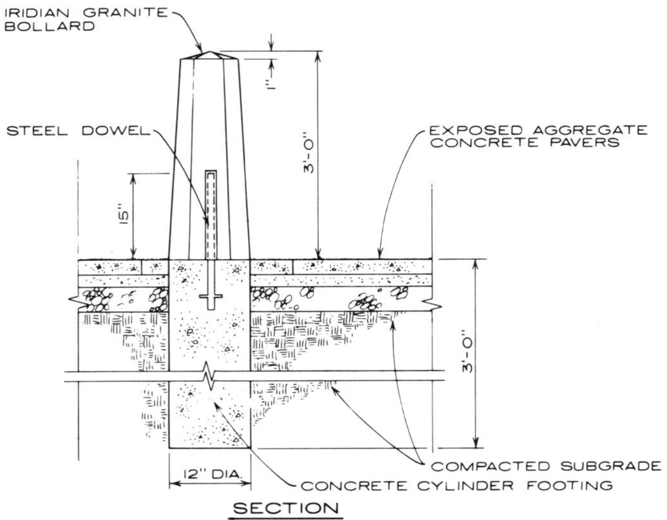

FIG. 9-168 Granite bollard detail.

FIG. 9-169 Granite bollards at Levi Plaza, San Francisco, California.

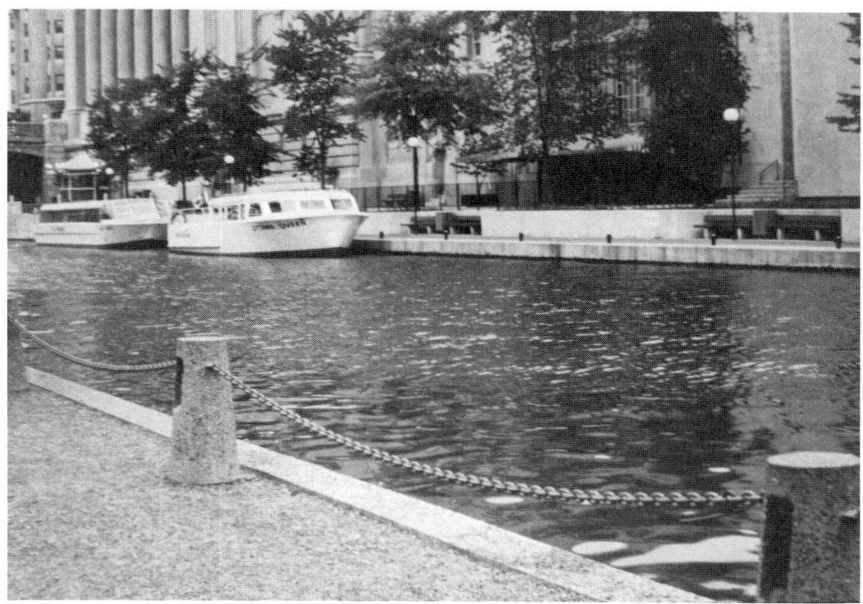

FIG. 9-170 Granite bollards and chain on Rideau Canal, Ottawa, Canada.

FIG. 9-171 Bollards at Riis Plaza, New York City.

Other Street Furnishings

Kiosks. Used as bulletin boards, directories, displays, and information booths, kiosks act as focal elements. They provide color, help give character to outdoor spaces, and often have night-lighting. (See Figs. 9-172 and 9-174.)

FIG. 9-172 Directory kiosk at Wyoming Avenue Plaza, Scranton, Pennsylvania, with medium bronze Kynar finish.

FIG. 9-173 Bronze anodized kiosk at Nicollet Mall, Minneapolis, Minnesota.

FIG. 9-174 Kiosk used on Essex Mall, Salem, Massachusetts.

Telephone Booths. Telephones are often placed in a variety of enclosures. Many contemporary units have been designed that provide partial weather and sound control, have vandal proof coin collection boxes, and are easily maintained. (See Fig. 9-175.)

FIG. 9-175 Telephone booths at Tampa City Center Esplanade, Tampa, Florida.

Bus Shelters and Canopies. These features are prevalent in urban areas such as pedestrian malls and provide shelter from inclement weather. Some bus shelters, for example, those used in Minneapolis on the Nicollet Mall, are also heated. (See Figs. 9-176 to 9-178.)

FIG. 9-176 Canopy used in downtown Mall, Allentown, Pennsylvania.

FIG. 9-176 Canopy used in downtown Wilkes-Barre, Pennsylvania.

FIG. 9-177 Covered kiosk type shelter at Levi Plaza, San Francisco, California.

FIG. 9-178 Bus shelters at the Nicollet Mall, Minneapolis, Minnesota.

Trash Receptacles. Trash containers may be designed in a variety of shapes and sizes, with many enclosing standard trash cans. Covers can be designed to keep rain out of the containers and weep holes can be provided for further drainage. (See Figs. 9-179 and 9-180.)

FIG. 9-179 Trash receptacle: Nicollet Mall, Minneapolis, Minnesota.

FIG. 9-180 Trash receptacle.

Drinking Fountains. As functional elements for pedestrian areas, drinking fountains are made of many materials, including precast concrete, metal, stone, or masonry. Some are specifically designed to accommodate wheelchairs. Freeze proof valves are desirable for use in cold climates. (See Figs. 9-181 and 9-184.)

FIG. 9-181 Drinking fountain for the handicapped.

FIG. 9-182 Precast concrete drinking fountain.

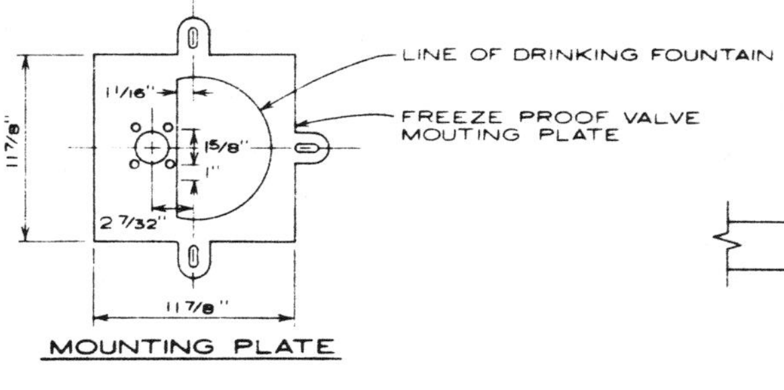

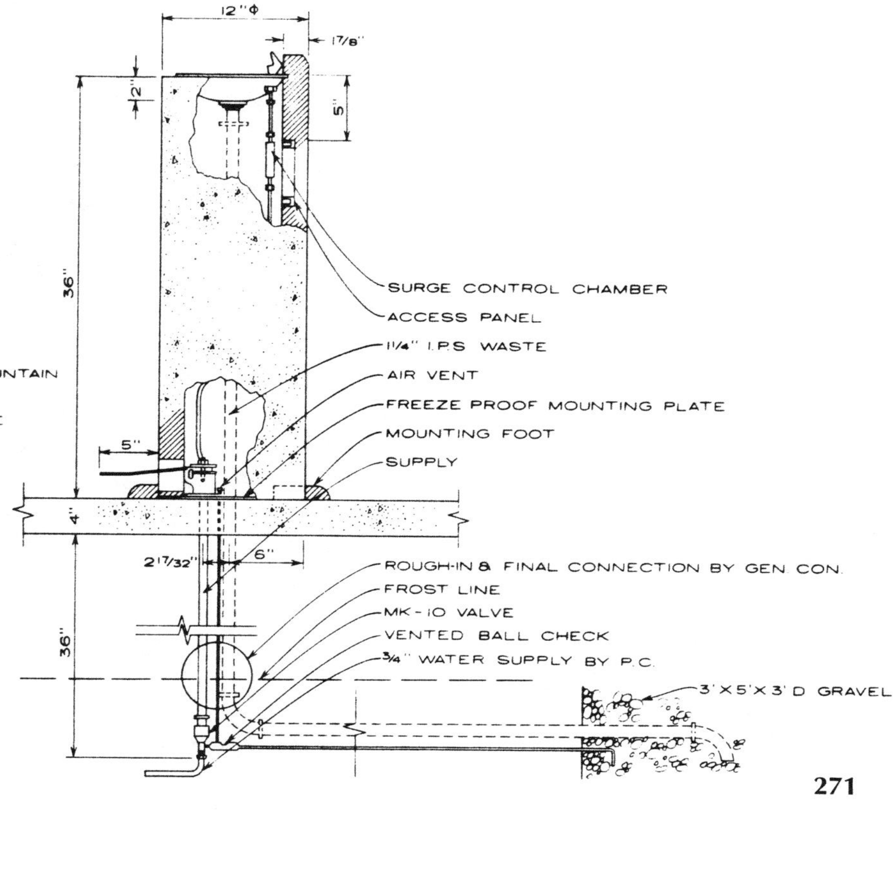

MOUNTING PLATE

LINE OF DRINKING FOUNTAIN
FREEZE PROOF VALVE MOUTING PLATE
11/16"
15/8"
1"
2 7/32"
11 7/8"
11 7/8"

12" Φ
1 7/8"
2"
5"
36"
SURGE CONTROL CHAMBER
ACCESS PANEL
1 1/4" I.P.S. WASTE
AIR VENT
FREEZE PROOF MOUNTING PLATE
MOUNTING FOOT
SUPPLY
5"
4"
2 17/32"
6"
ROUGH-IN & FINAL CONNECTION BY GEN. CON.
FROST LINE
MK-10 VALVE
VENTED BALL CHECK
3/4" WATER SUPPLY BY P.C.
36"
3' X 5' X 3' D GRAVEL

FIG. 9-183 Fountain detail.

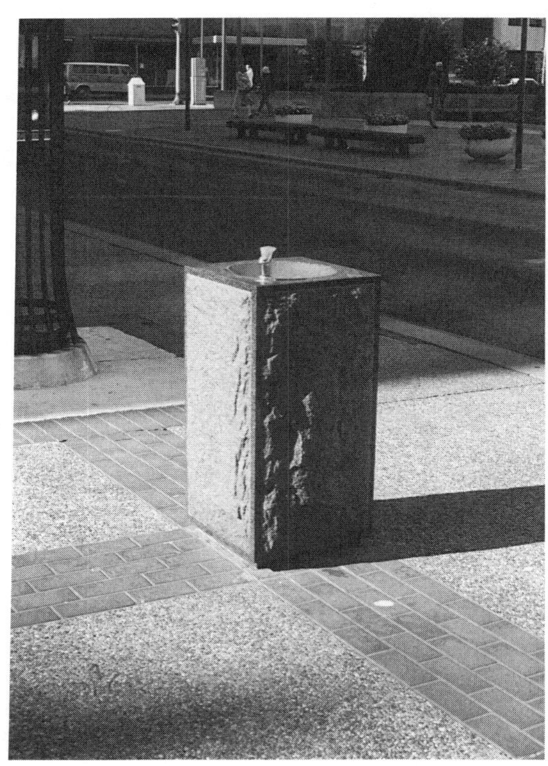

FIG. 9-184 Granite drinking fountain at Nicollet Mall, Minneapolis, Minnesota.

Clocks. Clocks serve as focal elements when used in plazas or pedestrian malls. If large enough, a clock can become a landmark; many are lighted for night viewing. (See Figs. 9-185 and 9-188.)

FIG. 9-185 Clock tower at Nicollet Mall, Minneapolis, Minnesota.

FIG. 9-186 Clock: Nicollet Mall, Minneapolis, Minnesota.

FIG. 9-187 Clock on polished granite pedestal at Lincoln Plaza, Dallas, Texas.

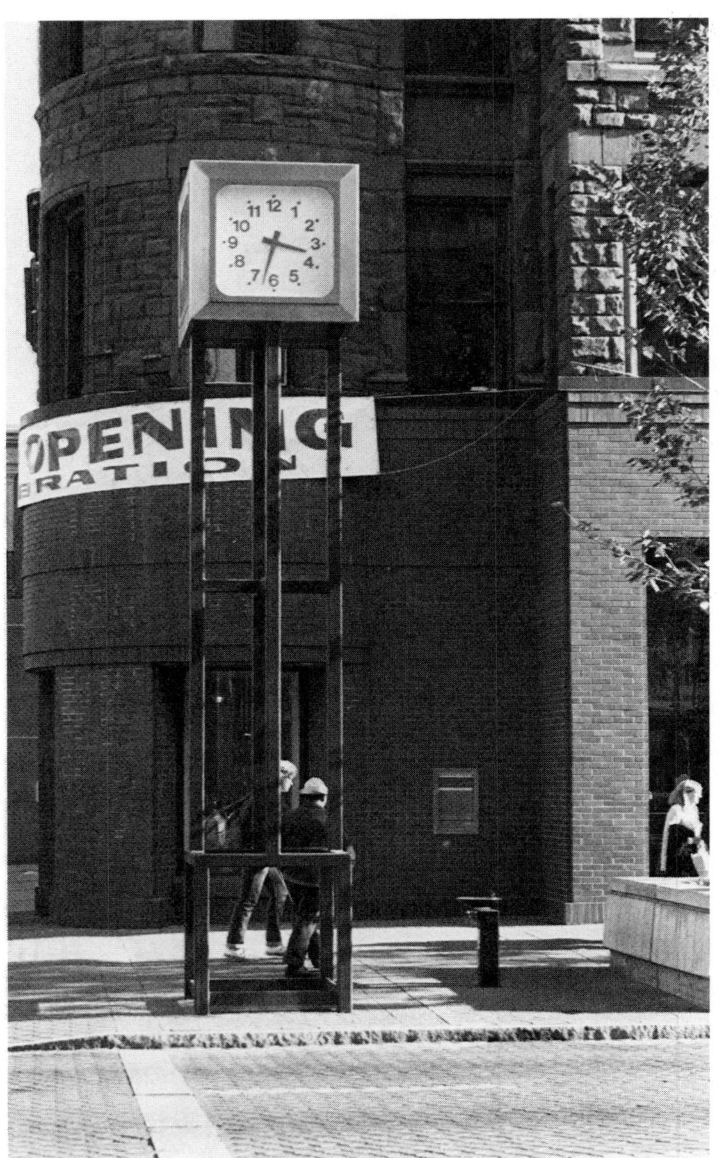

FIG. 9-188 Clock with stainless steel housing and bronze colored letters and base at Wyoming Avenue Plaza, Scranton, Pennsylvania.

Flagpoles. Flagpoles can serve as focal elements when used on plazas or adjacent to entrance areas. They also add color and can be lighted for night effect. Flagpoles are often placed in groups to give added impact and because they come in varying heights can be designed to work well with the scale of varying heights of buildings. (See Figs. 9-189 and 9-190.)

FIG. 9-189 Flagpoles at Zales Headquarters at Las Colinas, Irving, Texas.

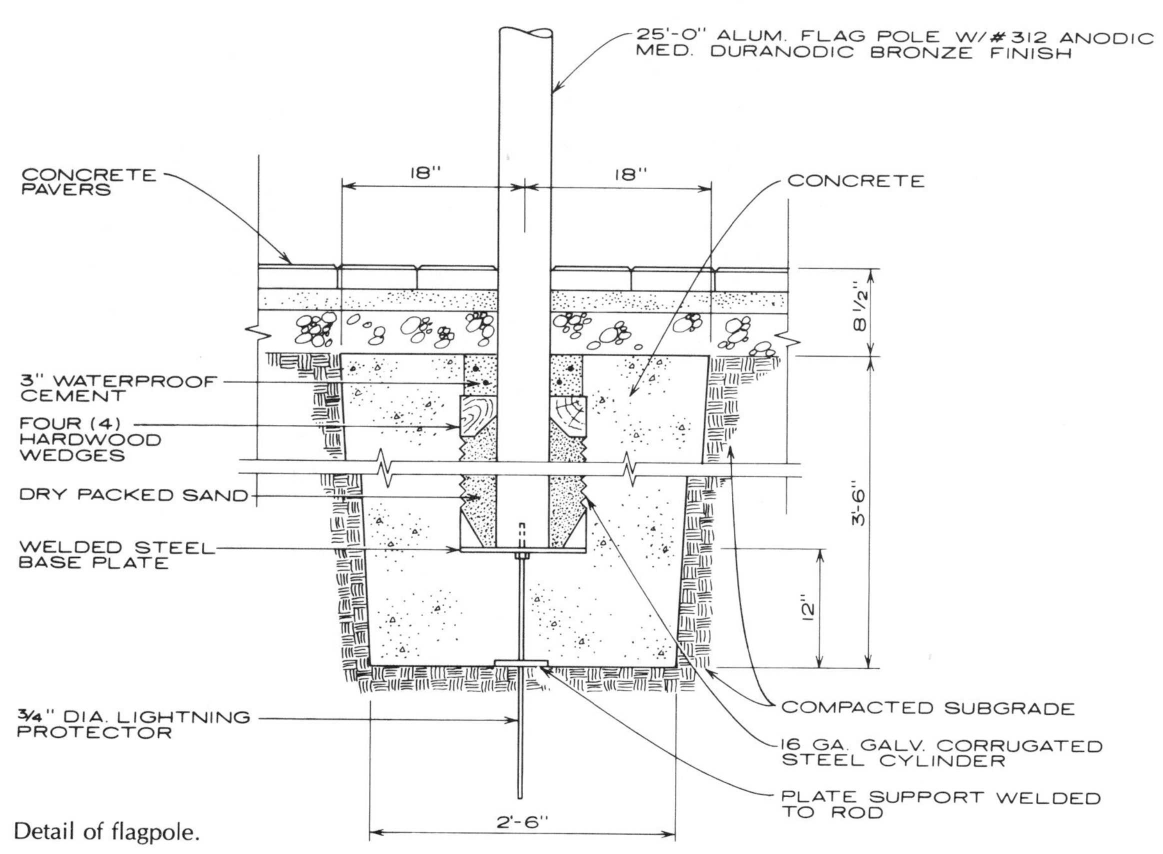

FIG. 9-190 Detail of flagpole.

Play Equipment. Small play structures can be designed for pedestrian mall areas in cities and can be a special feature or focal area in these streetscapes. Special attention should be given to the safety of these areas and the materials used for both the equipment and the surface of the area such as pea gravel. (See Figs. 9-191 and 9-192.)

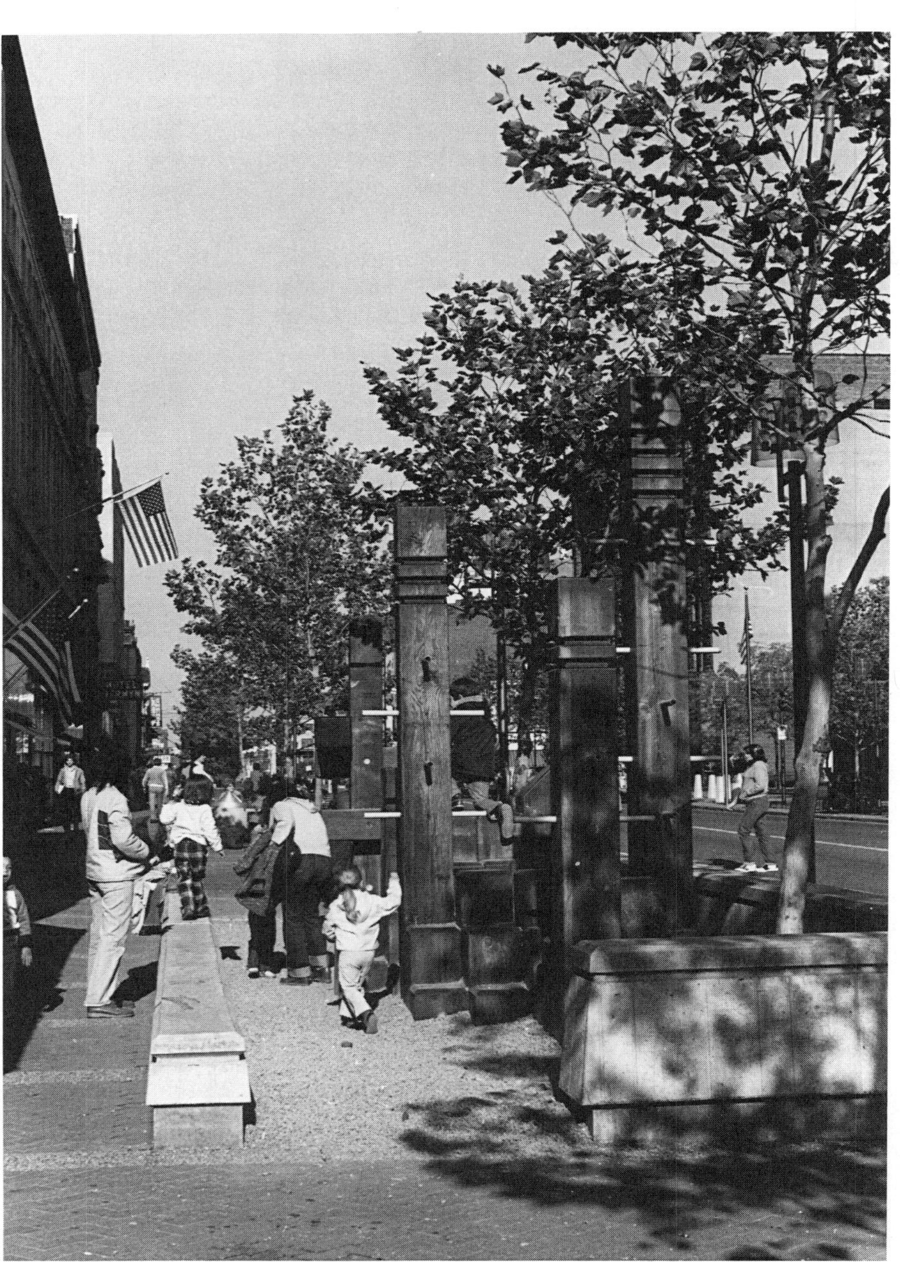

FIG. 9-191 An urban play area on Wyoming Avenue Plaza, Scranton, Pennsylvania.

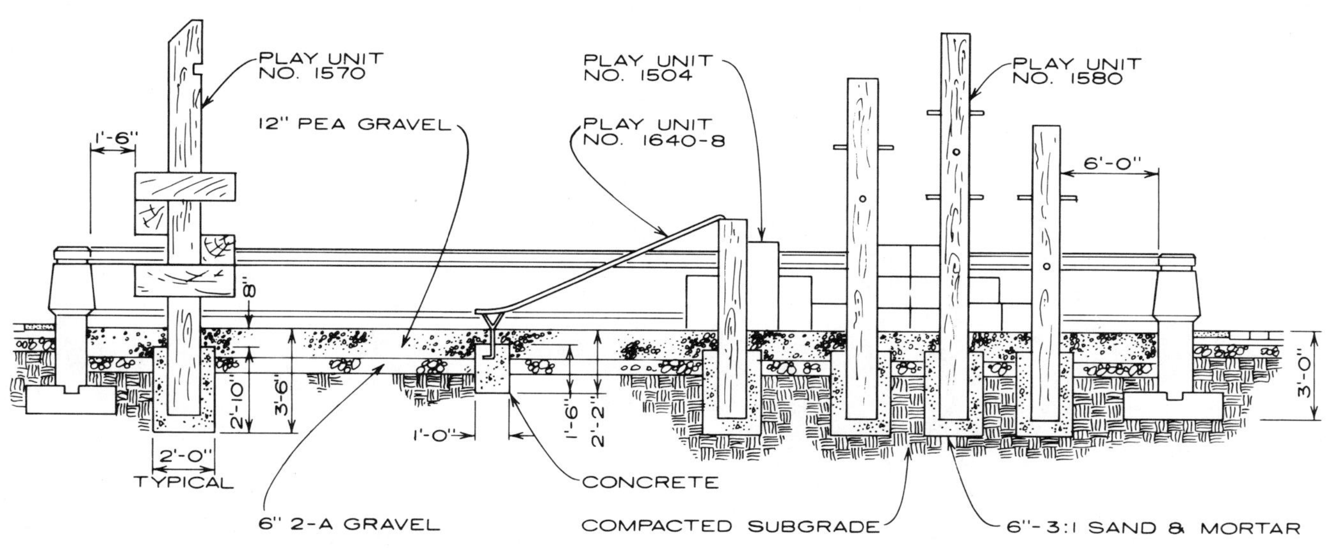

FIG. 9-192 Detail of play area.

FIG. 10-1 Trees used at Ithaca Commons, Ithaca, New York.

Chapter Ten
Plant Material in Site Planning

Research regarding the use of plant material has provided data on the importance of plants for climatic control, environmental engineering, and architectural and aesthetic uses as already mentioned. More detailed discussion follows.

CLIMATIC CONTROL

"Microclimate" refers to local variations in climate. Microclimatic factors that affect site planning are solar radiation, temperature, air movement, humidity, and precipitation.

Solar Radiation

Solar radiation provides light and heat—much of which is reflected back into space from clouds, with about 20% reaching the earth's surface. Part also is diffused by particles in the atmosphere; some is absorbed by oxides, water vapor, and ozone. Solar radiation warms the earth's surface, is reflected by paving and other objects, and can produce glare, especially from light colored paving. Trees are one of the best controls of solar radiation. (See Fig. 10-1.) They may block or filter sunlight. Temperatures are much cooler under shade trees, which provide natural air conditioning. This system operates with solar radiation, absorbing carbon dioxide, heat, and water and transpiring cool air in the form of water vapor.

University of Indiana scientists found that with an air temperature of 84° the surface temprature of a concrete street was 108°. Where shade trees were planted the surface temperature dropped 20°.

Wind

Wind helps to control temperature. Winds of low velocity may be pleasant, but as velocity increases they may cause discomfort and damage. Street trees can buffer winds in urban areas caused by convection and Venturi effects. Trees can also be planted in residential areas to provide protection from winter winds.

Precipitation

Plants help to control precipitation reaching the ground. By intercepting precipitation and slowing it down they aid in moisture retention and in the prevention of soil erosion. They also help the soil retain moisture by providing shade or protection from the wind.

ENVIRONMENTAL ENGINEERING

Air Purification

Plants clean the air through the process of photosynthesis and the emission of oxygen. Trees use carbon dioxide in photosynthesis. Auto exhausts account for much carbon dioxide, especially in urban areas. Trees also help filter out other pollutants, among them, sulfur dioxide, dust, pollen, and smoke.

Noise

Noise is a problem, particularly in urban areas. The level of sound is measured in decibels. The sound level of a normal conversation is about 60 decibels. A plane taking off produces 120 decibels at a 200 ft distance.

Sound energy usually spreads out and dissipates in transmission. Sound waves can be absorbed, reflected, or deflected. Plants absorb sound waves through their leaves, branches, and twigs, with those having thick fleshy leaves and thin petioles being best for this. A good example is the little-leaf linden. The trunks of trees deflect sound and it has been estimated that a 100 ft depth of forest can reduce sound by about 21 decibels.

Glare and Reflection

Plants reduce glare and reflection caused by sunlight. A light source received directly produces primary glare while reflected light is secondary glare. Plants may be used to filter or block glare by use of plant material with the appropriate size, shape, and foliage density. (See Fig. 10-2.)

Erosion Control

Plants are a primary means of preventing erosion from storm water runoff and of controlling erosion during construction. (See p 000.) Erosion is also minimized by plants, which intercept rain, decrease splashing, and increase water absorption.

FIG. 10-2 Plants filter glare.

ARCHITECTURAL AND AESTHETIC USES

For use in cities trees of large caliper such as 5 or 6 in. are in proper scale with buildings. It takes about 35 years for trees to reach maturity while the estimated life of many buildings is only 50 years.

Space Definition

Plants can be used in several ways: as walling elements to form outdoor spaces, canopies to provide shade, or as ground covers to provide color and texture on the base plane. (See Figs. 10-3 and 10-4.)

FIG. 10-3 Trees define spaces at Georgia Plaza, Atlanta.

FIG. 10-4 Trees can form a screen.

View Control

While trees and shrubs can screen out objectionable views, they can also provide backdrops for sculpture and fountains. Additionally, they may provide filtered views of buildings or spaces and frame a view, maximizing its effect.

Plants accent architecture, providing reinforcement at the entry to a building; or articulate space, setting up sequences where appropriate. (See Figs. 10-5 and 10-6.)

Mood

Plants also affect peoples' moods. The flowering cherries in Washington, D.C., announce spring's arrival.

Criteria Affecting Selection of Plant Material

Hardiness

1. Is a specific tree, shrub, or ground cover hardy in the region of the country where the site is located? Hardiness depends primarily on temperature and precipitation; however, such soil properties as degree of acidity or alkalinity are also important factors to consider. (See Figs. 10-7 and 10-8.)
2. Does the tree, shrub, or ground cover grow in or withstand moist or dry soil?
3. Will the plant tolerate city conditions if required? When the tree is too close to paved areas, will it die? When adjacent to paved areas, will the tree damage the paving?

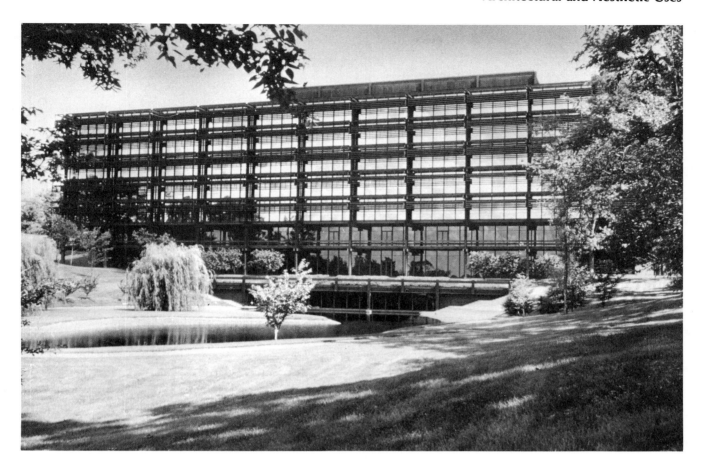

FIG. 10-5 Trees can provide a particular mood as done at John Deere, Moline, Illinois (Photograph courtesy of Kurt Youngstrom).

FIG. 10-6 A bosque of trees gives shade to the seating below.

4 Does the plant have light and airy foliage? Does it provide shade? Does it prefer south or north slopes? South slopes sometimes thaw in winter and this may cause damage to roots of some trees.

5 Is the tree, shrub, or ground cover free of or easily susceptible to disease?

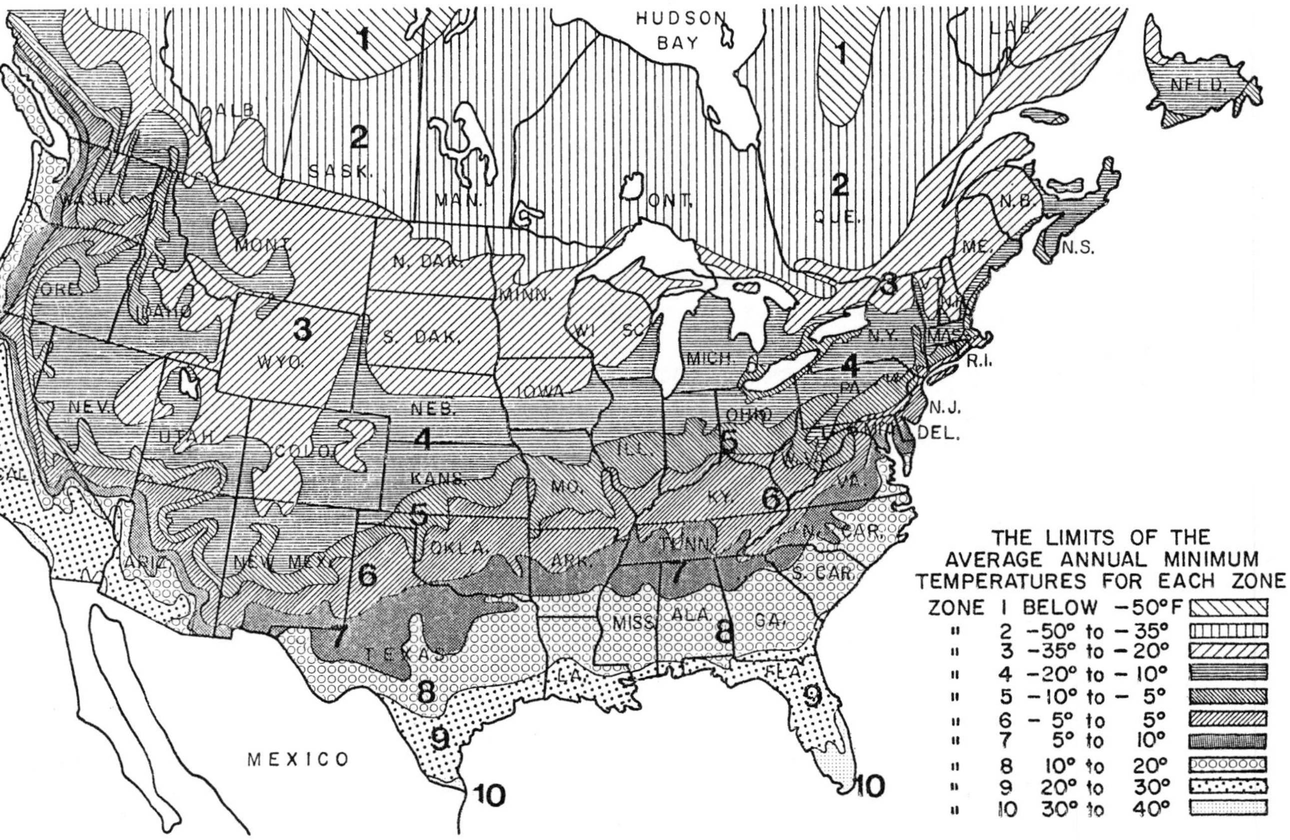

THE LIMITS OF THE AVERAGE ANNUAL MINIMUM TEMPERATURES FOR EACH ZONE

ZONE 1	BELOW	−50°F
" 2	−50° to	−35°
" 3	−35° to	−20°
" 4	−20° to	−10°
" 5	−10° to	−5°
" 6	−5° to	5°
" 7	5° to	10°
" 8	10° to	20°
" 9	20° to	30°
" 10	30° to	40°

FIG. 10-7 Hardiness zones of the United States and Canada. Compiled by the Arnold Arboretum, Harvard University, Jamaica Plain, Massachusetts, May 1, 1967.

FIG. 10-8 Yaupon hollies that are evergreen form a bosque and provide shade at the main entrance to the Kimbell Art Museum, Fort Worth, Texas.

Form and Structure

1 What is the height and spread of a particular tree or shrub at maturity? How long does it take to reach maturity?

2 Is the tree, shrub, or groundcover deciduous or evergreen? Deciduous trees may provide shade in summer and allow sunlight through in winter. Evergreen trees provide color year round and are good for windbreaks or screens.

FIG. 10-9 Form and structure are important in selecting plant material.

3 Does the tree have good branch structure and bark color? (See Fig. 10-9.)
4 Does the plant provide shade, have light and airy foliage?

Foliage, Flowers, and Fruit
1 What is the foliage size, form, texture, and color?
2 Is there autumn color and to what degree?
3 Are the flowers or fruits significant? When do they occur? How long do they remain effective on the plant? What is their color? Are the flowers fragrant?

Care
1 Is the tree, shrub, or ground cover easy or difficult to transplant?
2 Does the plant require much or little maintenance?

Arrangement

Provided plant selection criteria are met, plant material native to the site's region may be used or it may be imported from other areas. Both plant selection and arrangement must follow a planting plan developed to solve functional and aesthetic problems. Arrangement is based on the relation of plants in size, form, texture, and color. Site planners know which plants to group together by studying natural plant relationships (ecology) and trying to group them similarly in their schemes. Or after becoming familiar with the palette of plants and comprehending their size, form, texture, and color, they may form their own arrangements based on one or several of the plants characteristics. Site planners could, for example, group flowering trees by color and time of bloom.

Plant material may also be grouped in relation to topography or architectural structure. Or it may form a transition between ground and structure. It can become an enclosure or shelter, provide a screen, block wind, or offer shade. Particular trees serve to fulfill these needs much better than others, and it is the designers' knowledge and experience in using plant materials that serves best in the final analysis. (See Table 10-1.)

Table 10-1 Trees for Site Planning

Latin Name	Common Name	Zone	Height (ft)	Habit	Fall Color	Characteristics
		DECIDUOUS TREES				
Acer palmatum var.	Japanese Maple	5	10	R	Scarlet	Dense, green to red foliage
Acer palmatum atropurpureum	Bloodleaf Japanese Maple	5	10	R	Red	Red colored foliage
Acer palmatum atropurpureum Bloodgood	Bloodgood Japanese Maple	5	10	R	Red	Deep red foliage
Acer palmatum atropurpureum Oshiu-beni	Oshiu-beni Japanese Maple	5	10	R	Red	Red foliage in spring, green by summer
Acer platanoides var.	Norway Maple	3[a]	60	O[b]	Yellow	Dense
Acer platanoides Crimson King	Crimson King	3[a]	60	O[b]		Purple foliage
Acer platanoides Emerald Queen	Emerald Queen	3[a]	60	O[b]	Yellow	Rapid growth
Acer platanoides Summershade	Summershade	3[a]	65	O[b]		Dark green foliage
Acer platanoides pseudoplatanus	Sycamore Maple	5[a]	80	WS[b]		Winged fruit
Acer rubrum var.	Red Maple	3	75	R	Yellow; orange to red	Good fall color
Acer rubrum Armstrong	Armstrong Red Maple	3	35	U	Red to orange	Good fall color
Acer rubrum Autumn Flame	Autumn Flame Red Maple	3	60	R	Orange to red	Early fall color
Acer rubrum Bowhall	Bowhall Red Maple	3	40	P	Orange to red	Good fall color
Acer rubrum Gerling	Gerling Red Maple	3	35	U	Orange to red	Good fall color
Acer rubrum October Glory	October Glory Red Maple	3	60	R	Crimson to red	Good fall color, glossy foliage, holds leaves longer
Acer rubrum Red Sunset	Red Sunset	3	50	O	Orange to red	Good fall color
Acer rubrum Tilford	Tilford Red Maple	3	35	P	Orange to red	Good fall color
Acer Saccharum	Sugar Maple	3	65	O	Yellow to orange and red	Dense, good fall color
Acer saccharum Columnare	Columnar Sugar Maple	3	65	U	Yellow to orange and red	Brilliant fall color
Acer saccharum Green Mountain	Green Mountain Sugar Maple	3	65	O	Yellow to orange and red	Thick waxy leaves, dark green
Acer saccharum Monumentale	Sentry Sugar Maple	3	60	U	Yellow to orange and red	Dark green foliage, good fall color
Aesculus glabra	Ohio Buckeye	3	30	R	Brilliant orange	Small greenish flowers with 6 in. panicles
Aesculus hippocastanum	Horse Chestnut	3	65	O		White flowers, coarse foliage
Aesculus canea brioti	Ruby Horse Chestnut	3	65	O		Bright scarlet flowers with 6–8 in. panicles
Amelanchier canadensis	Shadblow Serviceberry	4	30	U	Yellow to red	White flowers, maroon/purple fruit
Betula alba	European White Birch	2	50	P	Yellow	White bark
Betula paprifera	Canoe Birch	2	40	P	Yellow	White peeling bark
Carya illinoensis	Pecan	5[a]	70	R		Texas state tree, adapted over the entire state
Carpinus betulus	European Hornbeam	5[a]	30	P[b]	Yellow	Dense
Cercidiphyllum japonicum	Katsura Tree	4	60	WS	Yellow to scarlet	Fine texture foliage, often several trunks
Cercis canadensis	Eastern Redbud	4	25	V	Yellow	Rosy pink flowers, heart-shaped foliage
Cladrastis lutea	American Yellowwood	3	40	R	Orange to yellow	Clusters of white flowers
Cornus florida	Flowering Dogwood	4	25	R	Scarlet	White flower clusters, red berries, lustrous foliage
Cornus floridarubra	Red Flowering Dogwood	4	20	R	Scarlet	Red flower clusters

Table 10-1 Trees for Site Planning *(contd.)*

Latin Name	Common Name	Zone	Height (ft)	Habit	Fall Color	Characteristics
		DECIDUOUS TREES				
Cornus kousa	Kousa Dogwood	5	18	R	Scarlet	Red fruit
Cornus mas	Cornelian Cherry	4	25	R	Red	Small yellow flowers, scarlet fruit, lustrous green foliage
Crataegus phaenopyrum	Washington Hawthorn	4[a]	25	R[b]	Scarlet to orange	White flowers and orange berries
Fagus grandiflora	American Beech	3	90	P	Golden bronze	Dense foliage, light gray bark
Fagus sylvatica var.	European Beech	4	70	P	Bronze	Dark gray bark, glossy dark green foliage
Fagus sylvatica atropunicea	Copper Beech	4	70	R	Bronze	Gray bark, purple foliage
Fagus sylvatica pendula	Weeping Beech	4	60	W	Bronze	Purple leaves, gray bark
Fagus sylvatica riversii	Rivers Purple	4	60	R	Bronze	Dark purple leaves, gray bark
Fraxinus americana	White Ash	3	80	R	Deep purple	Bark
Fraxinus pennsylvanica lanceolata var	Green Ash	2[a]	60	R[b]	Yellow	Rapid growth
Fraxinus p. lanc. Marshall's Seedless Ash	Marshall's Seedless Ash	2[a]	55	R[b]	Yellow	Dark green foliage
Ginkgo biloba var.	Ginkgo	4[a]	75	R[b]	Yellow	Disease resistant
Ginkgo biloba Autumn Gold	Autumn Gold Ginkgo	4[a]	45	U[b]	Yellow	Male
Ginkgo biloba Fairmount	Fairmount Ginkgo	4[a]	75	P[b]	Yellow	Male
Ginkgo biloba Lakeview	Lakeview Ginkgo	4[a]	50	U[b]	Yellow	Male
Ginkgo biloba Princeton Sentry	Princeton Sentry	4[a]	70	U[b]	Yellow	Male
Gleditsia triancanthos inermis var.	Thornless Honeylocust	4[a]	70	WS[b]	Yellow	Resistant to salt for winter use.
Gleditsia t. inermis Halka	Halka Honeylocust	4[a]	45	P[b]	Yellow	Straight trunk
Gleditsia t. inermis Imperial	Imperial Honeylocust	4[a]	35	WS[b]	Yellow	Dense foliage
Gleditsia t. inermis Majestic	Majestic Honeylocust	4[a]	65	V[b]	Yellow	Dark green foliage
Gleditsia t. inermis Moraine	Moraine Honeylocust	4[a]	80	V[b]	Yellow	Good green foliage, curved trunk
Gleditsia t. inermis Shademaster	Shademaster Honey-locust	4[a]	40	R[b]	Yellow	Disease resistant, holds leaves longer
Gleditsia t. inermis Skyline	Skyline Honeylocust	4[a]	45	P[b]	Yellow	Leathery foliage
Gleditsia t. inermis Sunburst	Sunburst Honeylocust	4[a]	35	WS[b]	Yellow	Yellow foliage on branch tip
Koelreuteria paniculata	Crape Myrtle	4[a]	30	R[b]		Yellow flowers
Lagerstroemia indica		7[a]	20	R	Orange-red to yellow	Shades of red, pink, white flowers all summer
Larix decidua	European Larch	2	60	P		Cones 2 in. long, needlelike foliage
Liquidambar styraciflua var.	Sweetgum	5[a]	60	P[b]	Scarlet	Disease resistant
Liquidambar styraciflura Burgundy	Burgundy Sweetgum	5[a]	60	P[b]	Purple	Holds leaves longer
Liquidambar styraciflua Festival	Festival Sweetgum	5[a]	60	U[b]	Red to yellow	Narrow upright form
Liquidambar styraciflua Moraine	Moraine Sweetgum	5[a]	60	O[b]	Scarlet	Fast growth
Liriodendron tulipifera	Tulip Tree	4	150	P	Yellow	Tulip-shaped green/yellow flowers
Magnolia soulangeana	Saucer Magnolia	5[a]	20	R[b]	Bronze	Shrublike, white flowers
Magnolia stellata	Star Magnolia	5[a]	20	R[b]	Orange	Shrublike, white flowers
Malus var.	Crabapple					
Malus American Beauty	American Beauty Crab	4[a]	20	U[b]		Red flowers, red fruit
Malus baccata	Siberian Crab	2[a]	25	U[b]		White flowers, red/yellow fruit
Malus floribunda	Japanese Flowering Crab	4[a]	25	P[b]	Yellow to orange	Pink-white flowers, red/yellow fruit
Malus hopa	Hopa Red Flowering Crab	4	25	R		China rose colored flowers, orange/red fruit
Malus hupensis	Tea Crab	4[a]	20	V[b]		Pink flowers, yellow/red fruit
Malus Radiant	Radiant Crabapple	4[a]	18	R[b]		Deep pink flowers, red fruit
Malus Red Jade	Red Jade Crab	4	12	W		White flowers, red fruit
Malus Red Jewel	Red Jewel Crab	4	15	WS		White flowers, red fruit, glossy foliage

Table 10-1 Trees for Site Planning *(contd.)*

Latin Name	Common Name	Zone	Height (ft)	Habit	Fall Color	Characteristics
		DECIDUOUS TREES				
Malus Royal Ruby	Royal Ruby Crab	4	15	U		Dark red double flowers
Malus sargenti	Sargent Crab	5[a]	8	R[b]		White flowers, dark red fruit
Malus Snowdrift	Snowdrift Crab	3[a]	20	R[b]		White flowers, orange/red fruit
Malus zumi calocarpa	Zumi Crab	4[a]	15	P[b]		White flowers, red fruit
Nyssa sylvatica	Black Gum	4	60	P	Scarlet to orange	Dense lustrous leaves
Oxydendrum arboreum	Sourwood	4	30	P	Scarlet	Small white flowers, lustrous leathery foliate
Phellodendron amurense	Amur Cork Tree	3[a]	45	WS[b]	Yellow	Corky bark
Pistacia chinensis	Chinese Pistachio	6	50	R	Red to yellow	Fine textured foliage
Platanus acerifolia var.	London Plane Tree	5[a]	80	WS[b]		Peeling bark.
Platanus acerifolia Bloodgood	Bloodgood London Plane Tree	5[a]	50	WS[b]		Disease resistant
Populus nigra italica	Lombardy Poplar	2	80	U	Yellow	Dense leaves, short-lived
Populus simoni fastigiata	Pyramidal Simon Popular	2	60	P		Glossy foliate, immunity to canker
Prunus cerasifera atropurpurea Pissardi	Pissard Plum	3	20	U		Reddish purple foliage, pink flowers
Prunus cerasifera Thundercloud	Purpleleaf Flowering Plum	3	20	U		Purple foliage, pink flowers
Prunus serrulata var.	Oriental Cherry	5–6	25	WS		Single white flowers, glossy red bark
Prunus serrulata Kwanzan	Kwanzan Cherry	5	40	R		Double pink flowers
Prunus subhirtella pendula	Weeping Japanese Cherry	5	30	W		Pink flowers, weeping
Pyrus calleryana var.	Callery Pear	5[a]	30	P[b]	Red	White flowers
Pyrus calleryana Aristocrat	Aristocrat Pear	5[a]	40	O[b]	Crimson	Larger foliage
Pyrus calleryana Bradford	Bradford Pear	5[a]	40	P[b]	Crimson	Thornless
Pyrus calleryana Chanticleer	Chanticleer Pear	5[a]	40	P[b]	Yellow	Rapid growth
Pyrus calleryana Fauriei	Fauriei Pear	5[a]	15	R[b]		Dwarf selection
Quercus alba	White Oak	4	90	WS	Purple red to violet purple	Massive specimen, resistant to salt for winter use
Quercus borealis	Red Oak	4[a]	75	R[b]	Red	Rapid growth, resistant to salt for winter use
Quercus coccinea	Scarlet Oak	4	75	R	Brilliant scarlet	Lustrous foliage
Quercus imbricaria	Shingle Oak	5	75	P	Yellow to russet	Lustrous, laurel-like foliage
Quercus laurifolia	Laurel Oak	7	60	R		Dense foliage
Quercus nigra	Water Oak	6[a]	60	R[b]	Yellow to brown	Acid and neutral soils only, good in southeast
Quercus palustris	Pin Oak	4[a]	75	R[b]	Red	
Quercus palustris var. sovereign	Soverign Pin Oak	4[a]	75	P[b]	Red	Branching horizontal or ascending
Quercus phellos	Willow Oak	5	50	R	Yellow	Willow-like foliage
Quercus robur	English Oak	5	75	O		Small dark green foliage
Quercus robur fastiagiata	Pyramidal English Oak	5	70	U		Small dark green foliage
Quercus shumardii	Shumard Oak	4[a]	60	R[b]	Red to yellow	Suited to alkaline soils, lustrous dark green foliage
Sabal palmetto	Cabbage Palmetto	8[a]	90	Palm[b]		
Salix babylonica	Babylon Weeping Willow	5[a]	40	W[b]	Yellow	Pendulus
Sapium sebiforum	Chinese Tallow Tree	7[a]	40	WS[b]	Red to yellow	Lustrous green foliage, fast growth
Sophora japonica	Japanese Pagoda Tree	4[a]	70	R[b]	Yellow	Foliage open, good shade tree
Stewartia koreana	Korean Stewartia	5	45	P	Orange to red	White flowers with yellow stamens, peeling bark
Stewartia pseudocamellia	Japanese Stewartia	5	60	P	Purplish	White flowers, peeling bark
Styrax japonica	Japanese Snowbell	5	30	WS		White pendulous flowers, fine textured foliage
Taxodium distichum	Bald Cypress	4[a]	70	P[b]	Russet	Feathery foliage, good in wet areas
Tilia cordata var.	Little-leaf Linden	3[a]	60	P[b]	Yellow	Disease resistant, leathery foliage

Table 10-1 Trees for Site Planning *(contd.)*

Latin Name	Common Name	Zone	Height (ft)	Habit	Fall Color	Characteristics
			DECIDUOUS TREES			
Tilia cordata Greenspire	Greenspire Linden	3[a]	60	P[b]	Yellow	Disease resistant, leathery foliage
Tilia cordata Chancellor	Chancellor Linden	3[a]	60	P[b]	Yellow	Dense foliage
Tilia europaea	European Linden	3[a]	60	R[b]	Yellow	
Ulmus americana var. Augustine	Augustine Ascending Elm	2[a]	90	V[b]		Susceptible to Dutch elm disease and necrosis
Ulmus carpinifolia Christine Buisman	Christine Buisman Elm	4[a]	60	V[b]		
Ulmus crassifolia	Cedar Elm	6[a]	60	U[b]	Yellow	Grows in alkaline soils, good bark
Zelkova serrata var.	Japanest Zelkova	5[a]	60	V[b]	Yellow to russet	
Zelkova Parkview	Parkview Zelkova	5[a]	60	V[b]	Russet	Disease resistant, consistent form
Zelkova Village Green	Village Green Zelkova	5[a]	60	V[b]	Russet	Disease resistant, rapid growth
			EVERGREEN TREES			
Acacia melanoxylon	Blackwood Acacia	10	40	P		Dark gray/green foliage, medium dark gray bark
Abies concolor	White fir	4[a]	100	P[b]		Blue/green foliage
Cedrus atlantica glauca	Blue Atlas Cedar	6	120	P		Light blue foliage
Cedrus deodara	Deodar Cedar	7	150	P		Pendulous branches, dark bluish, needlelike foliage
Ceratonia siliqua	Carob tree	10	40	R		Dark glossy foliage
Chamaecyparis lawsoniana	Lawson False Cypress	5	120	P		Evergreen foliage, shredding bark
Chamaecyparis obtusa	Hinoki False Cypress	3	120	P		Dark glossy green leaves
Chamaecyparis pisifera	Sawara False Cypress	3	150	P		Evergreen scalelike shredding bark
Cinnamomum camphora	Camphor Tree	9[a]	40	R[b]		Dense glossy foliage
Cryptomeria japonica	Cryptomeria	5	150	P		Evergreen, dagger-shaped needles, reddish bark
Cupressus macrocarpa	Monterey Cypress	7	40	P		Dense, dark green foliage
Eriobotrya japonica	Loquat	7	20	U		Long leathery leaves, fragrant flowers
Eucalyptus camaldulensis rostrata	Longbeak Eucalyptus	9	60	R		Reddish twigs, gray bark, dark green foliage
Ficus rubiginosa australis	Rustyleaf Fig	9	50	R		Dark green leathery foliage, rusty underside
Ilex vomitoria	Yaupon	7[a]	20	R[b]		Lustrous foliage, gray bark, bright red fruit on females
Ligustrum lucidum	Glossy Privet	7	25	R[b]		Glossy foliage, blue-black berries, rapid growth
Magnolia grandiflora	Southern Magnolia	7[a]	100	P[b]		White flowers
Olea europaea	Common Olive	9	25	R		Evergreen, gray/green silvery beneath, purple olives
Picea abies	Norway Spruce	2	150	P		Dark green needles less than 1 in. long
Picea omrika	Serbian Spruce	4	90	P		Needles, whitish on underside
Picea pungens	Colorado Spruce	2[a]	80	P[b]		Stiff green to blue foliage
Pinus nigra	Austrian Pine	4	90	P		Long dark green needles
Pinus resinosa	Red Pine	2	75	P		Long dark green needles
Pinus strobus	White Pine	3	100+	P		Long soft needles
Pinus sylvestris	Scotch Pine	2	75	P		Orange bark
Pinus thunbergi	Japanese Black Pine	4	90	P		Bluish-green needles
Pseudotsuga taxifolia	Douglas Fir	4–6	80+	P		Horizontal branching pendulous cones
Quercus agrifolia	California Live Oak	9	90	R		Evergreen, hollylike foliage
Quercus virginiana	Live Oak	7[a]	60	WS[b]		Fine textured foliage
Taxus cuspidata	Japanese Yew	4[a]	30	P[b]		Red berries
Tsuga canadensis	Canada Hemlock	3	90	P		Dense needlelike foliage
Tsuga canadensis pendula	Weeping Hemlock	3	10	W		Dense needlelike foliage
Tsuga caroliniana	Carolina Hemlock	4	75	P		Dense foliage, needlelike

[a]Zone: trees for city use.
[b]O = oval; P = pyramidal; R = round; U = upright; W = weeping; V = vase-shaped; WS = wide-spreading.

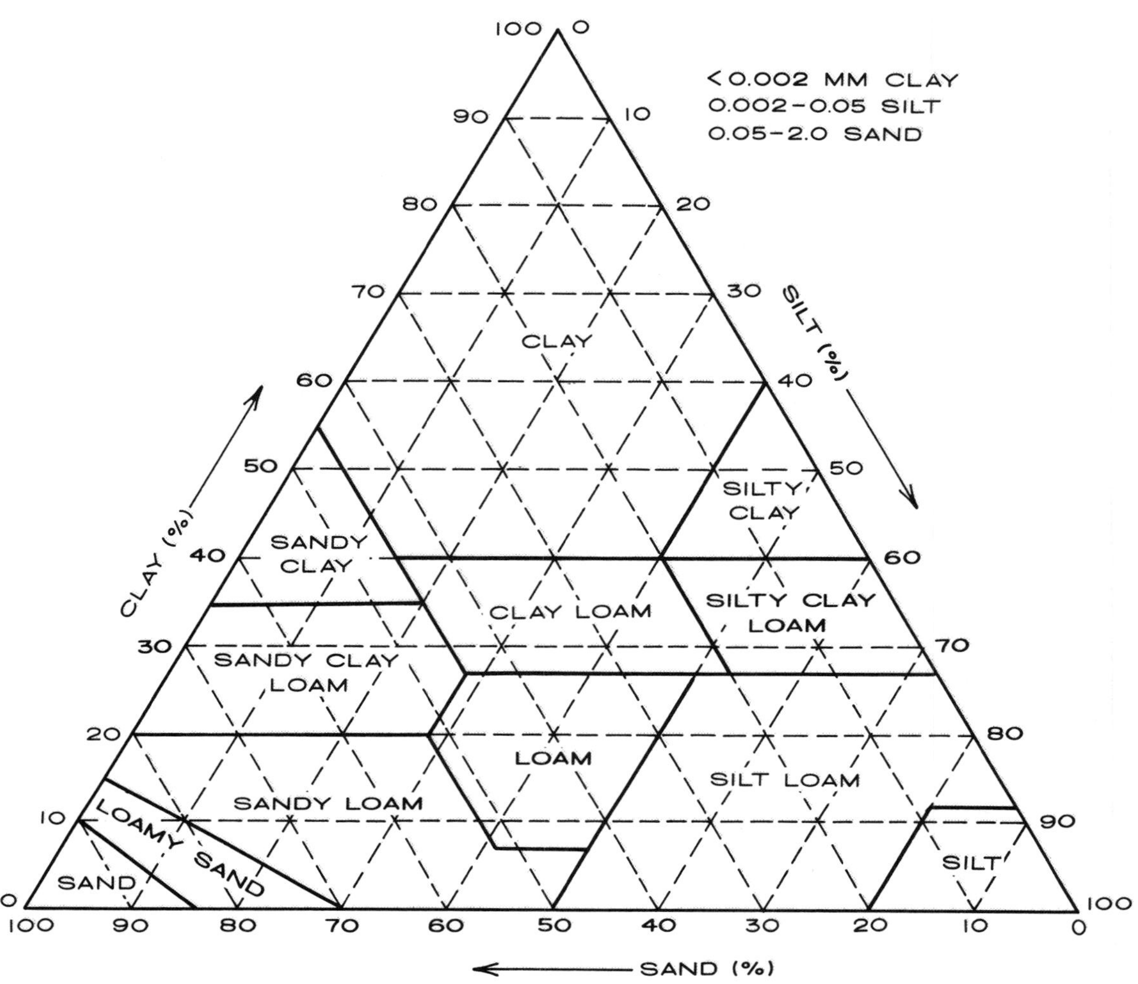

FIG. 10-10 Soil classification chart: U.S. Agriculture Department.

FACTORS RELATED TO INSTALLATION

Soil Composition and Testing

Soil is composed of mineral and organic matter, water, and air. (See Fig. 10-10.) Three mineral particles, as shown here, affect soil texture:

Sand	0.05 to 2.0 mm
Silt	0.002 to 0.05 mm
Clay	0.002 mm and smaller

Sand increases areation and drainage, but has little moisture holding capacity. Silt increases moisture holding capacity; clay increases nutrient holding capacity. Organic matter averages 3 to 5% in topsoil and keeps soil loose and porous.

Soil Test. Topsoil should be tested at a laboratory for pH and nutrient levels. The pH scale extends from 0 to 14, with a pH of 7 being neutral, below 7 acidic, and above 7 alkaline. The pH scale is logarithmic, and changing from a pH 7 to pH 8 means 10 times more alkaline soil. Going from a pH of 6.5 to 4.5 means the soil is 100 times more acidic. The majority of plants grow in a pH of 6 to 6.5; however, some plants will grow in more acidic soil. Nutrients are also most readily available in soil with a neutral pH.

When pH is tested, if the soil is too acidic limestone may be added to raise the pH level. Aluminum sulfate may be added if the soil is too alkaline to lower pH.

When soil is tested the organic content can be determined and nutrient deficiencies can then be corrected. In this manner it is possible to see if topsoil meets desired requirements. If not, nutrients may be added. The three major nutrients are nitrogen, potassium, and phosphorous; trace elements are magnesium, iron, sulfur, manganese, copper, zinc, boron, molybdenum, chlorine, and sodium.

Tree Pits

Tree pits should have a minimum diameter in paved areas of 5 ft and a minimum depth of 4 ft. The topsoil used for backfill should drain well. A typical mix would be one-third screened topsoil, one-third coarse sand, and one-third peat moss. Fertilizer such as manure is placed in the bottom of the pit at about 1 ft^3/ft diameter of the tree pit, except for evergreens.

Good drainage in a tree pit must be provided. Soil tests can be taken to check the need for a drainage system so that the trees do not become waterlogged.

Planting and Guying

Trees are generally dug at a nursery with a burlapped earth ball that has been tied with rope to prevent breakage. In planting the tree, the topsoil should be no higher than it was when the tree was growing at the nursery. This would be only an inch or two above the burlapped ball. After the tree is planted it should be well watered to remove air pockets in the soil. The tree is then guyed to prevent movement or breaking of the earth ball.

Next, a saucer about 3–6 in. high is placed around the tree to retain moisture from watering. A mulch of peat moss or wood chips about 3 in. deep is applied within the saucer to retain moisture. (See Figs. 10-11 to 10-16.)

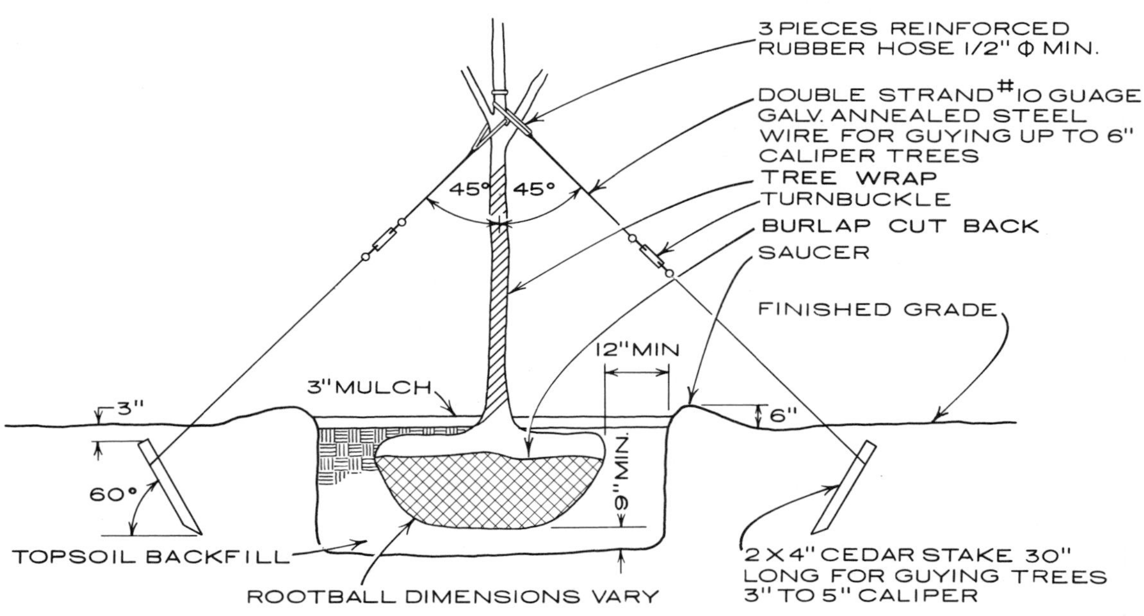

FIG. 10-11 Tree planting detail.

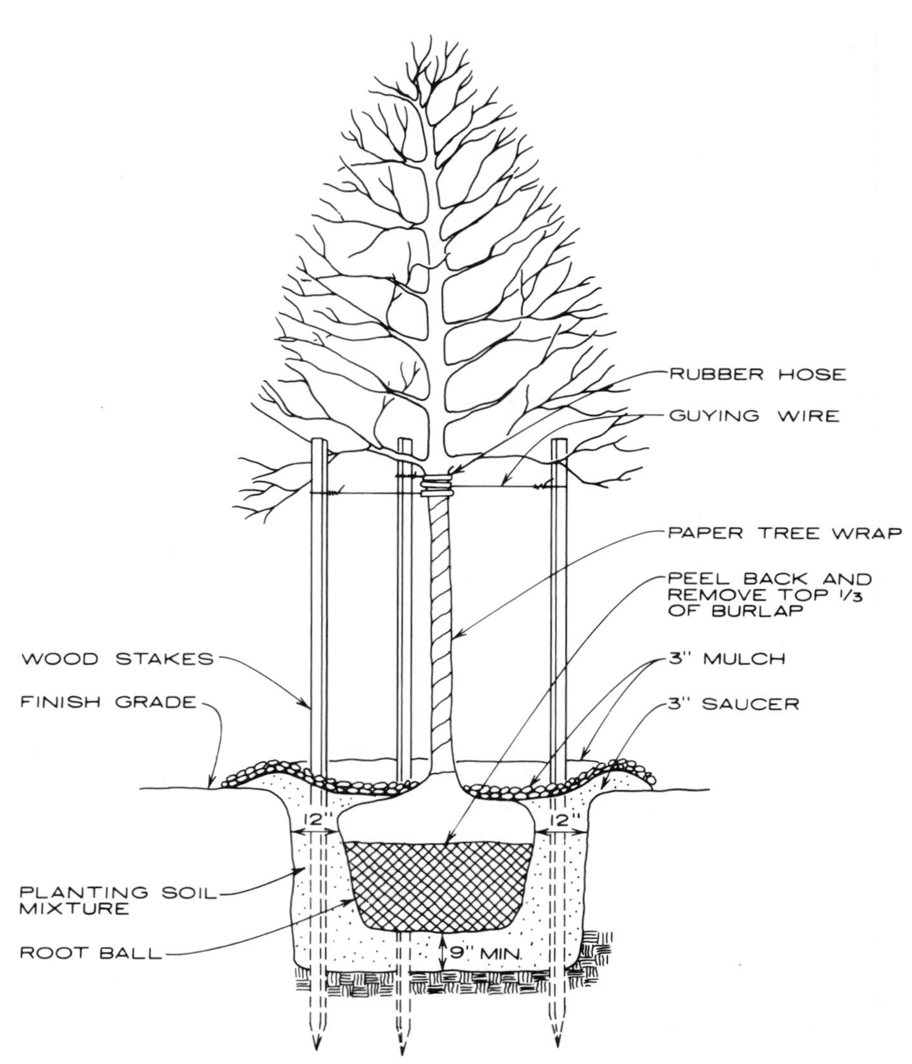

FIG. 10-12 Tree planting detail.

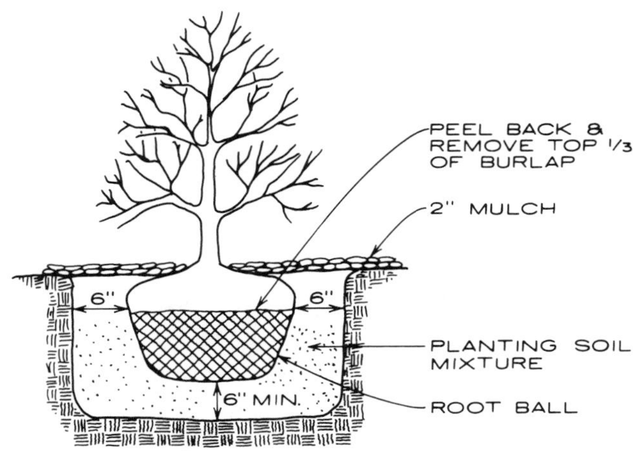

FIG. 10-13 Shrub planting detail.

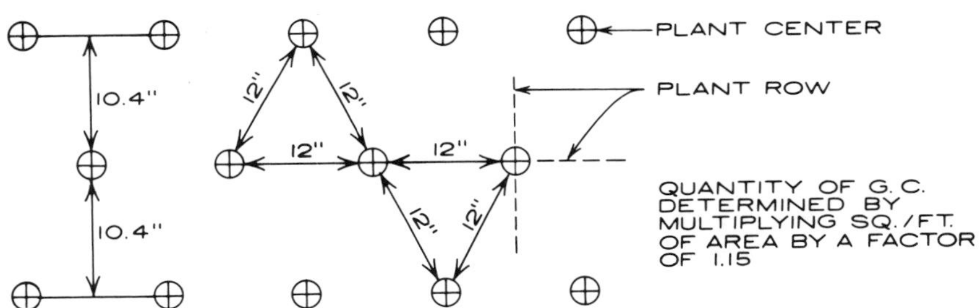

FIG. 10-14 Groundcover spacing.

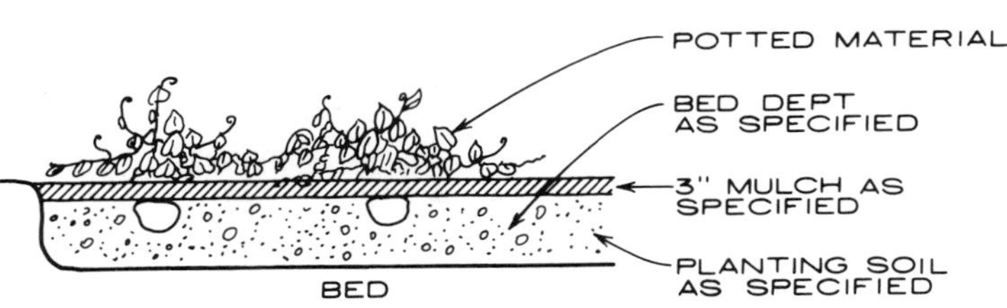

FIG. 10-15 Groundcover planting detail.

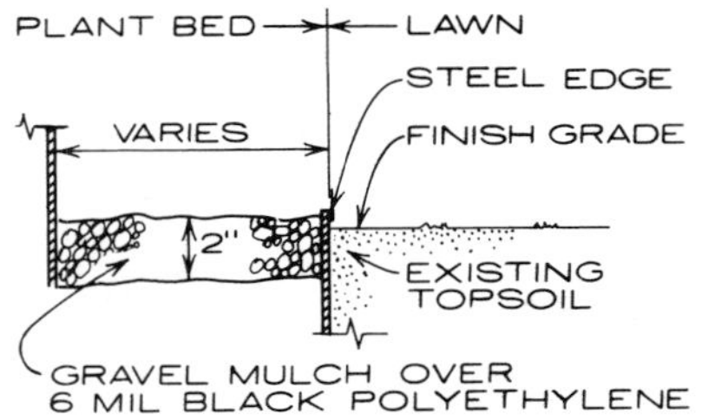

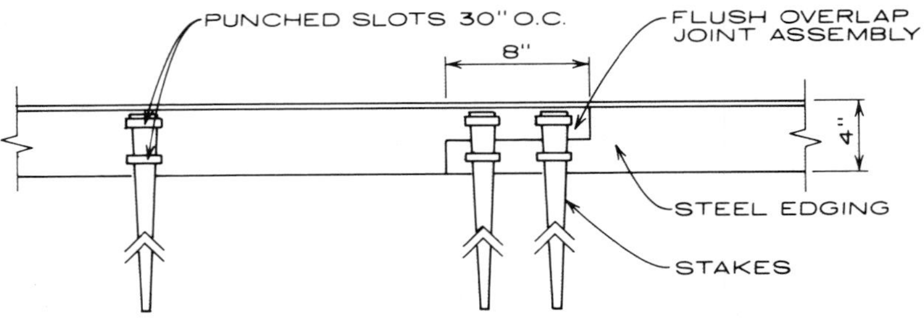

FIG. 10-16 Steel edge detail for plant beds.

Pruning

Pruning newly planted trees helps keep the evaporation of water in balance with the retention capacity of the roots, which have been cut back to the root ball. About one third of the branches are cut back.

Wrapping

After the tree is planted, the trunk should be wrapped with paper tree wrap or a good quality burlap up to the first major branch. The tree wrap prevents sun scald of some species and reduces evaporation through the trunk. Any wounds on the tree should be painted with tree paint.

Planting Dates

The dates for planting vary with each locality. Some trees do better when planted in the spring. In cool climates trees should be moved before new leaves come out. If trees are dug after leaves develop there is much greater chance that losses will occur. Deciduous trees can also be moved in the fall after the first hard frost. Evergreens can be planted in the late summer after new growth has hardened, temperatures have cooled, and soil is of good consistency for digging the earth balls. Evergreens are best moved in the early spring.

Maintenance

Trees planted in urban areas need care with pruning, watering, fertilizing, and spraying to prevent fungus or insects.

Maintenance problems also arise when trees undergo snow removal. When chemicals are used sodium nitrate is preferred to sodium or calcium chloride. Heavy use of salt can severely damage trees and other plant material and some trees are more resistant to salt than others, for example, red oak, white oak, and honey locust. Others such as linden, sugar maple, and hornbeam species are easily damaged.

Trees can also be raised above walk areas by the use of curbs. Where planters are used, winter injury to roots may be a problem. Insulation on the walls of the planter may help to prevent root injury. Planters must be well drained, particularly when on rooftop areas. The drain usually has about 3 or 4 in. of gravel above it with a fiberglass blanket separating topsoil from the gravel.

FIG. 11-1 Fountain at Tampa City Center Esplanade, Tampa, Florida.

Chapter Eleven
Specifications

In order to construct a project both construction drawings and written specifications must be developed. These are referred to as "construction documents." The documents above also contain contract forms, legal requirements for bidding, and conditions of the contract, while specifications cover the detailed requirements for products, materials, and workmanship.

In 1963 the Construction Specification Institute (CSI) developed a format for organizing the written documents. Most architectural specifications follow this system. Examples of some typical sections of specifications are given to show how the documents are written for site development portions of an architectural project.

THE PROJECT MANUAL

The title "Project Manual" originated with the American Institute of Architects in 1964. This was a more comprehensive title than calling it specifications because the manual contained the following:

1. Bidding requirements with contract forms, bonds, and certificates
2. Conditions of the contract
3. Specifications

The project manual format has a flexible system divided into 16 divisions. Also a system of numbering documents and specification sections has been standardized for various topics in each division and is described later in this chapter.

Introductory Pages

A typical project manual contains the following:

1. Cover Page with the following:
   a. Project Identification
   b. Name of Owner
   c. Architect/Engineer's Identification
   d. Date
2. Title Page with the following:
   a. Project Identification
   b. Name of Owner
   c. Contract Number
   d. Owner's Name and Address
   e. Architect/Engineer's Name, Address, and Telephone
   f. Consultants
   g. Date
   h. Certification, Signature, Seal, Registration of Architect/Engineer (when required by law)
3. Signature Page of Architect/Engineer, Owner, Contractor, and others as required
4. Table of Contents

Invitation to Bid

The invitation to bid is written to attract qualified bidders and to help prospective bidders make a decision on whether they should ask for a set of construction documents. The invitation to bid should be concise and contain the following (see Fig. 11-2):

1. Project identification
2. Description of work
3. Type of bids required
4. Time and place
5. Examination and obtaining documents
6. Bid security, references if required
7. Bidder's prequalifications
8. Owner's right to reject bids
9. Laws or regulations governing bids

Instructions to Bidders

The requirements that bidders must comply with both before and during the submission of their bids are contained in these instructions. The following information may be contained (see Fig. 11-3):

1. Project identification
2. Qualifications of bidders
3. Examination of project site
4. Examination of bidding documents
5. Addenda and interpretations
6. Substitutions
7. Taxes
8. Fees or permits
9. Required bonds such as performance bond, labor and material payment bond

INVITATION

INVITATION FOR PROPOSALS/LANDSCAPE IMPROVEMENTS

PROJECT: LANDSCAPE DEVELOPMENT PHASE 1
Fort Worth, Texas

PROJECT NO.: 4019

Gentlemen:

You are invited to submit proposals for the ______ Project Landscape Improvements work as required by the contract documents and briefly described as follows:

Planting, irrigation, and brick walks.

Sealed proposals from selected bidders will be received by the Owner's representative, ____________________

Place: ____________________
____

Attention: ____________________

Time: Until 2:00 P.M.

Date: Wednesday, January 30, 1987

Bidding Documents may be obtained from the office of the Architect.

Each set of Bidding Documents includes the following:

1 copy Project Manual/LANDSCAPE IMPROVEMENTS

1 set Drawings/Phase I Landscape Improvements

Call ____________________ at ____________________ if you have questions.

END OF INVITATION

FIG. 11-2 Invitation.

10. Contractor's representatives
11. Time of completion
12. Preparation of proposals
13. Submission of proposals
14. Withdrawal of proposals
15. Receipt and opening of proposals
16. Award of contract
17. Execution of agreement
18. Owner's right reserved

QUALIFICATION OF BIDDERS:

Proposals for work of this Contract may be submitted only by invitation.

The Owner may make such investigation as he deems necessary to determine the ability of the Bidder and his subcontractors to perform the work. Upon Owner's request, Bidder shall submit a completed AIA Document A305 to assist the Owner's investigation; submit completed form within 5 calendar days of request. The Owner reserves the right to reject any bidder if the evidence submitted by, or investigation of, such bidder fails to satisfy the Owner that such bidder is properly qualified to carry out the obligations of the Contract and to complete the work required therein.

EXAMINATION OF THE PROJECT SITE:

The Bidder, in order to fully understand the nature and scope of the work, must visit the site, familiarize himself with conditions under which the work is to be performed, and correlate his observations with the requirements of the Contract Documents. Such examination will be presumed to have been made and no allowance will be made to Contractor for extra labor and materials required or for conditions encountered that might have been foreseen had examination been made.

EXAMINATION OF BIDDING DOCUMENTS:

Should the Bidder, during examination of the Bidding Documents, find discrepancies, omissions, ambiguities, or conflicts in or among the documents, he shall bring such matters to the attention of the Architect.

Questions should be submitted to: ______________________________

____

____

ADDENDA AND INTERPRETATIONS:

Response to all questions, inquiries, and requests for additional information will be issued in the form of addenda to the Contract Documents. A copy of each addendum will be issued to all prospective bidders.

Bidder may, during the time allowed for bidding, be advised by addenda of additions, deletions, or changes in requirements of the Contract Documents.

Neither Architect nor Owner nor their representatives will be responsible for authenticity or correctness of oral interpretations or for information obtained in any manner other than by addenda.

Receipt of each addendum shall be acknowledged in the Bidder's proposal, and all addenda will be made a part of the Contract Documents.

SUBSTITUTIONS:

The Architect will not attempt to determine the acceptability of any product substitutions during the bidding period.

The Bidder is advised that inclusion of a substitution in any part of his bid is done at the Bidder's own risk with the understanding that, if awarded the Contract, he shall provide the specified product at no additional cost to the Owner, should the Architect find the substitute product not acceptable.

Refer to applicable portions of Supplementary Conditions and Division 1—General Requirements—which establish conditions under which substitutions will be considered.

Requests for substitutions received after 30-day period following execution of the Contract will not be considered and the specified product shall be provided at no additional cost to the Owner.

TAXES:

Include in the proposal sum, for each part of work, the cost of all sales, unemployment, old age pension, and other such taxes and expenses imposed by city, state, or federal government.

FIG. 11-3 Instructions to bidders.

FEES OR PERMITS:

Include in the proposal sum, for each part of the work, the cost of all fees, permits, licenses, deposits, and all other such expenses required for the completion of the work.

REQUIRED BONDS:

Performance Bond:

Bidder shall include, in his proposed sum for each part of the work, the cost of Performance Bond in amount of 100% of Contract Sum for each part of the work.

CONTRACTOR'S REPRESENTATIVE:

Bidder shall identify on his proposal a person who, in the event that Bidder is awarded Contract, is thoroughly familiar with the work and who may be contacted for duration of project during regular business hours to act as liaison between Contractor, Owner, and Architect.

TIME OF COMPLETION:

It is anticipated that the "Notice to Proceed" will be issued on or about February 15, 1987. The Bidder will be required to complete the work in 110 calendar days.

Bidder in submitting proposal thereby agrees, if awarded Contract, to commence work on date established by Owner in written "Notice to Proceed" and to fully complete work within the 110 days stated in Contract. Time will be computed from date on which Contract is signed.

PROPOSALS:

Preparation of Proposals:

Prepare proposals on forms provided by the Architect with all blank spaces fully completed, without interlineation, alteration, and erasure. All sums must be in both words and figures (if there is a discrepancy, the written sum will govern). Signatures must be in ink, executed by the principal, of the bidding firm, authorized to make contracts, attested by secretary, if corporation. Bidder shall state his full legal name.

Submission of Proposals:

Submit proposals in duplicate, in form as provided herein. This form may be photocopied only; retyping is not acceptable. Submit in sealed, opaque envelope, addressed as follows:

____

____

Attention: ________________________________

Clearly identify contents of the envelope by marking the lower left-hand corner as follows:

PROPOSAL/LANDSCAPE IMPROVEMENTS
Fort Worth, Texas

Withdrawal of Proposals:

The Bidder may withdraw his proposal, either personally or by telegraphic or written request, at any time prior to scheduled closing time for receipt of proposals.

After the opening of bids, proposals may not be withdrawn for a period of thirty (30) days from the bid date and will be subject to the Owner's acceptance during that time.

Receipt and Opening of Proposals:

The General Contractor will receive proposals until the appointed time of the appointed day and at the appointed place, all as designated in the "Invitation" and will open proposals privately.

Proposals received after the designated time and date will not be considered.

The Bidder is solely responsible for his proposal's arriving on time at the designated place.

No responsibility for the premature opening of a proposal that is not properly addressed and identified shall attach to the owner, the Architect, or their authorized representative.

AWARD OF CONTRACT:

The Owner will award Contract as soon as practical to the lowest responsible bidder, prices and other factors considered, provided low bid is reasonable, as judged by the Owner, and low bidder's proposal is in the best interest of the Owner.

The Owner may, at his option, award separate contracts for each part or parts of the work, as serves the best interests of the Owner. Therefore, the proposal sum for each part of Bidder's proposal must include all costs relative to that part.

EXECUTION OF AGREEMENT:

A copy of the form of Agreement, which the successful Bidder as Contractor will be required to execute, will be provided by the Owner.

The Bidder, if awarded Contract, shall, within ten (10) days after notice of award and receipt of Agreement forms from the Owner, execute and deliver to the Owner all copies of Agreement.

Within ten (10) days after notice of award by the Owner, the Contractor shall deliver to the Owner the Performance Bond, and policies of insurance or insurance certificates as required by the Contract Documents.

Failure or refusal to furnish bonds or insurance policies or certificates in a form satisfactory to the Owner shall subject the successful Bidder to loss of time from the allowable construction period equal to the time of delay in furnishing the required materials.

Contractor shall, within 15 calendar days after receiving "Notice to Proceed," submit a schedule for completing the work and shall complete the work within the time period specified in the proposal form.

OWNER'S RIGHTS RESERVED:

The right is reserved, as the interest of the Owner may require, to accept or reject any or all proposals, or to waive any irregularities or informalities in any proposal received.

END OF INSTRUCTIONS TO BIDDERS

Form of Proposal

The Form of Proposal is the document in which the bidder fills in the cost for one or more work items. The Form of Proposal may state the length of time the contractor has to complete the work, the date when bonds will be required, the name of insurance carrier of contractor, the length of time the proposal will remain in effect after receipt of bids, and owner's rights. (See Fig. 11-4).

FORM OF PROPOSAL

PROPOSAL/LANDSCAPE IMPROVEMENTS

Fort Worth, Texas

Project No.: 4019

Date: ______________________ 1987

Proposal of ______________________________ (hereinafter called "Bidder"), organized and existing under the laws of the State of ______________________________, doing business as [ ] a corporation, [ ] a Partnership, [ ], or [ ] an Individual.

TO: ______________________________

Attention: ______________________________

Gentlemen:

Having examined the Instructions to Bidders and Contract Documents, including the drawings, the specifications, and the following addenda.

Addendum No. __________, __________, __________, __________, __________
Dated __________, __________, __________, __________, __________

And being familiar with all conditions affecting the work, the Bidder proposes to provide all services, including superintendence; labor, materials and equipment required for completion of selected portions of the work, in accordance with Contract Documents, for separate bid sums indicated as follows:

Landscape work for the following items:

TOTAL BASE BID:

______________________________ Dollars, $ ______________________

Each separate bid sum includes its relative costs of insurance; bonds; and all sales taxes, excise taxes, and other taxes for materials, appliances, and services subject to and upon which taxes are levied.

UNIT PRICES:

The Bidder agrees that unit prices indicated on attached Schedule of Unit Prices, if accepted in the award of Contract, shall be used in establishing the adjustment of Contract Sums for additions and deletions from the Contract Work. Unit prices indicated shall include all costs, profit, and overhead, and no further surcharges shall be added.

EXTRA WORK:

If any change in the work is ordered and unit prices are not applicable, the Bidder proposes that the following percentages be applicable and added to the material and labor costs to cover overhead and profit.

FIG. 11-4 Form of proposal.

Percentage Markup to Payroll and Material Costs:

Combined percentage for taxes, insurance, overhead, and profit on Contractor's straight time payroll:

________________ Percent ________________ %

Percentage to be added to premium portion of overtime payroll expense:

________________ Percent ________________ %

Profit on Materials:

________________ Percent ________________ %

Percentage to be added for supervision of subcontractors:

________________ Percent ________________ %

ALTERNATE PROPOSALS:

The Bidder proposes to perform Alternate Work indicated on the Proposal for Alternates, attached herewith, for stipulated sums indicated therein, and which, if accepted, will result in additions to or deductions from the Base Bid price.

CONTRACT FORM:

The Bidder, if awarded Contract, agrees that he will have no objection to the proposed contract form, a sample copy of which is available from the Owner and is made a part of this proposal as fully and completely as if repeated word for word herein, and will execute same after the necessary information has been added thereto.

PERFORMANCE BOND:

The Bidder agrees, if awarded Contract, to deliver to the Owner, within ten (10) days after the date of written notice of award of Contract the required Performance Bond.

INSURANCE:

The Bidder agrees, if awarded Contract, to deliver to the Owner, within ten (10) days after the date of written notice of award of Contract and before proceeding with the work, the Certificate of Insurance as specified.

The Bidder proposes to use the following insurance carrier:

Name ________________

Address ________________

City ________________ State ________________ Zip ________________

Attach additional sheets if more than one insurance carrier is proposed and indicate type of insurance applicable to each carrier.

TIME OF COMPLETION:

The Bidder agrees, if awarded the Contract, to complete the work as within the period of time indicated in the Instructions to Bidders, commencing on the date of written notice to proceed.

OWNER'S RIGHTS:

The Bidder agrees that this proposal shall be good and may not be withdrawn for a period of sixty (60) days from the date established for receipt of bids.

The Bidder understands that the Owner reserves the right to reject any and all bids, to waive minor informalities in any bid, and to award the Contract in the best interest of the Owner.

CONTRACTOR'S REPRESENTATIVE:

The Bidder, if awarded Contract, proposes to provide services of the indicated person to act, during normal business hours, as liaison between Contractor, Architect and Owner.

Name ______________________________

Position ______________________________

Area Code __________ Telephone Number ______________________________

BIDDER'S CERTIFICATION:

The Bidder hereby certifies:

That this proposal is genuine and is not made in the interest of or on behalf of any undisclosed person, firm, or corporation, and is not submitted in the conformity with any agreement or rules of any group, association or corporation;

That he has not solicited or induced any person, firm, or corporation to refrain from bidding.

That he has not sought by collusion or otherwise to obtain for himself any advantage over any other bidder or over the Owner.

Bidder will not discriminate against any employee or applicant for employment because of race, creed, color, or national origin in connection with the performance of the work.

OWNER'S RIGHTS:

The Bidder understands that the Owner reserves the right to reject any and all bids, to waive minor informalities in any bid, and to award the Contract in the best interest of the Owner.

Respectfully submitted,

____
Name of Bidder

____
Signature

____
Title

____
Address

____
City State Zip

____
City State Zip

____
Area Code Telephone

SEAL
(If Bidder is a Corporation)

____
Attested By

____
Attested By

____
Date

Conditions of the Contract

The Conditions of the Contract in the project manual contain the General Conditions and the Supplementary Conditions that are supplemented by Division 1, General Requirements. The General Conditions for many architectural projects is AIA Document A201 General Conditions of the Contract for Construction. The latest edition of this document should be used (See Fig. 11-5).

The "General Conditions" of a construction contract outline the relationships, rights, and responsibilities of the signators of the contract. AIA Document A201 describes the following articles:

1. Contract documents
2. Architect
3. Owner
4. Contractor
5. Subcontractors
6. Separate contracts
7. Miscellaneous provisions, including bonds
8. Time
9. Payment and completion
10. Protection of persons and property
11. Insurance
12. Changes in the work
13. Uncovering and correction of work
14. Termination of the contract

Supplementary Conditions

Modifications needed to suit the requirements of the architect/engineer for a specific project are outlined in Supplementary Conditions. The changes required for deletions or modifications should follow the same order as in the general conditions.

General and Supplementary Conditions are contractual-legal portions of the contract. They should therefore be carefully prepared by persons knowledgeable in construction and should be reviewed by the owner's attorney. The architect/engineer should ask the owner to make sure his insurance agent reviews the project insurance coverage to make sure the owner is adequately protected. (See Fig. 11-6).

GENERAL CONDITIONS

The General Conditions of the Contract for Construction (AIA Document A201 Thirteenth Edition, August 1976), hereinafter referred to as the "General Conditions," are hereby made part of these Specifications to the same extent as if reproduced herein in full, except as modified, amended, revised, rescinded, or supplemented by the Supplementary Conditions, which shall take precedence in all cases of conflicting requirements. Those portions of the AIA General Conditions, which are not altered, modified, amended, or rescinded by the Supplementary Conditions shall remain in full force and effect as published. Copies of the Thirteen Edition of AIA Document A201 may be examined at the offices of the Architects or may be purchased, at a nominal charge, from any dealer in Architect's supplies, from the American Institute of Architects, 1735 New York Avenue, N. W., Washington, D. C. 20006, or from the AIA Bookstore, McKinney Ave., Dallas, Texas 75201.75201.

FIG. 11-5 General conditions.

SUPPLEMENTARY CONDITIONS

The following supplements modify, change, delete from, or add to the "General Conditions of the Contract for Construction," AIA Document A201, Thirteenth Edition, August 1976. Where any Article of the General Conditions is modified or deleted by these Supplementary Conditions, the unaltered provisions of that Article, Paragraph, Subparagraph, or Clause shall remain in effect.

ARTICLE 1; CONTRACT DOCUMENTS
1.1 Definitions

Add the following Subparagraph 1.1.5 to 1.1:

The Project Manual is the volume that includes the bidding requirements, sample forms, and certain elements of the Contract Documents such as the Conditions of the Contract and the Specifications.

ARTICLE 4; CONTRACTOR
4.4 Labor and Materials

Add the following Subparagraphs 4.4.3 and 4.4.4 to 4.4:

4.4.3 Not later than 30 days from the Contract Date, the Contractor shall provide a list showing the name of the manufacturer proposed to be used for the products identified in the General Requirements (Division 1) and, where applicable, the name of the installing subcontractor.

4.4.4 The Architect will reply within fifteen (15) days in writing to the Contractor stating whether the Owner or Architect, after due investigation, has reasonable objection to any such proposal. If adequate data on any proposed manufacturer or installer are not available, the Architect may state that action may be deferred until the Contractor provides further data. Failure of the Owner or Architect to reply promptly shall constitute notice of no reasonable objection. Failure to object to a manufacturer shall not constitute a waiver of any of the requirements of the Contract Documents, and all products furnished by the listed manufacturer must conform to such requirements.

Add the following Clauses 4.4.4.1 and 4.4.4.2 to 4.4.4:

4.4.4.1 After the Contract has been executed, the Owner and the Architect will consider a formal request for the substitution of products in place of those specified only under the conditions set forth in the General Requirements of the Specifications (Division 1).

4.4.4.2 By making requests for substitution based on Clause 4.4.4.1 above, the Contractor:

(a) represents that he has personally investigated the proposed substitute product and determined that it is equal or superior in all respects to that specified;

(b) represents that he will provide the same warranty for the substitution that he would for that specified.

(c) certifies that the cost data represented is complete and includes all related costs under this contact but excludes costs under separate contracts, and excludes the Architect's redesign costs, and waives all claims for additional costs related to the substitution which subsequently becomes apparent.

(d) will coordinate the installation of the accepted substitute, making such changes as may be required for the work to be complete in all respects.

ARTICLE 9; PAYMENTS AND COMPLETION
9.3 Applications for Payment

Add the following Clause 9.3.1.1 to 9.3.1:

9.3.1.1 Until Substantial Completion, the Owner will pay ninety (90%) percent of the amount due the Contractor on account of progress payments.

FIG. 11-6 Supplementary conditions.

ARTICLE 11; INSURANCE
Contractor's Liability Insurance

11.1.1 In the first line following the word "maintain", insert the words "in a company or companies licensed to do business in the state in which the project is located".

11.1.7 Liability Insurance shall include all major divisions of coverage and be on a comprehensive basis including:

1. Premises Operation (included X-C/U as applicable)
2. Independent Contractor's Protective
3. Products and Completed Operations
4. Personal Injury Liability with Employment Exclusion deleted
5. Contractual—including specific provisions for Contractor's obligation under Paragraph 4.18
6. Owned, nonowned, and hired motor vehicles
7. Broad Form Property Damage including Completed Operations
8. Umbrella Excess Liability

Add the following Clause 11.1.2.1 to 11.1.2:

11.1.2.1 The insurance required by Subparagraph 11.1.1 shall be written for not less than the following, or greater if required by law:

1. Workers' Compensation:

(a) State	Statutory
(b) Applicable Federal (e.g. Longshoremen's):	Statutory
(c) Employer's Liability	$100,000.

2. Comprehensive General Liability (including Premises Operations; Independent Contractors' Protective; Products and Completed Operations; Broad Form Property Damage):

(a) Bodily Injury:

$300,000.	Each Occurrence
$300,000.	Annual Aggregate

(b) Property Damage:

$100,000.	Each Occurrence
$100,000.	Annual Aggregate

(c) Products and Complete Operations to be maintained for 2 years after final payment.

(d) Property Damage Liability Insurance shall provide X, C, or U coverage as applicable.

3. Contractual Liability:

(a) Bodily Injury:

$250,000.	Each Person
$500,000.	Each Occurrence

(b) Property Damage:

$100,000.	Each Occurrence
$100,000.	Annual Aggregate

4. Personal Injury, with Employment Exclusion deleted:

$300,000.	Annual Aggregate

5. Comprehensive Automobile Liability:

(a) Bodily Injury:

$250,000.	Each Person
$500,000.	Each Occurrence

(b) Property Damage:

$100,000.	Each Occurrence

NOTE: State of Texas has a no-fault automobile insurance requirement. The Contractor shall be certain coverage is provided which conforms to any specific stipulation in the law.

6. Umbrella Excess Liability:

(a) $1,000,000.	Over Primary Insurance

11.2 Owner's Liability Insurance

Concerning the insurance described in Paragraph 11.2 of AIA Document A201, 1976 Edition.

1. The Contractor shall provide this insurance (normally under an Owner's Protective Liability Policy) with the following limits:

(a) Bodily Injury:

$500,000.	Each Occurrence
$500,000.	Aggregate

(b) Property Damage:

$100,000.	Each Occurrence
$100,000.	Aggregate

(c) Personal Injury, with Employment Exclusion deleted:

$500,000.	Aggregate

11.3 Property Insurance

Delete 11.3.1 in its entirety and substitute the following:

11.3.1 The Contractor shall purchase and maintain property insurance upon the entire Work at the site to the full insurable value thereof. Such insurance shall be in company or companies against which the Owner has no reasonable objection. This insurance shall include the interests of the Owner, the contractor, Subcontractors, and Sub-subcontractors in the Work and shall insure against the perils of fire and extended coverage and shall include "all risk" insurance for physical loss or damage including, without duplication of coverage, theft, vandalism, and malicious mischief. If not covered under all risk insurance or otherwise provided in the Contract Documents, the Contractor shall effect and maintain similar property insurance on portions of the Work stored off the site or in transit when such portions of the Work are to be included in Application for Payment under Subparagraph 9.3.2.

Add the following Clause 11.3.1.1 to 11.3.1:

11.3.1.1 The form of policy for this coverage shall be completed value.

Add the following Clause 11.3.1.2 to 11.3.1:

11.3.1.2 If by the terms of this insurance any mandatory deductibles are required, or if the Contractor should elect, with the concurrence of the Owner, to increase the mandatory deductible amounts or purchase this insurance with voluntary deductible amounts, the Contractor shall be responsible for payment of the amount of all deductibles in the event of a paid claim. If separate contractors are added as insureds to be covered by this policy, the separate contractors shall be responsible for payment or appropriate part of any deductibles in the event claims are paid on their part of the Project.

Delete Subparagraph 11.3.4 in its entirety and substitute the following:

Specifications

Division 1—General Requirements. Division 1 defines the scope of the contracts on which Bidding Requirements and Contract Forms are based. It also relates to provisions of the General Conditions: Its location at the beginning of the contents of the specifications signifies its relation to all sections of divisions 2–16. See Fig. 11-7, which is a typical section of the General Requirements.

01010	SUMMARY OF WORK	01010

PART 1—GENERAL

RELATED DOCUMENTS:

Drawings and general provisions of Contract, including General and Supplementary Conditions and Division-1 Specification sections apply to work of this section.

PROJECT/WORK IDENTIFICATION:

General: The name of the project is ______________________ and the project number, "4019", is shown on contract documents prepared by ______________________. Drawings and Specifications are dated ______________________.

Contract Documents indicate the work of Contract.

Summary by Reference: Work of contract can be summarized by reference to the Contract, General Conditions, Supplementary Conditions, Specification sections as listed in the "Table of Contents" bound herewith, Drawings issued separately, addenda and modifications to the contract documents issued subsequent to the initial printing of this project manual, and including but not necessarily limited to printed matter referenced by any of these. It is recognized that work of Contract is also unavoidably affected or influenced by governing regulations, natural phenomena including weather conditions, and other forces outside the contract documents.

ALTERNATES:

Definitions: Alternates are defined as alternate products, materials, equipment, installations, or systems for the work that may, at Owner's option and under terms established by Instructions to Bidders, be selected and recorded in the Contract (Owner-Contractor Agreement) to either supplement or displace corresponding basic requirements of contract documents. Alternates may or may not substantially change scope and general character of the work; and must not be confused with "allowances," "unit prices," "change orders," "substitutions," and other similar provisions.

General Provisions: A "Schedule of Alternates" is included at end of this section. Each alternate is defined by abbreviated language, recognizing that drawings and specification sections document the requirements. Coordination of related work is required to ensure that work affected by each selected alternate is complete and properly interfaced with work of alternates.

Notification: Immediately following award of Contract, prepare and distribute to each entity to be involved in performance of the work a notification of status of each alternate. Indicate which alternates have been 1) Accepted, 2) Rejected, and 3) Deferred for consideration at a later date as indicated. Include full description of negotiated modifications to alternates, if any.

PART 2—PRODUCTS (not applicable)

PART 3—EXECUTION (not applicable)

END OF SECTION 01010

FIG. 11-7 Summary of work.

Specification Sections. Each section of the specifications is divided into three major parts. (See Fig. 11-8).

PART 1—General, includes the following:
1. Related Documents
2. Quality Assurance
3. Submittals
4. Job Conditions

PART 2—Products, includes the following:
1. Descriptions
2. Proprietary name, ASTM number or classification

PART 3—Execution

This part describes how material or work is to be installed or carried out.

02930	LAWNS	02930

PART 1—GENERAL

RELATED DOCUMENTS:

Drawings and general provisions of Contract, including General and Supplementary Conditions and Division-1 Specification sections, apply to work of this section.

Section "Landscape Development, General" applies to work of this section.

DESCRIPTION OF WORK:

Extent of lawn work is shown on drawings.

Types of work required include following:

Fine grading and preparation of lawn areas.

Sodding of new lawn areas.

Replanting of unsatisfactory or damaged lawns.

SUBMITTALS:

Certification of Grass Seed:

Submit seed vendor's certified statement for each grass seed mixture required, stating botanical and common name, percentage by weight, and percentages of purity, germination, and weed seed for each grass seed species.

PART 2—PRODUCTS

GRASS MATERIALS:

Grass Seed: Provide fresh, clean, new-crop seed complying with tolerance for purity and germination established by Official Seed Analysts of North America. Provide seed of grass species, proportions, and minimum percentages of purity, germination, and maximum percentage of weed seed, as specified. Common Bermuda grass (*Cynodon dactylon*) of 98% purity, 82% germination.

FIG. 11-8 Lawn specification.

Sod: Provide strongly rooted sod, not less than 2 years old with a uniform thickness of not less than 2 inches and free of weeds and undesirable native grasses. Provide sod capable of growth and development when planted (viable, not dormant), composed with a minimum of 95% of the following:

Common Bermuda grass (*Cynodon dactylon*).

Deliver sod on pallets and protect root system from exposure to wind or sun.

Time delivery so that sod will be placed within 24 hours after stripping. Protect sod against drying and breaking of rolled strips. Keep sod stored under shade or covered with burlap.

PART 3—EXECUTION

SOIL PREPARATION:

Refer to Section "Landscape Development, General" for requirements for planting soil mixtures.

Limit preparation to areas that will be planted in immediate future. In areas with existing grass such as Hulen Street medians apply Roundup. After grass has died remove dead grass and begin work on subgrade.

Loosen subgrade of lawn areas to a minimum depth of 4 in. Remove stones over 1½ in. in any dimension and sticks, roots, rubbish, and other extraneous matter. RETAIN ABOVE AND BELOW IF ANY AREAS FOR LAWNS HAVE BEEN STRIPPED OF TOPSOIL.

Spread topsoil to a 4 in. minimum depth and meet thickness, grades, and elevations shown, after light rolling and natural settlement. Do not spread if material is frozen or if subgrade is frozen.

Allow for sod thickness in areas to be sodded.

Preparation of Unchanged Grades: Where lawns are to be planted in areas that have not been altered or disturbed by excavating, grading, or stripping operations, prepare soil for lawn planting as follows: Till to a depth of not less than 6 in.; apply soil amendments and initial fertilizers as specified in Section "Landscape Development, General"; remove high areas and fill in depressions; till soil to a homogeneous mixture of fine texture, free of lumps, clods, stones, roots, and other extraneous matter.

Prior to preparation of unchanged areas, remove existing grass, vegetation, and turf. Dispose of such material outside of Owner's property; do not turn over into soil being prepared for lawns.

Grade lawn areas to a smooth, even surface with loose, uniformly fine texture. Roll and rake, remove ridges and fill depressions, to meet finish grades. Limit fine grading to areas that can be planted within immediate future.

Moisten prepared lawn areas before planting if soil is dry. Water thoroughly and allow surface to dry off before planting of lawns. Do not create a muddy soil condition.

Restore prepared areas to specified condition if eroded or otherwise disturbed after fine grading and prior to planting.

SODDING NEW LAWNS:

Lay sod within 24 hours from time of stripping. Do not plant dormant sod or if ground is frozen.

Lay sod to form solid mass with tightly fitted joints. Butt ends and sides of sod strips; do not overlap. Stagger strips to offset joints in adjacent courses. Work from boards to avoid damage to subgrade or sod. Tamp or roll lightly to ensure contact with subgrade. Work sifted soil into minor cracks between pieces of sod; remove excess to avoid smothering adjacent grass.

Anchor sod on slopes with wood pegs as required to prevent slippage.

Hand seed any gaps between joints.

Water sod with fine spray immediately after planting.

PROTECTION:

Erect barricades and warning signs as required to protect newly planted areas from traffic. Maintain barricades throughout maintenance period until lawn is established.

MAINTENANCE:

Begin maintenance of lawns immediately after each area is planted and continue for the period specified under Section "Landscape Development, General."

Maintain lawns by watering, fertilizing, weeding, mowing, trimming, and other operations such as rolling, regrading, replanting as required to establish a smooth, acceptable lawn, free of eroded or bare areas.

Replant bare areas using same materials specified for lawns.

Watering: Install irrigation system before sodding to keep lawn areas uniformly moist as required for proper growth.

Mow lawns as soon as there is enough top growth to cut with mower set at specified height for principal species planted. Repeat mowing as required to maintain specified height. Do not delay mowing until grass blades bend over and become matted. Do not mow when grass is wet. Time initial and subsequent mowings to maintain following grass height:

Mow grass at 2 in. height. Do not mow lower than 1½ in.

Apply 15–5–10 fertilizer after second mowing and when the grass is dry.

ACCEPTANCE OF LAWNS:

Refer to Section "Landscape Development, General" for general requirements for inspection and acceptance of lawns.

Sodded lawns will be acceptable provided requirements, including maintenance, have been complied with, and healthy, well-rooted, even-colored, viable lawn is established, free of weeds, open joints, bare areas, and surface irregularities.

END OF SECTION 02930

NUMBERING SECTIONS

A specifications writer may use a system for numbering sections referred to as broadscope, mediumscope, and narrowscope sections. Broadscope section titles are typed in all capital letters in boldface if possible with 5-digit numbers. Mediumscope section titles are typed in upper- and lowercase and have hyphenated 3-digit numbers. Narrowscope sections are indented and unnumbered. For an example see the following:

02900 LANDSCAPING
-910 Shrub and Tree Planting
-930 Lawns and Grasses
    Hydro-mulching
    Seeding
    Sodding

The numbering system is flexible and all products can be specified in simple broadscope sections, or for example in separate mediumscope sections with 5-digit numbers as follows:

02900 Landscaping
02910 Shrub and Tree Planting
02930 Lawns and Grasses

The following table contains the broadscope numbers for "Documents" and "Sections."

Table 11-1 Broadscope Numbers for Documents and Specification Sections[a]

BIDDING REQUIREMENTS, CONTRACT FORMS, AND CONDITIONS OF THE CONTRACT

00010 PREBID INFORMATION

00100 INSTRUCTION TO BIDDERS

00200 INFORMATION AVAILABLE TO BIDDERS

00300 BID FORMS

00400 SUPPLEMENTS TO BID FORMS

00500 AGREEMENT FORMS

00600 BONDS AND CERTIFICATES

00700 GENERAL CONDITIONS

00800 SUPPLEMENTARY CONDITIONS

00850 DRAWINGS AND SCHEDULES

00900 ADDENDA AND MODIFICATIONS

Note: Since the items listed above are not specification sections, they are referred to as "Documents" in lieu of "Sections" in the Master List of Section Titles, Numbers, and Broadscope Explanations.

SPECIFICATIONS

DIVISION 1—GENERAL REQUIREMENTS

01010 SUMMARY OF WORK

01020 ALLOWANCES

01025 MEASUREMENT AND PAYMENT

01030 ALTERNATES/ALTERNATIVES

01040 COORDINATION

01050 FIELD ENGINEERING

01060 REGULATORY REQUIREMENTS

01070 ABBREVIATIONS AND SYMBOLS

01080 IDENTIFICATION SYSTEMS

01090 REFERENCE STANDARDS

01100 SPECIAL PROJECT PROCEDURES

01200 PROJECT MEETINGS

01300 SUBMITTALS

01400 QUALITY CONTROL

01500 CONSTRUCTION FACILITIES AND TEMPORARY CONTROLS

01600 MATERIAL AND EQUIPMENT

01650 STARTING OF SYSTEMS/COMMISSIONING

01700 CONTRACT CLOSEOUT

01800 MAINTENANCE

DIVISION 2—SITEWORK

02010 SUBSURFACE INVESTIGATION

02050 DEMOLITION

02100 SITE PREPARATION

02140 DEWATERING

02150 SHORING AND UNDERPINNING

02160 EXCAVATION SUPPORT SYSTEMS

02170 COFFERDAMS

02200 EARTHWORK

02300 TUNNELING

02350 PILES AND CAISSONS

02450 RAILROAD WORK

02480 MARINE WORK

02500 PAVING AND SURFACING

02600 PIPED UTILITY MATERIALS

02660 WATER DISTRIBUTION

02680 FUEL DISTRIBUTION

02700 SEWERAGE AND DRAINAGE

02760 RESTORATION OF UNDERGROUND PIPELINES

02770 PONDS AND RESERVOIRS

02780 POWER AND COMMUNICATIONS

02800 SITE IMPROVEMENTS

02900 LANDSCAPING

DIVISION 3—CONCRETE

03100 CONCRETE FORMWORK

03200 CONCRETE REINFORCEMENT

03250 CONCRETE ACCESSORIES

03300 CAST-IN-PLACE CONCRETE

03370 CONCRETE CURING

03400 PRECAST CONCRETE

03500 CEMENTITIOUS DECKS

03600 GROUT

[a] Reproduced from MASTERFORMAT—Master List of Sections Titles and Numbers, 1983, Alexandria, Virginia, Construction Specification Institute, United States and Canada.

03700 CONCRETE RESTORATION AND CLEANING

03800 MASS CONCRETE

DIVISION 4—MASONRY

04100 MORTAR

04150 MASONRY ACCESSORIES

04200 UNIT MASONRY

04400 STONE

04500 MASONRY RESTORATION AND CLEANING

04550 REFRACTORIES

04600 CORROSION-RESISTANT MASONRY

DIVISION 5—METALS

05010 METAL MATERIALS

05030 METAL FINISHES

05050 METAL FASTENING

05100 STRUCTURAL METAL FRAMING

05200 METAL JOISTS

05300 METAL DECKING

05400 COLD-FORMED METAL FRAMING

05500 METAL FABRICATIONS

05580 SHEET METAL FABRICATIONS

05700 ORNAMENTAL METAL

05800 EXPANSION CONTROL

05900 HYDRAULIC STRUCTURES

DIVISION 6—WOOD AND PLASTICS

06050 FASTENERS AND ADHESIVES

06100 ROUGH CARPENTRY

06130 HEAVY TIMBER CONSTRUCTION

06150 WOOD-METAL SYSTEMS

06170 PREFABRICATED STRUCTURAL WOOD

06200 FINISH CARPENTRY

06300 WOOD TREATMENT

06400 ARCHITECTURAL WOODWORK

06500 PREFABRICATED STRUCTURAL PLASTICS

06600 PLASTIC FABRICATIONS

DIVISION 7—THERMAL AND MOISTURE PROTECTION

07100 WATERPROOFING

07150 DAMPPROOFING

07190 VAPOR AND AIR RETARDERS

07200 INSULATION

07250 FIREPROOFING

07300 SHINGLES AND ROOFING TILES

07400 PREFORMED ROOFING AND CLADDING/SIDING

07500 MEMBRANE ROOFING

07570 TRAFFIC TOPPING

07600 FLASHING AND SHEET METAL

07700 ROOF SPECIALTIES AND ACCESSORIES

07800 SKYLIGHTS

07900 JOINT SEALERS

DIVISION 8—DOORS AND WINDOWS

08100 METAL DOORS AND FRAMES

08200 WOOD AND PLASTIC DOORS

08300 SPECIAL DOORS

08400 ENTRANCES AND STOREFRONTS

08500 METAL WINDOWS

08600 WOOD AND PLASTIC WINDOWS

08700 HARDWARE

08800 GLAZING

08900 GLAZED CURTAIN WALLS

DIVISION 9—FINISHES

09100 METAL SUPPORT SYSTEMS

09200 LATH AND PLASTER

09230 AGGREGATE COATINGS

09250 GYPSUM BOARD

09300 TILE

09400 TERRAZO

09500 ACOUSTICAL TREATMENT

09540 SPECIAL SURFACES

09550 WOOD FLOORING

09600 STONE FLOORING

09630 UNIT MASONRY FLOORING

09650 RESILIENT FLOORING

09680 CARPET
09700 SPECIAL FLOORING
09780 FLOOR TREATMENT
09800 SPECIAL COATINGS
09900 PAINTING
09950 WALL COVERINGS

DIVISION 10—SPECIALTIES

10100 CHALKBOARDS AND TACKBOARDS
10150 COMPARTMENTS AND CUBICLES
10200 LOUVRES AND VENTS
10240 GRILLES AND SCREENS
10250 SERVICE WALL SYSTEMS
10260 WALL AND CORNER GUARDS
10270 ACCESS FLOORING
10280 SPECIALTY MODULES
10290 PEST CONTROL
10300 FIREPLACES AND STOVES
10340 PREFABRICATED EXTERIOR SPECIALTIES
10350 FLAGPOLES
10400 IDENTIFYING DEVICES
10450 PEDESTRIAN CONTROL DEVICES
10500 LOCKERS
10520 FIRE PROTECTION SPECIALTIES
10530 PROTECTIVE COVERS
10550 POSTAL SPECIALTIES
10600 PARTITIONS
10650 OPERABLE PARTITIONS
10880 SCALES
10900 WARDROBE AND CLOSET SPECIALTIES

DIVISION 11—EQUIPMENT

11010 MAINTENANCE EQUIPMENT
11020 SECURITY AND VAULT EQUIPMENT
11030 TELLER AND SERVICE EQUIPMENT
11040 ECCLESIASTICAL EQUIPMENT
11050 LIBRARY EQUIPMENT
11060 THEATER AND STAGE EQUIPMENT
11070 INSTRUMENTAL EQUIPMENT
11080 REGISTRATION EQUIPMENT
11090 CHECKROOM EQUIPMENT
11100 MERCANTILE EQUIPMENT
11110 COMMERCIAL LAUNDRY AND DRY CLEANING EQUIPMENT
11120 VENDING EQUIPMENT
11130 AUDIO-VISUAL EQUIPMENT
11140 SERVICE STATION EQUIPMENT
11150 PARKING CONTROL EQUIPMENT
11160 LOADING DOCK EQUIPMENT
11170 SOLID WASTE HANDLING EQUIPMENT
11190 DETENTION EQUIPMENT
11200 WATER SUPPLY AND TREATMENT EQUIPMENT
11280 HYDRAULIC GATES AND VALVES
11300 FLUID WASTE TREATMENT AND DISPOSAL EQUIPMENT
11400 FOOD SERVICE EQUIPMENT
11450 RESIDENTIAL EQUIPMENT
11460 UNIT KITCHENS
11470 DARKROOM EQUIPMENT
11480 ATHLETIC, RECREATIONAL, AND THERAPEUTIC EQUIPMENT
11500 INDUSTRIAL AND PROCESS EQUIPMENT
11600 LABORATORY EQUIPMENT
11650 PLANETARIUM EQUIPMENT
11660 OBSERVATORY EQUIPMENT
11700 MEDICAL EQUIPMENT
11780 MORTUARY EQUIPMENT
11850 NAVIGATION EQUIPMENT

DIVISION 12—FURNISHINGS

12050 FABRICS
12100 ARTWORK
12300 MANUFACTURED CASEWORK
12500 WINDOW TREATMENT
12600 FURNITURE AND ACCESSORIES

12670 RUGS AND MATS

12700 MULTIPLE SEATING

12800 INTERIOR PLANTS AND PLANTERS

DIVISION 13—SPECIAL CONSTRUCTION

13010 AIR-SUPPORTED STRUCTURES

13020 INTEGRATED ASSEMBLIES

13030 SPECIAL PURPOSE ROOMS

13080 SOUND, VIBRATION, AND SEISMIC CONTROL

13090 RADIATION PROTECTION

13100 NUCLEAR REACTORS

13120 PREENGINEERED STRUCTURES

13150 POOLS

13160 ICE RINKS

13170 KENNELS AND ANIMAL SHELTERS

13180 SITE CONSTRUCTED INCINERATORS

13200 LIQUID AND GAS STORAGE TANKS

13220 FILTER UNDERDRAINS AND MEDIA

13230 DIGESTION TANK COVERS AND APPURTENANCES

13240 OXYGENATION SYSTEMS

13260 SLUDGE CONDITIONING SYSTEMS

13300 UTILITY CONTROL SYSTEMS

13400 INDUSTRIAL AND PROCESS CONTROL SYSTEMS

13500 RECORDING INSTRUMENTATION

13550 TRANSPORTATION CONTROL INSTRUMENTATION

13600 SOLAR ENERGY SYSTEMS

13700 WIND ENERGY SYSTEMS

13800 BUILDING AUTOMATION SYSTEMS

13900 FIRE SUPPRESSION AND SUPERVISORY SYSTEMS

DIVISION 14—CONVEYING SYSTEMS

14100 DUMBWAITERS

14200 ELEVATORS

14300 MOVING STAIRS AND WALKS

14400 LIFTS

14500 MATERIAL HANDLING SYSTEMS

14600 HOISTS AND CRANES

14700 TURNTABLES

14800 SCAFFOLDING

14900 TRANSPORTATION SYSTEMS

DIVISION 15—MECHANICAL

15050 BASIC MECHANICAL MATERIALS AND METHODS

15250 MECHANICAL INSULATION

15300 FIRE PROTECTION

15400 PLUMBING

15500 HEATING, VENTILATING, AND AIR CONDITIONING (HVAC)

15550 HEAT GENERATION

15650 REFRIGERATION

15750 HEAT TRANSFER

15850 AIR HANDLING

15880 AIR DISTRIBUTION

15950 CONTROLS

15990 TESTING, ADJUSTING, AND BALANCING

DIVISION 16—ELECTRICAL

16050 BASIC ELECTRICAL MATERIALS AND METHODS

16200 POWER GENERATION

16300 HIGH-VOLTAGE DISTRIBUTION (Above 600-Volt)

16400 SERVICE AND DISTRIBUTION (Above 600-Volt and below)

16500 LIGHTING

16600 SPECIAL SYSTEMS

16700 COMMUNICATIONS

16850 ELECTRIC RESISTANCE HEATING

16900 CONTROLS

16950 TESTING

10670 STORAGE SHELVING

10700 EXTERIOR SUN CONTROL DEVICES

10750 TELEPHONE SPECIALTIES

10800 TOILET AND BATH ACCESSORIES

FIG. 12-1 Tennis court for matches at Las Colinas Sports Club in Irving, Texas.

Chapter Twelve
Sports Facilities and Playgrounds

The objective of this chapter is to provide an understanding of different types of sports activities and their related sizes for site planning purposes. Since there are many different athletic authorities such as the NCAA, AAU, and so on whose standards may govern in specific situations, the data in this chapter are for preliminary planning purposes. The data presented here should be useful in planning outdoor recreation facilities for schools, parks, and private developments. (See Table 12-1 and Figs 12-1 to 12-39.)

ORIENTATION OF FACILITIES

Orientation of play fields is very important so that the sun is not providing a disadvantage by shining in a player's eyes. For example, one would not like to have a baseball or softball field oriented so that the southwest sun is shining into the batter's eyes in the evening. An indication of good orientation of fields is shown in the layout diagrams.

GRADING AND DRAINAGE

Properly designed grading and drainage of sports fields is essential for good use. Many of the same standards mentioned in Chapter Six on grading apply here. On surfaces paved with concrete it is possible to have minimum grades such as .5% grade to 1% grade and have surface drainage. Surfaces paved with bituminous-type materials generally need 1.5% grades to be built without low spots. Grass areas on football fields or baseball fields need a 2% grade for drainage while synthetic turf areas can be flatter with about .8%–1% Grade for drainage. On many fields underdrainage lines are required. These lines pick up water percolating through the soil so that the field does not stay soggy or have standing water especially where heavy use occurs such as on football fields or tracks. On some professional fields that have grass, a system can be designed that uses many underdrainage lines, special soil mixtures, and a pumping system that speeds up removal of drainage during rainy conditions.

Table 12-1 Sports Field Sizes[a]

Sports Activity	Dimensions	Play Area
Badminton		
Singles	17 ft × 44 ft	25 ft × 60 ft
Doubles	20 ft × 44 ft	30 ft × 60 ft
Baseball		
Little League	60 ft × 60 ft Diamond; Pitching Dist. 46 ft	Foul Lines 180–200 ft; CF 200 ft
Pee-Wee	60 ft × 60 ft Diamond; Pitching Dist. 38 ft	Foul Lines 180–200 ft; CF 200 ft
Pony League	80 ft × 80 ft Diamond; Pitching Dist. 54 ft	Foul Lines 200–250 ft; CF 200–300 ft
Babe Ruth	90 ft × 90 ft Diamond; Pitching Dist. 60½ ft	Foul Lines 250–320 ft; CF 250–400 ft
Professional	90 ft × 90 ft Diamond; Pitching Dist. 60½ ft	Foul Lines 300–350 ft; CF 300–400+ ft
Basketball	50 ft × 94 ft	60 ft × 100 ft Avg.
Boccie	8 ft × 62 ft	20 ft × 80 ft
Bowling (lawn)	14 ft × 100 ft per alley	120 ft × 120 ft (8 alleys)
Croquet	41 ft × 85 ft	50 ft × 95 ft
Field Hockey	150 ft × 270 ft Min. 180 ft × 300 ft Max	200 ft × 350 ft Avg.
Football	160 ft × 360 ft with end zones	190 ft × 420 ft
Golf		
Par 3 (pitch and put)	18 short holes	45–50 Acres
Nine-Hole Course	3000–3200 Yards	50–80 Acres
Flat Sites		50 Acres Min.
Gently Rolling		60 Acres Min.
Hilly Sites		70 Acres Min.
18-Hole Course	6200 Yards Min.; 6500 Yards Avg.; 7000 Yards Championship	110–200 Acres
Flat Sites		110 Acres Min.
Gently Rolling		120 Acres Min.
Hilly Sites		140–180 Acres
Handball (One Wall)	20 ft × 37 ft	37 ft × 45 ft
Handball (Four Wall) Racquetball	20 ft × 40 ft	20 ft × 40 ft
Ice Hockey	85 ft × 200 ft	115 ft × 230 ft
Lacrosse	Min. 180 ft × 330 ft Max. 210 ft × 330 ft	210 ft × 360 ft Avg.
Rugby	Min. 195 ft × 300 ft Max. 225 ft × 330 ft	225 ft × 450 ft
Shuffleboard	6 ft × 52 ft	10 ft × 57 ft
Soccer (men)	Min 195 ft × 330 ft Max. 225 ft × 360 ft	240 ft × 360 ft Avg.
Soccer (women)	Min 120 ft × 240 ft Max. 180 ft × 300 ft	200 ft × 320 ft Avg.
Softball	60 ft × 60 ft Diamond; Pitching Dist. 46 ft	Foul Lines 200 ft
Squash	25 ft × 45 ft	25 ft × 45 ft
Tennis		
Singles	27 ft × 78 ft	50 ft × 120 ft
Doubles	36 ft × 78 ft	60 ft × 120 ft
Tether Tennis	6 in. Diameter Circle	20 ft × 20 ft
Track	Lane Widths 42 in.; 6 Lanes Min.	300 ft × 700 ft Avg.
Volleyball	30 ft × 60 ft	50 ft × 80 ft

[a] The data are for preliminary planning purposes. For final design check with the athletic authority whose standards will apply.

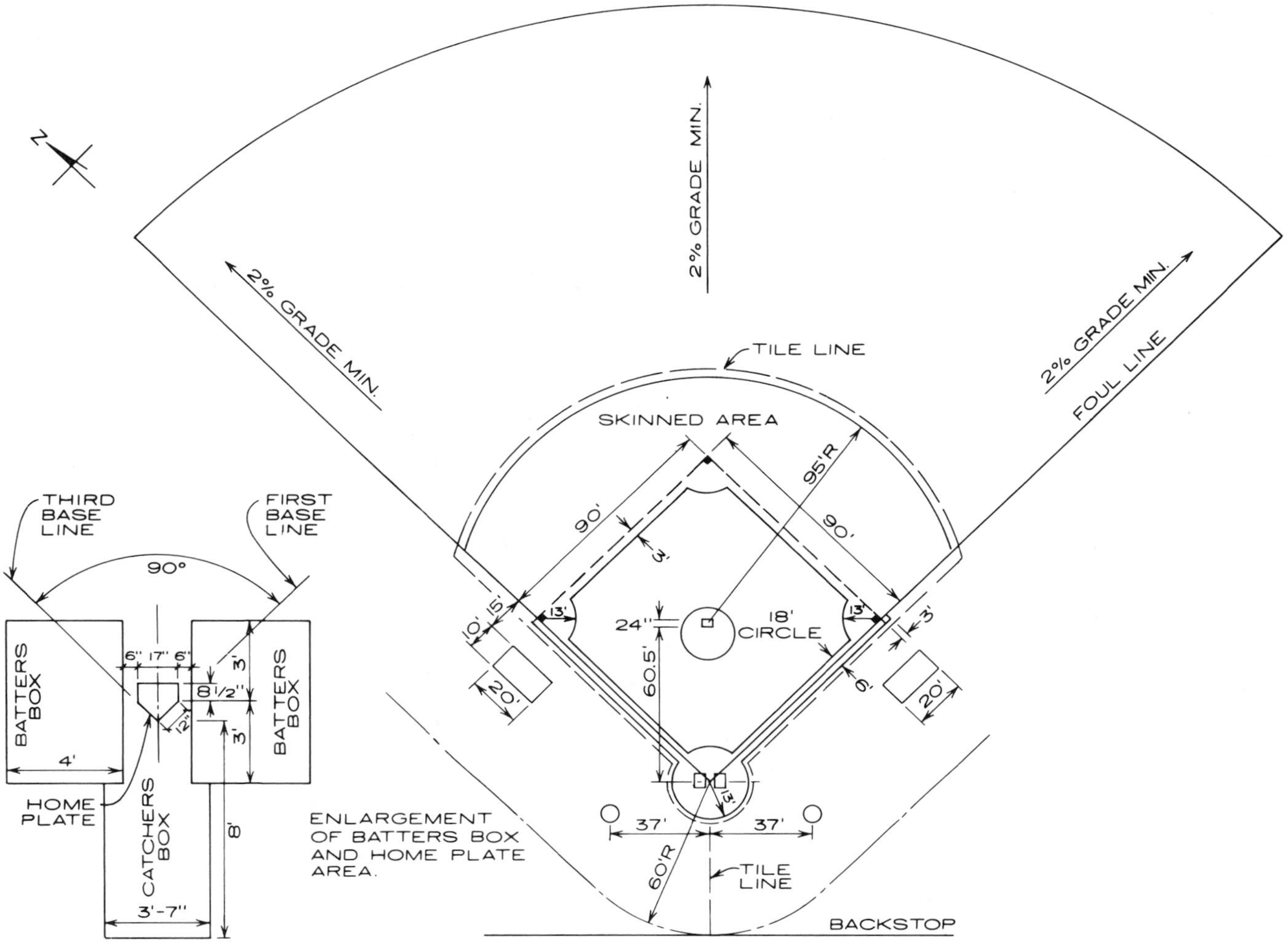

FIG. 12-2 Baseball field: baseball fields have foul lines of 300 ft or more. The best orientation has the batter facing north/northeast; however, other orientations have the batter facing south/southeast, or south. A southwest orientation puts the sun in the batter's eyes in the evening, which is not desirable.

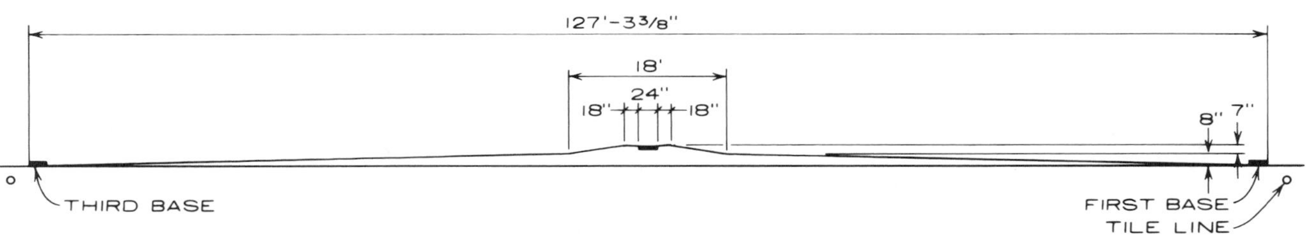

FIG. 12-3 Section showing grading of baseball field.

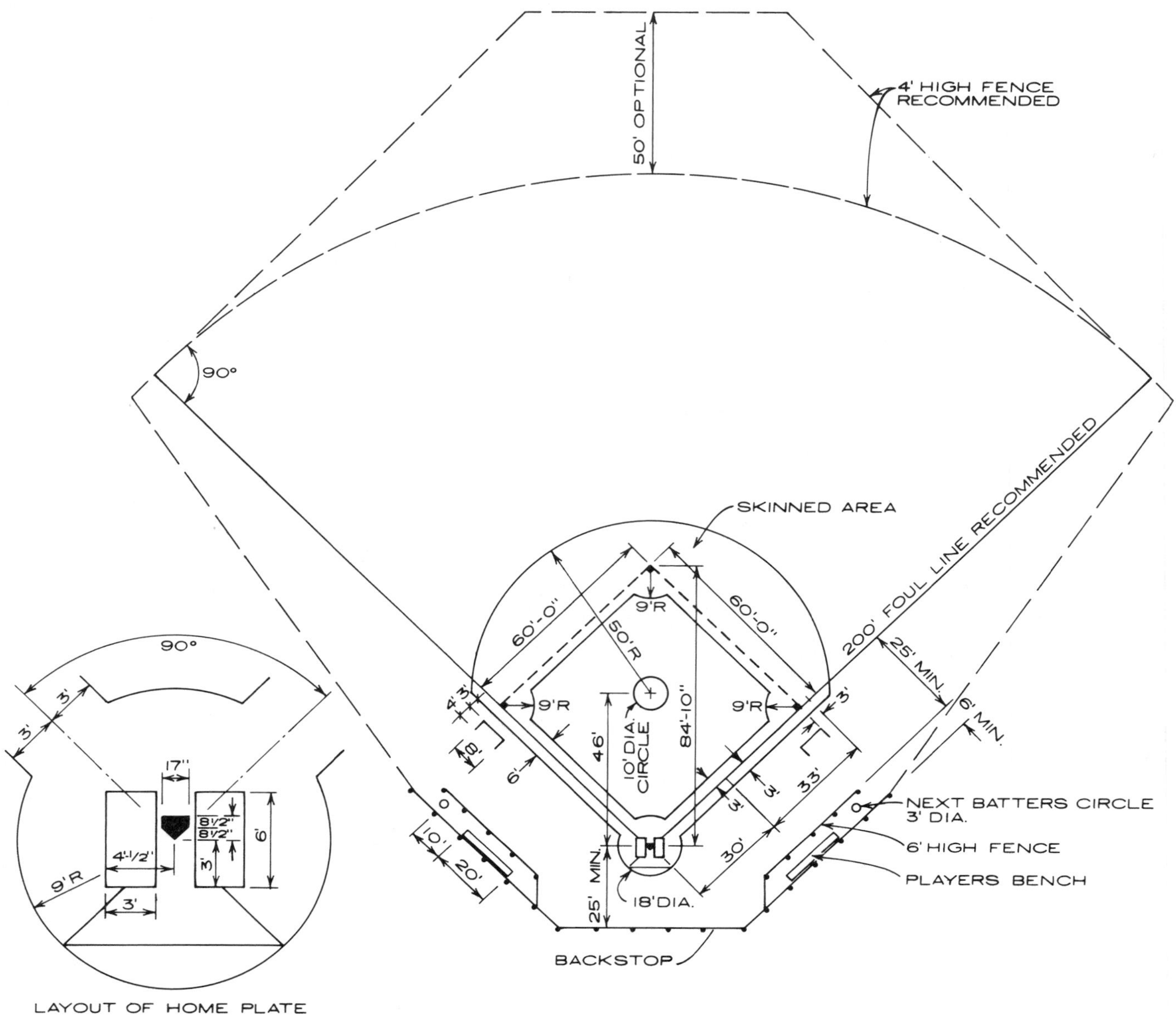

FIG. 12-4 Little league baseball field.

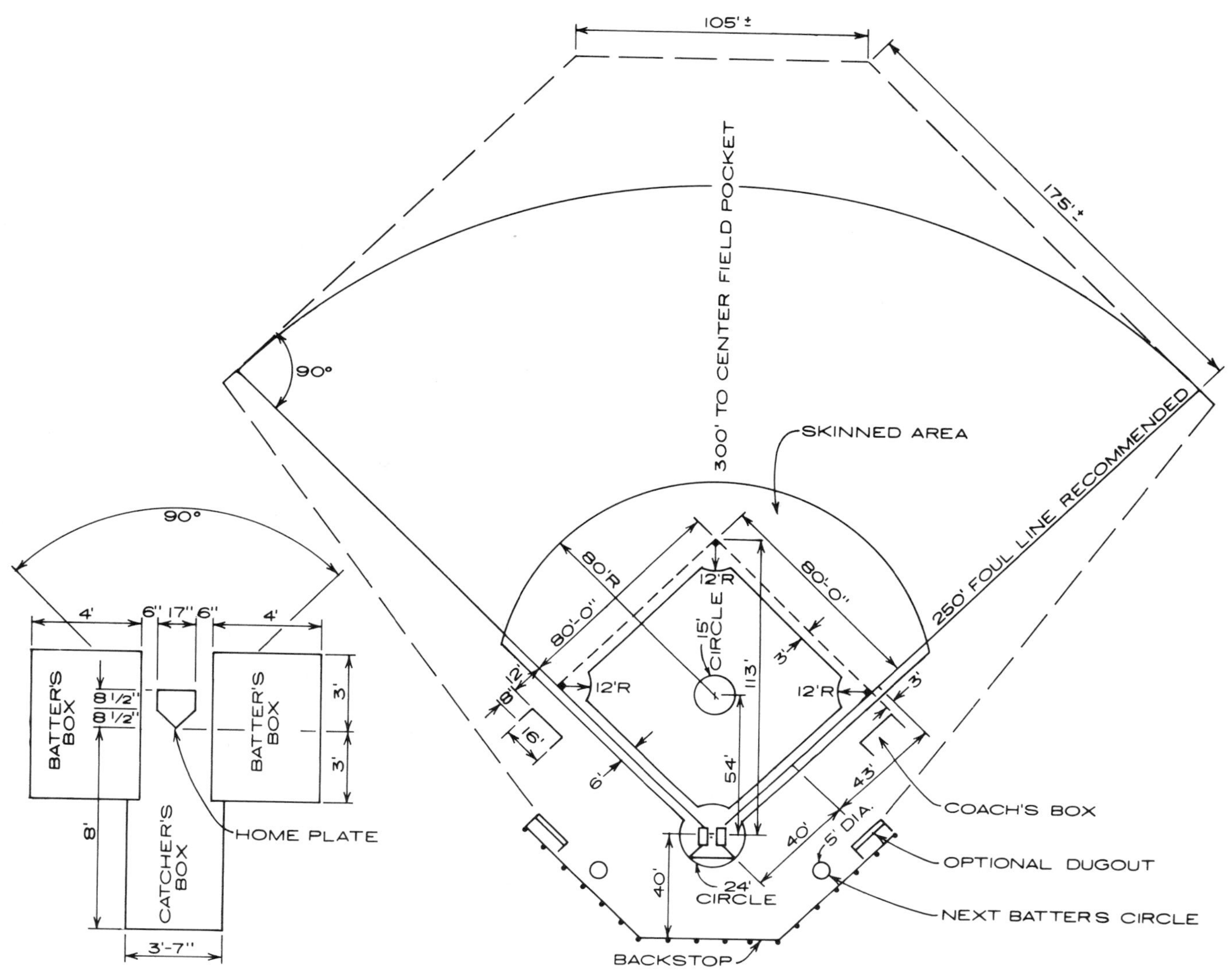

FIG. 12-5 Pony league baseball field.

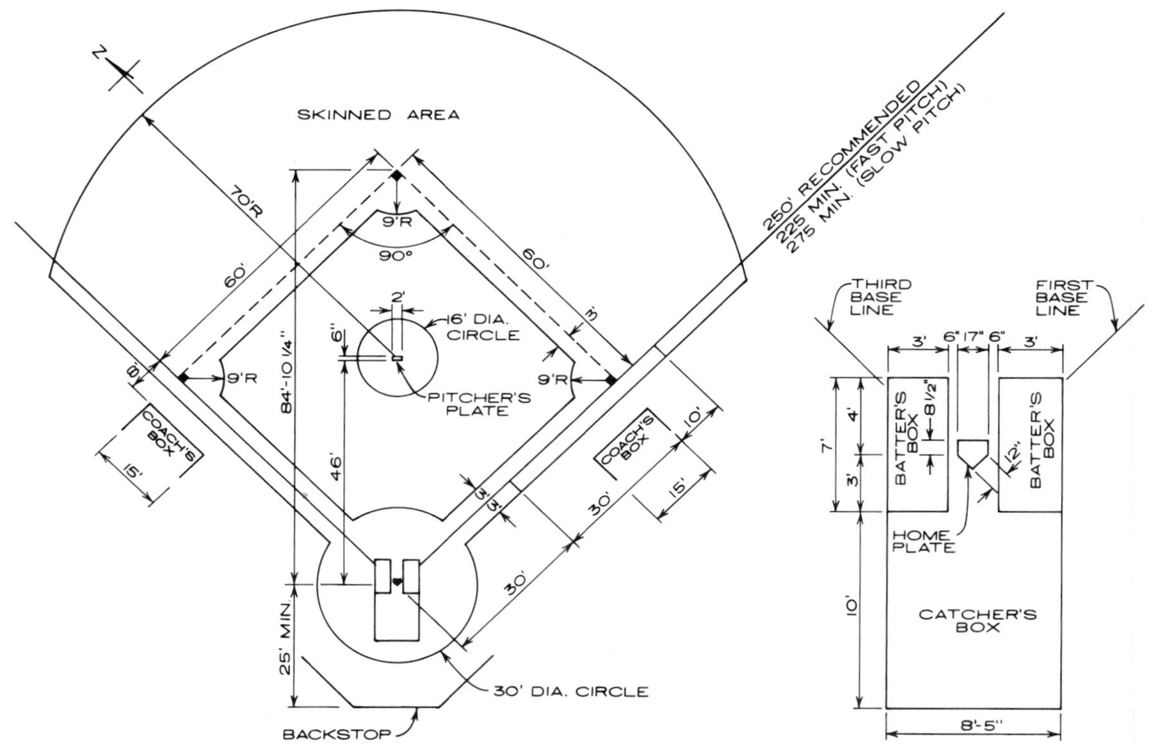

FIG. 12-6 Softball field (12 in. field layout).

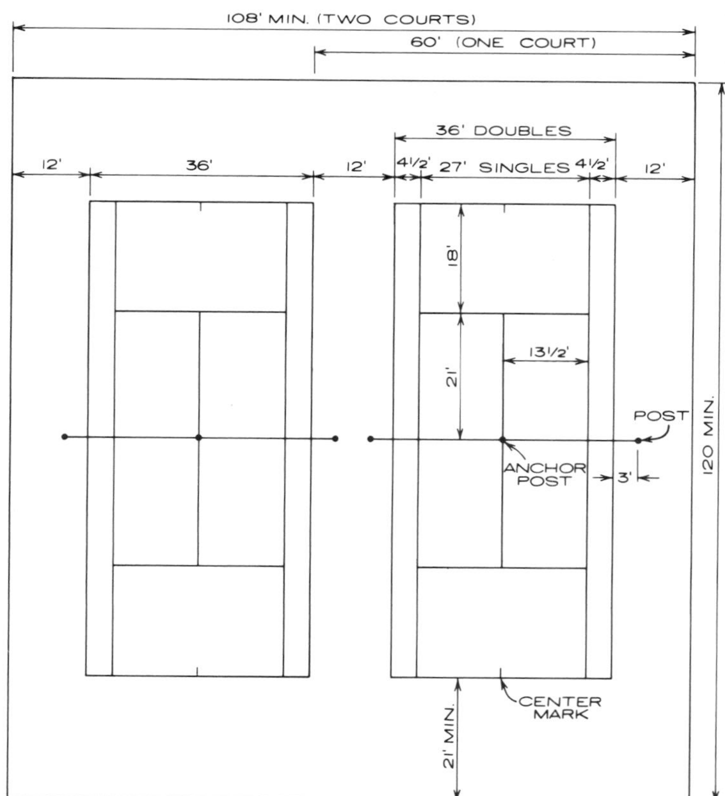

FIG. 12-7 Tennis courts: net is set a minimum of 3 ft 6 in. above the court surface. In some types of soils because of shrink-swell, bituminous-type courts could have problems with cracking, and reinforced concrete courts are more desirable. Pitch 1 in. per 10 ft. side to side or end to end or corner to corner. Do not drain to or from center net line.

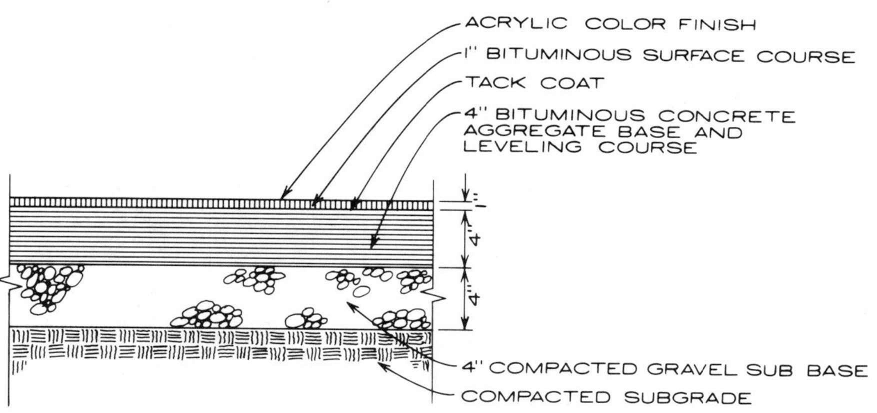

FIG. 12-8 Bituminous tennis court section.

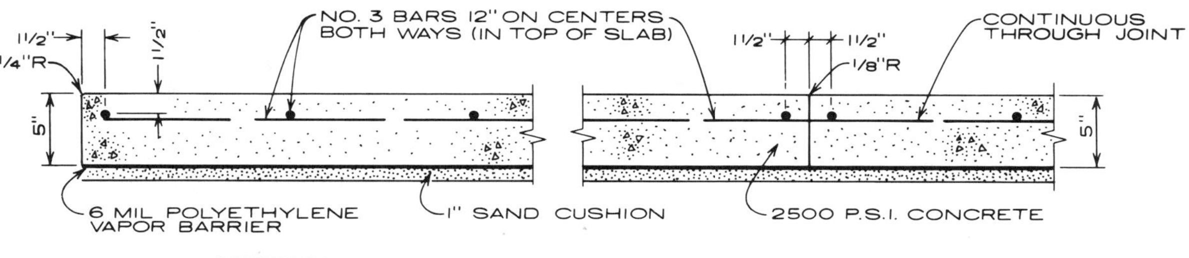

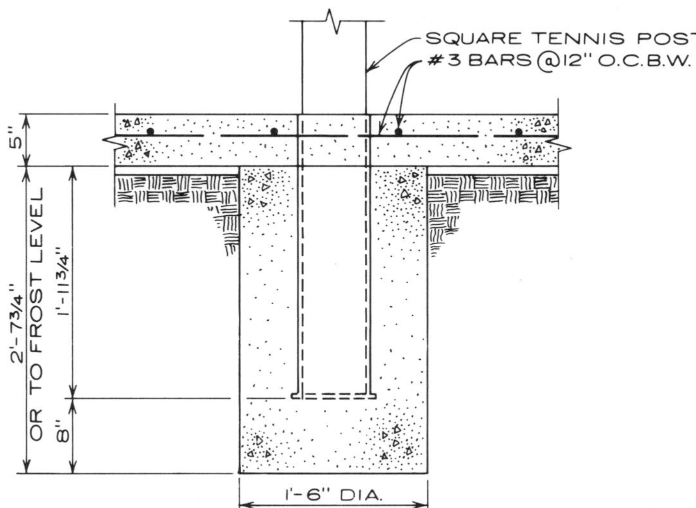

FIG. 12-9 Concrete tennis court section. Use 2500 psi concrete, which is more flexible in shrink-swell soil types. Place an expansion joint at the center of the court along net line and place saw cut outside of playing lines 1 in. deep.

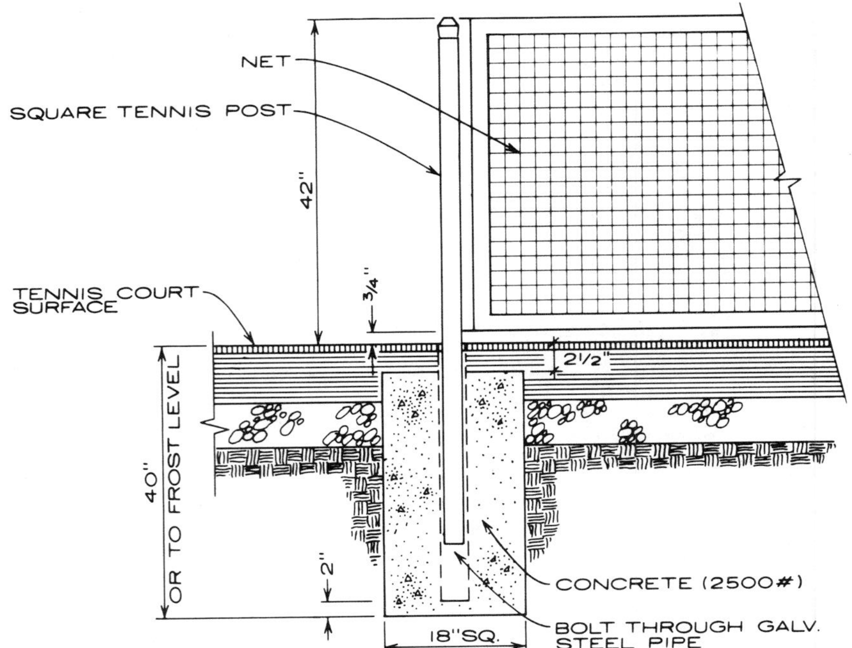

FIG. 12-10 Tennis net and post detail for bituminous courts.

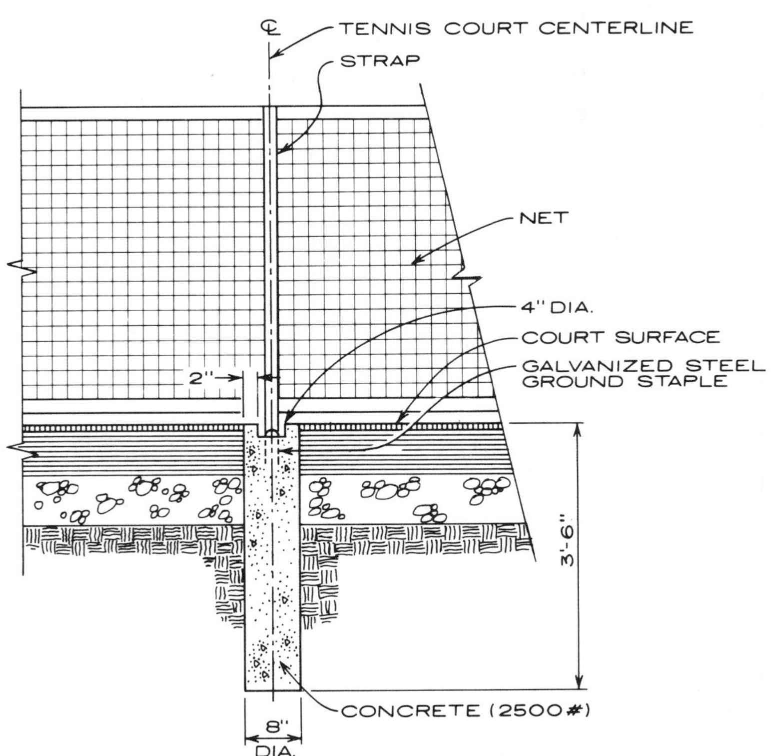

FIG. 12-11 Center anchor detail.

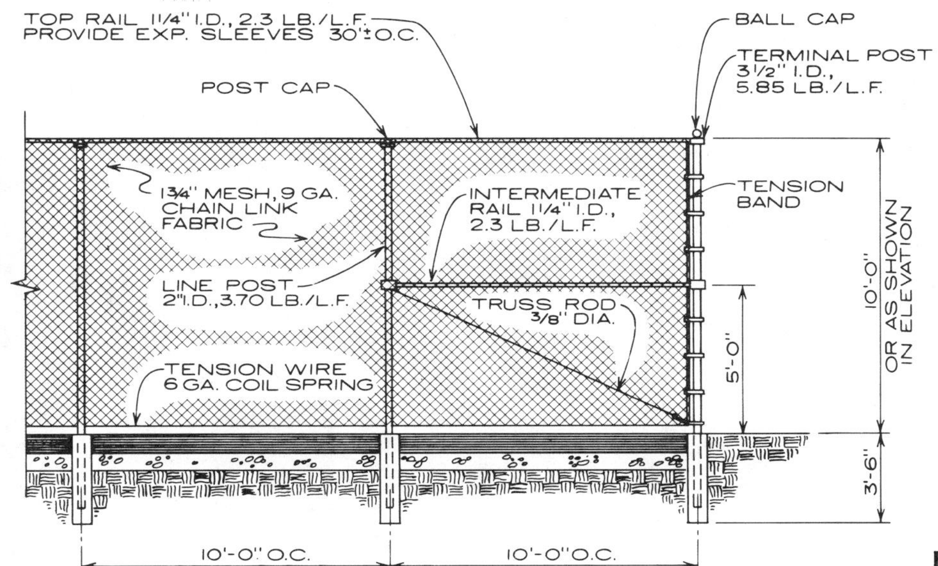

FIG. 12-12 Fence detail.

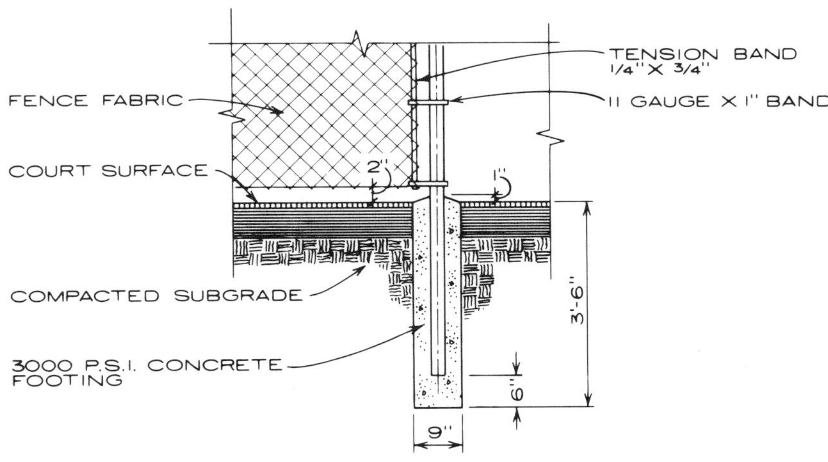

FIG. 12-13 Post and footing detail.

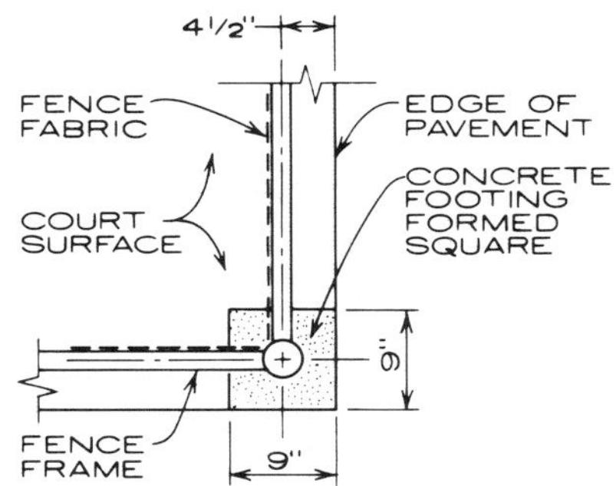

FIG. 12-14 Footing plan.

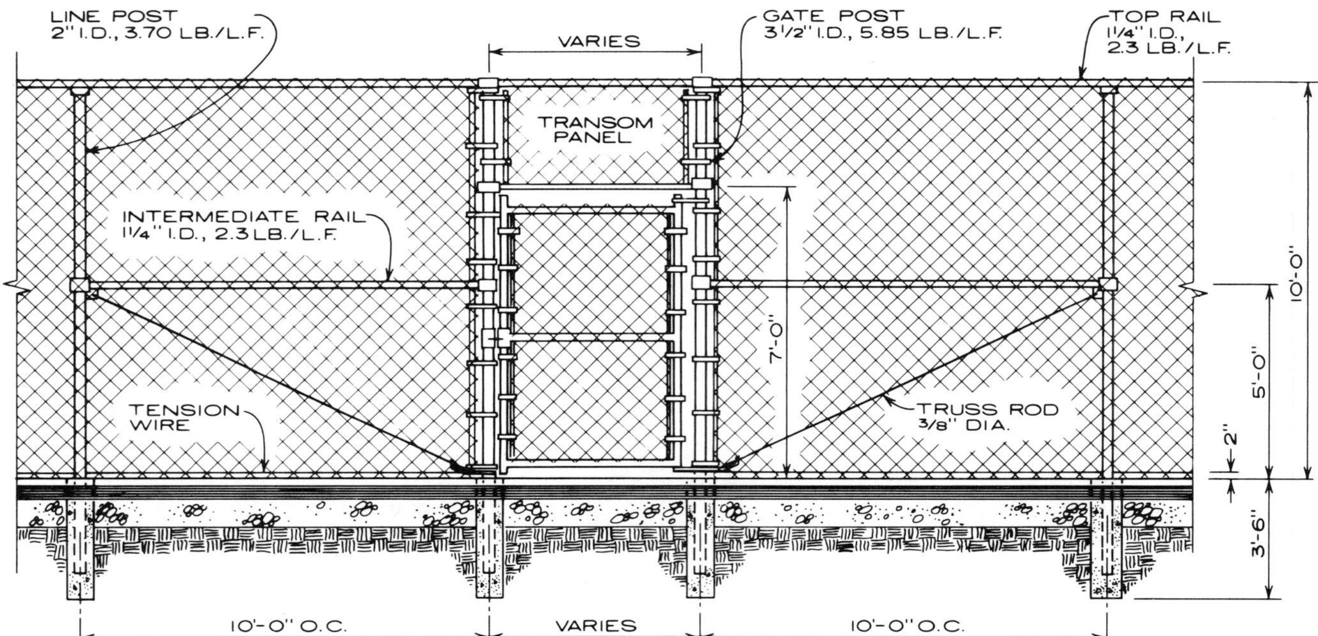

FIG. 12-15 Single gate.

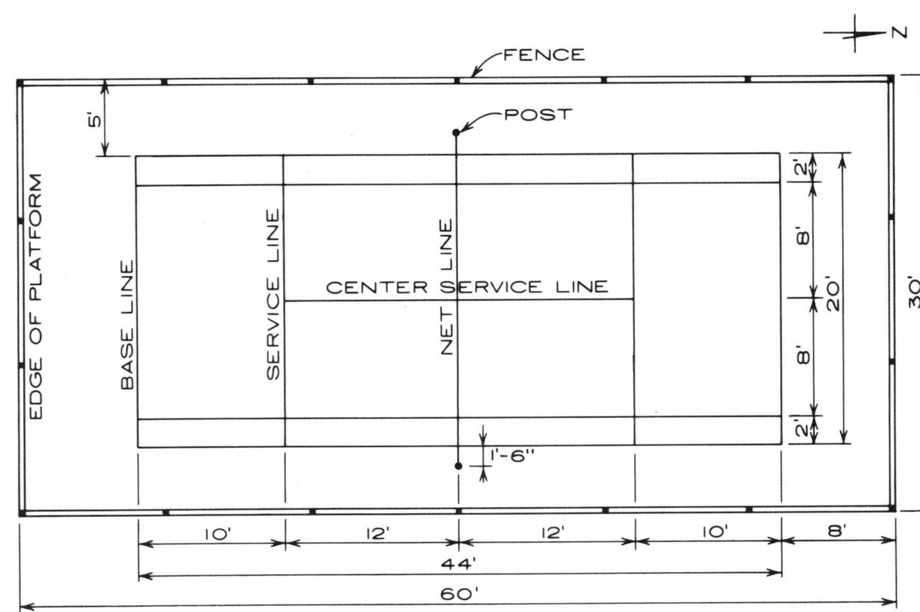

FIG. 12-16 Platform tennis: fence is 12 ft high 16 gauge 1 in. mesh and the net is 34 in. above the court.

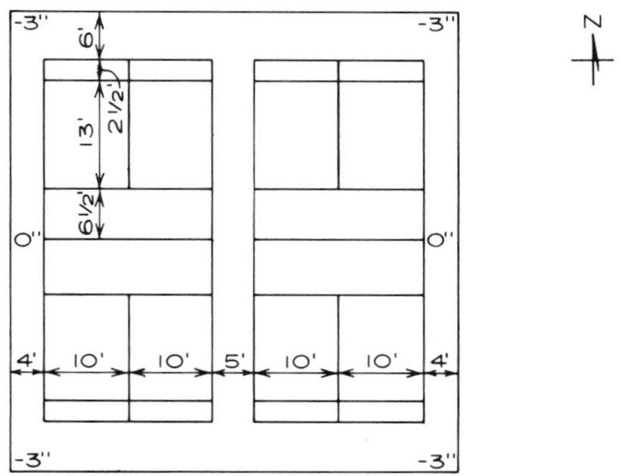

FIG. 12-17 Badminton: north-south orientation with net 5 ft high.

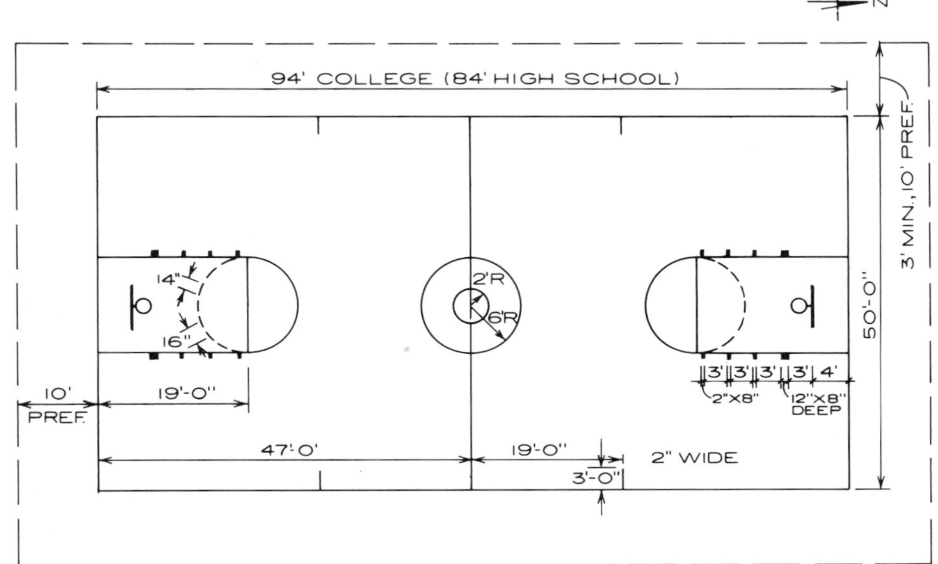

FIG. 12-18 Basketball: height of the basket is 10 ft above the floor or paving. The rectangular backboard is 4 ft × 6 ft and is used for college and/or high school. Fan-shaped backboards are also used in high schools.

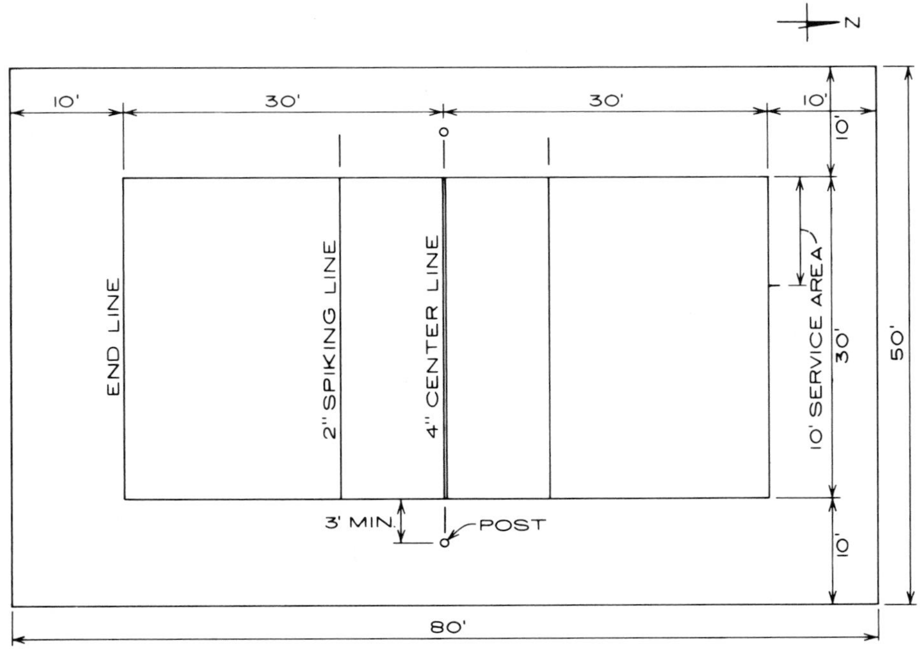

FIG. 12-19 Volleyball: top of 3 ft net is $8\frac{1}{4}$ ft above the court surface.

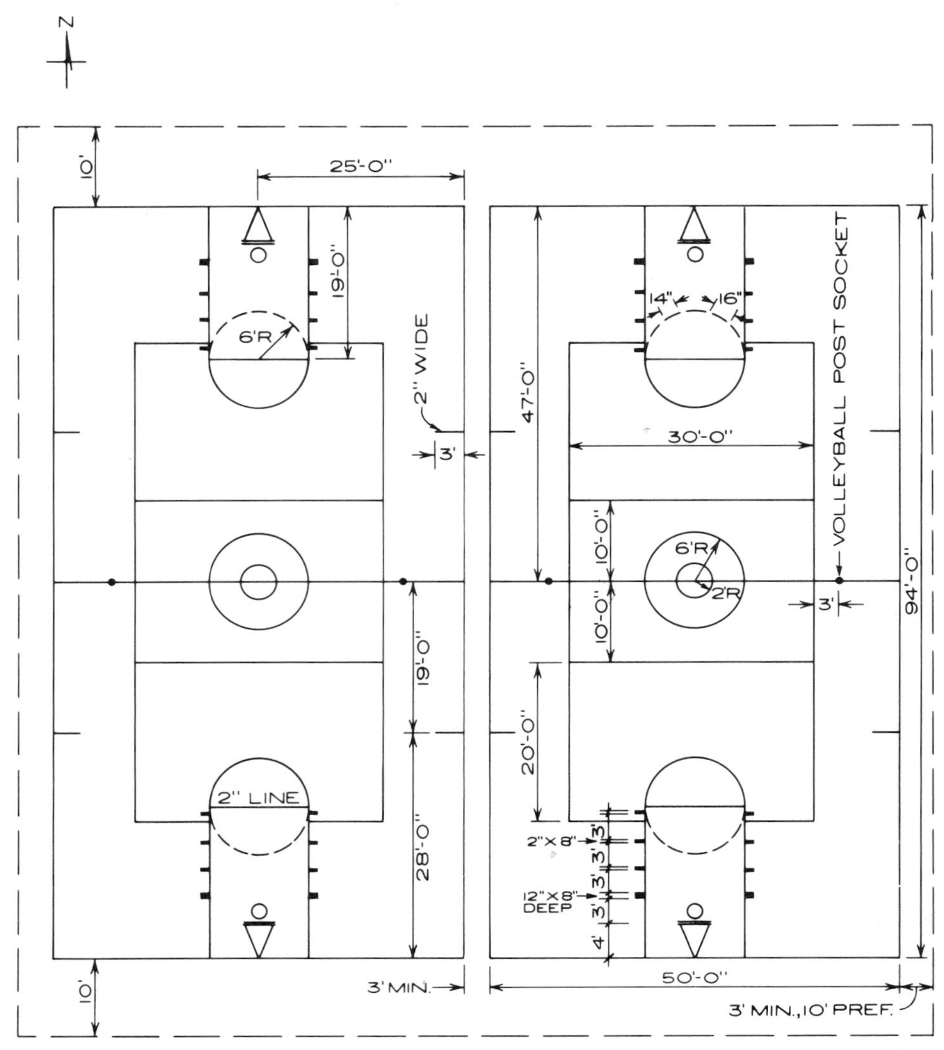

FIG. 12-20 Combination basketball/volleyball court.

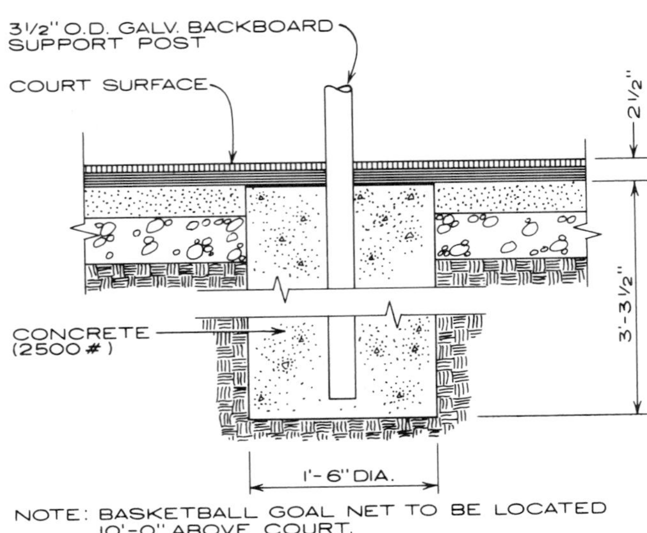

FIG. 12-21 Basketball goal support post detail.

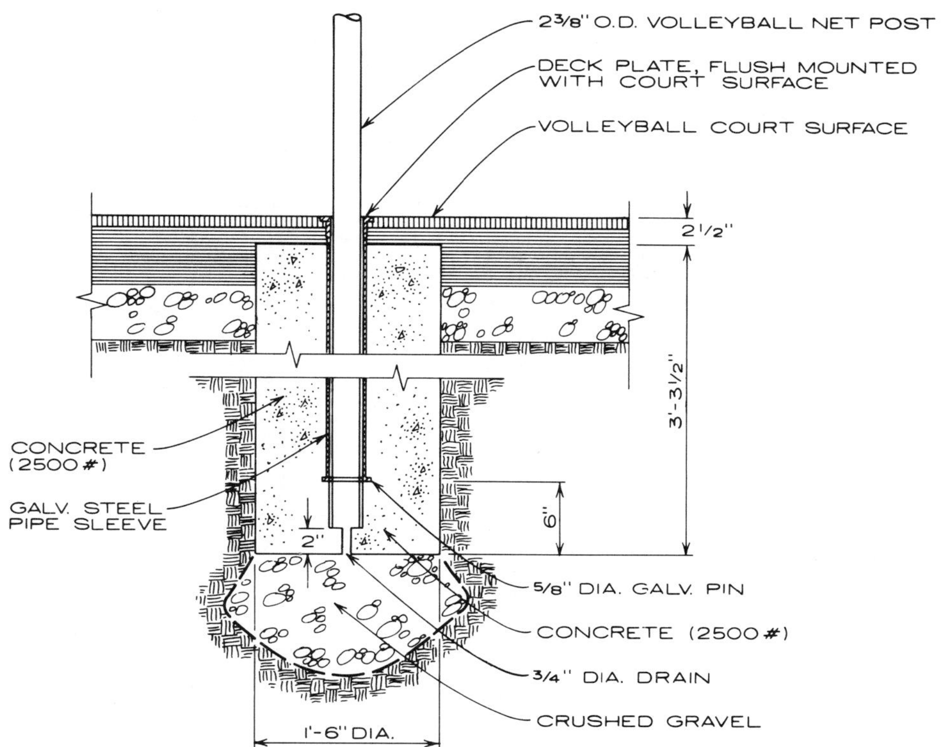

FIG. 12-22 Volleyball post detail.

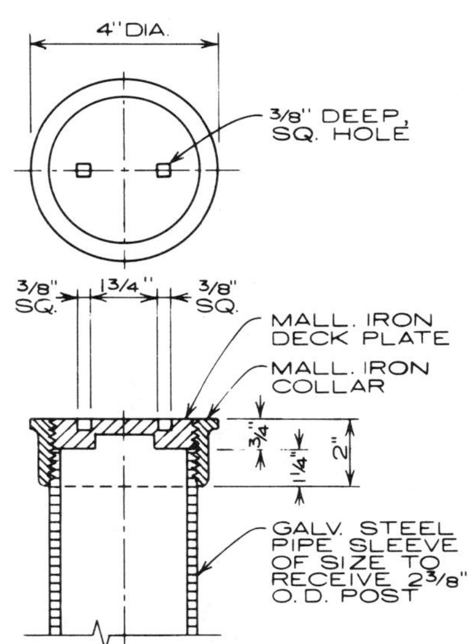

FIG. 12-23 Volleyball deck plate detail.

FIG. 12-24 Shuffleboard.

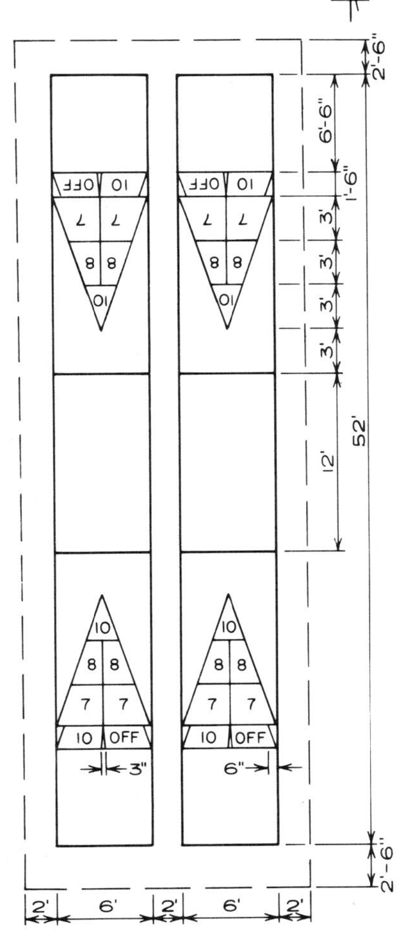

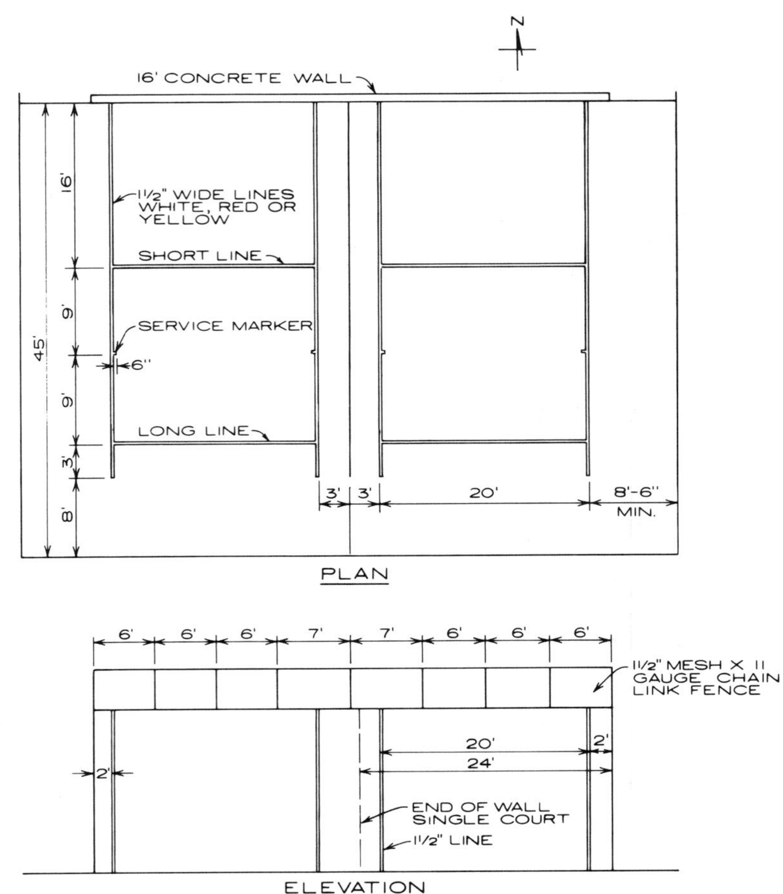

FIG. 12-25 One wall handball.

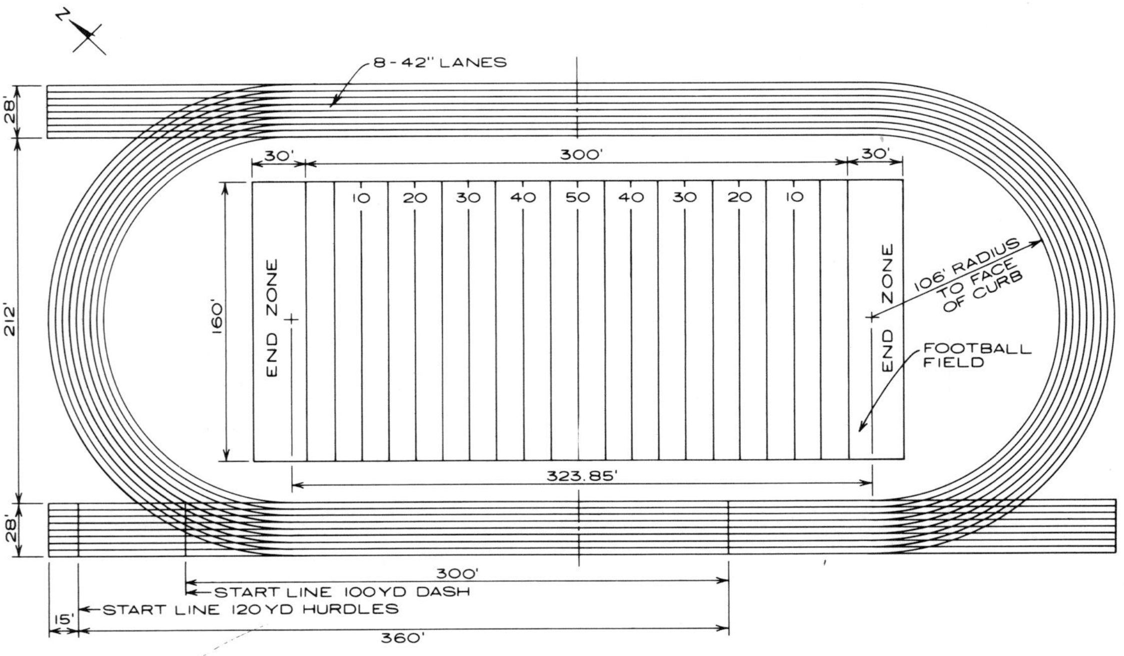

FIG. 12-26 Typical track with football field: the track has 4 laps per mile.

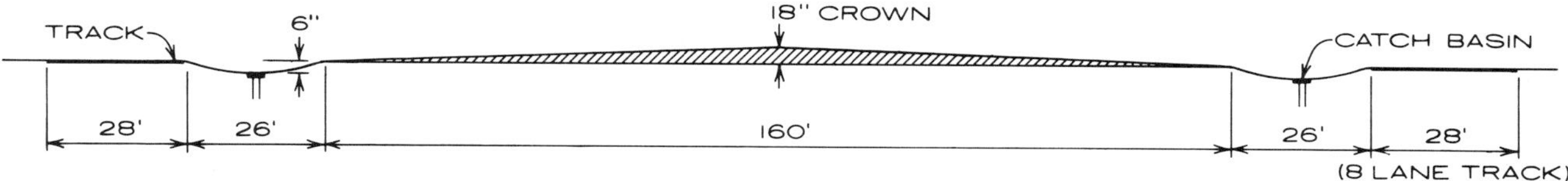

FIG. 12-27 Section showing the grading of a football field. The center of the field has a crown of 18 in. This is the minimum crown that should be used on natural grass.

FIG. 12-28 All-weather track, Plano, Texas.

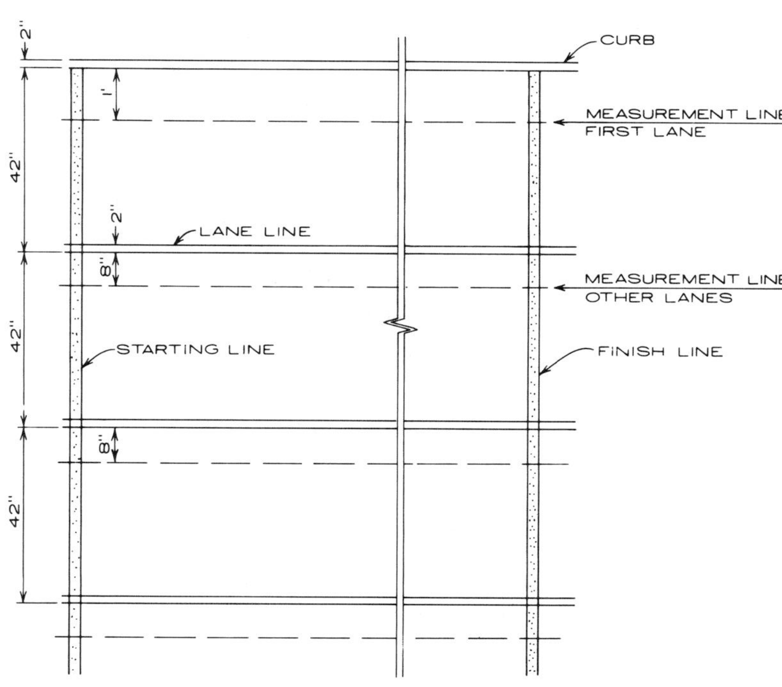

FIG. 12-29 Track running lane widths: 6 lanes are a minimum on synthetic tracks; one extra lane is used for cinder tracks.

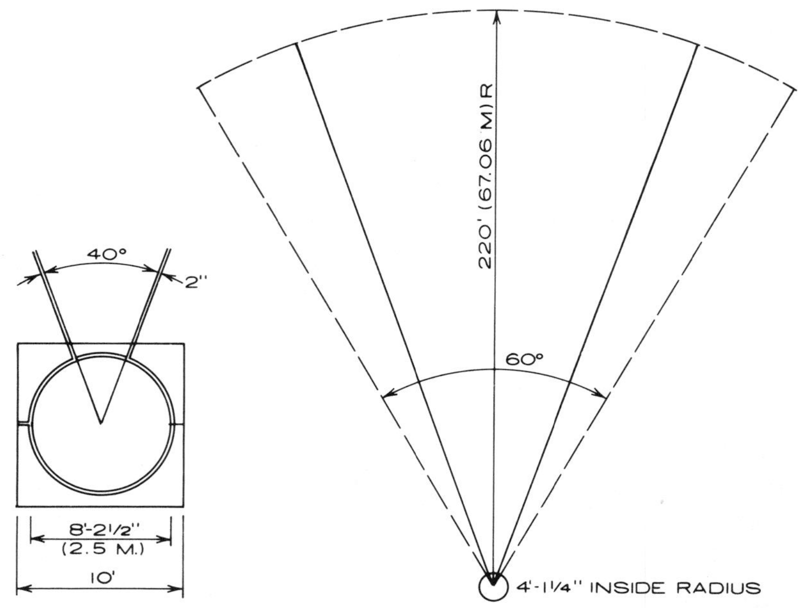

FIG. 12-30 Discus throw: a cage is used for limited safety, which is about 13 ft 1 in. high. The discus circle may be placed 1 meter in front of the hammer throw for use with the protective cage.

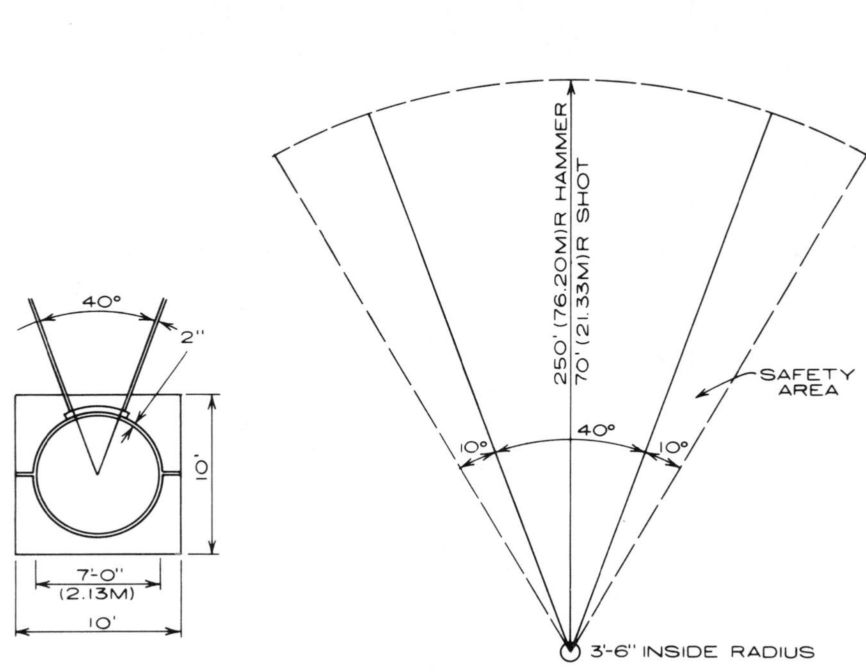

FIG. 12-31 Shot put and hammer throw: a cage is used for safety. The cage is centered on the hammer throw.

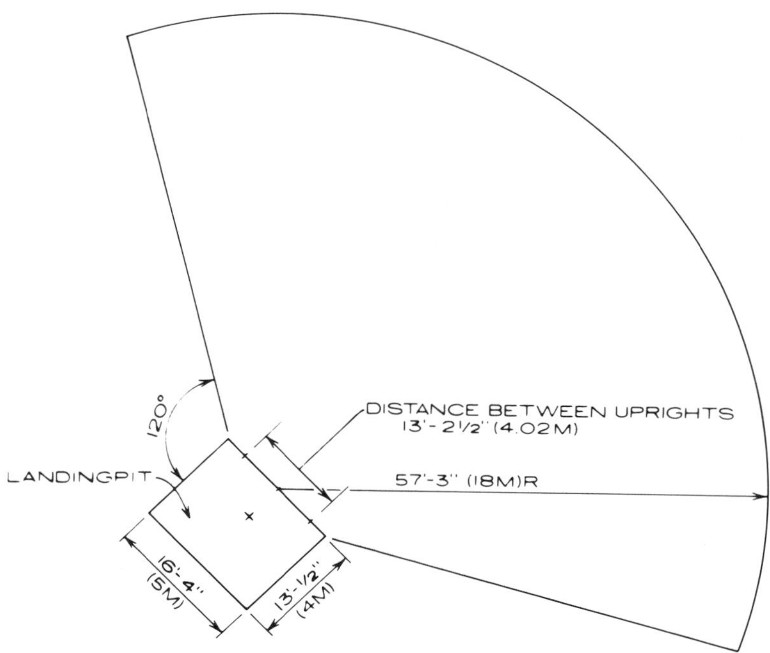

FIG. 12-32 High jump.

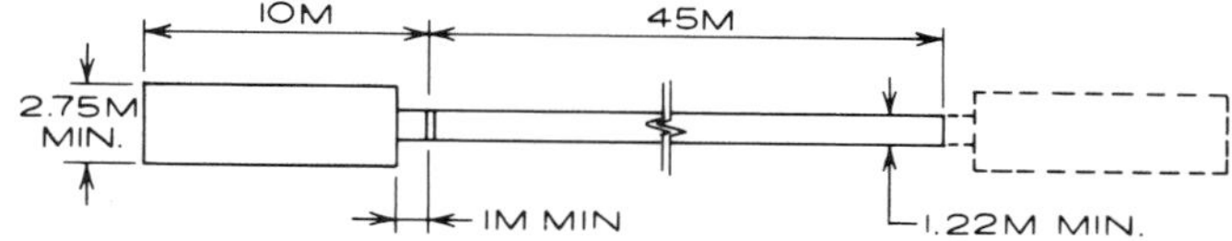

FIG. 12-33 Long jump: the landing pit is filled with sand.

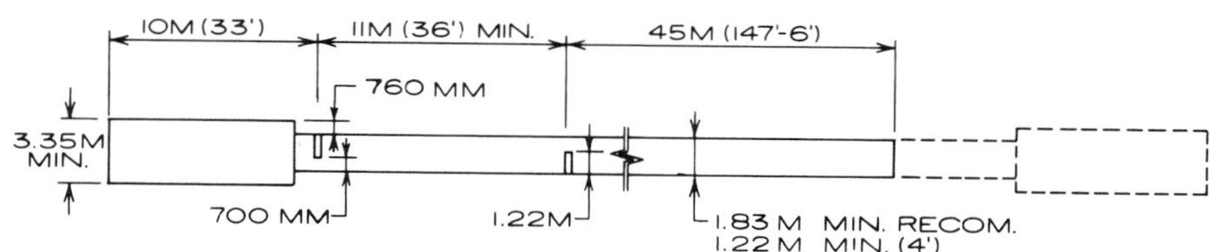

FIG. 12-34 Long and triple jump: the landing pit is filled with sand.

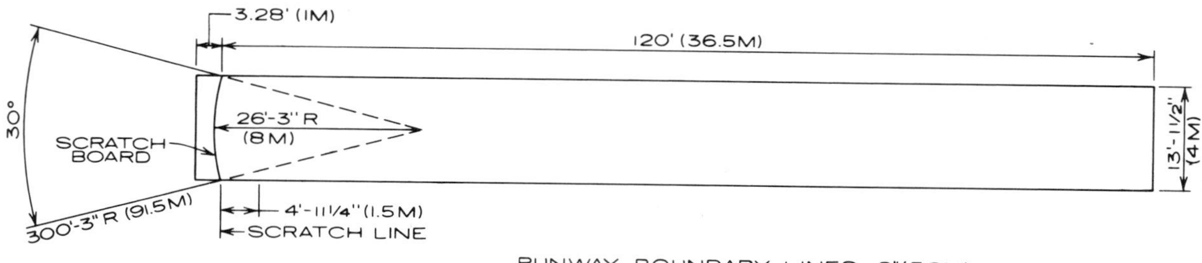

FIG. 12-35 Javelin throw.

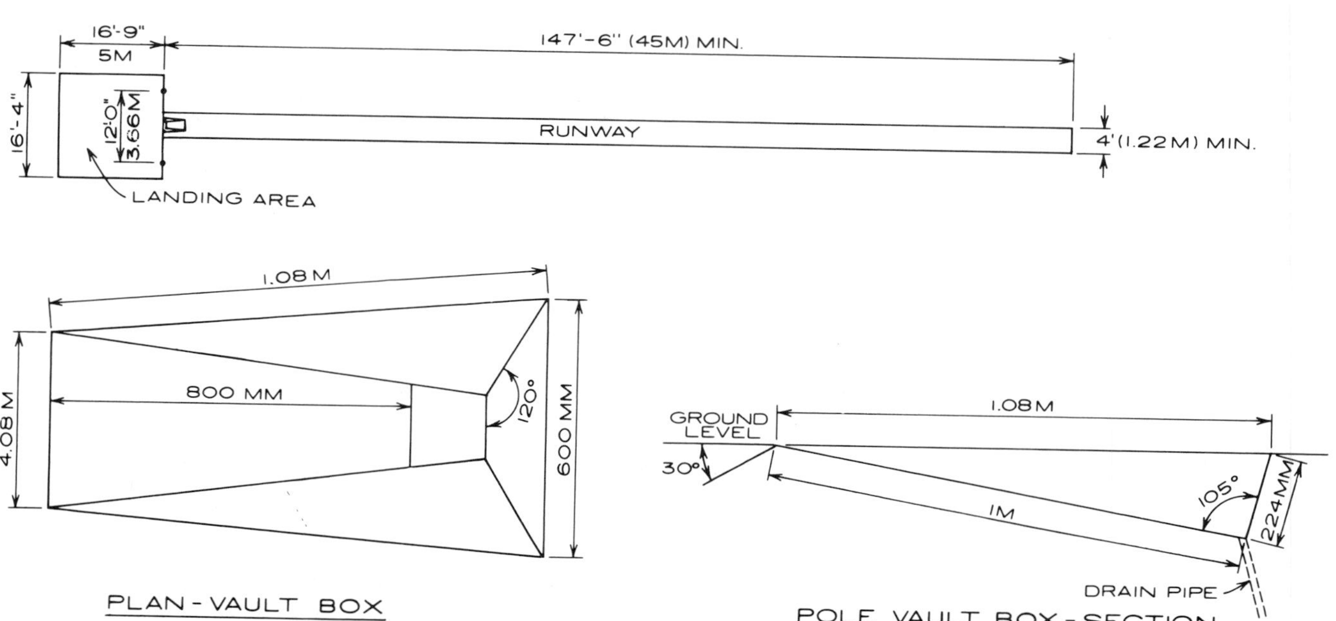

FIG. 12-36 Pole vault.

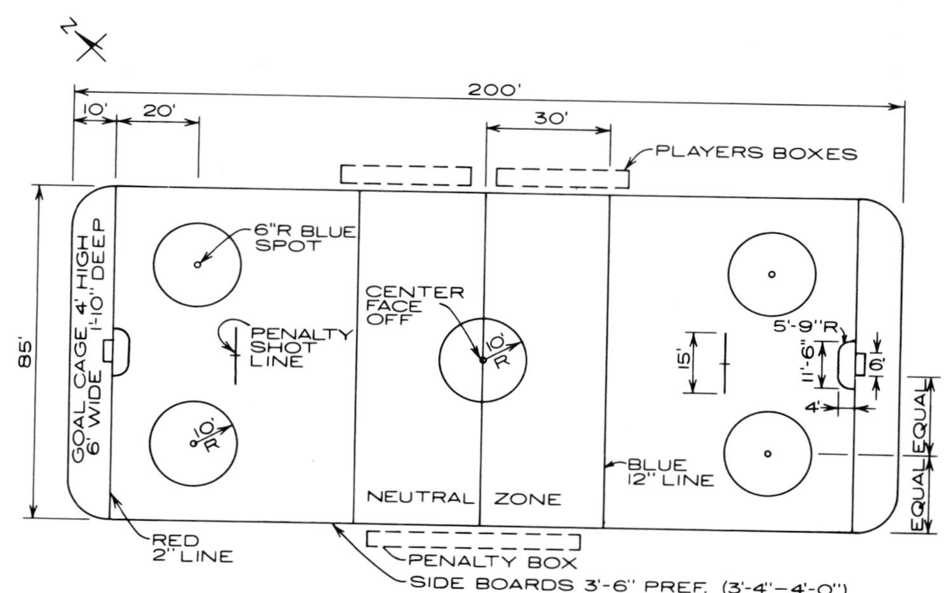

FIG. 12-37 Ice hockey.

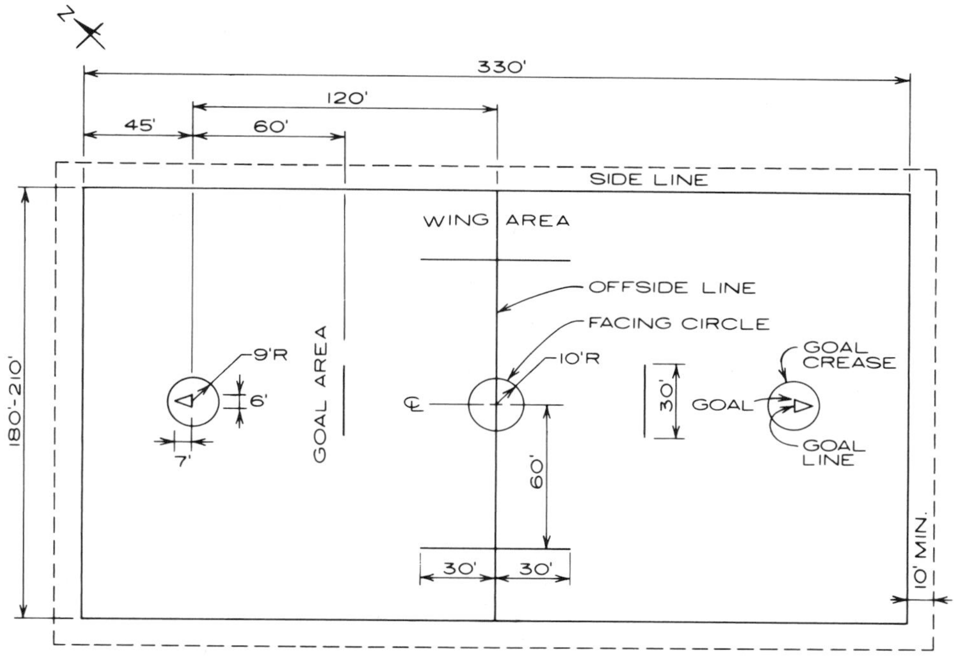

FIG. 12-38 Lacrosse.

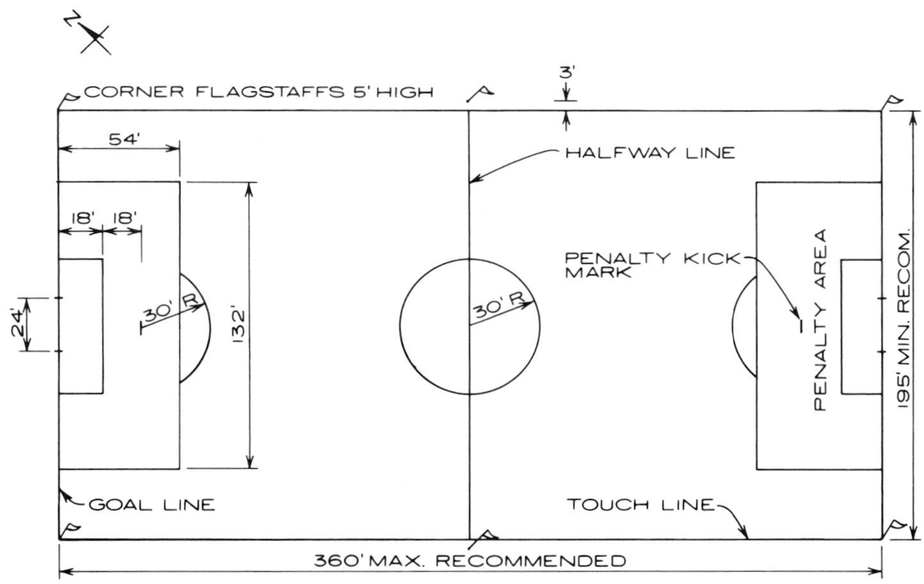

FIG. 12-39 Soccer.

Dimensions for Figures 12-2, 12-4, 12-5, 12-6, 12-18, 12-19, 12-24, 12-25, and 12-30–12-39 were provided by the Office of the Chief Engineers, U.S. Department of the Army, Washington, D.C.

GOLF COURSE DESIGN CRITERIA

An 18-hole golf course generally takes from 110 to 200 acres depending on the topography. Flat sites would be toward the lower end of the required acreage while steeper sites would need 140 to 200 acres. An average golf course is 6500 yards in length while championship courses are over 7000 yards. A typical course would be designed with four par 3 holes ranging from 130 to 250 yards; ten par 4 holes from 350 to 470 yards; and four par 5 holes from 471 to 550 yards.

Fairway width is generally 60 yards but can vary from 40 to 70 yards depending on the length of the fairway from the tee. Green sizes vary from 5000 to 10,000 ft^2 depending on the length of the hole and shot and whether there will be heavy play. Traps average four per green and are about 1000 ft^2 each and use about 25 tons each of clean white sand at a typical depth of 9 in. (See Fig. 12-40.) Ponds for irrigation also use much land with about a total of ten acres needed. Finally, golf cart paths require about 4500 lineal feet at an 8 ft width.

On flat sites where inadequate drainage is a problem, one approach would be to excavate enough fill material to create positive drainage and site features and in addition to build ponds for water storage. One hundred thousand to 300,000 yd^3 of material may have to be moved depending on site conditions and the features desired.

Drainage is also important for many sites located along floodplains or in marshy or low areas. With adequate drainage design good courses can be built, but they will have a greater construction cost. While swales can often handle small drainage areas storm drainage lines can be designed to carry water runoff from adjacent watersheds under fairway areas. This also helps to limit erosion.

Greens generally have a 10 to 12 in. soil mix over a 4 in. layer of gravel. A soil separator can be placed between the soil mix and the gravel bed. Beneath the gravel tile, PVC, or other types of drain lines can be used to remove percolation water. These lines can be connected to the storm drainage system or piped to irrigation ponds. (See Figs. 12–41 and 12–42)

FIG. 12-40 Golf course at Cove Cay, Clearwater, Florida.

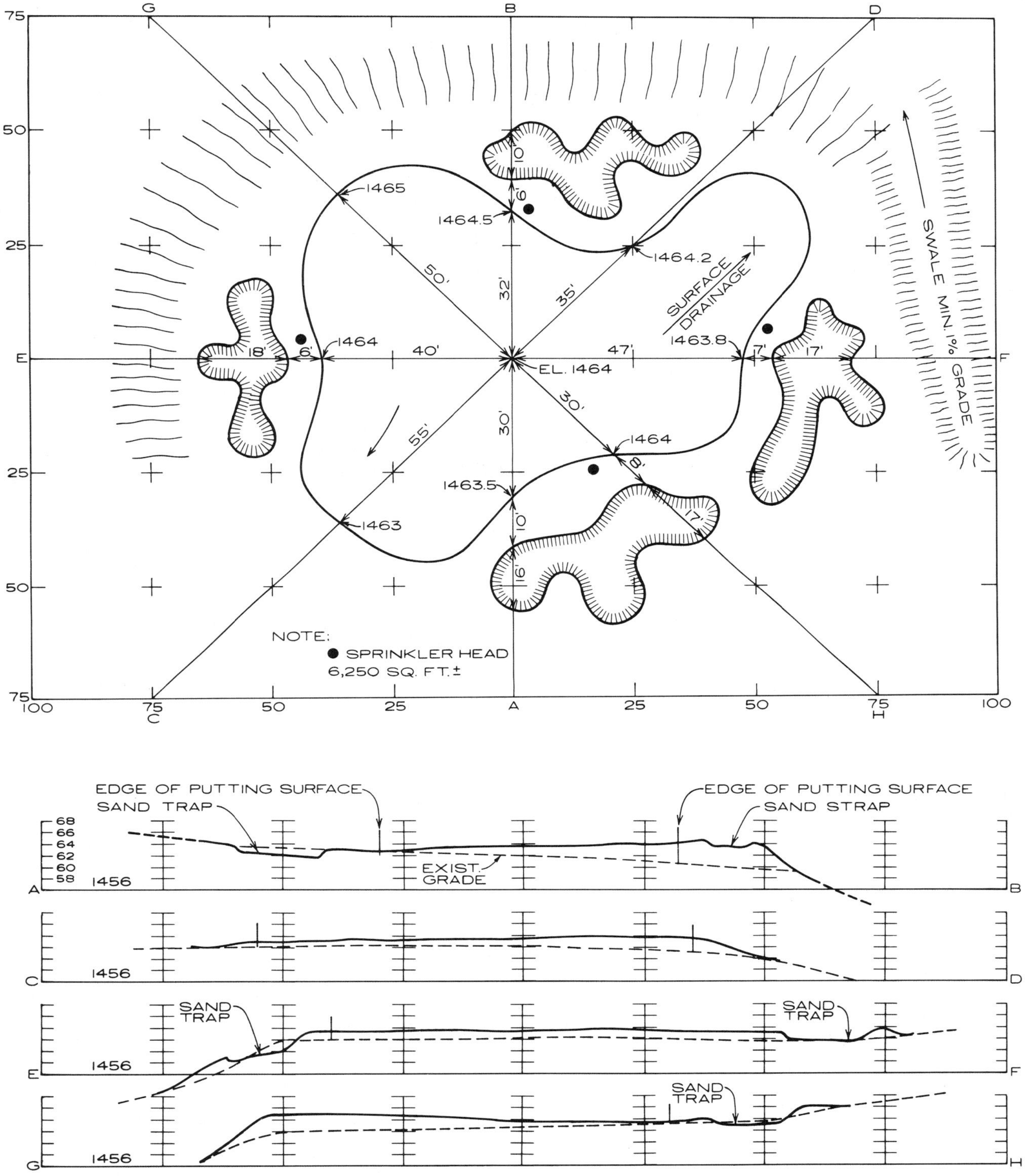

G B D

75 50 25 E 25 50 75

SWALE MIN. 1% GRADE

SURFACE DRAINAGE

1465
1464.5
1464.2
1464
1463.8
EL. 1464
1464
1463.5
1463

10' 6' 32' 35' 50' 18' 6' 40' 47' 7' 17' 30' 30' 55' 8' 17' 10' 16'

NOTE:
● SPRINKLER HEAD
6,250 SQ. FT. ±

100 75 50 25 A 25 50 75 100
C H

F

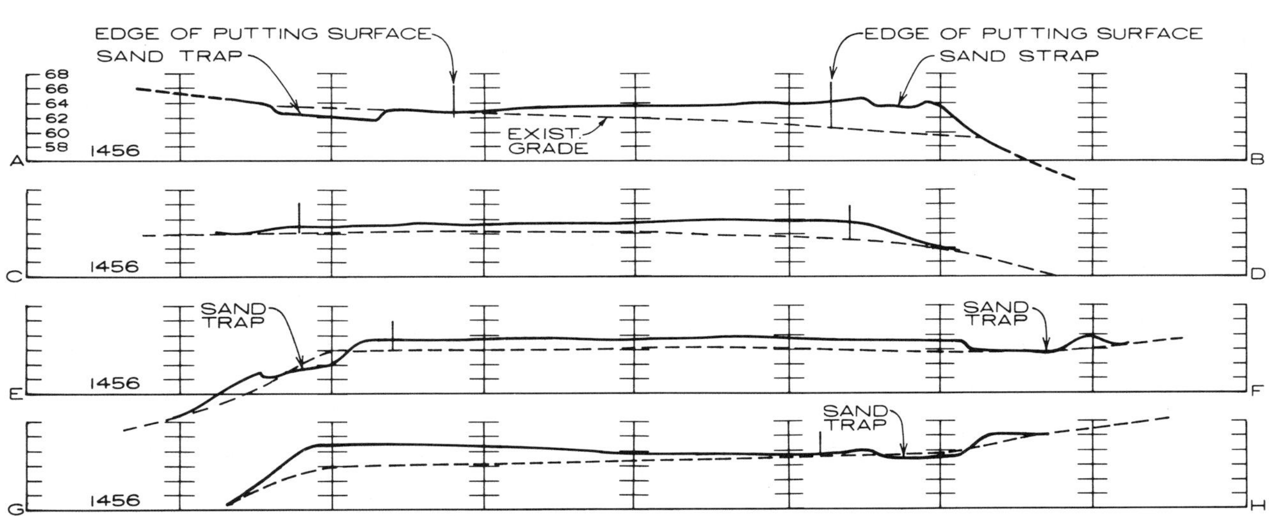

FIG. 12-41 Typical green layout and profiles.

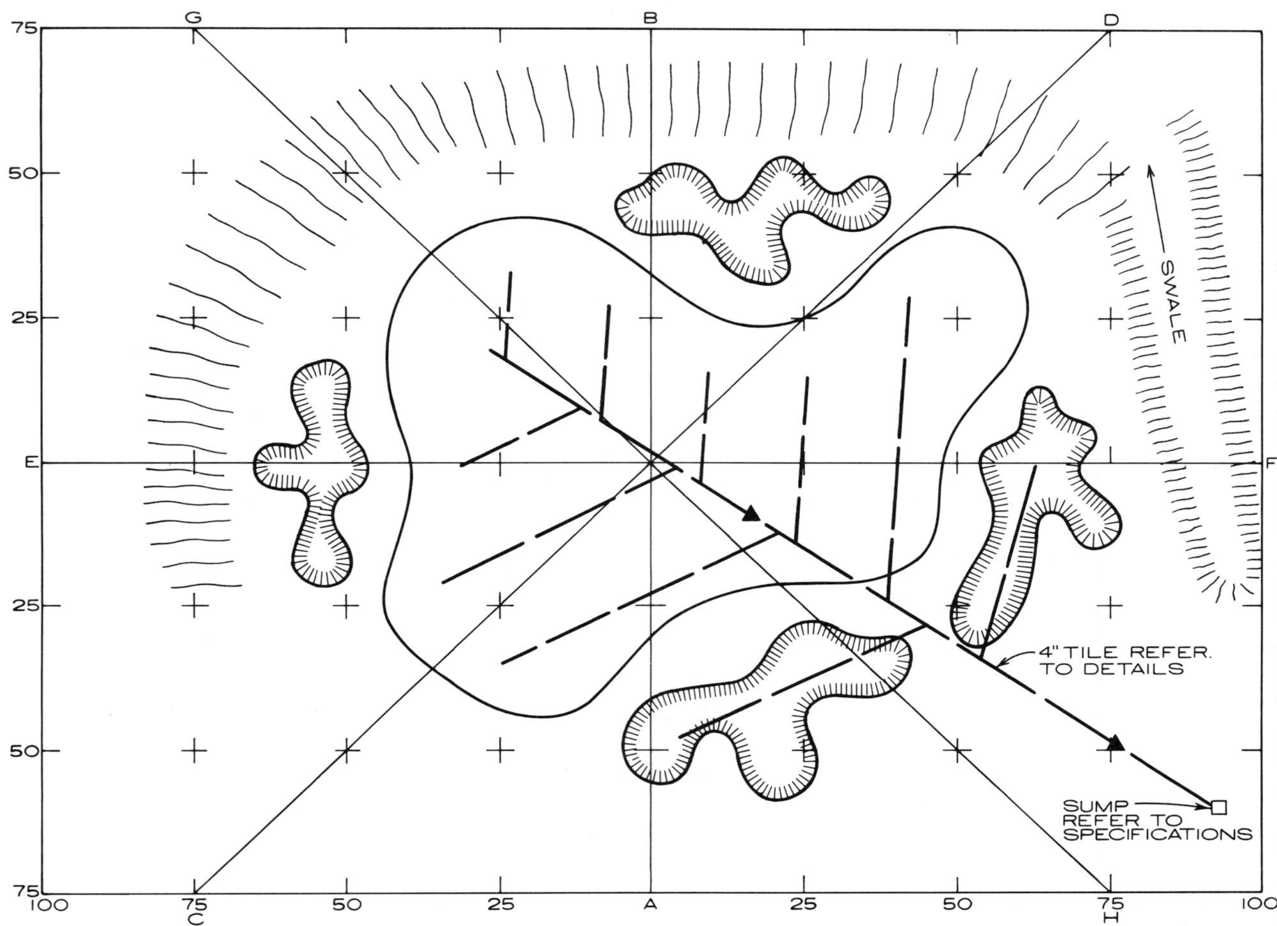

FIG. 12-42 Typical green underdrainage plan.

PLAYGROUNDS

Growth Characteristics

Playgrounds should be designed for various age levels and larger playgrounds should accommodate these age levels, each of which has its own characteristics as follows:

1. Ages 2 to 5 participate in basic physical skills such as sliding and swinging related to their hand grasp, muscle development, and coordination. They also enjoy crawling, throwing, and rolling. They are sensitive emotionally and can have sudden shifts in behavior.
2. Ages 5 to 6 need vigorous activity in games and stunts. They like running games and need climbing experience and some group play. These children have more of their large muscles rather than small muscles developed, hand grasp is fairly well established, and they tire easily. They are sensitive, dramatic, and can have extreme shifts in behavior. They also have short attention spans but are curious and eager to learn.
3. Age 7 to 8 need active, large muscle development. They enjoy climbing, simple stunts, and a minimal level of organized games. Their hands have grown larger, they have improved eye-hand coordination, and rapid growth in their arms and legs. They like competition, and their attention span has increased. They also participate with the opposite sex on an equal basis more in the second than in the third grade.
4. Ages 9 to 12 need a vigorous program of activities. They need an emphasis on sports skills, their muscle coordination is improving, and they are experiencing rapid growth. They like competition and desire to excel in skills and physical capacities. They are capable of understanding more complicated instructions, accept more responsibility, and need some knowledge of sports and game strategy. They have little interest in the opposite sex but have more need for group membership. These children also need a mixture of social settings. Children over 10 begin to outgrow playground equipment and as they get older wish to participate in sports such as softball and basketball or other social settings.

Safety

Designing playgrounds for safety should be a major priority of professionals. Hard surfaces such as concrete or bituminous that have no resilience should not be used because falls onto these surfaces can lead to severe injuries.

Materials like sand, pea gravel, or shredded tires have resilience and help to cushion a fall from play equipment. Each of these materials has its advantages; however, each has some problems. Sand generally gives a good surface, but it can lose its resiliency when wet or frozen and can also be contaminated by animals. Pea gravel is generally cleaner but needs maintenance to keep it contained in the play area. Shredded tires are resilient and are not affected by moisture but need maintenance for containment. Generally the depth of resilient material in the playground should be 1 in. deep for each foot of maximum height a child could fall. Also, underdrainage lines should be placed below the surface material to remove percolation water.

Play Structures. These structures should be designed so that falls will be away from other pieces of equipment. Heights above 8 ft are questionable. Equipment above a height of 4 ft should have a railing, and structures with platforms above 8 ft should have a barrier. Any height above 12 ft should be totally enclosed. When using higher equipment, it is safest to have no other equipment below in case of falls. This allows a resilient surface below to cushion the fall. (See Figs. 12-43 to 12-45.)

Spacing. Adequate spacing of play equipment is essential to prevent injuries. It is also best to separate such items as swings by age groups. By providing separation and adequate spacing, for example, small children may not be as likely to wander into larger children using swings or other apparatus. Swing seats should be made of soft materials such as rubber that cannot cause dangerous injuries due to battering. Buildings, paths, gates, fences, and other play areas should be at least 8 ft from an estimated use zone for pieces of equipment. Also there should be no protrusions or pinch points in play equipment.

Slide Design. Slides over 4 ft high should have sides at least 2½ in. in height. This prevents falls off the edges. At the top of slides over 4 ft high there should be barriers at least 38 in. high. Exit surface at the bottom of a slide over 4 ft high should be a minimum length of 16 in. The height of the exit above grade should be 9 to 15 in. and out of the way of other play equipment.

Stairways and ladders with steps should have handrails on both sides. Ladders with rungs should have a slope between 50° and 75° from horizontal grade, and stairways should have no greater than 35° slope from horizontal grade. Steps and rungs on slides should be evenly spaced with at least 7 to 11 in. between them for arm and leg reaches of children. Steps and rungs should be at least 15 in. wide and horizontal within 2° with permanent slip-resistant finish. Footings for play equipment should be placed below the resilient playground surface to eliminate potential injuries from falls. (See Table 12-2 and Table 12-3.)

FIG. 12-43 This play structure set in a resilient pea gravel bed has slides with protective sides and enclosed platforms for safety.

FIG. 12-44 This playground located in Goldengate Park, San Francisco, California has a resilient sand bed.

FIG. 12-45 Playground with fort: slide has protective sides and resilient sand bed.

Table 12-2 Manner in Which Injuries Occurred on Public Playground[a]

Type of Accident	Percent
Falls to surface	59
Falls—struck same piece of equipment	11
Falls—from one piece of equipment and struck other equipment	2
Impact with moving equipment	7
Contact with protrusions, pinch points, sharp edges, or points	5
Falls against, onto, or into stationary equipment	8
Unknown	8
Total	100

[a] Neiss emergency room-based special study April 10, 1978–May 1, 1978. U.S. Consumer Products Safety Commission Directorate for Hazard Identification and Analysis.

Table 12-3 Hazards Relating to the Most Common Types of Public Playground Equipment[b]

Type of Equipment	Percent Injuries	Percent Equipment in Use
Climbers	42	51
Swings	23	20
Slides	16	12
Merry-go-rounds	8	5
Seesaws	5	6
All other	6	6
	100	100

[b] Neiss emergency room-based special study, April 10, 1978–May 1, 1978, and Consumer Deputy Study of Playground Surfaces, September 13, 1978–October 16, 1978. U.S. Consumer Products Safety Commission, Directorate for Hazard Identification and Analysis.

FIG. 13-1 Constitution Plaza, Hartford, Connecticut (Photograph courtesy of Sasaki Associates).

Chapter Thirteen
Rooftop Gardens

With the growth of urban centers and their related land values open space in cities, often in the form of rooftop gardens, has become an important feature of both public and private development. While it is more costly to construct rooftop gardens because of waterproofing, special plant containers, soil mixes, and irrigation, almost any type of design can be carried out.

The need for pedestrian access in cities can also be met by providing rooftop open spaces that connect high-rise buildings above roadway noise and traffic. These open spaces can provide a "green oasis" feeling in the heart of the city. They also provide good views from tall buildings above the rooftop plazas.

These spaces can provide pleasant environments to gather in at lunchtime, with seating areas, fountains, sculpture, trees, shrubs, flowers, and for special events such as concerts. (See Figs. 13-1 to 13-24.)

The height of rooftop gardens above street level varies from those that are slightly above ground level, for example, on top of a parking garage of one or two stories to those that are on top of high-rise buildings. Ease of accessibility to the rooftop gardens affects the number of people who can use these open spaces. Gardens slightly above roadways are the easiest for access and may not require any steps or ramp areas. These obviously have advantages for handicapped users. Other types of gardens may need escalators or elevators for access. Depending on the height above street level various types of safety railings, walls, or other forms of physical or psychological protection may be needed for safety and for ease of mind of the user. (See Fig. 13–25.)

STRUCTURAL DESIGN

While the structural slab on which the garden is placed is designed by a structural engineer the building architect and landscape architect must carefully coordinate the design elements of the rooftop garden with the engineer so that the loads on the structural elements can be accommodated. Fountains, sculpture, and planting areas are heavy, while vertical elements such as light poles and flagpoles need enough depth for footings or for the deck to withstand wind loads.

Normally the structural engineer can modify the structural system to take some additional weight for feature elements. On the other hand, the landscape architect may have to use smaller types of plant material, lightweight concrete, or other paving materials, lightweight soil mixes, and special footing design for items like light fixtures.

WATERPROOFING

Since the slab on which the garden is developed is also the roof of the structure below, waterproofing of the slab becomes an item of the highest priority. There are several types of waterproofing membranes. Some can be applied in liquid form to provide a continuous sheet, some are rubber sheets with glued overlapped joints, and some are in sheets that are overlapped and adhere to one another. Usually the architectural specifications writer selects the waterproofing system and the protection board to prevent penetration of the membrane during construction. Also it is important to limit the number of penetrations of drain pipe, water pipe, electrical conduit, and items such as fountain equipment. Often installers certified by the waterproofing manufacturer are specified to install the waterproofing and a guarantee is provided. Water tests are also called for in the specifications to insure that there are no leaks before the garden construction continues.

FIG. 13-2 People using the buildings defining Constitution Plaza in Hartford, Connecticut, have a view of the plaza, with the fountain as a focal point, from upper stories and use it as pedestrians at the plaza level.

FIG. 13-3 This fountain integrates water with sculptural granite elements at Constitution Plaza, Hartford, Connecticut.

FIG. 13-4 This space is defined by vertical elements such as planters and trees at Constitution Plaza, Hartford, Connecticut (Photograph courtesy of Sasaki Associates).

Consideration must also be given to maintenance of the waterproofing in case a leak occurs. Open planting beds provide ease of access to repair waterproofing, but paving materials can also be designed for access. paving can be set on sand or sand asphalt, or the corners of pavers can be set above waterproofing on metal brackets or cones of concrete. The pavers can then be easily removed in the future if seepage occurs.

Often in larger architectural/engineering firms the landscape architect designs many of the waterproofing details along with details for planter walls, fountains, and other garden or plaza features. (See Fig. 13–26.)

FIG. 13-5 These mounds act as islands in this garden at Constitution Plaza, Hartford, Connecticut. The base plane of the garden is crowned to permit runoff water to flow toward the moat surrounding the garden where it is inconspicuously picked up in drains.

FIG. 13-6 Girardelli Square in San Francisco, California, by Lawrence Halprin and Associates.

FIG. 13-7 Railings provide safety along various areas at Girardelli Square in San Francisco, California.

FIG. 13-8 Plaza area with fountain as a focus at Girardelli Square, San Francisco, California.

FIG. 13-9 A sequence of spaces links areas together at Girardelli Square, San Francisco, California.

FIG. 13-10 Rooftop garden with fountain at the Spectrum Center, Addison, Texas.

FIG. 13-11 Sculpture exhibit by Arnaldo Pomodoro at Spectrum Center, Addison, Texas.

FIG. 13-12 Sculpture area at Spectrum Center, Addison, Texas.

FIG. 13-13 and 13-14 Henry Moore sculpture on rooftop plaza area at Dallas City Hall.

FIG. 13-15 This unique rooftop garden has a computerized fountain with 217-nozzles at Allied Bank Tower at Fountain Place, Dallas, Texas. Dan Kiley of Kiley-Walker designed the plaza and I.M. Pei & Partners designed the building.

FIG. 13-16 Another view of the fountain changing shape. This fountain also has a fiber-optic system of night lighting that allows the color of the water to change as the shape changes. All the fountains at Allied Bank Tower in Dallas, Texas have a recirculating system pumping 30,000 gallons of water per minute.

FIG. 13-17 Waterfalls and aerated jets are part of the plaza design which steps down the site. Also, cypress trees in waterproof precast concrete planters give rhythm to the design at Allied Bank Tower, at Fountain Place in Dallas, Texas.

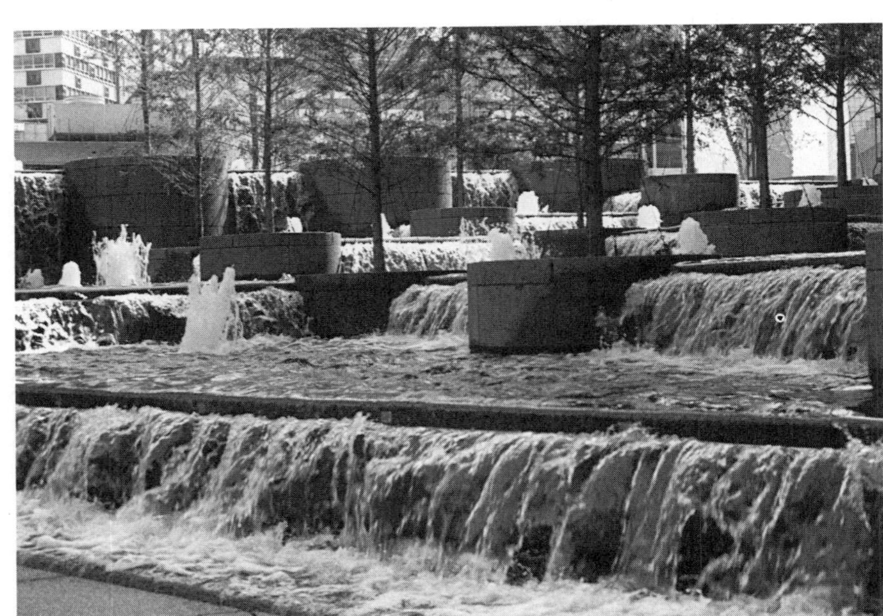

FIG. 13-18 A view of the waterfalls under a canopy of cypress trees at Allied Bank Tower, Fountain Place in Dallas, Texas.

FIG. 13-19 A view of the roof garden at the Oakland Museum, Oakland, California which is a three level structure integrated with roof gardens that cover it. Architect for the building Kevin Roche, Landscape Architect, Dan Kiley.

FIG. 13-20 Concrete planters on the roof garden at the Oakland Museum step up the site with views from the building at each level.

FIG. 13-21 Planters are at sitting height on the roof garden at the Oakland museum.

FIG. 13-22 The Kaiser Center Roof Garden in Oakland, California by landscape architect Theodore Osmundson, has a curvilinear pool integrated with mounding and planting.

FIG. 13-23 The walk system at the Kaiser Center Roof Garden connects to a pedestrian bridge which crosses the pool.

FIG. 13-24 A view of the water feature and adjacent mounding and planting at the Kaiser Center Roof Garden, Oakland, California.

FIG. 13-25 The entrance area to Citicorp in New York City terraces down to a plaza area. This fountain is the focus of the rooftop space.

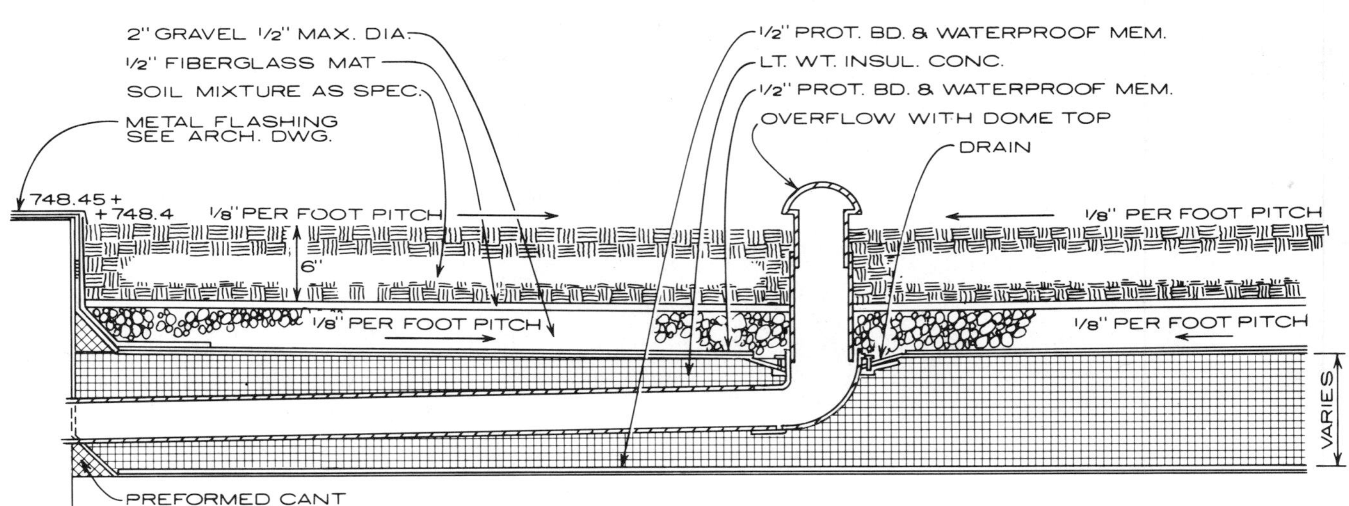

FIG. 13-26 Waterproofing section. Two waterproof membrane layers were used for additional protection over a computer area.

DRAINAGE

There are several ways to provide drainage on the rooftop garden. 1) Sometimes a slab is built with no pitch or slope. A lightweight material is then placed over the slab, which is sloped to drains set at the low points. Surface runoff can also be picked up by two level drains that reach the surface. In an open-joint paving system where water passes beneath plant beds or paved areas the water will flow directly to drains with the above system. 2) In other systems the concrete slab is sloped so that runoff passing through open-joint systems or plant beds can flow to drains in the slab. 3) In the third type of system the slab is flat with pitch developed on the surface paving and drains set on the surface at appropriate low points to pick up water runoff. Joints in the surface paving of the above type are sealed. It is also possible to place drains beneath the surface or to use two level drains, but since there is no pitch on the slab of this type of system seepage has a hard time reaching drains and in cold weather may freeze, causing damage.

Drainage in Tree Pits

In tree pits or shrub beds there should be a sloped floor with a drain at the low point. In many cases perforated pipe is used to help pick up water and carry it to the drain. Four in. of gravel is placed above the drain and entire planter bottom with a soil separator on top of the gravel to prevent clogging from the soil mix above. Another method is to use a material such as Enka-Drain in place of the gravel. Surface drainage in planters should also be considered in the design. (See Figs. 13-27 and 13-28.)

MECHANICAL EQUIPMENT

The mechanical/electrical engineer for the building designs the system to pick up storm water runoff in conjunction with the landscape architect. He also is involved in the design of equipment for fountains and the space for this equipment, irrigation controls, and electric supply for the fountain and garden lighting. Often it is desirable to have special mechanical consultants involved in the design of the fountain to help eliminate problems that easily develop where this specialized work is done.

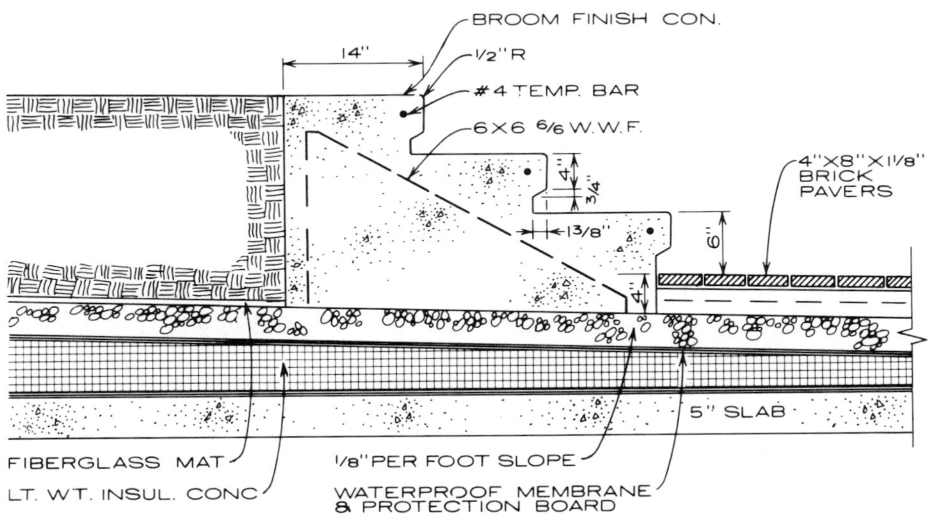

FIG. 13-27 Typical section through a planter at the Riverchase Galleria, Hoover, Alabama (Detail courtesy of the HOK Planning Group, Dallas, Texas).

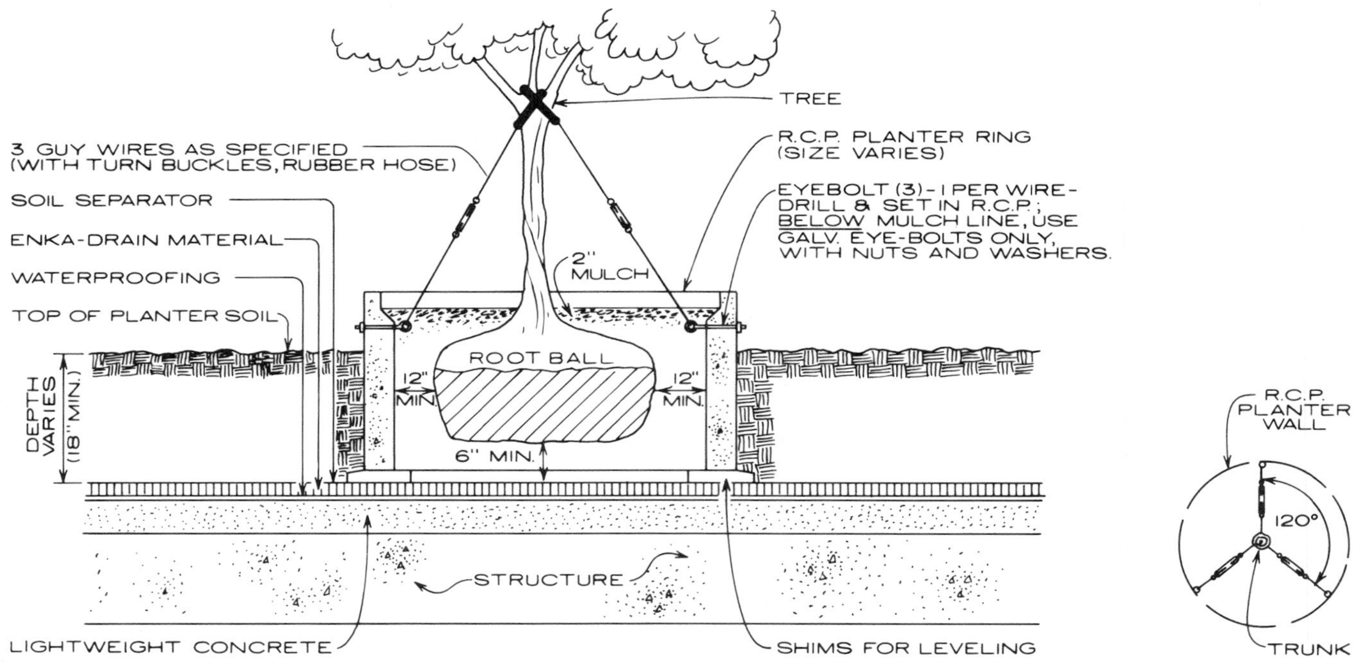

FIG. 13-28 Tree planting detail, Riverchase Galleria Motor Court, Hoover, Alabama (Detail courtesy of the HOK Planning Group, Dallas, Texas).

PLANTING AND IRRIGATION

Planting requirements for a rooftop garden can become unique when the issues of soil mixes, weight, irrigation, drainage, and plant material become concerns. The structural system must be designed to support the weight of trees where these are planted. The weight of the various materials such as concrete planter, soil mix, gravel, and tree must be calculated. The weight of these elements can total 10 to 15 tons. If the structure is not designed to allow for 3000 lbs/yd^3 of topsoil and 75 to 100 lbs/in. of caliper of a tree, for example, it may have to be modified to support the anticipated weight or a new design scheme may be needed. (See Figs. 13-29 to 13-32.)

PLANT CONTAINERS

Plant containers can be of any shape. They are usually above plaza grade, but where the floor of the slab can be depressed the containers can be set flush to the plaza. The following depths are desirable for plant containers:

1. A minimum depth of 4 ft is required for large trees for soil mix and gravel. A container width of 7 to 10 ft diameter or the tree pit extended to the crown of the tree is best.
2. A minimum depth of $2\frac{1}{2}$ to 3 ft is required for small trees with a container 4 to 6 ft in diameter.
3. A minimum depth of 24 to 30 in. for medium-sized shrubs with a container 30 to 48 in. in diameter.
4. A minimum depth for small shrubs of 18 to 24 in. and containers 18 to 24 in. in diameter.
5. Lawn areas require a soil depth of 6 to 12 in. with gravel recommended below the soil area.

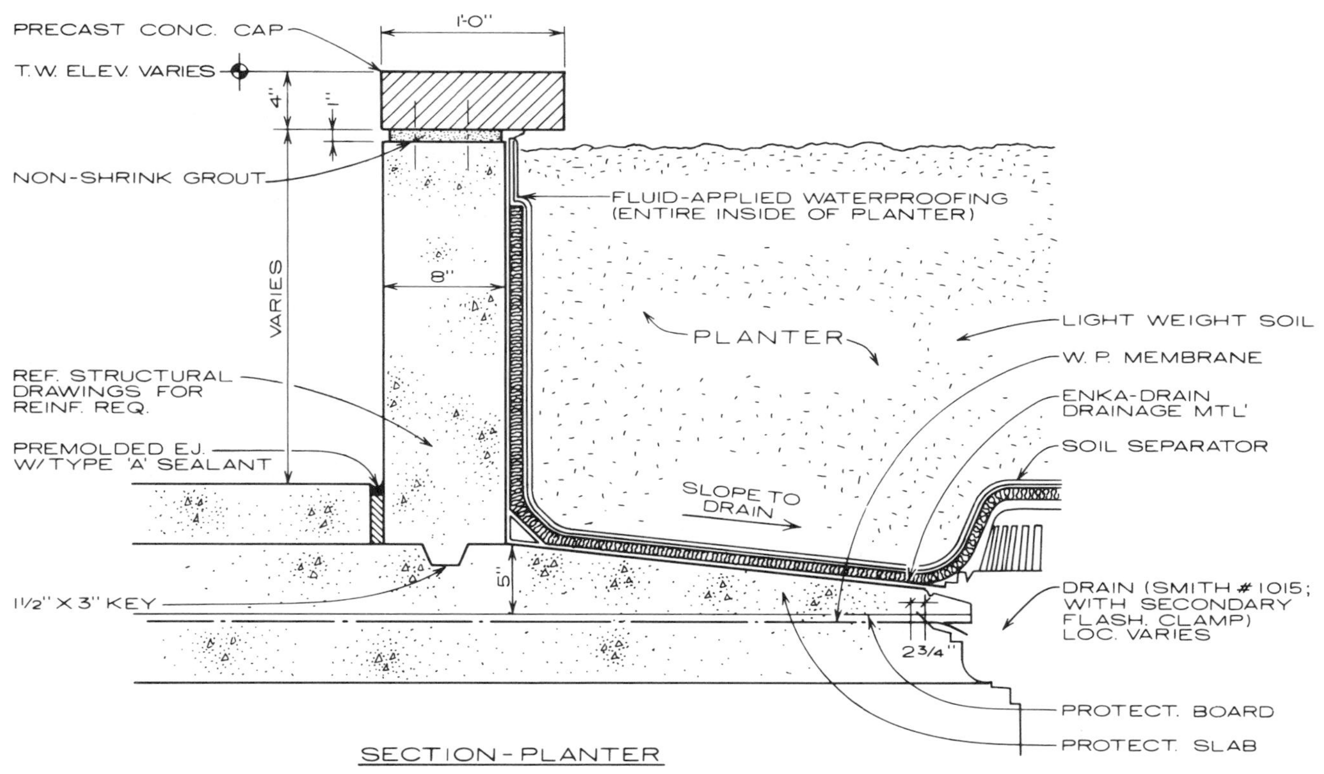

FIG. 13-29 Planter drainage detail.

FIG. 13-30 Fountain on rooftop area at Lincoln Plaza, Dallas, Texas.

FIG. 13-31 Rooftop garden with mounded areas for planting at IBM in the urban center area of Las Colinas, Irving, Texas.

FIG. 13-32 Fountain in rooftop garden at IBM in Las Colinas, Irving, Texas.

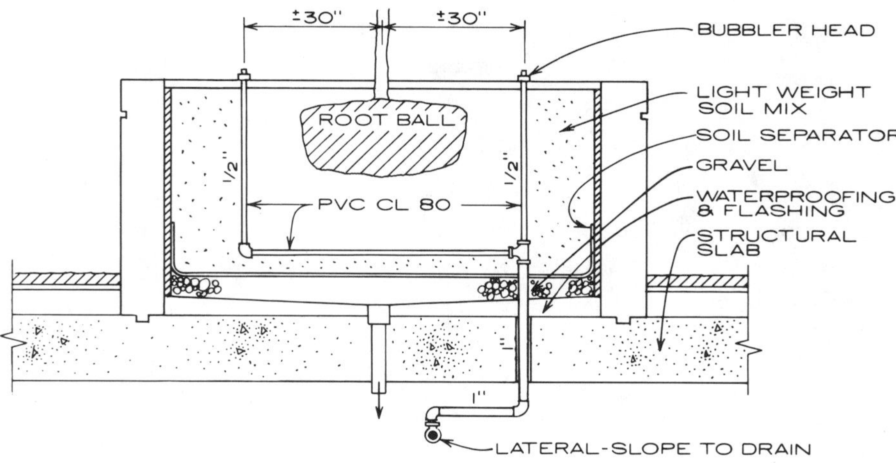

FIG. 13-33 Bubbler for planter.

IRRIGATION

Rooftop gardens should have provisions for both automatic irrigation and hose bibs for hand watering of trees and plants. It is best if trees can be watered individually on the surface of the planter rather than saturating from below. In this manner an oversaturated condition will be visible by maintenance personnel. In raised planters much more moisture is evaporated than when the planting is flush with the plaza. (See Fig. 13-33.)

SOIL MIX, GUYING, AND HARDINESS

Soil mixes vary with regional location. Therefore mixes and nutrient requirements should be checked with horticulturists in the specific area. State university agricultural extension departments can also be of assistance. Soil mixes for shade trees, for example, could be one-fourth to one-third by volume of screened topsoil, one-third to one-half by volume of coarse sand, and one-fourth to one-third by volume of peat moss. Lightweight materials such as perlite can also be used in the mixture or be substituted for part of another item such as sand.

Guying trees can be done by placing hooks in planter walls or with deadmen. If large trees are placed in windy areas where root growth is limited it may be necessary to permanently guy the trees with stainless steel or plastic-coated galvanized steel wire. (See Fig. 13-28.)

The plant material itself should be mostly hardy in the location it is to be planted. This is especially important since the plant material may be in stress conditions in its rooftop location. There may be extra heat from paving, evaporation of moisture in raised planters, limited room in which to grow roots to support its canopy, therefore requiring pruning, inadequate watering causing dieback, and added spraying needed for insect problems.

FIG. 14-1 Oakford Glen Condominiums, Abington Township, Pennsylvania (Photograph courtesy of Bellante, Clauss, Miller & Partners; Photographer, Otto Baitz).

Chapter Fourteen
Residential Development Concepts

In designing residential projects careful consideration must be given to how housing is placed on the land and the relationship of the units to each other, access, parking, and amenities. (See Fig. 14-1.) Several land planning and building site concepts are outlined in the discussion following.

LAND PLANNING CONCEPTS

Neighborhood Size

Neighborhood size has been studied since the Garden City concept was developed by Ebenezer Howard in 1898 in his book *Tomorrow: A Peaceful Path to Real Reform,* retitled *Garden Cities of To-Morrow* in 1902. A neighborhood has generally been considered as the size necessary to support one elementary school or about 1200 to 1500 families. Two neighborhoods are needed to support a junior high school and four to support a senior high school.

When the new town of Columbia, Maryland, was developed, five neighborhoods were used to form a village of 3000 to 5000 families (12,000 to 20,000 people). The new town has an anticipated population of 125,000.

The Superblock

The superblock has been used in place of the typical grid system of rectangular blocks. The elements of the superblock are (1) the separation of pedestrian and vehicular circulation by the use of service access lanes or cul-de-sacs serving groups of units and thereby eliminating through traffic; (2) housing with living areas and bedrooms oriented toward open space and garden areas forming park areas toward the center of the superblock; and (3) confining the use of roads of varying scale to one purpose, for example, as a service or collector street. These concepts, which originated with Radburn, New Jersey, have been further expanded by adapting the groups of units around an access drive for the cluster system described next.

Cluster Housing

This is a site development concept where houses are arranged in closely related groups. The use of housing clusters allows higher densities in suitable areas for development while preserving natural site features. These features may be natural drainage swales, steep wooded slopes, water features, rock outcrops, and so on. Site infrastructure costs may be lowered by this land planning method with additional savings in maintenance costs. Lots can be clustered around cul-de-sacs for example, and if made a smaller size, land can be provided for park belts or open space. Relief from standard rows of single family dwellings and freedom from through traffic can also be achieved. (See Fig. 14-2.)

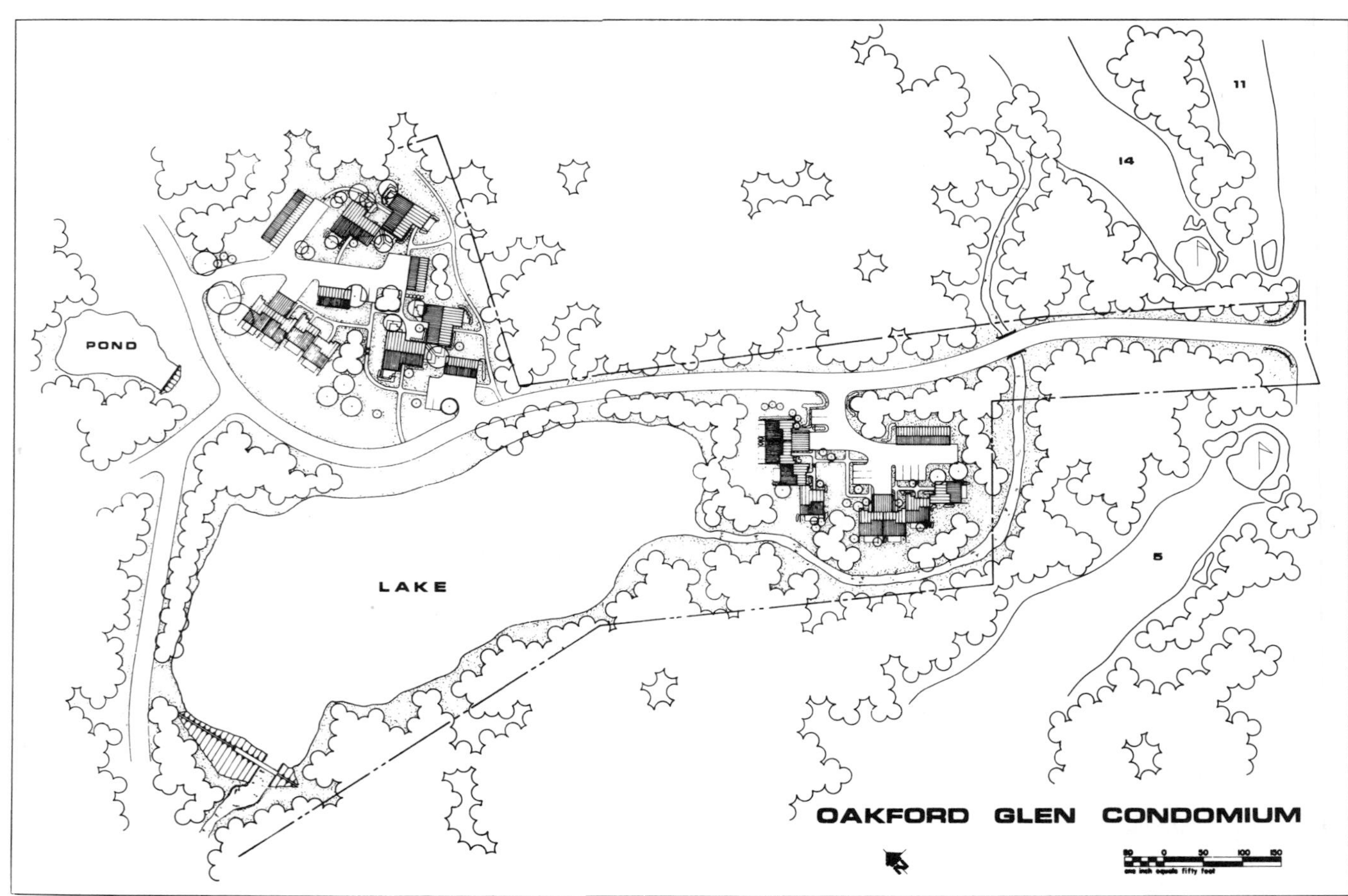

FIG. 14-2 Plan showing the cluster concept.

Planned Unit Development

The planned unit development (PUD) uses the cluster concept. It also may include a variety of dwelling units such as single family, duplex, townhouse, garden, multistoried, and high rise apartments.

The PUD can achieve flexibility in design without change in overall density. It encourages a more creative approach in the development of residential, commercial, and industrial land. It is also more efficient and economical in reducing roads and utilities. Sites are provided for parks, recreation areas, and, in large developments, golf courses. Neighborhood associations are often formed to administer the recreation and open space areas.

BUILDING SITE CONCEPTS

Public and Private Open Space

In the design of housing the relation of public and private areas is important to the interaction of residents and the degree of privacy desired.

Public Areas. Public areas are used by all residents of a residential development. They are the parking areas, roads, walks, parks, playgrounds, and trash collection facilities.

Semipublic Areas. Semipublic areas are the community swimming pool or other recreational facilities available only to residents or visitors of a particular planned unit development or apartment complex. Semipublic areas are also the entry areas, lobbies, and hallways of condominiums or apartment buildings. (See Figs. 14-3 to 14-9.)

FIG. 14-3 Entry court serving two units at Oakford Glen Condominiums, Abington Township, Pennsylvania.

FIG. 14-4 Swimming pool area at Lincoln Meadows, Fort Worth, Texas.

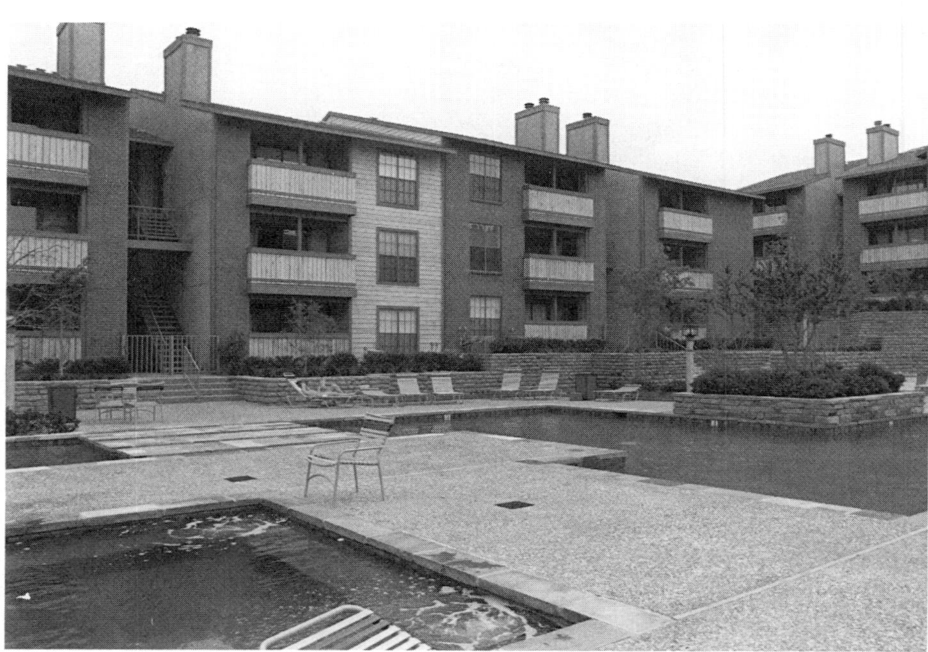

FIG. 14-5 Swimming pool area at Lincoln Meadows, Fort Worth, Texas.

FIG. 14-6 Swimming pool area at Lincoln Oaks, Fort Worth, Texas.

FIG. 14-7 Lincoln Oaks, Fort Worth, Texas.

FIG. 14-8 This swimming pool area has trellised sitting areas to provide shade at the Chesapeake Apartments, Fort Worth, Texas.

FIG. 14-9 Swimming pool area with trellised sitting area at Sterling Point Apartments in Woodhaven, Fort Worth, Texas.

Private Spaces. These spaces are enclosed or screened patio areas where people can eat outdoors, sunbathe, or entertain friends. They can also be screened balcony areas and porches. (See Figs. 14-10 and 14-11.)

FIG. 14-10 Screened patio area at Oakford Glen Condominiums, Abington Township, Pennsylvania.

FIG. 14-11 Private patio area at a condominium project.

Site Concepts

Developing a housing site concept requires a careful analysis of the sequence of events a visitor or resident follows in proceeding from the entrance of the development to a given unit. Is there a clear sequence of events from public to semipublic to private spaces? For example, one may drive from a minor road to a parking area and then move directly to a garage from which the unit is entered. Another sequence is to enter a semipublic carport and then follow a pedestrian walk to either a private entry court from which one proceeds into the unit or a semipublic transition area that serves two or more entries. Private entry courts are also generally good buffers between parking areas and dwellings.

In the superblock or cluster concept one can provide units with both an access or service side and a pedestrian-oriented side. To provide a transition area on the pedestrian side private courtyards or semipublic courtyard entrances can be developed. These courts can also serve to buffer noise.

Other factors to consider in developing housing layouts are temporary space for service vehicles, visitor parking, separation of children's play areas from service ones, visual privacy between units, minimum walking distance from parking areas to each unit, trash collection, and mail delivery.

Transition Areas or Linkages

Transition spaces are areas between public and semipublic spaces and between semipublic and private spaces. They may involve the widening of a public walkway where it meets the entrance court to a townhouse or they may be the steps to a housing unit. They may also be the space between a semipublic courtyard and the private space of an enclosed patio or balcony area.

These transition areas provide variety and interest in the landscape. They therefore must be given adequate attention during the design of housing projects.

SITE ANALYSIS FACTORS

Natural and Cultural Elements

As in other types of site planning a resource analysis is essential to understanding the natural and cultural features of a site and subsequently being able to determine the best opportunities for development. Topography generally is the principal natural factor in siting housing units, but depth of water table, bedrock, and water runoff patterns are also important.

In locating housing units one should review the best solar orientation for a particular climatic zone. (See Figs. 2-16 to 2-19.) This includes building placement in relation to solar orientation, warm and cool slopes, and wind direction. Other site features important in orienting units are views, existing vegetation, rock outcrops, and natural drainage swales. (See Fig 14-12.)

Alternate building site layouts can also be analyzed for energy efficiency. Does the site plan maximize solar orientation? Does it take advantage of summer breezes while affording protection against winter winds?

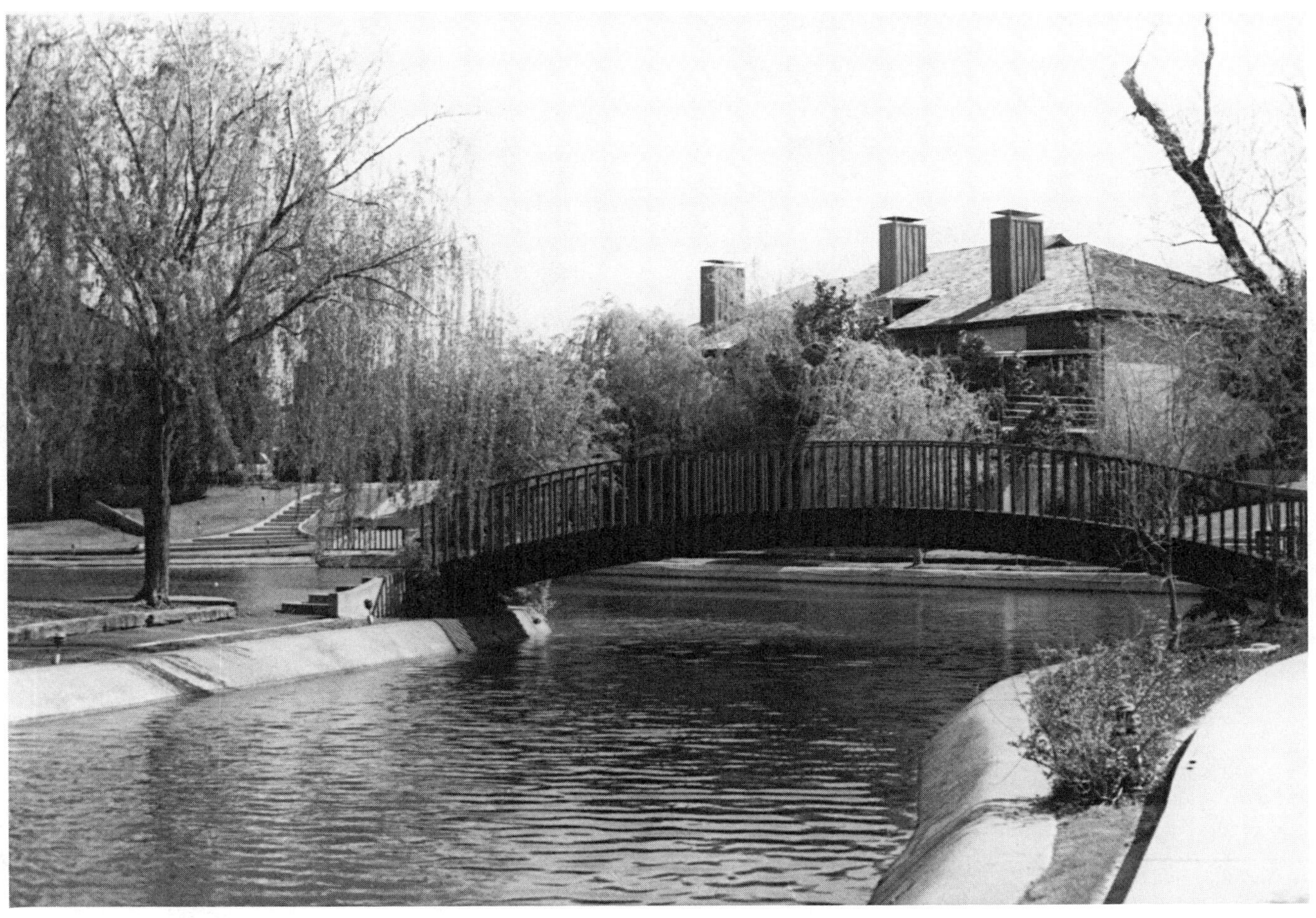

FIG. 14-12 Lake area at Willow Lake, Fort Worth, Texas.

Zoning and subdivision regulations for the local municipality where the project is located must also be reviewed. The requirements in these regulations must be followed so a project can receive approval as it progresses from a sketch plan through preliminary design and final design and construction drawings. If variations in zoning are desired an application to the local zoning hearing board is required. All procedures for approval of a housing development are usually described in the zoning and subdivision regulations.

In reviewing the components involved in developing a residential project it is apparent that many factors must be considered and balanced before a well-designed project can be achieved.

FIG. 15-1 Concrete monoliths and mounds are part of the landscape infrastructure at Preston Park South, Plano, Texas, by the HOK Planning Group, Dallas, Texas.

Chapter Fifteen
Development Design Guidelines

Development design guidelines, or architectural guidelines as they are often called, must set the concepts for the overall quality of a development. These documents are prepared for incorporation into articles of protective covenants and restrictions. The development guidelines concern a combination of landscape easements, building setbacks, and basic controls that provide direction to an applicant for his or her individual site and to insure the long-term development in a manner consistent with the developer's objective as to type, quality, image, and density of improvements.

DEVELOPMENT GOALS

The development goals should describe the intent and purpose of the proposed project. For example, some goals could be the following:

1. To develop a community with quality design standards and comprehensive support facilities that will establish it as a quality and unified environment.
2. To provide a variety of uses and tract sizes to permit development flexibility as well as amenities necessary to support business efficiency.
3. To provide direct access to the regional roadway network for connections to commercial centers, airports, and residential areas in a clean, congestion-free manor.
4. To establish a spatially sensitive environment of well-landscaped areas for a high-density urban center with a transition to medium-density development.

MASTER DEVELOPMENT PLAN DESCRIPTION

The master development plan should describe the various land uses and where they are located (See Fig. 15-2).

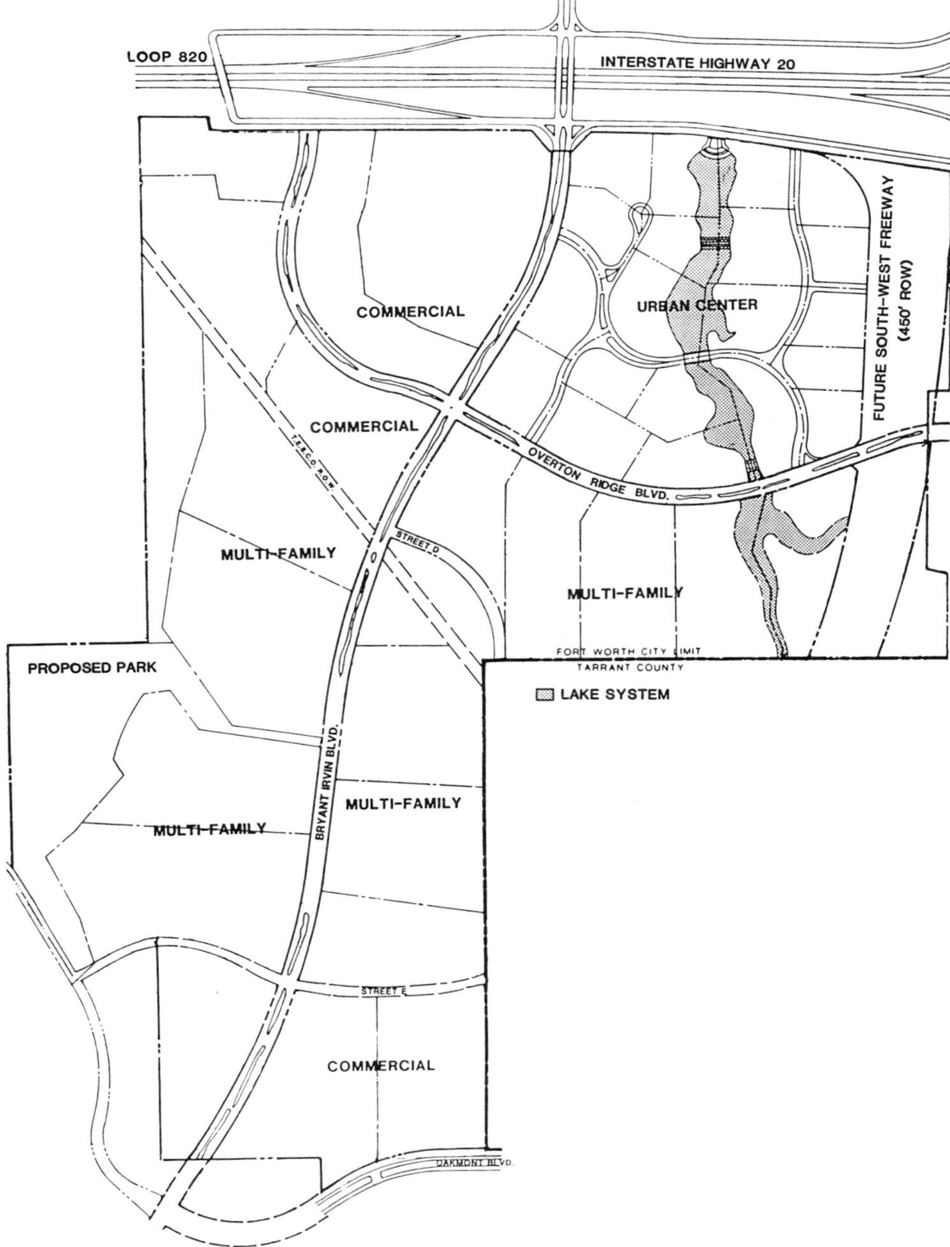

FIG. 15-2 This mixed use development plan shows parcels designated for commercial use, multifamily, and an urban center that will have office space.

Purpose of Document

All development guidelines and suggested procedures should be established to insure the developer's objectives for improvements to the development by individual parties. The document must also provide direction for the application of site-specific efforts.

Typical Definitions

The following words or phrases are often used in the text of development design guidelines.

1. *Applicant* means and refers to any individual or entity making application to purchase, lease, develop, or build upon any parcel of land within the project.
2. *Architectural Review Committee* (ARC) means and refers to the collection of individuals as detailed in this document who are charged with duties of design review and enforcement of standards for all building sites.
3. *Association* means and refers to the specific property owner's association as created by its articles of incorporation and by the covenants.
4. *Building Site* (SITE) means and refers to any severable development parcel available for sale, lease, development, or construction.
5. *Declarant* means and refers to members of the developer or its designates.
6. *Open Space* means any landscaped area included in any side, rear, or front yard or any unoccupied space on the lot that is open and unobstructed to the sky except for the ordinary projections of cornices, eaves, or canopies. Open space does not include motorcourt, drives, and parking.
7. *Owner* means and refers to any holder or valid title to any parcel of real estate in the project.
8. *Site Modifications* means and refers to any additions, alterations, changes to, or removal of any improvement to a building site or its attachments.
9. *Site Improvements* means and refers to any and all work necessary for and including construction or principal structures and their associated needs for particular building site.
10. *Structures* means and refers to all man-made edifices to be erected by any parties on any particular building site.

DEVELOPMENT CONCEPTS

In this section of the guidelines the development concepts should be described. To achieve a quality project, the following examples of concepts are outlined.

Visual Identity

A strong visual identity should be created that gives the development the appearance of high quality. The major boulevard with its intensive landscape right-of-way and easements can unify the entire development. Consistent design of site entrances, building locations, signage, and lighting can further enhance the visual identity of the project.

Development Plan

The development plan includes land uses provided under present zoning. The development plan must be sensitive to market conditions, and while maintaining basic integrity, the plan must also be responsive to change as allowed under the declaration.

These design guidelines should apply to each applicant for any site improvements, including but not limited to landscaping, parking, buildings, signage, and lighting. The Architectural Review Committee should have authority to review and render decisions as to the environment and aesthetic qualities relating to each building site.

Table 15-1 Setbacks

Roads	Surface Parking	Building Structure	Parking Structure
Road A Interstate	45 ft	45 ft	45 ft
Road B Collector	45 ft	45 ft	45 ft
Road C Primary Roadway	20 ft	20 ft	20 ft
Road D Secondary Roadway	10 ft	20 ft	20 ft

SITE PLANNING PRINCIPLES

The siting of structures strongly influences the desired character of a development. Requirements for building orientation and building setbacks from various roads can be described. For example, typical setbacks can be shown in table form (Table 15-1).

Site Grading and Drainage

Criteria for site grading as it affects water runoff must be developed so that drainage can be directed away from all buildings. Drainage should not be directed into adjacent sites. (See Fig. 15-3.) Slopes should be graded to a maximum of 3 : 1 in all cases. Drainage swales should have a minimum grade of 2%, and catch basins can be used in swales with a flatter than 2% grade to prevent standing water.

Vehicular Circulation

Circulation for employees, visitors, service and delivery, fire protection, and security is involved in this description. Parking lot entry drives, width of parking spaces, aisles, and angle of parking desired should be described here.

If separation of visitor and employee traffic at entrance or courts is envisioned it is described in this section. For example, special plazas, motor courts, or turnarounds can be encouraged to identify entrance areas. (See Fig. 15-4.)

Service or delivery areas should not be located along public roadways. They should be placed at the rear or side entrance of the structures for minimum visibility.

Parking

Parking requirements are described that set maximum walking distance to primary entrances. The type of curbs, paving, and water runoff collection should also be outlined. Parking is designed, for example, to handle employees occupying the structures as well as visitors, and any company cars without the use of on-street parking.

Pedestrian Circulation

Types, sizes, and linkages for pedestrian access should be described. Pedestrian circulation needs from parking areas or parking structures to building entries will be indicated. Walkways linking all buildings in the development can be required in the guidelines. Special features such as jogging paths may also be required in quality projects.

FIG. 15-3 Grading and drainage.

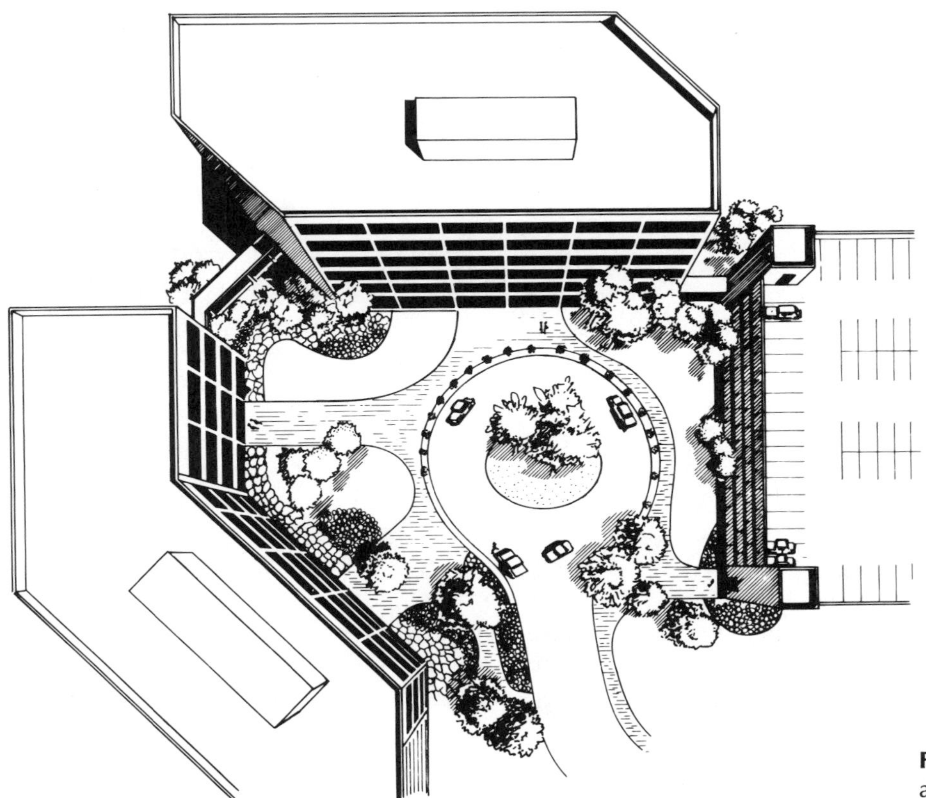

FIG. 15-4 Motor courtyards provide an address in a new development.

Easements

Easements are part of each tract of land sold and reserved for use by the development company as needed. An example is a landscape easement adjacent to road right-of-way that may be mounded, planted, and irrigated by the developer as part of the infrastructure of the project to create a quality image. (See Fig. 15-5).

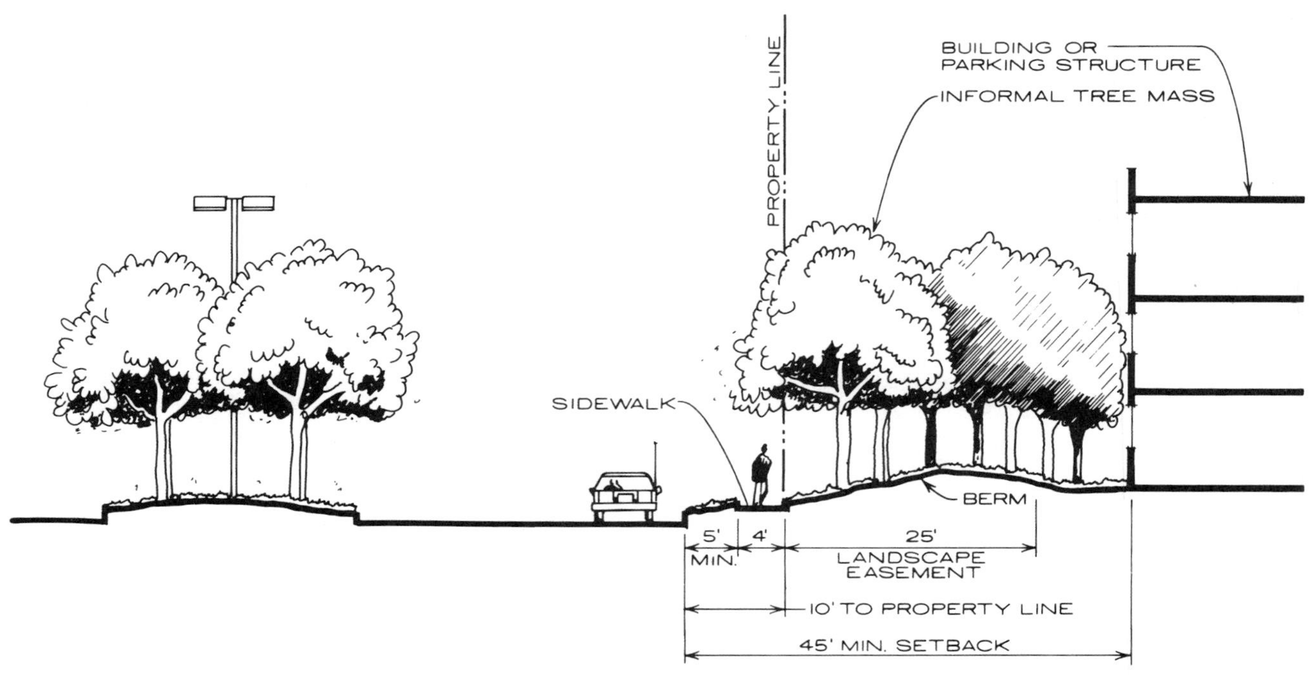

FIG. 15-5 Landscape easement.

Utilities

Utilities including water, sewer, electric, telephone, gas, communications, and so forth can be required to be placed underground from the nearest available source. If placed on the surface, screening of equipment from public view can be enforced.

Fences and Walls

Setbacks from walkways can be required for planting purposes. Chain link fence can be prohibited unless planted with shrubs or vines. The maximum height of fence such as 6 ft can be outlined as well as the location such as inside or across the back of a property for security.

ARCHITECTURAL DESIGN

Concepts

Examples of concepts for quality projects are described below. Building design should display thoughtful attention to quality of appearance and details that create harmony with the desired image of the total development. Purchasers should be given the latitude to present building designs that meet their needs to the Architectural Review Committee.

Review Criteria

The Architectural Review Committee can consider and evaluate all applications based on the character of the building and materials criteria as outlined in the following typical requirements:

1. The overall architectural design should present a quality image.
2. The exterior facade should incorporate no more, for example, than two or three building materials in addition to glass.
3. Use of glass should be limited to window application and should not form more than a certain percentage of the facade, for example, 80%.
4. Use of highly reflective materials should not, for example, be part of the building facade treatment.
5. Support structures should be of similar style, color, design, and materials as used for the principal structure.

Individual building design can exhibit a contrast in use of certain design elements such as color, materials, window spacing, and basic massing proportions. This can be permitted as long as such design contrasts are not in direct conflict with surrounding structures or the overall image of the development. Delineation of the building plane is encouraged. Window openings and other building elements can be recessed or delineated to define architectural elements and is encouraged.

Materials

All building materials proposed for use on individual building structures by each developer can be subject to review by the Architectural Review Committee. Material selection should be based on quality, durability, texture, color, method of application, and intended use.

Colors

The colors of all proposed buildings should be indicated on each submitted plan for review and approval of the Architectural Review Committee is required. Samples of materials may also be needed for submission. Color schemes should represent a quality expression consistent with the architectural character. Accent colors can be used to identify architectural detail and highlight features that are complementary to the design. Colors and intended application should be subject to approval by the ARC.

Roof Treatments

Roof design should be of quality appearance and be compatible with the overall architectural design of the structure. Mechanical equipment including vent stacks, elevator cabs, storage tanks, compressor units, water chillers, and the like must be located inside the building. Roof equipment on structures can be screened or hidden entirely by a parapet wall so as not to be seen from ground level from any point on the site or neighboring sites. (See Fig. 15-6).

Parking Structures

Parking structures and their relation to principal structures should be described and materials, color, and other elements approved by the ARC. For example, openings in the parking structure facades can resemble fenestration of the principal structure as shown in Fig. 15-7. A minimum of two entrances/exits are required per garage. A 35 ft setback between garage and building is required unless approved by the Architectural Review Committee.

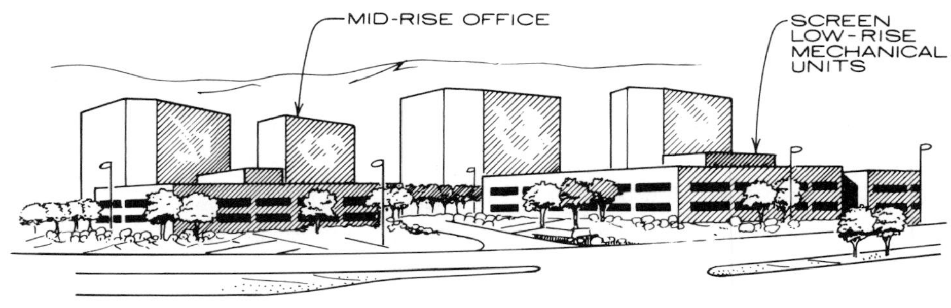

FIG. 15-6 Roof equipment should be screened.

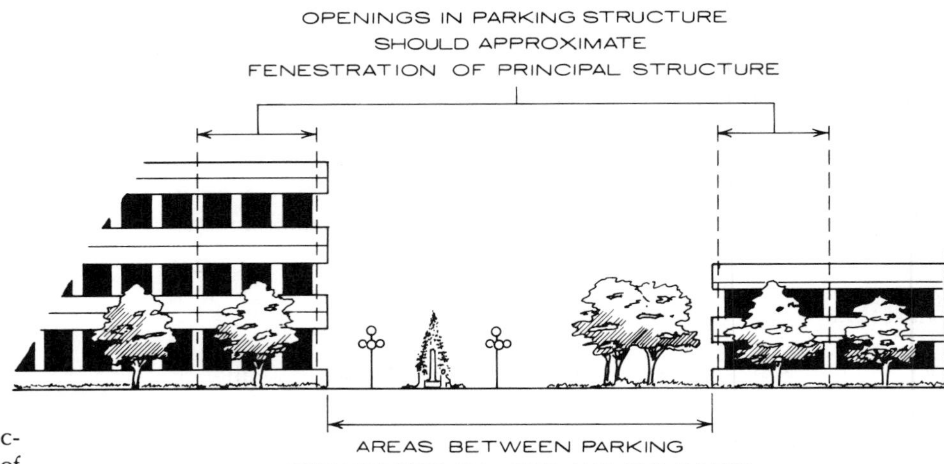

FIG. 15-7 Openings in parking structure should approximate fenestration of principal structures.

LANDSCAPE DESIGN PRINCIPLES

In order to maintain overall visual continuity it is important that the landscape treatment of individual spaces be consistent with the overall landscape development plan. A description of planting concepts follows below. The ARC should review all proposed landscape design plans to determine appropriateness and adherence to prescribed principles. For, example, plants should be arranged to highlight building entries, soften building masses, provide scale to site development, and define parcel edges. An approved project plant list should be included in an appendix to the guidelines.

Landscape Setbacks

Landscaping should occur within all setback requirements as determined for each parcel. Building site landscaping can present an attractive ground plane to pedestrians while screening building bases, service areas, parking structures, and surface parking lots as shown in Figures 15-8 and 15-9. Landscaping should be incorporated to be consistent with the desired image of the development.

When used, berms in setbacks can vary in height from 1 to 3 ft depending

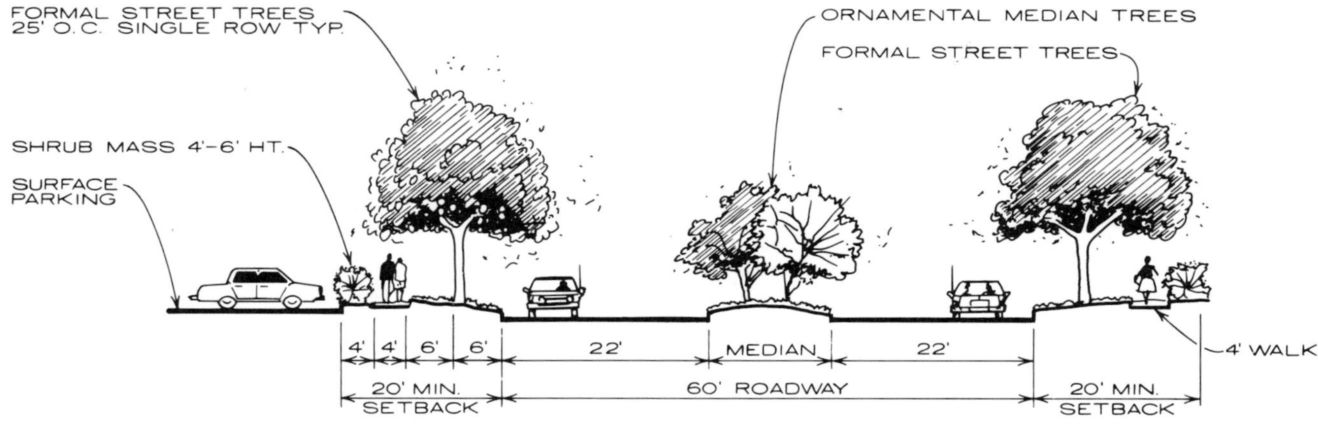

FIG. 15-8 Landscaping within setback requirements.

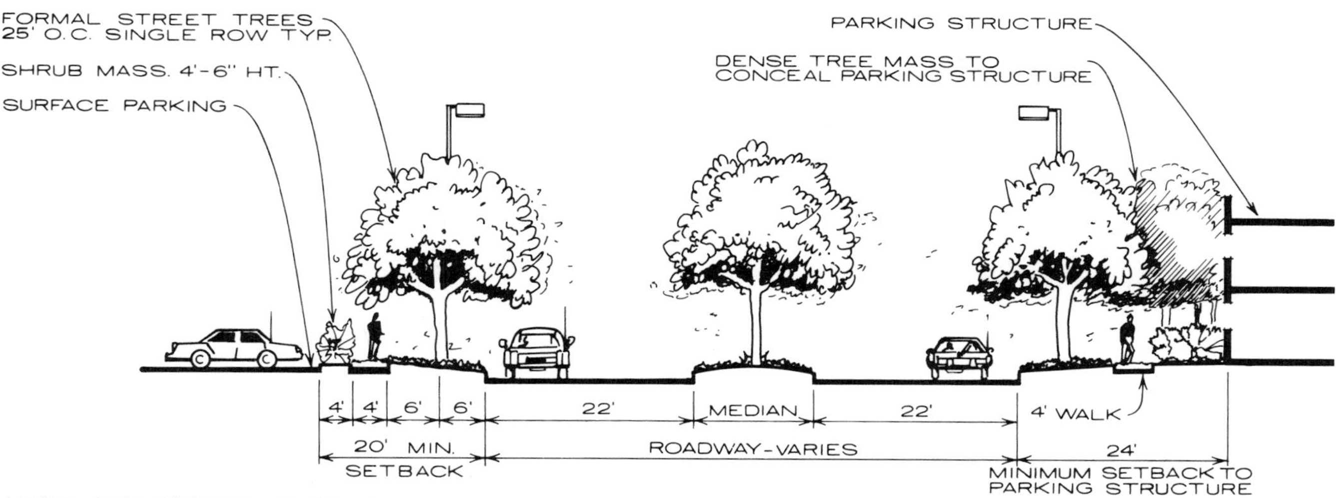

FIG. 15-9 Landscaping can screen service areas or parking or parking structures.

upon location and proximity of existing trees. The desired effect is one of smooth transition from the top of curb to the setback line with allowances made for placement of the sidewalk, if necessary.

Berms should have gentle transitions and soft, natural form. Grading of berms or mounds should not be lumpy or abrupt. (See Fig. 15-10.) A smooth transition should occur at the end of the berm. A smooth transition should also occur between existing trees and new trees and grades.

Entrances/Roadways

Entrances and roadways should be treated in relation to their function: entrances to individual parcels should be treated in a manner that reinforces the feeling of entry and is consistent in portraying the image of the development. (See Fig. 15-11.)

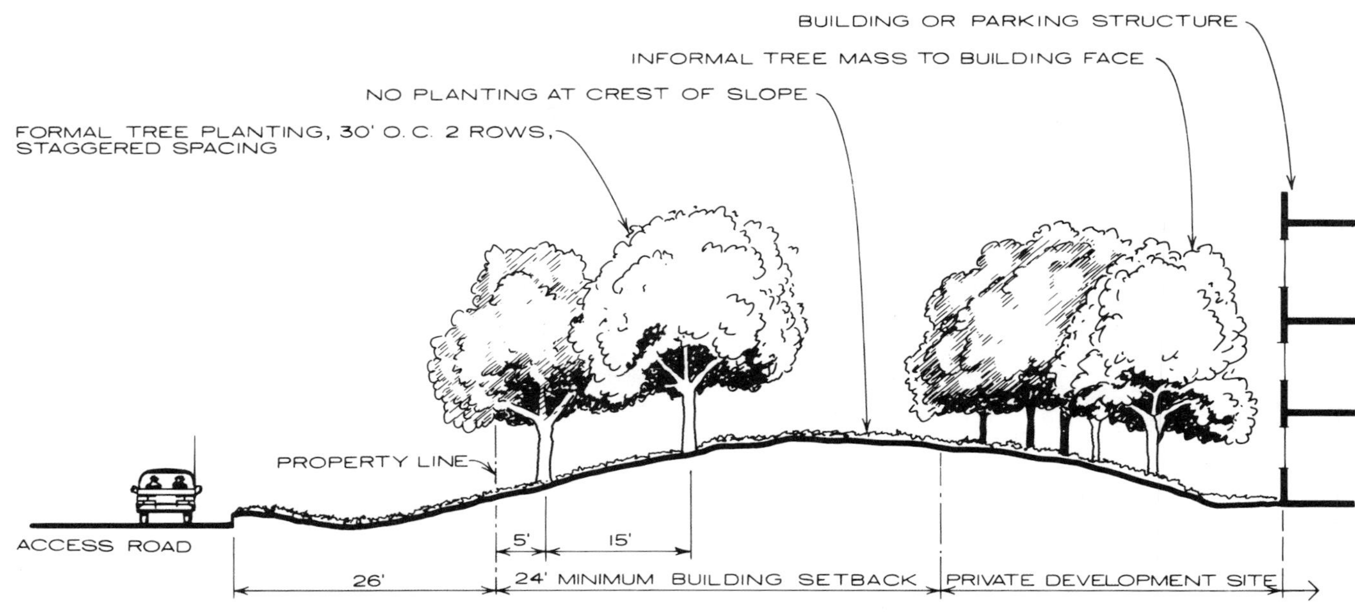

FIG. 15-10 Typical grading.

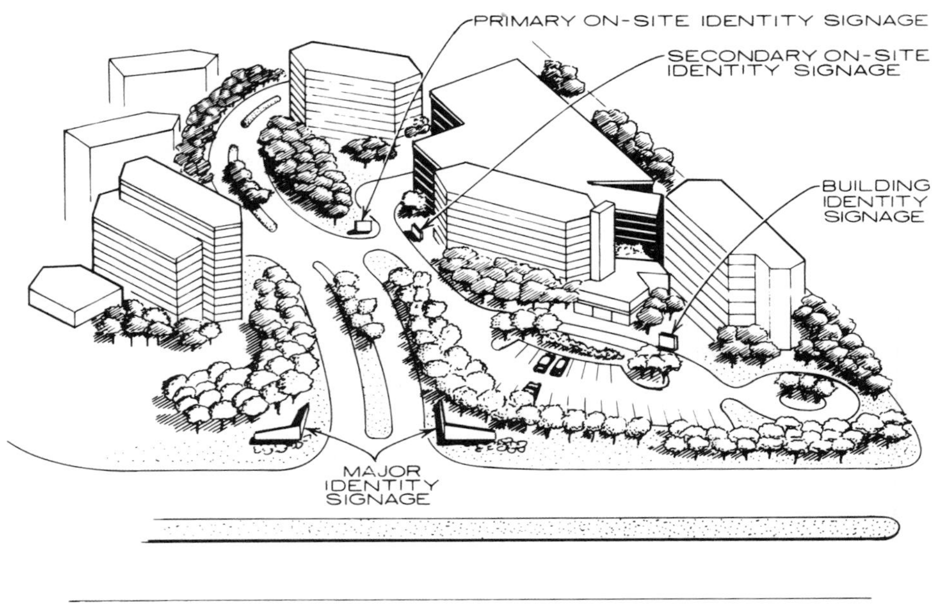

FIG. 15-11 Entrances are treated in relation to function.

Parking Areas

Parking facilities may include both parking structures as well as surface parking. In the case of surface parking, landscaping techniques should be used to alleviate the harsh visual appearance that accompanies paved parking lots. For example, a $3\frac{1}{2}$ ft hedge can be used for screening parking from public view.

Minimum cross-slope for parking areas should be 1% on concrete and 2% on bituminous. Catch basins should be provided to collect storm water runoff inside the parking lot as needed.

All surface parking must be screened from adjacent parcels with buffer planting. Trees can be used in combination with shrubs. (See Fig. 15-12.) A minimum of 5% of the parking/circulation area, for example, can be landscaped exclusive of setback areas. It is desirable that trees be planted in parking areas either in bays or planting islands of at least 5 ft by 5 ft. Irrigation should be installed in all planting areas. When use of existing trees is not possible, new trees should be planted in the parking areas. Trees should also be distributed throughout the parking area.

Parking structures, both below grade and above grade, should also receive landscape treatment to eliminate any conditions of the structure that might inhibit attractive views. All garages must be screened with heavy planting of trees; existing trees should be preserved wherever possible to screen garage structure. No part of the automobile below the hood-line should be exposed to public view from any point on the site, from adjacent sites, or public rights-of-way. The use of planters and vegetation for screening and enhancement of parking structures is also encouraged.

Loading Docks/Utility Areas

Loading docks and utility areas should be totally screened from views of principal streets, entry drives, parking areas, and building structures, and should not be located facing such areas. (See Fig. 15-13.)

Plant Materials

Landscaping outside setback areas should be from the approved plant material list. Choice of plant material can also be kept to a small number of species to provide a simple but well-designed landscape.

FIG. 15-12 Surface parking should be screened from adjacent parcels.

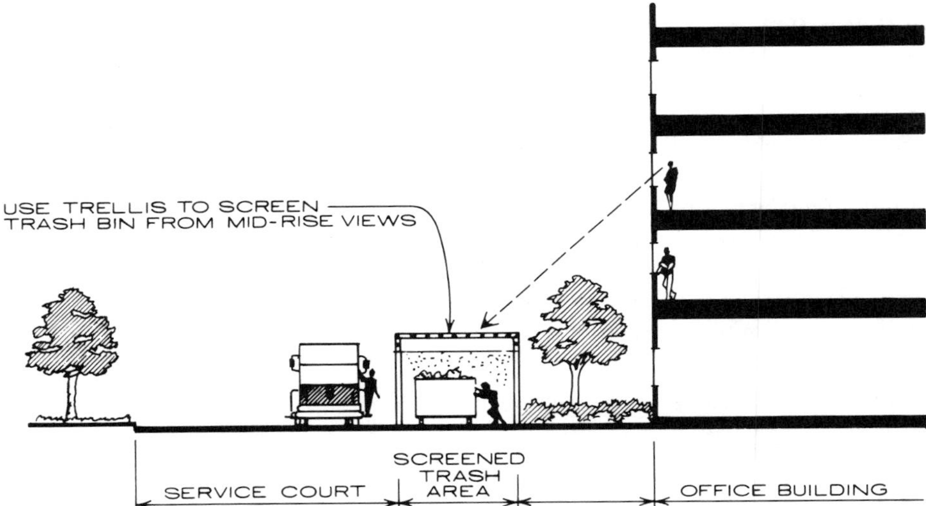

FIG. 15-13 Screening of trash areas.

Irrigation

All landscaped areas should be irrigated by an underground, automatic irrigation system of approved design. It should be a quality system requiring minimum maintenance.

Sprinkler heads should be located to effectively water areas intended with a minimum spray onto pavement and walks, and to insure effective even coverage.

Site Furniture

Site furniture and mechanical equipment visible from the street should be considered as landscape elements. All site furniture including exterior light fixtures should be subject to approval by the ARC.

SIGNAGE STANDARDS

The design intent of the signage program for a development should maintain a consistent quality image for the project as a whole while accommodating the individual purchaser's needs. This can be accomplished through a planned program of sign size, color, and message content, as well as a consistent typeface. (See Fig. 15-11.)

Project Identity Signage

The project identity signage can consist of words and/or be accompanied by a logo. Their comparative proportions should be maintained in all applications. The project identity sign should be placed at the primary entrances of the project. (See Figs. 15-14 to 15-17.)

Parcel Identity Signage

Each building site can have, for example, one ground mounted identity sign at the entry point of the individual site. General content of the sign should be limited to a company name and street address numerals. All identity signs should conform to construction and material restrictions established as appropriate.

FIG. 15-14 Project identity signage at Texas Highlands, a mixed use project on 107 acres in Carrollton, Texas, by the HOK Planning Group, Dallas, Texas.

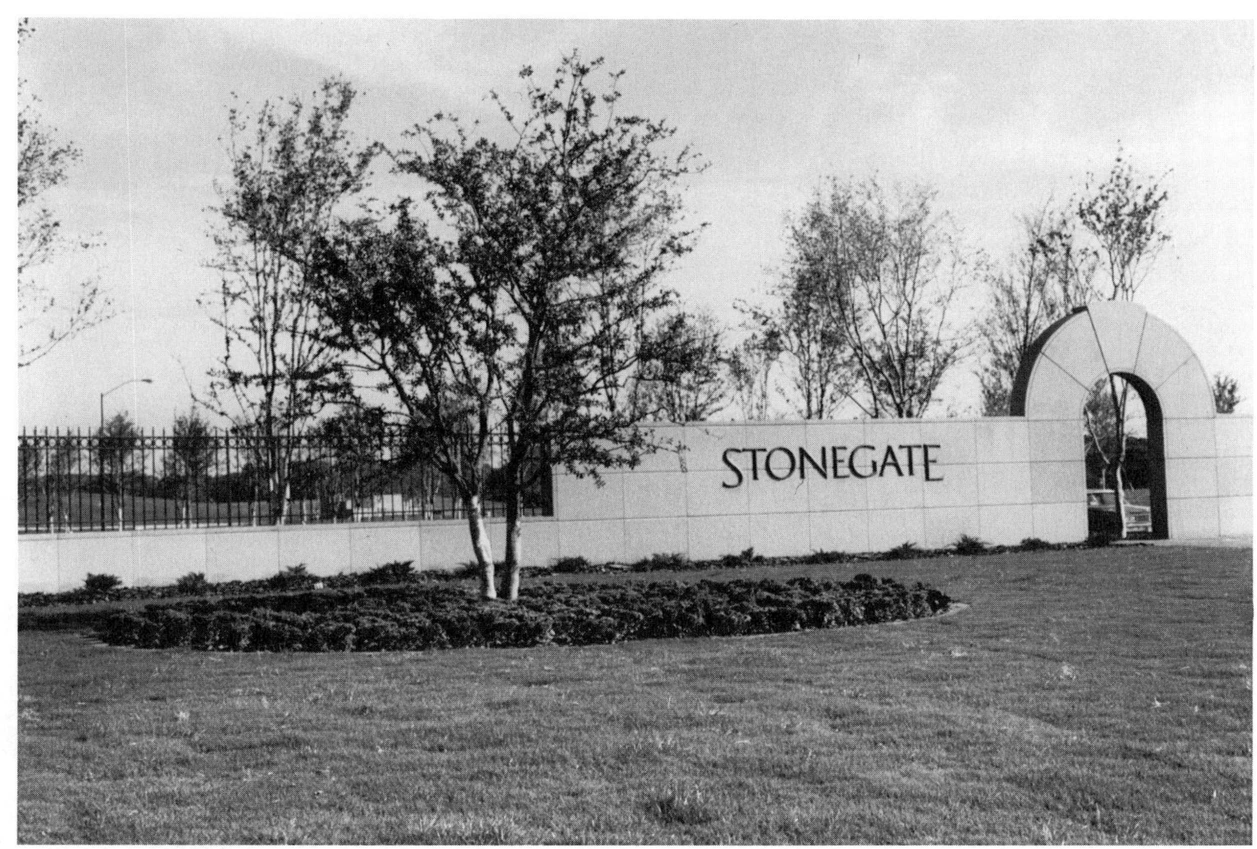

FIG. 15-15 Project identity signage at Stonegate, a mixed use project on 189 acres in Fort Worth, Texas, by the HOK Planning Group, Dallas, Texas.

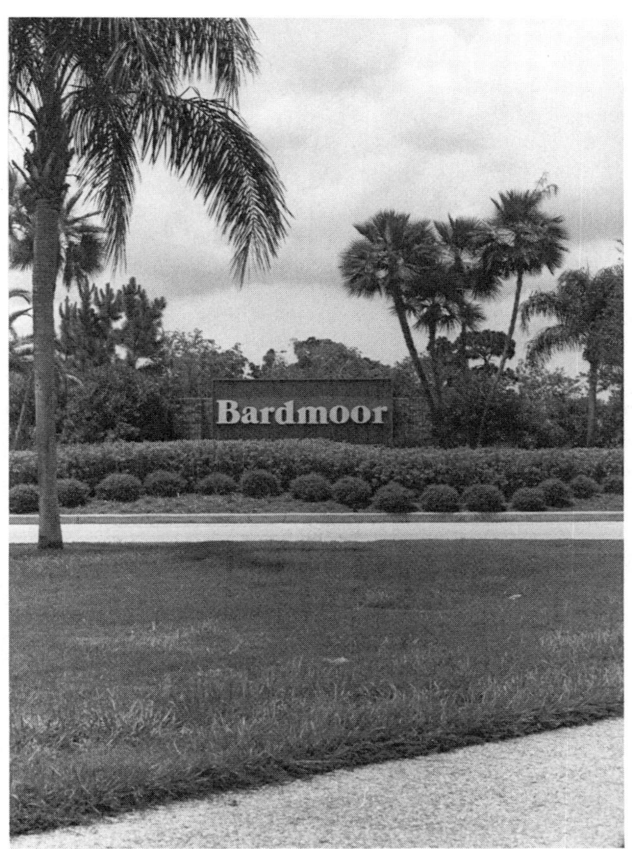

FIG. 15-16 Project identity signage at Bardmoor, a residential community in St. Petersburg, Florida.

FIG. 15-17 Project identity signage at Tampa Palms, a residential community in Tampa, Florida.

Secondary/Directional Signage

Secondary on-site signage should provide direction to specific buildings or building groups. These signs should be located on the site away from the site entry.

Building Identity Signage

Building identity signage should consist of one detached sign per building. Each sign should carry the logo and/or lettering for the major tenant in the individual building. Logo and letter design layout can be selected by the tenant. The message content, layout, colors, and/or finishes should be approved by the Architectural Review Committee.

Identity signs located directly on the building should carry the logo and/or lettering for the major tenant in the individual building. Logo and letter design and layout should be selected by the tenant. The message content, layout, colors, and/or finishes should be approved by the ARC.

Specialty Signage

Specialty signage involves signage for special services provided by tenants. Such services include restaurants, banks, and the like. Lettering and symbol design, layout, colors, and/or finishes should be approved by the ARC.

Building Address and Security Signage

Building address and security signage for office structures should be limited to building address and security information. No tenant identification should be allowed in a location inside the building that is conspicuously visible from outside the building. Sign color, size, and layout should be approved by the ARC. Signage should be limited, for example, to glass areas only.

Traffic, Street, and Parking Signage

Traffic, street, and parking signage throughout the site should consist of signs that conform to the state manual of uniform traffic control devices, as interpreted by a city engineer. Additional signage if required within private property should conform to the signage standards. No signs should be specified or installed in any area by a tenant without approval of the ARC.

LIGHTING STANDARDS

Appropriate night lighting improves safety and security for site users after dusk. Lighting should be provided for pedestrians, vehicles, and signage, and can be used for decorative accent purposes. Overall high levels of light are not desired; intensity should be no greater than required for automobile and pedestrian safety. Lighting schemes must be submitted for approval, including fixture types and finishes. The types of lighting such as sodium or mercury vapor should be indicated.

Pedestrian Lighting

Pedestrian walkways, plazas, and open spaces should be illuminated at sufficient levels by individual site developers. Pedestrian scale accent lighting is recommended. Public walkways at individual building sites should have lighting compatible with those used throughout the development. Fixtures should be installed by the site developer. Walkways and other pedestrian areas should be illuminated to a required minimum such as 0.25 footcandles. Height of fixtures should be called out such as 14 ft or 16 ft.

Vehicular Lighting

Fixtures selected for on-site driveways or surface parking should be consistent in type, style, and color with those used along the roadways in the development. These fixtures should be installed by each individual site developer. Fixtures located along the primary and secondary roadway within a specific area can also be installed by each site developer. Fixtures should be installed according to optimum spacing as recommended by the manufacturer and approved by the ARC. The pattern of lighting should be considered in order to provide a smooth, even lighting to eliminate glare or light flow intrusion into on-site structures or adjacent properties.

Parking structures should have appropriate interior lighting on each deck. Upper deck lighting fixtures should be consistent in maintaining a low profile image desired for parking structures. Fixtures should not be mounted to perimeter parapet walls. Wattage and spacing of fixtures should be designed, for example, to achieve a minimum of 0.50 footcandles and a maximum of 1.0 footcandles. Light poles can be limited to specific heights such as 30 ft. (See Fig. 15-18.)

Accent Lighting

Accent lighting of building, landscaping, and other special features should be encouraged; however, it should be subject to approval by the ARC in terms of placement of fixtures, fixture types, and methods of mounting or wiring. Concealed-source fixtures are generally preferred.

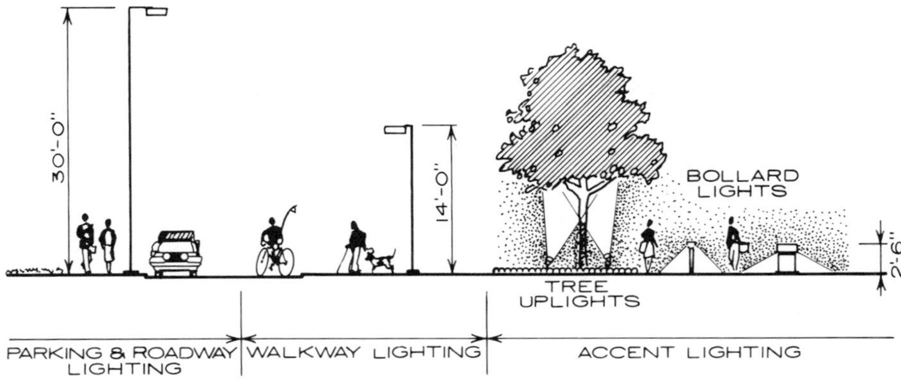

FIG. 15-18 Lighting treatments.

SITE OPERATIONS AND MAINTENANCE

Maintenance Standards of Building Sites

Maintenance requirements should be outlined in the guidelines. All building site owners and occupants including leases must be responsible for the continual maintenance of their buildings, improvements, and grounds in a safe, clean, and attractive condition at their own expense. The declarant should maintain the right of inspection and enforcement of maintenance conditions. The ARC and declarant should have the right, after proper notice of violation, to perform required maintenance and seek reimbursement from the owners. Following are typical descriptions of standards for maintenance of all building sites within the development. The ARC or declarant should reserve the right to modify these standards as necessary.

Grounds. In general, all litter, trash, refuse, and wastes must be promptly removed from a building site. A regular landscape maintenance program must be followed that includes arrangements for lawn mowing, tree and shrub pruning, weeding, fertilizing, watering, and plant material placement as needed.

Owners of improved building sites should be required to adhere to grounds maintenance standards for those areas visible to the general public or adjacent improved sites.

All driveways, walkways, courts, plazas, benches, light fixtures, signs, and so on affixed to a building site should be maintained in good working order and appearance. Refinishing should be undertaken prior to apparent deterioration and should comply with applicable health, safety, and ARC requirements.

Structures. Each individual building site owner or assigned designates is responsible for external maintenance of all structures affixed to the site. This should include but not be limited to painting, repair of surfaces, replacement of glass, and the like. The ARC and the declarant should retain inspection and enforcement rights.

Site Operations

The ARC should reserve the right to monitor site operations for emissions testing, effluent discharge, and so forth. Items that can be monitored are noise, odor, vibration, smoke, and dust. An example written for noise could be the following. Noise should be muffled so as not to be objectionable at any point along the purchaser's property line because of intermittence, beat frequency, shrillness, or intensity. The ARC should determine whether such noice is objectionable based on industry standards and opinions of adjacent property owners.

Enforcement

Enforcement of maintenance and operations of an owner's property affects the quality and image of the overall development. It is therefore necessary to have a description of enforcement policy in the guidelines. For example, if in the opinion of the developer, the association, or the ARC any owner has failed to properly maintain or operate his or her property, the developer, association, or ARC may give such person written notice of such failure. Within 10 days of such notice the owner must perform the care or maintenance required. Should the work not be performed within this time period, the developer, association, or ARC directly or through an authorized agent should have the right and power to enter into the owner's property and perform such care and maintenance without liability. The owner can be held liable for the cost of such work including the overhead cost of the administration of such a procedure. Should such bills not be paid within 30 days, this debt will constitute a lien against the property upon which the work was performed.

CONSTRUCTION PROVISIONS

Construction Site Requirements

Because of the large-scale nature of the project and marketing strategies established by the developer, development of individual building sites is expected to take a number of years. Therefore special construction provisions should be enforced by the ARC and the declarant to ensure that an attractive, nuisance-free setting is maintained during the extended period of construction. (See Fig. 15-19.)

The applicant, building, and/or contractor should submit a program that details proposed methods of compliance with the "construction operation standards" before actual construction begins. Such construction can begin only after notice to proceed has been granted by the ARC or declarant. Equipment access, parking and material storage, temporary utilities, clearing of vegetation, erosion and siltation control, on-site topsoil use, removal of construction debris, temporary signs, and temporary structures should be described.

DEVELOPMENT ADMINISTRATION

Guidelines including future modifications must be a part of every land sales agreement. The guidelines insure orderly, attractive, and lasting development that will preserve and enhance land values. An administrative organization

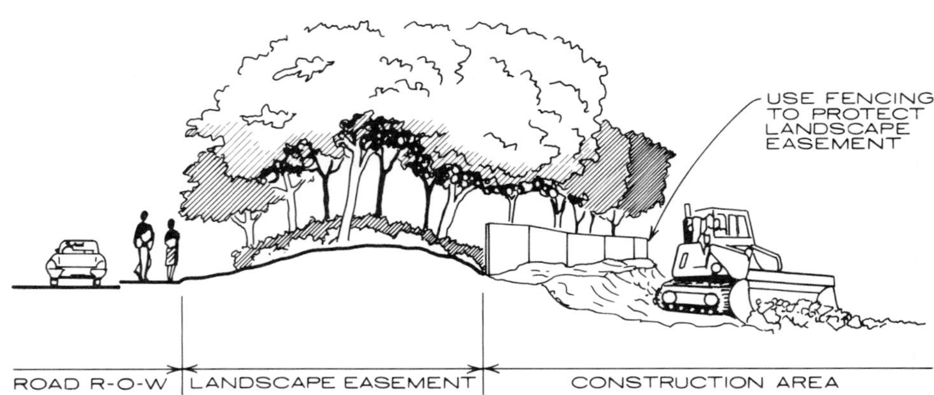

FIG. 15-19 Fencing to screen and protect landscape easements.

must be set up to administer and maintain the property until, for example, a property owner's association is formed. The following description illustrates how this can be done.

Administration

The development company, as the declarant of the covenants, conditions, and restrictions (CCR), should administer the development and maintenance of the property until the property owner's association ("association") is formed and incorporated as a nonprofit corporation. This should occur on or before the date on which the properties subject to the CCR are transferred. Furthermore, the association shall be so established and administered as to provide uniform treatment for all owners except that the development company may have a proportional number of votes in the association that is different from that accorded other owners. An "owner" means any person or entity other than an owner of residential property who is a record owner of a fee simple interest or undivided fee simple interest except, however, that the "owner" should not include any person or entity with only a security interest in the property. If any section of a property is used for residential development, the residential "owners" must select one member to represent their collective interest and vote their proportionate share. Each "owner" can designate a representative to the association.

Assessments

Every owner of property should pay to the declarant until such time as the association is established and thereafter to pay to the association:

1. Regular annual assessments to be used for designs, purchases, installations, maintenance, repair, and replacement of all improvements that are under the control and supervision of the declarant (or the association) along with the cost of any associated management or supervisory services, fees, labor, equipment, materials, and insurance coverage.
2. Special group assessments can be used on a one-time only basis to respond to unusual or emergency needs or to defray the cost of new construction, unexpected repair, or replacement of items covered by annual assessments.
3. Special member assessments can be used to defray costs of repair or replacement of improvements caused by the negligent act or omission of the specific owner.

Assessments should be rated and allocated among owners based solely upon the value of that portion of the properties (both land and improvements) held for record by each owner as assessed by the county for ad valorem tax purposes for the preceding year. A reserve fund can be established and maintained to be used for unexpected maintenance as determined by the declarant.

Enforcement

The declarant and the ARC should each have the right to enforce any of the convenant's conditions and restrictions. Enforcement should be by any proceeding at law or in equity against the owners of properties violating or attempting to violate any part of such restrictions.

DEVELOPMENT REVIEW COMMITTEE

Creation

In order to maintain consistent quality development for all building sites within the project over time, an Architectural Review Committee (ARC) should be established by the declarant or association. The size and composition of the ARC, its methods of election, and its duties and authorities should be determined, or amended, by the declarant or association.

Function

The ARC should establish and enforce quality design, development, and construction standards for the entire development. ARC members are charged with the duties of enforcing the protective design covenants as set forth in this document. The committee is responsible for review and approval of all plans and specifications for initial construction or alteration of existing improvements or conditions on all building sites within the project.

The ARC can also oversee compliance with maintenance and construction provisions as indicated in this document.

Factors Requiring Approval

All new construction, subsequent construction, modifications to exterior surfaces, and demolition of structures must be reviewed and approved by the ARC. Any improvements to the building site including grading, landscaping, setbacks, paving, signage, exterior lighting, and so on must also receive approval by the ARC.

Any changes in exterior color, shape, or finish of existing structures also requires approval from the ARC. Ordinary repairs and maintenance from normal use should not require approval if such repairs do not alter exterior appearance.

Enforcement

The Architectural Review Committee can enforce any and all conditions, design covenants, and restrictions in the interest of owners, applicants, and declarant, or the association. Violation of any condition, covenant, restriction, or reservation as determined by the ARC should allow prosecution against such person or persons.

Approval Process

Conceptual Site Plan. In step one the applicant or his or her designate should review the development guidelines and then prepare an easily readable but preliminary site plan that depicts building size and location, and parking structure or lot layout including capacity. The site plan should also include driveway size and location, building and parking setbacks, landscaped areas, and preliminary utility layout. The ARC should react to this submission in a timely manner and communicate its suggestions and comments.

Preliminary Plans. In step two a refinement of the site plan should be made. Elevations of the building, materials, and colors can be prepared. These plans should be in a format prepared by a registered architect/engineer. The ARC should review this submission in a timely manner.

Final Construction Plans. These plans represent finished site layout and complete architectural, structural, and design specifications. Included in these plans can be landscape development, signage, lighting, and so on. Processing time by the ARC can include referral to a qualified outside consultant.

The applicant should be required to engage a registered professional architect and engineer for the preparation of the project plans and specifications.

All components of building design must adhere to the city's building code and/or any other applicable codes or statutes. The foregoing procedures should prove reasonable and adequate for most situations. The ARC can, however, consider and react on special occasions in an effort to accommodate unusual situations where justified. These procedures should be part of the overall effort to insure that an acceptable quality level is attained in the development without the necessity of imposing unduly cumbersome regulations.

Williams Square, Las Colinas, Irving, Texas.

Appendix

FORMULAS

$$\text{Area of a circle} = \pi r^2$$

$$\pi = 3.1416$$

$$\text{Circumference of a circle} = 2\pi r \text{ or } \pi d$$

$$\text{Area of a triangle} = \tfrac{1}{2}\, b \times h$$

$$\text{Area of a trapezoid} = h \times \frac{(b_1 + b_2)}{2}$$

UNITS OF MEASURE AND CONVERSION FACTORS

U.S. Linear Measure to Metric

inch		=	25.4 millimeters or
		=	2.54 centimeters
foot	= 12 inches	=	0.3048 meters
yard	= 36 inches 3 feet	=	0.9144 meters
rod	= $16\frac{1}{2}$ feet or $5\frac{1}{2}$ yards	=	5.029 meters
furlong	= 660 feet or 40 rods	=	201.168 meters
mile	= 5280 feet or = 1760 yards or = 8 furlongs	=	1.609 kilometers

Nautical Measure

fathom = 6 feet
nautical mile = 6076.1033 feet (international)

Metric System of Linear Measure

1 millimeter	= 0.1 centimeter	=	0.0393	inches
10 millimeters	= 1.0 centimeter	=	0.3937	inches
10 centimeters	= 1.0 decimeter	=	3.937	inches
10 decimeters	= 1.0 meter	=	39.37	inches
10 meters	= 1.0 decameter	=	32.81	feet
10 decameters	= 1.0 hectometer	=	328.1	feet
10 hectometers	= 1.0 kilometer	=	0.621	miles
10 kilometers	= 1.0 myriameter	=	6.213	miles

Units of Area—U.S. Square Measure to Metric

square inch			=	6.452	square centimeters
square foot	=	144 square inches	=	929	square centimeters
square yard	=	9 square feet	=	0.8361	square meters
square rod	=	$30\frac{1}{4}$ square yards	=	25.29	square meters
acre	=	43,560 square feet or 160 square rods	=	0.4047	hectares
square mile	=	27,878,400 square feet or	=	259	hectares
		640 acres	=	2.59	square kilometers

Metric Square Measure to U.S.

square centimeter	= 100 square millimeters	=	0.15499	square inches
square decimeter	= 100 square centimeters	=	15.499	square inches
square meter	= 100 square decimeters	=	1549.9	square inches
square decameter	= 100 square meters	=	119.6	square yards
square hectometer	= 100 square decameters	=	2.441	acres
square kilometer	= 100 square hectometers	=	0.386	square miles

Volume Measure

1728 cubic inches	= 1 cubic foot	= 0.0383	cubic meters
27 cubic feet	= 1 cubic yard	= 0.7646	cubic meters

Metric Volume to U.S.

cubic centimeter	= 1000 cubic millimeters	=	.06102	cubic inches
cubic decimeter	= 1000 cubic centimeters	=	61.02	cubic inches
cubic meter	= 1000 cubic decimeters	=	35.314	cubic feet

Dry Measure

1 pint		= 33.60 cubic inches	=	0.5505 liters
2 pints	= 1 quart	= 67.20 cubic inches	=	1.1012 liters
8 quarts	= 1 peck	= 537.61 cubic inches	=	8.8096 liters
4 pecks	= 1 bushel	= 2150.42 cubic inches	=	35.2383 liters

Liquid Measure (Apothecaries)

60 minims	= 1 fluid dram	=	0.2256 cubic inches
8 fluid drams	= 1 fluid ounce	=	1.8047 cubic inches
16 fluid ounces	= 1 pint	=	28.875 cubic inches

U.S. Liquid

1 gill	= 4 fluid ounces	=	7.219 cubic inches
4 gills	= 1 pint	=	28.875 cubic inches
2 pints	= 1 quart	=	57.75 cubic inches
4 quarts	= 1 gallon	=	231 cubic inches
1 acre inch	= 27,154 gallons	=	3629.961 cubic feet
1 acre foot	= 325,851 gallons	=	43,559.942 cubic feet

Metric Fluid

1 centiliter	= 10 milliliters	=	.338 fluid ounces
1 deciliter	= 10 centiliters	=	3.38 fluid ounces
1 liter	= 10 deciliters	=	1.0567 liquid quarts
1 decaliter	= 10 liters	=	2.64 gallons
1 hectoliter	= 10 decaliters	=	26.418 gallons
1 kiloliter	= 10 hectoliters	=	264.18 gallons

Weight (Apothecaries)

1 grain		=	0.0648 grams
1 scruple	= 20 grains	=	1296 grams
1 dram	= 3 scruples	=	3.888 grams
1 ounce	= 8 drams	=	31.1035 grams
1 pound	= 12 ounces	=	373.24 grams

Weight (Avoirdupois)

1 grain		=	0.0648 grams
1 dram	= 27.34 grains	=	1.772 grams
1 ounce	= 16 drams	=	28.3495 grams
1 pound	= 16 ounces	=	453.59 grams
1 short ton	= 2000 pounds	=	907.18 kilograms
1 long ton	= 2240 pounds	=	1016.05 kilograms

Bibliography

American Association of State Highway Officials. "A Policy on Design Standards for Stopping Sight Distance," Washington, D.C.: AASHO General Offices, 1971.

American Association of State Highway Officials. *A Policy on Geometric Design of Rural Highways: 1965*. Washington, D.C.: AASHO General Offices, 1966.

American Society of Civil Engineers and the Water Pollution Control Federation. *Design and Construction of Sanitary and Storm Sewers*. New York, 1960.

Baker, Geoffrey, and Bruno Funaro. *Parking*. New York: Reinhold, 1958.

Bernatzky, Aloys. "Climatic Influences of Greens and City Planning," Anthos, No. 1, 1966.

Bernatzky, Aloys. "The Performance and Value of Trees," *Anthos*, No. 1, 1969.

Brinker, Russell C., and Warren C. Taylor. *Elementary Surveying*. 3d ed., rev. Scranton, Pa.: International Textbook, 1955.

Buckman, Harry O., and Nyle C. Brady. *The Nature and Property of Soils: A College Textbook of Edaphology*. 6th ed., rev. New York: Macmillan, 1960.

Carr, Stephen, Ashley/Myer/Smith. *City Signs and Lights*, for Boston Redevelopment Authority, Cambridge: MIT Press, 1973.

Chermayeff, Serge and Christopher Alexander. *Community and Privacy*. New York: Doubleday, 1963.

Church, Thomas D. *Gardens Are for People: How to Plan for Outdoor Living*. New York: Reinhold, 1955.

Community Builders Council. *The Community Builders Handbook*. Anniversary ed. Washington, D.C.: Urban Land Institute, 1968.

Eckbo, Garrett. *Landscape for Living*. New York: F. W. Dodge Corp., 1950.

Eckbo, Garrett. *Urban Landscape Design*. New York: McGraw-Hill, 1964.

Flawn, Peter T. *Environmental Geology*. New York: Harper & Row, 1970.

Frevert, Richard K. et al. *Soil and Water Conservation Engineering*. New York: Wiley, 1955.

Fruin, John J. *Pedestrian Planning and Design*. New York: Metropolitan Association of Urban Designers and Environmental Planners, Inc., 1971.

Halprin, Lawrence. *Cities*. New York: Reinhold, 1963.

Howard, Ebenezer. *Garden Cities of To-Morrow*. Cambridge: MIT Press, 1965.

Hubbard, Henry Vincent, and Theodora Kimball. *An Introduction to the Study of Landscape Design*. 2d ed., rev. Boston: Hubbard Educational Trust, 1929.

Kassler, Elizabeth B. *Modern Gardens and the Landscape*. New York: Museum of Modern Art, 1964.

Kemmerer, Harleigh. "Managing Outdoor Lighting," Grounds Maintenance, 1976.

Lehr, Paul E., Burnett, R. Will, and Zion, Herbert S. *Weather*. New York: Golden Press, 1965.

Lynch, Kevin. *The Image of the City*. Cambridge, Mass.: MIT Press, 1960.

Lynch, Kevin. *Site Planning*. Cambridge, Mass.: MIT Press, 1962.

Meter, Carl F. *Route Surveying*. 3d ed., rev. Scranton, Pa.: International Textbook, 1962.

McHale, John. *The Ecological Context*. New York: George Braziller, 1970.

McHarg, Ian L. *Design With Nature*. New York: Natural History Press, 1969.

Miller, Willard E. and George T. Renner et al. *Global Geography*, 2d ed., rev. New York: Thomas Y. Crowell, 1957.

Odum, Eugene P. *Fundamentals of Ecology*. 3d ed. Philadelphia, Pa.: W. B. Saunders Company, 1971.

Olgay, Victor. *Design with Climate*. Princeton, N.J.: Princeton University Press, 1963.

Parker, Harry, and John W. MacGuire. *Simplified Site Engineering for Architects and Builders*. New York: Wiley, 1954.

Ramsey, Charles G., and Harold R. Sleeper. *Architectural Graphic Standards*. 6th ed., rev. New York: Wiley, 1970.

Robinette, Gary O. *Plants/People/and Environmental Quality*. Washington, D.C.: U.S. Department of the Interior, National Park Service, in collaboration with the American Society of Landscape Architects Foundation, 1972.

Robinette, Margaret A. *Outdoor Sculpture: Object and Environment*. New York: Whitney Library of Design, 1976.

Rubenstein, Harvey M. *Central City Malls*. New York: Wiley, 1978.

Seelye, Elwin E. *Data Book for Civil Engineers: Volume I, Design*. 3d ed., rev. New York: Wiley, 1960.

Simonds, John Ormsbee. *Landscape Architecture: The Shaping of Man's Natural Environment*. New York: F. W. Dodge Corp., 1961.

Unterman, Richard K., and Robert E. Small. *Site Planning for Cluster Housing*. New York: Van Nostrand Reinhold, 1977.

U.S. Consumer Product Safety Commission, *A Handbook for Public Safety, Volume 1: General Guidelines for New and Existing Playgrounds*. Washington, D.C.: U.S. Government Printing Office, 1981.

Wyman, Donald. *Shrubs and Vines for American Gardens*. New York: Macmillan, 1958.

Wyman, Donald. *Trees for American Gardens*. New York: Macmillan, 1959.

Zion, Robert L. *Trees for Architecture and the Landscape*. New York: Reinhold, 1968.

Index